# A Government Reinvented

A Study of Alberta's Deficit Elimination Program

# A Government Reinvented

## A Study of Alberta's Deficit Elimination Program

**EDITED BY**

Christopher Bruce, Ronald Kneebone, and Kenneth McKenzie

**SPONSORED BY**

The Donner Canadian Foundation

Toronto  Oxford  New York
OXFORD UNIVERSITY PRESS
1997

Oxford University Press
70 Wynford Drive, Don Mills, Ontario  M3C 1J9

*Oxford  New York*
*Athens  Auckland  Bangkok  Bombay*
*Calcutta  Cape Town  Dar es Salaam  Delhi*
*Florence  Hong Kong  Istanbul  Karachi*
*Kuala Lumpur  Madras  Madrid  Melbourne*
*Mexico City  Nairobi  Paris  Singapore*
*Taipei  Tokyo  Toronto*

and associated companies in
*Berlin  Ibadan*

*Oxford* is a trademark of Oxford University Press


**Canadian Cataloguing in Publication Data**

Main entry under title:

A government reinvented : a study of Alberta's deficit
elimination program

Based on a conference held in Banff, Alta., Nov. 1995.
Includes index.

ISBN 0–19–541269–9

1. Budget deficits – Alberta – Congresses. 2. Government
spending policy – Alberta – Congresses. 3. Debts, Public –
Alberta – Congresses. 4. Fiscal policy – Alberta – Congresses.
5. Alberta – Politics and government – 1971–     . I. Bruce,
C.J. (Christopher J.), 1948–     . II. Kneebone, Ronald D.
(Ronald David), 1955–     . III. McKenzie, Kenneth J.
(Kenneth James), 1959–     .

HJ2056.5.A4G68 1997     336.3'097123     C97–930458–X


Design:  Max Gabriel Izod

Copyright © Oxford University Press Canada 1997

1 2 3 4 — 00 99 98 97

This book is printed on permanent (acid-free) paper ∞.

Printed in Canada

# Contents ∎

## Part IV  Public Opinion and Commentary

# CHAPTER 1

# Introduction ∎

*Christopher J. Bruce, Ronald D. Kneebone, and Kenneth J. McKenzie*

In December of 1992, Ralph Klein, former journalist, former mayor of Calgary, and then Minister of the Environment in the government of Premier Don Getty, won the campaign for the leadership of the Alberta Progressive Conservative Party. Six months later, in May 1993, the new Klein government tabled a budget calling for dramatic changes in provincial spending. It proposed a four-year plan to reduce the deficit, equal to $3.4 billion at the time, to zero by 1996/7. To do so, provincial expenditures would have to be reduced by approximately 20 per cent in nominal terms, no tax increases would be initiated, and there would be a fundamental restructuring of the public sector. Running on this election platform, the Conservatives were re-elected with a large majority on 15 June 1993. Two years later, in June 1995, the government announced that the $3.4 billion deficit it had inherited had been transformed into a $958 million surplus. By the end of fiscal year 1996/7, the spending cuts will be complete and it is projected that the government will have reduced provincial expenditures by $3.3 billion from their 1992/3 level, a nominal cut of 21 per cent. In real per capita terms, spending will have declined by a third (see Table 1), marking a massive withdrawal of government from the economy in a remarkably short period of time. Throughout all of this, Premier Klein and his Progressive Conservative government have managed to maintain an almost unprecedented level of popular support.

The so-called 'Klein revolution' has garnered a great deal of attention both nationally and internationally. The *Wall Street Journal* (23 February 1995) has referred to Ralph Klein as 'Canada's Reagan' and *The Globe and Mail* (21 February 1995) has talked of 'Ralphonomics' as perhaps being the way of the future. Others claim that the Conservatives have initiated a policy of 'slash and burn', signalling the beginning of the end of Canada's cherished social programs, particularly in health, education, and social services.

Most of those who praise and criticize what the Klein government has done concentrate almost exclusively on the broad fiscal figures. What has been the size of the cuts? What areas have been cut? What has happened to the provincial debt? Others concentrate on the question of whether the cuts have been beneficial or harmful. Have the cuts improved the way the Alberta

**Table 1:** Expenditure Reductions by Ministry, 1992/3 to 1998/9

| Ministry | 1992/3 Actual | 1993/4 Actual | 1994/5 Actual | 1995/6 Forecast | 1996/7 Estimate | 1997/8 Target | 1998/9 Target |
|---|---|---|---|---|---|---|---|
| Advanced Education and Career Development | 1,306.33 | 1,288.09 | 1,163.26 | 1,089.51 | 1,105.80 | 1,105.84 | 1,099.23 |
| | | *-1.40* | *-10.95* | *-16.60* | *-15.35* | *-15.35* | *-15.85* |
| | | *-3.69* | *-18.59* | *-26.29* | *-27.67* | *-30.07* | *-32.80* |
| Agriculture, Food and Rural Development | 1,075.56 | 654.98 | 350.05 | 437.251 | 471.702 | 464.67 | 485.357 |
| | | *-39.10* | *-67.45* | *-59.35* | *-56.14* | *-56.80* | *-54.87* |
| | | *-40.52* | *-70.25* | *-64.07* | *-62.53* | *-64.31* | *-63.96* |
| Community Development | 146.325 | 126.407 | 223.418 | 273.873 | 245.316 | 238.341 | 237.173 |
| | | *-13.61* | *52.69* | *87.17* | *67.65* | *62.88* | *62.09* |
| | | *-15.62* | *39.59* | *65.42* | *43.25* | *34.55* | *29.44* |
| Economic Development and Tourism | 104.351 | 97.606 | 76.844 | 85.225 | 70.952 | 67.682 | 52.016 |
| | | *-6.46* | *-26.36* | *-18.33* | *-32.01* | *-35.14* | *-50.15* |
| | | *-8.64* | *-32.68* | *-27.82* | *-41.90* | *-46.42* | *-60.19* |
| Education | 2,878.79 | 2,971.20 | 2,748.36 | 2,707.37 | 2,699.47 | 2,755.52 | 2,754.85 |
| | | *3.21* | *-4.53* | *-5.95* | *-6.23* | *-4.28* | *-4.31* |
| | | *0.81* | *-12.72* | *-16.88* | *-19.88* | *-20.93* | *-23.58* |
| Energy | 183.514 | 150.809 | 128.99 | 126.357 | 126.306 | 108.061 | 116.052 |
| | | *-17.82* | *-29.71* | *-31.15* | *-31.17* | *-41.12* | *-36.76* |
| | | *-19.73* | *-35.74* | *-39.15* | *-41.19* | *-51.36* | *-49.50* |
| Environmental Protection | 406.433 | 377.55 | 377.877 | 544.286 | 347.01 | 336.089 | 308.789 |
| | | *-7.11* | *-7.03* | *33.92* | *-14.62* | *-17.31* | *-24.02* |
| | | *-9.26* | *-15.00* | *18.36* | *-27.05* | *-31.69* | *-39.33* |
| Executive Council | 32.037 | 27.678 | 23.895 | 22.878 | 21.938 | 20.021 | 18.083 |
| | | *-13.61* | *-25.41* | *-28.59* | *-31.52* | *-37.51* | *-43.56* |
| | | *-15.61* | *-31.81* | *-36.89* | *-41.49* | *-48.38* | *-54.92* |
| Family and Social Services | 1,722.33 | 1,598.46 | 1,353.44 | 1,367.79 | 1,393.93 | 1,352.26 | 1,338.85 |
| | | *-7.19* | *-21.42* | *-20.58* | *-19.07* | *-21.49* | *-22.27* |
| | | *-9.35* | *-28.16* | *-29.81* | *-30.85* | *-35.14* | *-37.92* |
| Federal and Inter-governmental Affairs | 7.395 | 6.09 | 5.81 | 6.08 | 5.08 | 4.90 | 4.77 |
| | | *-17.67* | *-21.46* | *-17.77* | *-31.25* | *-33.73* | *-35.47* |
| | | *-19.59* | *-28.20* | *-27.32* | *-41.26* | *-45.25* | *-48.47* |
| Health | 4174.78 | 4038.75 | 3834.54 | 3667.67 | 3704.46 | 3644.57 | 3626.81 |
| | | *-3.26* | *-8.15* | *-12.15* | *-11.27* | *-12.7* | *-13.13* |
| | | *-5.50* | *-16.03* | *-22.35* | *-24.18* | *-27.89* | *-30.62* |
| Justice | 426.031 | 413.515 | 366.452 | 362.554 | 357.266 | 354.239 | 354.239 |
| | | *-2.94* | *-13.98* | *-14.90* | *-16.14* | *-16.85* | *-16.85* |
| | | *-5.19* | *-21.36* | *-24.79* | *-28.35* | *-31.32* | *-33.60* |
| Labour | 51.709 | 44.731 | 39.521 | 35.086 | 31.455 | 28.935 | 27.435 |
| | | *-13.49* | *-23.57* | *-32.15* | *-39.17* | *-44.04* | *-46.94* |
| | | *-15.50* | *-30.13* | *-40.03* | *-48.02* | *-53.78* | *-57.63* |
| Municipal Affairs | 836.315 | 663.568 | 515.791 | 310.442 | 282.13 | 274.146 | 229.278 |
| | | *-20.66* | *-38.33* | *-62.88* | *-66.27* | *-67.22* | *-72.58* |
| | | *-22.50* | *-43.62* | *-67.19* | *-71.18* | *-72.92* | *-78.11* |

**Table 1:** (Continued)

| Ministry | 1992/3 Actual | 1993/4 Actual | 1994/5 Actual | 1995/6 Forecast | 1996/7 Estimate | 1997/8 Target | 1998/9 Target |
|---|---|---|---|---|---|---|---|
| Public Works, Supply and Services | 598.886 | 565.437 | 476.322 | 495.32 | 469.395 | 454.835 | 442.75 |
| | | −5.59 | −20.47 | −17.29 | −21.62 | −24.05 | −26.07 |
| | | −7.78 | −27.29 | −26.90 | −33.03 | −37.26 | −40.96 |
| Science and Research | 47.575 | 45.834 | 41.757 | 38.64 | 37.942 | 38.802 | 38.537 |
| | | −3.66 | −12.23 | −18.78 | −20.25 | −18.44 | −19.00 |
| | | −5.90 | −19.76 | −28.22 | −31.86 | −32.63 | −35.31 |
| Transportation and Utilities | 802.589 | 804.828 | 782.575 | 769.357 | 671.14 | 661.887 | 663.04 |
| | | 0.28 | −2.49 | −4.14 | −16.38 | −17.53 | −17.39 |
| | | −2.05 | −10.86 | −15.28 | −28.55 | −31.88 | −34.03 |
| Treasury | 921.203 | 890.349 | 620.922 | 156.398 | 300.022 | 307.997 | 315.63 |
| | | −3.35 | −32.60 | −83.02 | −67.43 | −66.57 | −65.74 |
| | | −5.59 | −38.38 | −84.99 | −72.17 | −72.38 | −72.64 |
| Total Program Expenditures | 15,611.15 | 14,648.88 | 13,042.83 | 12,412.09 | 12,277.32 | 12,155.79 | 12,054.89 |
| | | −6.16 | −16.45 | −20.49 | −21.36 | −22.13 | −22.78 |
| | | −8.34 | −23.62 | −29.73 | −32.80 | −35.68 | −38.33 |

NOTE: Figures in the first horizontal row for each ministry are in millions of nominal dollars. Figures in the second row show the cumulative percentage reduction in nominal spending from 1992/3. Figures in the third row show the cumulative percentage reduction in real per capita spending. For these data, prices were assumed to increase by 2 per cent per year and population was assumed to grow by the average rate of the 10-year period 1984–93 (1.41 per cent per year).

SOURCE: *Agenda '96*, Alberta Government Budget, February 1996.

government provides services to its citizens or have they simply been an exercise in indiscriminate budget-cutting? While we think questions such as these are certainly interesting and important, and the chapters in this volume will touch upon all of them, we think an equally interesting question is: *How has the Klein government managed to do what it has done?* Specifically, how did the political and bureaucratic systems respond to the budget cuts? Did the government change the methods it used to allocate funds among departments? Did civil servants resist budget cuts? If so, how did the government deal with that resistance? If not, how was co-operation obtained? Was there a restructuring of the means by which government services were delivered? For example, were services privatized or contracted out; and, if so, were these changes the inevitable result of the budget cuts or were they the result of political decisions? Finally, how did the Klein government gain and maintain the acceptance of voters for such dramatic spending cuts?

It is our view that if Alberta's experience is to provide information for other governments, both within and outside Canada, the *processes* employed to obtain the budget cuts must be investigated. Hence, this study will provide very little grist for those Albertans who wish to argue that the cuts in any particular department were 'too large' or 'too small'. Our goal is the broader one of providing sufficient information concerning the techniques employed by the Alberta government that other governments will be able to determine whether they wish to adopt these techniques.

One might approach the central question from a number of directions. One approach is to ask how the government has convinced Alberta voters that a dramatic cut in provincial government expenditures and services was desirable. In particular, why has opposition been so muted? Another is to ask how the government has avoided the bureaucratic resistance that some economists and political scientists suggest would typically accompany dramatic cuts to government spending. Still another is simply to describe the 'nuts and bolts' of the spending cut-backs. What 'rules' were applied? What procedural changes were made? What role did the agency heads and bureaucracy play in the process? Finally, how and, indeed, why did the government manage these changes within such a short time frame? All of these approaches and perspectives are employed throughout the study.

Given the scope and magnitude of the changes taking place in Alberta, it quickly became apparent to us that no one or two or three individuals could do justice to all aspects of the reforms. As such, several individuals were invited to contribute to the volume by addressing specific aspects of the deficit elimination program. These experts are all from Alberta, specifically from the University of Calgary and the University of Alberta. To expand the perspective of the study, we also invited other individuals, for the most part, although not exclusively, from outside Alberta, to comment on some of these studies. Thus, the volume presents the views of both 'insiders' and 'outsiders', the latter perhaps less informed of the specifics regarding the changes taking place in Alberta but none the less knowledgeable in the areas in which they were asked to comment. Moreover, although most of the authors are economists, the volume also contains contributions by political scientists, experts in law, and experts in education. The result, we think, is a rather unique, multidisciplinary collection of views and analysis.

The volume is organized into four main parts. Part I (Chapters 2 through 4) contains contextual background for the study. In Chapter 2, Robert Mansell (University of Calgary) provides a brief fiscal and economic history of Alberta, focusing in particular on the environment just prior to the election of Ralph Klein as party leader at the end of 1992. A discussion of Mansell's chapter is provided by Kenneth Norrie (University of Alberta), who ponders the intellectual origins of the Alberta experiment. This is followed, in Chapter 3, by a summary written by Kenneth McKenzie (University of Calgary) of the public choice literature, which is relevant for understanding the reforms undertaken in Alberta. This chapter provides a microeconomic perspective of institutional design and public policy, focusing on both political and bureaucratic institutions. Stanley Winer (Carleton University) expands on some of the issues raised by McKenzie by proposing a general framework for studying the nature of institutional reform. In Chapter 4, Ronald Kneebone (University of Calgary) addresses some of the same issues, but this time from a macroeconomic perspective. He examines in particular the important impetus for change precipitated by a 'fiscal crisis'. In his comments on Chapter 4, Bryne Purchase (Queen's University) discusses the applicability of some of the insights provided by Kneebone to the federal government's fiscal situation. All three of these chapters, and the accompanying comments, provide a framework within which to view subsequent chapters that examine the details of the 'reinvention' of government specific to Alberta.

The three chapters in Part II analyse some of the details of the reforms undertaken in Alberta, but from a fairly broad perspective. In Chapter 5, Kneebone and McKenzie examine the process behind the institutional reforms in Alberta with a view to identifying some of the common themes, and highlighting some of the important differences, across departments and agencies. This chapter draws on interviews conducted in the spring of 1995 with 48 individuals, including Premier Klein, six cabinet ministers, seven MLAs, school board officials, Regional Health Authority executives, university and college presidents, and many other government and agency heads and officials. In his comments on this chapter, Michael Trebilcock (University of Toronto Law School) focuses on three aspects of the process identified by Kneebone and McKenzie: the across-the-board nature of the cuts; the role of 'voice' vs. 'choice'; and the speed and extent of the cuts. In Chapter 6, Paul Boothe (University of Alberta) discusses the new approach to budgeting in Alberta adopted by the Klein government. As part of the restructuring exercise, the government has instituted some unique innovations to the budget-making process and to the reporting of the government's fiscal affairs; Boothe describes these innovations and speculates on their implications. In Chapter 7, Kneebone and McKenzie examine how former governments in Alberta responded to unexpected changes in revenues and expenditures. They speculate as to the role this past experience has had in determining budgetary changes initiated by the Klein government.

Part III of this volume studies in detail the reforms associated with the 'big four' spending departments. Family and Social Services, Health, Career Development and Advanced Education, and Education together accounted for about 70 per cent of government expenditures in 1992/3. These departments and their associated agencies contributed, in varying degrees, to the elimination of the deficit and underwent structural reforms. (Note that 'Education' is also sometimes referred to as 'Basic Education' in this volume.)

M.S. Shedd (University of Calgary) analyses the Department of Family and Social Services in Chapter 8. With government welfare roles declining by almost 50 per cent within two years of the reforms, the experience in Family and Social Services deserves special attention. Shedd argues that the government's changes to social services can be considered from many different angles, but ultimately it is difficult to pass judgement given the normative nature of the reforms. Douglas Allen (Simon Fraser University) comments on Shedd's chapter and argues that although an evaluation of programs involving income transfers is difficult and inherently subjective, for the most part the government's approach to social service reform appears to be consistent with generally accepted guiding principles.

In Chapter 9, Richard Plain (University of Alberta) examines the changes in health care. Health care reforms have been perhaps the most contentious and controversial of the changes initiated by the government. Plain is rather critical of some aspects of the government's reforms in this area, arguing that they have moved quickly, and somewhat blindly, into uncharted waters. He advocates a somewhat more cautious and studied approach to health care reform. R.G. Beck (University of Saskatchewan) comments on Plain's paper, comparing some of the changes in Alberta to those that have taken place in Saskatchewan.

Herbert Emery (University of Calgary) examines changes within the post-secondary sector in Chapter 10. Focusing in particular on the University of Calgary, he uses university budget numbers to show that the post-secondary sector has been able to cushion itself to a large extent against the cuts. He also argues that post-secondary institutions in Alberta are in part facing budgetary challenges already faced by universities and colleges in other provinces. Jonathan Kesselman (University of British Columbia) follows with his thoughts on post-secondary educational reform. Picking up on Emery's argument that Alberta is somewhat behind the rest of Canada in cutting transfers to post-secondary institutions, he questions whether some of the changes in Alberta are transferable to other provinces.

In Chapter 11, Christopher Bruce (University of Calgary) and Arthur Schwartz (University of Calgary) look at changes to basic education in Alberta. Another potentially sensitive area from a political perspective, basic education experienced modest cuts to total revenue relative to most other departments and agencies, although these cuts were widely perceived as severe. Most of the restructuring in basic education was driven not so much by the fiscal imperative as by other factors. Stephen Lawton (Ontario Institute for Studies in Education) comments on Bruce and Schwartz's analysis, offering his own views on reform in basic education. He questions some of the conclusions of Bruce and Schwartz.

In Chapter 12, Christopher Bruce concludes Part III with a look at the contracting out and privatization initiatives undertaken by the Klein government. He concludes that the government's efforts in this regard have been somewhat disappointing, with a few high-profile exceptions such as licensing and liquor stores and the development of a new administrative structure with Delegated Administrative Organizations. Douglas West (University of Alberta) provides comments, offering some alternative explanations for the government's lack of initiatives in this regard.

Part IV contains two chapters. In Chapter 13, Keith Archer (University of Calgary) and Roger Gibbins (University of Calgary) report the results of an extensive telephone survey of Albertans conducted in the spring of 1995. They argue that Albertans seem to have adopted a sort of 'siege mentality' in response to the cuts. Albertans appear willing to accept the cuts because they think they are necessary, but they seem to have negative views on virtually every specific aspect of the cuts. Archer and Gibbins also point to various demographic cleavages within the population. Although virtually every demographic group seemed to favour the cuts, there are some marked differences in the degree of support. Archer and Gibbins also argue that Klein's agenda seems to have tapped into the inherent 'neo-conservatism' of the Alberta electorate. Linda Trimble (University of Alberta) comments on the Archer and Gibbins chapter, picking up in particular on the demographic cleavages, most specifically those related to gender. She argues that the government's agenda can also be viewed as having a strong 'neo-liberal' element.

In Chapter 14, we provide some concluding thoughts on the Alberta experience and a summary of some of the lessons learned from the study. Some of those thoughts are briefly presented here.

The past few years have been very busy ones in Alberta. As shown in the timeline in Figure 1, not a month has gone by without a major government budgetary announcement or restructuring initiative.[1] The tabling of the provincial budget in February 1996, which predicted a budgetary surplus over the coming fiscal year of between $23 million and $500 million, marked the culmination of a three-year process that saw a substantial reduction in real per capita government expenditures. Table 1 shows real per capita spending by government departments over the period from 1992/3 to 1998/9[2]. Overall, real per capita spending is expected to decline by 38 per cent over this period. This is a substantial reduction in the government's share of economic activity. As the table shows, in some areas the reduction was much greater than average and in others much less; however, no agency or department was left untouched.

There may be a tendency to equate a 38 per cent reduction in the size of the government with a similar reduction in the quantity and quality of services provided by the government. This need not be the case, particularly if service delivery can be reconfigured in a more efficient way. While it is too early to assess fully the impact of the spending reductions in this regard, we can examine the process underlying the reductions. Although it would be naïve and

**Figure 1:** From Deficit to Surplus under Ralph Klein: December 1992 to June 1995

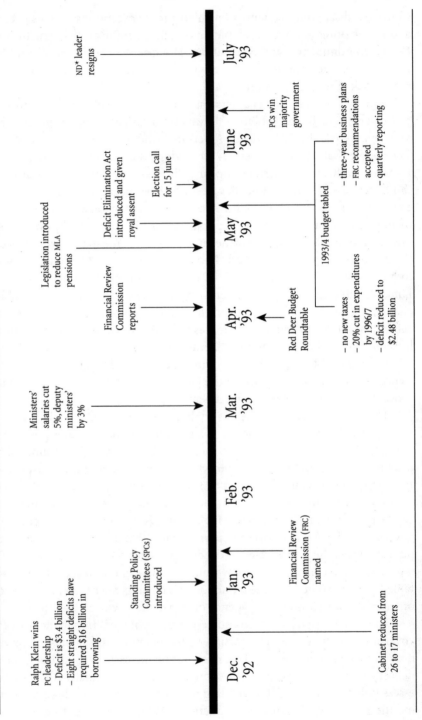

*In Alberta, 'ND' is the abbreviated designation of the New Democratic Party.

**Figure 1:** (Continued)

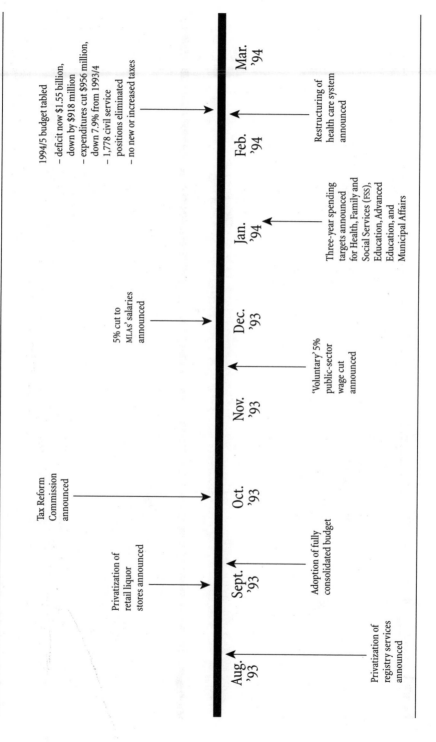

**Figure 1:** (Continued)

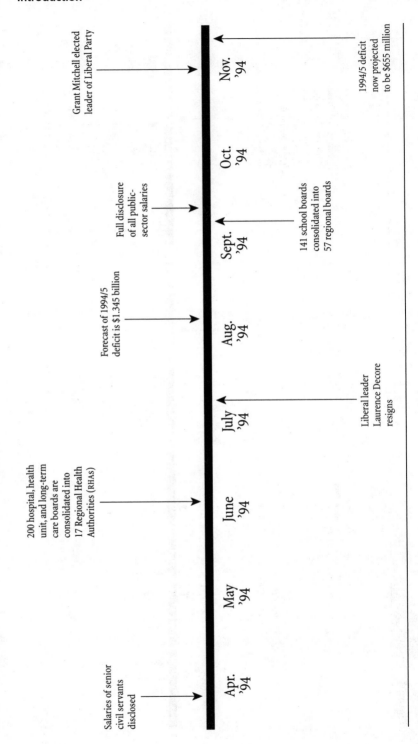

Salaries of senior civil servants disclosed

200 hospital, health unit, and long-term care boards are consolidated into 17 Regional Health Authorities (RHAs)

Forecast of 1994/5 deficit is $1.345 billion

Full disclosure of all public-sector salaries

Grant Mitchell elected leader of Liberal Party

Liberal leader Laurence Decore resigns

141 school boards consolidated into 57 regional boards

1994/5 deficit now projected to be $655 million

Apr. '94   May '94   June '94   July '94   Aug. '94   Sept. '94   Oct. '94   Nov. '94

**Figure 1:** (Continued)

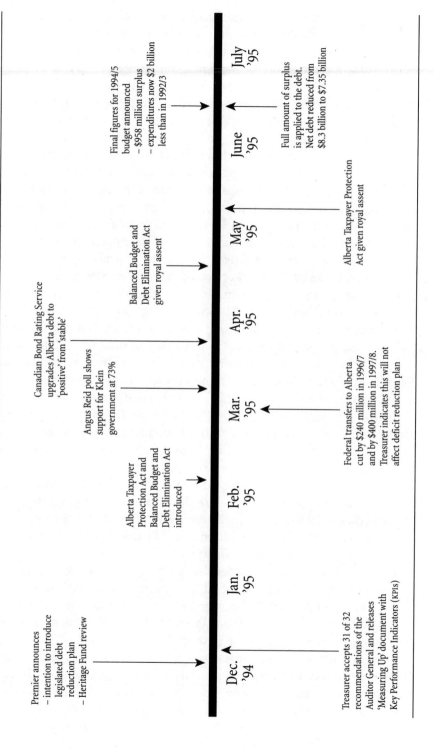

Premier announces
– intention to introduce legislated debt reduction plan
– Heritage Fund review

Canadian Bond Rating Service upgrades Alberta debt to 'positive' from 'stable'

Angus Reid poll shows support for Klein government at 73%

Alberta Taxpayer Protection Act and Balanced Budget and Debt Elimination Act introduced

Balanced Budget and Debt Elimination Act given royal assent

Final figures for 1994/5 budget announced
– $958 million surplus
– expenditures now $2 billion less than in 1992/3

Dec. '94    Jan. '95    Feb. '95    Mar. '95    Apr. '95    May '95    June '95    July '95

Treasurer accepts 31 of 32 recommendations of the Auditor General and releases 'Measuring Up' document with Key Performance Indicators (KPIs)

Federal transfers to Alberta cut by $240 million in 1996/7 and by $400 million in 1997/8. Treasurer indicates this will not affect deficit reduction plan

Alberta Taxpayer Protection Act given royal assent

Full amount of surplus is applied to the debt. Net debt reduced from $8.3 billion to $7.35 billion misleading to claim that the government's deficit elimination program has had no impact on service delivery in the province, after studying the program for the past year we feel confident that in many cases processes have been established that will act to minimize the impact on service delivery, and indeed in some cases service delivery may even have been enhanced. In other cases the reforms have not been well conceived, and service delivery likely will suffer to some extent. However, one thing that struck us time and time again was the remarkable resilience and flexibility of the public sector when it was asked to make substantial changes. Although we have observed the posturing, turf-protecting, and gamesmanship that one comes to expect of any large bureaucracy in transition, particularly, perhaps, a government bureaucracy, we also witnessed agencies and organizations and, most importantly, individuals responding to an often difficult situation with, if not enthusiasm (although in many cases there was that), then steadfast resolve and determination. In many cases it appears that the fiscal imperative provided the impetus to unleash creative and innovative energy that had been constrained by the status quo.

Will the changes stick? Only time will tell. Prior to the release of the February 1996 budget Premier Klein was talking about 'rewarding' Albertans for the 'sacrifices' they had made over the past three years. Some extra spending was announced, and a promise was made of widespread consultation as to what to do with the portion of the government surplus not earmarked by legislation for debt repayment. None the less, the slow speed with which public-sector institutions are often thought to change suggests that although major structural changes may take place only rarely and abruptly, the ramifications of these changes are likely to remain well into the future. Governments are defeated, prevailing ideologies change, and any number of exogenous events can affect government fiscal balances. Institutions, however, are long enduring. Even though the reforms were precipitated by the perception of a fiscal crisis, we have little doubt that the changes introduced by the Klein government have indelibly changed the institutional landscape in Alberta for some time to come. The decision-making structure within public institutions in the province differs substantially from what existed prior to 1993. From school boards to Regional Health Authorities, to agencies providing social services for children, the power structure has been altered, and the policy-making process in the future will reflect this. While the structure of these institutions will no doubt evolve over time, it may take another 'crisis' to precipitate a shift of the magnitude we have witnessed over the past three years.

Can the Alberta experiment act as a template for other governments? While many aspects of the reforms certainly are unique to Alberta, the processes underlying their implementation—both the good and the bad—can offer lessons to other governments. Here, too, only time will tell.

This volume owes its existence to many individuals. First and foremost, we owe a great debt to the Donner Canadian Foundation, which both encouraged and financed the project. In particular, we thank the Foundation's Patrick Luciani, who provided valuable input and support throughout the project. Our debt to the authors and discussants of the various chapters is obvious. On their behalf, we thank those who joined us for a conference in Banff, 3–5 November 1995, where preliminary versions of the chapters appearing in this volume were presented and discussed. Many of the participants were from other provinces and they greatly enhanced the debate by sharing the experience of budget-cutting in their own provinces and by offering differing points of view. We would also like to thank Devon Moodly, Andrew Bradford, and Doug McClintock for research assistance, and Moira Jensen for secretarial help. A special thanks is owed to Shelley Radway, who acted as a full-time research assistant for much of the project, but who went well beyond what was expected of her in that capacity. Finally, we would like to thank the many individuals working in the Alberta government and its related agencies, most particularly the cabinet ministers, civil servants, agency employees, and MLAs, who agreed to be interviewed for the project. Of this group, we owe special thanks to Premier Ralph Klein and Treasurer Jim Dinning, who not only agreed to be interviewed but also encouraged others to speak with us.

## NOTES

1. Figure 1 is adapted from a similar figure in *The Klein Government at Two: Staying the Course*. Government Policy Consultants (Edmonton, 1995).

2. The data in Table 1 show the fiscal plan as of February 1996. Since that time, the Klein government has announced plans to reduce the size of some of these expenditure cuts. Most of these cutback reductions have occurred in the area of Health. The budget presented in February 1997 revises the targets for 1998/9 to the following amounts:

Health: $4,018 million; a cumulative nominal cut of 3.8 per cent from 1992/3 and a cumulative real per capita cut of 23 per cent.

Total expenditures: $12,949 million; a cumulative nominal cut of 17 per cent from 1992/3 and a cumulative real per capita cut of 33.8 per cent.

# PART I

# Overview and Theory

# CHAPTER 2

# Fiscal Restructuring in Alberta: An Overview

*Robert L. Mansell*

## 1. INTRODUCTION

During Alberta's economic and fiscal boom of the 1970s, the size of the provincial government and its expenditures increased dramatically.[1] Even so, there was an accumulation of large fiscal surpluses, primarily as a result of burgeoning resource revenues. This comfortable situation quickly changed in the 1980s with, first the introduction of the National Energy Program and then, in 1986, the collapse of oil and grain prices. The faltering economy and the major declines in resource revenues led to a string of large deficits and a structural deficit of about $2.5 billion. By the 1991/2 fiscal year, the provincial government had exhausted its substantial net asset position and had accumulated a net debt of $2 billion. The deficit for the following year was $3.2 billion. In spite of some increases in taxes and attempts to reduce expenditures to more sustainable levels, the government was unable to close the large gap between annual revenues and expenditures. Put simply, there seemed to be the same inability in Alberta to resolve this deficit problem that was observed at the federal level and in other provinces.

In December of 1992, Ralph Klein won the leadership campaign of the Conservative Party and became Premier of Alberta. Within a few short months of this event it was becoming clear that his government was intent on waging a bold and aggressive attack on the fiscal deficit. The focus would be on a fiscal revolution involving major budget cuts and a restructuring of much of the public sector in the province.

The subsequent provincial election campaign focused on the elimination of the large fiscal deficits. The main combatants were the Conservatives and Liberals, with both arguing for massive spending cuts. On 15 June 1993 Klein's Conservative Party, receiving 44 per cent of the popular vote, was elected with a comfortable majority in the legislature. With the election out of the way, the fiscal revolution intensified. Targets were put in place involving cuts of about

20 per cent in spending by the government, with most of these occurring over a period of just two years. Other important initiatives included changes aimed at: improving the province's fiscal management, accounting, and reporting systems; rationalizing administration and reducing regulation; requiring government departments and agencies to operate more efficiently and be more accountable; privatizing the delivery of some government services; and implementing legislation to entrench the goal of balanced budgets and ensure that the province's debt would be reduced over time.

At the time, most governments had yet to admit that rapidly growing levels of public-sector debt were a serious problem and those that did recognize the seriousness of the problem were promoting gradualist approaches. That is, they argued that further increases in taxes and reductions in the rate of increase in expenditures was all that was really required to allow economic growth to solve the problem of growing debt levels.

The fiscal plan of the Klein government was quite different; there would be no further tax increases and expenditures would be cut substantially and quickly. This program has received considerable attention elsewhere in Canada and in the international press. Much of the national press has typically portrayed it as the agenda of a right-wing government primarily supported by the wealthy, a threat to all that is Canadian, and a program that is both unwanted and unneeded by other governments in Canada.[2] On the other hand, the international attention (for example, as reflected by articles in the *New York Times*, the *Wall Street Journal*, and *Barron's Magazine*) has typically focused on the imagination and originality in dealing with a difficult problem, the common-sense appeal, and the lessons for other deficit-ridden governments. Such large disparities in assessments alone provide adequate justification for a detailed analysis of the Alberta experiment.

The general objective in this paper is to provide the background, perspective, and context necessary to understand and evaluate the approach to fiscal problems by the Klein government. In addition to providing a review of Alberta's fiscal and economic history, I intend to summarize the nature of the province's fiscal problems at the time the new government came to power. Other objectives are to outline the specific elements of the fiscal restructuring by the Klein government, to discuss the political and economic logic of the program, and to compare the Alberta fiscal program with the approaches to deficit elimination in other jurisdictions.

The following section provides an abbreviated fiscal and economic history of the province. It begins with a summary of the pre-1970 period in an attempt to highlight certain themes relevant to understanding more recent developments. The period from 1970 to 1993 is examined in greater detail, with a focus on the causes of the fiscal problems and the earlier attempts to deal with them.

A summary of the landscape and alternatives facing the Klein government is then presented. It deals mainly with features such as the relative size of the deficit, the nature of the debt problem, the fiscal experiences in other jurisdictions, and the political environment. The next section provides a summary of the fiscal plan introduced by the Klein government, along with a general outline of the political and economic logic. Finally, some concluding observations are offered.

## 2. HISTORICAL PERSPECTIVE

### 2.1 The 1905–1971 Period

*Rapid Expansion and Debt*

The first two decades of Alberta's history after it achieved provincial status within Canada represented a period of rapid growth and considerable variability. Between 1906 and 1911 the population doubled and by 1929 it was almost four times the level in 1906, one year after Alberta became a province.[3] This growth created a rapid increase in the demand for basic infrastructure.

In the absence of financial assistance from the Dominion government, the provincial governments of the day felt they had to respond on their own. Without an income tax, they were forced to borrow substantial amounts of money relative to the province's output or Gross Domestic Product (GDP). However, these governments, beginning with the Liberal government of Alex Rutherford, which served until 1910, had visions well beyond basic infrastructure. Alberta was the first to develop a large-scale telephone infrastructure. The provincial government also provided many loan guarantees, most notably for the construction of railways, such as the Alberta and Great Waterways Railway from Edmonton to Fort McMurray. It also became indebted as a result of other initiatives like the Livestock Encouragement Act, the Seed Grain and Relief Acts, and irrigation projects. During this period the government was frequently accused of overzealous expansion.

It is noteworthy that this first attempt at province-building through loan guarantees, like similar attempts in the 1980s, was far from successful. Indeed, Premier Rutherford conveniently stepped down before the release of the report on the Alberta and Great Waterways Railway scandal. He was replaced by Arthur Sifton, who further expanded the government's involvement in railway construction.[4] Following a brief period under Charles Stewart, the Liberals were replaced by the United Farmers of Alberta in 1921.

By 1922, Alberta's debt was double that of Saskatchewan, even though Saskatchewan's population was about a third larger. During the 1920s large year-to-year variations in output and income continued, but there was a strong growth trend until the end of the period.[5] While the new government was able to reduce certain controllable expenditures by over $1 million, fixed charges (primarily those related to servicing the debt and loan guarantees) increased by $2 million. Net debt continued to rise (from $75 million in 1922 to $98 million in 1929), but net debt as a percentage of GDP was falling (from 34 per cent in 1922 to 22 per cent in 1929). According to some indexes of sustainability (see Boothe, 1994b), the government seemed to be successful in reducing the probability of default. However, in retrospect, it was already too late to avoid the default that would occur in 1936.

*Depression and Default*

By increasing taxes, reducing some expenditures, and, in 1929 and 1930, selling off its railroad assets to reduce the debt, the province was able to decrease the net debt by 1930 to what it had been in 1922. However, the slowing economy and the inability to reduce the main expenditures (on old age security and interest on the debt) meant a rapidly deteriorating fiscal situation. By 1933 Alberta GDP had fallen to just over 50 per cent of the level in 1929 and by 1935 it was still only 61 per cent of this level.[6] Between 1930 and 1932 alone, the provincial government's revenue dropped by 25 per cent. In 1933 an income tax was introduced and all other taxes were increased to achieve a primary surplus.[7] However, by 1936 interest on the debt was consuming 40 per cent of ordinary revenue and the Social Credit government of William Aberhart, which was elected in 1935, undertook a number of desperate actions. An Ultimate Purchaser's Tax was introduced in 1936 (but suspended in 1937); the government reduced the interest rates payable on bonds and savings certificates by 50 per cent; and bonds were not honoured for redemption except in cases of personal emergency. The Bank of Canada refused to provide any assistance and the province was forced to default on its debt in 1936.

As was the case immediately following its election, the Aberhart government continued its attempts to implement the monetary-reform ideas of Major C.H. Douglas, the Englishman whose doctrines formed the basis of the Social Credit movement, but these were thwarted by challenges under the British North America Act. With the election of the government of Ernest Manning in 1944, the province gradually moved away from the Social Credit dogma of Major Douglas and towards more conventional ideas and policies.

Over the period 1937–45, the economy continued to improve, largely as a result of the war-induced recovery of grain prices, but it was still subject to considerable variability. As noted by Hanson (1952), policies such as those by the federal government that froze wheat prices below world levels and an embargo on imported cattle by the United States further accentuated the swings in the economy. Over this period there was little additional agricultural settlement. Rather, the main change was an acceleration of the mechanization of agriculture and the shift of the population from rural to urban areas. Since other parts of the provincial economy were unable to absorb this exodus from agriculture, there was an increasing net outflow of people from the province, mainly to Ontario, British Columbia, and the US.

### The Dynamic Decade and Beyond

As noted by Hanson (1958), the provincial economy was dramatically transformed over the period 1946–56 with the emergence of the petroleum sector. Although there were significant discoveries of oil and gas in Alberta in earlier periods, this new industry only came of age after the Leduc No. 1 oil discovery in 1947. This was quickly followed by a string of other major finds, leading to a sevenfold increase in investment in the province between 1946 and 1956.[8] Over this decade, the share of provincial output associated with mining (which includes the petroleum sector) went from 10 to 26 per cent, the share of the construction sector grew from 14 to 26 per cent, and agriculture's share fell from 54 to 27 per cent (Hanson, 1958).

The growth of the petroleum industry had a number of important impacts on the provincial economy. It quickly led to a reversal of the population net outflow so that the province entered another period of rapid population growth. Except for three years in the mid-1960s, net migration to Alberta remained positive and significant over this era. And, taking account of the direct and indirect effects, by 1971 the petroleum sector accounted for about one-half of the Alberta economy.[9]

The development of this sector had other impacts as well. The high capital intensity of the oil and gas industries, combined with the specialized and technological nature of the input requirements, provided for the development of important backward and forward industrial linkages in the province. As such, it quickly became a key or propulsive industry capable of generating large impacts on most sectors and regions in Alberta. As noted by Norrie (1984), this pattern of development closely followed that predicted by the staple or export theory and would likely mean continued dominance by the primary sector. That is, such development leads to a large primary sector that exports most of its output, an underdeveloped manufacturing sector, and an industrial sector based on providing inputs for the extractive sector or processing raw materials prior to export.

Nevertheless, as emphasized by Hanson (1958), the high productivity of the petroleum sector and the requirements for a highly skilled labour force translated into above-average wage levels in petroleum and related activities, the development of a highly skilled labour force in the region, and an impetus for urbanization. By speeding up the rural-to-urban population shift and providing the base for a large managerial/entrepreneurial class, the petroleum sector also played a major role in the political transformation of the province, marked by the election of the Conservatives in 1971.[10] As described by Richards and Pratt (1979), this involved the replacement of a populist-agrarian political regime with one embodying the values and methods of a new managerial urban élite.

Alberta's fiscal situation showed marked improvement with the development of the petroleum sector after 1947. It provided large resource revenues for the government, and other tax revenues increased as a result of the economic growth generated by oil. Total revenues for the provincial government rose from $45 million in 1946/7 to $250 million in 1956/7 (about one-half of the latter amount coming from royalties, leases, and rentals). Over this same period, the government's net asset position went from a net debt of $118 million to a net asset of $253 million.[11]

By 1956/7 expenditures were beginning to catch up to revenues, largely because of the transfers to local governments to assist them in meeting the rapidly growing infrastructure demands in the urban centres. Nevertheless, under the careful and conservative stewardship of the Manning governments, the province had managed this period of rapid growth and development in the province while maintaining relatively low tax levels and generally balanced budgets.

During the 1960s, the Alberta economy exhibited relative stability, largely due to the stabilizing impacts of the petroleum sector. Except for the early part of the decade, the economy grew at a rate at or slightly above the national average, net migration to the province was significant and positive, and the unemployment rate remained well below that for Canada.[12] With the end to the boom levels of investment in the 1950s, the province became more and more reliant on increasing levels of oil and gas production to provide the stimulus for growth since oil and gas prices remained low and steadily declined in real terms.

## 2.2 The 1971–1993 Period

*Another Boom: 1971–1981*

Alberta entering the 1970s was very much a product of the history previously described. It had become a modern, largely urban society. The residents had achieved a standard of living and per capita income about equal to the Canadian average. Almost half were born in other provinces or countries and came to the province in search of economic opportunity. This self-selection meant that a high proportion of the population could be classified as risk-takers: entrepreneurial, mobile, and economically motivated. Their values and the overall character of the province had also been profoundly shaped by Alberta's industrial heritage. Both the agriculture and petroleum industries tend to be typified by capital-intensive production processes, a high degree of risk, externally determined and highly variable prices and policies, and a large number of independent producing units. The development of the petroleum sector simply enhanced the basically rural conservative values of rugged individualism, risk-taking, entrepreneurship, and a unique mix of self-reliance and co-operation.

The capital intensity of agriculture and petroleum and the large number of independent producing units generally meant that there was not a broad base in Alberta for organized labour or the associated values. There was a wide-spread respect for and acceptance of market forces and the need to adjust to shifts in the market. At the same time, this vulnerability to the vagaries of inter-national markets and nature would generate a keen awareness that the threats were primarily external rather than coming from within the province. This, combined with the reality or perception that national policies would typically favour the industrial heartland at the expense of the hinterland, could explain the widespread sense of economic alienation and the appeal of politicians emphasizing the need to 'circle the wagons' to face the enemy, keeping backs exposed only to those within the province. It is possible that these characteris-tics can also help explain the tendency for Albertans to prefer long-serving gov-ernments with little effective opposition in the legislature.[13]

Within this general environment, the Conservative government of Peter Lougheed was elected in 1971, terminating the reign of Social Credit, which had been in power since 1935. This has been characterized by Richards and Pratt (1979) as the inevitable outcome of the urbanization of Alberta and the growth of an indigenous managerial class. Although almost all of the expertise and finance associated with the development of the oil and gas industry had initially been from outside the province, by the end of the 1960s there was a growing managerial and professional class with strong Alberta roots. Peter Lougheed was an exemplary member of this class and he captured the senti-ment that it was time for a change, that the province needed to become less reliant on a depleting resource, that diversification and industrial development were essential to break the cycle of boom and bust, and that more of the deci-sions affecting Alberta's economic future needed to be made in Alberta. As noted by Tupper and Urquhart (1992), Alberta seems to have a traditional paradox concerning the government's role. That is, the provincial government must be rhetorically *laissez-faire* but interventionist in practice, particularly with respect to policies aimed at escaping the cycles of boom and bust. The Lougheed governments would seem to fit this classification.

Shortly after the election, the OPEC oil embargo in 1973 initiated a dramatic upward spiral in the international price of oil. One of the first acts of the Lougheed government was to increase its share of energy rents, first by intro-ducing a new mineral tax and then by replacing that tax and the 16⅔ per cent statutory royalty of the Social Credit governments with a new scheme whereby royalties were tied to the energy prices. Royalties collected by the government increased from $260 million in 1972 to $560 million in 1974. The stated purpose of these additional revenues was to bring about industrial diversification.[14] The view of the government at the time was that Alberta had perhaps a decade to accomplish this before an inevitable and substantial decline occurred in the province's production of oil and gas.

Shortly after the initial increases in oil prices, the federal government implemented a number of policies involving price controls on oil and gas, export taxes, restrictions to exports, and increased federal taxes on energy producers, all over the strong objections of the provincial government. While these greatly reduced the province's share of the energy rents, the total amount of resource revenue flowing to the government of Alberta still increased sharply. As shown in Figure 1, there was a steady increase to 1980, at which time per capita resource revenue (measured in 1971 dollars) reached over $1,000.

The budgets over the 1972–81 period brought in a number of tax reductions. These included a reduction in property taxes in 1973, a reduction in gasoline, other fuel, and property taxes in 1974, a 28 per cent decrease in personal income taxes in 1975, elimination of taxes on motor fuels and further reductions in property taxes in 1978, an increase in the tax exemption levels for

**Figure 1:** Real Per Capita Natural Resource Revenue, Alberta (in 1971 dollars)

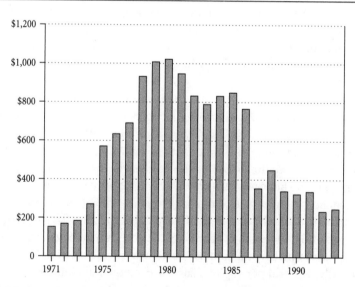

NOTE: In comparison, the average real per capita resource revenue for the other provinces has typically been less than $50.

SOURCE: Population figures from Cansim matrices 6369–72 and 6219–23. Provincial CPI indexes from matrices 1860–9. Financial Management System (FMS) data for resource revenues from matrices 2808–17.

**Figure 2:** Real Per Capita Provincial Government Revenue for Alberta and Other Provinces (in 1971 dollars; average is for provinces excluding Alberta)

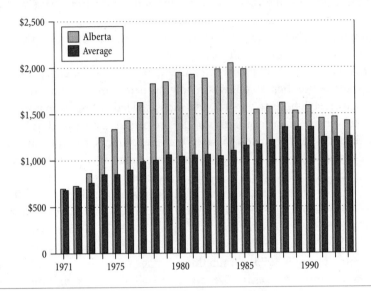

SOURCE: FMS revenue figures from Cansim matrices 6769–78. See Figure 1 for population and price index sources.

lower income groups, and a decrease in the small business corporate tax in 1979 (Smith, 1991: 252). In spite of these tax reductions, the growth in resource revenues and the increases in other revenues as a result of the rapid growth in the economy generated a steady rise in real per capita revenues. As indicated in Figure 2, by 1980 these were about double the average for the other provinces.

Real per capita program spending by the provincial government increased slightly in the years to 1974. Thereafter it began to increase sharply with every election but with some partial downward corrections after the election spending spree.[15] As indicated in Figure 3, there was a series of unusually large increases in 1979. Boothe (1990: 14) noted that the increase in real per capita program spending between 1979 and 1982 was 62 per cent, 'an increase probably unmatched elsewhere in Canada in peace-time.' His experiments also suggest that 1978 was the final year of sustainable spending levels in Alberta.

In spite of the increases in spending, the government began running large fiscal surpluses, which by the mid-1970s were averaging between $2 and $3 billion annually. The real per capita balances are shown in Figure 4. In 1976, the Alberta Heritage Savings Trust Fund (AHSTF) was established. The three goals of this fund were to save for the future, to strengthen and diversify Alberta's economy, and to improve the quality of Alberta life.[16] From 1976 to 1982, a total of $8.3 billion was transferred to the AHSTF and all income earned by the fund

**Figure 3:** Real Per Capita Provincial Government Expenditures for Alberta and Other Provinces (in 1971 dollars; average is for provinces excluding Alberta)

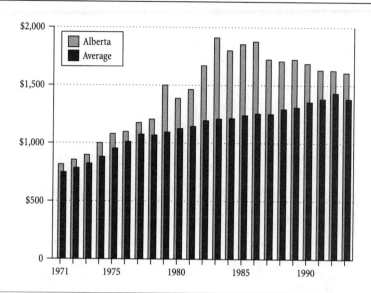

SOURCE: FMS expenditures for provincial governments from Cansim matrices 6769–78.

was reinvested in it. The annual transfer was equal to 30 per cent of resource revenue. After September 1982, the investment income earned by the AHSTF was transferred back to the General Revenue account. In 1982/3 the annual contribution was reduced to 15 per cent of resource revenues, and in 1987/8 no further transfers were to be made to the AHSTF and all investment income continued to flow to General Revenues. The contributions to the fund from 1983 to 1987 amounted to just $3.72 billion. The annual transfers from the AHSTF peaked at $1.7 billion in 1985/6 and have declined fairly steadily to about $1 billion for the current budget year.[17]

It is useful to note some similarities and differences between this and earlier boom periods. As with the initial boom at the beginning of the century, provincial government expenditures increased dramatically. A large percentage of these expenditures involved capital projects that, because they entail ongoing operating expenditures and obligations, would have a lasting effect on future expenditure levels. A similarity with the initial boom period after Alberta became a province is that the provincial government was very interventionist. Also, like the earlier period, the financial obligations incurred by the government to maintain expenditure levels and prime the economy after the end of the boom of the 1970s would lead to large losses and a rapid build-up of

**Figure 4:** Real Per Capita Provincial Government Balances for Alberta, 1971–1993 (in 1971 dollars)

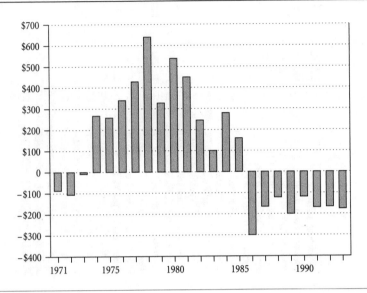

SOURCE:  See Figures 2 and 3.

debt. An important difference is that, unlike the first major boom, the government had accumulated a large net asset position. In contrast to these booms, the degree of intervention and the increases in government expenditures during the rapid expansion of the post-war dynamic decade appear to have been much more contained and sustainable. Nevertheless, in all cases there seems to be evidence that increases in revenues invariably lead to increases in expenditure levels.

Several other points are noteworthy. First, the boom of the 1970s, like the case of previous booms, was never really seen by the government as an economic boom but, rather, as a permanently higher growth path. This view prevailed until the subsequent economic bust was well entrenched. That is, in spite of the historical evidence that periods of rapid growth are typically relatively short-lived and almost always end in 'bust', there seems to be great difficulty in containing the psychology of extrapolation. It might be recalled that even well into the 1980s, after there was ample evidence of a softening in world oil prices, the common projections called for continued and dramatic long-term increases in energy prices. Within this context, the difficulties of the provincial government in containing increases in expenditures can be appreciated. Some might argue that the creation of the AHSTF was necessary if only because it would have been impossible for the provincial government to increase spending further without creating excessive inflationary pressures. However, it could also be viewed as the product of a few who actually recognized the situation as a boom and the need to resist the pressure for even higher spending.

A second point is that there is a fundamental conflict even for governments that recognize a boom and see an increased need to diversify or otherwise achieve a more stable and sustainable economy. As emphasized by Norrie, in the case of a small, open, resource-based economy such as Alberta's, a booming resource sector will tend to result in an economy even more specialized in, and dependent on, that sector.[18] For example, in the case of Alberta, by 1980 the petroleum sector's direct contribution alone to the province's GDP increased to almost 25 per cent and resource revenues amounted to $4.5 billion or almost 80 per cent of total revenues (of $5.7 billion).[19] At the same time, however, this increased specialization and volatility 'provided the incentive, along with the revenue and regulatory powers to achieve exactly the opposite outcome' (Norrie, 1984: 75).

### Hard Times and Recovery: 1981–1993

Although some of the seeds for an economic bust were sown in the 1970s by predictable market forces and adjustments, a major turning point in the Alberta economy occurred with the introduction of the National Energy Program (NEP) towards the end of 1980. Within a year it generated a massive shift of investment out of the province and further increased the large transfers out of Alberta by the federal government. In combination with high interest rates and a slowdown in other regions, the effect was a sharp reversal in Alberta's economic fortunes.[20] Figures 5 and 6, which show net migration (a sensitive measure of relative regional economic performance) and the Alberta unemployment rate for the 1971–94 period, illustrate the magnitude of the downturn.

After a partial recovery in 1984 and 1985, the provincial economy was hit with another major shock. Almost immediately after the deregulation of domestic oil prices (which allowed domestic prices to rise to the international price), in 1986 the world oil price fell to about half the level in the previous year. In addition, grain prices dropped dramatically. Consequently, the value of Alberta's exports fell by almost 25 per cent. This downturn in the provincial economy triggered another wave of net out-migration and, in spite of the reduction in the labour force, the unemployment rate rose above the national average for the first time in many decades. Total employment in the province did not reach the 1981 level until the summer of 1987 and the growth rate for GDP remained below the national average from 1982 to 1988.

As indicated in Figure 1, resource revenue for the provincial government fell sharply with the introduction of the NEP in late 1980 and then again in 1986

**Figure 5:** Net Migration to Alberta, 1971–1993

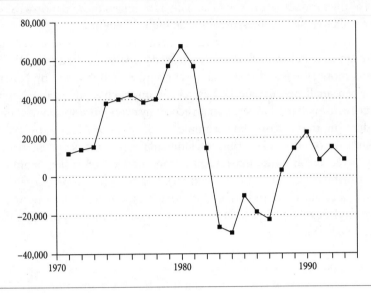

SOURCE:  Statistics Canada, Cat. No. 91–002.

**Figure 6:** Alberta Unemployment Rate, 1971–1993

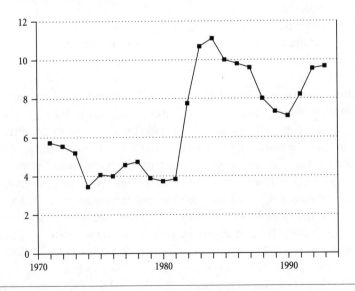

SOURCE:  Statistics Canada, Cat. No. 71–201.

with the drop in oil prices. Resource revenues fell from about $4.5 billion in 1980/1 to $1.4 billion in 1986/7. While there was some recovery in crude oil prices in subsequent years (but only to about two-thirds the level of domestic prices in 1985), natural gas prices began a significant decline following the deregulation of gas markets and prices. However, with the expansion in oil and gas production resulting from market and price deregulation, resource revenues showed some recovery from the levels in 1986/7. Over the period 1989/90 to 1993/4 they have averaged $2.4 billion annually, well below the levels during the late 1970s and early 1980s.[21]

As shown in Figure 2, total budgetary revenue (on a real per capita basis) dropped in 1986 by about 25 per cent from what it was in the previous seven or eight years. Although it was still somewhat above the average in other provinces, it exhibited a pattern of secular decline. This was in spite of a number of tax increases, including: an almost quadrupling of the cigarette tax, a 47 per cent increase in health premiums, and increases in liquor control board mark-ups in the 1983 budget; an increase in personal income tax rates from 38.5 to 43.5 per cent of basic federal tax effective 1 January 1984; and, in the 1987/8 budget, a further increase in personal tax rates to 46.5 per cent of basic tax, the imposition of an 8 per cent surtax, the addition of a 1 per cent flat rate tax on taxable income, the reintroduction of taxes on motor fuels, further increases in liquor control board mark-ups, another doubling of the tobacco tax, the introduction of a hotel room tax, an increase of 25 per cent in health insurance premiums, and an increase in the general corporate tax rate from 11 per cent to 15 per cent.[22] Also, as noted earlier, by 1987/8 there were no further transfers of resource revenue to the AHSTF and all income generated by the fund was transferred to General Revenues.

As indicated in Figure 3, real per capita expenditures by the Alberta government increased dramatically from 1981 to 1983 and then stabilized at these higher levels until 1987. The expenditure plans outlined in the budgets over this period can be summarized as follows:

1980/1: Major increases in most operating and capital budgets.

1981/2: Major increases in most operating and capital budgets.

1982/3: The introduction of an Alberta Economic Resurgence Plan to deal with the negative effects of the NEP on the petroleum sector and the downturn in the economy (this plan was estimated to cost about $1 billion in the first year and involved a variety of measures to restore oil and gas activity, increases for advanced education, interest shielding programs, and so on).

1983/4: A 'hold-the-line' approach involving a reduction in the growth rate for expenditures from 7.5 per cent to 2.3 per cent.

1984/5: Another 'hold-the-line' budget.

1985/6: An increase of 14 per cent in expenditures, with major increases in support for farmers and livestock producers and a substantial royalty reduction and incentive program for the petroleum sector.

1986/7: A plan for a slight reduction in expenditures.

1987/8: The plan was to reduce program expenditures by 6.3 per cent and move to a balanced budget by 1990/1.

1988/9: The expenditure plan was to increase program spending slightly.

1989/90: Program expenditures were to increase by 5.5 per cent.

1990/1: Program spending was to be up only slightly and the government stated that it was more than halfway towards meeting the target of a balanced budget by 1991/2.

1991/2: Program spending was to fall by about 2.7 per cent (while there were planned increases in Health, Education, and Social Services, the budgets for many other departments were to be significantly reduced) and a small surplus was forecast for 1991/2: the actual deficit for 1991/2 ballooned to about $1.5 billion.

1992/3: Program spending was expected to increase by about 2.3 per cent and there was a plan to introduce spending control legislation to limit annual increases to 2.5 per cent, 2.25 per cent, and 2 per cent over a three-year period.

The revenue and expenditure policies led to surpluses until 1982/3, at which time there was a small deficit, then a small surplus in 1983/4 and a surplus of about $1.6 billion in 1984/5 (see R. Smith, 1991: 240). However, after 1985/6 the provincial government ran substantial deficits until the surpluses recorded by the Klein government in 1994/5. The first large deficit occurred in 1986/7 and amounted to almost $3.5 billion, equal to about 6 per cent of GDP. For the period 1986/7 to 1992/3, the annual deficit averaged $2.3 billion. The projected budget balances and the actual or realized balances are shown in Figure 7.

In summary, it would appear that the provincial government's response to the growing downturn in the economy in the early 1980s was to increase expenditures dramatically. The Alberta Economic Resurgence Plan in 1982 exemplifies the attempt to reverse the direction of the economy through aggressive application of Keynesian policy. The expectation at the time seemed to be that there would be a fairly quick recovery once the worst features of the NEP were corrected and the other sectors of the economy pulled out of recession. The improvements in 1983 and especially in 1984 seemed to point in this direction. With the election of the Mulroney government at the federal level and the promise to end the NEP, a full recovery of the economy and the province's

**Figure 7:** Projected and Actual Surpluses/Deficits in Alberta, 1984/5 to 1994/5 (millions of dollars)

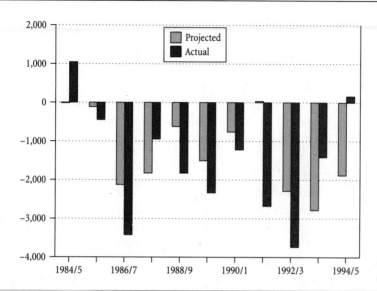

SOURCE: Data from Alberta Treasury, *Financial Summary and Budgetary Review and Budget Address* (various years). Actual deficits are estimated using subsequent information from the provincial budgets and accounts, with adjustments to reflect variations over time in accounting methodology used by the Provincial Treasurer.

resource revenues seemed likely.[23] In 1986, after Premier Lougheed stepped down, the government of Don Getty faced the dramatic decline in revenues associated with the collapse of oil and grain prices. As Getty noted later, he 'inherited an economy and budget based on $40 oil—and the price of oil was $13' (Boothe, 1994: 7).

Even after the collapse of oil and grain prices in 1986 it would appear that the dominant view within the government was that oil prices would rebound and resolve the growing deficit problem. A common expectation for many years was that oil prices would follow a hockey stick pattern. That is, they might remain flat for a period but would soon resume the ascent to much higher levels. Under this scenario it was just a matter of tolerating deficits until this price recovery occurred in the near future. By the latter part of the 1980s there seems to have been a shift in the plan. The fact that the government was prepared to increase taxes significantly suggests that the deficits were no longer seen as a transitory phenomenon. However, the view seems to have been that, with these increases in revenues and some control over the rate of increase in expenditures, the province would be able to grow out of the problem. Eventually, the revenue trajectory would meet the expenditure trajectory. As illustrated in Figure 4, this was not to be.

## 3. THE ENVIRONMENT IN 1993

### 3.1 The Economy

Ralph Klein won the Conservative leadership in December 1992 and became the Premier of Alberta. This new government almost immediately began working on a plan to deal with the province's serious fiscal deficit problem. Then, after winning the election in June 1993, a program that would become known as the Klein Revolution was quickly implemented. The economic environment at the time the new government was planning the restructuring of the province's finances was significantly different from that a decade earlier when the fiscal deficits became a major problem.

*Structural Changes*

The values for the location quotients[24] in Table 1 indicate that the structure of the Alberta economy in 1993 had changed markedly from that which existed a decade earlier when it still exhibited the extreme specialization in petroleum and related activities as a result of the energy boom. The location quotient for 'other primary' (a category dominated by oil and gas) suggests that by 1993 the petroleum sector, relative to the overall economy, had declined to about what it was in the late 1960s and early 1970s. Further, the relative contributions of this sector to provincial government revenues had fallen back to the levels several decades earlier.[25] The other notable changes included a decline in the relative size of the construction sector and gains in the relative size of the manufacturing sector.

Also, beginning in the late 1980s, there was significant growth in forestry and related activities. In general, as outlined in Mansell and Percy (1990), the end of the energy boom brought about a reversal of the trend of increased specialization in petroleum production. By 1993, the economy was more

**Table 1:** Location Quotients for Alberta Sectors (selected years)

| Sector | 1973 | 1983 | 1993 |
|---|---|---|---|
| Agriculture | 2.45 | 1.51 | 1.87 |
| Other Primary | 2.63 | 3.74 | 2.78 |
| Construction | 1.18 | 1.50 | 1.16 |
| Manufacturing | 0.41 | 0.43 | 0.51 |
| Transportation, Communications, and Utilities | 1.00 | 1.05 | 0.95 |
| Retail and Wholesale Trade | 1.09 | 1.05 | 0.99 |
| Finance, Insurance, and Real Estate | 1.06 | 0.98 | 0.81 |
| Community, Personal, and Business Services | 1.03 | 1.04 | 0.96 |
| Public Administration | 0.96 | 1.04 | 0.87 |

SOURCE: Calculated using employment data from Statistics Canada, Cat. No. 71–001.

**Figure 8:** Variability of GDP for Canadian Provinces

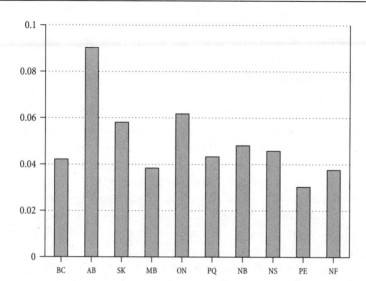

SOURCE: See Mansell and Percy (1990: 68–70) for the measure of Regional Economic Instability (REI). Index values are computed using data for the period 1961–93. The trend value used as the benchmark in computing annual variations is calculated using the Hodrick-Prescott filter. This filter allows the trend to follow the actual series without restricting the shape of the trend. The lambda value used is 100.

diversified and inherently more stable than it was in any period since the mid-1970s.

Nevertheless, the petroleum sector was still a key element of Alberta's economy. For example, in 1990 it directly accounted for almost 20 per cent of GDP, about 30 per cent of total investment, approximately 60 per cent of Alberta's exports, and roughly 30 per cent of provincial government revenues.[26] As such, the performance of oil and gas activities would continue to play a major role in determining the overall performance of the economy and the state of the province's finances.

Although the diversification achieved after the economic bust in the 1980s no doubt served to reduce the degree of variability, Alberta has typically had one of the least stable regional economies in Canada. For example, as shown in Figure 8, the values for a regional instability index indicate significantly higher variability of GDP for Alberta than for the other provinces over the period 1961–93.

Much of the diversification of the Alberta economy since the energy boom years has been achieved through the operation of market forces.[27] However, the provincial government had also engaged in aggressive attempts to assist in the development and expansion of new and existing industries in the period since the establishment of the AHSTF. Initially, this mainly involved a variety of projects and programs aimed at infrastructure development, assistance for research, and improvements in access to financial resources.[28] With the desperation of the early and mid-1980s, the government shifted to more direct methods of encouraging industrial development through the provision of loans, equity, and loan guarantees. There were many such interventions involving direct assistance to specific companies or private-sector projects. While there has not been an objective or comprehensive assessment of the benefits and costs to the province of these projects, any such study would be unlikely to endorse the approaches taken by the government. For example, since 1980 the government has written off almost $2.4 billion as a result of the failure of these types of projects and initiatives.[29] Such large losses would undoubtedly play a role in the decision of the Klein government to change direction dramatically in terms of the role of government in the business of the private sector.

Another important aspect of structural change concerned the dramatic restructuring within many Alberta industries that had already occurred by 1993. Much of this was in response to the lower energy prices (and lower primary commodity prices generally), as well as the increasing competitive pressures associated with freer trade and globalization. This restructuring involved many elements of downsizing, consolidation of assets, reductions in overheads, and streamlining to allow faster adjustment to a rapidly changing market environment. It is notable that over this period the provincial government, like most other governments, had to a large extent felt immune from these types of restructuring. With the launch of the Toward 2000 Together initiative,[30] the government of Alberta appears to have recognized that, if not because of market pressures, fiscal pressures alone would eventually require similar responses by governments.

It would seem that in 1993 the structure and basic character of the labour force and population were still much as they had been historically. Most of the population growth during the 1970s and 1980s had been through net in-migration. In spite of the out-migration following the NEP and the collapse of energy and grain prices, Alberta remained very much a province populated by people who had come in search of economic opportunity.[31] It also remained at or near the top in terms of education and skill levels of the labour force and had the lowest rate of unionization.[32] As described earlier, all of these characteristics, plus the dramatic adjustments at great cost during the downturn of the economy in the 1980s, point to a population that placed a high value on economic opportunity, recognized the need to adjust to external changes, and had the skills and experience at adjusting. These characteristics are particularly important in the context of the fiscal restructuring approach adopted by the provincial government.

*Performance of the Economy*

As shown in Figure 9, after a long and slow recovery, the Alberta economy expanded at a higher rate than the national average in 1988 and since then has managed in most years to maintain this distinction. A number of factors are behind this better-than-average performance. These include: a modest recovery in oil and gas prices (see Figures 10a and 10b), combined with adjustments in 1992 to make royalty rates more competitive and sensitive to the level of energy prices; a low value of the Canadian dollar (relative to the US dollar), which has meant increased Canadian dollar prices for oil, gas, and other exports, along with significant growth in foreign demand for these products; a stable level of oil production and rapid growth in gas production (see Figure 11); the increased competitiveness resulting from the restructuring, particularly after 1986; the growth of new primary sectors such as forestry and growth in sectors such as manufacturing.

In late 1992 and early 1993, however, it was far from clear that the performance of the Alberta economy would improve from the modest levels achieved in the first part of the 1990s. Most forecasts had been overly optimistic about the rate of recovery after the 1990–1 recession in Canada generally. At the time, Alberta's economic performance was typically seen as fragile. Consequently, while in retrospect it can be observed that the plans for large reductions in spending by the provincial government were well timed in terms

**Figure 9:** Growth Rates for Alberta and Canadian Real GDP, 1971–1993

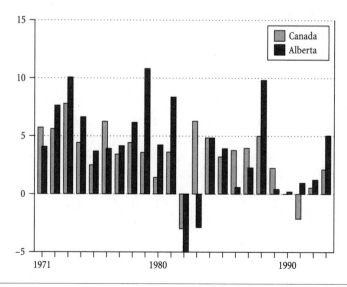

SOURCE: Data from Statistics Canada, Cansim matrix 6102.

**Figure 10a:** Real Oil Prices, 1993 US Dollars per Barrel, 1971–1994

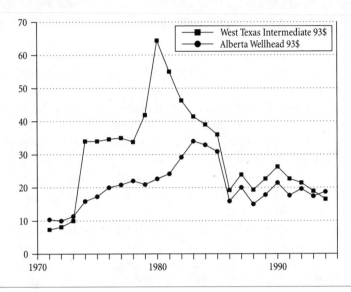

SOURCE: Data from Canadian Association of Petroleum Producers, *Statistical Handbook.*

**Figure 10b:** Real Gas Prices, 1993 Canadian Dollars per Million Cubic Feet, 1971–1994

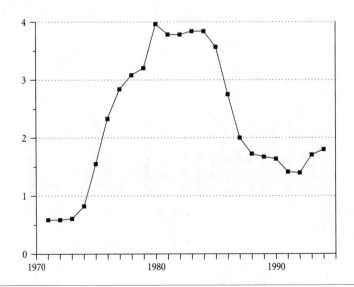

SOURCE: Data from Canadian Association of Petroleum Producers, *Statistical Handbook.*

**Figure 11:** Alberta Production of Oil and Gas, 1971–1994

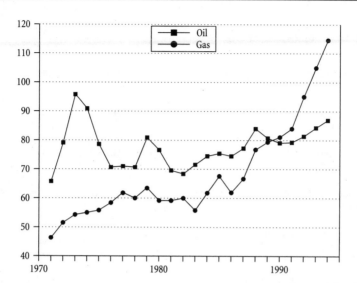

NOTE: Oil production is measured in millions of cubic metres. Gas production is measured in billions of cubic metres.
SOURCE: Data from Statistics Canada, Cat. No. 26–213.

of the economic cycle, this was far from obvious at the time. In fact, the common assessment by the Keynesian establishment in the intellectual heartland was that such cuts would almost certainly throw the economy into a 'made-in-Alberta' recession.

### 3.2 Fiscal Situation

*Deficits*

The 1992/3 budget prior to Ralph Klein becoming premier estimated a General Revenue Fund deficit of almost $2.3 billion and forecast additional deficits totalling $6.5 billion over the period to 1996/7.[33] The budget included plans for a continuation of salary and hiring freezes for some components of the civil service, increased contributions to pension plans administered by the government, the elimination of some committees and boards, and the introduction of legislated spending limits. There was no indication of how the government would eliminate the projected deficit of $1.1 billion in 1996/7 to meet its balanced budget target.

While the expected deficit was already large by most standards (taking into account population size and the level of GDP; see Table 2), the actual deficit would turn out to be much larger. Since the early 1980s there had been a pronounced tendency, as a result of both overestimation of revenues and

**Table 2:** Provincial Fiscal Comparisons (for 1992/3 unless noted otherwise)

|  | BC | AB | SK | MB | ON | PQ | NB | NS | PE | NF |
|---|---|---|---|---|---|---|---|---|---|---|
| 1. Prov. taxes as % of revenue | 60.1 | 40.4 | 52.9 | 54 | 71.9 | 67 | 47.8 | 46.5 | 41.5 | 41.6 |
| 2. Fed. transfers as % prov. rev. | 15.6 | 16.1 | 28.9 | 37.4 | 18.1 | 22.0 | 43 | 38.9 | 44.7 | 42.9 |
| 3. Prov. deficit as % of revenue | 12.2 | 20.1 | 13.6 | 6.8 | 28.5 | 14.0 | 11.9 | 22.2 | 12.1 | 8.3 |
| 4. Prov. debt service as % revenue | 5.0 | 10.5 | 16.8 | 10.6 | 12.7 | 13.6 | 13.2 | 23.1 | 14.6 | 15.0 |
| 5. Expenditures per capita ($) | 5,333.0 | 5,418.0 | 5,018.0 | 4,950.0 | 5,070.0 | 5,656.0 | 6,183.0 | 5,314.0 | 6,178.0 | 5,998.0 |
| 6. Non-supporting debt/GDP ratio (%) |  |  |  |  |  |  |  |  |  |  |
| 1988/9 | 11.0 | 18.7 | 33.7 | 29.5 | 17.1 | 35.3 | 28.7 | 38.5 | 31.4 | 51.5 |
| 1992/3 | 17.8 | 29.4 | 42.9 | 34.3 | 27.5 | 45.4 | 33.1 | 44.0 | 32.9 | 50.2 |
| 7. Credit rating (Moody's) |  |  |  |  |  |  |  |  |  |  |
| 1988 | Aa2 | Aa1 | A1 | A1 | Aaa | Aa3 | A1 | A2 | A3 | Baa1 |
| 1993 | Aa1 | Aa2 | A3 | A1 | Aa2 | A1 | A1 | A3 | A3 | Baa1 |
| 8. Basis point spread on 10-year provincial bonds relative to Canada 10-year bonds |  |  |  |  |  |  |  |  |  |  |
| 1988 | 55 | 50 | 52 | 61 | 55 | 60 | 70 | 80 | 90 | 93 |
| 1992 | 61 | 59 | 120 | 79 | 100 | 99 | 80 | 96 | 115 | 132 |
| 1995 (August) | 15 | 13 | 34 | 24 | 30 | 75 | 71 | 31 | 45 | 50 |
| 9. Personal income tax rates |  |  |  |  |  |  |  |  |  |  |
| Basic rate (% of fed.) | 52.5 | 45.5 | 50.0 | 52.0 | 58.0 | na | 62 | 59.5 | 59.5 | 69 |
| Top marginal rate (fed. + prov.)* | 51.1 | 46.1 | 52.0 | 50.4 | 53.2 | 52.9 | 50.7 | 50.3 | 50.3 | 51.3 |
| 10. Corporate tax rates |  |  |  |  |  |  |  |  |  |  |
| Small business | 10 | 6 | 9 | 10 | 9.5 | 5.8 | 9 | 5 | 7.5 | 5 |
| Large corp. (top marginal rate) | 16.5 | 15.5 | 17 | 17 | 15.5 | 16.2 | 17 | 16 | 15 | 16 |
| 11. Retail sales tax (%) | 7 | 0 | 9 | 7 | 8 | 8/4 | 11 | 11 | 10 | 12 |
| 12. Tax on unleaded gas (cents/litre) | 11 | 9 | 15 | 11.5 | 14.7 | 14.5 | 10.7 | 13.5 | 11.2 | 15.7 |

* Includes surtaxes.

SOURCES: Data from Wood Gundy, *1994 Provincial Profiles* (Economics Department) and *1995 Provincial Profiles* (Economics Department); Nesbitt Burns, Economic Research, *Provincial Handbook*; and Canadian Tax Foundation, *Provincial and Municipal Finances* (various issues).

**Figure 12:** Variability of Provincial Government Revenues and Expenditures

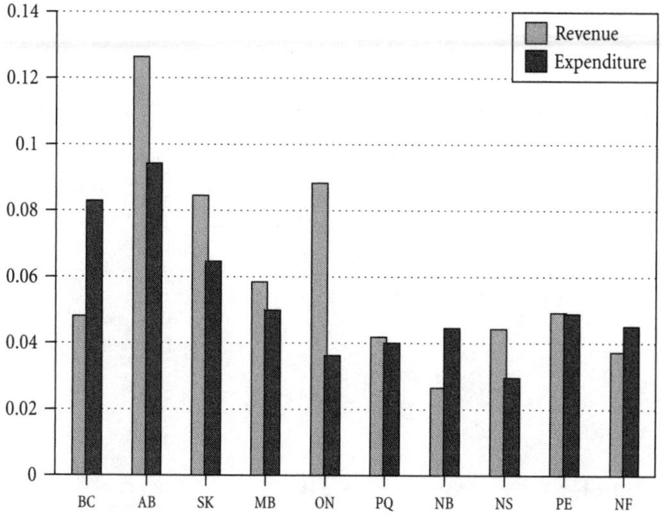

SOURCE: See Mansell and Percy (1990: 69) for index of variability, notes to Figure 8 for methodology, and notes to Figures 2 and 3 for data source. Index values are computed using data for the period 1961–93.

underestimation of expenditures, for the actual deficits to be much larger than those projected by the government (see Figure 7). Part of this can be traced to the much greater volatility of revenues and expenditures for the Alberta government compared to the situation in other provinces (see Figure 12). The credibility of the government's budget estimates was further in doubt because of the year-to-year changes in accounting methodology (a common practice among governments) and the absence of consolidated accounts to capture the changes in other funds such as the AHSTF.

The major causes of these deficits included the dramatic drop in revenues after the mid-1980s (see Figure 2), continued declines in real per capita revenues after this period, and the inability to aggressively bring real per capita spending back down to the provincial average or to levels consistent with the new reality in terms of Alberta's revenues (see Figure 3). In retrospect, the much higher per capita expenditures inherited from the policies of the 1970s and 1980s had become deeply entrenched. Not only had the 'expectations benchmark' been raised, but the capital expenditures (especially on such things as hospitals) had put in place a fairly rigid stream of operating cost obligations. In addition, as noted in Boothe (1994a), the traditional budgetary processes made it very difficult to achieve anything more than modest reductions in constant dollar expenditures through keeping expenditure increases below the rate of inflation.

**Table 3:** Provincial Employees per 1,000 Population, 1974, 1984, and 1990

| Province | 1974 | 1984 | 1990 | 1984 Population (millions) |
|---|---|---|---|---|
| Ontario | 12.8 | 12.8 | 13.1 | 9.21 |
| Québec | 14.0 | 15.6 | 18.6 | 6.65 |
| British Columbia | 16.4 | 16.9 | 14.9 | 2.96 |
| Alberta | 24.2 | 28.7 | 28.6 | 2.40 |
| Manitoba | 14.3 | 16.7 | 18.1 | 1.07 |
| Saskatchewan | 22.3 | 23.2 | 23.9 | 1.02 |
| Nova Scotia | 22.5 | 26.7 | 27.9 | 0.88 |
| New Brunswick | 36.7 | 44.4 | 52.9 | 0.72 |
| Newfoundland | 28.7 | 36.8 | 39.4 | 0.58 |
| Prince Edward Island | 34.5 | 35.9 | 40.2 | 0.13 |

SOURCE: Calculations are based on data from Statistics Canada, Provincial and Territorial Government Employment, Cat. 72–007 and Cansim matrices 6369–72 and 6219–23.

It is also worth noting that in 1992 Alberta still had a provincial government that was large relative to governments in other provinces, in spite of attempts in some budgets in the late 1980s and early 1990s to bring about a reduction, primarily through attrition. Table 3 presents data on the number of provincial employees per 1,000 population. The provinces are ordered by population size (from largest to smallest) so as to highlight the economies of scale inherent in public-sector employment. These data show that the number of provincial employees per 1,000 population in Alberta increased significantly between 1974 and 1984. By 1990 (the last year for which comparable data are available), the ratio for Alberta was still much higher than what would be expected, taking account of population size and the situation in other provinces. Indeed, Alberta's ratio was essentially the same as that in Nova Scotia despite having three times the population.

The above-average severity of Alberta's deficit problem in the late 1980s and early 1990s can be related to policy and economic factors unique to the province. However, it is important to note that there were also a number of other, more general factors that had created an underlying tendency for governments to run large and growing deficits. As indicated in Table 4, federal government deficits had become a very significant problem by the early 1980s and have continued to be a major concern for most of the period since then. Although less severe initially, aggregate provincial deficits increased

**Table 4:** Deficits in Canada: Selected Years (billions of dollars)

| Year | Provincial | Federal | Total | Total as % of GDP |
|---|---|---|---|---|
| 1981/2 | 5.4 | 15.6 | 21.0 | 7.5 |
| 1984/5 | 8.2 | 38.6 | 46.8 | 13.4 |
| 1987/8 | 7.7 | 28.3 | 36.0 | 8.4 |
| 1990/1 | 9.5 | 32.1 | 41.6 | 8.0 |
| 1991/2 | 22.2 | 34.5 | 56.7 | 8.4 |
| 1992/3 | 25.8 | 41.0 | 66.8 | 9.7 |
| 1993/4 | 19.8 | 42.0 | 61.8 | 8.7 |
| 1994/5 | 15.3 | 37.9 | 53.2 | 7.1 |
| 1995/6 (forecast) | 13.1 | 29.4 | 42.5 | 5.4 |

SOURCES: Data from Department of Finance, Government of Canada, *Canada's Economic and Fiscal Challenges*, Jan. 1994; and Nesbitt Burns, Economic Research, *Provincial Handbook*, Sept. 1995.

dramatically in the early 1990s. More recently they have shown significant declines, particularly in relation to the federal government's deficit.

A number of factors underlie this tendency for growing deficits. Many of the largest expenditure programs were put in place during the 1950s and 1960s when it appeared that a long-term trend of rapid economic growth and low real interest rates would continue. In such a situation, even without increases in taxes, government revenues would grow fast enough to keep up with the expansions in expenditures and with the cost of servicing any debt. It has been noted by Eltis (1995), for example, that from 1960 to the late 1970s, the growth rates in GDP were substantially above the interest rates on public debt. From that time on, however, the opposite has been true. This has meant substantial growth in debt-servicing costs in absolute terms and as a percentage of total output. A consequence has been an escalation in the proportion of government expenditures and revenues allocated to debt servicing.

This tendency for increasing debt-servicing costs to create large deficits could have been contained or eliminated through increasing revenues and/or decreasing program expenditures to create large primary budget surpluses.[34] Most governments in Canada substantially increased taxes, particularly after the mid-1980s. Total government revenue as a percentage of GDP in Canada increased from just under 34 per cent in 1985/6 to more than 36 per cent by 1991/2. Although program spending declined from about 38 per cent of GDP in 1982/3 to about 35 per cent (or equal to the revenue share) in 1987/8, it remained high by historical standards and by the standards of all G-7 countries except Italy and France. The resulting large primary deficits and high interest rate levels caused government deficits in Canada to soar even after, in 1987/8, Canadian governments (in the aggregate) began running primary surpluses.[35]

Several other factors have complicated these deficit problems. First, there has been little or no growth in real per capita incomes in Canada for almost a decade. In fact, real after-tax incomes have tended to decline. This, combined with the fact that by the early 1990s the total tax burden in Canada (measured as a percentage of the economy) was already well above that in important competitor countries like the US and Japan, made it increasingly difficult to deal with the deficits through even higher taxes. Second, there has been a deterioration in elements such as unemployment rates and employment security, which has increased demands on governments. Third, in 1993, the dominant view by the federal government and most provincial governments was that the deficits were not a major problem, that once the economy rebounded they would be automatically resolved and that, in the absence of a major campaign by the relatively silent majority of net fiscal contributors in the population, they had no political interest in dealing with the deficit problem.

## Debt

A government's gross debt is just the accumulation of deficits. As such, the large deficits in Alberta outlined in the previous section caused a dramatic increase in the province's debt. For example, between 1986 and 1991, the per capita debt of the Alberta government increased by 340 per cent. The next largest increase over this period was for Quebec, where the increase was 42 per cent. As outlined later, the increase for Alberta was even larger when proper accounting was applied to such things as loan guarantees and unfunded pension liabilities.

The existence of the AHSTF helped accommodate this rapid increase in gross debt. In its absence, Alberta's credit rating would have been downgraded much faster and further than it was, providing the motivation for policies to reduce quickly and substantially the fiscal deficits. However, even with the sizeable assets in the AHSTF, the province's net debt position (measured as assets minus liabilities) went from net assets of $12.6 billion in 1985/6 to an estimated net debt of almost $5.5 billion at the end of 1992/3. Over this period, debt-servicing costs went from less than 1 per cent of revenues to over 10 per cent.[36] As indicated in Table 2, by 1992/3 Alberta had reached, and was poised to surpass quickly many other provinces in terms of the percentage of revenues going to debt service and the ratio of non-supporting debt to GDP.

It is important to put these debt levels into perspective through some comparisons. First, as shown in Table 2, prior to the first Klein government, Alberta's debt relative to the size of the economy was less of a problem than for the other provinces except British Columbia. Rather, the major problem was the rate at which it was growing. Second, Alberta had suffered a downgrading by all four major credit rating agencies but the interest premium over comparable government of Canada debt instruments was still at the low end among provincial governments. However, it must be emphasized that the interest premiums for government of Canada bonds were rising and, since mid-1993, the average premiums for provincial 10-year bonds have fallen to below-average levels. In other words, the markets have viewed Canadian bonds less favourably and have improved their opinions of provincial government bonds relative to federal government bonds (see Nesbitt Burns, 1995: 6).

Third, each province's debt must be viewed within the context of that for all governments in Canada. For example, Albertans are affected not just by the level of provincial debt but by the level of total government debt in the country. Primarily because of the dramatic increase in federal debt, by 1993 government debt in Canada was just slightly under 100 per cent of GDP. Among the G-7 countries, only Italy had a worse ratio (108.4 per cent in 1992) and the next highest countries compared to Canada (Japan at 64.9 per cent and the US at 63.0 per cent in 1992) were well below. Of equal concern was the fact that Canada had already achieved the distinction of having by far the largest net foreign debt relative to GDP, even far surpassing Italy.[37] The dependence on foreign financing has also meant a soaring current account deficit, which by the early 1990s reached an extremely high level equal to 4 per cent of GDP. Since other countries have hit the wall in circumstances similar to those facing Canada, a number of international agencies had begun flagging Canada as an 'OECD suspect' and a 'soft default prospect'.[38]

### Revenue and Expenditure Levels

As shown in Figure 2, in 1992 and 1993 real per capita revenue for the government of Alberta was much lower than it was during the late 1970s and early 1980s, but it was still significantly above the provincial average. This above-average revenue was achieved through the increases in provincial tax rates in the late 1980s as well as the increases in federal tax rates over the period since the mid-1980s.[39] These partially offset the declines in resource revenues so that, in 1992/3, real per capita revenue to the provincial government was still 17 per cent above the average in the other provinces. As indicated in Table 2, this was achieved even though the contribution of federal transfers and own-source tax revenues remained among the lowest in terms of the share of total provincial government revenues.

As shown in Table 2, in Alberta the rates for most of the main provincial taxes were significantly below those in other provinces in 1992/3. Further, as estimated by McMillan and Warrack (1995: 14–15), when local and provincial taxes are considered, Alberta still had an above-average tax capacity and below-average tax effort. Using data for 1990/1, they note that Alberta's fiscal capacity (or the size of the tax base) was 33 per cent above the provincial average, with about half of this above-average position due to oil and gas revenues. In addition, the tax effort in Alberta (measured as the ratio of what is actually raised to what could be raised if tax rates were set at average provincial levels) was only 75 per cent. If average provincial tax rates were applied to Alberta's tax base, revenues in 1990/1 would have been about $1.5 billion greater, or an increase of over $600 per capita.

Although they had fallen slightly in the period since the mid-1980s, in 1992/3 real per capita expenditures by the provincial government were still 15 per cent above the average for the other provinces (see Figure 3). However, the appropriate benchmark is not necessarily the average for the other provinces. As shown in Figure 3, real per capita expenditure by the other provincial governments followed a trend of increase and it is far from clear that even the levels in 1992/3 could be considered sustainable.

### 3.3 Political Environment

By the late 1980s and early 1990s there were signs that Albertans had become very concerned with the fiscal situation in the province and within Canada. The Mulroney government was first elected in September 1984 with strong support from Alberta voters. Two important planks in the platform from an Alberta perspective were the promises to dismantle the hated NEP and to deal with the large fiscal deficits. The NEP was eventually eliminated, but the best the government could do on the fiscal front by the end of Mulroney's first term was to achieve a modest operating surplus (the overall deficit remained in the $30 billion range). Although Alberta voters endorsed the Mulroney government in the subsequent election, this support appears to have been based heavily on the promise of the free trade agreement between the US and Canada, the strength of Alberta representation in the cabinet, and a lingering distrust of the Liberals. The lack of success in dealing with the deficit, the rapidly escalating federal debt, doubts about the promised 'sacred trust', and the perception that the Conservatives were continuing the Liberal tradition of pork-barrel politics (exemplified by the CF-18 aircraft maintenance contract scandal) prevented enthusiastic support.

By 1990 the support in Alberta for the federal Conservatives was in rapid decline. The continued concerns noted above, the substantial increases in taxes, and the unpopularity of the Goods and Services Tax (GST) were all factors. At the same time, the Reform Party of Canada under the leadership of Preston Manning was signing up members at the rate of 3,000 per month; it had the support of well over 30 per cent of voters in Alberta according to polls, and its lead over the other federal parties in the province was growing.[40] The Reform platform included such things as support for the notion of fundamental equality of all provinces, parliamentary reform (a triple-E Senate and free votes in the House of Commons), and the general move to bottom-up (versus top-down) policy-making. However, a key element was a bold plan to cut 10 to 15 per cent across the board in program spending and to do this over a relatively short period of time. This was in sharp contrast to the gradualist deficit plans of the other parties, which relied on reductions in the rate of increase in program spending and optimistic projections of economic growth to possibly eliminate the deficit at some future date.

At about the same time, Albertans were becoming increasingly discontented with the Getty government. For example, a poll in November of 1990 indicated that only 15 per cent of the respondents would vote for the Conservatives, compared to 57 per cent who said they would vote for a provincial wing of the Reform Party of Canada.[41] In the same poll, those surveyed were asked to indicate how they would like the government to eliminate the long-standing $2 billion deficit. The responses indicated 54 per cent for cutting spending, 17 per cent for raising taxes, 9 per cent for ignoring the deficit, and 20 per cent undecided. Additional evidence of an underlying discontent in Alberta with the handling of the fiscal situation by the provincial and federal governments could be seen in the rapid growth in membership in organizations like the Canadian and Alberta Taxpayers Associations. Further, conferences on government deficits and debt seemed to be particularly good draws in Alberta.

In retrospect, as early as 1990 an astute political observer would have concluded that a majority of Albertans would support the type of aggressive action on deficits through expenditure cuts at the provincial level that the Reform Party was advocating at the federal level. Viewed in this light, the election of the Ralph Klein government on such a platform should not have been surprising. Indeed, it is useful to note that in the election of 1993, the Conservatives and Liberals both campaigned for 'brutal' and 'massive' cuts, and together they obtained 84 per cent of the vote.

## 4. THE KLEIN PROGRAM

### 4.1 Origins of the Plan

It would appear to an outsider that the fiscal program implemented by the Klein government was more evolutionary than revolutionary at the beginning. There may have been a general outline of the types of changes desired but the details of how to accomplish them still needed to be worked out after the election in 1993. However, by the time he became Premier in December of 1992, Ralph Klein and those who would become key ministers possibly already had a reasonably well-formed game plan. Many of the ideas being generated at the grassroots by those involved with the Reform Party and other groups would have been available to those interested in developing new provincial policies.

In addition, Lisac (1995: 65) notes that in late October of 1992, Ralph Klein signed a letter responding to a survey by the Canadian Manufacturers' Association dealing with various aspects of provincial government policy. The response outlined the need to: reduce the number and size of government departments and decrease overlap and regulation; privatize some government services, cut government expenditures, and improve productivity of program delivery before considering new taxes; maintain low taxes as a key element of competitive advantage; appoint an independent commission to review Alberta government finances; and focus economic policy on global trade, attracting international investment, linking education more closely to employer require- ments, and upgrading resources rather than attempting to establish new indus- tries. It is particularly interesting that many of these policy directions appear to have emerged from the Department of Economic Development and Trade and would later be the themes of the Toward 2000 Together initiative.[42] It is also of note that, since these positions would later be key elements of the Klein gov- ernment, Ralph Klein may have formed the outline of the fiscal and economic plan much earlier than commonly thought.

It is possible, but unlikely, that all of the strategies and details of how to accomplish the broad objectives outlined in the response to the Canadian Manufacturers' Association survey were in place before Klein became Premier. A more probable scenario is that they evolved in a logical or common-sense fashion and have only recently gained the appearance of a detailed and well- orchestrated plan. This is the assumption adopted below in the description of the fiscal restructuring program as of late 1995. Many details concerning the fiscal restructuring are discussed by Paul Boothe in Chapter 6. The discussion in the next section is intended as an overview.

### 4.2  Accounting, Reporting, and Budgeting
*Problems*
As described earlier, by the early 1990s there were serious concerns about the integrity of the government's accounts and some of the budgetary methodolo- gy. This seemed to come to a head with the 1991/2 budget, which projected a small surplus but ended up with a deficit of almost $3 billion. As shown in Figure 7, the actual deficit was larger than that projected in the budgets in seven of the eight years between 1985/6 and 1992/3. Further, at the very least, there was considerable confusion concerning the amount of unfunded liabilities associated with loan guarantees, the consolidated budget position (taking account of the interrelationships in terms of assets and liabilities in the various

separate accounts), the value of the assets in the AHSTF, and the net asset or debt position of the provincial government.

## Financial Review Commission

A logical first step in the fiscal restructuring was to get a better picture of the government's fiscal situation. Almost immediately after assuming the position of provincial treasurer, Jim Dinning appointed a financial review commission. The Alberta Financial Review Commission (AFRC), chaired by Marshall Williams and including other business leaders, was to inquire into and report on the appropriateness of the accounting principles and methods used and on the overall financial position of the province.

The report subsequently filed by the commission indicated that, as of 31 March 1993, the forecast consolidated deficit was $3.17 billion, consolidated provincial debt was $25.5 billion (including unfunded pension liabilities and the province's share of school board debt), there were net consolidated financial assets of $14.5 billion, and the net debt was $11 billion. It estimated that the government had moved from a net asset position of about $12 billion in 1985/6 to a position of net debt by 1991/2.

Among other things, the AFRC concluded that: (i) the annual deficit was serious and getting worse and action was required immediately as every delay would mean a more painful solution ultimately and a higher burden of servicing the debt; (ii) accounting and reporting needed to be provided on a consolidated basis using generally accepted accounting principles (GAPP) in all areas, with the information provided in a more timely fashion; (iii) budget estimates of revenues and expenditures should be developed on the basis of realistic and conservative assumptions; (iv) there was a need to establish long-term goals and specific program objectives and then develop budgets and reporting systems so that performance could be measured, as well as a need to review overall fiscal accountability; (v) there should be a general downsizing of the entire government infrastructure, including a reduction in the 150 government-owned or controlled agencies, funds, boards, and corporations, many of which have mandates considerably expanded from those originally intended; (vi) the assets of the AHSTF should be transferred to the General Revenue Fund to reduce management overhead and reduce the false sense of security arising from the reporting of assets in isolation from liabilities; (vii) the government should properly account for all loans and loan guarantees and recognize the high risk of such initiatives, de-emphasize the use of such approaches, and ensure that any further use is approved by the legislature or an all-party committee; (viii) the government should provide the Audit Committee under the Auditor General with the responsibility for reporting on the progress in implementing the recommendations.[43]

*Reporting and Budgeting Changes*

Many of the AFRC's recommendations were quickly implemented by the provincial treasurer. Beginning with the 1992/3 *Budget Update* released in January 1993, quarterly reports were implemented to provide information on a consolidated basis and for individual funds, agencies, programs, and revenue sources. Also, budget projections would now be done on a more conservative basis (for example, resource revenue estimates for budget planning were now done on the basis of a moving five-year average of actual resource revenue).[44] It will be recalled (see Figure 12) that revenues for the Alberta government have been particularly variable from year to year and difficult to forecast accurately. The use of the new approaches would serve to reduce significantly the tendency towards overestimation. As described later, the adoption of three-year spending plans would have similar effects on the ability to forecast expenditures.

It will suffice to note here that, with respect to accounting, reporting, and budgeting, Alberta arguably now has the most accurate and complete accounting among senior governments in Canada. Further, to this point the budget projections have proven to be conservative, leaving significant room to accommodate most unforeseen and unforeseeable revenue and expenditure variations.[45]

### 4.3 Redefining and Downsizing Government

*Reducing Administration Costs*

The first concrete notice that there would be a serious redefinition and downsizing of the provincial government occurred in early February of 1993 with the announcement of the elimination of six deputy minister positions and a plan to cut about 1,000 positions out of a civil service of about 30,000. This was followed, in March, with an announcement of a 5 per cent cut in the basic ministerial salaries for members of the cabinet and a freeze of all grants to hospitals, schools, post-secondary institutions, and municipal governments. Then, just before the election of 15 June, the Treasurer presented the 1993/4 budget, which included plans to cut about 20 per cent from overall spending.

In a news release in late 1993, a series of initiatives to downsize and restructure the operations of the provincial government were noted. These included the reduction of MLA salaries by 5 per cent, the elimination of the MLA pension plan, the reduction of the salaries for deputy ministers and senior officials by 5 per cent, a decrease in the number of departments from 26 to 16, a salary freeze and then a reduction of 5 per cent in the public service payroll budget, and a decrease of 2,575 full-time government positions (bringing the decrease since 1986 to 23 per cent).[46]

As part of the attempt to reduce administration costs, in January of 1994 the government announced plans to reduce the number of operating school boards from over 140 to about 60. In addition, it would begin administering the education portion of municipal taxes in order to reduce the variations across the province in per student education expenditures. In the case of health care, the government created 17 Regional Health Authorities (RHAs) in order to rationalize hospital administration costs and planning. A further potential benefit would be the ability to establish efficiency benchmarks based on the experience of the most successful RHAs and to allow some bidding among RHAs for the provision of selected services.

## Bottom-Up Decision-Making

There was also a reduction from 26 cabinet and caucus committees to four standing policy committees (SPCs). In addition to the dollar savings, this was a concrete example of the attempt to broaden the decision-making base and make better use of the talents and input of backbench MLAs. All of the Conservative MLAs serve on these SPCs, which are responsible for proposing legislation and approving budget allocations in four broad policy areas before any cabinet decisions are made. This initiative has been particularly important in terms of providing greater grassroots input to policy-making, constraining the power of cabinet ministers and senior bureaucrats, and allowing decision-makers to have a less departmentalized and better overall view of government policy.

## Core Businesses and Business Plans

Following on the recommendations of the AFRC, in February of 1994 the government spelled out the core areas it would focus on and introduced three-year business plans for government departments and agencies.[47] The core businesses defining the key role of the government were: investing in people and ideas; building a strong, sustainable, and prosperous province; providing essential services for the health and well-being of Albertans; maintaining a quality system of roads and highways, telecommunications, and utilities; and providing law, order, and good government. These categories were used in reviewing each of the programs offered by the government and represented an attempt to draw a line between 'essential' and 'non-essential' and between 'appropriately provided by government' and 'appropriately provided by the private sector'. Any activity of the provincial government that did not clearly fit into one or more of these categories would be a candidate for elimination or privatization. The privatization of liquor sales and registry offices had been announced in September of the previous year. Other initiatives to remove the government from non-core areas included the sale of interests in energy projects and plans to privatize such things as regional airports, the Alberta Opportunity Company, and Vencap Equities Alberta Ltd.

The lessons concerning government attempts at forced growth should have been learned before similar initiatives were taken by the provincial government in the 1970s and 1980s.[48] They were not, however, and one result has been the long list of embarrassing write-offs of industrial development project investments in the province. This has no doubt provided substantial motivation for the Klein government to avoid additional misadventures in the business of the private sector. Viewed in this light, the establishment of the core business guidelines might also be partly interpreted as an attempt to reduce the likelihood of repeating past mistakes.

The business plans applied to every government department and agency. They set out the missions, mandates, objectives, actions, results, and spending targets over a three-year period for every unit. They afforded an opportunity to examine the need for each program and, if it was an essential part of the core business, how it could be best provided. By focusing attention on outcomes, they would also allow departments to learn and adjust in terms of the design and delivery of programs.

These plans were also important as the first step in improving accountability. First, each plan would have to be examined by the appropriate SPC before being released, thus providing a layer of oversight by those in closest contact with the population. Second, it would make it more difficult than in the past for departments or other units to make ad hoc spending decisions since any sharp deviations from the plans and targets would invite considerable scrutiny. Third, these plans would form the basis of a system of performance measures to keep track of the progress relative to a set of benchmarks or targets. This would allow a variety of actions—including adjustments to reward or punish units on the basis of their performance—aimed at increasing accountability, efficiency, and effectiveness of departments and agencies.

*Performance Measures*

The first annual report on performance measures was released in June 1995.[49] It provided the baseline data and information and set out 22 measures of overall performance in the core areas of people (educational attainment, life expectancy, income distribution, etc.), prosperity (taxation, net debt, per capita output, job creation, etc.), and preservation (crime rates, quality of air, water, and land, resource sustainability, etc.). In a number of cases, targets were also indicated. By the fall of 1995, each government department was to provide a report outlining measures of performance tied to the three-year business plans. Beginning with the 1996 budget process, these were to be supplemented with a 'watch list' based on performance measures for areas of high priority, those undergoing major changes, those where performance is lagging, and those where there is concern about the quality of service.

## 4.4 Consultation and Leadership

*Setting an Example*

The attempts by governments in Canada to cut expenditures have often been met with cynicism, in large part because the politicians have been seen as following a different standard. That is, they ask others to take cuts or pay higher taxes while maintaining or enriching their salaries, pensions, and other benefits.

In 1979 the pension plan benefits for MLAs were approximately doubled and there was a further 30 per cent increase in 1989. This set the stage for a key decision by Premier Klein in terms of cementing support for his fiscal agenda. After intense negotiation with former MLAs benefiting from earlier decisions on pensions, the government was able to announce prior to the election in 1993 a cut to pension benefits, but it only applied to the new beneficiaries over the previous four years. After a less than favourable public reaction, the premier announced that, henceforth, there would be no MLA pension plan. This, combined with the 5 per cent cuts to salaries for ministers, other MLAs, and senior officials in the government, represented an important symbol of leadership by example.

*Roundtables*

Another important milestone in the development and implementation of the fiscal plan was the consultation process involving a series of roundtables. The first was a Budget Roundtable with about 140 participants held in Red Deer on 29–30 March 1993.[50] It was to reach much the same conclusions as the Alberta Financial Review Commission (AFRC) in its report released a short time later.[51] The consensus seemed to be that: Alberta must act quickly on eliminating the deficit; the first priority should be on reducing expenditures before raising taxes; the pain should be shared fairly; the best approach would be to leave the decisions on how the cuts were to be carried out to those organizations closest to the point of delivery of government services; governments must work to increase efficiency and accountability; government must lead by example; and special interest groups must give way to the collective interests of Albertans.

It will remain for others to debate the real significance of this consultation. However, the outcome appeared, at a minimum, to confirm for the government the popularity of an aggressive approach to the deficit much as was suggested by the growth in support for the Reform Party and the Canadian Taxpayers Association. Along with the report of the AFRC, it also served to increase significantly the general understanding among community leaders throughout the province of the causes and implications of continued high deficits and the possible solutions. Further, this roundtable approach would be carried over into other areas. For example, similar consultations were organized to examine and recommend actions to deal with health care and education in the province.

At the risk of some oversimplification, it would also appear that these consultations, especially the Budget Roundtable, represented a way to undercut the special interest groups and the system of political patrons and clients that have always made it extremely difficult to cut expenditures. In particular, it imposed a visible budget constraint on all participants with regard to allocation recommendations. In such circumstances it becomes much more difficult for a special interest to argue for its favourite program if it must also explain who among those around the table must make the sacrifice to pay for it. Similarly, it is difficult for a special interest to refuse to volunteer to reduce demands when others have offered to make sacrifices for the common good.

## 4.5 Adjust Taxes or Expenditures?

One alternative available to the Klein government in early 1993 was to simply maintain the status quo. Although the result would be a continuation of large deficits and a rapidly growing level of debt, Alberta's ratio of net debt to GDP and the proportion of revenues going to service the debt were still fairly low by the standards of the federal government and other provincial governments (see Table 2). Further, the province's credit rating was still quite high. As such, it would have been possible simply to delay action, as was the norm elsewhere, until discipline was exerted externally by bond markets.

This was not considered a viable alternative for several reasons. As noted previously, it was becoming obvious that Albertans wanted the deficit problem fixed and any party not prepared to make changes in search of a solution would be discounted. Clearly, not many in the province understood the finer points of deficit and debt mathematics, such as the conditions for a steady debt to GDP ratio.[52] Nevertheless, there seemed to be a recognition of the main implications based on common-sense propositions. For example: rising interest payments to service a growing debt must mean less is available to finance spending on government services; so long as the interest rate on borrowed money exceeds the (social) rate of return associated with the use of the money (or the growth in the productive capacity to cover the interest and repay the principal), there must be a reduction in sustainable living standards;[53] under these circumstances the deficits amount to a continual shifting of tax burdens to 'our children' and future generations and a shifting of consumption benefits from them to present generations; the longer the delay in dealing with the large deficits, the larger and more costly will be the tax increases and/or expenditure cuts; and the growing debt will negatively affect the distribution of income to the extent that, in combination with the upward effect on interest rates, the revenues coming from a broad cross-section of income groups are increasingly returned to the net savers, who are disproportionately from the highest income groups.

## The Tax Alternative

Another alternative was to raise taxes, perhaps in combination with some reductions in expenditures, as a way of dealing with the large deficits. The Financial Review Commission did not rule out such an approach and many participants of the Budget Roundtable seemed to accept that it might be necessary to increase existing taxes in the province or introduce a sales tax.[54] One of the most salient aspects of the approach adopted by the Klein government was that there would be no further tax increases even though there remained considerable tax room.[55] For example, McMillan and Warrack (1995) have estimated that something over $1.5 billion in additional revenue could be raised by introducing a 5 per cent sales tax on all personal expenditures or by increasing other existing taxes to the average levels observed in other provinces.

There were some proponents of this alternative at the Budget Roundtable. Not only had the other governments in Canada raised taxes as part of their attack on deficits, but this would greatly reduce the size of the required cuts in expenditures. In the absence of higher taxes, the required cut in spending was estimated to be about 20 per cent. Given the difficulties of other governments in achieving even minor decreases in expenditures, such cuts seemed outside the range of possibilities.

However, there were also arguments against significant tax increases. The public, having endured substantial increases in federal and provincial taxes (see Section 3.3), was not in a mood for additional taxes. It would appear that Albertans, and Canadians in general, had been pushed to the point of tax exhaustion. Another interpretation noted by Ruggeri, Van Wart, and Howard (1995) is that, by the mid-1980s, a large and stable coalition had formed against further tax increases. This consisted of households with above-average income, voter turnout, and education. In contrast, those who favoured tax increases rather than expenditure cuts represented a more heterogeneous group, with some factions benefiting from a variety of transfer payments and others primarily affected through changes in the level of government service. Although potentially large, such a group could not attain the cohesiveness necessary to form a strong voting block.

However, there seemed to be more practical arguments against further tax increases to deal with the deficit in Alberta. These are summarized as follows.

(1) The increases in taxes by other governments (for example, the federal government) have tended to remove or substantially reduce the pressures to reduce expenditures. The experience of Alberta would suggest that, throughout the 1970s and 1980s, expenditures were driven to a large extent by available revenues and access to credit.

(2) Per capita expenditures by the Alberta government were already above the average for the other provinces and even the levels for the other provinces

were likely above sustainable levels. Consequently, raising taxes would entrench Alberta's high expenditure levels, which were not sustainable, and the province would end up, like other governments, with the worst possible combination of high expenditure levels, high taxes, and little or no fiscal flexibility to accommodate expected or unforeseeable events. The lack of a revenue cushion would be particularly problematic for Alberta given the expected long-term reductions in resource revenues, the high degree of variability of revenues and expenditures (see Figure 12), and the continued downloading by the federal government.

(3) Hikes in tax rates often do not generate the predicted increases in revenues, in part because of the erosion of tax bases as tax rates reach unacceptably high levels. While the introduction of a sales tax would boost revenues, the absence of a provincial tax has come to be viewed by the population almost as a birthright. Even without a sales tax and given the levels of other taxes, per capita revenues already exceeded the average for other provinces. Adding a further tax would eliminate any tax advantage associated with the province's petroleum rents and eliminate an advantage helping to offset other locational disadvantages facing the industries needed to diversify and develop the economy. It has also been argued that to maintain a stable pattern of government services over time, some tax room must be preserved so that it can later be used to offset the expected decrease in revenues from the petroleum sector as resource rents decline.

(4) There has been increasing evidence that taxes, especially once they reach the higher levels now common in Canada, are not as costless as typically assumed in the past. For example, analyses by Scarth (1994) and by Dahlby (1995) suggest that such levels of taxation involve considerable distortions and a large cost in terms of reductions in overall output and income. Consequently, the high tax levels imposed by other governments in Canada would not be an appropriate benchmark for a province like Alberta with the option of not increasing taxes further.

### The Expenditure Alternative

In the September 1993 *Budget Update*, a plan was announced involving a decrease in program expenditures from $13.0 billion in 1992/3 to $10.2 billion in 1996/7, at which time the government was committed to achieving a balanced budget. This represented a decrease of 21.7 per cent over just four years. McMillan and Warrack (1995: 12) have calculated that when population growth and inflation are taken into account, this translates into a decrease in real per capita program spending of 27 per cent.

Such a decrease in spending, especially over a short period, must be considered extraordinary by almost any standard. One instance where government even more aggressively reduced spending has been New Zealand, where a major financial and fiscal crisis loomed. The reductions planned by the Klein government were also notable in that, unlike even cases like Saskatchewan, Alberta was not facing any such crisis in the near future (although further credit downgrades would have occurred) and the province still had considerable room to increase tax revenues. Further, the reductions represented a major shift in how the government viewed expenditure policy. The typical approach has been to set policy primarily on the votes for expenditures, with determination of how to finance the expenditures, through tax increases or borrowing, being mainly the secondary decision. In contrast, the Alberta program would now first involve a determination of the votes for tax and borrowing levels, with expenditures to be decided mainly within this budget constraint.

The main arguments against cutting expenditures, especially by such a large amount, have generally focused on the expenditure levels in other provinces. Using this approach, it is suggested that per capita spending should be adjusted downward only to the average for the other provinces. However, there are two problems with such arguments. First, the provincial average is based on widely differing population sizes, economic conditions, and views concerning the role of government. For example, simply because of economies of scale alone, one would expect per capita expenditures for many provincial government programs to be much higher in the provinces with small populations than in the larger provinces. Such factors are not taken into account with a simple average for the provinces. Second, it is far from clear that the average for the other provinces represents a sustainable benchmark. In fact, as of 1993, this average, being dominated by provinces like Ontario and Quebec with clearly unsustainable expenditure levels, was almost certainly well above any level that could be maintained without continually rising taxation levels. Another typical argument against large expenditure cuts has been that they would result in a large negative Keynesian multiplier effect that would create a 'made in Alberta' recession. The consequent decreases in revenues and increases in spending would lead to a larger rather than a smaller deficit.

There are a number of serious weaknesses in these types of arguments. First, if they were valid it would be hard to explain the lack of growth in employment and the soaring deficits given the generous application of deficit-financed Keynesian stimulus in Alberta and other parts of the country. Second, it is now much more commonly recognized that, through positive effects on private-sector expectations and spending, through reductions in the large distortions associated with high tax levels, and through the reallocation of resources to more productive uses, decreases in government spending may have little or no negative multiplier impacts. For example, as noted by Giavazzi and Pagano (1990), Denmark and Ireland seemed to have reduced government expenditures without any significant negative impacts on the economy and, indeed, those economies seemed to thrive during the cuts in spending.[56] It is now apparent that, given the negative impacts of high taxation and deficit levels, there is the possibility that reductions in government spending can provide a stimulus to the economy.

A third point is that the extent of any negative expenditure effects will depend on the credibility of the fiscal plan and the timing of the cuts in relation to the economic cycle. In general, the negative impacts on the economy are likely to be much smaller if it is widely believed that the fiscal restructuring plan will be followed and will be permanent. Unlike the case where the fiscal plan is less credible and considered temporary, businesses and consumers are likely to make more of the required adjustments (through changes in expectations, labour market behaviour, saving decisions, and so on) that will minimize the short-term costs associated with expenditure cuts. A further point made by Robson and Scarth (1994: 37) is that 'The longer a government waits during its elected period of office [to make budget cuts], the less credible are its promises about major cuts, and the less likely it is that deficit reduction will involve costs that are small in relation to the benefits.' It can also be noted that the negative impacts of expenditure cuts will be smaller the more they are timed to occur during a period of strong economic growth.

The final common argument against expenditure cuts is that they will lead to a reduction in the amount and quality of social infrastructure. In turn, this will generate a decline in overall productivity and the returns on private investment, both of which will mean a further drop in the level of economic welfare.

It is entirely possible that major cuts could mean decreases in the amount and quality of social infrastructure. However, it can be noted that rising debt levels that decrease the revenues available for program and capital spending can have the same effect. Further, it must be recalled that much of the increase in spending in recent decades has been more on consumption than capital formation or upkeep. In addition, for cases such as Alberta where, even after the cuts, per capita program spending would still be quite high by most First World standards, it remains to be demonstrated that there is necessarily a close relationship between variations in expenditures and variations in outcomes in areas like education and health.

## 4.6 Cutting Quickly and Deeply

### The Gradualist Alternative

Most attempts at dealing with fiscal deficits and debt in Canada have been gradualist. At the federal level, for example, the plan since 1984 has been to reduce the rate of growth in expenditures and allow the expected growth in revenues to catch up. This has been continued under the Chrétien government, where the date at which a balanced budget is to be achieved is simply 'sometime in the future'. This gradualist approach has a long Canadian tradition based on the view that it is either not possible or too costly to have individuals and businesses adjust over shorter periods of time. Along with the federal deficit reduction plans, examples include the policies during the 1970s and 1980s to avoid the need to adjust quickly to energy prices and the long-standing policies to mitigate the need for economic adjustment by the 'have not' regions.

A major problem with the gradualist approach in general, and in the specific case of fiscal deficits, is that the required adjustments are never likely to be made because of a lack of incentives and credibility. The tendency is to avoid adjustments because the signal being given is that adjustments are very difficult and there are no clearly defined benefits such as the avoidance of further tax increases or expenditure cuts. Indeed, by delaying adjustments in an environment of low growth rates for output and high real interest rates, the burden of the debt will continue to rise, causing further pressure for higher taxes and/or expenditure cuts. Moreover, such a plan requires adherence over a period of many years, but any given government has a term of only about four years. This also works against the credibility of a deficit reduction plan.

### The Cold-Turkey Alternative

The Klein government rejected the traditional gradualist approach and implemented a program of deep and quick reductions in expenditures. The plan announced in the September 1993 *Budget Update* called for decreases in program spending of $2.2 billion, or a reduction of 17 per cent in three years (1993/4 to 1995/6), compared to a total decrease of just under 22 per cent over the four-year period. The cuts in just the first two years were to amount to $1.6 billion.

Given the gradualist tradition, it is not surprising there have been many criticisms of the approach taken. One, dealt with in the previous section, is that such large and quick cuts would certainly create a major economic recession in the province. Another common criticism has been that, because such an approach does not allow sufficient time to plan and adjust, there is the danger of doing serious harm to government programs.

At the same time, however, the cold-turkey approach has considerable common-sense appeal. First, it is consistent with maintaining credibility and, as noted above, this is an important factor in maximizing the chances of achieving the reductions and minimizing any dislocations to the economy. The cuts would be completed well within the government's expected minimum term of office and, equally important, would allow people to see 'light at the end of the tunnel' before the next election. Second, given the relatively short length of periods of strong growth, particularly for a highly variable economy like

Alberta's, the cuts could take place over the part of the economic cycle where any short-term pain could be more easily accommodated and where adjustment costs would be minimized. Third, if a significant reduction in expenditures is required, it is more likely that a credible plan of large cuts will trigger the fundamental changes to institutional behaviour necessary to actually achieve them. For example, it is generally accepted that the likelihood of innovative and major shifts by institutions is small unless there is a major shock to the operating and planning paradigm. Fourth, from a purely political perspective, fast cutting makes it more difficult for special interests to mobilize and form coalitions to threaten the program.

## 4.7 Sharing and Managing the Cuts

### Sharing the Pain

It has long been observed that individuals will react differently in most situations depending on whether they are asked to make a sacrifice in isolation for the common good or to make the same sacrifice for the common good knowing that others will also make sacrifices.[57] In general, they are much more willing to do so in the latter case.

This observation underpins another important distinction of the fiscal plan by the Klein government. That is, unlike the traditional approach where the government attempts to reset priorities and then cut vertically (that is, selectively eliminate certain programs that serve specific constituencies), the method adopted involved across-the-board cuts, with some variations to reflect relative priorities in broad policy areas. Following the 5 per cent cuts to labour resource payments for provincially funded departments and organizations, at the beginning of 1994 the government announced the planned cuts by each major program area in order to achieve the overall spending reduction of 20 per cent.[58] These included reductions of: 12.4 per cent to Education, almost all of which was to take place in 1994/5; 17.6 per cent to Health, spread fairly evenly over five fiscal years beginning with 1992/3; 14.2 per cent to Advanced Education and Career Development, concentrated in 1994/5 and 1995/6; 18.3 per cent to Family and Social Services, spread mostly over two years beginning in 1993/4; and 77.9 per cent to the Municipal Assistance Grant, primarily over three years beginning in 1994/5. To reach the 20 per cent target, the budgets in most other areas were to be cut by considerably more than those for Education, Health, Social Services, and Advanced Education.

It would appear that this broad sharing of the pain has played an important role in minimizing any widespread opposition to the cuts. Put simply, it is difficult for any one group to form major opposition to cuts when they will be revealed as a 'special interest' by the willing sacrifices of other groups in the common interest. In addition to the isolation of many special interest groups, there is a greater tendency for all groups to more clearly recognize the existence of an aggregate budget constraint.

## Managing the Cuts

The traditional approach to budget cutting has generally been based on the notion that the government is ultimately responsible for the types, quantities, and quality of government services and how they are produced and delivered. As such, the government has the right and the responsibility to micro-manage any expenditure reductions. However, this approach has come under increasing attack for a variety of reasons. First, it has been apparent for some time that the direction of change has been towards decentralization and towards having decisions made closer to where the actual production and consumption of the services take place. Second, developments in areas such as principal-agent and asymmetric information theory suggest that the top-down approach to decision-making is not effective or optimal. For example, within this theory, the principal (the provincial government in this case) decides what the objectives are to be. The goal then is to find the best way to get the agents (school boards, hospital boards, etc.) to meet these objectives using their superior information concerning production and cost functions, the key trade-offs, and so on.

It would appear, at least in broad outline, that the Klein government has adopted this approach of setting overall targets for various program areas and then allowing the cuts to be managed at lower levels. Following a statement made by Michel Belanger, a former chair of the National Bank, this came to be affectionately referred to as the 'stupid approach' during the Budget Roundtable.[59] However, the government has attempted some micro-management in certain areas. An example is the Access Fund created by withdrawing funds from Advanced Education. This has been used to create competition among post-secondary institutions for a return of some funding based on specific educational objectives set by the provincial government.[60]

## 4.8 Legislating Discipline

### Deficit Elimination

The enactment of legislation to require the achievement of a balanced budget has been fairly common. A good cross-section of such legislation in a provincial context can be found in the proposed or implemented deficit elimination acts in Alberta, British Columbia, Manitoba, and New Brunswick.

Alberta's Act, among other things, sets out the maximum deficit allowed in each year, with a zero deficit required in 1996/7 and every year thereafter.[61] It also stipulates: that the maximum amounts for deficits must be adjusted downward for the subsequent year if the actual deficits in any year exceed the established amount; that the maximum deficit amounts for subsequent years are not to be adjusted if there is overachievement in any one year; that if actual revenues exceed the budgeted amount, the difference can only be used to reduce the debt; that the resource revenues and corporate taxes used for budgetary purposes shall not be greater than the lesser of the average amount for the previous five years or 90 per cent of the forecast; that restrictions be imposed on the issuance of special warrants and on supply votes; and that the Audit Committee (established under the Auditor General Act) and the Provincial Treasurer shall, respectively, report on progress with respect to the elimination of the deficit and on the accuracy of budgetary revenue and expenditure estimates.

Experience in other jurisdictions suggests that such legislation is not a panacea in the battle to eliminate deficits and the growth of debt. Rather, it would appear that the main role is in adding credibility and assisting in the entrenchment of discipline. As legislation, it can be altered or eliminated by future governments. However, the longer such legislation remains in place, the more difficult and risky it will be for any future government to depart substantially from the main intent of the Act.

### Taxpayer Protection and Debt Retirement

Two other noteworthy pieces of legislation in the context of the government's program are the Alberta Taxpayer Protection Act (Bill 1) and the Balanced Budget and Debt Retirement Act (Bill 6).[62] Bill 1 requires that a referendum be conducted on the imposition of a general provincial sales tax before any legislation implementing such a tax is introduced. In addition to reaffirming the main elements of the Deficit Elimination Act outlined above, with some modifications,[63] Bill 6 requires that the Crown debt be paid down in an orderly fashion according to a schedule so that the net financial debt is zero by the 2021/2 fiscal year, that in any given year at least $100 million must be applied to the debt, and that any excess of revenues over expenditures in a fiscal year must be used to pay down the Crown debt.

## 5. CONCLUDING OBSERVATIONS

### 5.1 Summary

#### Historical Perspective

The rapid growth in spending during Alberta's first two decades as a province represented the initial exercise in province-building. The associated deficits, combined with the guarantees and other commitments to industrial projects, were unsustainable and the province was forced to default on its debt during the Great Depression.

The period of rapid growth from the late 1940s to the late 1950s was different, partly because it was a case of extensive growth associated with the development of the petroleum sector rather than intensive growth associated with a large increase in regional terms of trade. In addition, the Manning governments were successful in constraining the growth of spending beyond levels that could be maintained. During the next boom phase beginning in the early 1970s, the previous pattern of rapid growth in government spending re-emerged and would prove to be a major cause of the large structural deficits over most of the period since the mid-1980s.

A review of the historical record suggests four main factors relevant to the causes of and solutions to Alberta's deficit problem. First, it would appear that fiscal deficits invariably arise from rapid growth. In the case of other regions and nations this is usually attributed to the 'soft' budget constraints when the real growth rate exceeds the real interest rate by a significant margin. In an Alberta context there is another factor. Given the narrow economic base and the high degree of variability of the economy, there is usually a strong incentive for governments to get involved in province-building exercises. This typically involves infrastructure and industrial diversification/development projects. Consequently, there seems to be a tendency for governments in the province to be rhetorically *laissez-faire* but quite interventionist in practice. The fiscal difficulties seem to arise when there are rapidly growing resource revenues that provide the fiscal capacity to grease the propensity for large-scale intervention.

Second, in spite of the long history of booms and busts, governments, like individuals and businesses, seem subject to the psychology of extrapolation. That is, boom periods seem to be typically viewed as a transition to a new, permanently higher growth path rather than something that is invariably followed by an economic bust. As a result, government spending programs have tended to be based on income gains that are viewed as permanent but in fact are transitory. Third, there has usually been a tendency to underestimate greatly the costs of lowering expectations and government spending once it is clear that neither is sustainable under average growth conditions.

The fourth point relates to the structure of the economy and the character of the province. Many of the unique characteristics observed in the province can be traced back to Alberta's general history and industrial heritage. The economic base has developed around agriculture and petroleum. Both of these are capital-intensive, involve many small, independent production units, are export-oriented and subject to the vagaries of internationally determined prices and national policies, and entail high risk and entrepreneurship. The addition of the petroleum sector also provided the impetus for the development of a highly skilled, educated, and adaptable labour force. As well, the substantial growth via in-migration has meant a large proportion of the population consists of those who came in search of economic opportunity.

In combination, these factors have tended to produce a population with values more disposed towards smaller government and self-reliance, with experience at adjusting to major shifts in external factors, and with a perception that the main threats come from outside rather than from within the province. These characteristics may help explain why a majority of Albertans would encourage and support the type of tough fiscal program associated with the Klein government.

### The Fiscal, Economic, and Political Environment in 1993

At the beginning of 1993, the Klein government faced a structural deficit of about $2.5 billion, the fastest growing debt in the country (by a wide margin), real per capita expenditures significantly above the average in other provinces, and the likelihood of further downgrades in the province's credit rating. On the positive side, net debt relative to the size of the economy was still quite small compared to that in most other provinces and that of the federal government. Also, although they were substantially below what they were in the late 1970s and early 1980s, real per capita revenues were still above the provincial average. Moreover, there was no provincial sales tax and other taxes were still somewhat lower than in other provinces.

By 1993, the petroleum and related sectors had become less dominant factors in the economy compared to the situation in the 1970s and 1980s, and other sectors like forestry and manufacturing were increasing in importance. In combination with the dramatic restructuring of the petroleum and related sectors and the reasonable levels of energy prices and demand, this meant that the Alberta economy was as fundamentally sound as it had been for a long time. While there was perhaps less downside risk than in the previous decade or so, it still had the distinction of being the most variable regional economy in Canada. In terms of overall performance, the Alberta economy had established a solid pattern of being able to consistently outperform the national average. However, the halting economic recovery elsewhere meant that, during the period when much of the Klein fiscal program was developed, it was far from clear that Alberta would continue to show such a solid performance.

There were a number of important indicators in 1992 and 1993 that Albertans were ready for major change. There was real disappointment with the failure of the Mulroney government to arrest the soaring federal debt. This, along with the tax exhaustion, was producing rapidly growing support for the Reform Party and other groups with plans to attack the deficit problem through aggressive spending cuts. Polls in Alberta indicated that if the Reform Party ran in the next provincial election, it would win by a large margin.

### The Klein Revolution

The Klein revolution, then, appears to have come about through a confluence of events.[64] The fundamental characteristics of the population noted above had generated the base of support for an aggressive approach to the deficit problem. The feedback from the Budget Roundtable, from the Financial Review Commission, and from the growth in support for Reform and for groups like the Canadian and Alberta Taxpayers Associations all seemed to confirm this support. The premier and his key ministers provided the broad outline of a plan to eliminate the deficit without raising taxes and, in general, to lower expectations with respect to the role of government and to subject much of the public sector to the types of restructuring and adjustment that had been taking place in the private sector for some time. Within a year of taking office, the Klein government had turned the initial commitment and broad outline into a fairly complete and convincing program.

Important elements of this program include: major improvements in accounting, reporting, and budgeting; the adoption of conservative budgetary assumptions that are appropriate for a province like Alberta with highly variable revenues and expenditures; consolidation of administration and reductions in administration costs; redefining the business of government and subjecting government departments and agencies to planning, performance, and accountability principles; setting an example through cuts at the top; public consultation and more public input through empowerment of backbench members of the government; large spending cuts without significant tax increases despite the existence of significant tax room; a departure from the traditional approach so that expenditures are now driven by the primary decision of how much to tax rather than the reverse; adoption of the cold-turkey approach and rejection of the more common gradualist approach; the use of broad-based cuts, with some variations to reflect priorities in terms of broad policy areas, and pushing the management of the cuts in most cases to levels where the expertise and better information for effective micro-management should exist; and measures to increase credibility of the promise to eliminate deficits, to encourage adjustments in behaviour and expectations, and to encourage, through legislation, the fiscal discipline of this and future governments.

There can be little doubt about the significance of the Alberta experiment in restoring fiscal balance. The sheer magnitude of the cuts, the speed with which they have been applied, and the way in which they have been accommodated suggest a strong alternative to the traditional approaches to deficit cutting. In addition, the Klein revolution is notable in that the adjustments have been almost entirely on the expenditure side. Most governments have not demonstrated the discipline to cut expenditures until external constraints (such as credit ratings) have become very binding. Perhaps most importantly, the Alberta program seems to have been very effective. The targets for expenditure reductions have been met, a surplus was recorded ahead of the 1996/7 date for achieving a balanced budget, the economy has continued to expand at rates well above the national average, the province maintains a tax advantage, and it maintains considerable fiscal room to provide flexibility and manoeuvrability.

## 5.2 Challenges

At this point it would appear that the logic and results are more on the side of the program adopted by the Klein government to deal with fiscal deficits than on the side of the more traditional approaches.[65] Nevertheless, it will take considerable time before a complete and thorough assessment is possible. Moreover, there remain significant shorter-run challenges and risks that are addressed in the other chapters in this volume.

Here the focus is on the external challenges and those that are longer term in nature. The almost desperate fiscal situation at the federal level, not to mention the complications arising from the Québec problem, is a major issue for Albertans, as it is for Canadians in other provinces. The achievement of a sterling fiscal performance in Alberta could ultimately be tantamount to securing the best seat on the *Titanic*. A related concern is that to deal with its fiscal deficits, the federal government will simply increase the rate at which it downloads the problem to the provinces. The latest federal budget shows that Alberta, along with British Columbia and Ontario, will continue to bear the brunt of the reductions in transfers when account is taken of equalization payments. In fact, the net transfers to all of the other provinces except Québec will increase. To the extent this downloading continues primarily to the 'better-off' provinces, Alberta is at risk and even at greater risk when the political factor is included.

Another challenge will be an assessment of the longer-term implications of the expenditure cuts. For example, it may well be that many of the cuts were accomplished by diverting capital replacement and maintenance expenditures to operating expenditure categories. This 'running down' of capital would not be entirely obvious over shorter periods and could be extremely costly to reverse. Furthermore, unlike the case for the private sector, the standard accounting procedures used by governments do not allow a ready determination of the existence or extent of such problems. The consequences of the cuts in terms of other aspects of government services may also occur only slowly over longer periods of time and may also be difficult to measure and address in a timely fashion.

A further challenge will be sticking to the program after a series of substantial surpluses or when the provincial economy next experiences a major shock, particularly of the negative type experienced with the introduction of the National Energy Program and the collapse of grain and oil prices in 1986. Notwithstanding the legislated requirements to maintain a balanced budget (and make annual contributions to paying down the debt), such a negative shock could have the potential to undermine dramatically the commitment to the program in the absence of further cushions such as a substantial revenue stabilization fund. Similarly, one would expect the government's resolve to stick to the program to be seriously tested once it is clear that substantial surpluses will be achieved even under normal circumstances. Put simply, in the absence of a deficit problem and with a decline in debt levels, it will be more difficult politically to maintain the tight control on expenditures embodied in the program.

## NOTES

1. A grant from the Donner Canadian Foundation to support this research is gratefully acknowledged. Andrew Bradford provided invaluable research assistance. Any views expressed in this paper are those of the author alone and should not be interpreted as reflecting the views of the Donner Canadian Foundation.

2. Recently, however, there has been a noticeable softening of this assessment, particularly as even the central Canadian governments have recognized the need to deal with the deficit problem.

3. The population in 1929 was 690,000, compared to 185,000 in 1906. These and other data for this section are from Government of Alberta (1938).

4. See Lisac (1995: 230–9) for an interesting comparison of this period of Alberta's fiscal history with that of the 1980s.

5. The values for Alberta GDP (in millions) for the period 1920 to 1930 (with percentage changes from the previous year) are: 1920 = 376.4; 1921 = 223.6 (–40.5); 1922 = 221.9 (–0.8); 1923 = 301.1 (35.7); 1924 = 298.6 (–0.8); 1925 = 360.6 (20.8); 1926 = 383.2 (6.3); 1927 = 462.3 (20.6); 1928 = 439.5 (–4.9); 1929 = 409.6 (–6.8); 1930 = 330.9 (–19.2). Data from Government of Alberta (1938). See also Hanson (1952).

6. The values for Alberta GDP (in millions) over this period are: 1929 = 409.6; 1930 = 330.9; 1931 = 255.5; 1932 = 214.2; 1933 = 207.0; 1934 = 255.6; 1935 = 251.0. Data from Government of Alberta (1938).

7. That is, the revenues exceeded the expenditures, excluding interest payments.

8. Investment, mostly financed externally, increased from $122 million in 1946 to $909 million in 1956. Hanson (1958).

9. It is interesting to compare this to the situation in Saskatchewan. In 1941, the respective populations of Alberta and Saskatchewan were 818,000 and 896,000. Both provinces were suffering increasing net outflows of population prior to 1946. By 1950 the net flow reversed in the case of Alberta but remained an outflow for Saskatchewan. By 1971, Alberta's population was 1,628,000 compared to 926,000 for Saskatchewan. Similarly, whereas total personal income in Alberta was only slightly higher than that in Saskatchewan in 1941, by 1971 it was more than twice as large. See Mansell (1987).

10. In 1946, 56 per cent of the population was classified as rural. By 1951, the rural population had fallen to 48 per cent. Statistics Canada, census data.

11. See Hanson (1958).

12. See Mansell and Percy (1990: 8–13).

13. See Levesque and Norrie (1979).

14. The main elements of the government's industrial strategy were set out in the Premier's Policy Statement (Alberta Hansard, 23 Oct. 1974, 3133–4). It emphasized secular stability and the need to become less dependent on the sale of unprocessed resources. See also MacGregor (1981) for a summary of the policies during this period.

15. In Chapter 7, Kneebone and McKenzie present measures of the magnitude and significance of the effect of elections on Alberta's fiscal choices.

16. The second goal was later changed to 'strengthen or diversify'. For a history of this fund, see P. Smith (1991).

17. Figures for the AHSTF are from Alberta Treasury, *Budget Address* (various years).

18. This tendency is referred to as Dutch Disease.

19. Figures from Alberta Treasury, *Financial Summary and Budgetary Review*, 1980–1.

20. A diagnosis of this downturn and that following in 1986 can be found in Mansell and Percy (1990).

21. Figures from Alberta Treasury, *Budget Address* (various years).

22. See Smith (1991) for details.

23. It is interesting to note that the projections for oil prices were very optimistic until well after the mid-1980s. For example, the National Energy Board projections in 1981 were that real oil prices would be about 60 US$/bbl (measured in 1993$) by 1990. In 1984, real prices in 1990 were projected to be almost 40 US$/bbl with significant increases thereafter. In 1986, real oil prices were projected to increase to about 25 US$/bbl by 1995. Data from National Energy Board, *Canadian Energy Supply and Demand* (various issues).

24. A location quotient is defined as the percentage of activity in sector i in the region divided by the percentage of activity in sector i in the nation. A quotient of greater than one generally indicates that the region specializes in that activity and, hence, is a net exporter, while a value of less than one usually indicates that the region is a net importer of production associated with that activity.

25. For example, by 1989 royalties, rentals, and land bonuses had declined to a level equal to about 4 per cent of Alberta GDP. These revenues amounted to between 4 and 5 per cent of GDP over the period 1960 to 1973 and were less than half that in the late 1970s and early 1980s. See Wright Mansell Research Ltd. (1991).

26. See Wright Mansell Research Ltd. (1991).

27. See Mansell and Percy (1990).

28. For example, this included irrigation and flood control projects, the establishment of the Alberta Opportunity Company and Vencap Equities Alberta Ltd., investments in Syncrude, and the development of various research and development operations. These are listed in the various annual reports of the Alberta Heritage Savings Trust Fund.

29. The largest 10, with the write-offs in millions of dollars in brackets, include NovAtel ($646), Swan Hills Waste Treatment Plant ($410), Lloydminster Bi-Provincial Upgrader ($392), Gainers ($209), Millar Western ($199), Magnesium Company of Canada ($164), Syncrude (loan write-off, $81), Chembiomed ($58), Northern Lite Canola ($51), and General Systems Research ($31). Data from Alberta Taxpayers Association (mimeograph).

30. This was the government's attempt to update its overall industrial development strategy. A summary can be found in Toward 2000 Together, Premier's Conference on Alberta's Economic Future, Moderator's Report, May 1992.

31. By 1981, 46 per cent of Alberta's population was born outside the province. As a comparison, the figure for Ontario was 34 per cent. Only BC and the Territories had higher percentages. Statistics Canada, census data.

32. By 1986, only 30 per cent of the paid workers in Alberta were unionized, a percentage significantly below that in the other provinces. See M.L. Coates, D. Arrowsmith, and M. Courchene, *The Labour Movement and Trade Unionism Reference Tables* (Kingston, Ont.: Industrial Relations Centre, Queen's University, 1989).

33. The projected deficits were $2.2 billion in 1993/4, $1.8 billion in 1994/5, $1.4 billion in 1995/6, and $1.1 billion in 1996/7. Figures from Provincial Treasurer, *Budget Address 1992.*

34. A primary or basic surplus requires that revenues exceed expenditures, excluding the cost of debt servicing.

35. Data from Department of Finance, Government of Canada, *Canada's Economic and Fiscal Challenges*, Jan. 1994.

36. Data from Provincial Treasurer, *Financial Summary and Budget Review* and *Budget Address* (various years), and Alberta Financial Review Commission (1993).

37. See Neufeld (1993).

38. For example, 'Soft Options Leading to Debt-Default in the OECD', *The International Bank Credit Analyst* (Dec. 1994): 26, suggests that Canada's 'dependence on external borrowing remains excessive and its interest burden consumes a large portion of national savings. This implies that the country is on the edge of serious instability.'

39. The increases in provincial tax rates are described in Section 2.2. The increases in federal income tax rates also increase tax revenues for the provinces even in the absence of increases in the basic provincial rates (expressed as a percentage of the federal rate).

40. For example, a Gallup poll in Oct. 1990 indicated that in Alberta 36 per cent supported the Reform Party, with 20 per cent support in BC and 15 per cent across the Prairies.

41. Poll results reported in *Alberta Report*, 12 Nov. 1990: 7–11.

42. Toward 2000 Together involved a process initiated by Premier Getty in Aug. 1991 to solicit opinions from Albertans on a broad range of issues and strategies, many dealing with the economic future of the province.

43. See Alberta Financial Review Commission, *Report to Albertans*, 31 Mar. 1993.

44. This was subsequently changed to the lesser of the five-year average or 90 per cent of the forecast for resource revenue. A similar approach was adopted for corporate income tax revenues.

45. Primarily because of better than expected levels of economic activity and resource revenues, the actual deficits have been considerably smaller than the budget projections in 1993/4 and 1994/5. See Figure 7.

46. Government of Alberta, *News Release,* 24 Nov. 1993.

47. Government of Alberta, *A Better Way: A Plan For Securing Alberta's Future,* 24 Feb. 1994.

48. For example, see Mathias (1971).

49. Government of Alberta, *Measuring Up, First Annual Report By The Government of Alberta,* June 1995.

50. This was referred to as *Right on the Money, A Budget Roundtable,* 29–30 Mar. 1993.

51. The conclusions were summarized in *Summary, Budget Roundtable 'Right on the Money',* issued by the co-chairs Norm Wagner and Ralph Young (dated 6 Apr. 1993).

52. For example, the general condition that the steady debt to GDP ratio equals the basic fiscal deficit as a percentage of GDP, divided by the difference between the real growth rate and the real interest rate.

53. It might be noted that most of the borrowing was essentially to finance consumption (in the form of government services) rather than to finance capital (including social infrastructure) that would increase productive capacity.

54. The consensus seemed to be that a 10 to 15 per cent cut in provincial government expenditures was possible and should be attempted first, but that it might be necessary to eliminate the remainder of the deficit through increases in revenues.

55. However, some user fees have been introduced and some existing fees have been increased.

56. On these issues, see the articles by Johnson, Bayoumi and Laxton, Barry and Devereaux, and James in Robson and Scarth (1994).

57. An example of this is the 'isolation paradox' in the literature on cost-benefit and market failure.

58. See Government of Alberta, *News Release*, 18 Jan. 1994.

59. 'There are two ways to cut expenditures. There is the intelligent way—which involves going through each department and questioning each program. Then there is the stupid way: announcing how much will be cut, and getting each department to cut that amount. I favour the stupid way.' From *Right on the Money, A Budget Roundtable*, 1993, p. 24.

60. See Emery's discussion in Chapter 10.

61. See 1992–3 Bill 67 of the Legislative Assembly of Alberta, *Deficit Elimination Act*.

62. See 1995 Bill 1 of the Legislative Assembly of Alberta, *Alberta Taxpayer Protection Act* and 1995 Bill 6, *Balanced Budget and Debt Retirement Act*.

63. For example, under Bill 6, in calculating resource revenues for budgetary purposes, the provincial treasurer can now use the lesser of the five-year average for non-renewable resource revenues or 90 per cent of the forecast amount for these revenues. In the recent Bill 47 (Reinvestment Act), additional changes are introduced, including an acceleration of the paydown of Alberta's net debt to eliminate it by the year 2010.

64. Further to this, see the discussion by Kneebone and McKenzie in Chapter 5.

65. As a result of the cuts and unexpected revenue gains, particularly in natural resource and corporate income tax revenues, the provincial government achieved surpluses of $958 million in 1994/5 and $1.1 billion in 1995/6. A large surplus is also forecast for 1996/7.

## REFERENCES

Alberta Financial Review Commission (1993), *Report to Albertans* (31 Mar.).

Barry, F., and M.B. Devereux (1994), 'The Macroeconomics of Government Budget Cuts: Can Fiscal Contractions Be Expansionary?' in W. Robson and W. Scarth, eds, *Deficit Reduction—What Pain, What Gain?* Toronto: C.D. Howe Institute.

Bayoumi, T., and D. Laxton (1994), 'Government Deficits, Debt and the Business Cycle', in W. Robson and W. Scarth, eds, *Deficit Reduction—What Pain, What Gain?* Toronto: C.D. Howe Institute.

Boothe, P. (1990), 'Public Sector Saving and Long-Term Fiscal Balance in a Resource-Based Economy: Alberta 1969-1989'. Research Paper No. 90-13, Department of Economics. Edmonton: University of Alberta.

———— (1994a), 'Economic Reality and the Perceptions of Budget Makers'. Research Paper No. 94-7, Department of Economics. Edmonton: University of Alberta.

———— (1994b), 'A Comment on Government Deficits: Measuring Solvency and Sustainability', in W. Robson and W. Scarth, eds, *Deficit Reduction—What Pain, What Gain?* Toronto: C.D. Howe Institute.

Dahlby, B. (1992), 'Sustainable Fiscal Policy and Fiscal Adjustment in Alberta'. Research Paper, Department of Economics, University of Alberta (28 July).

———— (1994), 'The Distortionary Effect of Rising Taxes', in W. Robson and W. Scarth, eds, *Deficit Reduction—What Pain, What Gain?* Toronto: C.D. Howe Institute.

Eltis, W. (1995), 'The Transformation of the World Economy in the 1990s', *The International Bank Credit Analyst* (Jan.).

Giavazzi, F., and M. Pagano (1990), 'Can Severe Fiscal Contractions Be Expansionary? Tales of Two Small European Countries', in O.J. Blanchard and S. Fisher, eds, *NBER Macroeconomics Review*. Cambridge, Mass.: MIT Press.

Government of Alberta (1938), *The Case for Alberta. Part I, Alberta's Problems and Dominion-Provincial Relations*. Edmonton: King's Printer.

———— (1993), *Seizing Opportunity: Alberta's New Economic Development Strategy* (22 Apr.).

———— (1994), *A Better Way: A Plan for Securing Alberta's Future* (24 Feb.).

———— (1995), *Measuring Up, First Annual Report By The Government of Alberta* (June).

Government of Canada, Department of Finance (1994), *Canada's Economic and Fiscal Challenges* (Jan.).

Hanson, E.J. (1952), 'A Financial History of Alberta, 1905-1950'. Ph.D. dissertation (Clark University).

———— (1958), *Dynamic Decade: The Evolution and Effects of the Oil Industry in Alberta*. Toronto: McClelland & Stewart.

*The International Bank Credit Analyst* (1994), 'Soft Options Leading to Debt-Default in the OECD' (Dec.).

James, S. (1994), 'Debt Reduction with Distorting Taxes and Incomplete Ricardianism: A Computable General Equilibrium Analysis', in W. Robson and W. Scarth, eds, *Deficit Reduction—What Pain, What Gain?* Toronto: C.D. Howe Institute.

Johnson, D.R. (1994), 'Ricardian Equivalence: Assessing the Evidence for Canada', in W. Robson and W. Scarth, eds, *Deficit Reduction—What Pain, What Gain?* Toronto: C.D. Howe Institute.

Levesque, T.J., and K.H. Norrie (1979), 'Overwhelming Majorities in the Legislature of Alberta', *Canadian Journal of Political Science* 12 (3): 451–70.

Lisac, M. (1995), *The Klein Revolution*. Edmonton: NeWest Press.

MacGregor, J.G. (1981), *A History of Alberta*. Edmonton: Hurtig Publishers.

McMillan, M.L. (1991), *Provincial Public Finances: Plaudits, Problems and Prospects*. Canadian Tax Paper No. 91. Toronto: Canadian Tax Foundation.

————, and A.A. Warrack (1995), 'Alberta's Fiscal Update: One-Track (Thinking) Towards Deficit Reduction'. Information Bulletin Number 28. Edmonton: Western Centre for Economic Research, University of Alberta.

Mansell, R.L. (1987), 'Energy Policy, Prices and Rents: Implications for Regional Growth and Development', in W.J. Coffey and M. Polese, eds, *Still Living Together: Recent Trends and Future Directions in Canadian Regional Development*. Montreal: Institute for Research and Public Policy.

————, and M.B. Percy (1990), *Strength in Adversity: A Study of the Alberta Economy*. Edmonton: University of Alberta Press.

Maslove, A.M. (1989), *Budgeting in the Provinces: Leadership and the Premiers*. Monographs on Canadian Public Administration—No. 11. Toronto: The Institute of Public Administration of Canada.

Mathias, P. (1971), *Forced Growth*. Toronto: James Lorimer.

Nesbitt Burns (1995), *Provincial Handbook, Economic Research*. vol. II (Sept.).

Neufeld, E.P. (1993), 'Canada's Looming Fiscal Crisis: How Bad is it?' The C.D. Howe Institute Conference on Deficits and Debt, Palliser Hotel, Calgary (1 June).

Norrie, K.H. (1984), 'A Regional Economic Overview of the West Since 1945', in A.W. Rasporich, ed., *The Making of the Modern West*. Calgary: University of Calgary Press.

Richards, J., and L. Pratt (1979), *Prairie Capitalism: Power and Influence in the West*. Toronto: McClelland & Stewart.

Robson, W.B.P., and W.M. Scarth (1994), *Deficit Reduction—What Pain, What Gain?* Toronto: C.D. Howe Institute.

Ruggeri, G.C., D. Van Wart, and R. Howard (1995), 'Fiscal Incidence as an Indicator of Voter Preference', *Canadian Business Economics* 3 (3): 42–53.

Smith, P.J. (1991), 'The Politics of Plenty: Investing Natural Resource Revenues in Alberta and Alaska', *Canadian Public Policy* 17 (2): 139–54.

Smith, R. (1991), 'Alberta: Provincial Public Finances', in M. McMillan, ed., *Provincial Public Finances: Provincial Surveys*, vol. 1. Canadian Tax Paper No. 91. Toronto: Canadian Tax Foundation.

Tupper, A., L. Pratt, and I. Urquhart (1992), 'The Role of Government', *Government and Politics in Alberta*.

Wood Gundy (1994), *1994 Provincial Profiles*. Economics Department.

——— (1995), *1995 Provincial Profiles*. Economics Department.

Wright Mansell Research Ltd. (1991), *The Role of the Oil and Gas Industry in the Alberta Economy and the Macroeconomic Impacts of Royalty Adjustments*. A Study Prepared for the Independent Petroleum Association of Canada. (Oct.).

# Comments on Chapter 2　　　　　　　　　　■

*Kenneth Norrie*

The organizers of this study are to be congratulated on their choice of author for the overview chapter. Professor Robert Mansell is, without question, the ranking expert on Alberta's economic development and the role of government policies, federal and provincial, in that development. His expertise is amply demonstrated in this chapter. Professor Mansell provides an interesting historical perspective stretching back to the very beginnings of the province in 1905, sets out the economic and political environment for the election year 1993, and discusses the components of the Klein program and their apparent rationale in considerable detail. I can recommend this chapter as a comprehensive and well-written introduction to the subject.

I had considerable difficulty deciding how to proceed with an overview of an overview. In the end, I decided to focus my comments around four general questions that arose in reading this chapter.

The first question is perhaps an obvious one: what is the 'Alberta experiment' exactly? From Mansell's chapter, and from other sources, it seems that there are at least three answers to this query. One, it is aggressive deficit and debt reduction, largely taking the form of quick and deep expenditure cuts. Two, it is a rethinking (read: downsizing) of the role of government in the economy. Three, it is a reconsideration of the way in which the government manages the functions it does maintain. Departments now operate with multi-year business plans, their performances are judged according to explicit performance criteria, and fiscal discipline is enforced through legislation.

Mansell discusses each of these aspects of the Klein agenda in detail, but he does not comment on the connections among them. Thus we are left wondering if there is one Alberta experiment with three interrelated parts or three separate Alberta experiments. In other words, how necessary is any one part of the agenda to any other part? In particular, is deficit and debt reduction driving the others? To what extent are the spending cuts motivated by deficit considerations, and to what extent by a preference for smaller government? To what extent are the managerial initiatives intended to cut administration costs, and to what extent are they driven by a concern to improve visibility and accountability? Where does the oft-stated objective of maintaining the lowest rates of personal and business taxation in Canada fit into all this?

The second general question follows from the first. What are the origins of the Klein agenda? Mansell looks for these in Alberta's economic and political history, and he is certainly correct to do so. But it would be interesting to cast the net wider and ask, as well, what the intellectual roots are. Chris Bruce has spoken about how the Alberta experience provides a rare 'laboratory' setting for testing theories of political and bureaucratic behaviour. But surely the reverse phenomenon is equally interesting, that is, the role that theory plays in informing policy. Is there any evidence that particular theories, philosophies, writers, or research institutes played an important role in shaping the Klein strategy? If so, by what process did these ideas become practical guides to action? As a corollary, is there any evidence that economic theory, however simple, is being used to guide the implementation of the strategies? For example, have public finance principles had any role in the decision to meet deficit targets by cutting spending rather than by raising taxes, or in deciding which government functions to privatize?

One might also ask about precedents in other jurisdictions. Premier Klein's international media attention notwithstanding, Alberta is not alone in the world in cutting deficits and debts, downsizing government, and reforming bureaucracies. For a while, it seemed that every time I turned on the radio in Edmonton I heard someone with a New Zealand accent talking about 'leaping canyons'. How important was the New Zealand experience, or other international initiatives, to the framers of the Alberta experiment? I suspect that there are politicians and bureaucrats in Regina, Saint John, and St John's who wonder why Alberta gets all the attention. Let us not forget that even the Mulroney Tories, who are best remembered for their annual $30–$40 billion deficits, cut program spending, privatized government operations, and merged departments and agencies.

The third question, an extension of the second one really, is whether the Alberta experiment can be transplanted to other provinces. One might interpret Mansell as suggesting that it cannot. He argues forcefully that the inherent instability of the Alberta economy in general, and of resource rents in particular, have much to do with the quick run-up of deficits and debt. He also argues, more positively, that the province's industrial structure, its experience at dealing with economic instability, and its high proportion of economically motivated migrants have given it a population 'more disposed to smaller government and more self-reliance', a majority of whom 'would encourage and support the type of tough fiscal program associated with the Klein government'. Yet, as noted above, Alberta is not the only jurisdiction, nor indeed even the first one, to embrace fiscal austerity. The progress of Ontario's 'Common Sense Revolution' will provide an interesting test of this intriguing hypothesis.

The final question is whether we (academics, journalists, others) have devoted enough attention to the potential pitfalls of the Alberta experiment. Mansell does not attempt any such evaluation, nor should we expect him to in an overview chapter. The tone of the long section on the Klein program, however, suggests that he is largely supportive of the measures and the procedures. He expresses some concerns about the long-term implications of running down social capital, and doubtless he would add others if probed. The chapters on health, education, and welfare that appear later in this volume will add some further qualifications and reservations. Since economic development is not one of the areas covered, I can take this opportunity to note my own concern with the apparent objective of removing government completely from this area. We will avoid future 'NovaTels' with this strategy, but we might miss some future 'Syncrudes' as well. The policy implications of some of the new growth theories are worth studying, I believe.

In closing, let me once again congratulate the organizers for putting together this volume, and Bob Mansell for producing this overview chapter.

# CHAPTER 3

# Institutional Design and Public Policy: A Microeconomic Perspective

*Kenneth J. McKenzie*

## 1. INTRODUCTION

The purpose of this chapter is to summarize some of the research concerning the design and implementation of public policy in order to provide a theoretical framework within which to evaluate the institutional reforms undertaken by the Klein government. The literature in this area is immense; as such, the summary will be selective. The focus will be on studies considered, perhaps somewhat arbitrarily, to take a microeconomic perspective; Kneebone discusses macroeconomic issues in the following chapter. Although the discussion is largely, and intentionally, devoid of any specific references to the Alberta situation, the issues addressed and the studies summarized have been chosen because of their relevance to the changes currently taking place in the province.[1]

## 2. THE PUBLIC CHOICE APPROACH TO POLICY ANALYSIS

The standard approach to analysing government policy is based on the traditional neoclassical paradigm. It is presumed that economic agents are rational and self-interested and make decisions that maximize their well-being. In an environment where information is costless and symmetric (though not necessarily perfect), there are no transaction or bargaining costs, property rights can be costlessly defined and enforced, and there is no market power, the allocation of resources in the economy achieved in market equilibrium will be Pareto efficient—it will not be possible to reallocate resources in a way so as to make one group of individuals better off without making another group worse off. This, of course, is the first theorem of welfare economics.

In this environment, government intervention in the economy may be justified from a social welfare perspective only on distributional or equity grounds. When the market equilibrium results in an outcome that is considered to be socially inequitable, the government may play a redistributive role in the economy.

It is possible, however, that the economy fails to achieve an efficient alloca-tion of resources, in which case government intervention may be justified on efficiency grounds. This can occur if there are *market failures*—i.e., if informa-tion is not symmetric or its acquisition is not costless, transacting and/or bar-gaining costs are not zero, property rights cannot be costlessly defined and/or enforced, or if there is market power. When this is the case, there may be scope for government policy to move the economy closer to an efficient outcome.[2] Most economists would agree that, in the presence of market failures, there is good reason for some government institutions to exist on efficiency grounds.

Under the traditional neoclassical approach to public economics the gov-ernment is typically treated as 'institution neutral' and benevolent. That is, the efficiency of government policy is analysed independently of the political and bureaucratic institutions through which it is conceived and implemented. It is thus implicitly assumed that government institutions are efficient in their own right, and the government is presumed to maximize some (not always well-defined) social welfare function. Public choice theory, on the other hand, makes no such presumptions—it explicitly allows for potential inefficiencies due to failures in political and bureaucratic institutions, and recognizes that govern-ments and bureaucracies are composed of utility-maximizing individuals whose objectives may not always be well aligned with the 'public good', how-ever it might be defined.

Both approaches to public policy analysis recognize the importance of transaction costs, information costs and asymmetries, difficulties in defining and enforcing property rights, etc., and their implications for the efficiency of the equilibrium outcome. While market failures in the private sector imply *scope* for government intervention, similar failures in the public sector suggest that this intervention may give rise to other inefficiencies.

The genesis of the public choice approach to policy analysis can be found in the writings of Bowen (1942), Black (1948), Buchanan (1949), Arrow (1950, 1951), and Downs (1957), among others. This was followed by Buchanan and Tullock's seminal work, *The Calculus of Consent* (1962). The current literature in the area is very large, and growing.

The public choice approach focuses on the relationships between the elec-torate, legislators, and bureaucrats, and the implications of these relationships for the formulation of public policy. As illustrated in Figure 1, even when reduced to their bare essentials, these relationships are complicated. The schematic shows in a simplified way how the preferences of the electorate, politicians, and bureaucrats interact within political and bureaucratic institu-tions to produce policy outcomes.

Voters elect politicians to represent their interests. Through their member-ship in cabinet and various committees, politicians formulate government

**Figure 1:** Lines of Communication

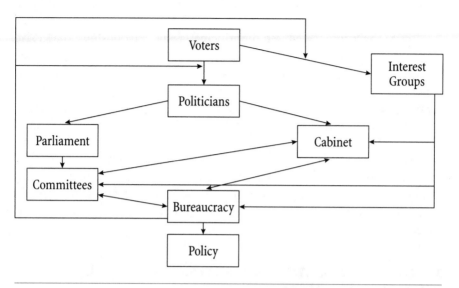

NOTE: The arrows represent lines of communication or directions of influence among the participants in the democratic/bureaucratic process.

policy. This policy is carried out by the bureaucracy, who are able to influence the final product through their implementation of the policy, through their participation in the policy-making process itself via their interaction with politicians, and through their influence on political outcomes in their roles as consumer-voters. Throughout the process, special interest groups may influence government policy by lobbying individual politicians, members of cabinet, committees, and the bureaucracy; indeed, the bureaucracy can be viewed as an interest group itself.

The schematic also serves to illustrate the multitude of *principal-agent* relationships that exist throughout the policy process. At various stages principals (e.g., voters, politicians) rely on agents (e.g., politicians, bureaucrats) to act in a way that reflects the wishes and interests of the principals. Monitoring and information collection costs can give rise to an asymmetry of information between principals and agents. This means that the principals are not able to perfectly or costlessly observe the actions of the agents, who may have different preferences and/or objectives. This, it is argued, is one of the key reasons that political and bureaucratic institutions may be inefficient. Principal-agent theory suggests that a way to reduce this potential inefficiency is to reward (or punish) the agent based on some *ex post facto* measure of performance. In this way, the agent can be induced to act in the best interests of the principal. Much of the public choice literature relies (sometimes implicitly) on principal-agent theory as the basic analytical framework within which to study the efficiency of political and bureaucratic institutions.

Given the complicated set of principal-agent relationships that exist throughout the policy process, there is no generally accepted 'grand unified' model of the political and bureaucratic process. Although there are some important exceptions, researchers have tended to focus on different aspects of the policy-making process independently of each other. So, for example, there is a body of literature that deals primarily with the principal-agent relationship between voters and politicians, largely abstracting from the role of the bureaucracy; another body of research focuses primarily on the relationship between legislators and civil servants, for the most part abstracting from the electorate. Although this distinction is somewhat artificial, and at times forced, it does allow the various studies to be grouped together in a reasonably coherent manner.

## 3. VOTERS AND POLITICIANS: THE EFFICIENCY OF THE POLITICAL MARKETPLACE

Most democratic societies employ some form of representative democracy whereby citizens do not decide on public policy directly, but rather choose representatives to do so on their behalf. In this section some of the literature dealing with the normative characteristics of political outcomes in this environment will be briefly summarized. A particularly important question concerns the conditions under which a political outcome determined under representative democracy is efficient.

Arguments about the normative characteristics of the political process are inevitably slippery because there are no obvious standards against which to measure outcomes. Economists naturally appeal to the notion of Pareto efficiency. That is, policies enacted by politicians are efficient if an alternative set of policies cannot be introduced so as to make one group of citizens better off without making another group worse off. Strictly speaking, then, Pareto 'improving' policies should be able to garner unanimous support. Yet modern democracies rarely, if ever, rely on the principle of unanimity. Moreover, most policy decisions do not involve Pareto improving outcomes, as one group is almost inevitably made worse off. A somewhat different notion of political efficiency, rooted in the majority voting tradition, is thus often employed. This notion focuses on the extent to which the policies enacted by politicians represent the wishes of their constituents. According to this notion, a policy is efficient if it is preferred by the majority. If politicians enact policies that would not receive the support of a fully informed majority, they are 'shirking' on their constituents, and the resulting outcome is not politically efficient. This approach to political efficiency reflects the view that in a democratic society the voters are the ultimate source of authority.

Another efficiency concept that will arise in the ensuing discussion is *second-best* efficiency. The idea here is that a Pareto efficient (first-best) outcome may not be attainable because it is too costly, or even impossible, to overcome the market failure, typically because of information or transaction costs. In this case, a second-best efficient outcome is the 'most efficient' of all outcomes attainable subject to the presence of the existing market failure.

## 3.1 The Median Voter Model

Much of the public choice literature that studies outcomes under majority rule employs the median voter model conceived by Hotelling (1929) and refined by Downs (1957). The starting point for the model is the presumption that 'parties formulate policies in order to win elections, rather than win elections in order to formulate policies' (Downs, 1957: 28). The idea is that if a politician wants to maximize the likelihood of being elected, and if election outcomes are decided by a majority voting rule, then (under some conditions) he/she will choose a policy position at the centre (median) of the distribution of policy preferences of the constituents. In this model, policy choices that reflect the preferences of the median voter are efficient according to the second notion of efficiency described above.

A limiting feature of the median voter result is that it holds only under fairly stringent assumptions, although these are not as restrictive as suggested by the original Hotelling-Downs formulation. The original formulation assumed that individual voter preferences were 'single-peaked' and expressed over one-dimensional policy outcomes, and that the distribution of preferences among voters was unimodal and symmetric. In a careful survey of spatial models of political competition, Osborne (1995) shows that some of the assumptions made in the original formulation can be relaxed without sacrificing the basic result. For example, when the analysis is extended to allow for multidimensional policies the median voter theorem survives, although it is less likely that an equilibrium will exist. The symmetry assumption can also be generalized. Moreover, the basic idea behind the model continues to hold 'even if each candidate, like each citizen, cares about the policy enacted, rather than [just] whether or not she wins [the election]' (Osborne, 1995: 271). The one assumption that appears vital to the median voter result is that of single-peaked preferences. This means that for each voter there exists an *ideal position*, such that policies that are further and further away from this position, in any direction, make the voter worse and worse off. When this condition does not hold, it is possible to get 'vote-cycling', where pair-wise voting among alternatives does not yield an unambiguous ranking. In this case majority voting does not result in a stable equilibrium (Comanor, 1976). Although much of the public choice literature seems to take the assumption of single-peakedness for granted, there is no reason to expect preferences to satisfy this condition. The assumption of single-peakedness thus imposes considerable structure on preferences. This makes it difficult to make general judgements about political outcomes using the model.

Another problem with the standard model is that it presumes no uncertainty on the part of either voters or candidates regarding each other's preferences over policy positions. Osborne shows that under conditions of certainty, the median voter model predicts that candidates choose *identical* policy positions. Although casual observation suggests that candidates and parties often choose *similar* platforms, they are not typically identical. Extensions that account for this will be discussed in section 3.3.

### 3.2 Arrow's Theorem
The remarkable insight of Arrow (1950, 1951), suggests that the two notions of political efficiency discussed above—Pareto efficiency and the ability to garner majority support for the policy—may not be reconcilable. Arrow shows that, in general, unless we are willing to make very restrictive assumptions about individual preferences, there is no democratic voting mechanism (majority rule or otherwise) that can be used to aggregate the preferences of individual constituents in a way that will guarantee a Pareto efficient outcome. As such, even if we presume that politicians cater to the preferences of the median voter, we cannot be sure that the resulting policy outcome will be Pareto efficient. For example, in an illustration of Arrow's general result in a specific context, Shepsle and Weingast (1984) show that the provision of public goods in a median voter model will not generally be efficient.

### 3.3 Uncertainty and Imperfect Information
From a modelling perspective the median voter model gives rise to several problems. As mentioned, the fact that candidates do not typically choose identical platforms cannot be explained by the standard model. Moreover, median voter outcomes are not generally Pareto efficient, which is a thorn in the side of those who believe, perhaps somewhat dogmatically, in the ultimate authority of the political marketplace. Finally, there is the problem of vote-cycling and the general instability of equilibrium if one is not prepared to assume single-peakedness. Introducing uncertainty into the political process, whereby candidates are uncertain about the preferences of voters and/or voters are uncertain about the true policy platforms of candidates, not only makes for a more realistic model but addresses some of these difficulties.

Osborne (1995) shows that when candidates have their own preferences about policy outcomes, and therefore do not care only about winning or losing, they may choose different policy positions if they are uncertain about the distribution of the citizens' ideal policy positions. Mueller (1989) discusses a class of models known as *probabilistic voting models*, whereby voters are uncertain about the true policy positions of the candidates. Depending on the form of the function determining the probability that a voter will vote for a particular candidate, the outcome of a majority-rule electoral process will be one that maximizes some social welfare function that aggregates the expressed preferences of the voters over political outcomes. Coughlin (1982) shows that as long as the probability that an individual will vote for a candidate is an increasing function of the voter's expected utility from that candidate's platform, the resulting political equilibrium will be Pareto optimal. This is a remarkable result, analogous to the 'invisible hand' of the market yielding an efficient outcome in the economic marketplace. Here, political competition under a majority voting rule gives rise to the same type of result. This would appear to restore the faith of those who believe in the sanctity of the political process.

## 3.4 Costly and Asymmetric Information

There are, however, several reasons why one should not be too sanguine about this result. The role of information is again key. Information about public policy issues and politicians is costly to obtain and often unreliable. Moreover, the benefits to individual voters of obtaining this information are typically quite low, because each individual, by virtue of his/her single vote, has only a negligible impact on the outcome of any election. Also, if candidates tend to 'cluster' around similar platforms, it may not be worthwhile to vote because policy positions are effectively indistinguishable from each other, particularly if there are costs associated with the act of voting itself (e.g., time costs). As such, if they choose to vote at all, utility-maximizing consumers may choose to be 'rationally uninformed'.[3]

This 'rational ignorance' on the part of voters was pointed out by Downs (1957); intimately associated with it is the idea that information-gathering costs can give rise to an asymmetry of information across voters[4] because some policies have important consequences for certain groups within society. For these groups, information costs may be quite low and/or the benefits of information acquisition quite high. Furthermore, when the benefits of a policy are concentrated but the costs diffuse, the beneficiaries have a greater incentive to become informed and to involve themselves in the political process than those bearing the costs (Demzetz, 1982). Ferejohn (1990) argues that in this environment the distribution of knowledge across the electorate is likely to be quite uneven.

In an environment where information is costly and asymmetric, politicians have an incentive to provide it. They may also have an incentive to use information strategically, perhaps through false or misleading advertising. There are several implications of this. One, pointed out by Breton and Wintrobe (1992), is that asymmetric information regarding the 'quality' and honesty of politicians may give rise to an adverse selection problem in the market for politicians. Since voters cannot tell 'good' (honest) politicians from 'bad' (dishonest) ones, all politicians tend to get lumped together, tarred with the same brush so to speak. As such, high quality is undervalued in the political marketplace and low quality is overvalued. In much the same way that 'lemons' in the used car market can drive out good cars because consumers have difficulty in costlessly distinguishing between them, the presence of low-quality politicians can drive out high-quality politicians.

Notwithstanding the adverse selection problem, the presence of costly information may manifest itself in other ways. For example, it may provide an incentive for parties to run 'non-issue'-oriented campaigns to economize on the information-gathering costs imposed on the electorate. Thus, the *perceived* trustworthiness, honesty, and credibility of party leaders can play a key role in election outcomes simply because rational voters do not want to go to the time and expense of researching complicated policy positions; they are content to rely on a leader they believe will 'do the right thing'.

Brennan and Buchanan (1984) offer another explanation for why political outcomes in the presence of 'rational ignorance' may not have desirable normative characteristics. They draw the analogy between the act of voting and fan participation at a sporting event. By cheering, an individual expresses a preference for a particular team. While recognizing that the collective voice of fans *may* affect the outcome, fans realize that their *individual* support is inconsequential. As such, factors other than their impact on the outcome determine individual fan behaviour. So it is with voting. Given the irrelevance of the individual vote, voting behaviour is likely affected by factors that have nothing to do with the desire to influence the outcome—peer pressure, catchy campaign slogans, the personal appeal of the candidate, etc. Noting that the Pareto efficiency of the probabilistic voting models is based on the *expressed* preferences of voters, which may well reflect factors other than the actual policy positions of the candidates, Brennan and Buchanan question the significance of any positive or normative conclusions that may be drawn. Their view seems to be that the political equilibrium in these models can be considered efficient only in a very unsatisfactory second-best sense.

Another issue in an environment with costly and asymmetric information that has important implications for the efficiency of the political marketplace is the extent to which political representatives ignore the wishes of their constituents. Kalt and Zupan (1990) investigate the presence of such shirking in the US Congress using a political ideology rating scale. They find some evidence of 'principal-agent slack' and 'ideological shirking' on the part of Congress, whereby members of Congress do not seem to be representing the interests of their constituency. This contrasts with the findings of Peltzman (1984, 1990), who questions the empirical importance of Downsian 'rational ignorance' and, by implication, principal-agent slack. Peltzman (1984: 210) concludes that the presence of ideological shirking on the part of Congress 'is more apparent than real'. Peltzman (1990) seeks to determine whether or not voters use available economic information when making voting decisions, in particular whether voters use information on the economic performance of incumbents to punish or reward them at the voting box. The approach is consistent with the principal-agent approach to policy analysis, which suggests that principals (voters) compensate agents (incumbent politicians) based on some measure of past performance. On the basis of his investigation, Peltzman concludes 'that the voting market is a surprisingly good aggregator of . . . information' (p. 29), and, 'indeed, one would be hard put to find nonpolitical markets that process information better than the voting market' (p. 63). His results call into question those who feel the efficiency of political markets is suspect because of costly and asymmetric information.

## 3.5 Interest Groups and Rent-Seeking

Another implication of costly information is that it can give rise to an opportunity for interest groups to influence political outcomes. Coughlin, Mueller, and Murrell (1988) incorporate interest groups into a probabilistic voting model. They define an interest group as a group of individuals with identical preferences and incomes. In their model, interest groups play a purely passive role—they do not lobby or try to influence political outcomes directly. None the less, the mere presence of these like-minded individuals can affect the outcome of political competition. In particular, they show that under some conditions the political outcome is still Pareto efficient, but with the interests of individual groups weighted more heavily the larger their membership.

Of course, interest groups are not typically passive, as they have an incentive to take advantage of asymmetric and costly information to influence political outcomes, for example, by providing campaign funds to politicians or by advertising on their own. Many authors have captured this idea by developing models in which the number of expected votes depends not only on candidate platforms but also on campaign expenditures.[5] As such, interest groups play an active role in influencing political outcomes through their campaign contributions. See, for example, Kau, Keenan, and Rubin (1982); Mueller (1989) presents a similar model.

The so-called 'Virginia School' of public choice, typically associated with Buchanan, Tollison, and Tullock, among others, focuses on the inefficiencies arising from special interest group behaviour.[6] The presence of interest groups has implications for the efficiency of the political outcome for two reasons. First, groups may lower efficiency directly by financing candidates whose positions regarding the provision of, say, some public good most closely matches their own. If the number of votes a candidate receives increases relative to the amount spent on campaigning, this can result in an equilibrium outcome where the level of public good provision is not Pareto efficient. So, for example, park lovers may contribute funds to elect a candidate who is in favour of more parks than would be dictated by pure efficiency considerations.

Interest groups may also contribute to candidates in order to encourage a straight transfer of wealth from one group to another. An important point to realize is that even if this transfer is lump sum—i.e., independent of personal characteristics or circumstances—and therefore apparently irrelevant from an efficiency perspective, it may still have efficiency implications. This is because this *rent-seeking* on the part of individuals to secure and collect the transfer involves the use of resources that could otherwise be put to productive use— the time, effort, and money devoted to pursuing a purely redistributive goal could be devoted to other, more socially productive activities. Indeed, under some conditions the wealth received by the group benefiting from the transfer can be completely dissipated by these rent-seeking costs.[7]

Stigler (1971) and Peltzman (1976) have investigated the role of interest groups in a regulatory context in their seminal studies of 'regulatory capture.' The thrust of their argument is that regulations arise as the result of the demand from interest groups for government intervention. That is, government regulators can be 'captured' by an interest group when the regulatory outcome is favourable to that group. This is in stark contrast to the (neoclassical) notion that government regulation exists to protect the interests of the general public. Although both Stigler and Peltzman are primarily concerned with the positive aspects of regulation and interest groups, the idea that government policies can benefit certain groups to the possible detriment of the citizenry at large has obvious normative implications for the efficiency of political markets.

The focus on interest groups as a way of generating wealth transfers à la Stigler and Peltzman has been the impetus for what has come to be called 'Chicago Political Economy' (CPE). Although it is difficult to provide a precise description of CPE, at the risk of oversimplifying the matter we can say that the unifying concept seems to be similar to that of their counterparts in economics—a belief in the primacy of markets, in this case the political marketplace. The school is also distinguished methodologically by its emphasis on equilibrium models and its strong empirical focus. Although CPE is often viewed as focusing on issues of a positive nature—Stigler is often cited as saying that he is out to understand the world, not change it—one cannot deny the normative implications of much of their work. Indeed, CPE is often contrasted with the Virginia School; again, at the risk of oversimplifying, the former are proponents of the view that political markets are efficient, while the latter question this contention.

Becker (1983) has been somewhat less reticent than Stigler in making normative evaluations. He makes the point that if the amount of political pressure applied by an interest group is an increasing function of their gain in well-being, then interest groups provide a way for the intensity of preferences to enter the political process. He goes on to argue that the presence of lobbying and interest groups thus minimizes the efficiency costs of redistribution.[8] Wealth transfers due to pressure groups are efficient because other ways of redistributing wealth would be more costly.

Wittman, another researcher in the Chicago tradition, argues that the presence of interest groups can enhance, or at least not detract from, the efficiency of the political marketplace. He contends that competition among interest groups for legislative favour mitigates many of the detrimental effects of such groups. Wittman also argues that the influence of interest groups over politicians is naturally limited because if a candidate adopts a policy position too far from the median voter in order to attract campaign contributions from interest groups, the number of votes lost from informed voters will eventually exceed those gained from marginally uninformed voters due to increased advertising (Wittman, 1989: 1408).

### 3.6 Decision Externalities

Hettich and Winer (1993, 1995) discuss the efficiency implications of what they call 'decision externalities' in political institutions. Legislators are often elected by distinct constituencies or coalitions and are thus primarily interested in policies that benefit those constituencies, ignoring costs imposed on others. This gives rise to a decision externality whereby legislators do not take full account of all of the social costs and/or benefits associated with their decisions—another consequence of the concentrated benefits and diffuse costs associated with some policies. The result can be excessive pork-barrelling and overspending (see, for example, Weingast, Shepsle, and Johnson, 1981). This need not be a geographic phenomenon, as other sorts of constituencies also benefit from government spending or the lack thereof. For example, the Canadian parliamentary system invests a great deal of authority with cabinet ministers. These ministers may have an incentive to institute policies that benefit certain groups, while not fully accounting for the more diffuse costs possibly associated with those policies. This can be thought of as another manifestation of the regulatory capture idea developed by Stigler (1971) and Peltzman (1976). In this case, cabinet ministers are captured by, or become advocates for, the clientele served by their ministry.

Von Hagen and Harden (1995) examine how different budget processes may serve to moderate the tendency for governments to overspend due to decision externalities. They suggest that 'spending ministers' (SMs) have an incentive to consider only the net benefit of spending on activities that benefit their constituencies, ignoring the costs imposed on taxpayers at large. They refer to the resulting tendency for individual SMs to overestimate the marginal benefit of certain activities as *fiscal illusion*—of course, it is nothing more than a decision externality arising from the concentrated benefits and diffuse costs associated with many government spending programs. They show that how budget decisions are decided in cabinet has important implications for the size of the budget. For example, if each SM merely submits the budget for his/her own ministry, treating all other ministry budgets as given, with a simple vote taken on the resulting budget, the Nash equilibrium outcome is a budget in excess of the social optimum. They go on to argue that budget processes that lead to a 'strengthening [of] the collective interest of the government'—i.e., that internalize the decision externalities—moderate this spending bias (von Hagen and Harden, 1995: 774). For example, if the budget process starts with negotiations among SMs over binding limits on their allocations, the spending bias decreases. Also, if ministers without portfolio, including the first minister and finance minister (treasurer), are vested with 'special strategic powers in the budget process'—such as veto power, agenda control, control over information flow among the SMs—the spending bias decreases because these ministers' interests are not tied as closely to narrow constituencies. Von Hagen and Harden empirically investigate some of the implications of their model by examining the spending patterns of 12 European Union countries. They find that countries investing a great deal of power with the first minister or finance minister tend to have lower deficits and debt.

Some have argued that parliamentary committees may exacerbate the decision externality problem. A cynical view of these committees is that they are only a mechanism to appease backbenchers who helped get the government elected. However, Hettich and Winer (1993: 19) argue that 'to the extent that [such committees] actually influence legislation, the "you scratch my back and I'll scratch yours" atmosphere in such committees will tend to produce overexpansion of government budgets'. Thus, the committee system may facilitate logrolling, whereby members support each other's favourite spending programs. Hettich and Winer also argue that agenda control by parliamentary committees can worsen the agency problem between politicians and the bureaucracy. Although these issues will be discussed in more depth below, the idea is that the committee structure can turn a simple principal-agent relationship (between cabinet and the bureaucracy) into a multiple principal-agent relationship (between cabinet, committees, and the bureaucracy), allowing agencies to play the two principals against each other and making it more difficult to control the bureaucracy.

## 3.7 The Reform of Political Institutions

Purchase and Hirshhorn (1994: 190), in their summary of a project studying government and competitiveness in Canada, point out that if we take as given the parliamentary structure of government as enshrined in the constitution, there is little in the way of reforms to the fundamental structure of our political institutions that might be contemplated. They argue that 'the most central accountability device of representative democracy is the election', and that 'one has ultimately to believe in the efficacy of the democratic process, the intelligence of Canadians, and the entrepreneurial capacities of political activists and partisans.'

None the less, the literature summarized above suggests some changes to political institutions that may serve to facilitate this process. Some of these are considered here. The focus is on mechanisms that may help internalize decision externalities and increase the accountability of governments by increasing the information flow. Of course, implementing any of these mechanisms requires the political will to do so. So long as governments feel that the political costs of undertaking institutional reform outweigh the political benefits, they are unlikely to initiate changes. Ultimately, there must be a perceived desire on the part of the electorate for change.

### Internalizing Decision Externalities

Some possible problems with the strong executives (cabinets) associated with parliamentary governments were discussed above. As noted by Hettich and Winer, Parliament can act as a monitoring, evaluation, and review mechanism for cabinet policies. Parliamentary committees can play an important role in this regard. Yet, as discussed above, these committees can also give rise to problems of their own. Quoting Franks (1987), Hettich and Winer (1995: 25 n. 13) caution that these committees must result in 'government in parliament, not by parliament'. Thus, Parliament and its committees must act as a check on the government, not as the government itself.

Yet it is important not to lose sight of the positive role that parliamentary committees can play in their oversight capacity. These positive attributes may be enhanced, and the negative ones reduced, if the committees are structured in light of the above considerations. For example, if the oversight responsibilities of the committees encompass broadly related policy areas, this may result in an exchange of information across policy areas allowing members of the committees, including the cabinet ministers, to better view the 'big picture' and perhaps internalize some of the decision externalities. This suggests a committee structure that is not too specialized, with not too many committees. This overlap may also allow the committees to 'benchmark' the departments against each other, possibly leading to a sort of competition among departments and agencies, again increasing the amount of information available to policy-makers. Fewer and larger committees may also reduce the scope for 'backscratching'; committees that are fluid in nature, changing membership and composition periodically, may also help in this regard by preventing members from staking out and protecting turf in certain policy areas. Finally, while a multiple principal-agent relationship may make it easier for the bureaucracy to play the principals off against each other, it also increases the amount of monitoring the bureaucracy is subjected to. Thus, in some circumstances multiple principals may lower the asymmetry of information and lead to a more efficient outcome. A related possibility is that these committees may serve as another line of defence against the tendency of cabinet ministers to overspend on the beneficiaries of their department's services. As discussed by Kneebone and McKenzie in Chapter 5, and Boothe in Chapter 6, some of the changes to the committee structure in Alberta may well capture some of these positive features.

Breton (1991) and von Hagen and Harden (1995) emphasize the role of the finance minister or treasurer in the parliamentary system as another internal mechanism that may offset some of the decision externality problems. As discussed above, the argument is that the finance minister can serve (at least partly) to balance the demands of the spending ministers against the capacity of the treasury. Breton also argues that the tradition of budget secrecy may help to strengthen the position of the treasurer in this regard. The role of the provincial treasurer in the budget-making process is discussed at length by Boothe in Chapter 6 (and also by Kneebone and McKenzie in Chapter 5).

### Increasing Government Accountability

Much of the previous discussion has focused on the importance of information in the political process.[9] Intimately associated with information is the issue of government accountability. Stanbury (1994: 87) holds the rather pessimistic view that 'the present system of cabinet government is seriously flawed with respect to one of its most widely-cited virtues—accountability,' and that 'the ability of Parliament and voters to hold accountable the cabinet . . . is highly limited . . . [because] little useful information is disclosed that would permit voters to properly assess the performance of the government.'

Yet some steps can be taken to increase the amount of information and, therefore, the accountability of the government. Even those who lean towards the Chicago view that political markets are relatively efficient would presumably favour initiatives that make government actions more transparent and visible.

For example, the auditor general can play an important role as watchdog on the government. The annual report of the auditor general not only makes government extravagances public, but often emphasizes problems with government accounting and reporting conventions. A similar role may be played by citizen review commissions, which may be charged with reviewing some aspect of government operations, either on an *ad hoc* or on a continuing basis. It is important that these commissions be at arm's length from the government in order to enhance their credibility.

Other changes involve government accounting and reporting practices. Ip (1991), along with many others, criticizes governments for being less than transparent in the accounting of their activities. Under current conventions, governments are able to move items 'off-budget', making them less visible and therefore less accountable. Governments may also manipulate the public accounts by moving items between years, by over- or underestimating revenues and/or expenditures to make improvements appear more dramatic (or blame previous governments for problems), by using tax expenditures or loan guarantees to reduce the visibility of subsidies, etc. All of these activities enable the government to manipulate its financial statements for its own ends.

While not all of these problems can be eliminated, some steps can be taken to minimize them. For example, many have stressed the need for governments to present a *consolidated budget*, which encompasses all government activities and reduces the ability to move items off-budget. Publishing tax expenditure accounts and properly accounting for loan guarantees may also increase the visibility of government subsidies. Some have also called on governments to employ *capital budgets* for expenditures that involve capital formation (Auld, 1994). Although many conceptual difficulties are involved, such as determining what is capital, properly accounting for depreciation, etc., such an approach would focus attention on expenditures that may justifiably be financed by borrowing. Others feel that these difficulties may actually allow for more deception (Boothe, 1993).[10] Boothe discusses the Alberta government's move to consolidated budgeting in Chapter 6.

Another issue that may be important is accounting for the highly cyclical nature of some revenue sources. Resource revenues in particular may be highly volatile, generating large budgetary windfalls or losses. Developing budgetary mechanisms to account for this volatility would be challenging, but may help increase government accountability. As discussed by Kneebone and McKenzie in Chapter 7, the Alberta government has made some important changes to its budget-making process to account for this volatility.

Finally, various legislative restrictions may be placed on the ability of the government to tax and borrow. Kneebone discusses the relevant issues in this regard in the following chapter.

## 4. POLITICIANS AND BUREAUCRATS: THE THEORY OF BUREAUCRACY

The previous section focused primarily on the principal-agent relationship between voters and their elected representatives and on some of the normative characteristics of the political outcomes. For the most part ignored in the discussion was another important actor in the public policy arena, one who is not elected at all—the public-sector bureaucrat.

### 4.1 Niskanen's Budget-Maximizing Bureaucrat

The first systematic examination of the role of the bureaucracy in the policy-making process was William Niskanen's seminal work, *Bureaucracy and Representative Government* (1971). Although some previous work on bureaucracy had been undertaken as early as Weber (1947), with useful contributions by Tullock (1965) and Downs (1967), Niskanen was the first to model formally the role of the bureaucracy in a public choice framework. It is impossible to overstate Niskanen's influence in this area. Bendor (1988: 354), for example, acknowledges Niskanen's work as 'the forerunner of numerous formal models and . . . even today it is probably the single most cited study.' Citing Goodin (1982), Blais and Dion (1991) report that Margaret Thatcher assigned Niskanen (1975) as required reading for British civil servants. Moreover, Ronald Reagan appointed Niskanen to his Council of Economic Advisors.

In his model of the bureaucracy Niskanen views the relationship between the bureaucracy and the legislature (which he treats as a single principal) as one of bilateral monopoly—a single seller offering output to a single buyer. In this case a bureau offers an output (some package of government services and/or public goods) to the legislature in exchange for a budget. He argues that 'the relative incentives and available information, under most conditions, give the bureau the overwhelmingly dominant monopoly power' (1971: 30). In other words, because the bureau has superior information regarding the costs and/or benefits of programs it offers, it is difficult for the legislature to monitor the efficiency of production. Moreover, as monopoly providers, most bureaus are freed from competitive pressures to be efficient; this lack of competition also deprives the legislature of an important benchmark against which to measure the efficiency of the bureau. Given the difficulty of measuring the output of some bureaus, it is also difficult to link bureaucratic salaries and/or budgets either directly or indirectly to the efficient production of output. Thus, bureaucrats rarely have a financial incentive to act efficiently. Finally, inefficient operations in the private sector are often the targets for takeovers. This can act as an important disciplinary device for private-sector managers. No such possibility exists for public-sector bureaucrats. For all of these reasons, Niskanen perceives the legislature (the principal) as operating in a largely 'passive' manner, accepting or rejecting take-it-or-leave-it budget offers from a bureau (the agent) that is pursuing its own self-interest in an environment largely devoid of both internal and external pressure to strive for efficiency.

If bureaucrats in Niskanen's model do not pursue efficiency, what do they pursue? Niskanen (1971: 38) lists a number of variables that may enter the bureaucrat's utility function: 'salary, perquisites of the office, public reputation, power, patronage, output of the bureau, ease of making changes, and ease of managing the bureau'. It is important to note that most of these variables are non-pecuniary and are therefore difficult to measure. He notes, however, that all but the last two variables are likely to be positively related to the total budget, thus his characterization of the budget-maximizing bureaucrat.

Niskanen's model of the budget-maximizing bureaucrat gives rise to stark predictions regarding the efficiency of bureaucratic choices, the gist of which can be illustrated in a very simple framework.[11] The bureau receives a budget that is a function of the *revealed* demand for the output (G) of the agency by the legislature, B(G). This function, which can also be viewed as a public benefit function as revealed by the political authority, is presumed to be increasing at a decreasing rate, therefore the *marginal* benefit schedule, MB(G), is depicted as downward sloping in Figure 2. The bureau in turn faces a cost function C(G) that is increasing at an increasing rate; therefore, the *marginal* cost schedule in Figure 2, MC(G), is upward sloping. It is presumed that although the bureau knows the form of both the benefit and cost schedules, the legislature knows only the former. Thus, the legislature can observe output but cannot determine whether or not that output is at the Pareto efficient level.

The Pareto optimal level of output for the agency is the level of output where the marginal public benefit equals the marginal public cost, denoted G* in Figure 2. Budget-maximizing bureaucrats, by virtue of their superior information regarding the costs of providing the services, are able to expand output up to point $G^0$, where the budget just covers the cost of production—i.e., $B(G^0)=C(G^0)$. At $G^0$, the consumer surplus on the inframarginal units up to G* (area E) is exactly offset by the excess of marginal costs over marginal benefits on the units produced in excess of G* (area F). Thus, the monopoly bureau is able to capture the consumer surplus by overproducing. Area F is the agency cost of an unchecked bureaucracy due to asymmetric information. Niskanen's model thus predicts an outcome that is not Pareto efficient because of the larger-than-optimal output (in terms of the demand revealed by the political

**Figure 2:** Niskanen's Budget-Maximizing Bureaucracy

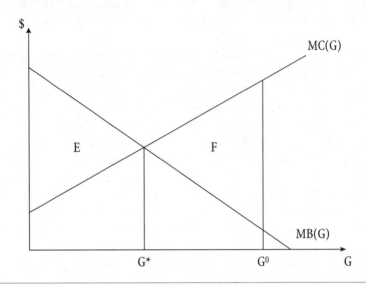

authorities), but where the output that is produced is done so efficiently in the sense that it is produced at minimum cost.

### 4.2 Some Extensions and Empirical Investigations

McGuire (1981: 315) notes that an important implication of Niskanen's model is that at the budget-maximizing level of output the total budget rises with a decrease in the cost of the output. Thus, in equilibrium, the 'demand [for the government service] always *appears* to be elastic'. Indeed, McGuire shows that if Niskanen's model is correct, the price elasticity of demand for government services will equal −1 (therefore, a 1 per cent increase in the price of a government service will cause a 1 per cent reduction in demand). Although McGuire does not test this hypothesis himself, he reviews several previous studies of the elasticity of demand for public services and notes that they tend to find inelastic demands. He thus concludes that the hypothesis receives little empirical support. This conclusion may be a bit cavalier. None of the studies he surveys explicitly calculates the price elasticity of demand for government services, and the one that probably comes the closest, Borcherding and Deacon (1972), actually tends to support the hypothesis of unitary elasticity—they find that for four of seven non-federal government services in the US, the elasticity of demand with respect to the marginal tax price is very close to −1, and for another is about −.9. A later study by Wyckoff (1988) tests the unitary elasticity hypothesis directly and finds that the elasticity of demand for capital expenditures is close to −1, but for current expenditures it is only −.34. Borcherding (1985) reports that Ott (1980) has also found evidence in support of a unitary elasticity. Niskanen (1991) reports that his preliminary (unpublished) findings on the demand for defence, which applies the Borcherding and Deacon methodology, suggests a high (negative) price elasticity. As such, there does seem to be some evidence of high negative elasticies of demand for government services, which is consistent with the oversupply hypothesis from Niskanen's original model. As pointed out by Niskanen (1991), however, although these studies are suggestive they do not constitute a direct test of the budget-maximizing model because there is no way of knowing what the underlying population demand function is.

Migue and Belanger (1974) provide an early theoretical extension of Niskanen's model. They replace the assumption of budget-maximizing bureaucrats with one where bureaucrats maximize their *discretionary* budget, which is the difference between the total budget and the minimum cost of producing the output expected by the political authority. This 'surplus' is spent on additional staff, perquisites, capital, etc. While Niskanen (1971) predicts that output will be too large (relative to the Pareto efficient level) but will be produced efficiently (i.e., at minimum cost), in Migue and Belanger's model, output can be either too high or too low but will always be produced inefficiently (i.e., at higher than minimum cost). Thus, while the Niskanen and the Migue and Belanger models share the prediction that bureaucrats will seek budgets that are too large, they differ in how the surplus budget will be distributed. Niskanen (1975, 1991) has subsequently endorsed Migue and Belanger's approach as one 'that both generalizes and simplifies' his original model (1991: 18).

Many studies have sought to analyse the extent to which the public sector suffers from the productive inefficiency predicted by Migue and Belanger. The typical approach is to compare the unit cost of government output to the unit cost of private firms who supply a comparable output. Niskanen (1975) cites several such papers, including studies of garbage collection, electricity production, fire-fighting, and airlines. Trebilcock (1994) reports that many studies find government-provided services cost from 30 per cent to 90 per cent more than equivalent services provided by the private sector. Borcherding (1977: 62) talks about the 'Bureaucratic Rule of Two', whereby 'removal of an activity from the private sector will double its unit costs of production.' In a survey of studies of government waste, Savas (1982: 111) concludes that 'it is safe to say, at least, that public provision of services is not superior to private provision, while those who believe on *a priori* grounds that private services are best can find considerable support for their position.'[12]

Although many studies seem to show that government production is inefficient, there are several reasons why one should be cautious in interpreting this evidence as providing support for the inefficiency of bureaucracy. First, in many cases it is difficult to measure the outputs produced by the public sector. How can we compare the costs of public vs. private-sector production when we cannot measure output properly? Second, in many cases a competitive benchmark simply does not exist. Third, as noted by Rosen (1995), the efficiency of an enterprise—public or private—depends to a large extent on the market environment in which it operates. A publicly run enterprise facing a lot of competition may be very efficient, while a privately owned monopoly may be very inefficient. An example of how competition can overcome bureaucratic inefficiency is provided by Caves and Christensen (1980). They compare Canada's two railways, one private and one public, and find no evidence that the public system is more inefficient. They conclude that 'any tendency toward inefficiency resulting from pubic ownership has been overcome by the benefits of competition' (p. 974). Finally, evidence that government bureaus are inefficient relative to the private sector may not be evidence of *bureaucratic* inefficiency, but rather of *political* inefficiency. Fiorina (1977) and Fiorina and Noll (1978) present the somewhat cynical view that politicians actually promote bureaucratic inefficiency so that they can intervene on their constituents' behalf and reap the political benefits—'in a very real sense each [politician] is a monopoly supplier of bureaucratic unsticking services for his district' (Fiorina, 1977: 43). Yet another possibility is that politicians promote inefficiency to facilitate transfers to groups who benefit from it.

In a series of important papers, Romer and Rosenthal (1978, 1979, 1982) investigate the role of agenda control in the budget process. They examine the implications of 'base budgeting' for school districts in Oregon. In Oregon, each school district has a legally set base budget. School boards can obtain additional funds, however, by proposing larger budgets in a referendum. If the referendum passes, the proposed budget becomes the new base budget. If the referendum fails, the budget reverts back to its old base.

Referendums on budgetary proposals provide a unique opportunity to test the theory of the budget-maximizing bureaucracy. Under direct democracy the monopoly power and informational advantage of the bureaucracy are likely to be at their greatest. Moreover, the bureaucracy is in a much better position to control the budgetary agenda under direct democracy than when budget proposals are presented to a political authority. To see how agenda control can affect the outcome, consider a standard median voter model. Figure 3 portrays the utility function of the median voter, defined over school expenditures, G. If the electorate were allowed to vote over the entire range of expenditures, the outcome would be $G^*$, the most preferred expenditure level of the median voter. Under the Oregon scheme, however, this is not done. Rather, a base level, $G^r$, is set by law. This gives rise to the possibility that a school district can hold

**Figure 3:** Base Level Budgeting

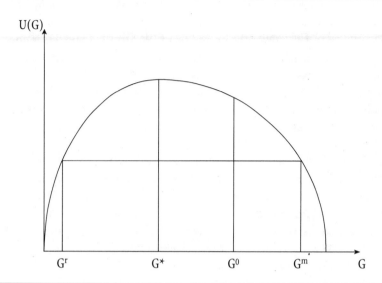

a referendum for any budget between $G^r$ and $G^m$, say $G^0$, and receive the approval of the median voter, because she prefers any of those budgets to $G^r$. Thus, whenever the base budget is less than the median voter's most preferred outcome, the school board can hold a referendum and force an expansion in the budget beyond the most preferred level of the median voter.

In a cross-sectional analysis of per student spending Romer and Rosenthal (1982) find that for districts where the base budget exceeds the preferred budget, average spending per pupil is virtually identical to the base budget, while for districts where the base budget is less than the preferred budget, the average spending per pupil is more than 15 per cent higher. While these findings provide convincing support for the bureaucratic model, the results illustrate more generally the power that rests with those who set the budget agenda, whether they are bureaucrats, cabinet ministers, or committees. In particular, if the agenda setter has a higher preference for government expenditure than the relevant median voter, spending is likely to be higher.[13]

### 4.3 How Does a Budget-Maximizing Bureaucrat Respond to Budget Cuts?

Niskanen presumes a utility-maximizing bureaucrat who seeks to maximize the size of the budget (or, perhaps, the discretionary budget). Yet in many jurisdictions, the recent trend has been to cut government expenditures. How, then, will a utility-maximizing bureaucracy respond to budget cuts? Some have suggested that an implication of Niskanen's model is that agency heads will react to cuts by reducing the quantity and/or quality of programs and services rather than personnel. Laband (1983) investigates this possibility in connection with the across-the-board reductions in the US imposed by the Reagan administration in 1983 and 1984. Over the period from 1982 to 1984 budgets in the agencies studied by Laband fell by an average of about 21 per cent, while the average decline in employment was only about 5 per cent. Moreover, in 91 per cent of the agencies examined, the budget cut was proportionately greater than the reduction in personnel. Laband thus concludes that bureaucrats seek to 'trim the meat, not the fat', when faced with budget cuts (1983: 311).

De Groot and Van Der Sluis (1987) develop a formal model that predicts similar behaviour. They argue that bureaucrats try to avoid 'social conflicts' within the agency and therefore that 'the goal of conflict minimization, and in particular that of avoiding forced layoffs, is an important additional objective that has to be incorporated into models of bureaucracy behaviour in periods of declining budgets' (p. 104).[14] De Groot and Van Der Sluis conjecture that to avoid conflicts within the organization, agency heads will rely as much as possible on attrition to meet budget cuts, resisting forced lay-offs beyond this. The extent to which agency heads are successful in this regard is an indication of the power of the bureaucracy. De Groot and Van Der Sluis hypothesize that the reduction in employment should be higher in agencies where the turnover of the workforce is naturally high, because in these agencies personnel cuts are easier to make without precipitating social conflict. They test this hypothesis using data on a large economics department at a Dutch university facing cutbacks. They find that the size of the workforce reduction is indeed positively related to the turnover rate. Although the relationship is relatively weak, the results are consistent with the idea that bureaucrats seek to minimize social conflict by avoiding forced lay-offs in the face of a declining budget.

Bureaucrats facing a looming decline in the size of their budget may also attempt to change the composition of the workforce within the agency. Perhaps the most well-known statement of this phenomenon is from Parkinson, who observed that between 1914 and 1928, following World War I, the number of ships in the British navy declined by about 67 per cent while the number of officers and enlisted men declined by about 32 per cent. Over this same period, administrative personnel increased by about 78 per cent, prompting Parkinson to note that Britain had 'a magnificent navy on dry land' (Parkinson, 1957: 7). This sort of administrative expansionism has come to be known as 'Parkinson's Law'.[15]

McKee and Wintrobe (1993) offer an explanation for Parkinson's Law based on the idea that managers seek to build informal 'vertical networks' with subordinates. These networks establish trust and build a sort of 'network capital' within the organization, which increases productivity and lowers monitoring costs.

McKee and Wintrobe hypothesize that promoting line workers to administrative positions is a way for agency managers to protect from dismissal employees with whom they have built up this capital, based on the premise that administrative personnel are less likely to be laid off. Using data from the Ontario public school system, they find strong evidence supporting the presence of Parkinson's Law. Indeed, they find that Parkinson's Law is not restricted to the public sector, as they present similar empirical evidence for the US steel industry.

Another important aspect of budget-cutting and the institutional change that often accompanies it concerns the conditions under which the central actor in the decision-making process delegates the responsibility for implementing the cuts to subsidiary, or local, actors. For example, if the Ministry of Advanced Education must allocate a budget cut within the post-secondary sector, should the decision be centralized, with the ministry deciding which departments and programs are cut, or should the ministry decentralize the decision, leaving it to individual post-secondary institutions to decide on their own?

This question is addressed by De Groot (1988).[16] He formulates a principal-agent model under asymmetric information, where the central actor is the principal and the local actor is the agent. He identifies two benefits of decentralized decision-making in this environment: (1) because of the asymmetry in information, the central actor may lack the specific information required to allocate the cuts efficiently within and across local agencies, and thus decentralization avoids the efficiency loss associated with making uninformed decisions; and (2) since local actors must ultimately implement the changes and operate in the new environment, they are more likely to be more committed to changes that they make themselves, or at least that they participated in. An example of the first type of benefit from decentralization arises if tastes differ across local regions but are homogeneous within regions. Local decision-makers may be better able to make choices reflecting local preferences than are the central authorities.

Breton (1990) identifies other benefits that may arise from decentralization. Devolving decision-making responsibilities to local agencies may give rise to 'horizontal competition' between agencies. This allows different agencies to experiment with different policies. A sort of policy diffusion may result, as a successful policy innovation in one agency may be copied by others. Horizontal competition among decentralized agencies may also provide the central authority, and voters, with benchmarks against which to compare the efficiency of their regional decision-maker. This, too, could lead to more efficient policies.

De Groot also identifies two costs of decentralization: (1) local actors are likely to be more sensitive to the social conflict arising from things like forced lay-offs resulting from the budget cuts, and may therefore seek to avoid them; and (2) decentralization may increase the amount of time required to implement the decisions. One might add two other potential costs of decentralization to De Groot's list: (3) local actors may ignore the impact of their decisions on other jurisdictions, resulting in a type of decision externality; and (4) decentralization could lead to replication of services and/or lost economies of scale.

To test his model empirically De Groot investigated the process involved in the reduction in hospital beds in the Netherlands from 1982 to 1984. Despite the obvious data difficulties in carrying out this type of study—the biggest problem is measuring the degree of decentralization—his results tend to confirm that the level of decentralization depended on the types of trade-offs described above. In particular, he finds that the greater the information deficiency at the central level, the higher is the level of decentralization.

## 4.4 The Bureaucracy and the Demand for Government Expenditures

To this point the discussion has focused on the impact of bureaucrats on the *supply* of government services. Another possibility is that bureaucrats affect the *demand* for government services through their impact on electoral outcomes in their role as voters-consumers. Buchanan (1977) raises this possibility in a discussion of the conflict of interest that exists when bureaucrats vote in elections.

Many hypothesize that bureaucrats will have a higher preference for government expenditures than the typical voter because not only do they benefit from the provision of the public services as consumers, but also from the increased prestige, power, job security, and (possibly) salaries associated with higher expenditures in their role as government employees. Others hypothesize that bureaucrats possess greater voting power than their numbers suggest because 'their costs of information and political participation are relatively low due to problems of public affairs being their daily "business"'; therefore 'they participate much more in all types of political activities, and particularly in voting' (Pommerehne and Frey, 1978: 100).

Although the influence of government employees on the size of government through their voting behaviour does not require that the voter turnout among bureaucrats be higher than average, the likelihood that they will influence the outcome is enhanced if this is the case. Most studies show that voter participation is indeed higher for bureaucrats than for the electorate as a whole (see, for example, Bush and Denzau, 1977; Frey and Pommerehne, 1982; Bennett and Orzechowski, 1983).[17]

Even if voter participation by public employees is higher than average, an important question is whether their preferences regarding government expenditures differ significantly from the rest of the population. An early study by Rubinfeld (1977) concludes that the probability of voting for an increase in local school expenditures in a Detroit suburb was higher if the individual was employed as a teacher in the public sector. Courant, Gramlich, and Rubinfeld (1980) find that public-sector employees in Michigan tended to favour lower reductions in state expenditures than did private-sector employees. Both of these studies try to control for other socio-economic and demographic factors, and therefore provide some evidence that the preferences of government employees do indeed differ from the population as a whole regarding the size of government.

Santerre (1993), building on Pommerehne and Frey (1978), investigates whether school employee voting power has a greater impact on school spending in districts in the US where expenditures are voted on directly than in districts that elect representatives to decide such issues. His hypothesis is that the elimination of the 'middle man' in direct democracy districts increases the voting power of school employees. He finds that the impact of school employee voting power on expenditures is marginally (but statistically significantly) higher in the direct democracy districts. This has two important implications. First, it provides further evidence in support of the hypothesis that bureaucratic preferences regarding government expenditures differ from the general populace, and that those preferences can manifest themselves in larger government. Second, and perhaps more importantly, it suggests that 'political institutions matter given certain circumstances' (Santerre, 1993: 196). In other words, the institutional framework within which policy decisions are made can indeed affect the outcome.

Finally, Blais, Blake, and Dion (1991) investigate the hypothesis that budget-maximizing bureaucrats have a tendency to vote for left-wing parties because these parties tend to favour government expenditures. In numerous elections in several countries, including Canada, they find evidence of a public-sector/private-sector cleavage in voting patterns, with civil servants expressing a marked relative preference for left-wing parties. The authors conclude that their findings suggest 'qualified' support for the budget-maximizing bureaucrat model.

## 4.5 Legislative Control Theories of the Bureaucracy

An important element of Niskanen-type models of the bureaucracy is the largely passive role played by the political authority—legislators are effectively limited to either accepting or rejecting the bureau's budget proposal. Many authors have questioned this passive depiction of the legislature, arguing that the political authority has an incentive to monitor and 'bargain' with the bureaucracy to secure an outcome that is superior for the legislature. Budget proposals are commonly vetted by the minister, treasury board, cabinet, and various *ad hoc* and standing committees. The outcome is likely to be a compromise between the desires of a budget-maximizing bureaucracy and those of a legislature pursuing its own political ends. Niskanen assumes that the bureaucracy has the upper hand in this bargaining game. Others argue to the contrary—that legislatures have the leverage in the bargaining process by virtue of their control of the purse and their ability to gather information and monitor outcomes. Following Carroll (1993), we will refer to the latter as the 'legislative control theory' of the public sector.

Legislative control theory can be thought of as the counterpart in the theory of bureaucracy to the Chicago approach to political economy discussed earlier, insofar as both suggest that efficient political and bureaucratic institutions evolve endogenously. Wittman, for example, argues 'that the principal-agent problem of bureaucracies has been greatly exaggerated since there are numerous methods of reducing the potential for opportunism,' and moreover, 'it is truly impossible to find any alternative structure that is more technically efficient' (1990: 12).

Numerous authors have investigated the extent to which outcomes reflect the preferences of the political authority rather than those of the bureaucracy. Proponents of legislative control theory contend that the tendency of researchers to focus on formal monitoring mechanisms and explicit bureaucratic guidelines and incentives is misplaced. For example, many have observed that the political authority is only rarely and sporadically involved in the explicit monitoring and control of agencies. Some have interpreted this sporadic intervention as suggestive of a Niskanenesque environment where the bureaucracy is allowed to run amok, until it finally goes too far and must be reined in by the political authority. Others, such as Weingast and Moran (1983), Weingast (1984), and McCubbins and Schwartz (1984), have argued that this interpretation may be inappropriate. They claim that political control over the bureaucracy works through more subtle mechanisms than direct and explicit control. They point out, for example, that politicians are in almost continuous contact with their constituents, who use the services provided by the various agencies. Thus, legislators are able to monitor agency actions indirectly, and cheaply, simply by listening to their constituents. McCubbins and Schwartz refer to this as *fire alarm oversight*, as opposed to *police patrol oversight*. Also, the political authority controls the allocation of money across agencies. The politicians are more likely to direct funds to and otherwise reward agencies that further their political ambitions. Bureaucrats know this, and therefore have an incentive to act in a way that is desired by their political masters. As such, 'competition for budget increases . . . substantially mitigates asymmetries in information about bureaucratic production' (Weingast, 1984: 155). Thus, although they do not claim that bureaucratic shirking does not exist, these authors argue that there is good reason to question the extent of shirking suggested by Niskanen-type models. Moreover, the lack of direct political surveillance and participation in agency decisions may not be indicative of shirking but rather of a well-functioning bureaucracy that is merely carrying out the wishes of its political principal.

In two careful case studies of congressional oversight committees in the US, Weingast and Moran (1983) and Weingast (1984) seek to determine the validity of the legislative control model. Weingast and Moran examine a substantial change in the policy direction of the Federal Trade Commission (FTC) in the late 1970s, and Weingast studies sweeping changes in the jurisdiction of the Securities and Exchange Commission (SEC) in the early 1960s. The authors argue that in both cases the policy changes were precipitated neither by bureaucratic initiative nor by the need to sanction a bureaucracy run amok. Rather, the evidence suggests that the policy changes reflected a change in the political climate and/or a change in the membership of the congressional oversight committee. In both cases the authors conclude that the evidence is consistent with an environment where Congress controls the agency rather than the other way around.

Spillar (1990) offers evidence against legislative control theory. He considers a three-player multiple principals-agent game involving Congress (representing broad consumer interests), a bureaucratic regulator, and an industry interest group. Congress and the regulator have a principal-agent relationship, whereby the actions of the regulator are not perfectly observed by Congress. Of course, there is some scope for Congress to influence regulator behaviour if the right incentives are offered. However, Spillar argues that the industry interest group may be able to influence the regulator as well. He observes that bureaucrats often leave the civil service for a position in the industry they previously regulated and conjectures that this potential pay-off (or 'bribe') may influence the regulator's behaviour. Spillar empirically implements his model by estimating the determinants of the conditional probability that regulators in three regulatory agencies work for the industry following their tenure with the government. He shows that the higher the discretionary budget granted a regulator while working for the government, the lower the probability that he or she will subsequently work for a regulated industry. He also shows that previous public employment increases the probability of obtaining a regulated-industry job. On the basis of these findings, he 'does not reject the existence of an agency problem between Congress and its regulatory agencies'; moreover, 'while Congress seems to use its budget to discipline regulators, congressional control does not seem to be perfect' (Spillar, 1990: 98).

## 4.6 Reforming, Rethinking, Remaking, Revamping, and Reinventing the Bureaucracy

There has been a veritable explosion of researchers and commentators calling for bureaucratic reform. The study of bureaucracy has become positively New Age, as illustrated by the popularity of Osborne and Gaebler's *Reinventing*

*Government* (1992), no doubt the only book to make the best-seller list on what McKee and Wintrobe (1993: 309) refer to as the 'notoriously dull subject of public administration'.[18] This zeal for bureaucratic reform has been a boon not only to the publishing industry. Various states in the US have instituted major bureaucratic reforms. The American federal government is in the midst of a 'reinvention' of its own, arising from the National Performance Review under Vice-President Gore; this was preceded by the Canadian federal government's Public Service 2000 initiative in 1990.

As discussed above, most studies suggest that the potential inefficiency of the bureaucracy arises for two basic reasons: (1) the monopoly position of bureaus implies a lack of competitive pressure to be efficient; and (2) asymmetric information implies that the political authority cannot costlessly monitor and control the bureaucracy. Virtually every bureaucratic reform discussed in the popular literature and elsewhere can be related to these two factors. Although space considerations preclude a complete discussion of the scope for bureaucratic reform, some of the key issues suggested by the literature can be briefly summarized.

### Choice vs. Voice

Albert Hirschman (1970) emphasizes the distinction between 'choice vs. voice' as alternative ways for consumers to communicate their preferences for goods and services; this distinction is also useful when thinking about bureaucratic reform. Hirschman's main point is that some markets are characterized by free mobility (and other important characteristics), which allows consumers to communicate their preferences through acts of choice (what Hirschman calls 'exit')—if consumers do not like the price and/or quality of the service offered by one provider, they simply choose another. In these markets, the competition that arises from the ability of consumers to exercise choice leads to efficient outcomes. In other cases choice is not possible (or permitted), and consumer preferences can only be conveyed through non-market means, for example, via the expression of views through the political process—the exercise of voice.

Many advocates of bureaucratic reform argue that there is more scope for choice (i.e., competition) in public-sector activities than has traditionally been the case and that by increasing choice, efficiency will be enhanced. Indeed, some argue that the apparent inefficiency of the bureaucracy is not due to public provision at all but rather to the lack of competition. For example, in their study of Canada's private and public railway systems, Caves and Christensen (1980: 974) conclude 'that the oft-noted inefficiency of government enterprises stems from their isolation from effective competition rather than their public ownership per se.'

Of course, there is not always scope for private-sector competition; indeed, one may well question the presence of government provision when this scope does exist. But this does not mean that the benefits of competition need be lost. For example, many advocate creating competition among bureaus and agencies to simulate the pressure of a competitive market and achieve the associated efficiencies. The creation of 'horizontal competition' among agencies has potentially widespread applications. One type of horizontal competition occurs when agencies have overlapping jurisdictions, so that clients are able to go to more than one agency for a service. The efficiency gains arising from this type of competition may more than offset losses due to the duplication of services. It is important to keep these considerations in mind in light of recent efforts to eliminate overlap and redundancy both within and between governments as a way of saving money and supplying common services more efficiently (Purchase and Hirshhorn, 1994: 8). While these efforts are laudable, one should be aware of the possible trade-offs. A more centralized and co-ordinated system is not necessarily more efficient. As Landau (1969: 356) points out: 'If there is no duplication, if there is no overlap, if there is no ambiguity, an organization will neither be able to suppress error nor generate alternative routes of action.' Duplication and overlap may in some instances act as a control device to reduce the inefficiency inherent in the bureaucratic provision of goods and services. To the extent that this is true, the consolidation of agency functions and/or jurisdictions may actually increase expenditures because there will be fewer competitive incentives and higher monitoring costs. As such, the gains from intergovernmental and interagency co-operation *may* be short-lived; costs may be higher in the long run due to the lack of horizontal competition.[19]

Horizontal competition among agencies need not be explicit with multiple agencies providing the same services to the same people. Another type of horizontal competition arises when similar agencies provide services to different people. This type of horizontal competition may encourage policy innovation and help address some of the information problems endemic in principal-agent relationships by providing the political authority with 'benchmarks' or standards against which to judge efficiency (Breton, 1990). Rose-Ackerman (1986) advocates the use of 'tournaments', whereby agencies receive 'prizes' based on performance as a way of encouraging competition among agencies.

Benchmarking and horizontal competition need not be restricted to agencies in a particular political jurisdiction. Comparisons with agencies in other jurisdictions, both nationally and internationally, can do much to convey information regarding the efficiency of the bureaucracy. Data are often a problem in comparing performance across jurisdictions—as Purchase and Hirshhorn (1994: 49) point out, there does not yet exist 'an accepted set of international scorecards and benchmarks for the public sector'.

Creating competition for internal government services also has the potential to generate efficiency improvements. Many government bureaus do not provide services to the public but rather to other government bureaus—government printing, office supplies and procurement, and maintenance and janitorial services are obvious examples. To the extent that these internal service agencies enjoy a monopoly position as sole providers of government services one might expect high prices and low quality. Of course, one possibility is to privatize or contract out these services, but introducing competition may accomplish much the same purpose.

It is not always feasible to introduce choice through competition in the public sector. Many public-sector activities exist precisely because market imperfections are such that the activity would not be efficiently undertaken in a competitive environment. Bureaucratic reforms need not concentrate only on the 'choice' in the 'choice vs. voice' framework. The most obvious outlet for 'voice' is the ballot box. Yet registering preferences through voting is cumbersome: the opportunities to do so are infrequent, and one typically votes for a policy package rather than individual items. None the less, steps may be taken to facilitate the revelation of consumer preferences via voice. Recall that the cornerstone of the legislative control theory of the bureaucracy is the ability of consumers or clients to monitor agencies cheaply on behalf of the political authority. One of the weaknesses of this theory is the presumption that this monitoring simply takes place naturally. Yet institutions and mechanisms can be established to facilitate this process. School councils, roundtables, and consumer, business, labour, and academic advisory groups not only facilitate bureaucratic monitoring and convey consumer preferences but can encourage the formation of partnerships among the various actors in the process, allowing knowledge, expertise, and other resources to be shared. Osborne and Gaebler (1992), for example, stress the importance of establishing an ongoing relationship between government and the community, what they call 'community-owned government'. This not only allows services to be more flexible and better tailored to community needs (preferences), but may also save money by deprofessionalizing service delivery. Thus, decentralization may not only facilitate choice via horizontal competition, it may also facilitate voice by moving agencies closer to consumers.

An important question that has not been addressed concerns the conditions in which efficiency gains should be pursued by enhancing choice or by enhancing voice. Moreover, within each category there are many possible approaches and institutional arrangements. The question of instrument choice, though important, is somewhat beyond the scope of this chapter. However, one point that should be made is that dogmatically applying one approach across all government agencies is not likely to yield substantial efficiency gains, and, indeed, may make matters worse. Market, technological, institutional, and political factors all bear on the question of instrument choice. Given the myriad goods and services offered by the public sector, this suggests that, although many goals and principles may be broadly applicable, a case by case, agency by agency, service by service approach is likely to yield the greatest gains. 'One-size-fits-all' institutional reform is unlikely to be successful. See Hirschman (1970), Trebilcock (1994), Purchase and Hirshhorn (1994), and Trebilcock, Hartle, Pritchard, and Dewees (1982) for more on this point.

Some of the institutional reforms undertaken in Alberta have served to enhance both choice and voice. Kneebone and McKenzie provide an overview of some of these changes in Chapter 5. Changes in health care, particularly the encouragement of horizontal competition, are discussed by Plain (Chapter 9). Bruce and Schwartz (Chapter 11) discuss changes in basic education, including the centralization of funding with the province, the role of charter schools, and the creation of parent councils. Emery (Chapter 10) explains structural changes (or the lack thereof) in advanced education.

### Delegation, Monitoring, and Incentives

The protestations of Niskanen notwithstanding, it seems clear that the political authority is not completely impotent with regard to monitoring and controlling the civil service. The monitoring role played by parliamentary committees was discussed in sections 3.6 and 4.5. Performance measures—the public-sector equivalent of management by objectives—are another mechanism gaining favour in the public sector.

Performance indicators in the public sector can play three roles. First, they can act as a way of conveying information to the public to facilitate choice. Consumers can make informed decisions and choices regarding health care and education, for instance, only if they are able somehow to compare the various agencies that provide the services. Second, in a similar way performance indicators may facilitate voice by providing consumers with more information to help them bring pressure to bear on politicians. Third, performance indicators can play an important role in monitoring and controlling the bureaucracy. Again, this may be done for purely information purposes, but most advocates of the use of performance indicators argue that their real benefits arise when they are linked with incentives.

Many are sceptical of the scope for increasing bureaucratic efficiency by implementing performance measures. The problem is that it is often difficult to develop meaningful output measures for the public sector, and even if output is measurable, relevant benchmarks often do not exist (although see the discussion on horizontal competition above). In these cases there may be a tendency to measure inputs (effort) rather than outputs. But this can be problematic. In many public-sector activities the link between effort and performance is poorly understood. In section 4.3 a version of Parkinson's Law was stated to the effect that administration increases even when agencies are in decline. A perhaps more popular version of Parkinson's Law is that *work expands so as to fill the time available for its completion*. This suggests that in many bureaucracies there is no clear relationship between inputs and outputs—bureau employees are inevitably busy, no matter how many of them there are or how much work they have to do.

Although there may be some merit in this view of bureaucracy, it seems to miss a key point. Principal-agent theory is predicated on the assumption that the principal cannot directly evaluate the quality (or quantity) of an agent's input in the first place. When this is the case, efficiency can be enhanced by rewarding the agent on the basis of some measure of past performance. It need not be the case that the agent's effort is the only determinant of the output, nor that the output be measured perfectly. So long as there is some correlation between effort and performance and between the possibly imperfect performance measure and the underlying 'unobservable' output, it is possible to design an incentive scheme that will increase efficiency. This is not to say that effort should not be devoted to developing good performance measures, because the size of the efficiency gain is inversely related to the accuracy of the performance measure. Moreover, steps can be taken to alleviate at least some of the measurement problems. Carroll (1993), for example, recommends segmenting bureau functions into parcels that produce more readily identifiable outputs. Cassidy (1994) discusses some initiatives by the federal government in Canada to develop 'special operating agencies', which are spin-offs of well-defined activities from broader agencies.

The emphasis placed by those who argue for the increased use of performance measures in the public sector on the importance of measuring outputs, even imperfectly, rather than inputs, is thus consistent with the basic idea behind principal-agent theory. Moreover, an ill-conceived attempt to measure inputs can lead to perverse incentives, such as the 'what gets measured gets done' phenomenon (Gaebler and Osborne, 1992).

Another example of this can be found in the traditional line-item budgeting approach used by many governments. Presumably this approach is taken so as to monitor bureau expenditures and ensure that they are going where they are supposed to. It is usually difficult to move money between categories, as requests to do so may result in a loss of funds. For fear of losing some of their budget, agency managers may adopt a 'spend it or lose it' attitude, which encourages bureaus to waste money. Some local and federal governments are moving toward what Osborne and Gaebler (1992: 122) call 'mission-driven' budgeting. Under this approach, bureaucrats are given a 'global' budget and may allocate funds at their discretion; any budgetary savings stay in the agency.

Rather than focusing on measuring budgetary inputs, mission-driven budgeting is more concerned with measuring budgetary outcomes.

The delegation of discretionary authority implicit in mission-driven budgeting also makes it more likely that agency personnel will 'buy into' the system. Purchase and Hirshhorn (1994: 18) talk about the need to encourage 'an internalized commitment to a common objective on the part of those in an organization'; Thompson and Fryer (1994) refer to the importance of respecting the organizational or corporate culture, on the premise that understanding this culture is the first step in changing or redirecting it. A movement towards deployment and empowerment, along with the associated changes to organizational culture, has been an important part of bureaucratic reform movements in Canada and the US. For example, Thomas (1993) reports that the Canadian federal government's Public Service 2000 exercise is said to involve 10 per cent legislative change, 20 per cent system change, and 70 per cent change in organizational culture. The Strive Toward Excellence in Performance (STEP) program instituted by the government of Minnesota places a great deal of emphasis on delegation and empowerment. It is important, however, not to get too caught up in the rhetoric of delegation and empowerment—there are costs as well. Increasing the discretionary authority of the bureaucracy also increases the opportunity for the bureaucracy to pursue its own objectives, which may not be compatible with the political authority. As Thomas (1993: 56) points out, 'philosophies of decentralization must recognize the constitutional requirements of ministerial responsibility'. In the extreme, entrepreneurial public-sector managers may undermine ministerial responsibility. Trebilcock (1994: 66–7) argues that there may also be 'political problems' associated with an outcome-oriented, decentralized bureaucracy. He points out that the more flexible personnel policies implicit in this approach 'may create a serious tension with established job security conventions in the public service' and are 'likely to be strongly resisted by a major organized interest group, which has a significant capacity to disrupt government activities if its concerns are not at least to some extent accommodated.'

Finally, as pointed out by Hettich and Winer (1995: 28–9), another method for controlling public-sector bureaucracies is the politicization of senior agency appointments. While this helps ensure bureaucratic compliance by 'tying [senior bureaucrats] into the reward and punishment structure of the party in power', Hettich and Winer point out that there are social costs associated with politicization, particularly in a parliamentary system. The use of political appointments may inhibit the formation of long-term contractual relationships between the private and public sectors.

Boothe discusses the implementation of performance measures in Alberta in Chapter 6; Kneebone and McKenzie also address the issue in Chapter 5.

*Incrementalism and Path Dependency*

The pace of reform is another important consideration. DiIulio, Garvey, and Kettl (1993: 6) argue for an 'incremental, evolutionary, experimental process', apparently on the grounds that bureaucratic traditions have evolved slowly over time and therefore must be modified slowly over time. They argue that 'policymakers mostly delude themselves when they think that "comprehensive study" or "bold inventive action" can produce useful, enduring change', concluding that 'once-and-for-all efforts at structural reforms must fail' (p. 2). Trebilcock (1994: 72) concurs, arguing that 'system-wide changes' should be carefully considered because 'we often cannot know all the efficiency, distributional, and social effects of these changes in advance.'

Yet incrementalism is not without its problems. Jackson (1982) discusses the tendency of governments to rely on incremental budgeting whereby only decremental *changes* in agency budgets are subjected to the scrutiny of the political authority. One possible reason for this is that legislators have more knowledge and information regarding the costs and benefits of *additional* operations and programs than they do about current or past operations—the informational asymmetry between legislators and the bureaucracy is less pronounced. There are several problems with this approach. First, when decisions are made incrementally and sequentially, some opportunities may be lost because they come late in the decision process—order and agenda counts. Second, decisions may be fragmented, giving rise to the possibility that incompatible and inconsistent decisions are made.[20] Third, to the extent that a previous budget (or policy) takes on the aura of the *de facto* default, the analysis of Romer and Rosenthal (1978, 1979, 1982) on benchmark budgeting becomes relevant, as they suggest that the bureaucracy can present budgets that differ from the legislators' most preferred choice and still gain approval. Although framed in a budgetary context, this reasoning is applicable to any type of policy change. This point is very important, because it emphasizes the role the bureaucracy can play in influencing the direction of reform via agenda control, particularly under incrementalism. Finally, given the postulated preference of the bureaucracy for 'ease of managing the bureau' (Niskanen, 1971: 38) and the hypothesized propensity of agency managers to avoid social conflict (De Groot and Van Der Sluis, 1987), it is not obvious that an incrementalist approach provides the necessary impetus for change. Perhaps a 'crisis environment' forces the social conflict required for real change. Coupled with incentives and the appropriate delegation of discretionary authority, crisis may better release the creative juices and entrepreneurial spirit of the bureaucracy than an incremental approach.

The role of crises in forcing institutional reform is related to the notion of path dependency in the evolution of public policy, whereby policy reforms tend to be autocorrelated in the sense that current changes reflect previous policy decisions. This idea has been discussed by Wilsford (1994) and North (1990), among others. North argues that because there are sizeable set-up costs and significant transaction and information costs associated with large institutional reforms, there is a tendency to conceive of policy changes within the context of existing structures and institutions—policy movement tends to be incremental, following a path determined in large part by previous decisions. Wilsford argues that in this type of environment strong conjunctural forces, which tend to occur only rarely and exceptionally, are required to move policy onto a new path. Based on an analysis of health care reforms (or the lack thereof) in major industrialized countries, Wilsford suggests that these policy conjunctures tend to be typified by the following elements: (1) the perception of a crisis, typically fiscal in nature; (2) the presence of a relatively centralized, somewhat hierarchical political system that is able to move quickly in the typically narrow window of opportunity offered by the confluence of events; (3) strong and determined political leadership, typically in the persons of the first minister and other major ministers, most particularly the finance minister or treasurer; (4) the basic elements of reform that will constitute the 'big change' should already have been thought out and prepared; (5) the electorate must be receptive to innovation—i.e., the political climate must be ripe for change; and (6) the opponents of change, and those who benefit from the status quo, must be fragmented.

While there is no claim that these are the only elements that can constitute a major policy conjuncture, or that they are either necessary or sufficient to move policy onto a new trajectory, the presence of at least some of these elements no doubt increases the probability that a major policy change will take place. In particular, the presence of a perceived fiscal crisis plays a prominent role in precipitating major policy innovations. Yet the path dependency argument emphasizes that a fiscal crisis alone may not be enough—some of the other elements must also be present at the conjunctural moment for a major policy initiative to occur. Kneebone and McKenzie argue in Chapter 5 that Alberta may well be in the midst of a major conjunctural moment coinciding with the perception of a fiscal crisis.

## 5. CONCLUSIONS

Based on this rather selective survey of the literature, it is apparent that a consensus has yet to emerge among economists and other social scientists regarding the efficiency of political and bureaucratic institutions. Supporters of the Chicago School of political economy and legislative control theory seem to be of the opinion that existing institutions are efficient simply because they exist. Under this view, equilibrium political outcomes are efficient because 'policies that raise efficiency are likely to win out because they produce gains rather than deadweight costs' (Becker, 1983: 396), and any observed tendency for legislators to shirk on their constituents is 'more apparent than real' (Peltzman, 1984: 210). In a similar vein, Wittman (1989: 1413 n. 33) argues in the second-best tradition that 'the aggregation of preferences [under majority rule] may be imperfect in comparison with a situation of zero transaction costs and perfect (or costless) information, but this is an inappropriate standard by which to judge the efficiency of either economic or political markets.' Bureaucracies, too, are efficient, because even in the presence of costly and asymmetric information no other institutional form will be better—'if it is truly impossible to find any alternative structure that is more technically efficient because individuals lie and shirk and monitoring is costly (or because any structure has inherent problems of coordination), then the bureaucratic form is, in fact, efficient' (Wittman, 1990: 12).

An implication of this view is that economists (and other social scientists) have nothing useful to contribute to public policy simply because efficient policies and the institutions to implement them arise endogenously as a part of the political process. Thus, as in Becker (1976: 248): 'economists are no more able to discover better ways to redistribute than they are able to discover better ways to produce the products of business'; or as in Stigler (1982: 14, 15–16): 'if we look at any important economic policy of the state, we shall find that it takes account of whatever established knowledge economists possess', and therefore it cannot be the case that public policy would be improved if politicians only listened to economists' advice, because 'what the economists had to say that was relevant was heard and [already] acted upon.'

Others disagree. Among conventional public choice researchers there is 'widespread agreement that there is no reason to presume that government policies will be efficient' (Hahn, 1990: 61). Advocates of this view hold that the institutions that arise in response to inefficiencies and the demand for redistribution in the public sector may be inefficient in their own right because of the existence of failures in political and bureaucratic markets. Moreover, unlike the private economy in the absence of market failures, the political process does not have an invisible hand that turns private self-interest into the social good (Mitchell, 1988: 107). An implication of this view is that social scientists have important contributions to make to the policy-making process by pointing out the nature of the inefficiencies, and suggesting institutional reforms that minimize them.

Both schools can refer to an impressive array of empirical studies to support their position. So what is one to conclude? Perhaps the best approach is to take a moderate view, granting the remarkable ability of the democratic process to generate institutions that achieve relatively efficient outcomes, while recognizing that these institutions are the product of an imperfect market process in their own right. As such, although some political institutions are very efficient, others may not be; some bureaucratic arrangements act to minimize agency costs, others do not. The literature stresses the importance of monitoring and information costs, competition, and the structural characteristics of the institutions in determining the efficiency of the outcome.

Accepting the reality that political and bureaucratic reform will not occur unless there is a desire for reform on the part of the electorate, and this desire is conveyed to politicians, economists can play an important role in educating the public about the scope for inefficiency in the public sector. Moreover, economists can provide some general insights into how to address the problems caused by political and bureaucratic market failures.

## NOTES

1. In Chapter 7 Kneebone and McKenzie relate the changes in Alberta to some of the issues raised here.

2. Of course, I am speaking somewhat loosely here. More precisely, in the parlance of welfare economics, a welfare-improving intervention on the part of the government is called a Pareto Improvement—where some groups are made better off and none worse off. A broader notion of welfare improvement is a Potential Pareto Improvement. This means that a government policy yields an outcome that is 'more efficient' if under the reallocation the 'winners' could potentially compensate the 'losers' and still be better off.

3. The so-called 'voting paradox'—that individuals vote despite all of this—is often resolved by postulating a sense of patriotic or civic duty, so that the act of voting itself gives rise to benefits independent of the impact the individual may have on the outcome. Rational voters trade all of these benefits and costs off against each other when deciding whether or not to vote and how much effort to devote to information acquisition. See Riker and Ordeshook (1968) and Ashenfelter and Kelley (1975).

4. The rational ignorance idea also suggests that voters may be myopic, paying more attention to recent than past information. Some have argued that this may manifest itself in political business cycles. See Blais and Nadeau (1992) for a recent study in a Canadian context. This issue is also discussed by Kneebone in the following chapter.

5. The hypothesis that money can buy votes has been empirically investigated by many authors and has generally not been rejected. In a recent Canadian study, for example, Palda and Palda (1985) show that the number of votes received by challengers in federal elections in Ontario was an increasing function of the size of their

campaign expenditures. Interestingly, although the same was true for incumbents, the effect was substantially smaller, implying that challengers benefit more from campaign spending than do incumbents.

6. See, for example, Buchanan (1988), Buchanan and Tollison (1970), and Buchanan, Tollison, and Tullock (1980).

7. Early research on rent-seeking, such as Tullock (1967) and Posner (1974), was motivated by low welfare cost estimates of monopoly (for example, by Harberger, 1954), which did not include rent-seeking costs. It has now become a well-established part of economics in many other contexts. For more recent work on the costs of rent-seeking, see Katz and Rosenberg (1989), Scully (1991), and Dougan and Snyder (1993).

8. Although these costs are minimized in Becker's model, this is not to say that they are not large in relation to the wealth transfer they help sustain. See also Becker (1985).

9. This section draws on Purchase and Hirshhorn (1994: ch. 10).

10. See Mintz and Preston (1994).

11. The following closely follows Mueller (1989).

12. For a more recent survey in a Canadian context, see Kitchen (1993).

13. See Filimon, Romer, and Rosenthal (1982).

14. It is not clear that Niskanen did not consider this 'additional objective' himself. He allows, for example, that the 'ease of making changes, and ease of managing the bureau' (Niskanen, 1971: 38) are possible arguments in the bureaucratic utility function that do not increase the size of the budget.

15. See section 4.6 in this chapter for another statement of Parkinson's Law.

16. The literature on fiscal federalism also bears on this issue. See, for example, Boadway and Hobson (1993).

17. For a dissenting view, see Jaarsma, Schram, and van Winden (1986), who find little evidence that bureaucrats in the Netherlands have higher voting participation than non-bureaucrats.

18. It may be relevant to note that neither author is an economist or a political scientist—Osborne is an author/journalist and Gaebler is a former city manager. This no doubt accounts for the readability and immense popularity of their book.

19. A related concept is the Tiebout hypothesis, which relates to the efficiency aspects of competition among local governments. See the discussion by Ron Kneebone in Chapter 4.

20. I would like to thank Chris Bruce for bringing these two points to my attention.

## REFERENCES

Arrow, K. (1950), 'A Difficulty in the Concept of Social Welfare', *Journal of Political Economy* 57 (Aug.): 328–46.

———— (1951), *Social Choice and Individual Values*. New York: John Wiley & Sons.

Ashenfelter, O., and S. Kelley (1975), 'Determinants of Participation in Presidential Elections', *Journal of Law and Economics* 18 (Dec.): 695–733.

Auld, D. (1994), 'Public Investments, Accountability and Optimal Capital Stocks', in B. Purchase, ed., *Policy Making and Competitiveness*. Government and Competitiveness Project Seminar Series. Kingston: School of Policy Studies, Queen's University.

Becker, G. (1976), 'Comment: Toward a More General Theory of Regulation', *Journal of Law and Economics* 19: 245–8.

———— (1983), 'A Theory of Competition Among Pressure Groups for Political Influence', *Quarterly Journal of Economics* 98 (Aug.): 31–40.

———— (1985), 'Public Policies, Pressure Groups, and Dead Weight Costs', *Journal of Public Economics* 28: 329–47.

Bendor, J. (1988), 'Review Article: Formal Models of Bureaucracy', *British Journal of Political Science* 18: 353–95.

Bennett, J., and W. Orzechowski (1983), 'The Voting Behaviour of Bureaucrats: Some Empirical Evidence', *Public Choice* 41: 271–83.

Black, D. (1948), 'On the Rationale of Group Decision Making', *Journal of Political Economy* 56 (Feb.): 23–34.

Blais, A., and S. Dion (1991), 'Introduction', in A. Blais and S. Dion, eds, *The Budget-Maximizing Bureaucrat: Appraisals and Evidence*. Pitt Series in Policy and Institutional Studies. Pittsburgh: University of Pittsburgh Press, 3–12.

Blais, A., and R. Nadeau (1992), 'The Electoral Budget Cycle', *Public Choice* 74 (4): 389–403.

Boadway, R., and P. Hobson (1993), *Intergovernmental Fiscal Relations in Canada*. Canadian Tax Paper No. 96. Toronto: Canadian Tax Foundation.

Boothe, P. (1993), 'Capital Budgeting in the Public Sector: Lessons from Alberta's History', in J. Mintz and R. Preston, eds, *Capital Budgeting in the Public Sector*. Policy Forum Series 30. Kingston: John Deutsch Institute, Queen's University.

Borcherding, T., ed. (1977), *Budgets and Bureaucrats: The Sources of Government Growth*. Durham, NC: Duke University Press.

———, and R. Deacon (1972), 'The Demand for the Services of Non-federal Governments', *American Economic Review* 62: 891–900.

Bowen, H. (1943), 'The Interpretation of Voting in the Allocation of Resources', *Quarterly Journal of Economics* 58 (Nov.): 27–48.

Brennan, G., and J. Buchanan (1984), 'Voter Choice: Evaluating Political Alternatives', *American Behavioural Scientist* 28 (Nov./Dec.): 185–201.

Breton, A. (1990), 'Centralization, Decentralization and Intergovernmental Competition', Reflections Paper No. 4. Kingston: Institute for Intergovernmental Relations, Queen's University.

——— (1991), 'The Organization of Competition in Congressional and Parliamentary Governments', in A. Breton, G. Galeotti, Pierre Salmon, and R. Wintrobe, eds, *The Competitive State*. New York: Kluwer Academic, 13–38.

———, and R. Wintrobe (1992), 'Freedom of Speech vs. Efficient Regulations in the Market for Ideas', *Journal of Economic Behaviour and Organization* 17.

Buchanan, J. (1949), 'The Pure Theory of Government Finance: A Suggested Approach', *Journal of Political Economy* 57 (Dec.): 496–505.

——— (1977), 'Why Does Government Grow?', in T. Borcherding, ed., *Budgets and Bureaucrats: The Sources of Government Growth*. Durham, NC: Duke University Press.

——— (1988), 'Market Failures and Political Failure', *The Cato Journal* 8: 1–13.

Buchanan, J., and R. Tollison (1972), *The Theory of Public Choice*. Ann Arbor: University of Michigan Press.

———, and ———, eds (1980), *The Theory of Public Choice II*. Ann Arbor: University of Michigan Press.

Buchanan, J., R. Tollison, and G. Tullock (1980), *Toward a Theory of the Rent-Seeking Society*. College Station: Texas A&M University Press.

Bush, W., and A. Denzau (1977), 'The Voting Behaviour of Bureaucrats and Public Sector Growth', in T. Borcherding, ed., *Budgets and Bureaucrats: The Sources of Government Growth*. Durham, NC: Duke University Press.

Canada (1990), *Public Service 2000: The Renewal of the Public Service of Canada*. Ottawa: Supply and Services Canada.

Carroll, K. (1993), 'The Effects of Multiple Objectives in the Theory of Public Sector Supply', *Public Choice* 74 (1): 1–20.

Cassidy, G. (1994), 'Contracting Out', Government and Competitiveness Project Discussion Paper 94–06. Kingston: School of Policy Studies, Queen's University.

Caves, D., and L. Christensen (1980), 'The Relative Efficiency of Public and Private Firms in a Competitive Environment: The Case of Canadian Railways', *Journal of Political Economy* 88: 958–76.

Comanor, W. (1976), 'The Median Voter Rule and the Theory of Political Choice', *Journal of Public Economics* 5 (Jan.–Feb.): 169–77.

Coughlin, P. (1982), 'Pareto Optimality of Policy Proposals with Probabilistic Voting', *Public Choice* 39 (3): 427–33.

Courant, P., E. Gramlich, and D. Rubinfeld (1980), 'Why Voters Support Tax Limitation Amendments: The Michigan Case', *National Tax Journal* 33 (Mar.): 1–20.

Crowley, R.W. (1994), 'The Public Sector and Public Provision in Economic Theory', Government and Competitiveness Project Discussion Paper 94–08. Kingston: School of Policy Studies, Queen's University.

De Groot, H. (1988), 'Decentralization Decisions in Bureaucracies as a Principal-Agent Problem', *Journal of Public Economics* 36: 323–37.

———, and J. Van Der Sluis (1987), 'Bureaucracy Response to Budget Cuts: An Economic Model', *Kyklos* 40: 103–9.

Demzetz, H. (1982), *Economic, Legal and Political Dimensions of Competition*. DeVries Lectures in Economics: Theory, Institutions and Policy, No. 4. Amsterdam: North-Holland.

DiIulio, J., G. Garvey, and D. Kettl (1993), *Improving Government Performance: An Owner's Manual*. Washington: The Brookings Institution.

Dougan, W., and J. Snyder (1993), 'Are Rents Fully Dissipated?', *Public Choice* 77: 793–814.

Downs, A. (1957), *An Economic Theory of Democracy*. New York: Harper & Row.

———— (1967), *Inside Bureaucracy*. Boston: Little, Brown.

Ferejohn, J. (1990), 'Information and the Electoral Process', in J. Ferejohn and J. Kulkinske, eds, *Information and the Democratic Process*. Champaign: University of Illinois Press, 3–19.

Filimon, R., T. Romer, and H. Rosenthal (1982), 'Asymmetric Information and Agenda Control: The Bases of Monopoly Power in Public Spending', *Journal of Public Economics* (Feb.): 51–71.

Fiorina, M. (1977), *Congress: Keystone of the Washington Establishment*. New Haven: Yale University Press.

————, and R. Noll (1978), 'Voters, Legislators and Bureaucracy: Institutional Design in the Public Sector', *American Economic Review* 68: 256–60.

Frey, B., and W. Pommerehne (1982), 'How Powerful are Bureaucrats as Voters?', *Public Choice* 38: 253–62.

Hahn, R. (1990), 'The Political Economy of Environmental Regulations: Towards a Unifying Framework', *Public Choice* 65 (Apr.): 21–47.

Harberger, A. (1954), 'Monopoly and Resource Allocation', *American Economic Review* 44: 77–87.

Hettich, W., and S. Winer (1992), 'Economic Efficiency, Political Institutions and Policy Analysis', paper prepared for the International Institute of Public Finance Meetings, Leningrad (mimeograph).

————, and ———— (1993), 'Institutional Mechanisms for Efficient Policy', Government and Competitiveness Project Discussion Paper 93–10. Kingston: School of Policy Studies, Queen's University.

————, and ———— (1995), 'Decision Externalities, Economic Efficiency and Institutional Responses', *Canadian Public Policy* 21 (3): 344–61.

Hirschman, A. (1970), *Exit, Voice and Loyalty: Responses to Decline in Firms, Organizations and States*. Cambridge, Mass.: Harvard University Press.

Hotelling, H. (1929), 'Stability in Competition', *Economic Journal* 39: 41–57.

Ip, I. (1991), *Big Spenders*. Toronto: C.D. Howe Institute.

Jaarsma, B., A. Schram, and F. van Winden (1986), 'On the Voting Participation of Public Bureaucrats', *Public Choice* 48: 183–7.

Jackson, P. (1982), *The Political Economy of Bureaucracy*. Oxford: Philip Alan.

Kalt, J. and M. Zupan (1990), 'The Apparent Ideological Behaviour of Legislators: Testing for Principal-Agent Slack in Political Institutions', *Journal of Law and Economics* 33 (Apr.): 103–31.

Katz, E., and J. Rosenberg (1989), 'Rent-seeking for Budgetary Allocation: Preliminary Results for 20 Countries', *Public Choice* 60: 133–44.

Kau, J., D. Keenan, and P. Rubin (1982), 'A General Equilibrium Model of Congressional Voting', *Quarterly Journal of Economics* 97 (May): 271–93.

Kitchen, H. (1993), 'Efficient Delivery of Local Government Services', Discussion Paper 93–15. Kingston: School of Policy Studies, Queen's University.

Laband, D. (1983), 'Federal Budget Cuts: Bureaucrats Trim the Meat, Not the Fat', *Public Choice* 41: 311–14.

Landau, M. (1969), 'Redundancy, Rationality and the Problem of Duplication and Overlap', *Public Administration Review* 29: 346–58.

McCormick, R., and R. Tollison (1981), *Politicians, Legislation, and the Economy*. Boston: Martinus Nijhoff.

McCubbins, M., and T. Schwartz (1984), 'Congressional Oversight: Police Patrols versus Fire Alarms', *American Journal of Political Science* 28: 165–79.

McGuire, T. (1981), 'Budget-maximizing Governmental Agencies: An Empirical Test', *Public Choice* 36: 313–22.

McKee, M., and R. Wintrobe (1993), 'The Decline of Organizations and the Rise of Administrators: Parkinson's Law in Theory and in Practice', *Journal of Public Economics*: 309–27.

Mintz, J., and R. Preston, eds (1995), *Capital Budgeting in the Public Sector*. Policy Forum Series 30. Kingston: John Deutsch Institute, Queen's University.

Mique, J., and G. Belanger (1974), 'Towards a General Theory of Managerial Discretion', *Public Choice* 17 (1): 24–43.

Mitchell, W. (1988), 'Virginia, Rochester and Bloomington: Twenty-five Years of Public Choice and Political Science', *Public Choice* 56: 101–19.

Mueller, D. (1989), *Public Choice II*. Cambridge: Cambridge University Press.

Niskanen, W. (1971), *Bureaucracy and Representative Government*. Chicago: Aldine Autherton.

———— (1975), 'Bureaucrats and Politicians', *Journal of Law and Economics* 18 (3): 617–44.

———— (1991), 'A Reflection on *Bureaucracy and Representative Government*', in A. Blais and S. Dion, eds, *The Budget-Maximizing Bureaucrat: Appraisals and Evidence*. Pitt Series in Policy and Institutional Studies. Pittsburgh: University of Pittsburgh Press, 13–31.

North, D. (1990), *Institutions, Institutional Change and Economic Performance*. (Political Economy of Institutions and Decisions Series). Cambridge: Cambridge University Press.

Osborne, D., and T. Gaebler (1992), *Reinventing Government: How the Entrepreneurial Spirit is Transforming the Public Sector*. New York: Addison-Wesley.

Osborne, M. (1995), 'Special Models of Political Competition Under Plurality Rule', *Canadian Journal of Economics* 27 (May): 261–301.

Palda, K., and K. Palda (1985), 'Ceilings on Campaign Spending: Hypothesis and Partial Test with Canadian Data', *Public Choice* 45 (3): 313–31.

Peltzman, S. (1976), 'Towards a More General Theory of Regulation', *Journal of Law and Economics* 19 (Aug.): 211–40.

———— (1984), 'Constituent Interest and Congressional Voting', *Journal of Law and Economics* 27 (Apr.): 181–210.

———— (1990), 'How Efficient is the Voting Market?', *Journal of Law and Economics* 33 (Apr.): 27–63.

Pommerehne, W., and B. Frey (1978), 'Bureaucratic Behaviour in Society: A Case Study', *Public Finance* 33: 99–112.

Posner, R. (1975), 'The Social Costs of Monopoly and Regulation', *Journal of Political Economy* 83: 807–27.

Purchase, B., ed. (1994), *Policy Making and Competitiveness*. Government and Competitiveness Project Seminar Series. Kingston: School of Policy Studies, Queen's University.

————, and R. Hirshhorn (1994), *Searching for Good Governance*. Final Report of the Government and Competitiveness Project. Kingston: School of Policy Studies, Queen's University.

Riker, W., and P. Ordeshook (1968), 'A Theory of the Calculus of Voting', *American Political Science Review* 62 (Mar.): 25–42.

Romer, R., and H. Rosenthal (1978), 'Political Resource Allocation, Controlled Agendas, and the Status Quo', *Public Choice* 33: 27–43.

————, and ———— (1979), 'Bureaucrats versus Voters: On the Political Economy of Resource Allocation by Direct Democracy', *Quarterly Journal of Economics* 93 (Nov.): 563–87.

————, and ———— (1982), 'Median Voters or Budget Maximizers: Evidence from School Expenditure Referenda', *Economic Inquiry* 20 (Oct.): 556–78.

Rose-Ackerman, S. (1978), *Corruption: A Study in Political Economy*. New York: Academic Press.

———— (1986), 'Reforming Public Bureaucracy Through Economic Incentives', No. WSIV-12, Law and Economics Program, Faculty of Law, University of Toronto.

Rubinfeld, D. (1977), 'Voting in a Local School Election: A Micro Analysis', *Review of Economics and Statistics* 59 (Feb.): 30–42.

Santerre, R. (1993), 'Representative vs. Direct Democracy: The Role of Public Bureaucrats', *Public Choice* 76: 189–97.

Savas, E. (1982), *Privatizing the Public Sector*. New Jersey: Chatham House.

Scully, G. (1991), 'Rent-seeking in U.S. Government Budgets: 1900–88', *Public Choice* 70: 99–106.

Shepsle, K., and B. Weingast (1984), 'Political Solutions to Market Problems', *American Political Science Review* 78 (June): 96–111.

Spiller, P. (1990), 'Politicians, Interest Groups, and Regulators: A Multiple-Principals Agency Theory of Regulation, or "Let Them Be Bribed"', *Journal of Law and Economics* 33: 65–101.

Stanbury, W. (1994), 'Holding Government Accountable: Insights from Efforts to Reform the Federal Regulation-Making Process', in B. Purchase, ed., *Policy Making and Competitiveness*. Government and Competitiveness Project Seminar Series. Kingston: School of Policy Studies, Queen's University.

Stigler, G. (1971), 'The Economic Theory of Regulation', *Bell Journal of Economics and Management Science* 3.

——— (1982), 'Economists and Public Policy', *Regulation* (May/June): 13–17.

Thomas, P. (1993), 'Coping with Change: How Public and Private Organizations Read and Respond to Turbulent External Environments', in L. Siedle, ed., *Rethinking Government: Reform or Reinvention?* Montreal: Institute for Research on Public Policy, 31–62.

Thompson, M., and J. Freyer (1994), 'Collective Bargaining in Canada's Public Sector', Government and Competitiveness Project Discussion Paper 94–15. Kingston: School of Policy Studies, Queen's University.

Trebilcock, M. (1994), *The Prospects for Reinventing Government*. Toronto: C.D. Howe Institute.

Trebilcock, M., D. Hartle, R. Pritchard, and D. Dewees (1982), *The Choice of the Governing Instrument*. Ottawa: Economic Council of Canada.

Tullock, G. (1965), *The Politics of Bureaucracy*. Washington: Public Affairs Press.

——— (1967), 'The Welfare Cost of Tariffs, Monopolies and Theft', *Western Economic Journal* 5: 224–32.

von Hagen, J., and I. Harden (1995), 'Budget Processes and Commitment to Fiscal Discipline', *European Economic Review* 39: 771–9.

Weber, M. (1947), *The Theory of Social and Economic Organization*. New York: Free Press.

Weingast, B. (1984), 'The Congressional-Bureaucratic System: A Principal-Agent Perspective (With Applications to the SEC)', *Public Choice* 44: 147–91.

———, and M. Moran (1983), 'Bureaucratic Discretion or Congressional Control? Regulatory Policymaking by the Federal Trade Commission', *Journal of Political Economy* 91 (Oct.): 765–800.

———, K. Shepsle, and C. Johnston (1981), 'The Political Economy of Benefits and Costs: A Neoclassical Approach to Distribution Politics', *Journal of Political Economy* 89 (Aug.): 642–64.

Wilsford, D. (1994), 'Path Dependency, or Why History Makes It Difficult but Not Impossible to Reform Health Care Systems in a Big Way', *Journal of Public Policy* 14 (3): 251–83.

Wittman, D. (1977), 'Candidates With Policy Preferences: A Dynamic Model', *Journal of Economic Theory* 14 (Feb.): 180–9.

——— (1989), 'Why Democracies Produce Efficient Results', *Journal of Public Economics* 97 (6): 1395–1424.

——— (1990), 'Why Government Bureaucracies are Efficient and Not Too Large: The Endogeneity of Institutional Design', Political Economy Research Group Papers in Political Economy, Paper No. 8, University of Western Ontario.

Wyckoff, P. (1988), 'A Bureaucratic Theory of Flypaper Effects', *Journal of Urban Economics* 23: 115–29.

# Comments on Chapter 3    ∎

*Stanley Winer*

Ken McKenzie's chapter ('Institutional Design and Public Policy: A Micro-economic Perspective') is a rich and interesting survey of literature on the relationship between political institutions, policy outcomes, and economic efficiency. The normative perspective taken by many of the contributors to this literature is important because even a good description of what Premier Klein is doing in Alberta or what Premier Harris is doing in Ontario does not tell us what they should be doing. This is a rather obvious point, but it is worth recalling from time to time.

Rather than comment on the chapter directly, I intend in these brief remarks to introduce yet another approach to the welfare analysis of public policy in the presence of political institutions, one that my colleague Walter Hettich and I have been pursuing. In this approach we attempt to combine several of the ideas discussed in the chapter within a unified framework.

An examination of the foundations of normative theory in economics points to three steps needed to construct an appropriate framework for the assessment of budgetary and other policy processes and outcomes. To begin, an analysis is required that places the first theorem of welfare economics (the 'invisible hand' theorem) in the context of a political economy. Put differently, a set of ideal conditions in a representative democracy must be formulated that serves as a counterfactual to existing institutional arrangements, and a proof must be provided that under these conditions budgetary outcomes will be, in some well-defined sense, optimal. The second necessary step is development of an analogue to the analysis of the failure of private markets. Cases where the basic theorem does not hold must be identified and examined to give guidance to policy analysts. Third, measurement is required to make the analysis complete. One must formulate ways of assessing the consequences for welfare, or other specified social objectives, of suggested policy reforms so that comparisons across alternative proposals become feasible. In what follows I briefly discuss some of the issues and problems associated with the first two of these steps, by way of introduction to the kind of work that will be required to complete such an approach to the welfare analysis of the public sector. These remarks rely to some extent on our recent paper (Hettich and Winer, 1995).

## STEP ONE: EXTENDING THE FIRST THEOREM OF WELFARE ECONOMICS

In the first theorem of welfare economics, the outcome of ideal, perfectly competitive private markets is an efficient allocation of resources—an allocation where it is not possible to increase one person's welfare without reducing someone else's. Allocations that depart from this standard of reference are considered to be suboptimal or inefficient. Development of an analogue to the first theorem for situations involving collective choice requires that this standard be expanded in a manner appropriate for the evaluation of public decisions. In particular, it is desirable to incorporate transaction costs into the analysis as an explicit element.

Much of traditional economic analysis has relied on a frictionless world to represent the ideal reference solution. Keith Acheson and Stephen Ferris (1991: 46) have nicely characterized the nature of the frictionless world. With some obvious additions that place their work in the context of this volume, their description may be paraphrased in the following way (my changes are enclosed in square brackets):

> . . . assume that mechanisms exist that costlessly make all information about resources available to all individuals [including to Premier Klein and his cabinet]. All political and other promises are also costlessly enforceable. For public goods, the unanimity principle rules. Complex contracts between government and private citizens are costless to make and enforce. [Disputes with Ottawa over the distribution of resource rents are costlessly resolved.] In this world, an optimal allocation of resources results from contract and exchange.

Some reflection will indicate the problems arising from adoption of a standard defined in this manner. In reality, it is expensive to obtain relevant information and to enforce legal arrangements, while public choices are based on some version of majority rule rather than on the unanimity principle. If deviations from a frictionless world are deemed to be inefficient, all costs associated with the gathering of information, the drafting and enforcement of contracts, and the making of collective decisions must be considered to be improper uses of economic resources. On the other hand, if such transaction costs are accepted as necessary elements of the analytical framework, the emphasis is changed. Analysis must now focus on whether these costs are minimized in particular situations and on whether existing institutions and policies are a rational response to their existence.

Acheson and Ferris point out some of the implications for efficiency analysis of theoretical work incorporating transaction costs into the standard of reference:

> The broader analysis revealed that competition could be excessive, could be bad and needed to be socially controlled. It justified for efficiency reasons making political decisions by majority rule and other non-unanimity voting schemes. It also provided the possibility of an efficiency defense for government involvement in the economy. (1991: 54)

The reluctance to accept the full implications of the broader standard probably helps to explain why comparison with a frictionless world continues to play a role in most economic evaluations of public policy.

While the literature on transaction costs alerts us to the dangers of judging the public sector against an optimal standard appropriate for a frictionless world (in which there really is no need for government), it focuses primarily on private contracts and markets and does not pursue the public-sector aspects of the analysis in detail. A separate literature has developed, dealing primarily with additional theoretical questions that arise when the political process plays an integral part in the design of economic models. A question that has been of much concern to those analysing the economic consequences of public choices is whether majoritarian choices can yield stable equilibrium outcomes and whether such outcomes will be located on the Pareto-efficiency frontier, where all feasible changes that would increase the economic welfare of at least one individual, without reducing the well-being of someone else, have been implemented. This question leads directly to the search for a democratic process that may serve as an analogue to Adam Smith's invisible hand.

Recent work by Peter Coughlin and others (reviewed in Coughlin, 1992) demonstrates that political competition in a representative democracy can in fact lead to stable and efficient equilibrium outcomes under certain conditions. This may be the case as long as candidates continually maximize expected plurality or expected votes while being uncertain of how voters will respond to their platforms.[1] Theoretical results derived from a probabilistic voting model correspond to an intuitive understanding of the political process. In such a model, one in which potential entry of new parties or candidates forces existing parties to search continually for new platforms that will ensure electoral success, there are strong pressures to offer efficient policies to voters. As long as inefficiency persists, there remains the possibility that some party will be able credibly to promise Pareto improvements and thus capture more support from voters who care primarily about their own welfare, regardless of which party satisfies them. In turn, this implies that competitive political pressures will push the society toward an efficient equilibrium allocation of its resources.

Although it is not apparent from my brief description, the standard of reference used in voting models remains the same as in most economic models of private markets—the efficient allocation in a frictionless world. However,

while much work remains to be done for this and other reasons, the probabilistic voting literature suggests that it may indeed be possible to formulate an
analogue to the first theorem of welfare economics for situations that include
collective choice.

## STEP TWO: ANALYSING POLITICAL MARKET FAILURE

In a framework that includes ideal conditions under which the political
process results in an optimal allocation of resources, analysis of the systemic
factors that lead to failure of the political marketplace—the second step in the
proposed welfare analysis—is an appropriate and clearly defined analytical
task.

As Ken McKenzie's survey indicates, many scholars have attempted to formulate reasons why public policy outcomes will not be efficient. One approach
that several authors have explored is based on an extension of the concept of an
externality in the private sector. As a general rule, inefficiency in the allocation
of resources may arise as a result of the operation of the public sector whenever we have what may be called 'decision externalities', that is, when decision-
makers fail to take account of all costs or all benefits relevant to society in making allocational choices. In private markets, as Ronald Coase (1960) has
pointed out, individual maximizing decisions will fully internalize all social
costs and benefits as long as property rights are fully specified and can be
enforced at reasonable cost. Similarly, there is efficiency in political markets if
incentives and constraints for public decision-makers are formulated in an
optimal manner. When this is not the case, decision externalities will occur,
leading to choices that may fall short from society's point of view.

A case study on the use of benefit-cost analysis within Transport Canada,
conducted some years ago by Walter Hettich (1979), illustrates how decision
externalities may arise. The policy question concerned approval of a short take-
off and landing system (STOL) for Toronto, Montreal, and Ottawa, with
Transport Canada supporting a positive regulatory decision while other groups
pushed for a negative outcome. Both sides attempted to buttress their positions
with benefit-cost studies. While the analysis presented by a consultant for the
opposing side followed the principles established in the economic literature for
such studies, the one submitted by Transport Canada deviated in important
respects from accepted economic practice. Measured costs focused only on
items creating budgetary responsibilities for Transport Canada. Other items,
such as the opportunity cost of Toronto Island, which is government-owned
land, and outlays that would have to be borne by Hydro-Québec, were not
included. On the other hand, secondary benefits to the industry manufacturing
aircraft suitable for this type of service were overemphasized. As a result, the

analysis supported establishment of a STOL service, while the report based on established principles did not.

The Transport Canada study reflects a type of decision externality that occurs in all types of public institutions and agencies at all levels of government and, for that matter, in the operation of bureaucracies in the private sector. Since managers are often evaluated on the basis of how well they use agency budgets, they have little incentive to take account of costs that fall outside their purview. In addition, it is rational for them to emphasize benefits that accrue to groups providing the agency with political support in the budgetary process, even though such benefits may be primarily distributional in nature and may not represent an economic gain.

While the concept of a decision externality as a basis for analysing 'market failure' seems promising, it is not without problems. In the first place, it is easier to identify a decision externality than to suggest reforms that clearly lead to an improvement in the allocation of resources. This is especially so in view of the roles played by transaction costs and political competition in determining the evolution of existing institutions. In thinking about decision externalities in the public sector, the policy analyst must acknowledge that public bureaucracies do not have a bottom line like private firms, and that one cannot be provided at any reasonable cost (which is perhaps the main reason why most of their activities remain in the public domain). Thus it is not unreasonable for politicians and voters to judge bureaucratic performance in part on the basis of what a bureau can do with a given budget, leading to incentives for public servants to stretch their financial resources as far as possible. Moreover, under the pressure of political competition, various institutional arrangements may have already evolved to attenuate suitably the undesirable consequences for welfare of such an evaluation process. In the STOL case, such arrangements may include the requirement that large projects be assessed by quasi-independent tribunals.

There is a second general problem that faces the policy analyst who wants to use the concept of the decision externality as an analytical tool. It remains to be shown how this type of political market failure may arise and be analysed within a formal model of political equilibrium, such as the probabilistic voting model referred to above.

I will leave the third step—empirical measurement of departures from an ideal standard of reference in a democracy—aside, except to say that it has so far received the least attention in the literature, and conclude by restating my basic point of view. To make judgements about policy outcomes and processes, it is desirable to use a framework that acknowledges the existence of both transaction costs and collective choice, that establishes conditions under which policy outcomes in a representative democracy are ideal, and that allows the formal analysis of reasons for and measurement of departures from that ideal.

As Ken McKenzie's survey shows, there has been a great deal of interesting and useful work on the various pieces of such a welfare analysis. An important next step will be to combine this work within a comprehensive framework like the one that I have briefly discussed.

## NOTE

1. The existence of uncertainty about how each voter will cast a ballot plays a key role in ensuring that an endless vote-cycle over alternative budgets will not occur. See Coughlin (1992) for the technical details.

## REFERENCES

Acheson, K., and S. Ferris (1991), 'Origins of Theories of Organization', in T.K. Rymes, ed., *Welfare, Property Rights and Economic Policy: Essays and Tributes in Honor of H. Scott Gordon*. Ottawa: Carleton University Press, 39–64.

Coase, R.H. (1960), 'The Problem of Social Cost', *Journal of Law and Economics* 3 (Oct.): 1–44.

Coughlin, P.J. (1992), *Probabilistic Voting Theory*. Cambridge: Cambridge University Press.

Hettich, W. (1983), 'The Political Economy of Benefit-Cost Analysis: Evaluating STOL Air Transport for Canada', *Canadian Public Policy* 9 (4): 487–99.

———, and S.L. Winer (1995), 'Decision Externalities, Economic Efficiency and Institutional Response', *Canadian Public Policy*.

Wittman, D. (1995), *The Myth of Democratic Failure: Why Political Institutions Are Efficient*. Chicago: University of Chicago Press.

# CHAPTER 4

# Institutional Design and Public Policy: A Macroeconomic Perspective

*Ronald D. Kneebone*

## 1. INTRODUCTION

The purpose of this chapter is to review economic research on the implications of the nature of institutions for the design and implementation of public policy. The chapter will focus on reviewing macroeconomic research. In particular, I will examine how certain processes and rules that govern public policy choices affect outcomes as measured by the size of budget deficits and debt, the allocation of government functions between levels of government, and government decisions regarding broad expenditure and taxation choices.

In section 2, I review the literature on how the institution of democracy influences the choices governments make. Section 3 examines the role of fiscal federalism—the allocation of government functions between levels of government. Section 4 reviews the role played by what we might call 'commitment technologies', that is, rules and restrictions placed on government by agents both outside and inside the policy-making process. Finally, section 5 looks at how the recent choices made by the Alberta government fit into these theories. That is, has the Alberta government initiated changes to any of these institutions? If so, how will the changes that have been made affect the likely long-term success of its budget-cutting exercise?

## 2. THE DEMOCRATIC PROCESS

Governments of Western economies operate under the restriction of democracy. Governments are elected and decisions are made within the constraint that elected officials face re-election in the near future. There are at least two favourable implications of the democratic process: it controls the policy choices made by elected policy-makers by threatening them with a future loss at the polls and it allows for the election of policy-makers whose preferences most closely mirror those of the majority. In these ways the institution of democracy constrains policy-makers to implement policies that voters deem appropriate. The literature has, however, also identified three potential ways in which democracy may exert unfavourable influences on decision-makers—a bias towards deficit financing of government expenditures, a bias towards timing government expenditures so as to curry favour with voters, and a bias towards delaying inevitable policy changes. I will discuss each of these in turn.

## 2.1 The Deficit Bias of Democracy

Governments must finance public expenditures by taxation, by deficit financing, or by some combination of the two. The literature identifies three ways by which the democratic process may create a bias in favour of government deficit financing.

### Differing Time Horizons

Democracy creates a deficit bias because the costs and benefits associated with spending and revenue decisions are evaluated over different time horizons. In particular, the benefits from spending public money are often obtained immediately whereas the costs of raising funds via borrowing are felt only in the longer run.

Both politicians and the public contribute to the deficit bias that results from these different time horizons. Taxpayers do so if they discount the future tax liabilities implied by current deficits at a rate higher than the interest rate government pays on public debt. This will typically be the case since individuals face more stringent credit constraints than those faced by government and thus pay higher rates on borrowing. Many taxpayers may also be liquidity constrained and thus vote for deficits as a way of relaxing that constraint. Politicians contribute to the deficit bias due to their uncertainty about remaining in office. This uncertainty causes them to discount the future even more heavily than taxpayers and causes them to value most highly those expenditure and revenue choices that yield the most immediate political pay-offs. As a result of these differing time horizons, there occur an undervaluation of future tax liabilities and an underestimation of the future economic cost of financing today's expenditures with borrowing. The consequence is a bias towards deficit financing for current expenditure.

Von Hagen and Harden (1994) suggest that another way of looking at the problem of differing time horizons is to interpret the deficit bias inherent in the democratic process as resulting from an underrepresentation of future taxpayers in today's decisions. If those bearing the burden of future tax liabilities had a full voice in current decisions, this burden would be counted fairly and governments would be less inclined to use deficit financing.

This argument, however, assumes the current generation ignores the interests of future generations when making current decisions. The Ricardian equivalence hypothesis suggests this may not be the case. This hypothesis suggests that the current generation of taxpayers is concerned about the higher future taxes implied by current deficits because the next generation of taxpayers consists of their children. An implication is that taxpayers are indifferent towards financing government expenditures with taxes vs. deficits. Deficits imply future taxes to be paid by the current generation's children. Since they care about the welfare of their children, parents react to a current deficit by saving an amount exactly equal to that deficit and plan on leaving this as a bequest. In this way, the current generation is made indifferent towards deficits vs. taxes because its consumption possibilities are reduced equally regardless of the choice. In a Ricardian world, then, the democratic process does not induce a deficit bias by failing to consider the needs of future generations.

Cukierman and Meltzer (1989) point out that not all families are identical with respect to their current and expected future economic situation, and thus resurrect the idea of there being an inherent deficit bias in the democratic process even in a Ricardian world. In their model, agents seek to balance concern for their own welfare with concern for the welfare of their children. Those of the current generation who are 'poor' in the sense that their own income is low relative to the expected income of their children do not find it optimal to leave bequests and in fact would prefer to borrow from their children by voting for current government deficits. In a growing economy, or in an economy where real interest rates are expected to be higher for the next generation, the proportion of poor parents grows. Conversely, the 'rich' find it optimal to leave positive bequests. Now suppose a vote is held on whether to finance government expenditures with a deficit or with an increase in current taxes. Poor parents vote for a deficit because this enables them effectively to borrow from their children. Rich parents are indifferent towards voting for either taxes or deficits because they can adjust the size of their bequest to compensate their children for a current deficit. With some of the population indifferent and the rest preferring deficits, the democratic process will favour deficits.

### Minimizing Political Costs

Hettich and Winer (1988) construct a model that suggests another source of deficit bias emanating from the democratic process is the strategic behaviour of politicians. Building on the work of Downs (1957), they assume the objective of democratically elected policy-makers is to set a budget in a way that maximizes political support.[1] Support for the government is an increasing function of government expenditures and a negative function of the level of taxation (including deadweight losses). Within this framework, the politically optimal tax structure is one where each revenue source is used up to the point where the marginal political opposition per dollar of tax revenue raised is equalized across all revenue sources. Gillespie (1991) extends the model to allow explicitly for deficit financing. Consistent with the results of Hettich and Winer, he finds that where it has the constitutional right a government will find it optimal to choose its mix of borrowing and money creation on the same basis as that on which it chooses its mix of taxes—by equating marginal political costs across revenue sources. In this framework, then, balanced budgets are inefficient from the viewpoint of governments since the total political cost of collecting a given amount of revenue is not minimized.

A corollary of Gillespie's extension would seem to be that deficit reduction will be favoured by politicians only when the 'political price' of raising revenue via deficit finance becomes greater than that from taxation or from expenditure cuts. Since at some point a growing debt/GDP ratio must become large enough that the cost of servicing that debt either crowds out other types of government expenditure or demands an unbearable level of taxation, eventually the political price of further deficits becomes prohibitive. At this point, the political benefits of deficit reduction overwhelm the benefits of deficit increases and politicians will propose programs of deficit reduction.

In some sense, then, there may be a maximum level of debt beyond which political expediency will demand adoption of a more fiscally prudent course. Since, as Gillespie notes, an important part of the cost of issuing debt is the debt-servicing cost, the political costs of debt financing fall as interest rates fall and rise with the size of the debt. Thus he would argue that the deficit bias is especially acute during periods of low interest rates coupled with small debt and is least pervasive when debt and interest rates are high. The recent proliferation of balanced budgets among the provinces, and the federal government's recent efforts to get serious about its own deficit, all at a time of high interest rates and debt, would seem to provide support for the idea that the maximum level of politically viable debt has been reached. If so, a period of politically expedient, fiscally prudent government budgets may be at hand.

Gillespie argues that another corollary of the Hettich and Winer model is that the fewer the revenue sources available to a government the greater will be the tax rates on the remaining revenue sources to which it has access. Thus, he suggests that an implication of banning deficit finance by constitutional or legislative edict is that it creates an incentive for governments to impose higher tax rates on those revenue sources that remain. It should also be noted, however, that banning deficits may also cause governments to opt for reduced expenditures rather than increased tax rates, if the political costs of doing the latter exceed those of the former.

It is interesting to compare the predictions of the Hettich and Winer model with those generated by the theory of optimal taxation. The optimal taxation literature takes as its departure from political economy models of tax design the assumption that the motive of tax designers is to minimize the excess burden suffered by taxpayers. Thus, the optimal tax system equates the marginal excess burden per dollar of revenue across all revenue sources. A revenue system satisfying this criterion will not, in general, resemble that which maximizes political support for democratically elected decision-makers seeking to maximize political support. In fact, the nature of the revenue system predicted by the optimal taxation literature is invariant to the nature of the political system. None the less, the two approaches make similar predictions regarding the use of deficit finance. That is, deficit finance is also part of the revenue system suggested by optimal tax considerations and, because increases in debt-servicing costs increase the excess burden associated with a given dollar of revenue raised by bond sales, its use will be inversely related to the interest rate.

Hettich and Winer note that the tax system described in their model can be considered globally efficient if it is interpreted as reflecting a long-run equilibrium generated by a competitive political system. In this sense, the revenue system is optimal for a given set of political institutions. Recognition of this suggests that reform of the way government collects revenue must go hand in hand with a redesign of political institutions. This prediction serves as an important point of departure from the optimal tax literature.

### The Strategic Use of Debt

A third way the literature has identified that the democratic process may create a bias favouring deficits arises out of consideration of possible strategic behaviour by ideologically opposed constituencies. Tabellini and Alesina (1990) present a model to show how competition between such constituencies will generate a deficit bias. The basic idea is that the current majority of voters face an asymmetry. If revenue is raised by borrowing, the current majority has control over how the proceeds will be used. In the future, when expenditures must be cut or taxes raised to repay the accumulated debt, the current majority knows it may not hold power. The future costs of debt repayment are thus not taken into account as fully as are the current benefits, and the current majority therefore votes for deficit financing of expenditures. Borrowing is a way of shifting the costs of current budget changes on a future majority of voters having what might be a different ideology. The greater the ideological differences between majorities, and the more often power changes hands, the greater will be the deficit bias.

Persson and Svensson (1989) present a similar model except here the focus is on potential strategic behaviour of ideologically opposed political parties.

They show that a fiscally conservative government expecting defeat by a less fiscally conservative party may use the size of the government's debt as an instrument to influence the next government's budgetary choices. The essential idea is that by leaving it with a high debt service, the fiscally conservative predecessor can force a greater degree of fiscal conservatism on the more expansionary government. Whether the fiscally conservative government adopts such a policy depends on the attractiveness of a trade-off between imposing on the economy the costs of what it perceives to be an inappropriate fiscal policy and constraining what it perceives to be the inappropriate fiscal choices of the next government. The trade-off becomes more favourable toward running up the current deficit the greater the ideological differences between parties. Persson and Svensson argue their model explains the large deficits incurred during the Reagan presidency. An oft-quoted editorial in the *New York Times* (25 Jan. 1987) offers some anecdotal support: 'This deficit is no despised orphan. It's President Reagan's child, and secretly, he loves it, as David Stockman has explained: The deficit rigorously discourages any idea of spending another dime for social welfare.'

Finally, a number of analysts have noted incentives for incumbent governments to manipulate the size of government deficits in order to influence future election results. An example is Aghion and Bolton (1990), who suggest that right-wing governments may choose to increase debt to make a larger fraction of voters debt-holders and hence less likely to support left-wing parties that might default on debt. Similarly, Milesi-Ferretti and Spolaore (1994) suggest that in the 1980s the Republican Party in the US was struggling to find favour with voters whose preference for social spending was closer to that of the Democratic platform. In light of this, the purpose of the Reagan deficits was to limit the importance of social spending in electoral decisions by increasing debt-servicing costs and thereby shrinking the budget available for social spending. Thus, when the median voter weighed the importance of various issues for determining which party to vote for, he/she placed a lower weight on social spending because little could be afforded in this area. In these sorts of models, then, debt is used not to tie the hands of a possible successor but to manipulate the weighting scheme in the median voter's list of preferences.

## 2.2 Political Business Cycles

The same sort of strategic behaviour between political parties and voters described above as creating a deficit bias has also been identified in the literature as giving rise to what have become known as 'political business cycles'. This literature has its origins in anecdotal evidence suggesting that just prior to elections, governments stimulate aggregate demand via tax cuts, increases in expenditure, and/or reallocations of expenditures into highly visible areas.[2]

Thus, the size and composition of government budgets are a function of the timing of elections.

In a seminal article, Nordhaus (1975) presented a theoretical model to explain this behaviour. A crucial assumption of his model is that voters form their expectations 'adaptively'. That is, movements in economic variables observed in the recent past are assumed by voters to be good predictors of future movements in these variables. Economic agents are therefore said to be 'backward-looking'. In this framework, an incumbent policy-maker has an incentive to boost aggregate demand and generate an expansion of output. Voters reward this behaviour with votes because they fail to recognize the expansion is temporary—in the long run, rates of growth in economic activity return to natural rates.[3] Thus, voters reward incumbent policy-makers in the mistaken belief that post-election economic outcomes will closely resemble pre-election economic conditions. Because policy-makers can engineer favourable pre-election economic conditions, they have an incentive to manipulate budgets to do so. A prediction of this model is that government deficits and the level of economic activity will increase just prior to elections.

Recent contributions to this literature emphasize that individuals have 'rational', or 'forward-looking', rather than adaptive expectations. Rational voters recognize that aggregate demand shocks, such as those that can be engineered by manipulating government spending and taxation, are indeed temporary in their effect on economic activity. The question posed by this literature is why rational voters would allow their expectations regarding post-election behaviour to be influenced by pre-election machinations. Rational voters should disregard policy-induced pre-election deviations from long-run rates of growth in economic activity as irrelevant information for predicting post-election economic activity. No reward would be granted to policy-makers who engineer a pre-election economic boom. Why, then, do governments seem to engage in such pre-election budgetary manoeuvres?

Rogoff (1990) presents a model in which voters can, at any point in time, observe government consumption spending and taxes. Voters cannot observe the competence of elected officials, nor can they observe government spending on public infrastructure until some later period. Voters desire to elect a competent decision-maker because that person can produce public goods more cheaply (that is, with lower tax burden) than an incompetent decision-maker. The problem for the competent decision-maker is how to signal competence to voters.

In the model, voters cannot tell whether an increase in government consumption spending is due to a more efficient use of taxes (which can only be engineered by the competent decision-maker) or due to a shift of expenditures towards consumption and away from public infrastructure spending. For given taxes, increasing government consumption spending has smaller costs for the competent decision-maker since he/she can finance this with a smaller decrease in public infrastructure spending than can be managed by an incompetent decision-maker. Assuming candidates, like all agents in the model, suffer from the loss of public infrastructure, an incompetent decision-maker will shy away from pre-election budget manoeuvres more so than will the competent decision-maker. This leaves the door open to the competent decision-maker to signal competence to voters by increasing government consumption spending and lowering taxes. Although rational voters know that pre-election budget manoeuvres are costly (because of a loss in public infrastructure spending) and are designed only to garner votes, they none the less reward this behaviour because doing so elects a decision-maker who is competent for making future decisions during the period of his/her mandate.

An interesting implication of Rogoff's model is that constitutional or legislated rules designed to prevent the use of costly fiscal policy distortions to signal the competence of an incumbent may not be desirable. The reason is that it is unlikely that such rules can completely stifle the incumbent's incentive to signal his competence. Since in the absence of restrictions it benefits the incumbent to signal using those ways that minimize the social costs of his signalling, restricting the range of signalling options will exacerbate these costs.

Alesina (1987) presents an earlier variation on Rogoff's model in which the political landscape is populated by politicians and political parties differing ideologically. Thus we might imagine two political parties, a right-wing party that attributes a high cost to inflation relative to unemployment and a left-wing party that attributes a relatively higher cost to unemployment and relatively little to inflation. In the model, changes in government occur unexpectedly due to swings in the preferences of the electorate. As a result of nominal rigidities, a change in government causes temporary expansions in economic activity followed by slowdowns (if the left-wing party is elected and attempts to stimulate economic activity) or slowdowns followed by expansions (if the right-wing party is elected and attempts to reduce inflation).

Key differences between the predictions of this model and that of Rogoff (1990) is that here, politically induced cycles occur *after* elections, and government policies change not because politicians alter their platforms in a bid to curry favour with voters but because the majority of voters switch support between sets of politicians who stay true to their principles. Like Rogoff's model, the cycles in Alesina's model are costly to society, but so long as ideological differences exist among voters they may be an unavoidable price to be paid for adopting the democratic process.

## 2.3 Delaying the Inevitable

A third implication of the institution of democracy is the potential for elected representatives to delay inevitable, urgent, and necessary policy changes. An obvious example is the fact economists have for a long time been warning Western governments that economic conditions are such that the choice of deficit finance had put their debts on an explosive path.[4] The simple accounting calculation involved in this warning has been clear to Canadian policy-makers since the early 1980s and yet, until the 1995 budget, little has been done to make a serious dent in the size of the federal deficit. The result has been a rapid increase in debt-servicing costs so that they are now the largest single expenditure item in the federal budget. Due to the explosion in these costs, the cost of reducing the deficit is far larger now than it was just five years ago. If adjustment was clearly inevitable, why did policy-makers not make the policy adjustment immediately and avoid these higher costs?

This is the question addressed by Alesina and Drazen (1991). Their thesis is that major policy changes generally recognized as necessary by all political groups are none the less delayed because, although it is known that the costs of adjustment will be shared across these groups, the cost borne by each group is known only to that group. In this situation, a 'war of attrition' must be fought during which the costs of adjustment are increased and each politically represented socio-economic group tries to wait the others out. Each group has an incentive to delay concession in the hope the others give in and absorb the larger portion of the adjustment costs.

Alesina and Drazen show that the war of attrition is likely to be longer the more unequal the distribution of adjustment costs across groups. Thus, delayed policy responses are especially long for the most contentious of policy changes. Within a governing party, the speed with which adjustments are made increases with the degree of homogeneity within the party. Coalition governments composed of parties from a wide span of the political spectrum are therefore especially vulnerable to policy paralysis.

Neil Wallace (cited in Sargent, 1986) suggests that decision-making in the United States often follows this pattern of hard, but inevitable, policy changes being delayed by wars of attrition. He notes that the President, Congress, and the Federal Reserve System each controls a separate element of the aggregate government budget constraint. Although separate, the three players must, formally or informally, co-ordinate their actions due to the arithmetic of the government budget constraint. Successful monetary policy requires a co-operative fiscal policy and vice versa. If one or more players is unco-operative and intransigent, they must play what Wallace refers to as a 'game of chicken' to determine who will have to adapt to whose policy. He uses this model to explain the conflict between the monetary authority's policy of tight money and the fiscal authority's policy of large deficits during the Reagan presidency.

Drazen and Grilli (1993) extend the Alesina and Drazen (1991) thesis to argue that an economic crisis may be beneficial in that it puts an end to wars of attrition by enabling necessary but politically unpopular changes to be made. Applying their model to the current situation in Canada, the explosive federal government debt requires large tax increases and/or expenditure cuts. The distributional impact of these changes has seemingly paralysed successive federal governments as the economy has settled into a welfare-inferior equilibrium in which a war of attrition is being fought between affected voting coalitions. In this situation, the threat of an economic crisis, wherein the welfare loss that agents can expect to suffer as a result of the crisis dwarfs the loss resulting from the unpopular tax and spending policy changes, may be beneficial by forcing an end to the war of attrition and thereby facilitating transition to a welfare-superior equilibrium. The downgrade of the federal government's Canadian dollar-denominated debt in April 1995 might therefore be viewed as having provided the evidence of a forthcoming fiscal crisis necessary to make the spending cuts announced in the 1995 budget palatable.

A common thread runs through all the hypotheses suggesting a bias favouring deficit financing of government expenditures. The common thread is that of a trade-off. For example, although in their preference functions current voters may weigh the interests of future generations less heavily than their own, when the costs imposed on future generations by current deficits become great enough, voters will none the less demand change. Similarly, an incumbent government will find it advantageous to impose inappropriate fiscal choices in order to constrain the actions of an incoming government only to the extent it perceives the trade-off to be attractive. At some point, the costs of purposely introducing inappropriate fiscal choices must become large enough that they exceed the benefits of discouraging the introduction of, say, a new spending program by an incoming government. Finally, although for low levels of debt and debt-servicing costs the political price of raising revenue via deficit finance may be less than that from taxation, at some point the costs of servicing debt become so large that the political price becomes prohibitive. At this point, the political benefits of deficit reduction overwhelm the benefits of deficit increases and politicians will find it beneficial to propose programs of deficit reduction.

Recognition of these trade-offs indicates that the bias towards deficits can be overcome; deficits are not an inevitable part of democracy. Elsewhere (Kneebone, 1996), I have reviewed four decades of deficits and debts in Canada and have shown that fiscally imprudent behaviour by the federal and provincial governments is a relatively recent phenomenon. It is useful to keep in mind that prior to 1975, provincial and federal budget imbalances were consistently small and as often positive as negative. If in the latter half of the 1990s governments in Canada return to balanced budgets, they will be returning to what was the norm for most of Canada's fiscal history.

## 3. FISCAL FEDERALISM

Generally speaking, what makes budgetary decisions difficult in a democracy is the fact that conflicting needs and aspirations must be satisfied via a political process that rewards reaching some sort of broad consensus. The more disparate are points of view, the more difficult, costly, and time-consuming it is to reach consensus and hence implement major policy changes. The possibility of strategic behaviour on the part of socio-economic groups and their political representatives means inevitable policy changes may be delayed and the costs of adjustment may be increased. In this section, I discuss the implications for budget-making of another source of conflict—that which arises due to there being more than one level of government.

Canada's is a federal system of government. The public sector of the Canadian economy consists of an independent central bank, a federal government, ten provincial governments, some 2,000 city, town, and village governments, and some 3,000 rural municipalities. Provincial and local governments together currently control roughly one-half of the aggregate public-sector budget. As Figure 1 shows, however, the relative shares of the total public sector have varied widely over time. The federal government controlled only 39 per cent of total government spending in 1926 but by the 1950s it was controlling

**Figure 1:** Government Spending Shares, 1926–1993

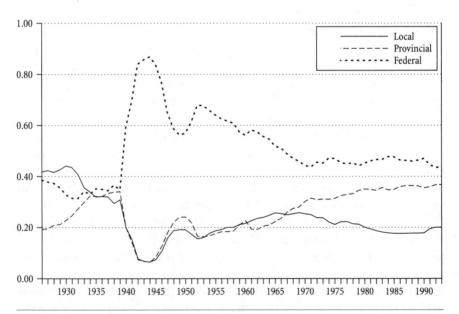

SOURCE: Statistics Canada Cat. Nos. 13–531 and 13–201.

an average of 63 per cent. Since then the federal share has fallen—to 41 per cent as of 1995. Also interesting is the fact that if we compare 1926 to 1993, there has been a complete reversal in the relative sizes of the provincial and local levels of government. Clearly the Canadian federation has been, over the past 70 years, a very dynamic institution.

Table 1 presents the major revenue sources and the major spending areas of the federal and provincial government sectors in Canada in fiscal year 1991/2. The table illustrates the large economic role played by provincial governments and shows that in virtually all major tax fields and areas of spending responsibilities the federal and provincial governments both play very substantial roles. An implication is that both tax reform and the reform of expenditure programs require the co-operation of these two levels of government. This not only makes reform more difficult than otherwise, but it also provides a breeding ground for intergovernmental conflict and, possibly, wars of attrition. Another important potential source of intergovernmental conflict is government transfers. In 1991/2, transfers were equal to 3.8 per cent of GDP, 15 per cent of federal government expenditures, and 17.5 per cent of provincial revenues. Transfers in 1991/2 were also almost exactly equal to the size of the increasingly politically unpopular federal deficit. Put in this way, the potential for intergovernmental conflict during a period of fiscal restraint seems obvious.

In the remainder of this section, I review the hypotheses that economists have put forward to describe how the degree to which government is decentralized might influence budgetary choices. To put these hypotheses in context, I begin with a brief review of the pros and cons of government decentralization.

**Table 1:** Canadian Federal and Provincial Government Revenues and Expenditures as a Fraction of GDP, Fiscal Year 1991/2

| | Revenues | | | Expenditures | |
| | Provincial | Federal | | Provincial | Federal |
|---|---|---|---|---|---|
| Personal Income Tax | 6.1 | 9.9 | Health | 6.5 | 1.1 |
| Corporate Income Tax | 0.8 | 1.6 | Social Services | 4.1 | 8.1 |
| Consumption Taxes | 4.2 | 4.6 | Education | 4.5 | 0.6 |
| Health Insurance Premiums | 1.5 | 2.3 | Debt Service | 2.8 | 6.4 |
| Intergovernment Transfers | 3.8 | — | Intergovernment Transfers | — | 3.8 |
| Total | 21.7 | 20.4 | Total | 24.0 | 24.9 |

SOURCE: *Public Finance Historical Data* 1965/6–1991/2: *Financial Management System*, Statistics Canada, Cat. No. 68–512.

## 3.1 The Costs and Benefits of Decentralization

The most basic argument in favour of decentralization is that it enables government to better tailor public expenditures to meet the needs and desires of local communities. Thus the claim is often made that the local community knows better than the provincial government in Edmonton or the federal government in Ottawa how to spend taxpayers' dollars. The judgement that centralized decision-making tends to impose uniformity on how, and in what quantity, goods and services are provided to communities with different preferences is the very reason why a federal system of government is chosen over a unitary state. Support for decentralized government therefore rests on the assumption that people of similar tastes gather together into a local community. If those with different preferences were evenly spread across the country a unitary state could satisfy the median voter in each locality with the exact same package of goods and services.

The incentive for people with particular wants for government-provided goods and services to gather with others of similar wants, and for those people to attract others with similar wants to their community, is clear; the outcome of votes on public provision will more likely satisfy one's own preferences. The explanation of how people with similar tastes for these goods and services can see to it that their preferences are satisfied is due to the Tiebout hypothesis, which states that if there exist local governments, each with a different tax and public expenditure package to offer their citizens, and if citizens are mobile between these jurisdictions, then an optimal set of such packages will result. Put another way, by 'voting with their feet' a mobile citizenry will influence the taxation and spending decisions of government. Those citizens who prefer a minimum of government involvement in the economy will locate in a jurisdiction offering low taxes and minimal public expenditures. Citizens valuing greater government involvement in the economy will migrate to relatively high tax and public spending jurisdictions. In this way, people with like preferences for government-provided goods and services will gather into local communities. Once this occurs, a centralized government is unable to satisfy the demands of all local communities by providing a uniform set of goods and services.

The Tiebout hypothesis is the basis for the claim that decentralized government is more efficient than centralized government. There are two sources for this claim. The first is the idea that decentralization offers a market solution to the problem of determining the true demand for 'public goods'. A public good is a good or service that can be enjoyed by person A without person B's enjoyment of that good being affected. In addition, neither person can prevent the other from enjoying that good once it is provided. It should be apparent from this definition that the optimal provision of public goods is problematic because of what has been called the 'free rider' problem; that is, people have an incentive to feign indifference when asked how much they would be willing to pay for public goods. As a result, private firms are unwilling to provide public goods and it is left to government to provide them. However, unless government is better able than private firms to divine the true willingness to pay for public goods, such goods will tend to be under-provided relative to the amount taxpayers truly desire. Hence there is a market failure and inefficient amounts of public goods are provided. Decentralization enables local governments to offer alternative amounts of public goods. If citizens are mobile across localities, they will locate in those jurisdictions offering what they judge to be the optimal provision of public goods. In this way, local government jurisdictions can determine the demand for public goods by observing how citizens 'vote with their feet' and public goods will be provided in optimal amounts in each community. In this way, then, decentralized government can be judged to be more efficient than centralized government.

The second way in which a decentralized system of government is hypothesized to be more efficient is by encouraging innovation. Here again the Tiebout hypothesis is important because it suggests that the mobility of citizens will encourage efforts to find ways of minimizing the costs of providing government goods and services. Thus, the discovery of a cost-effective method of sewage treatment in region A will force the government of region B to adopt that approach or risk the wrath of its citizens and perhaps lose tax base due to their moving. The larger the number of local jurisdictions experimenting in the provision of government goods and services, the greater the likelihood of innovation and technical progress.

The major problem inherent in a decentralized system of government arises when we consider programs to redistribute income to satisfy equity goals. An example might be a local government alleviating poverty by implementing a more generous social welfare program. Such a program encourages the poor from other jurisdictions to move into its jurisdiction. An alternative response is to lower the generosity of welfare provisions and thereby encourage the poor to move to a different community. In these ways local governments can 'free-ride' on other jurisdictions. Unfortunately if all local communities respond in this second way the result is a level of welfare provision that is less than what voters in local communities would deem appropriate if welfare recipients were not mobile. Inefficiency thus results and there is a case for enforcing national standards to prevent interjurisdictional competition from driving provision of the redistributive program below socially optimal levels. National standards can be enforced in two ways. One is to have centralized provision of redistribution programs. The drawback to this approach is that we lose the opportunity for experimentation and innovation obtained with decentralized provision. The other option is to have decentralized provision but national funding. This solution requires the use of intergovernmental grants. The budgetary implications of grants will be discussed in the next section.

Another problem for a decentralized system of government arises in those cases when the benefits derived from consuming public goods extend to those outside the jurisdiction of the government providing the good. For example, since water pollution abatement in Calgary not only benefits Calgarians but also all citizens living in communities downriver from Calgary, taxpayers in Calgary will vote for spending less on water pollution abatement than would be demanded if all voters who were affected by the decision had a vote. By not taking into account the so-called 'spillover' effects of their decision, the taxpayers of Calgary vote for a less than optimal amount of the public good.

The implication of this spillover problem is that when the level of government chosen to provide a particular public good does not control a jurisdiction that includes all those who realize benefits from the provision of that good, it will fail to provide the optimal amount of the public good. When this is the case, three solutions are possible. One is to shift responsibility for that good's provision to the next higher level of government so that all who are affected by the decision of how much public good to provide have a vote in the matter. Unfortunately, this solution to the spillover problem involves losing the interjurisdictional competition that both offers a solution to the free-rider problem and generates innovation.

A second solution to the spillover problem—*the Coase theorem*—involves allowing local jurisdictions to negotiate compensation with one another. Referring to our example above, since communities downriver of Calgary want Calgary to spend more on water treatment than Calgarians are willing to pay, they should be willing to contribute to the cost of further treatment.[5] Thus, negotiations can solve the spillover problem so long as the number of agents involved in negotiations does not become so large that the bargaining costs of this solution become prohibitive.

The third solution to the spillover problem is to leave responsibility for providing public goods at the local jurisdiction but use matching conditional grants to partially finance its provision. The idea is that individuals outside a local jurisdiction that is providing a public good with spillover effects should contribute to the cost of providing that good an amount equal to the benefits they receive from its provision. Citizens outside the local jurisdiction make this contribution by paying taxes to a more senior level of government, which in turn provides grants to the local jurisdiction. By making the grant conditional on it being spent on the good or service generating the spillover effect, citizens outside the local jurisdiction can encourage the optimal provision of that good.

To summarize, the desirability of government decentralization rests on the existence of local public goods and on citizens having differing preferences for such goods. When these conditions are satisfied, decentralization enables inter-regional migration to reveal preferences for local public goods and thus lead to their optimal provision. Innovation in the provision of government-provided goods and services is also encouraged by decentralizing government. For these reasons, economists generally favour decentralized government. Spillover effects and the implementation of income redistribution programs, however, call for central government involvement via the use of intergovernmental grants.

## 3.2 The Budgetary Implications of Decentralization

This section considers four ways that the degree of government decentralization has been cited as having a possible impact on budgetary decisions.

### Scale Economies and Program Duplication

There are two oft-cited disadvantages of decentralized government that have direct budgetary implications. One is that it means losing the opportunity to take advantage of economies of scale. However, this claim has little empirical evidence to support it. In fact, Bird and Hartle (1972) suggest most government-provided goods and services are characterized by constant, not increasing, returns to scale so that there is no advantage to assigning their provision to higher levels of government. To the extent that governments provide true public goods there is no denying that per capita costs decrease with the number of taxpayers who finance it so that larger jurisdictions realize a cost advantage. Even here, however, it does not necessarily require that communities be amalgamated into larger government units to take advantage of cost economies. For example, if consumers of the public good live in adjacent communities, one community could produce the public good in amounts sufficient to realize scale economies and sell output to the other (Bird and Slack, 1993).

The second oft-cited disadvantage of decentralized government is that by saving on duplication of effort centralization may offer an important cost saving by requiring fewer bureaucrats to administer programs. While such cost savings may be available from centralizing government programs, this argument and, indeed, that for economies of scale miss the point. The reason for adopting a federal system is precisely because the close co-ordination of government services that may come with centralized provision fails to satisfy the disparate preferences of local communities.

### Budget Interdependence

All governments face a budget constraint. At any point in time total expenditures, including the cost of paying interest on outstanding debt, must equal total revenues raised from taxes and from the sale of bonds. In a federation, the budget constraints of the federal and provincial/state government sectors are closely intertwined. One reason for this is due to institutional arrangements. Cost- and revenue-sharing, intergovernmental grants and transfers, and, in Canada, the fact that provincial income taxes are 'piggybacked' onto the federal tax rate[6] are all reasons why budgetary decisions made by one level of government have a direct impact on the budget of the other. An additional reason is that the two levels of government spend and collect revenues from the same private sector. Thus, any fiscal policy change by one level of government must, by affecting the tax base, interest rates, and inflation, give rise to what the other level of government sees as an exogenous shock to its budget position. The way this second level of government responds to the budget disturbance must feed back into the private sector and thereby into the budget of the first. In this way, then, an interesting dynamic arises from the interdependence of budgets that complicates any attempt to forecast the economic impact of fiscal policy changes.

Some idea of the magnitude of this interdependency between federal and provincial budgets in Canada is provided by Wilson, Dungan, and Murphy (1994), who use a macroeconometric model to simulate the effects of fiscal policy changes. In one simulation, they report that over the 1989–91 period several federal tax increases had the effect of *reducing* the federal deficit by $4.25 billion while simultaneously *increasing* the deficit of the provincial government sector by $1.48 billion—an amount equal to 35 per cent of the federal deficit reduction.[7] These estimates of federal/provincial budgetary interdependence are important for they indicate that since changes in the *total* government sector budget matter for macroeconomic variables, fiscal policies in general, and efforts to control deficits and debt in particular, would be most effective were they co-ordinated between these two levels of government.

Having said this, there are few reasons why one should expect a great deal of budgetary co-operation and co-ordination in a federation. Earlier I reviewed theories suggesting that governments endeavour to minimize the political price to be paid for tax increases or program cuts. If so, then intergovernmental transfers make an attractive source of expenditure cuts for a federal government. As these transfers fund the provision of programs provided by the provinces, the provinces likely will be on the receiving end of the anger of voters when these programs are eliminated. If the federal government acts on these incentives—and a reading of 1995/6 provincial budget papers suggests the provincial governments are almost unanimous in expressing the opinion that this is exactly what the federal government is doing—it clearly does not create an atmosphere conducive to intergovernmental co-operation.

The provinces also face incentives to act in a non-co-operative fashion. Each province benefits from being a member of a larger monetary union that gives it access to a larger pool of savings than otherwise. For this reason, provinces pay lower interest rates on money they borrow than would be the case if they had to borrow only from their own citizens. Provinces thus have an incentive to borrow and thereby impose higher interest rates on other members of the federation. If there is a perception that other members of the union will not allow a fellow member to default on its debts, the incentive for profligate spending is greater still.[8]

For the most part, the economic history of intergovernmental relations in Canada suggests incentives for non-co-operative behaviour have dominated any recognition of a need to co-ordinate fiscal choices. For example, in recent years the federal and provincial governments have had very different views regarding the urgency with which deficits must be brought under control and the most appropriate way of doing so; compare the response of Alberta, which over the period 1992/3 to 1994/5 eliminated a large deficit almost solely via expenditure cuts, and the federal government, which during 15 years of a fast-growing debt responded almost exclusively with tax increases and only now has begun to implement serious expenditure cuts. The federal and provincial governments are also increasingly in conflict over what the provinces perceive to be unwarranted large cuts in federal transfers to the provinces; the so-called offloading of the federal deficit onto the provinces. Tensions between provincial governments have come about due to perceptions that loose fiscal policy by Ontario during the mid-1980s caused the Bank of Canada to impose a more restrictive monetary policy than would otherwise have been necessary. Since by necessity any monetary policy is imposed on all members of a currency union, Ontario's fiscal decisions are thought by some to have had a substantial negative impact on the other provinces.

The decentralization of economic policy-making thus greatly complicates budgetary choices. But is that all? Would a supranational government body designed to co-ordinate fiscal choices solve the problems due to the existence of a second level of government? I have shown elsewhere (Kneebone, 1989) that with respect to what will likely be the most important public policy question in Canada for the next 10 (or more) years—deficit and debt control—the existence of a second level of government significantly restricts the available policy options under all but the most rigid schemes for intergovernmental co-ordination. In that paper two degrees of co-operation were compared. In the first, the two levels of government were assumed to co-ordinate fully their fiscal choices so that they effectively acted as a single government. In the second, the other level of government was assumed to react passively to the policy initiatives of the first, in the sense that it did not intentionally offset or supplement the other's initiatives but instead simply issued or retired debt to finance the disturbance to its budget wrought by the other's actions. Although recent history suggests non-co-operative behaviour might be a more realistic modelling choice than this, it turns out that even such passive behaviour significantly restricts the option of fiscal authorities to deficit finance. It turns out that deficit financing is viable under a much more restrictive condition when governments are assumed to respond passively to one another's initiatives than when their actions are closely co-ordinated. Thus, unless a supranational body causes the two levels of government to behave in a way that effectively creates a unitary state, the existence of two levels of government significantly affects an important budgetary policy option.

### Intergovernment Grants and Transfers

The budgetary implications of intergovernmental grants and transfers are fairly straightforward. As noted earlier, when local provision of government-provided goods and services generates spillover effects, matching grants offer a way of causing the local government to internalize the external benefits of the spillover. If the matching rate can be set equal to the marginal benefit that accrues to residents outside the jurisdiction receiving the grant, matching grants effectively reduce the cost to the receiving government of providing the local public good and thus encourage its production in an optimal amount. Similarly, unconditional grants, typically used for equalization purposes, aim to equalize the capacity of lower-tier governments to provide a certain level of goods and services. Such grants produce a straight income effect that will have a differential effect on local provision of government-provided goods and services depending on their income elasticity of demand.

A different view of the budgetary implications of grants and the role they play in a federation is offered by economists such as Brennan and Buchanan (1980). According to their Leviathan hypothesis, the public sector is a monolith that seeks to exploit its citizenry systematically by maximizing the tax revenue it extracts from the economy. In this approach decentralization of the public sector into many lower-tier governments constrains the budget choices of government (Leviathan) to reflect more closely the wishes of voters. This is so because of the disciplining effects of a mobile citizenry; a lower-tier government that fails to reflect voters' wishes suffers a loss of local tax base.

A corollary of the Leviathan hypothesis is that governments will seek to secure institutional arrangements to offset the constraints placed on it by a mobile citizenry. Brennan and Buchanan identify intergovernment grants as such an institutional arrangement. By collecting revenues nationally and then transferring the revenue via grants to lower levels of government, governments evade the disciplining effects of interjurisdiction migration. Citizens can no longer escape high tax burdens by moving to other local jurisdictions, with the result that government grows larger than it would otherwise. Thus, according to the Leviathan hypothesis, grants and transfers weaken constraints on government spending.

One problem with the Leviathan hypothesis is that it is difficult, if not impossible, to distinguish it from other hypotheses of government behaviour. For example, governments that are hypothesized to be able to collude successfully in such a way as to use intergovernment grants to circumvent the constraining effects of migration might also conspire to complicate the tax system sufficiently to cause taxpayers to be unaware of their true tax burden. Thus a complicated tax system would be viewed as evidence of a Leviathan government sector seeking to maximize the tax revenue it extracts from citizens. Unfortunately, a tax system with many different tax rates is also consistent with a theory of government behaviour where bureaucrats seek to minimize the excess burden of taxation by imposing a set of non-uniform excise taxes in a way consistent with the Ramsey rule of optimal taxation. Similarly, the use of intergovernment grants is consistent with an effort by government to finance local public goods in a way that provides for their efficient level of provision—by financing the provision of local public goods that have spillover effects to prevent fiscally induced migration or to meet equity objectives. Hence, it is difficult to attach a reliable explanation to *why* transfers have evolved.

It is also interesting to note that the Leviathan hypothesis is at odds with more recent descriptions of how governments interact. Rather than envisioning intergovernmental conflict and distrust between eleven fiscal authorities and the Bank of Canada wherein wars of attrition are fought to determine whose preferred policy option will be imposed on whom, the Leviathan hypothesis suggests these governments co-operate with one another to maximize the revenue they can extract from taxpayers. The rancour between governments over any proposals to change the division of powers is not terribly supportive of this view of the world.

A final budgetary influence of intergovernmental grants results from the possibility of a stabilization component to transfers. An important reason why a regional economy may choose to join into monetary union with other regions is that its business cycle differs from that in the other regions. Thus, regions may find it beneficial to join a union that includes intergovernmental transfers designed to transfer revenue from booming regions to those in recession. In this way, regions effectively buy into an 'insurance policy' that smooths out revenue fluctuations. Bayoumi and Masson (1995) provide evidence that in Canada intergovernmental grants play only a small role, both absolutely and relative to their effect in the United States, in smoothing the revenues of provincial governments. As well, Mansell and Schlenker (1995) suggest even this small influence is unevenly felt across provinces. Indeed, those provinces with the most volatile economies seem to receive the least amount of interregional 'insurance'.

*Voting and Budget Choices in a Decentralized State*

If inefficient amounts of government-provided goods and services and lack of innovation in the provision of such goods and services are the result of the lack of competition between government units, it follows that decentralized provision of such goods and services should be vigorously pursued. Bird and Slack (1993) suggest, however, that there are problems with relying on Tiebout effects to enforce competition between government units. In particular, they note that while 'voting with one's feet' might act to discipline government and encourage competition between them, this may not be the preferred type of citizen protest. Suppose, for example, relatively wealthy citizens end up on the losing side of a democratic vote on government-financed education. By establishing private schools the wealthy can express dissatisfaction with the result of the vote but by doing so they create a two-tier system that is less equitable than was judged to be reasonable by the community as a whole. Thus, as Hirschman (1971) argues, the exit alternative undermines the political 'voice' mechanism. This is important because 'voting with one's feet' can be a rather blunt tool of citizen protest. Most parents cannot afford private schools and few will find it optimal to move to new public school jurisdictions in protest against the curriculum offered in their current community. For reasons such as these, Hirschman suggests that the political process must serve as the ultimate disciplining device on government and no amount of decentralization can substitute for this.

Having said this, it is clear that voting is a blunt tool as well. The opportunity to vote is infrequent and votes are usually limited to broad packages of choices rather than specific choices. What's more, as discussed by McKenzie in Chapter 3, the incentives for citizens to participate in elections or other manner of public debate (letters of complaint to newspaper editors, legislators, and bureaucrats) are not overwhelming and the incentives for bureaucrats to make government decisions opaque are strong. Recognition of these points suggests another argument favouring decentralized government. That is, by reducing the number of voters that can be involved, local elections may cause the average citizen to increase the subjective value placed on the vote. In this way, decentralization may increase participation in elections, making smaller government units more politically efficient (Bird and Slack, 1993).

Persson and Tabellini (1994) have pursued the question of how centralizing government might affect political choices. They abstract completely from issues arising from possible economies of scale and Tiebout effects and ask how centralization might affect political outcomes. They conclude that whether centralization leads to larger or smaller government depends on the nature of the government program under consideration and the distribution of voter preferences.

To take an example, consider an economy with two regions, one with a higher mean income than the other but that are otherwise identical. The income distributions in both regions are skewed to the right so that the mean income is greater than the median. Taxation and government spending are determined via democratic votes and preferences are such that voters become worse off the further they move, in either direction, from their preferred choice. Thus, the preferences of the median voter prevail. Voters whose income is to the left of the voter with the mean income favour income redistribution; voters to the right do not. Since the median voter is to the left of the mean, majority voting leads to income redistribution in both regions. Now suppose that the redistribution scheme is to be centralized. Since the mean incomes in the two regions differ, integration of the two sets of voters causes some voters in each region to change their votes. For example, a voter in the rich region whose income is just to the left of the mean income in that region will find on integration that he/she is now richer than the majority of voters in the integrated federation and will now vote against redistribution. Similarly, some voters who were relatively rich in the poorer region will now be relatively poor nationally and will now favour redistribution. Because of the rightward skew in the income distributions, there will be more voters from the poor region who switch to voting against redistribution than there will be voters from the rich region who switch to voting for redistribution. Thus centralizing the redistribution program leads to a smaller program.

For other types of programs, the effect of centralization will have the opposite effect. Persson and Tabellini show this to be the case with social insurance programs such as unemployment insurance. The essential reason for this is that now the critical determinant of voting patterns becomes the probability of lay-off rather than one's income level. Assuming that the probability of lay-off is skewed to the left, so that the minority of people suffer most of this risk, then centralizing such a program leads to a larger program than otherwise.

## 4. COMMITMENT TECHNOLOGIES

Governments may be constrained in the budget choices they make by financial markets, by fiscal rules of behaviour, and by the nature of the institutions within which legislators make decisions. The common theme in this section is that, because of these factors, governments may be forced to commit to certain fiscal choices or actions they might not otherwise adopt.

### 4.1 The Discipline of Financial Markets
Even in the absence of constitutional or legislative rules, governments are subject to penalty should their budgetary choices be found wanting by lenders.

**Table 2:** Relative Bond Yields

|  | New Brunswick | British Columbia | Ontario |
|---|---|---|---|
| 31 March 1991 | 101 | 61 | 58 |
| 31 March 1992 | 82 | 71 | 87 |
| 31 March 1993 | 76 | 53 | 81 |
| 31 March 1994 | 55 | 33 | 66 |

SOURCE: John Sheriff, Midland Walwyn Capital Inc.

This penalty is imposed in two closely related ways. First, as debt grows to levels high enough to cause lenders to become concerned about the possibility of default, they demand a higher interest rate to compensate for the increasing risk of default. Because demanding a higher interest rate itself increases the risk of future default by increasing the cost of carrying debt, the interest rate premium lenders demand will increase at an increasing rate with debt. If debt continues to grow, lenders must eventually reach the point that no further interest rate increases can entice them to hold this government's debt; to buy debt at such high interest rates will guarantee default.

In Canada there are substantial spreads in the yields paid on provincial government bonds in Canada. In addition, these spreads appear to be responsive to relative debt levels and current budget policies. Table 2 shows the difference, measured in basis points, between the interest rate paid on new issues of 10-year bonds sold by the New Brunswick, British Columbia, and Ontario provincial governments, and the interest rate paid on similar bonds sold by the Government of Canada. Over the period shown in the table, both New Brunswick and British Columbia reduced their deficits and announced their intentions to achieve balanced budgets by 1995/6. Ontario's deficit remained high with little hope of large reductions in the near future. What the table indicates is that New Brunswick and British Columbia were rewarded for their efforts with a significant reduction in the interest rates they had to pay on their debts.

The fact that New Brunswick and British Columbia should be so rewarded is consistent with the findings of Capeci (1994), who showed, in a study of New Jersey municipalities, that current period fiscal decisions have a significant impact on the cost of borrowing. Capeci found that a one standard deviation increase in the amount borrowed is associated with a 66 basis point increase in annual bond yields. Goldstein and Woglom (1992), also looking at US municipal bond yields, similarly found that governments that reined in deficits and reduced debt were rewarded by reduced bond yields. As well, they found that the interest rate penalty imposed on profligate governments increased at an

**Figure 2:** Debt vs. Bond Rating, Saskatchewan

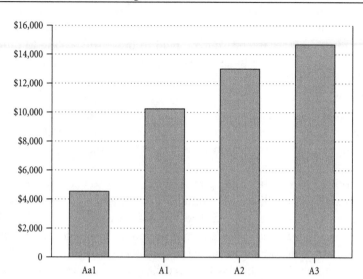

SOURCE: Bond ratings are from *Moody's Bond Record* (various issues). Gross debt data are from Statistics Canada, matrix 3209. Population data are from Statistics Canada, matrix 6375.

increasing rate, reflecting the concern of lenders that higher yields also increase the risk of default.

The second way in which financial markets impose penalties on profligate governments is through credit ratings. Credit-rating agencies serve financial markets by evaluating and publishing objective measures of default risk. A credit downgrade imposes discipline on profligate borrowers not only by signalling the need for interest rate increases but, more importantly, by causing certain lenders who are subject to capital adequacy standards to cut off new credit to such borrowers. As such lenders are typically large, a downgrade requires that the risk premiums rise to induce the remaining lenders to absorb new debt. Further downgrades lead to more severe consequences as more and more lenders are required to cut off this borrower. Consequently, default risk becomes an increasing function of one's debt and imposes an increasingly more stringent penalty. In this way, credit-rating agencies cause financial markets to impose penalties on governments that run large deficits for prolonged periods of time.

This relationship is illustrated in Figure 2, which graphs the average value of gross debt per capita in Saskatchewan against Moody's rating on that debt under four periods of different credit ratings between 1981 and 1993.

The figure illustrates the non-linear relationship suggested above; as debt grows, the marginal additions to debt necessary to prompt a credit downgrade diminish. Boothe (1993) speculates that the pool of prospective lenders allowed to purchase Saskatchewan debt diminished from between 125 to 140 institutions when its rating was high to only 25 or 30 at the lower rating. Thus, not only must a higher interest rate be paid to those still willing to purchase debt, but greater attention must be paid to the preferences and concerns of those remaining lenders. Government becomes more and more captive to the demands of a dwindling number of lenders.

The ability of financial markets to discipline profligate government borrowers is limited, however.[9] One reason is that the ability of credit-rating agencies to impose such penalties on a profligate borrower is a function of the central bank's reputation with respect to the question of its willingness to purchase (monetize) the debt of that government. This is so because if the central bank has exhibited a willingness to purchase the debt of a government, holders of that debt face a much reduced threat of default risk; the central bank has effectively announced it stands ready to print money to enable the government to meet its debt obligations. The holders of such debt face only currency risk— the risk that a surprise inflation will reduce the real value of debt—and in compensation they demand a risk premium that is reflected in a higher nominal interest rate payable on this debt. For this reason, the discipline on profligate borrowers imposed by credit-rating agencies is most strongly applied to states/provinces and local governments—issuers of government debt that central banks refuse to buy.

In Canada, another important way in which governments circumvent the discipline of financial markets is to provide themselves with privileged access to public pension funds. For example, each province has access to the Canada/Quebec Pension Plan contributions made by citizens of their province.[10] A further benefit of this privileged access to CPP/QPP funds is that the provinces pay a rate of interest on this debt equal to the rate paid on federal government bonds, a rate Table 2 shows to be sometimes substantially lower than what would otherwise have to be paid.

Governments can also circumvent market discipline by not making information freely or easily available. Pushing spending programs and borrowing off the balance sheet is one way of doing this. Finally, a government may simply have such a short time horizon that market signals have no effect on its behaviour. Moreover, as discussed earlier with respect to political business cycles, failure to heed market signals may be done on purpose to saddle a successor government with a debt crisis. It may also reflect an ongoing war of attrition.

It is difficult to measure how well financial markets discipline borrowers. With respect to the disciplining effects of credit downgrades, simply being threatened by a downgrade may prompt action, thus making a relationship difficult to observe. Another reason is that bond ratings reflect an appraisal of long-term risks so that the rating need not correlate well with a government's current or near-term budget position. As well, credit ratings reflect a judgement based in part on non-financial factors. Thus, the mere election of a government pledged to a program of large spending increases, for example, may prompt an immediate credit downgrade so that a relationship between credit ratings and budget policy becomes difficult to observe.

None the less, there is anecdotal evidence to suggest that credit ratings have influenced budgetary choices among Canadian governments. Maslove, Prince, and Doern (1986), for example, note the frequency with which 'preserving the province's credit rating' is given as a rationale for austerity measures. Kneebone (1994) observes that during the 1980s, credit-rating agencies were quick to downgrade provincial governments that allowed their deficits to grow too quickly, and speculates that, possibly as a consequence, the provincial debt/GDP ratios of those provinces remained under control despite trying economic conditions.

## 4.2 Tax and Expenditure Limits and Deficit Restraints

In the United States the use of tax and expenditure limits (TELs) and balanced budget requirements are popular ways of constraining state government budget choices.[11] Since 1977, 18 states have implemented binding TELs. Most of these impose limits on state expenditures; only five states impose limits to taxation. The TELs of 10 of these states are enshrined in state constitutions; the remaining eight are statutory requirements. The most common form of restriction among US states is a limit on revenues or expenditures as a fraction of personal income. California, for example, requires that real per capita tax revenue be held constant, while Arizona limits state taxes to 7 per cent of personal income. Twenty-nine states are subject to constitutional or statutory restrictions that prevent the state from carrying a deficit into the next fiscal year. Another seven states are subject to constitutional or statutory restrictions that prevent them from carrying a deficit forward into the next biennium.

Outside of the US, interest in constitutional restrictions on government budget policy has been sparked by the proposal of designers of the proposed European Monetary Union (EMU) that member states be required to satisfy deficit (3 per cent of GDP) and debt (60 per cent of GDP) restrictions. In Canada, neither the federal government nor the provinces face constitutional restrictions on the size of the deficits and debts they may incur. Only very recently have some provinces introduced statutory requirements for balanced budgets. New Brunswick was first off the mark with legislation requiring a balanced budget on the current account (omitting the capital account) in 1993. In 1995 this was amended to require a balanced consolidated budget over every four-year period. Also in 1995, Alberta passed, and Manitoba proposed, legislation requiring balanced consolidated budgets. Manitoba's legislation is interesting in that it specifies substantial financial penalties to be incurred by members of cabinet (20 per cent of salary) should a deficit occur. The penalty doubles if a deficit is incurred in a second consecutive year.

In 1991 British Columbia passed legislation (the Taxpayer Protection Act) calling for limits on spending growth with the intention of achieving a balanced budget by 1995. This attempt to implement a TEL was short-lived, however, and it was repealed in 1992 following the election of a new government. Alberta's Taxpayer Protection Act (1995) introduces a different type of TEL in that it prohibits the introduction of a provincial sales tax without the question first being approved in a referendum. The Manitoba Balanced Budget Act similarly constrains government by requiring a referendum before it can increase tax rates on any of four tax types. New Brunswick's Act specifically states there shall be no limits on taxes or spending, so long as the balanced budget goal is met.

The effectiveness of TELs and deficit limits has been the subject of a number of recent studies. In a study of US state budgets, Stansel (1994) reports that the five-year growth rate of per capita spending in states with TELs fell from 0.8 percentage points above the US average in the five years before TEL enactment to 2.9 percentage points below the US average in the five years after. Judging effectiveness from a different perspective, Poterba (1994) finds that US state rules on deficits and tax/spending limits are correlated with more rapid fiscal adjustment to unexpected deficits. In addition, the nature of the response is affected by the existence of fiscal rules. In particular, states with deficit and tax/spending limits are more likely to respond to unexpected deficits with spending cuts and less likely to respond with tax hikes than are states without such limits. Similarly, von Hagen (1991) finds that fiscal restraints on US state budgets significantly increase the probability of a state exhibiting a lower per capita debt and lower debt-to-income ratio.

Yet another way of measuring the effectiveness of TELs is to examine how self-imposed fiscal restrictions affect bond yields. This is the approach of Eichengreen and Bayoumi (1994). Using data from 37 US states covering the period 1981–90, they find that self-imposed fiscal constraints lower the interest rate that must be offered on general obligation bonds by upwards of 50 basis points. They also find that this benefit of self-imposed constraints grows with the level of debt, so more heavily indebted jurisdictions benefit most from imposing fiscal rules designed to control future growth in their debts.

Analysts have found that the effectiveness of TELs and deficit restrictions is increased by certain critical features of their design and by features of the political landscape. Stansel (1994) notes that since TELs are designed to restrict the choices available to legislators, they will become less effective over time if they are not designed in such a way as to minimize the ability of legislators to circumvent their purpose. Thus, he notes the importance of preventing the movement of expenditures 'off-budget' in order to free them from the TEL cap. Von Hagen (1991) similarly finds that when it is not prevented by the design of the fiscal restraint, restraint leads to a change in debt composition; governments substitute unrestricted for restricted debt instruments. All of these results support the idea that administrators will seek, and likely find, ways to obfuscate and circumvent fiscal restraints if doing so services their own interest. These findings, then, are suggestive of the pervasive influence of the political economy issues discussed earlier.

When rules and restraints are imposed to limit the menu of budgetary policy choices, it is perhaps not surprising that the benefits of such restraints come only at a cost. The major source of these costs is the fact that TELs and deficit restrictions put limits on the automatic stabilizer role played by deficits, taxes, and expenditures. That is, if taxes and expenditures are 'progressive' in the sense that net transfer tax revenues paid by the average taxpayer decrease during a recession, then state budgets will provide a 'fiscal offset' to temporary reductions in private incomes.

In a study of US state budgets, Bayoumi and Eichengreen (1995) find that state budgets provide about 14 per cent of the total fiscal offset to income fluctuations supplied by all government budgets and social security funds. They further show that the cyclical responsiveness of state budgets is affected by self-imposed fiscal restraints and that, in particular, these restraints lowered the fiscal offset to income fluctuations supplied by state budgets by about 40 per cent. Their estimates for Canada suggest that the provincial/local government sector provides roughly one-half of the fiscal offset to income fluctuations coming from government and public pension funds. This suggests that imposing restrictions on the size of provincial deficits (local government deficits are already subject to control) might have a very significant negative impact on the automatic stabilizer role of government budgets in Canada.

As Alesina and Perotti (1995) note, evaluating the costs and benefits of fiscal restraints is difficult because it involves comparison of second-best outcomes. A balanced budget law, for example, is clearly suboptimal since it prohibits the use of beneficial 'tax-smoothing' and automatic stabilizer roles of budget imbalances. On the other hand, the lack of such a constraint is also suboptimal since politically induced second-best budget outcomes often result. In general, the more indebted a government the more attractive are financial restraints. That this is so is suggested by the findings of Eichengreen and Bayoumi (1994) that heavily indebted jurisdictions are rewarded with larger interest rate reductions when such restraints are put in place than are less indebted jurisdictions.

## 4.3 The Budget Process

The process by which governments arrive at a budget is essentially a collection of rules and conventions that govern how decisions are made. This collection of rules can, by constraining the flexibility of decision-makers, by limiting the input of special interest groups, and so on, have substantial impact on budget outcomes.[12] In some sense, then, the rules that govern the budget process can be thought of as complements to balanced budget amendments or similar fiscal restraints. Indeed, given the incentives politicians have to try to circumvent fiscal restraints, changes in the budget process may be a useful, or even necessary, way by which the integrity of fiscal restraints can be maintained.

The nature of the incentives that govern the interrelationships between participants in the budget-making process and the effect these have on allocations of the total budget across departments are dealt with in detail by McKenzie in Chapter 3. In this section, then, I will only touch on how the nature of the institutions within which legislators make decisions are thought to affect certain macroeconomic outcomes.

A very basic aspect of any budget-making process is a government's accounting practices. Poterba (1995) compares US states that maintain separate budgets for capital and operating expenditures with those that do not. He finds that states that maintain separate budgets spend more on capital projects than states with unified budgets. Poterba argues that this is inconsistent with the argument sometimes advanced that public accounting practices are a veil with no impact on policy outcomes.

In an effort to quantify the degree to which governments have committed to a budgetary process conducive to fiscal discipline, von Hagen (1992, 1994) constructs two indices for each of the 12 governments in the European Community (EC). The first index (SI) is intended to measure a government's commitment to establishing a fiscally responsible budget. To that end, the SI index is established by assigning a number between 0 and 4 to indicate the degree to which a government's budget process (i) assigns a strong strategic position to the prime minister or the finance minister in establishing a general constraint on the overall size of the budget, (ii) involves a parliamentary process with strong limits on budget amendments, (iii) involves a large degree of budget transparency, and (iv) assigns a strong position to the finance minister *vis-à-vis* the spending ministers. The second index (CON) attempts to measure a government's commitment to a long-term budget plan. To that end, the CON index again assigns a number between 0 and 4 to indicate the strength of a government's commitment to (i) a multi-annual fiscal target embedded in a consistent economic forecasting framework, (ii) a high degree of budget monitoring, (iii) limited amendment power of parliament, and (iv) limited flexibility of budget execution. High values for the SI and CON indexes thus indicate a high degree of commitment to limiting the overall size of the budget and to a long-term plan from which the government is not likely to deviate to meet short-term political interests. To establish the importance of these features of the budget process, von Hagen matches the SI and CON indexes to broad measures of fiscal performance. He finds that the three EC countries with the highest SI and CON indexes had, on average, considerably lower deficit/GDP and debt/GDP ratios than did the three countries with the lowest SI and CON indexes. Although, as Alesina and Perotti (1995) note, these results are tentative and further comparative empirical work needs to be done, the general lesson seems to be that budgetary institutions matter for determining fiscal policies.

In general, the available evidence suggests that all of these commitment technologies appear to be effective at reducing government deficits and debts. As our discussion of the effects of TELs and deficit limits on the automatic stabilizer role of government deficits suggests, however, it is another question whether the goals or targets that commitment technologies are to satisfy are *desirable*. Thus, if the efficacy of TELs and balanced budget requirements are firmly established in future empirical work, it will be imperative that these goals and targets be carefully considered and their costs and benefits weighed.

## 5. THE ALBERTA EXPERIENCE

In this final section I will try to paint, in broad strokes, a picture of how the election of Ralph Klein, how the changes introduced into Alberta government budgeting, and how other institutional changes that are part of the so-called 'Klein revolution' can be analysed within the various models surveyed. Other chapters in this volume will examine these questions more closely.

In section 2, I reviewed a literature that essentially argues that voters get the level of taxes, expenditures, and deficits they demand because politicians typically opt for the most politically attractive budget choice. A corollary of this approach is that when the preferences of voters change, so, too, will the size and/or composition of government budgets. A useful place to start in describing the Alberta experience might therefore be to ask whether the changes introduced by the Klein government can be associated with a shift in voter preferences.

In Alberta, as throughout North America, it seems obvious that an ideological shift to the right has occurred, with popular opinion demanding that governments behave in a more fiscally prudent way than they have in the recent past. The size of this shift has undoubtedly been smaller in Alberta than elsewhere due to what seems to be the inherent fiscal conservatism of Albertans; evidence of this is presented by Archer and Gibbins in Chapter 13.[13] None the less, the changes the Klein government has introduced involve a substantial shift from what Albertans had been getting from their provincial government over the past 20 years under Premiers Lougheed and Getty. The fact that, like Klein currently, Lougheed enjoyed a high level of popular support suggests a substantial shift in the preferences of Albertans.

The source of this shift of preferences can likely be attributed to the rapid deterioration of Alberta's public finances following the fall in energy prices in 1986 (see Mansell, Chapter 2, for further discussion). The speed with which Alberta's net asset position turned into a large net debt position undoubtedly prompted a perception among voters of a fiscal crisis. If so, this perception may have been responsible for Albertans coming to the conclusion that the potential losses they might expect to suffer if the growth of the debt was left unchecked were large relative to the costs associated with cuts to provincial expenditures and/or increases in provincial tax rates. Thus, as Drazen and Grilli (1993) suggest, a perception of a fiscal crisis may have been responsible for making substantial expenditure cuts and/or tax rate increases palatable.

If this interpretation of a significant shift in Albertans' preferences is correct, then an important part of the success of the fiscal changes initiated by the Alberta government was its ability to gauge and respond to this shift in popular sentiment. The first step in this process was, of course, to get elected. In a speech during the 1992 election campaign, Ralph Klein laid out a fiscal plan for significantly reducing the size of the provincial government. His promise was to eliminate Alberta's large provincial deficit by fiscal year 1996/7 and to do so solely via expenditure cuts. He warned that the implication was that there would be a sizeable reduction in the provincial government. Klein was elected and his party returned with 51 of 83 seats in the provincial legislature.

In an interview conducted as part of this project,[14] the provincial treasurer indicated that the next step for the government was to ask the public for a list of priorities so as to enable it to establish its own political priorities. The government-sponsored public roundtables on major issues such as health, education, and the deficit were an important part of this effort. These roundtables, conducted prior to the announcement of the budget cuts, provided a way for the government to gauge public opinion regarding where the cuts should be made. In a very real sense, then, the Alberta government simply responded to the shift in public preferences, a shift so strong and prevalent that both the major political parties in the province ran on a platform of spending cuts in the 1992 election. Given this shift in preferences, the government behaved in a politically optimal way—an interpretation that finds support in the public opinion survey presented in Chapter 13.

In section 4, I reviewed a literature that suggests that commitment technologies and the nature of the budget process are important for determining the likelihood of fiscal changes being made permanent. What has the Klein government done in this regard?

If process is important, then many of the more important changes introduced by the Klein government may be the most subtle and least talked about. A way of quantifying these changes is to try to make a judgement regarding what has happened to the value of von Hagen's (1992, 1994) so-called SI index for Alberta. The changes made to the budgeting process are discussed more fully by Boothe in Chapter 6, but we can note here that this index has been increased in value by the government's efforts to increase budget transparency and to increase the power of the Treasurer *vis-à-vis* the spending ministers. Similarly, von Hagen's CON index has been increased by the introduction of a high degree of budget monitoring, limited flexibility in budget execution, and a multi-annual fiscal target embedded in a consistent and conservative forecasting framework. Based on von Hagen's analysis of the EC budgets, these changes in process should increase the likelihood that Alberta will maintain lower deficit and debt/GDP ratios than it would otherwise.

As well as these changes in the budgetary process, the Klein government has passed three pieces of legislation designed to prevent future governments from undoing what it has done. The Balanced Budget and Debt Retirement Act (1995) and the Deficit Elimination Act (1993) commit governments in Alberta to reaching a balanced budget, prohibit deficits in the future, and establish a gradual pay-down of the outstanding provincial debt. The Alberta Taxpayers Protection Act (1995) prevents this and future governments from introducing a provincial sales tax without a referendum to approve it. As well, in February 1996 the government announced its intention to introduce legislation prohibiting this and future governments from making loans to private businesses. With these pieces of legislation in place, this and future governments will be significantly restricted in the range of budget choices open to them.

The attraction of such legislation is that the scope for using the budget for political ends is reduced, and the likelihood that deficits may persist due to wars of attrition being fought is lessened. Unfortunately, the survey of political business cycle models suggests that many of the possible 'cures' to these problems of democracy—problems such as wars of attrition and budget manipulations at election time—may be worse than the 'disease'. Thus, an interesting implication of the political business cycle model presented by Rogoff (1990) is that TELs or balanced budget legislation designed to prevent the use of fiscal policy distortions to signal the competence of an incumbent policy-maker may not be desirable if they force the policy-maker to signal using ways that generate larger social costs. Even abstracting from concerns such as these, the review of the effects of TELs and balanced budget legislation suggested that, while they appear to be effective at reducing the size of budgets and budget deficits, they also substantially reduce the beneficial role of budgets as automatic stabilizers. In a province often subject to wide variations in economic activity (see Mansell, Chapter 2, for a discussion), this is an important consideration.

Some implicit recognition of the potential negative effect of the government's budget rules on the budget's automatic stabilizer role seems to have been made by the decision to build large revenue cushions into forecasts. The Balanced Budget and Debt Retirement Act requires that the budgeted amounts of resource and corporate income tax revenues be the lesser of 90 per cent of the government's forecast or the five-year average of actual revenue. Thus, for fiscal year 1996/7 the government expects resource revenue of $2,646 million but has budgeted for $2,381 million, providing a cushion of $265 million. This, plus the corporate income tax cushion, leaves $545 million of revenue out of the budget to be used to finance unexpected increases in expenditures and decreases in revenues without threatening the government's balanced budget promise or its plan to meet minimum debt repayments each year. Whether or not the revenue cushion, equal to 4 per cent of total revenues, will be sufficient to keep the government from having to adjust spending and/or tax rates in the face of an economic downturn remains to be seen.

Some information on this question comes from Kneebone and McKenzie (Chapter 7), who calculate that over the period 1970/1 to 1993/4, the average unexpected increase in the deficit was only $38.7 million (1994 dollars). The revenue cushions therefore would appear to be more than sufficient to handle the average deficit shock. Unfortunately, this average shock comes with a large standard deviation and had a maximum value of $1,745 million (1994 dollars). These latter values are the result of the oil and gas price shocks that intermittently rock Alberta's finances. They indicate that this government's fiscal rules may force it to impose pro-cyclical tax and spending policies, should such shocks strike in the future.

Finally, in section 3, I discussed how a decentralized government offers solutions to the free-rider problem, may encourage innovation in the delivery of publicly provided goods and services, and may enable the public sector to provide goods and services that more closely reflect the wants of citizens. One of the most emphasized aspects of government reforms in Alberta has been the effort to decentralize government provision of goods and services. During the interviews conducted as part of this project, ministers stressed that decentralization was intended to encourage innovation and to enable the public sector to provide goods and services that more closely reflect the wants and needs of citizens. This emphasis was especially strong in the area of Family and Social Services, where it was stressed that it was counterproductive to try to apply the same rules and conditions for the provision of social services across all of Alberta—the needs of the urban poor differ substantially from the needs of poor aboriginals living on rural reserves, for instance. The hope that decentralization might encourage innovation and cause local wants to be better served has also been emphasized in the area of health with the introduction of Regional Health Authorities (RHAs) and in basic education with the encouragement of school councils.

The details of how and why decentralization of government has occurred in these areas will be discussed in later chapters in this volume. For now I will only draw attention to the fact that although this government has stressed decentralization, it has not fully committed to the ideal of decentralization. A good deal of control remains with the central authority. In part, this may reflect a recognition that 'voting with one's feet', while economically efficient, is not necessarily consistent with the goal of equity. An example of where this is apparent is in the government's treatment of school taxes. As will be described in more detail in Chapter 10, the government now collects all school tax revenue and allocates it to school boards on a needs-adjusted per capita basis. When asked in an interview if it was necessarily bad for school tax bases to differ significantly across regions, a minister noted that 'education is fundamentally different from building bridges'. That is, although it may be acceptable that certain areas are not able to develop certain types of infrastructure because of a small tax base, it is not acceptable that the education of children should suffer for this reason. This kind of limit placed on decentralization may thus reflect an implicit recognition of the problem of 'voice' versus 'exit' raised by Hirschman (1971) and discussed earlier. Whether or not the degree of decentralization adopted by this government will be sufficient to spark the innovation and the preference revelation that decentralization is designed to promote remains to be seen and will need to be the subject of future research.

## NOTES

1. A simplification of this model worth noting is that no independent role is assigned to the government bureaucracy. Thus, only the motives of politicians are modelled as a determinant of the structure of the revenue system. See McKenzie, Chapter 3, for a discussion of the role of the bureaucracy and its relationship with the government.

2. Evidence regarding the question of whether a political business cycle has existed in Alberta is presented by Kneebone and McKenzie in Chapter 7.

3. A necessary condition for the existence of political business cycles is the existence of nominal rigidities. Such rigidities enable the growth rate in real output to vary from its natural rate in the short run. Without nominal rigidities, changes in fiscal

policy cannot generate the expansions in economic activity with which policy-makers hope to curry favour with voters.

4. This was the lesson of Sargent and Wallace (1981).

5. Alternatively, if the downstream communities are deemed to hold the right to clean water, Calgary taxpayers should be willing to compensate downstream communities for the pollution caused by Calgary's less than 100 per cent effective water treatment plants. This will be an economically efficient arrangement if the cost of improving Calgary's treatment plants is greater than the compensation demanded by downstream communities.

6. For all provinces but Québec, provincial personal income tax rates are defined as a percentage of the federal rate. Thus, changes in the federal tax rate have a direct effect on provincial revenues.

7. See, as well, Wilson and Dungan (1993), who use the same simulation model to investigate the impact of a hypothetical, gradual reduction in federal expenditures under alternative monetary policy regimes. Given a non-accommodating monetary policy, they find a $5.4 billion improvement in the federal deficit comes at the cost of a $3 billion worsening of the budget balance of the provincial government sector.

8. Concern about incentives for unco-operative behaviour are not unique to Canada. The Maastricht Treaty's minimum standards of fiscal prudence for potential entrants into the proposed European Monetary Union are due to concerns that each member will have an incentive to act in such a way as to impose costs on others.

9. See Lane (1993) for a thorough discussion.

10. Kitchen (1991) reports that Ontario has historically met almost all of its borrowing requirements from this source and from access to the provincial school teachers' pension fund. As a result, as of the late 1980s, only 3.5 per cent of Ontario's debt was held by the general public.

11. The following description of TELs in the United States is based on Stansel (1994). The description of state balanced budget requirements is from Eichengreen (1990) and von Hagen (1991).

12. In Chapter 6, Paul Boothe reviews these issues and the budget-making process in Alberta.

13. Archer and Gibbins conclude that although there may be varying hues of neo-conservatism among Albertans, they tend to be neo-conservatives none the less. Kneebone and McKenzie (Chapter 7) provide empirical estimates suggesting governments in Alberta have responded to this inherent fiscal conservatism by generating a political business cycle.

14. See Kneebone and McKenzie, Chapter 5, for an analysis of these interviews.

## REFERENCES

Aghion, P., and P. Bolton (1990), 'Government Debt and the Risk of Default: A Political Economic Model of the Strategic Role of Debt', in R. Dornbusch and M. Draghi, eds, *Public Debt Management: Theory and Practice*. Cambridge: Cambridge University Press.

Alesina, A. (1987), 'Macroeconomic Policy in a Two-Party System as a Repeated Game', *Quarterly Journal of Economics* 102: 651–78.

———, and A. Drazen (1991), 'Why are Stabilizations Delayed?', *American Economic Review* 81: 1170–88.

———, and R. Perotti (1995), 'The Political Economy of Budget Deficits', *IMF Staff Papers* 42 (1): 1–31.

Bayoumi, T., and B. Eichengreen (1995), 'Restraining Yourself: The Implications of Fiscal Rules for Economic Stabilization', *IMF Staff Papers* 42 (1): 32–48.

———, and P. Masson (1995), 'Fiscal Flows in the United States and Canada: Lessons for Monetary Union in Europe', *European Economic Review* 39: 253–74.

Bird, R., and D. Hartle (1972), 'The Design of Governments', in R. Bird and J. Head, eds, *Modern Fiscal Issues: Essays in Honour of Carl S. Shoup*. Toronto: University of Toronto Press.

———, and E. Slack (1993), *Urban Public Finance in Canada*. Toronto: John Wiley & Sons.

Boothe, P. (1993), 'Provincial Government Debt, Bond Ratings and the Availability of Credit', in R. Harris, ed., *Deficits and Debt in the Canadian Economy*. Kingston: John Deutsch Institute for the Study of Economic Policy, Queen's University.

Brennan, G., and J. Buchanan (1980), *The Power to Tax: Analytical Foundations of a Fiscal Constitution*. Cambridge: Cambridge University Press.

Capeci, J. (1994), 'Local Fiscal Policies, Default Risk, and Municipal Borrowing Costs', *Journal of Public Economics* 53: 73–89.

Cukierman, A., and A. Meltzer (1989), 'A Political Theory of Government Debt and Deficits in a Neo-Ricardian Framework', *American Economic Review* 79 (4): 713–32.

Downs, A. (1957), *An Economic Theory of Democracy*. New York: Harper & Row.

Drazen, A., and V. Grilli (1993), 'The Benefit of Crises for Economic Reforms', *American Economic Review* 83 (3): 598–607.

Eichengreen, B. (1990), 'One Money for Europe? Lessons from the US Currency Union', *Economic Policy* 10: 118–87.

———, and T. Bayoumi (1994), 'The Political Economy of Fiscal Restrictions: Implications for Europe from the United States', *European Economic Review* 38: 783–91.

Gillespie, W.I. (1991), *Tax, Borrow and Spend: Financing Federal Spending in Canada, 1867–1990*. Ottawa: Carleton University Press.

Goldstein, M., and G. Woglom (1992), 'Market-Based Fiscal Discipline in Monetary Unions: Evidence from the US Municipal Bond Market', in M. Canzoneri, V. Grilli, and P. Masson, eds, *Establishing a Central Bank: Issues in Europe and Lessons from the US*. Cambridge: Cambridge University Press.

Hettich, W., and S. Winer (1988), 'Economic and Political Foundations of Tax Structure', *American Economic Review* 78: 701–12.

Hirschman, A. (1971), *Exit, Voice and Loyalty*. Cambridge, Mass.: Harvard University Press.

Kitchen, H. (1991), 'Ontario: Provincial Public Finances', in M. McMillan, ed., *Provincial Public Finances, Volume 1*. Ottawa: Canadian Tax Foundation.

Kneebone, R. (1989), 'On Macro-Economic Instability Under a Monetarist Policy Rule in a Federal Economy', *Canadian Journal of Economics* 22: 673–85.

——— (1994), 'Deficits and Debt in Canada: Some Lessons from Recent History', *Canadian Public Policy* 20: 152–64.

——— (1996), 'Four Decades of Deficits and Debt', in P. Fortin and L. Osberg, eds, *Unnecessary Debts*. Toronto: James Lorimer & Company.

Lane, T. (1993), 'Market Discipline', *IMF Staff Papers* 40 (1): 53–88.

Mansell, R., and R. Schlenker (1995), 'The Provincial Distribution of Federal Fiscal Balances', *Canadian Business Economics* 3 (2): 3–22.

Maslove, A., M. Prince, and G. Doern (1986), *Federal and Provincial Budgeting*. Volume 41 of the Royal Commission on the Economic Union and Development Prospects for Canada. Toronto: University of Toronto Press.

Milesi-Ferretti, G., and E. Spolaore (1994), 'How Cynical Can An Incumbent Be? Strategic Policy in a Model of Government Spending', *Journal of Public Economics* 55: 121–40.

Nordhaus, W. (1975), 'The Political Business Cycle', *Review of Economic Studies* 42: 169–90.

Persson, T., and L. Svensson (1989), 'Why a Stubborn Conservative Would Run a Deficit: Policy with Time-Inconsistent Preferences', *Quarterly Journal of Economics* 104: 325–45.

———, and G. Tabellini (1994), 'Does Centralization Increase the Size of Government?' *European Economic Review* 38: 765–73.

Poterba, J. (1994), 'State Responses to Fiscal Crisis: The Effects of Budgetary Institutions and Politics', *Journal of Political Economy* 102 (4): 799–821.

——— (1995), 'Capital Budgets, Borrowing Rules, and State Capital Spending', *Journal of Public Economics* 56: 165–87.

Rogoff, K. (1990), 'Equilibrium Political Budget Cycles', *American Economic Review* 80: 21–36.

Sargent, T., and N. Wallace (1981), 'Some Unpleasant Monetarist Arithmetic', *Federal Reserve Bank of Minneapolis Quarterly Review* (Fall).

——— (1986), 'Interpreting the Reagan Deficits', *Federal Reserve Bank of San Francisco Quarterly Review* (Fall).

Stansel, D. (1994), 'Taming Leviathan: Are Tax and Spending Limits the Answer?' *Policy Analysis*, No. 213, CATO Institute.

Tabellini, G., and A. Alesina (1990), 'Voting on the Budget Deficit', *American Economic Review* 80: 37–49.

von Hagen, J. (1991), 'A Note on the Empirical Effectiveness of Formal Fiscal Restraints', *Journal of Public Economics* 44: 199–210.

———— (1992), 'Budgeting Procedures and Fiscal Performance in the EC', Commission of the European Communities Directorate for Economic and Financial Affairs, Economic Papers 96, Oct.

————, and I. Harden (1994), 'National Budget Processes and Fiscal Performance', mimeograph.

Wilson, T., and P. Dungan (1993) *Fiscal Policy in Canada: An Appraisal.* Ottawa: Canadian Tax Foundation.

————, P. Dungan, and S. Murphy (1994), 'The Sources of the Recession in Canada: 1989–1992', *Canadian Business Economics* 2 (2): 3–15.

# Comments on Chapter 4 ∎

*Bryne Purchase*

## 1. INTRODUCTION

At the heart of Chapter 4, and the one preceding, is acceptance of the proposition that institutions matter. How we organize our economic and, in this instance, political affairs matters to the outcomes that we get. I agree with that proposition. Indeed, it would be difficult for an economist not to agree. It is the basis of modern economics, owed to the genius of Adam Smith, that in the presence of certain institutional structures each individual's steadfast pursuit of self-interest none the less leads to the collective or public interest. Although this is a proposition developed in respect of essentially private activity, it clearly has great import for the political marketplace as well. We do not have to trust one another, or even in God, as long as we have a competitive market with complete information, well-defined and defensible property rights, and no externalities. And it is where those institutional features are not present in the private sector that economists have found a necessary, if not sufficient, condition for the growth of the public sector. Curiously, the same set of generic frailties in governments—relating to competition, information, and externalities—now lead us to question the efficiency and effectiveness of these institutions. However, where we can restore the basic principles of good organizational design to the public sector we can hope to improve its performance. Chapter 4 looks particularly to the question of institutional design and the implications for deficits and debt financing.

## 2. THE POLITICAL MARKETPLACE

The chapter begins its investigation where it matters most—in the political marketplace. This makes sense. If the political marketplace is fundamentally flawed, then it is almost certain to derail the rest of the governmental system.

Professor Kneebone reviews the theoretical literature on an alleged bias in democracies towards deficit financing. And I must say that I am impressed by the enormous ingenuity of the theorists in developing models to explain why individual citizens and their political agents might be inclined in that direction.

None the less, the term 'democracy' carries with it such a huge variety of institutional structures that it is difficult to test some of the more simple hypotheses relating to majority rule voting. Moreover, on balance I side with Professor Kneebone in suggesting that the historical evidence on the federal government does not support the notion of a financing bias. Nor have all democratic jurisdictions done as poorly as our own federal government in recent years. Provincial governments in Canada have had different performances, yet with very similar institutional structures. (It would, however, be interesting to see an institutional explanation of why Italy and Canada have done so much worse than other G-7 countries in respect of debt financing.)

From an outsider's perspective, Alberta does not have, nor has it had in recent years, a serious debt problem. But the federal government is a far different story and is the focus of my attention. If one rejects the notion of an ingrained bias in democratic institutions, why, then, did it take so long for the federal government to respond with determination to its own spiralling debt?

One thing is certain—it was not a lack of institutional power, of ideological preference, or of knowledge of the size of the problem. A Tory government had all the institutional power that back-to-back majority governments in a parliamentary democracy can give. It even had a public mandate to tackle the deficit.

Nor was it a problem of ideology. This was a government that deregulated in large sectors of the economy, negotiated free trade with the US, and introduced a tax that only economists could love. It had a finance minister from Bay Street and a Finance Department that was intellectually and bureaucratically powerful.

Yet they continued to underperform relative to their own deficit targets and even more so relative to their rhetoric. Why? I can think of a number of reasons, some of which I would lay at the feet of economists and their inability to predict accurately the course of the economy. But it was primarily, of course, a problem of politics. Politicians do not have to take the forecasts of economists seriously, and in fact do not when it suits them. The specific political blockage involved the prime minister and the regional coalition and constitutional promises that made his electoral victories possible. The promises that gave him so much power apparently also tightly constrained that power.

In short, the failure to act aggressively was tied to federal-provincial and constitutional politics. And while, in the end, the federal Progressive Conservative Party collapsed along with its regional coalition, the regional-constitutional issues just do not seem to lessen, much less go away. Indeed, in most ways they are now represented by their own essentially regional parties on the national stage.

## 3. FEDERAL-PROVINCIAL STRUCTURE

It is appropriate, then, to consider the federal structure of government in Canada. And Professor Kneebone's chapter moves to such issues. He outlines the major theoretical explanations for why we have this structure. To put it in a nutshell, the federal structure is either a reflection of a search for institutional efficiency in the provision of public goods or for institutional monopoly. As to which it is, again I tend to align myself with Professor Kneebone on the side of a search for more efficiency; but I can certainly appreciate the collusive potential of governments as well.

Whatever the primary motives for a federal structure, once it is in place there are externalities and problems of a lack of co-ordination. Professor Kneebone deals with these in his chapter. But let me continue to reflect on intergovernmental finance and some of the macroeconomic problems it has helped to create.

In my experience the provinces never saw the federal debt as their problem, or even potentially their problem. Even the terminology of 'offloading' implies that a spiralling federal debt and a poorly performing national economy really are the federal government's problem to deal with, somehow without affecting provincial governments.

There is only one taxpayer, but where the debt resides in the system does, in my view, influence real decisions. Had the feds offloaded more aggressively and earlier in the 1980s, Canada's debt problem would have been addressed much sooner by real program change. And it would have disciplined the provincial governments in a way that an equivalent amount of debt did not affect the federal government. I am quite sure, for example, that Ontario would not have expanded its spending quite so aggressively, even under the Liberal–NDP accord.

As I see it, the problem was an inability federally to acknowledge that the economy was not only structurally weaker, but also much less stable than it had been. The government also stuck for too long with the Keynesian view, however attenuated, that the centre was the proper financial cushion for the entire intergovernmental structure. And it retained, again for too long, the notion that long-term commitments were a viable way of doing federal-provincial business. In the future I would be looking for institutional designs that change these presumptions and that result in much quicker feedback from the economy into program spending.

When the federal government finally did renege on its commitments it did not share the pain across all provinces, thereby breaking one of the rules that Professor Kneebone suggests works well in gaining acceptance for change. The federal timing wasn't good either. The federal cap on the Canada Assistance Plan (CAP) hit Ontario in the midst of its deepest, most prolonged recession since the 1930s. In short, they waited too long to act and when they did act there was not a sense of fairness to their actions. It will cost them in the long run.

## 4. REGULATING GOVERNMENTS

We are all familiar with the problems of trying to regulate the private sector. It seems to me that it is just as difficult to regulate the public sector, but it is also worth trying to regulate it. There are, of course, constraints on governments running deficits. Professor Kneebone deals with these in his chapter. And I have some comments on all of these constraints.

Let me begin with the budget process. We know that political agents will suppress or distort financial information that will reflect badly on their performance. I have seen it first hand. To the degree that we can make this more difficult we will improve both accountability and performance. I strongly support accounting changes that force a consolidated view of government activities as well as the move to more accrual accounting. Incidentally, we should not just look at actual outcomes but also forecast outcomes. One area that we need to review more carefully is fiscal forecasts, particularly on the revenue side. Unlike economic forecasts, there are no external benchmarks to judge whether they are being manipulated.

The most important external constraints on debt financing by governments are the financial markets and the rating agencies. Certainly if there is a democratic bias it will be reflected in their sober assessments. For highly indebted governments these are powerful external accountabilities. No doubt it is one reason why the provincial governments are in much better financial shape than Ottawa. They simply would not be allowed to get themselves as deeply into the financial quagmire without some external reaction.

Ultimately, the financiers must make some dispassionate judgements about politics. So their pronouncements and/or reactions are political acts. Certainly the governments that I have worked for in Ontario have been very much aware of and constrained by the attitudes and opinions of their financiers. I can only think it is infinitely more so now.

Finally, one is inevitably drawn to the question of whether by institutional design the federal government, for example, might have been forced to take dramatic action sooner on its deficit problem. This raises the question of statutory or constitutional requirements for balanced budgets and/or other tax and expenditure limits (TELs). We have an enormous amount of evidence from the United States that they do have an influence.

And we have provincial governments across Canada now that are willing to commit themselves through legislation to meeting their deficit reduction targets. I take these commitments seriously. I think they are an entrepreneurial response to the lack of public credibility that afflicts all politicians. One can find similar devices to establish credibility in the private sector.

But these committed governments cannot commit future governments. And I do not think it would have saved Ontario in 1990–91, for example, if a Liberal government had left behind such a statutory requirement. I am quite sure that any statute would have been repealed by the incoming NDP government.

As noted earlier, the problem of debt financing is particularly acute at the federal level. It is also proving to be more difficult to tackle in an aggressive fashion. Therefore, I think we should take another serious look at a constitutional provision limiting the federal deficit. Even now, however, one will run into opposition within the economics profession concerned with stabilization objectives. I myself tend to discount this concern. In the first instance I do not believe that governments in Canada have the technical capacity to stabilize the economy; and, in any case, they do not, even now, seriously attempt to do so.

## 5. CONCLUSION: A CAVEAT

I said at the outset that I agree with the basic premise in Professor Kneebone's chapter that institutions matter and that we should give careful consideration to their design. But I would add a caveat.

Perfect public institutions, as with perfect private markets, are difficult to find in practice, if not to conceive in theory. Therefore, in reality we may be more dependent than we would like on our fellow citizens' or our politicians' built-in sense of commitment, loyalty, fair play, and self-restraint.

It is also something to keep in mind in deciding how to treat one another, even if unconstrained by institutional design. Civilization is more than a collection of organizations and rules. And, I suspect, much more fragile.

# PART II

# The Process Behind the Reforms

# CHAPTER 5

# The Process Behind Institutional Reform in Alberta

I

*Ronald D. Kneebone and Kenneth J. McKenzie*

## 1. INTRODUCTION

The purpose of this chapter is to take a broad look at the process underlying the cuts and institutional reforms in Alberta, with a view to identifying some of the common themes and highlighting some of the important differences across departments and agencies. Subsequent chapters will focus individually on the budget cuts in each of the four largest spending ministries—Education, Advanced Education, Health, and Social Services.

The chapter draws on interviews conducted in the spring of 1995. Interviews were held with 48 individuals, including members of the government (the premier, cabinet ministers from the four largest departments, as well as with the treasury minister and some backbench MLAs); civil servants and bureaucrats (deputy ministers and other senior officials within the four big-spending ministries); and various stakeholders: Regional Health Authority (RHA) administrators, school board trustees and superintendents, presidents and senior administrators of post-secondary institutions, and some non-governmental organizations receiving provincial funding. While common questions were asked in all of the interviews, the conversations were fairly open-ended, as we followed up on potentially interesting avenues of discussion as they arose.

Although the interviews covered many issues, the overriding theme that guided our inquiries was the *process* behind the budget cuts and institutional changes. As such, the issue of how justified the cuts may or may not be will not be dealt with in this chapter.

The remainder of the chapter is organized as follows. Sections 2 through 6 are largely descriptive, devoted to summarizing the key points made in the interviews. Although there is some analysis contained in these sections, the bulk of the discussion is reserved for section 7, where the analysis will draw on the theoretical background laid out in Chapters 3 and 4. Section 8 presents our conclusions.

## 2. THE SIZE AND SPEED OF THE CUTS

The overall reduction in the province's budget will amount to about 20 per cent over the three-year period beginning in 1993/4. An interesting issue concerns how this 20 per cent figure was arrived at and how the cuts were allocated across the various departments and agencies. For example, the Family and Social Services budget will fall by 19.3 per cent over this period, Health by about 17 per cent, Advanced Education by 15.5 per cent (after adding back the Access Fund), and Education by 12.4 per cent.[1] At the same time the budgets for Economic Development and for Treasury will decline by amounts in excess of 40 per cent and 50 per cent, respectively. In this section, we review the issues of why it was deemed appropriate that the cuts should amount to 20 per cent of the budget, why it was considered important to implement the cuts in only three years, and why cuts were larger in some areas than others.

### 2.1 Why 20 Per Cent?

Most of the ministers and their senior officials claimed that the 20 per cent figure was chosen simply because it was the cut in expenditures required to eliminate the deficit without increasing tax rates. These statements are consistent with the oft-stated view of this government that the source of Alberta's deficit problem was that it had a spending problem, not a revenue problem. In follow-up questions we asked how far this government would be prepared to go in this regard. One minister suggested that if the deficit was 30 per cent of expenditures, then that is how much they would have cut expenditures. However, another key minister stressed that 'we are not libertarians' and complained about commentators who suggested the government is ideological. In general, we found it difficult to direct discussion toward the question of the appropriate size of government and away from discussion about eliminating the deficit.

It is also clear from the interviews that the 'political optics' of the 20 per cent figure are considered important. Premier Klein first mentioned this figure in a speech in Leduc in 1992, in the run-up to the Conservative leadership convention. Many of those interviewed suggested that one of the keys to the political success of Premier Klein has been the consistency he has displayed in presenting his fiscal agenda. Many stressed that from his speech in the Leduc high school in 1992, through the 1993/4 budget that laid out the details of the government's fiscal agenda, to the almost $1 billion windfall surplus in 1994/5, Klein has never deviated from his commitment to reduce spending by 20 per cent: 'he has never blinked, never wavered'. A tightly focused goal and unshakeable resolve were thus generally deemed to be crucial by the politicians we interviewed.

## 2.2 The Importance of a Big Cut

The importance of the 20 per cent cut was also brought home from a different perspective when we asked if the institutional reforms could have taken place without the pressure resulting from very substantial budget cuts.

There was a recognition on the part of both politicians and administrators that the fiscal imperative was critical for focusing attention on the need for structural change. There was widespread agreement that although some of the changes may have eventually occurred, the institutional reforms were very much a product of the fiscal agenda. Many emphasized that the request for 20 per cent and 40 per cent budget cut scenarios forced departments and agencies to think carefully about what they were doing, how they did it, and whether or not they should be doing it at all. One senior bureaucrat opined that a cut in excess of 10 per cent was necessary for real reform to take place.

One minister indicated that a lot of reforms had been 'put aside' for some time and that many individuals both in and out of government were frustrated with the status quo; the spending cuts freed these people to implement reforms they had wanted to make for a long time, as the fiscal imperative eliminated the 'inertia' in various departments. Another minister made a similar observation, noting that the budget-cutting initiative had the effect of 'unleashing innovation' and 'creating positive energy' within departments and agencies. Many also expressed the feeling that the cuts signalled that there was the political will to implement reforms that many bureaucrats had been waiting to make. One minister observed that the fiscal situation gave various stakeholders 'a soapbox to talk about fundamental issues of restructuring'. Another remarked that 'coming to the fiscal wall did us a favour by forcing us to make changes.' Agency administrators expressed similar opinions. The CEO of one RHA felt that 'without the big cuts, we could not have got past the barrier to change that results from people defending their hospital.'

Another way in which some of the ministers expressed the importance of a big cut was to express the opinion that there was a need to address the fundamental reasons the budgets got so big in the first place, for otherwise expenditure increases would begin to 'sneak back in'. One minister used an analogy to a small business in serious financial difficulty. A manager doesn't just go in and slash costs indiscriminately; he or she examines the business operation and asks how you can do things differently. Budget cuts without the accompanying structural changes would not 'stick' and structural change would occur only with large cuts.

## 2.3 The Need for Speed

Although most of those interviewed agreed that the fiscal agenda has provided the impetus for much needed institutional reforms that may not otherwise have been made, there was concern on the part of some administrators and stake-holders with the speed at which the cuts and the associated reforms are being implemented. The expenditure cuts started very shortly after Klein became premier and are being implemented over just three years. Why so fast?

On the question of why the cuts were started so quickly after Klein became premier, one senior minister remarked that 'if one waits until all of one's ducks are lined up, it means you wait forever.' The same minister stressed that it was thought important to 'get the pain and anguish over with as quickly as possible'.

On the question of why the cuts have been imposed over just a three-year period, one minister offered the explanation that 'the premier made that promise, he keeps his promises, it's that simple.' Another posed the rhetorical question, 'Is it kinder to cut a dog's tail off one inch at a time?' A senior bureaucrat offered a similar view, arguing that the alternative to cutting fast is to squeeze institutions slowly over time without indicating to them when the squeezing will stop. This is not conducive to the institution implementing real reform.

Opinions regarding the pace of the cuts among those charged with actually implementing them varied to some extent. Concerns over the speed at which the cuts are taking place were most pronounced in the area of health care. One RHA administrator expressed the opinion that 'too much has happened far too fast'. The speed and front-end-loaded nature of the cuts have often been at the top of the agenda at the meetings of the Council of RHA Chairs (consisting of chairpersons of the 17 RHAs). One official indicated that 'some of the concern over pace is valid', and that they are 'monitoring' the situation. The speed of the cuts to health care seems to be particularly problematic in Edmonton and Calgary, which are about a year ahead of the rural RHAs in terms of reducing their budgets; indeed, they have already been provided some additional 'transitional money' for acute care in response to concerns of this nature.[2] The CEO of one RHA cautioned that large cuts present a double-edged sword in the sense that although he felt that the fiscal downsizing was required to create a restructuring 'mindset', the cuts may now be getting in the way of the reforms as the RHAs lose some of their flexibility due to lack of funds.

Although administrators in other areas also expressed concern over the pace of the cuts, overall the protests seemed muted in comparison with opposition to cuts to health care. Indeed, a senior administrator at one post-secondary institution was supportive of the 'fast-track' approach, indicating that they wanted to 'do it once, do it up front, and do it well'. He said that they would rather face 'one big surprise' than a series of smaller ones, and that 'if you have to swallow a frog, it's best to swallow it in one gulp.' Many administrators, then, seemed supportive of the opinion of many ministers that one large, fast cut was preferable to many smaller ones.

## 3. THE ROLE OF POLITICS

Virtually all of the ministers and their senior officials emphasized that some of the groundwork for institutional change in their departments had been in place prior to the election of the Klein government. For example, Family and Social Services was looking at welfare reform as early as 1985, at a time when the reforms were not conceived as a budget-cutting exercise. Similarly, health care reforms were on the table well before the Klein government was elected. In Education, it also appears that an agenda for reform existed within the department before 1992; officials indicated that they were just looking for the 'right time' to implement the changes. In Advanced Education there was a 'recognition', pre-Klein, that an examination of the post-secondary system was required, but no clear ideas had emerged as to what changes might be made. Thus, to varying degrees, the key ministries had done some of the work required to institute fairly major reforms even before the Klein Conservatives took power. What, then, spawned the across-the-board reforms associated with the Klein government? Why did they happen now and not before? Would the changes have occurred eventually?

There is little doubt in talking to both ministers and senior officials that the philosophical shift among voters that seemed to accompany, and possibly explain, the election of the Klein Conservatives was an important factor in precipitating the reforms.[3] As one minister put it, at any particular 'slice in time' one would observe many policies under consideration in the civil service. Some of these policies may stay on the 'back burner' for some time if they do not fit into the political agenda. To initiate major reforms, he argued, one needs a 'buy-in at the political level ... politics is key'. Virtually all of the politicians emphasized the importance of the 'grassroots' and 'common-sense' nature of the government's fiscal agenda. They stressed to us that Conservative Party conventions, beginning in 1983 but especially since 1986, had been pushing platforms stressing balanced budgets, downsized government, and institutional reform focusing on moving government closer to the community (more on this below). It was also stressed to us that the public roundtables preceding the 1993 budget—particularly the Red Deer Roundtable in March of 1993—reaffirmed to the politicians the desire for change at the grassroots level. These roundtables apparently played a key role in reaffirming to the politicians that the public was supportive of their general policy direction. Indeed, the politicians we interviewed remarked that the participants at the Red Deer Roundtable turned out to be more ardent budget-cutters than the government itself.[4]

The political will to reduce and reform government that comes from a united caucus also seems to have been another crucial factor. The MLAs that form the Calgary caucus were particularly adamant on this point, claiming that at various times each of them had faced 'tremendous pressure' from their constituents, but that they were able to withstand this pressure because they 'bought into' the general philosophy behind the cuts and reforms, and were convinced that if 'one breaks, we all fall'. One backbencher referred to the fiscal agenda and the accompanying need for reform as the 'glue that binds caucus together'. Another important factor in this regard was the fairly large turnover in the Conservative caucus as a result of the election. This injection of 'new blood' served to further unite caucus. Also helpful in this regard was that elimination of MLA pensions and MLA salary cuts were revealed to Progressive Conservative candidates before the election. As a result, those who none the less chose to run in the election held a rather common point of view regarding the appropriateness of the cuts and the way of implementing them.

All of the politicians we interviewed stressed the importance of Ralph Klein. Indeed, MLAs typically remarked that none of the changes could have happened without Klein. Two major reasons were provided for this prevailing opinion. First, ministers and MLAs alike noted that Klein's leadership style, described as 'allowing everyone to speak' even if this means allowing someone 'to dig a hole from which they must escape', was critical. On this issue, one MLA noted that in previous governments, MLAs were handed the budget at press time but that under Klein, MLAs are much more informed and involved in the policy-making process. An important way in which backbenchers have become more involved in the decision-making process is via this government's introduction of Standing Policy Committees (SPCs), something we discuss further below. This management style seems to have had the affect of maintaining caucus support. A senior minister also noted that the strong support Klein gives his ministers has proven to be very important in their ability to push reforms through. The second explanation ministers and MLAs provided for their assertion that Klein was a critical part of the success this government has had in imposing large expenditure cuts was simply the high degree of trust Albertans seem to have in Ralph Klein.

Our interviews with RHA administrators brought to our attention a politics of a different kind. Some of the largest cuts have come in the area of health and these cuts have been accompanied by an emphasis on community care and giving consumers better access to alternative health care treatments. One RHA administrator noted that this has resulted in a 'power shift' away from physicians and toward the community at large and other health care providers. He noted that whereas physicians dominated hospital boards for decades, during which time it was impossible to 'manage against the will' of physicians, this has now changed and they are proving reluctant to accept the change. Expressing similar sentiments, another administrator argued that trying to get certain groups to change, physicians in particular, was 'like herding cats'. Nothing from our interviews indicated whether or not this was an intended outcome of the creation of the RHAs.

## 4. THE ALLOCATION OF THE CUTS ACROSS DEPARTMENTS

Concerning the question of how the cuts were allocated across departments, ministers and senior officials described an iterative process, involving a lot of 'give and take'. None the less, there is little doubt that throughout it all, Alberta Treasury and its minister, Jim Dinning, were firmly in control of the budget agenda.[5]

Dinning related to us that the government started by asking what the people's priorities were—and hence, what the government's priorities should be. Having established these priorities it was clear that it would not be possible to apply a 'one size fits all template' to the budget-cutting process across all departments. Still, some general principles could be employed. Dinning provided us with a copy of the flow chart used as a part of this review (see Appendix 1). The flow chart required each department to undertake a program/service review, addressing questions such as 'Is the program/service a core requirement?' and 'Should the provincial government be responsible for the service?' All non-core programs were candidates for termination and every program and service was subjected to this scrutiny. Moreover, no department or agency was left with the illusion that it could escape cuts altogether. Each department, including the big four, was asked by Treasury to assess the feasibility of 20 per cent and 40 per cent budget-cut scenarios. As such, right from the beginning departments were put in a position to justify why they *should not* receive a budget cut of 20 or 40 per cent.

Although some of the ministers described early pre-budget consultations with various stakeholders, solid numbers were not typically discussed at these meetings. Instead, they only served to lay the groundwork for the cuts looming on the horizon, and helped establish areas of priority within the departments and get stakeholders involved right from the beginning. The final budget cut for each department was arrived at via negotiation with Treasury. As one minister put it, 'there is no easy answer' to why his department ended up with a certain percentage cut other than it was determined in discussions with Treasury to be a cut 'which could be coped with'.

An important element of the Conservatives' budget-cutting approach has been to ensure that although the cuts are differential, they were none the less across-the-board—every department and agency has taken a significant cut. This 'share the pain' and 'gore every ox' approach was identified by many as being an important factor in muting opposition to the cuts, both inside and outside of the government. For example, one MLA indicated that the fact that everyone was sharing in the cuts enabled her to tell constituents that the government was not playing favourites. The move very early on to cut MLA salaries and pensions added further credibility to this claim. The across-the-board nature of the cuts also provided some political assistance to agency heads. The head of one agency indicated that his job became substantially easier after these cuts were mandated. He found that people were more willing to accept reductions when they perceived that they were not being singled out. Finally, this sentiment was echoed at a higher level by the ministers. All ministers indicated that they doubted they would have been able to reduce their departments' budgets by as much as they did, or to implement the institutional reforms that accompanied the cuts, if they had moved in isolation.

## 5. THE BUDGET PROCESS

Although Paul Boothe will deal specifically with the budget-making process in Chapter 6, a brief discussion is included here to highlight some of the key factors that surfaced during the interviews.

A common theme throughout the interviews, which was briefly alluded to earlier in the chapter, was the key role play by Alberta Treasury under Jim Dinning. Treasury's presence lurks in the background of virtually every aspect of the reforms. As discussed in Chapters 3 and 4, a strong Treasury Department is often cited as providing a way to offset the spending proclivities of the traditional 'spending departments'. That is, there can be a tendency for the ministers of these departments to overspend due to the presence of a 'decision externality'—they have an incentive to consider only the benefit of spending on activities that benefit their constituencies, ignoring the costs imposed on taxpayers at large. A budget process that *begins* with the departments effectively bargaining with Treasury, which represents the broader constituency of all taxpayers, over the allocation of the cuts can help internalize this decision externality and offset the spending bias. Our interviews suggest that this is exactly what has happened in Alberta. The process *started* with each department budgeting for both 20 and 40 per cent cuts; they were immediately put on the defensive and had to justify to Treasury why they should not face these cuts. The final allocation of the cuts was then a matter of negotiating with Treasury.

Another important element of the policy-making process highlighted during the interviews was the role of the Standing Policy Committees. A month after becoming premier, Klein replaced 26 government committees with four SPCs. Each SPC is responsible for overseeing four of the government's 16 departments and each is chaired by a non-cabinet minister. Every government MLA is assigned to an SPC, but backbenchers can attend any SPC meeting with full voting privileges (opposition members do not sit on SPCs). It was very apparent throughout the interviews that the politicians viewed the SPCs as extremely important. One minister indicated that the committees are 'very tough on ministers', and that it is difficult to get anything through cabinet without first taking it through the relevant SPC. The same minister went on to describe the SPCs to be 'like castor oil—it is good for you but you take it grudgingly'.

All of the ministers we interviewed described the SPCs as playing an important co-ordination role across related ministries. They seem, then, to have forced ministries to internalize some of their decision externalities. One minister described the SPCs as having 'an intense focus on policy', as being a good 'vetting place', and to have proven useful in facilitating intergovernment communication. It was emphasized to us, however, that the role of the SPCs has not been limited to reviewing policies put forward by the relevant departments. They seem also to have played a role in initiating policy. One backbench MLA went so far as to say that the SPCs are on a par with the cabinet in this regard. Another remarked that this feature made her experience as a backbencher in this government as different from her experience in previous governments 'as night is different from day'. From these and other similar sentiments expressed to us, it is evident that the SPCs have gone a long way towards pacifying government backbenchers and making them feel 'part of the team'.

Interviewees also stressed the importance of three other changes to the budget process introduced by the Klein government: the introduction of three-year business plans, Key Performance Indicators (KPIs), and three legislative acts restricting taxing and spending.

With respect to the three-year business plans, one minister argued that they were key to moving planning away from the 'spend it or lose it' philosophy that is encouraged by planning on an annual basis.[6] The minister remarked that the business plans also provide the benefit of there being far less micromanagement by cabinet; all departments have a plan and day-to-day decisions are expected to adhere to that plan. Another senior minister noted that the business plans were valuable tools for keeping tabs on how well performance measures were being met. The introduction of three-year business plans met with universal approval by the administrators we interviewed. They were described as an invaluable aid to planning and as a way of ensuring some stability to funding.

The government's use of Key Performance Indicators was also often identified as a crucial innovation. Each department and agency has been asked to establish measurable performance indicators and publish them as a part of its three-year business plan. We were told that their purpose is simply 'to encourage better performance.' The hope seems to be that this better performance will come about for two reasons. First, voters will know better what they are getting (one senior minister put it this way: 'we get $13 billion of Albertans' money and we want them to know what they are getting for it') and can thus better judge the government's performance. Second, KPIs will improve monitoring (or as one MLA put it; 'if you can't measure it, you can't manage it'). Almost all of the ministers and senior bureaucrats noted, however, that KPIs were just that—indicators. Typically, concern was expressed regarding the ability to translate the department's goals into adequate performance measures. One senior bureaucrat stressed that the purpose of the KPIs was *not* to have 'government by autopilot'. Interestingly, however, backbench MLAs with whom we spoke felt that KPIs would play a much more important role than did ministers and bureaucrats. The backbenchers felt that, rather than acting simply as targets and planning tools, budgets would eventually be closely tied to the KPIs.

Outside of the government, the KPIs were often accepted as inevitable and even desirable. The head of a major provider of social services remarked that although he had yet to see KPIs issued by the Ministry of Family and Social Services, his organization had long used its own set of KPIs and these proved useful for evaluating the effectiveness of programs. The president of a post-secondary institution expressed a similar sentiment and emphasized the need for KPIs because the current system of allocating grants 'operates in a vacuum' with respect to the question of productivity. He also indicated that he felt KPIs would prove to be a valuable aid to planning; they will enable his institution to better choose between financing program A versus program B without relying solely on 'gut feelings'. Despite the general support for KPIs by those outside government, there were concerns expressed, especially from the presidents of post-secondary institutions. One feared that KPIs might be used as a political tool while another expressed the concern that because caucus does not understand the need for university research the KPIs may fail to consider this function adequately.

The government has passed three pieces of legislation designed to affect the budget process both now and in the future: the Alberta Taxpayer Protection Act (requiring a referendum to approve the introduction of a sales tax), the Deficit Elimination Act (requiring that the deficit be reduced to zero by fiscal year 1996/7), and the Balanced Budget and Debt Retirement Act (requiring a gradual reduction of the province's debt until its elimination in fiscal year 2021/2). These were judged by a senior minister as important for ensuring that fiscal responsibility will be the hallmark of future governments in Alberta. When an interviewer remarked that legislation can be changed by future governments, the minister agreed but argued that voters would punish such acts and were not likely to allow things to slip back to how they were done before.

Finally, the Financial Review Commission (FRC) was cited by many of the ministers as a key factor in making government more accountable and therefore more credible. The FRC was composed of several Alberta business and financial executives who were asked to provide recommendations to make government financial statements more transparent and accountable. The resulting report made numerous recommendations regarding the reporting of the financial activities of the government, and the government quickly implemented virtually all of them, most notably the use of consolidated budgeting. As one minister put it, after the FRC there was 'no more booga booga' associated with the provincial government accounts. It was stressed to us by the politicians that the implementation of the recommendations of the FRC signalled a fresh start in the area of government reporting and accountability.

## 6. DECENTRALIZATION AND COMPETITION

A reading of government budget documents and departmental business plans reveals an emphasis on decentralization and competition. In particular, many departmental business plans emphasize the empowerment of local units and authorities to make crucial decisions on how to implement the budget cuts and policy reforms. In some cases these local units will be competing directly against each other for clients, in others the competition will be for government funding. What is the rationale behind this emphasis? What are the implications? We found from our interviews that the answers to these questions differed substantially depending on whether we were interviewing people from Advanced Education, Basic Education, Health, or Social Services. We therefore consider each in turn.

### 6.1  Advanced Education

The minister and senior bureaucrats in Advanced Education expressed the view that the ministry's role is one of encouraging institutions to examine the way that they operate, rather than imposing major structural changes on the institutions 'from above'. They also explained that they see themselves as facilitating a reform process undertaken by the institutions themselves rather than leading them down a well-defined path. In particular, officials stressed that they were not interested in telling institutions which programs to eliminate, consolidate, or specialize in because 'they know more about it than we do'. Rather, it was intended that the institutions would work with each other in this regard.

Although for the most part the ministry has indeed delegated the implementation of the budget cuts to the post-secondary institutions, it has at the same time put in place numerous controls. These include enrolment corridors, limits on how much and with what speed tuition fees will be allowed to increase, some edicts early in the process regarding program closures in nursing and certain 'expensive' apprenticeship programs at the colleges, and the creation of an 'Access Fund'.[7] The ministry has also been studying the use of KPIs, with an eye to linking them to a funding mechanism for post-secondary institutions. Early on in the process, the ministry 'hinted strongly' that the post-secondary institutions should seek a 5 per cent compensation cut from faculty and staff (a similar cut was requested of most government employees) and for the most part this cut was implemented. The minister and senior bureaucrats in the ministry defended these controls to us as being necessary to prevent institutions from 'taking the easy way out' by merely decreasing enrolment and/or increasing tuition. In their view, they are maintaining a high degree of decentralization in the provision of post-secondary education with a minimum of centralized control.

Perhaps not surprisingly, many of the post-secondary administrators we interviewed interpreted these actions as a decided increase in the 'intrusive' nature of the ministry. A president of one post-secondary institution indicated that the freedom of institutions such as his to design and implement programs has been significantly curtailed. Of particular concern to many of the university and college administrators was the creation of the Access Fund, through which the government has a direct input into post-secondary program design. The priorities for the Fund have been established and implemented largely independently of the post-secondary institutions. Although the institutions have been encouraged to co-operate in applications to the Fund, there is a definite element of competition associated with the Access Fund. Indeed, the president of one institution described the Access Fund as 'raw competition'.

Most of the administrators anticipate that this sort of competition for funds between institutions will increase as the ministry develops a mechanism that ties funding to performance criteria as measured by KPIs. Like the Access Fund, it is anticipated by the administrators with whom we spoke that this will be a 'zero-sum game' whereby some institutions gain and others lose.

Somewhat paradoxically, at the same time the ministry has, via the Access Fund, created an environment where the institutions effectively compete with each other for government funding, the ministry has emphasized co-operation, consolidation, and specialization among post-secondary institutions as a part of the budget-cutting process. It has done so by encouraging the development of 'centres of specialization' and by stressing the need to reduce program duplication. The administrators of post-secondary institutions we interviewed indicated that both the universities and the colleges have had numerous discussions regarding program specialization, and some progress has already been made. These administrators typically remarked that although the ministry does not appear to have a well-defined plan regarding rationalization and specialization, it has been a strong advocate of the institutions co-operating with each other in this regard.

## 6.2 Basic Education

While for the most part post-secondary institutions have retained their autonomy in the face of the budget cuts and the reductions have been implemented in a largely decentralized manner (with the exceptions noted above), in many respects exactly the opposite has happened in the area of basic education.[8] The Ministry of Education has put in place a very specific and detailed funding formula that specifies exactly how much money each school district receives, primarily on the basis of the number and type of students in the district. Moreover, local school boards, the number of which has been reduced by about two-thirds, are no longer able to levy property taxes to help finance local school expenditures. Rather, these property taxes are centrally collected by the provincial government and allocated to school districts according to the funding formula. The funding formula also specifies how the money given to the school boards must be allocated across broad expenditure categories. For example, large urban boards are allowed to allocate a maximum of 4 per cent of their budget to non-school-based administration, 82 per cent to teaching, etc. The cuts to administration include curriculum development, which is being centralized at the ministry to avoid duplication of effort. While reducing the discretionary authority of school boards, the ministry has at the same time empowered teachers and parents to have a greater say in how individual schools are run by implementing school-based management, increasing the potential role of parent councils, and allowing for the creation of charter schools. Thus, while centralizing and controlling budgeting and funding decisions, as well as basic curriculum development, the ministry has decentralized other types of decision-making by delegating some authority to individual schools.

What appears to be the more centralized and intrusive tack of the Ministry of Education, relative to that taken by Advanced Education, seems to have been motivated in part by a concern that certain school boards would not react 'appropriately' to the budget cuts. A senior administrator at the ministry level indicated that 'history has shown that [leaving school boards to their own devices] might not work at some boards.' The greatest concern expressed to us was that cutting grants to boards without controls would result in certain boards simply 'offloading onto taxpayers' by increasing local taxes. A senior bureaucrat reiterated this concern in a separate interview. He related how in 1984, when the province demanded a 3 per cent budget cut from school boards and gave the boards *carte blanche* as to how to handle the cut, some boards responded 'well' but others did not. In particular, he charged that some boards chose to direct their cuts to politically sensitive areas like special education in an effort to embarrass the government. He argued the government was anxious to avoid a repeat of this experience.

Those we interviewed from the ministry indicated that another motivation for the changes they introduced was to eliminate funding discrepancies between school districts due to divergent property and business tax bases while encouraging competition among school boards for students along the quality or service dimension. Ministry officials indicated that under the old system only about 33 per cent of the total funding school boards received from the province was based on enrolment; under the new system this has increased to about 75 per cent. As such, under the new system boards have an incentive to try to attract students. Officials indicated that this was done specifically to encourage competition among school boards.

The reforms did not completely eliminate the ability of the boards to raise money independently of the province. Individual boards are allowed to hold plebiscites on local tax increases to fund specific programs (a special school levy). However, additional taxes raised in this manner cannot exceed 3 per cent of the board's budget. Virtually all of the school board officials interviewed indicated that they did not envision holding such a plebiscite in the near future. The reasons varied, but two were predominant. First, there was a feeling that the money would somehow be lost due to an offsetting cutback in the provincial grant; one urban board representative expressed concern that the funds 'would flow out of the city to the rural areas', which is reflective of the view of some that the reforms were partly motivated by a desire to redistribute funds to rural areas. Second, there was a feeling that such a plebiscite would not be successful in the current political climate.

Ministry officials were reluctant to endorse the view that local school boards have been circumvented under the new system. Indeed, one senior official responded with an emphatic 'no' to our question about whether our impression that there has been an apparent decrease in the discretionary authority of local school boards was correct. Change requires direction and leadership, he argued, and it 'does not imply a long-term centralist approach'. School board trustees and superintendents displayed no such reluctance; for the most part they see their discretionary authority and flexibility as having been substantially reduced. One school board official indicated she had no problem with a 12.5 per cent budget cut but was, rather, concerned with the way the ministry was trying to control the spending choices of school boards. This was a common sentiment among school board officials.

With respect to the question of promoting school competition, the prevalent view was again one of apprehension. One official opined that the ministry is offering parents 'an illusion' when it tells them they will have greater say in course design and program offerings via parent councils and charter schools. Province-wide curriculums currently in place mean there are very few options for dropping or adding courses. Another noted that school principals are 'fit to be tied' over the idea of interschool competition. Their concern is that a 'black cloud' can settle over a school's reputation and it can take a long time to rid the school of that reputation even after changes have been made. Principals also complain that it is unfair to judge a school when so much of students' performances depends on the degree of parental support.

## 6.3 Health

A key element of the health care reforms in Alberta has been the creation of 17 Regional Health Authorities (RHAs), each charged with overseeing the provision of health care services in a specified region.[9] The idea for RHAs first arose in the Alberta context in the *Rainbow Report*, a government document on health care reform released in 1989. Prior to the introduction of the RHAs, acute care delivery in Alberta was the responsibility of about 200 separate hospital boards. While the replacement of 200 hospital boards with 17 RHAs may appear on the surface to be a move to a more centralized system, the RHAs have much broader responsibilities for health care than did hospital boards. Moreover, officials with Alberta Health and representatives of the RHAs agreed that the sort of 'competition' between hospitals under the old system tended to be wasteful, as each hospital was more concerned with enhancing and/or protecting its own position than with looking at the 'big picture'. Those interviewed also indicated that there was very little co-ordination among providers of acute care, long-term care, and community health, which did not always generate desirable or cost-efficient outcomes. There is a perceived need on the part of both ministry officials and RHA administrators for a more holistic approach to health care, and this is seen to be best achieved through the creation of RHAs responsible for all of the health care needs in their region. As one official put it, the goal is to provide a 'continuum of care' within each region.

Officials within the ministry described Alberta Health's main role now as setting standards and targets, establishing guidelines and general policies, monitoring the overall health care system, and allocating the health care budget across RHAs. One official indicated that 'we are out of the business of delivering health care services', which is now the responsibility of the RHAs. For the large bulk of the expenditures managed by the RHAs, Alberta Health has provided little in the way of specific guidance. For the most part, the RHA administrators concurred that the ministry has not given specific guidelines. One administrator indicated that aside from general philosophical guidance, Alberta Health just gave them the budget numbers and said 'go to it, folks'; another noted that 'Alberta Health's major strategy has been to put a stamp on an envelope containing instructions to cut more.'

As was the case with both Advanced and Basic Education, an often talked-about aspect of the health care reforms seems to be to encourage co-operation and co-ordination among RHAs, but in a competitive environment. There are two formal mechanisms to facilitate co-operation: the Council of Chairs and the Provincial Health of Alberta Association. However, there seemed to be a feeling among RHA administrators that neither of these mechanisms is really doing much to encourage co-ordination on the 'day-to-day' and 'nuts-and-bolts' issues, as most of the discussion is at 'high levels'. One RHA administrator indicated that given the lack of communication among the RHAs it is surprising how similarly the various authorities have evolved. Moreover, what communication that has taken place has not been due to 'the guiding hand of government'.

While both Alberta Health and RHA officials indicated to us their belief that the new system is at least partially designed to encourage competition, neither side expressed a clear vision of how this would occur. Administrators noted that while consumers are able to obtain health care in any region they want, they were sceptical that the availability of this type of choice really mimics competition between RHAs in a meaningful way. How individual RHAs might encourage competition in the provision of health care services *within* their regions was also unclear to administrators. The problem seems to be that there is no clear view of exactly what is the fundamental role of the RHAs. Most of the administrators interviewed perceive the RHAs as the *providers* of health care services within their regions, not as *purchasers* of health care services on the behalf of consumers. Others did not recognize the distinction. Perhaps for this reason, there has been a very limited amount of 'subcontracting' by hospitals to private clinics.[10] Officials from Alberta Health were similarly unclear about how competition would be promoted. A senior ministry official expressed the hope that publishing comparisons of the operating costs of each RHA would promote competition by fostering an atmosphere conducive to innovation and experimentation. However, this official indicated that the seemingly necessary prerequisite for this to occur—tying RHA funding to performance indicators—was not in the cards at this point.

## 6.4 Family and Social Services

Although the bulk of the 19.3 per cent reduction in Family and Social Services (FSS) spending has been achieved by a reduction in welfare caseloads, there have been some important institutional changes.[11] FSS has always done a lot of contracting out rather than providing services directly. Everything from foster home care to shelters, to boys and girls clubs, is funded by the ministry but provided by private-sector interests. In total, FSS funds about 150 agencies, most under contractual arrangement, many of which are competitively tendered. The contracts are monitored and evaluated periodically by contract managers. For the most part the agencies are given a free rein in how they spend their money; there are no specific guidelines with respect to administrative spending, etc.

However, departmental officials indicated to us that they keep a close watch on how the money is spent as a part of the general monitoring process.

Ministry officials indicated that part of the rationale for the reforms being introduced by the Klein government was to give front-line social workers more leeway to be innovative in terms of designing 'individualized' plans for each client. Career counselling and the design of individual job-training programs are now to be among the more important duties of social workers. Officials told us that this is possible because while welfare caseloads have been reduced, staffing has not declined by the same proportion, thus enabling caseworkers to spend more time on each case. Officials indicated that this increased emphasis on counselling reflects the general objective of moving clients off passive welfare roles to more active, training-oriented programs. One official described this as being a drastic change from the past, when FSS 'just gave money away'.

The most significant changes in FSS relating to the theme of decentralization will be in the area of Children's Services. The ministry plans to create 17 Regional Social Assistance Authorities (RSAAs), each charged with delivering social services to children in a specified geographic area (the regional boundaries coincide with those of the RHAs). The motivation behind the changes to the delivery of Children's Services is similar to that behind RHAs: there is a desire to achieve a more holistic and co-ordinated approach to social service delivery for children within specified regions. Moreover, departmental officials, including the minister, expressed a strong belief that needs vary significantly across the province and that a 'one-size-fits-all' template does not result in the best delivery of services. The intention is to have six regional directors, each responsible for two or three of the 17 RSAAs. Each RSAA will have one departmental staff member and one community staff member who will act as facilitators between FSS, the communities, and clients. The desire is for each region to develop a community service plan that is culturally sensitive to local needs.

The individuals involved in running agencies funded by FSS all welcomed the move to more holistic, community-centred services for children. They lamented the lack of co-ordination under the old system and felt that it couldn't get any worse and will almost certainly get better under the new system. The head of one agency indicated that the government finally saw the wisdom in relying on the private sector to provide Children's Services. It is his feeling that the private sector is more community-based and can deliver a higher quality of service at lower costs.

## 7. DISCUSSION

The summary of our interviews presented in sections 2 through 6 reveals some common threads, as well as some apparent inconsistencies and contradictions.

In this section, we try to pull some of the common threads together and analyse some of the inconsistencies within the framework of the theories of government and organizational behaviour reviewed in Chapters 3 and 4.

In section 2 we summarized the responses to our questions regarding why the overall budget cut was 20 per cent and why it was judged by the politicians we interviewed that the cuts had to occur over such a short period of time. The unanimous response from the politicians was that 20 per cent was what was required to balance the budget and they were elected on a platform of balancing the budget without tax increases. Another often-heard explanation of why a government might choose an accelerated approach to deficit elimination and restructuring, an explanation that was not, however, offered by those we interviewed, is the idea that if the cuts are implemented early in the government's mandate, voters may 'forget' some of the transitional costs associated with the cuts when it is time to go to the polls in 1997 or 1998.

Both of these explanations are consistent with optimal political choices made by a government operating in an environment typified by what is often referred to as 'rational ignorance' on the part of voters. That is, if voters face high information acquisition and processing costs, it is rational for governments to advocate easy-to-understand, common-sense policy platforms. As well, in such an environment voters may have short memories, giving rise to the possibility of 'political business cycles' whereby voters reward governments only for what they have done lately. This encourages governments to impose policies that have unpleasant transition costs early in their mandates so as to leave time in which to endure the transition costs and begin to enjoy the benefits of a lower deficit before they must seek re-election.[12] Thus, it is not surprising that governments elected on a mandate of deficit reduction will find it optimal to reduce or eliminate the deficit very quickly.

We also suspect that the single-minded pursuit of deficit reduction had the benefit of providing very little ammunition for the Liberal opposition. Klein effectively derailed the standard criticism directed at politicians, of not keeping election promises, by making one very simple-to-understand and very visible promise, running for election on that promise, and then sticking to it. The speed with which the cuts have been imposed was often referred to in our interviews as being conducive to minimizing opposition from special interest groups. Hitting on all fronts simultaneously can diffuse opposition and make it difficult for interest groups to mobilize. Archer and Gibbins, in Chapter 13, present evidence to support this supposition.

At a general level, most of those we interviewed agreed that the institutional restructuring in Alberta has been, if not caused by, then certainly accelerated by the fiscal agenda. The fact that in many areas restructuring had been talked about for some time within the government, but only initiated under the pressure of deep expenditure cuts, suggests that fiscal pressure did indeed act as an important catalyst for change. Although the magnitude and speed of the cuts have been a matter of some concern, for the most part agency administrators in the RHAs, school boards, post-secondary institutions, and so on indicated that they have been able to manage the changes, at least up to the time of our interviews. A number of administrators expressed concern over low employee morale in an environment of wage roll-backs and lay-offs. That they should do so is supportive of the idea postulated by De Groot and Van Der Sluis (1987) that bureaucrats will try to avoid 'social conflicts' within the agency by avoiding large structural changes, including forced lay-offs. In such an environment, the pressure resulting from the size and speed at which the budget cuts are being implemented can force the social conflict within the bureaucracy required for institutional restructuring.

The idea that deep expenditure cuts may be necessary to force the social conflict necessary to restructure a bureaucracy is interesting as it is closely related to the idea from the macroeconomic literature that a fiscal crisis may be necessary to force an end to wars of attrition between politicized socioeconomic groups. That is, as reviewed by Kneebone in Chapter 4, Alesina and Drazen (1991) present a model in which major policy changes are delayed because the costs of adjusting to the new policy are borne unequally by different groups. Each group knows the costs of adjustment falling on themselves, but not on others. In such a situation, a war of attrition may result, wherein each group delays supporting the policy initiative in the hope that others will give in by accepting a solution that involves them absorbing a greater portion of the costs.

This sort of model seems to be particularly applicable to government deficit reduction efforts. Most groups recognize the need to eliminate (or at least reduce) persistent government deficits. Yet, as one might expect, there is also a tendency for stakeholders to view the cuts to their own agency or group as the most devastating and thus to resist these cuts. Drazen and Grilli (1993) note that the perception of an economic crisis may prove to be beneficial in this environment by putting an end to the war of attrition and enabling necessary but politically unpopular changes.

The opinion survey conducted by Archer and Gibbins, discussed in Chapter 13, suggests that this description contains some merit for describing the situation in Alberta in the past few years. While Albertans strongly support the cuts in general, there is significantly less support for cutting specific areas. Similarly, in our interviews with administrators and stakeholders, there was a virtual universal recognition that the deficit needed to be eliminated or at least drastically reduced, yet many expressed displeasure with the size of the cuts they were asked to endure. What seems to have caused both voters and administrators to grudgingly accept the cutbacks was the perception of an impending fiscal crisis and the recognition that something needed to be done.

Not all analysts support the fast-track approach to institutional change; some favour a more incremental, evolutionary reform process. Yet, as discussed by McKenzie in Chapter 3, there are difficulties associated with incrementalism. For example, an incremental approach may give the bureaucracy more control of the policy agenda. If the status quo becomes the *de facto* policy default, this may allow those who control the policy agenda to present reforms that may be superior to the status quo but globally inefficient. The results of our interviews suggest some recognition of this problem by politicians, senior bureaucrats, and administrators. Recall, for example, the comment of the RHA administrator that a large cut was necessary to get past the problem of people defending their own hospital, and the comment made by a number of the ministers we spoke with that the large cuts eliminated 'inertia' and 'unleashed innovation'.

In section 4, we summarized the responses to questions regarding how it was decided that the overall budget cut of 20 per cent would be allocated across departments. We were told that the emphasis throughout the process was on establishing core areas, both within and across departments, with non-core areas expected to absorb higher-than-average cuts. The treasurer was clear in indicating to us that the starting point of budget-cutting was to determine the people's priorities and in this way the government's political priorities were established.

This differential approach to budget-cutting is consistent with a government that perceives different political costs and benefits associated with reducing spending across different functional areas. Hettich and Winer (1988) suggest that a 'politically optimal' tax structure will use each revenue source up to the point where the marginal political opposition per dollar raised in taxes is equalized across all sources. Similar reasoning suggests that a government seeking to minimize the overall political cost associated with budget cuts will equate the marginal political cost per dollar of expenditure reduction across agencies and departments. With this interpretation, the fact that the cuts were fairly uniform across the high-profile areas implies that the government views the marginal political cost of cutting budgets in the key areas as relatively equal, although apparently education was determined to be somewhat more politically sensitive than other areas.

Another interesting aspect of the approach taken by this government is that in determining the political costs of imposing expenditure cuts in particular areas, the government seems to have ignored the political opposition of special interest groups. The effort seems instead to have been directed towards appealing directly to the voter. This was done via a number of public roundtables where a cross-section of Albertans were brought together to examine and debate specific issues.[13] As indicated earlier, the pre-budget roundtable in Red Deer in 1993 was particularly important in terms of reaffirming the public's acceptance of the government's platform. Further to this point, the government's policy of cutting quickly and simultaneously across all areas of government spending and selling the cuts as being shared by all seems to have had the effect of stifling organized opposition from special interest groups. The approach of circumventing 'intermediaries' and appealing directly to individual voters and consumers is also present in many of the reforms. For example, the role of school boards has been reduced and direct parental involvement has been increased by providing an opportunity to establish charter schools and by expanding the role of school councils.

In section 5, we summarized the responses to our questions regarding changes to the government's budget and decision-making process. Backbench MLAs expressed a common enthusiasm for the introduction of Standing Policy Committees (SPCs) and ministers expressed a grudging acceptance that the SPCs represented a healthy restraint placed on their freedom. All whom we interviewed agreed that the power of the SPCs lies not only in the vetting of ideas coming from the ministries, but also in their ability to introduce new ideas into the policy process.

Hettich and Winer (1995) caution that powerful legislative committees such as these can result in government *by* parliament, rather than government *in* parliament. That is, they argue that if these committees are too powerful, it can result in parliament abandoning its traditional role as a monitoring, evaluation, and review mechanism for cabinet policies. Yet it is clear from our interviews that the SPCs have played a major role in the monitoring and review of the government's policies. In addition, it is apparent that the SPCs have forced ministries to internalize the external costs of some of the choices they consider. This is so because with only four committees, the oversight responsibilities of the SPCs encompass many broadly related areas. This results in an exchange of information across policy areas—perhaps internalizing some of the decision externalities that can occur if cabinet ministers become 'captured' by their constituencies—and better co-ordinating policies across departments. This sort of overlap may also allow committees to 'benchmark' departments against each other, giving rise to the sort of horizontal competition and policy diffusion discussed earlier with respect to decentralization. While critics of these committees talk about the increased scope for 'back-scratching' and 'logrolling', which can lead to excessive spending, up to this point exactly the opposite seems to have happened with the Alberta SPCs; the committees seem to have reined in the spending tendencies of cabinet ministers. So far, at least, the SPCs seem to have worked quite well and offer support for the hypothesis put forward by von Hagen (1992, 1994) that putting procedural limits on the choices of ministers is correlated with greater fiscal discipline.

Another innovation this government has introduced into the budget process is the use of three-year business plans and Key Performance Indicators (KPIs). This is a relatively recent innovation in the public sector in Canada, and government officials readily admitted to us that they are not yet sure exactly what role they will play. KPIs can act as a mechanism to facilitate not only governmental monitoring of the bureaucracy, but also public monitoring. The use of KPIs has three potential benefits.[14] First, they can act as a way of conveying information to the public to allow them to make informed decisions regarding health care, education, etc., by allowing them to compare various agencies that provide the services. This can facilitate and encourage innovation and competition among agencies (more on this below). Second, KPIs can provide more information to consumers to help them bring pressure to bear on politicians and therefore on the bureaucracy. Finally, KPIs can increase public-sector efficiency if they are appropriately tied to incentives—i.e., performance-based funding. At this point business plans and KPIs seem to be primarily playing the role of an additional monitoring device. No one we interviewed indicated that specific plans are in place to tie funding directly to the KPIs, although the government is still considering the possibility. Indeed, recent documents released by the Department of Advanced Education indicate that some portion of post-secondary funding may in future be tied to performance.

Based on what we heard in our interviews, however, we suspect that KPIs will have limited scope. One reason is that although there seems to be an understanding within the government that it is important when measuring performance to focus on *outputs* rather than *inputs*, the government appears to be struggling with defining appropriate output measures. This, of course, is because many public-sector outputs cannot be easily measured. There also seems to be a recognition, if not an understanding, of the 'what gets measured gets done' phenomenon whereby the presence of KPIs can lead to perverse incentives. In other words, agencies may focus more on achieving the indicators than on providing the appropriate service. For these reasons we suspect that the forcibly put conclusion of one senior minister, that KPIs will *not* be used to 'govern by autopilot', will prevail.

Finally, in section 6, we summarized the responses to our questions regarding the government's apparent attempts to decentralize the provision of health care, education, advanced education, and social services. A common theme that arose from our interviews was that while the government has put in place institutional reforms designed to decentralize and to encourage competition, it has at the same time introduced other reforms designed to restrict the nature of the competition that might result. For example, in the area of advanced education, at the same time as the province introduced the Access Fund—which was characterized by a president of a post-secondary institution as 'raw competition'—the province also imposed enrolment corridors to prevent universities and colleges from reducing enrolment to help meet the budget cuts and restrictions on the level and rate of increase in tuition fees. As well, the universities and colleges were encouraged to look into amalgamating and rationalizing program offerings. Thus, at the same time that post-secondary institutions were told to compete for scarce resources, they were also prevented from competing in certain ways. Something similar can be observed in the area of basic education. At the same time that the government is encouraging the establishment of school councils to bring education choices closer to parents and teachers and to foster competition across school boards, it has also implemented an exhaustive set of restrictions on how local school boards can spend tax dollars and substantially restricted their ability to obtain independent funding. Once again, schools and school boards are told to compete for scarce resources, but only in specific ways.

To understand why a government might choose to encourage decentralization and then seek to stifle the competition it introduces—with the result that different aspects of the reforms appear to work at cross purposes—it is useful to review the costs and benefits of competition and decentralization and perhaps in this way explain some of the apparent contradictions and inconsistencies.[15]

One of the benefits of decentralization is that local, or decentralized, authorities may have better information regarding the needs and preferences of their clientele, enabling the more efficient delivery of services. Indeed, one of the stated objectives of many of the reforms has been to bring the decision-making process 'closer to the people'. If preferences and needs vary across regions within the province, this approach can enhance efficiency. Many of the reforms in Health (the creation of RHAs), Basic Education (the emphasis on site-based management and parent councils), and Family and Social Services (the creation of RSAAs) reflect the desire to realize this benefit of decentralization.

Another benefit of decentralization and local decision-making is that it more directly involves local agencies in the decisions about and implementation of the reforms. The idea is that individuals are more likely to be committed to changes they make themselves. Many of the ministers we talked to stressed this point, as they referred to the release of 'innovative energy' from the civil service that has accompanied the changes.

Devolving decision-making responsibilities to local units can give rise to another benefit via the creation of a sort of 'horizontal competition', whereby agencies 'compete' with each other not only for clientele and government funds, but also for ideas and policy approaches. In this environment, a sort of policy diffusion may result, where successful policy innovations in one agency or district may be adopted by others. The 17 Regional Health Authorities and the Regional Social Assistance Authorities seem to be particularly well set up for this to occur.

On the other hand, there are costs associated with decentralization, and many aspects of the reforms seem to be specifically designed to curb some of these costs. Perhaps the biggest problem is that decentralization may give rise to agency and bureaucracy problems due to costly monitoring. That is, local or decentralized agencies may pursue different objectives than the provincial government wants them to pursue. In some instances the government has dealt with this problem by moving towards a more centralized, more intrusive institutional setting. This is particularly true in Basic Education, where the government seems to believe that the decisions made by local authorities have not represented the interests of all Albertans but rather those of teachers, school board officials, and perhaps parents of school-aged children. This could be due to the presence of a decision externality arising in the context of local school board elections, where these groups have a disproportionate influence on outcomes because of a largely disinterested general populace. Initiatives such as formula- and enrolment-based budgeting and removing the taxing authority of local school boards have been instituted specifically to limit the discretionary authority of the school boards, and perhaps to circumvent the decision externality problem.

Even in areas where the government has devolved a great deal of authority, it has instituted mechanisms to encourage certain types of spending, for example, the Access Fund in Advanced Education. This type of competition, whereby institutions compete for funds on the basis of defined criteria, can help overcome informational and agency problems on the part of the government. Quite simply, it is a way of inducing agencies to do what the government wants them to do. Although the institutions may not like it, the Access Fund definitely provides a means for Advanced Education to play a more direct role in program development and to ensure that certain priorities are met. Whether the priorities are 'correct' is a matter open to debate. Finally, in Health there are maximum and minimum constraints on broad categories of spending, such as acute care, long-term care, lab services, community care, and so on.

Another possible cost of decentralization is a lack of co-ordination across agencies. For example, different post-secondary institutions may offer similar programs, or there may be similar facilities in different RHAs. The government has dealt with this by encouraging the relevant agencies and institutions to co-operate with each other in matters such as the development of 'centres of specialization'. This approach was particularly visible in Advanced Education and Health. It is unclear exactly how this co-operation is supposed to take place in an environment where institutions are effectively competing for funding. Moreover, while developing centres of specialization may well eliminate overlap and redundancy, there is a downside. Duplication and overlap may in some instances act as an important control and disciplinary device. Competitive markets are full of duplication and redundancy, yet the outcome is efficient essentially because the presence of this redundancy keeps providers' 'feet to the fire'—if they don't offer a high-quality good at a reasonable price, someone else will. The elimination of duplication inherent in the development of centres of specialization may not lead to efficient delivery in the long run.

Finally, while competition between localities and regions can lead to the efficient provision of public services—most particularly if a mobile citizenry 'votes with their feet' and seeks out the tax/service mix that most closely matches their preferences—this can sometimes come at the cost of equity. This issue was raised by McKenzie and Kneebone in Chapters 3 and 4, where Hirschman's (1971) alternative forms of expression—voice and exit—were discussed. Exit can lead to inequitable solutions, and reliance on it must be tempered by recognition of the role of voice. Some recognition of this issue seems to have been at least implicitly made in the design of school reforms. It was made clear to us in the interviews that the school tax reform was an equity issue. Thus, the fact that the ability of school boards to compete with each other along the tax dimension has been virtually eliminated is again consistent with a government trying to balance efficiency with equity. Similarly, while school boards are encouraged to compete for students through enrolment-based budgets, nothing has been done to encourage individual schools to do the same thing. This, combined with the empowerment of school councils, suggests an attempted trade-off between efficiency and equity and a recognition of the merits of both voice and exit.

Although it appears that there are some inconsistencies and contradictions in the government's approach to decentralization, an alternative interpretation is that the government has tried to reach a compromise in attempting to capture the benefits of decentralization while avoiding some of the costs. Only time will tell whether or not they have succeeded.

## 8. CONCLUSIONS

An interesting question that arises in light of the budget cuts and institutional reforms taking place in Alberta is whether the Alberta experience can be repeated or replicated in other jurisdictions. In Chapter 2, Mansell relates some aspects of the political and economic history of Alberta that may bear on this issue. In Chapter 13, Archer and Gibbins provide further insight into the feasibility of other jurisdictions doing what Alberta has done by concentrating on the current political environment.

Still other insights come from 'path dependency' models of economic and institutional innovation. Some commentators have observed that public policy-making can be viewed as a process dominated by path dependency (see, for example, North, 1990; Wilsford, 1994), whereby there is a tendency to conceive of policy changes within the context of existing structures and institutions; policy movement then tends to be incremental, following a path determined in large part by previous decisions. In this environment it is argued that strong conjunctural forces, which tend to occur only rarely and exceptionally, are required to move policy onto a new path. In a study of health care reforms (or the lack thereof) in five major industrialized countries, Wilsford (1994) concludes that these policy conjunctures tend to be typified by some common elements: (1) the perception of a crisis, typically fiscal in nature; (2) the presence of a relatively centralized, somewhat hierarchical political system that is able to move quickly in the typically narrow window of opportunity offered by the confluence of events; (3) strong and determined political leadership, typically in the persons of the first minister and other major ministers, most particularly the finance minister or treasurer; (4) the basic elements of reform that will constitute the 'big change' should already have been thought out and prepared; (5) the electorate must be receptive to innovation; that is, the political climate must be ripe for change; and (6) the opponents of change, and those that benefit from the status quo, must be fragmented.

While there is no claim that these are the only elements that can constitute a major policy conjuncture, nor that they are either necessary or sufficient to move policy onto a new trajectory, the presence of at least some of these elements no doubt increases the probability that a major policy change will take place. In particular, as with the 'war of attrition' models discussed previously, the presence of a perceived fiscal crisis plays a prominent role in precipitating major policy innovations. Yet the path dependency argument emphasizes that a fiscal crisis alone may not be enough; some of the other elements must also be present at the conjunctural moment for a major policy initiative to occur. In our view, virtually all of the above elements were in place following the election of the Klein Conservatives in 1993. Let's consider each in turn.

(1) *The perception of a crisis.* There is little doubt that in Alberta there was the perception of impending fiscal crisis and that this perception had been building for some time. Indeed, with all three major political parties, including the New Democrats, stressing the need for action on the deficit during the 1993 election campaign, this perception was fuelled and cultivated by the political parties themselves. Moreover, subsequent polls have confirmed that Albertans perceive a serious fiscal problem.[16] Despite interviewing 46 individuals, from the premier to school trustees to the heads of charitable agencies, we came across no one who challenged the need to reduce the provincial deficit.

(2) *The presence of a relatively centralized political system able to move quickly.* Despite popular perceptions to the contrary, the Canadian parliamentary system, with its strong executive and tradition of party unity, can move relatively quickly to implement policy reforms once the decision to move is made.

By way of comparison, consider the somewhat fragmented political system in the US, where numerous checks and balances make it very difficult to institute major policy changes. Wilsford (1994) argues that the institutional make-up of the US is such that an extremely strong conjuncture is likely required to precipitate major policy reform. The fact that the grassroots of the Conservative Party and the party caucus are firmly behind the cuts and the reforms has no doubt facilitated the changes.

(3) *Strong and determined leadership*. Premier Ralph Klein has clearly provided powerful political leadership. As indicated earlier, Klein has displayed a consistent and steadfast resolve to eliminate the deficit via expenditure cuts right from the beginning. Moreover, he has proven to be very popular with voters in general, as poll after poll confirms an almost unprecedented popularity rating for the premier; up to this point at least, it seems that he can do no wrong. Our interviews with ministers and MLAs confirmed that Klein's leadership style has also been crucial in maintaining the party's resolve during the budget-cutting process.

Interestingly, although Klein's role in keeping the government, and the public, focused on the fiscal situation has been very important, his role in the reform process itself seems to have been less so. His leadership approach and his role as a conjunctural force might be contrasted with that of Margaret Thatcher, who as prime minister presided over major policy reforms in Britain. Thatcher's leadership style was somewhat autocratic, if not exclusionary. She eschewed widespread consultation and directed the reform process personally and centrally.[17] Klein's approach seems to be much more inclusionary, and less detail-oriented. The task of working out the details of the reforms seems by and large to have been left to the major ministers.

A key individual in this regard had been the treasurer, Jim Dinning. Klein has been given a powerful assist by his treasurer, who is no less determined to stay the fiscal course than the premier. The role of Alberta Treasury in pushing the other ministries not only for expenditure reductions, but for structural change, was alluded to throughout the interviews. Treasury has played a key role both in setting the budget agenda and in establishing performance measures and three-year business plans, which are key parts of the reform process. The important point here is thus not so much that a particular style of political leadership is required at the conjunctural moment, but rather that the leadership is unwavering and consistent. Both Klein and Dinning are extraordinarily determined, and the importance of this determination in staying the fiscal course and in encouraging structural reform at the conjunctural moment should not be overlooked.

(4) *Basic reforms were thought out and prepared*. As noted earlier, in many departments the basic elements of reform had been under discussion for some time. The policy soil had been particularly well cultivated in Health, Education,

and Social Services. Health care reforms had been on the table for some time, at least since 1989. Although incremental changes had been made prior to Treasury's demand for a 17 per cent budget cut, nothing had been done in the way of fundamental structural reform. Senior officials in Education indicated during our interviews that they, too, had the basic elements of a reform package in place for some time, but were frustrated by their inability to move forward with the changes. Welfare reforms had also been under discussion for some time prior to 1992. Family and Social Services had a basic agenda in mind as early as 1985, but only with the election of the Klein government in 1993 were they able to move forward in earnest. Interestingly, it is in these three departments—Health, Education, and Social Services—that the most fundamental structural reforms appear to have been instituted. Advanced Education, despite facing a budget cut of a similar size, has not as yet implemented structural changes of the same magnitude. This may well reflect the fact that although officials at the Department of Advanced Education indicated there was a recognized need for a policy review prior to the election of the Klein government, little specific groundwork had been laid. This provides evidence, then, that a fiscal crisis alone does not a policy reform make. To take advantage of the other conjunctural elements, the basic elements of reform that will make up the 'big change' must be prepared in advance.

(5) *A receptive electorate.* There are strong indications that the political climate was ripe for change. Already mentioned above was the fact that Conservative Party conventions had put forward platforms focusing on balanced budgets and fundamental reforms to health and education for at least eight years. Moreover, after 15 years of big spending under Peter Lougheed, followed by six years under Don Getty during which the status quo was essentially maintained despite deteriorating fiscal balances, the electorate was no doubt ready for a fundamental change in policy direction.[18] Although the Conservatives had already been in power for 21 years prior to Klein's election, and he himself was a minister in the previous government, Klein was able to convince voters that he would embark on a fundamentally different path.

(6) *A fragmented opposition.* Up to this point at least, opposition to the reforms has been relatively weak and ineffectual. For example, the Liberal opposition has been able to score relatively few 'hits' on the government. Important in this regard may be the fact that the Liberals themselves ran on a platform of deficit elimination and reform in the 1993 election campaign. This has made it difficult for them to criticize the government cuts with any credibility. The traditional defenders of the status quo in areas like health and education have been no more effective. Health care workers have not as yet presented a united front opposing the changes, primarily because, as with most reforms, there are winners and losers. As we noted earlier, many of those interviewed indicated that the health care reforms have resulted in a power shift

away from traditional doctors and hospitals. At the same time, non-traditional health care workers, and health care administrators, have witnessed an increase in their power. None the less, the Alberta Medical Association, which represents the province's physicians, has become more vocal since the fall of 1995 as attention has begun to shift towards questioning the viability of the fee-for-service system and payments to physicians. Indeed, there is a perception that the AMA managed to cause the government to back down from efforts to restrict physicians' remuneration. More generally, the civil service, teachers, post-secondary faculty and staff, etc., who, perhaps arguably, benefited from the status quo, have not been able to mount rigorous opposition to the changes. Indeed, these groups have been remarkably passive in the face of widespread wage cuts and lay-offs.

Further to this point, in Chapter 3 McKenzie notes there is an important distinction to be made between legislative control theory and Niskanen-type theories of bureaucracy. The former postulates that agency actions reflect the preferences of legislators, the latter that they reflect the preferences of the bureaucracy. The evidence suggests that on a macro level at least, the institutional changes implemented in Alberta reflect the political preferences of the legislators. That is, despite the fact that the bureaucracy was contemplating reforms in some areas internally, only when the political winds changed, driven by the fiscal agenda, were the reforms initiated. A number of ministers related to us during our interviews how the 'first run' at the business plans was not satisfactory because the bureaucracy was sceptical that they were serious about the size and speed of the cuts. We were told, however, that 'they soon got the message' and 'bought in . . . big time'. One potential danger of this enthusiastic espousal of change is that there may be a tendency for the civil service to neglect its traditional role of warning the government against ill-conceived policies.[19] Civil servants may become 'can-do' enthusiasts, which, while facilitating the reform process, may result in a less cautious approach to policy-making. From this perspective, then, the lack of opposition to the reforms creates dangers as well as opportunities for a reforming government.

In sum, we think that a good case can be made that a number of elements have come together to form a rather unique policy conjuncture in Alberta, resulting in an environment both receptive to major policy reform and able to move forward with that reform. Whether the changes have been good or bad for Alberta is a matter open to debate, and indeed it is likely too early at this point to do more than speculate. However, it seems clear that the province is in the midst of an important policy conjuncture, precipitated by a rather unique confluence of events, not the least of which is the perception of an impending fiscal crisis. Whether other jurisdictions are approaching a similar conjuncture remains to be seen.

**<u>Appendix 1:</u>** A Framework for Program/Service Review

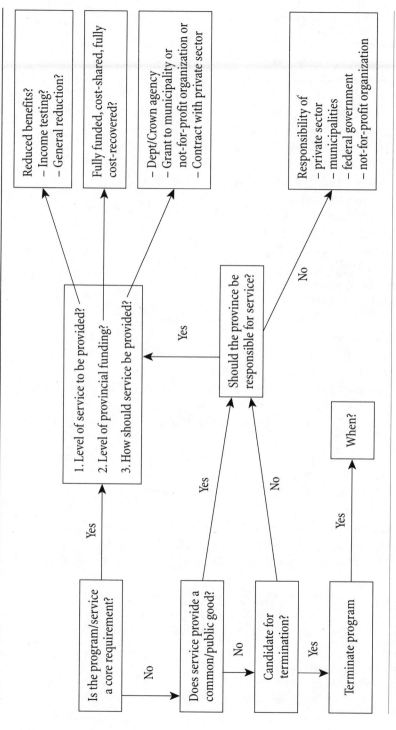

SOURCE: Alberta Provincial Treasurer.

## Appendix 2: List of Interviewees

**Politicians**

The Honourable Ralph Klein, Premier
The Honourable Jack Ady, Minister of Advanced Education and Career Development
The Honourable Mike Cardinal, Minister of Family and Social Services
The Honourable Jim Dinning, Treasurer
The Honourable Halver Johnson, Minister of Education
The Honourable Gary Mar, Minister of Culture and Recreation
The Honourable Shirley McClellan, Minister of Health
Jocelyn Burgener, MLA
Yvonne Fritz, MLA
Jon Havelock, MLA
Denis Herard, MLA
Bonnie Laing, MLA
Stan Schuemacher, MLA
Shiraz Sheriff, MLA

**Civil Servants**

Aslam Bhatti, Assistant Deputy Minister, Health
Reno Bosetti, Deputy Minister, Education
Pat Boynton, Assistant Deputy Minister (Children's Programs), Family and Social Services
Archie Clark, Director of Strategic Planning and Research, Advanced Education
Bob Dawson, Executive Assistant to the Minister, Advanced Education
Bernard Doyle, Acting Deputy Minister, Health
Lynne Duncan, Deputy Minister, Advanced Education and Career Development
Mick Farrell, Assistant Deputy Minister (Planning), Family and Social Services
Don Flemming, Deputy Minister, Family and Social Services
Mat Hanrahan, Assistant Deputy Minister (Adult Programs), Family and Social Services
Greg Moffatt, Executive Assistant to the Minister, Treasury
Paul Taylor, Ministerial Projects and Liaison, Treasury
Brian Wik, Executive Assistant to the Minister, Education

**Agency Representatives**

Robert Bigsby, President, Olds College
Larry Bryan, CEO, Calgary Regional Health Authority

Sharon Carrey, Olds College
Dan Cornish, President, Red Deer College
Murray Fraser, President, University of Calgary
George Ghitan, Hull House, Calgary
Monsignor William Irwin, President and CEO, Catholic Social Services, Edmonton
John Keenan, Hull House, Calgary
Dale Landry, President, Southern Alberta Institute of Technology
Brian Lemon, CEO, Capital Regional Health Authority
Ken Little, Budget Director, Edmonton School Board
David Lynn, Superintendent of Finance, Foothills School District
Al Martin, CEO, Red Deer Regional Health Authority
Ursula Mergney, Superintendent of Finance and Treasurer, Calgary Board of Education
Dwight Nelson, CEO, Headwaters Regional Health Authority
Keith Pedersen, Vice-President, Southern Alberta Institute of Technology
Dean Powers, Treasurer, Edmonton Board of Education
Christopher Smith, Program Director, Edmonton Social Planning Council
Roger Smith, Vice-President (Academic), University of Alberta
Peggy Valentine, Trustee and Chair, Calgary Board of Education
Lou Zanglanelli, Managing Director, Hull House, Calgary

## NOTES

1. For Basic and Advanced Education these figures refer to the percentage decline in the government grant. As institutions have other sources of revenues—property taxes in the case of Basic Education and tuition in the case of Advanced Education—total revenues will fall by less. For more details, see Emery, Chapter 10, and Bruce and Schwartz, Chapter 11. It should also be noted that the percentages cited refer to cuts in nominal dollars from the 1993/4 budget. In real, per capita terms, the cuts have been larger than this.

2. In the 1994 budget, Calgary and Edmonton received an additional $100 million in 'transitional' money.

3. See Archer and Gibbins, Chapter 13, for evidence of such a philosophical shift among Alberta voters. In Chapter 4, Kneebone discusses political economy models that emphasize the importance of such shifts.

4. Both authors attended the Red Deer Roundtable. For a further discussion of the role played by the roundtables, see Boothe, Chapter 6.

5. The crucial role of the Treasurer in budget-cutting was discussed in Chapters 3 and 4. This issue will be revisited below in the discussion of the budget-making process. See also the discussion in Boothe, Chapter 6.

6. On this issue, see the discussion relating to line-item budgeting in McKenzie, Chapter 3.

7. For details of all these features, see Emery, Chapter 10.

8. For a more in-depth discussion of how Basic Education has been affected by institutional reforms and budget cuts, see Bruce and Schwartz, Chapter 11.

9. For more detail on how budget cuts and restructuring have affected health care in Alberta, see Plain, Chapter 9.

10. An example of such contracting out has occurred in the area of some eye surgery.

11. For a more in-depth discussion of the reforms in Family and Social Services, see Shedd, Chapter 8.

12. For a discussion of all these issues, see McKenzie and Kneebone in Chapters 3 and 4, respectively.

13. We can't vouch for the sampling integrity of the roundtables, but most observers feel that disparate points of view were represented. It is worth noting that at the Budget Roundtable attended by the authors, the opposition party was represented by its current leader, Grant Mitchell.

14. For further discussion of the costs and benefits of using KPIs, see McKenzie, Chapter 3.

15. See McKenzie and Kneebone in Chapters 3 and 4, respectively, for a more complete discussion.

16. See the survey conducted by Archer and Gibbins, Chapter 13.

17. See Wilsford (1994).

18. For a discussion of this issue, see Mansell, Chapter 2.

19. Butler, Adonis, and Travers (1994), in their analysis of the failed poll tax in Britain, cite an abandonment of the traditional cautionary role of the civil service as one of the reasons that this ill-advised policy was able to go ahead.

# REFERENCES

Alesina, A., and A. Drazen (1991), 'Why Stabilizations are Delayed', *American Economic Review* 81: 1170–88.

Butler, D., A. Adonis, and T. Travers (1994), *Failure in the British Government: The Politics of the Poll Tax*. Oxford: Oxford University Press.

De Groot, H., and J. Van Der Sluis (1987), 'Bureaucracy Response to Budget Cuts: An Economic Model', *Kyklos* 40: 103–9.

DiIulio, J., G. Garvey, and D. Kettl (1993), *Improving Government Performance: An Owner's Manual*. Washington: The Brookings Institution.

Downs, A. (1957), *An Economic Theory of Democracy*. New York: Harper & Row.

Drazen, A., and V. Grilli (1993), 'The Benefits of Crises for Economic Reforms', *American Economic Review* 83 (3): 598–607.

Hettich, W., and S. Winer (1988), 'Economic and Political Foundations of Tax Structure', *American Economic Review* 78: 701–12.

———, and ——— (1993), 'Institutional Mechanisms for Efficient Policy', Government and Competitiveness Project Discussion Paper 93–10, Kingston: School of Policy Studies, Queen's University.

———, and ——— (1995), 'Decision Externalities, Economic Efficiency and Institutional Responses', *Canadian Public Policy* 21 (3): 344–61.

Jackson, P. (1982), *The Political Economy of Bureaucracy*. Oxford: Philip Alan.

Kneebone, R. (1995), 'Institutional Design and Public Policy: A Macroeconomic Perspective' (mimeograph).

McCubbins, M., and T. Schwartz (1984), 'Congressional Oversight: Police Patrols versus Fire Alarms', *American Journal of Political Science* 28: 165–79.

McKenzie, K. (1995), 'Institutional Design and Public Policy: A Microeconomic Perspective', mimeograph.

North, D. (1990), *Institutions, Institutional Change and Economic Performance: The Political Economy of Institutions and Decisions*. Cambridge: Cambridge University Press.

Romer, R., and H. Rosenthal (1978), 'Political Resource Allocation, Controlled Agendas, and the Status Quo', *Public Choice* 33: 27–43.

———, and ——— (1979), 'Bureaucrats versus Voters: On the Political Economy of Resource Allocation by Direct Democracy', *Quarterly Journal of Economics* 93 (Nov.): 563–87.

———, and ——— (1982), 'Median Voters or Budget Maximizers: Evidence from School Expenditure Referenda', *Economic Inquiry* 20 (Oct.): 556–78.

Trebilcock, M. (1994), *The Prospects for Reinventing Government.* Toronto: C.D. Howe Institute.

von Hagen, J., and I. Harden (1995), 'Budget Processes and Commitment to Fiscal Discipline', *European Economic Review* 39: 771–9.

Weingast, B. (1984), The Congressional-Bureaucratic System: A Principal-Agent Perspective (With Applications to the SEC)', *Public Choice* 44: 147–91.

———, and M. Moran (1983), 'Bureaucratic Discretion or Congressional Control? Regulatory Policymaking by the Federal Trade Commission', *Journal of Political Economy* 91 (Oct.): 765–800.

Wilsford, D. (1994), 'Path Dependency, or Why History Makes It Difficult but Not Impossible to Reform Health Care Systems in a Big Way', *Journal of Public Policy* 14 (3): 251–83.

# Comments on Chapter 5　　　　　　　　　　　■

*Michael J. Trebilcock*

My very pleasurable task for this volume has been to review three superb chapters: Kenneth McKenzie's 'Institutional Design and Public Policy: A Microeconomic Perspective'; Ron Kneebone's 'Institutional Design and Public Policy: A Macroeconomic Perspective'; and Kneebone and McKenzie's 'The Process Behind Institutional Reform in Alberta', and to present short comments on the third of these chapters, viewing the other two as a backdrop. I commend all three chapters to readers, all of them vastly insightful and illuminating—the first two providing immensely valuable reviews of large and complex bodies of literature, and the third providing some applications of this literature to the institutional reform process in Alberta. In focusing on the themes developed by Professors Kneebone and McKenzie, I want to single out three for comment.

## 1. THE EXPENDITURE-CUTTING PROCESS: ACROSS-THE-BOARD VERSUS SELECTIVE CUTS

Governments in the past in many jurisdictions, when faced with a need to cut public expenditures, have typically undertaken across-the-board cuts of government spending, as opposed to selective expenditure cuts. Across-the-board expenditure cuts are perhaps politically less painful than selective cuts, but they entirely ignore the differential importance of policy objectives, current program performance, and the potential for substituting superior governing instruments. The Alberta experience seems to have reflected an intermediate course between across-the-board expenditure cuts and selective cuts. According to Kneebone and McKenzie, the government's operating premise was that the total expenditure budget had to be cut by 20 per cent to eliminate the deficit, although the aggregate expenditure cut was not distributed equally over various departments and agencies.

The authors point out, for example, that the Family and Social Services budget will fall by 19.3 per cent over the three-year period beginning in 1993/4, Health by about 17 per cent, Advanced Education by 15.5 per cent, and Basic Education by 12.4 per cent. The authors also describe the decision-tree that the treasurer and his officials in the review process required each department or agency to follow. However, how the particular percentage cuts were arrived at for each area of government expenditure is not clear to me. In particular, it is not clear to me whether these percentages were the *result* of program-by-program reviews or were the *a priori* targets given to each of the ministries in the light of which they themselves undertook program-by-program review. The recently elected government of Ontario, like the Alberta government in 1993/4, has announced that public expenditures in Ontario must be cut by 20 per cent over the term of its mandate in order to eliminate the current budget deficit. In generating this level of aggregate expenditure reductions, the Ontario government appears to be proceeding by applying a presumptive 20 per cent cut to all of its major sectors—in other words, something very close to an across-the-board expenditure cut.

Professors Kneebone and McKenzie argue that the across-the-board nature of the cuts in Alberta was a critically important element in its political acceptance. They state that the 'share the pain' and 'gore every ox' approach was identified by many people they interviewed in the course of their research as being an important factor in muting opposition to the cuts ('getting buy-in'); if everyone is seen to be sharing the cuts in a reasonably equal manner, there is likely to be less opposition. People were more willing to accept reductions when they perceived that they were not being singled out. I accept the political potency of the equality of sacrifice, while recognizing that this also reduces the political costs for politicians in making much more discriminating or selective cuts. However, I am not at all persuaded that in the long run this is a rational approach to the reduction and reallocation of public expenditures, despite political imperatives pushing in this direction.

For example, well-managed private-sector firms or well-functioning families, facing a need to cut costs, are highly unlikely to cut all costs by the same margin across-the-board. In work that I undertook for the Management Board Secretariat of the Ontario government in May 1995, before the change of government, I outlined what seemed to me to be a more rational approach to expenditure reductions and reallocations than an across-the-board or semi-across-the-board cut. In brief, my approach would cluster programs in broadly related areas and require relevant ministries to rank programs by reference to (1) their integral/peripheral importance to identified core policy objectives; (2) where integral, the efficacy of existing instruments in advancing policy objectives; (3) the potential for substituting more cost-effective instruments. A central agency of government would then choose which low-ranking programs in each area to eliminate in order to meet overall deficit reduction targets.

## 2. THE ROLE OF VOICE AND EXIT IN INSTITUTIONAL ACCOUNTABILITY

In their chapter, Kneebone and McKenzie detail a number of institutional changes that at least on the surface reflect a strong commitment to decentralization or devolution of government decision-making functions—in the health sector through the creation of Regional Health Authorities (RHAs); in the school system, through greater reliance on school-based management and the role of parent councils; and in the Family and Social Services area through the creation of Regional Social Assistance Authorities (RSAAs) charged with delivering social services to children in specified geographic areas. In the case of the post-secondary sector, the government, while imposing major expenditure reductions, has left the individual institutions with the responsibility of determining how to meet the cuts while issuing strong directives that more co-ordination among these institutions is needed to reduce overlap and duplication.

The authors' description of these institutional changes suggests some significant measure of confusion as to the respective roles of competition and co-ordination among the decentralized institutions, or to put the issue another way (following Albert Hirschman), the respective roles of exit (choice) on the part of citizens (the discipline of competition) and the role of voice on the part of citizens in holding these public-sector institutions accountable for their performance. The authors note that in the case of the school system, all budget allocations are now to be made by the provincial budget, local school boards have largely lost their ability to raise local school taxes, and the school curriculum is to be determined centrally. Similarly, the way in which individual RHAs are to encourage competition in the provision of health care services within their regions is unclear. Most of those in this sector interviewed by the authors view the RHAs as the *provider* of health care services within their region, not as the purchaser of health care services on behalf of consumers, and indeed some did not recognize this distinction. In the university sector, enrolment numbers and tuition fees are still tightly regulated.

I believe that much more careful thinking is required as to the respective roles of competition and co-ordination, and citizen choice and citizen voice, in publicly financed or operated institutions. For example, in the case of the RHAs and the RSAAs, how are these institutions held accountable to citizens for the quality of their performance? Do citizens have some role in the decision-making processes of these agencies, given that board members are apparently appointed by government and not locally elected by citizens? Can citizens elect to be serviced by other agencies (exit) and take some per capita share of government funding with them? In the case of the school system, what is the objection to schools being given a significant amount of discretion in setting their own curricula, subject to local parental oversight? What are the objections to local schools or school boards having the ability to raise additional local taxes to support a higher quality or more expensive range of educational services (given that local municipalities presumably have this ability now with other local taxes)? Why should the universities be required to co-ordinate their offerings pursuant to either some government or collectively generated central plan? What is the objection to universities competing both over course offerings and levels of tuition fees (subject to the availability of adequate income contingent loan facilities for needy students)? In these various respects, it is not clear to me that the government's policies reflect a clearly worked-out view of the respective roles of competition and co-ordination, and of individual citizen choice and effective citizen voice.

## 3. INCREMENTAL VS. CONVULSIVE CHANGE

Professors Kneebone and McKenzie argue that the Alberta experience refutes the position of commentators such as myself who have argued in the past that political and bureaucratic processes will typically only accommodate marginal or incremental rather than fundamental institutional changes. However, even I have acknowledged that a fiscal catharsis may substantially relax the political and bureaucratic constraints on major public-sector institutional reform (or, if one process, undermine path dependency).

Nevertheless, this view of the catalysts of institutional change is disturbing in several respects. Well-functioning institutions in the public and private sector are continuously innovating or adapting to changes in their environment on a host of (typically) small margins, which cumulatively over time are often likely to have a major transformatory effect on such institutions. On the theory of change described by Professors Kneebone and McKenzie, in the public sector we must resign ourselves to long periods of institutional stasis or inertia punctuated occasionally by cathartic paradigm shifts in response to crises. But well-functioning institutions would not have allowed self-inflicted crises of the kind we are addressing to develop in the first place. What we most of all need to be assured of now is that current institutions have governance structures and face dynamic incentives so as to be able to respond or adapt to changes in their environment without being driven to a state of crisis.

That is to say, rather than congratulating ourselves on the fact that fundamental institutional reforms were finally provoked by the fiscal deficit crisis, I note with disappointment that a number of the reform proposals recently implemented had been under consideration by various ministries since the early 1980s, but were viewed as politically inexpedient. But if 20 per cent of the government's expenditures are now widely viewed as not warranting the government's borrowing costs associated with financing them, even in the absence of a deficit or debt it might be argued that well-informed taxpayers would equally not have viewed their tax dollars as wisely spent on these activities. Is the implication of deficit-driven reforms that in the absence of a deficit the expenditure reductions and institutional reforms undertaken by Alberta would not have been warranted? Does it follow that now that the deficit has been eliminated, the impetus for policy and institutional innovation is over? This seems to imply a binary institutional response function of 0 or 10 (but nothing in between). This seems a very odd and unappealing concept of public governance, which, as with governance in dynamic successful private-sector corporations, should be a continuous process. In this sense our aspiration must be to evolve a process of incremental rather than convulsive policy change.

CHAPTER 6

# The New Approach to Budgeting in Alberta ■

*Paul Boothe*

## 1. INTRODUCTION

In 1993, the government of Alberta embarked on a program to eliminate the
deficit over three years by reducing government spending.[1] As part of the
government's overall strategy for achieving its goal, the budget process was
changed substantially. Defining the budget process broadly, the changes the
government made covered a wide range of activities, including: public consultations (the roundtables); the use of expert panels (the Financial Review
Commission and the Tax Reform Commission); the use of legislative constraints on budgeting (the Deficit Elimination Act, the Taxpayer Protection Act,
and the Balanced Budget and Debt Retirement Act); new methods of developing budgets at the department level (department business plans) and of arriving at budget decisions by caucus (Standing Policy Committees) and cabinet
(Treasury Board); and new methods of evaluating performance and monitoring results flowing from budget initiatives.

Previous academic work examining changes in Canadian government
budget practices casts serious doubt on whether changes in budgeting have a
significant effect on the level or mix of spending.[2] However, government spending in Alberta has declined substantially and there is a widely-held view among
politicians and government officials that changes in the budget process have
contributed in an important way to attaining the government's goal of eliminating the deficit.

Changes in the broadly-defined budget process are ongoing in Alberta and
it is much too early to provide a full evaluation of their impact. Thus, the more
modest purpose of this chapter is to describe the new approach to budgeting
(as it currently exists) and to contrast it with past practices in Alberta.

The remainder of the chapter is organized as follows: In the next section,
I present a chronological description of the budget cycle. The role of public
consultation and expert panels is described in the third section, followed in the
fourth section by an examination of the impact of constraining legislation.

**Table 1:** Budget Cycle Chronology

| Month | Event |
|---|---|
| | Deficit limits set by legislation. |
| July–August | Caucus sets new business plan themes, principles, and directions. |
| July | Treasury Board sets fiscal parameters (revenue forecasts, revenue assumptions, expenditure limits). Budget Call Memo sent to departments. |
| August–September | Departments develop business plan scenarios based on alternative spending reduction scenarios. |
| September | Department business plans reviewed by Standing Policy Committees. |
| October | Departments meet with Treasury Board and Standing Policy Committee chairs to review business plans. |
| November | Treasury Board issues three-year spending targets to departments. |
| December–January | Departments finalize business plans based on Treasury Board directions. Treasury finalizes budget documents to be tabled in legislature. |
| February–March | Budget speech. |
| March–April | Budget debate (20–30 sitting days). |
| May–June | Royal assent. |

In the fifth section, the business planning approach to developing department budgets is discussed. The role of the Standing Policy Committees, which evaluate and monitor department business plans, is considered in section six. The final section presents some brief conclusions and explores directions for future research to evaluate the impacts of changes to Alberta's budget process.

## 2. THE BUDGET CYCLE

The main elements of the budget cycle are outlined in Table 1. In all cases, dates are approximate and may vary from year to year. The budget cycle is underpinned by legislative constraints on budgeting—in the current environment, the Deficit Elimination Act.

The budget cycle begins in July when caucus meets to decide on the overall directions for business plans based on government priorities—which themselves may be reviewed and debated at that time. At the same time, the cabinet committee responsible for financial matters, the Treasury Board, develops aggregate fiscal parameters and transmits these to individual departments through the Budget Call Memorandum.

Departments begin to develop their business plans for the next fiscal year in late summer.[3] Plans are developed based on the alternative spending scenarios included in the Budget Call, as well as the departments' own forecasts of demand and proposals regarding the best method to deliver their core services. Department plans are reviewed in September by the Standing Policy Committees of caucus.

By mid-fall, departments (usually the minister and deputy minister) have met with Standing Policy Committees and discussed the policy implications of the business plans. The financial implications of business plans are then reviewed by the Treasury Board. Standing Policy Committee chairs are included in Treasury Board meetings with departments (as well as any cabinet discussions of the particular committee's policy area). After attempting to reconcile the financial implications of the business plans at an aggregate level, the Treasury Board issues firm spending targets to departments, which in turn finalize their business plans.

December and January are generally devoted to resolving last-minute issues and the preparation by Treasury of detailed budget documents and the budget speech to be tabled in the Legislative Assembly. The budget speech is typically delivered in February or March (depending on the timing of the spring session of the Assembly) and then debated by the legislature (sitting as Committee of Supply) for 20–30 sitting days (7–10 weeks). Royal assent is given to supply bills by the Lieutenant-Governor in May or June.

The new budget cycle differs from past practice in a number of important ways. While some of these changes will be discussed in more detail below, it is useful to draw attention to two main changes in the process:

1. *The business planning approach to department budgeting.* Requiring departments to define their core business, and to develop goals, strategies to meet those goals, and performance measures to monitor progress, represents a fundamental shift in the budget process.

2. *Review of department business plans by Standing Policy Committees.* The policy overview and co-ordination function performed by committees dominated by backbench MLAs is another fundamental shift.

We now turn to an examination of the impact that public consultations and the advice of expert panels have on the budget process.

## 3. PUBLIC CONSULTATION AND EXPERT PANELS

The government faced a difficult political problem in the spring of 1993. The leadership of the Progressive Conservative Party had just changed following the retirement of Premier Getty as party leader. The new leader, Premier Klein, was facing an imminent general election with government popularity at an extremely low level. The new leadership needed to put its stamp on government by outlining a new, more appealing direction to voters. The government began to renew itself by gathering advice and building support through a two-track process of consulting the public and commissioning expert panels. The first public consultation, called the Budget Roundtable, was conducted by Alberta Treasury in March 1993, and other government departments soon followed suit. Two expert panels were commissioned: the Alberta Financial Review Commission, which reported in March 1993, and the Alberta Tax Reform Commission, which reported in February 1994.

The first Budget Roundtable, which became known as the Red Deer Roundtable, brought together more than 100 participants selected to represent a broad spectrum of opinion in Alberta. Representatives from large and small business, labour, education, health, and agriculture were included. An attempt was made to include people who were not traditional supporters of the government as well as its traditional allies. Government MLAs attended to listen, but not to participate in the proceedings. Opposition MLAs were also invited and attended. The roundtable was co-chaired by two private-sector business executives, Norman Wagner from Calgary and Ralph Young from Edmonton, and group discussion leaders were drawn from Alberta business, education, and labour.

The government had two main purposes in initiating the roundtable process. The first was to begin to educate the public regarding Alberta's fiscal situation, including the fact that Alberta had recently become a net debtor after 40 years as a creditor. The second was to gauge public support for measures to deal with the deficit. The government was surprised at the strength of public discontent over the deterioration in Alberta's finances and the public's willingness to address the deficit issue. A strong message was sent that Albertans (at least as represented by the roundtable participants) were willing to support harsh measures to eliminate the deficit over a short time horizon.

In retrospect, the Red Deer Roundtable (along with the Financial Review Commission recommendations) contributed significantly to the development of the government's May 1993 budget and the subsequent election platform.[4] The success of the Red Deer Roundtable led other government departments to hold their own roundtables—with varying degrees of success. However, all departments used input from the roundtables to develop their business plans. Alberta Treasury repeated the Budget Roundtable process in 1994, when participants looked mainly at the issue of performance measurement in government.

At least as important as the Red Deer Roundtable in shaping the government's approach to budgeting was the input from expert panels, especially the Financial Review Commission. The commission was chaired by Marshall Williams, a Calgary business executive, and included nine senior executives (mostly accountants) from Calgary (6), Edmonton (2), and Lloydminster (1). The commission's mandate was to look into the appropriateness of government accounting procedures and to give an independent assessment of the province's financial position as of 31 March 1993. The government hoped that the commission would restore confidence in the reporting of Alberta's finances and convince citizens of the seriousness of Alberta's financial position.

The commission made a number of recommendations that soon found their way into the government's fiscal plan and motivated changes in the budget process. Commission recommendations included:

1. That a fiscal plan be established on an urgent basis to eliminate (not simply reduce) the deficit (which the commission renamed 'overspending').
2. That the use of loan guarantees to business be reduced.
3. That economic and fiscal assumptions used in budgeting be 'conservative'.
4. That government finances be reported on a consolidated basis to improve accountability. While the consolidated measure of the deficit was higher, in the commission's view it presented a more accurate picture of the true state of affairs.
5. That financial reporting be more frequent and more timely.

With the release of its report, the commission sounded the alarm on the urgency of eliminating the deficit and reinforced the message of the Red Deer Roundtable. The government respond quickly and positively to the Financial Review Commission report and promised fast implementation of its recommendations. Many of the recommended changes were adopted as early as the May 1993 budget.

A second expert panel was also commissioned by the government to advise on the revenue side of the province's finances. The Alberta Tax Reform Commission was established in September 1993 and reported in February 1994. This commission was chaired by Jack McDonald, a Red Deer business executive, and included four members from the Alberta business community and one mayor. The commission's mandate included eight questions whose basic thrust was to examine the Alberta tax system and make recommendations to improve Alberta's competitive position.

After holding public hearings and accepting written submissions, the commission made a number of short- and long-term recommendations. Short-term recommendations included:

1. Move to province-wide, market-value property assessment.
2. Phase out the Machinery and Equipment Tax as a source of municipal and school district revenue and replace it with a new property tax on the province-wide property tax base.

Longer-term recommendations included:

1. Move to the lowest possible personal and corporate income tax rates after the deficit was eliminated.
2. Move to a modest, broad-based sales tax to permit lower personal and corporate income tax rates, but only after the deficit was eliminated and the sales tax was approved by referendum.

The government adopted the low-tax message as a key element of its competitiveness strategy and used it to bolster its case that the deficit had to be dealt with through expenditure reduction. It also moved quickly to adopt the province-wide, market-value property assessment as a base for property tax to fund municipal and school district expenditures. However, the government dissociated itself from the recommendation to move towards a modest sales tax and passed the Alberta Taxpayer Protection Act of 1995 to ensure that no sales tax would be imposed without a provincial referendum.

Together, the Red Deer Roundtable and the Financial Review Commission had a significant impact on the government's direction, the budget process, and the province's financial reporting. The Alberta Taxpayer Protection Act was only one of the legislative constraints the government was to impose on budgeting. We now turn to the two other constraints.

## 4. LEGISLATIVE CONSTRAINTS ON BUDGETING

Two important pieces of legislation, the Deficit Elimination Act of 1993 (DEA) and its successor, the Balanced Budget and Debt Retirement Act of 1995 (BBDRA), now impose significant constraints on both the expenditure and revenue sides of Alberta's budget. The DEA, which forms the cornerstone of the government's fiscal plan, lays out the three-year timetable to eliminate the deficit mainly through expenditure reductions. In addition, the DEA addresses the problem that has plagued budgeting in Alberta for the last 40 years—the volatility of revenues.

The DEA contains a number of elements related to expenditure:

1. Annual deficit targets for 1993/4: $2.5 billion; 1994/5: $1.8 billion; 1995/6: $0.8 billion.
2. If a deficit target is missed in a given year, it will be added to the next year, i.e., a deficit of $3.0 billion in 1993/4 (over target by $0.5 billion) would make the 1994/5 target $1.3 billion (rather than $1.8 billion). To date, all deficit targets have been achieved by a comfortable margin.
3. Smaller than targeted deficits in past years cannot be used to offset a missed target in the current year.

4. Higher-than-planned revenues cannot be used to increase expenditure. Extra revenue must be used to reduce debt.
5. No special warrants may be authorized in the absence of a clearly-defined emergency.

The DEA imposes strict constraints on allowable deficits. Coupled with the government's commitment not to raise taxes (some fees and health insurance premiums have been raised) and the constraint that positive revenue surprises cannot be used to increase spending even if the deficit target has been met, the DEA *requires* that deficit elimination be achieved largely through expenditure reduction.

A key element of the DEA on the revenue side deals with the volatility of revenues. Natural resource revenue projections used in budgeting must be the lesser of forecasted revenue or a five-year moving average of past natural resource revenue. This measure is designed to avoid basing expenditure decisions (which tend to be difficult to reverse) on temporarily high revenues. A number of times in Alberta's history, the province has delayed dealing with structural imbalances in its budget because of temporarily high resource revenues.[5] In reality, the structural imbalances themselves were created by treating large natural resource windfalls as stable, permanent sources of revenue.[6]

The move to budgeting revenues based on prudent assumptions rather than current forecasts has been advocated recently by Robson (1994). Using the federal budget as an example, Robson shows how using probabilistic forecasts that centre on best-guess estimates of key determinants of revenue and statutory expenditure exposes budget-makers to a significant probability of missing deficit targets. Robson's proposed solution is to base budget projections on prudent assumptions, which will generally underestimate revenues and overestimate statutory expenditures in order to provide some protection from missing deficit targets because of random forecasting errors.[7]

The final element of the DEA concerns reporting. In keeping with the recommendations of the Financial Review Commission, the DEA commits the government to provide quarterly financial reports on spending and revenue by department within 60 days of the end of a quarter. This represents a substantial improvement over past annual reporting, which was sometimes provided almost a full year after the end of the year in question. Thus, accountability is significantly enhanced. In addition, departments that are off track meet with Treasury Board to outline the mid-course corrections they will make to meet targets. Thus, the DEA improves overall compliance with voted budgets.

The Balanced Budget and Debt Retirement Act of 1995 lays out the government's plan to eliminate the province's net debt over a 25-year period beginning in 1997/8. The following elements make up the BBDRA:

1. The government cannot run a budgetary deficit.
2. The government must provide an audited statement of net debt as of 31 March 1997.
3. Net debt must be reduced by 20 per cent of the 1996/7 total in each succeeding five-year period.
4. Minimum annual reductions of net debt of $100 million must be made unless the province is ahead of its net debt target for the current five-year period.
5. Budget surpluses must be used to reduce debt, not to increase expenditure beyond voted budgets.
6. Special warrants will only be authorized for clearly defined emergencies.

On the revenue side, the BBDRA contains the following provisions:

1. The provincial treasurer must report annually on the economic assumptions, forecasted revenue, and 'excess' (difference between forecasted and budgeted) natural resource and corporate tax revenue.
2. Natural resource revenue will be budgeted to be the lesser of: 90 per cent of forecast or the five-year moving average of natural resource revenue.
3. Corporate tax revenue will be budgeted to be the lesser of: 90 per cent of forecast or the five-year moving average of corporate tax revenue.

Finally, the BBDRA continues the practice of quarterly financial reporting on a by-department basis.

When it comes into force in the 1997/8 fiscal year, the BBDRA will constrain government budgeting even further than the DEA. In addition to laying out an orderly schedule for net debt reduction, the BBDRA prohibits annual deficits. Since government accounting has shifted substantially towards full consolidation, there will be little opportunity to follow the time-honoured practice of circumventing budgetary constraints by moving items off budget.

In Chapter 4, Kneebone reviewed some of the debate in the academic literature over the efficacy of legislated constraints to budgeting. To date, the Alberta government has lived within the imposed constraints. However, it has benefited from a substantial increase in revenues that allowed it to meet its targets with ease. It may be argued that this is exactly the kind of situation in which legislated limits to spending are required, although the true test will probably come only when revenues decline substantially.

In a game-theoretic framework, the value of legislated budget constraints is clear. Legislating budgetary rules is a mechanism for building credibility—

governments voluntarily designing mechanisms that will impose political costs if budgetary commitments are not honoured. Credibility is also enhanced by building a track record of meeting budgetary commitments. In this sense the DEA has provided a series of benchmarks for the government to use to prove its credibility over time.

## 5. THE BUSINESS-PLANNING APPROACH TO BUDGETING

Volumes have been written about the business-planning approach to public-sector budgeting.[8] Major federal commissions in Canada (the Nielsen Task Force) and the US (the Gore Commission) have included private-sector participants in their efforts to reform and streamline government. Several US states, notably Oregon and Texas, have devoted considerable resources to monitoring and evaluating public-sector results.

Despite the contentions of some critics, the motivation behind this trend in public-sector management is not to turn government into a business but rather to make government more business-like in its delivery of services. In practical terms, more *business-like* means: (1) focusing on goals, (2) efficiency in delivery, and (3) monitoring and evaluating performance. An important implication of this approach is that government departments that are accountable for results require a reasonable degree of autonomy to develop and implement strategies for their achievement.

Rather than budgeting for a single year as in the past, departments are now required to prepare plans over a three-year horizon. This fits well with the government's original fiscal plan as put forth in the DEA, which committed to eliminate the deficit over a three-year period. Although plans are updated annually, to date the three-year planning horizon has lent added predictability to department budgets and has helped the planning process of client agencies and groups. A key difference between the new approach and past attempts at multi-year budgeting is that the focus was explicitly on the final year target, rather than on the next budget year. Indeed, budgeting for intervening years was simplified once the end-point budget target was set.

The business-planning approach to public-sector budgeting has not been confined to government departments. Government agencies and boards governing public institutions such as post-secondary institutions and regional health authorities[9] have also been required to develop business plans over the same planning horizon. This requirement has served to force consistency over a longer period and to expose agencies that were assuming changes in government policy to ensure the success of their plans in later years.

Although the first set of business plans[10] tabled with the 1994 budget varied substantially across departments, all plans contained the following six elements:

1. Assessment of the operating environment.
2. Mission and vision for the organization.
3. Goals of the organization.
4. Strategies for the achievement of goals.
5. Financial plan.
6. Measures of performance.

The assessment of the environment (sometimes referred to as 'environmental scan') is designed to identify all 'exogenous factors' related to the delivery of services. These factors might include: demand for services, availability of alternative providers, and future trends that might affect the demand or cost of services. Mission and vision for the organization define the core businesses of the organization and set down the long-term desired results. The goals of the organization set out the short-term results to be achieved in pursuit of the long-term objectives outlined in mission and vision. Action plans for the achievement of short-term goals are set forth in the strategies section of the business plan, and are accompanied by the financial plan. Finally, measures of performance are proposed both to facilitate an evaluation of the success of the business plan and as a specific incentive mechanism.[11]

The greater degree of department autonomy required in a business-planning approach to budgeting is manifest in a number of ways. For example, net budgeting is now permitted and even encouraged as departments look for alternative resources to fund programs and use market tests to evaluate the demand for services. Formerly, net budgeting was tightly controlled and actively discouraged by Alberta Treasury because it was thought to erode central agency and legislative control and accountability.

Other indicators of the increased autonomy of departments include: the transfer of disbursement control and payroll functions to departments, central agencies billing departments for the services they provide, and the transfer of personnel administration and purchasing to individual departments. A reduction in the number of legislative votes required to approve a departmental budget gives departments more scope to reallocate resources internally within a fiscal year to meet unexpected challenges or opportunities to accomplish their business plan goals.

One of the most fundamental changes to budgeting that comes as a result of the business-planning approach is the use of performance indicators to measure and evaluate departments' progress in implementing their business plans and achieving their stated goals. Although some jurisdictions (notably in the US) have worked in this area for several years, it is fair to say that this work is still in its early stages and the jury is still out on the feasibility of judging the success of all government activities using performance measures. However, it is clear that the publication of performance measures is already having effects within government departments and agencies.

Alberta's first set of performance measures was proposed in 1994 (Alberta, 1994) and reported on in 1995 (Alberta, 1995). Grouped under three headings[12]—people, prosperity, and preservation—the 22 measures were selected through a public consultation process. Measures under the 'people' heading include such things as: educational attainment, literacy and numeracy, life expectancy, and distribution of family income. Prosperity measures include tax burden, net debt, provincial GDP, and job creation. Preservation measures include crime rates, air quality, and health status.

Co-ordination between the government's 22 core measures and the additional measures used by departments to monitor their individual progress will require further study and work. In principle, there should be close links between the measures used to evaluate performance in each department and those that summarize the government's overall performance and against which government wishes to be measured.

The requirement for performance measurement has also been extended to government agencies and boards. For example, Regional Health Authorities were asked to include performance measures in their business plans submitted to the minister of health. Recently, the Capital Health Authority released its first performance report,[13] which included measures of customer satisfaction, volume and quality of service, and access (waiting lists and times). In addition, the Capital Health Authority announced its intention to publish performance reports each quarter. Other Regional Health Authorities are expected to follow suit.

## 6. THE ROLE OF STANDING POLICY COMMITTEES

One of the key changes in the budget process that goes hand in hand with the business-planning approach is the use of large caucus committees to review department budgets. Department budgets are reviewed for policy implications by the Standing Policy Committees and are integrated into the government's overall fiscal plan by the Treasury Board.

The five Standing Policy Committees are: Agriculture and Rural Development, Community Services, Financial Planning, Health, and Natural Resources and Sustainable Development.

All 16 government departments are assigned to one of these committees. Each is comprised of 17 or 18 government members chaired by a backbench MLA. In reality, Standing Policy Committee chairs are junior cabinet ministers, with a substantial pay supplement and other cabinet perquisites. The Standing Policy Committee chair attends all cabinet and Treasury Board meetings that discuss matters in his/her policy area. Cabinet ministers (six or seven) sit on each Standing Policy Committee as members, and each cabinet minister is a member of at least two Standing Policy Committees.

The main function of the committees is to examine departments' policy directions to ensure that they fit into the government's overall policy plan and to monitor the implementation of business plans. Standing Policy Committee reviews, which do not encompass the fiscal implications of business plans (that role is reserved for Treasury Board), try to answer three questions: (1) Is the department doing the right things (i.e., do the department's core businesses fit with government direction and priorities)? (2) Is the department's business plan implementation successful and can success be measured (i.e., with a focus on outcomes, are the right measures being used to gauge success)? (3) Are the methods used to implement the plan appropriate and technically feasible?[14]

Annual budget cycle reviews of departments by Standing Policy Committees focus on three main areas: the department's draft annual report from the previous year, the current year status report, and the three-year business plan for the upcoming budget. The first area allows the committee to render a final judgement on the department's performance. The second area allows the committee to monitor current implementation and to account for current successes and problems in judging the new business plan. The final area provides an opportunity for committee input into the future directions of the department over the next three years.

The use of Standing Policy Committees represents an important innovation in the budget process in Alberta. One implication of Standing Policy Committee review of department business plans is that backbench MLAs are much more involved in policy-setting aspects of budgeting than in past years. Given that cabinet ministers from different departments serve on the same Standing Policy Committees, opportunities to co-ordinate policy initiatives between departments are enhanced. Finally, cabinet ministers, who must present and defend department business plans before Standing Policy Committees, are more accountable to caucus, and backbench MLAs themselves have a greater accountability for the success or failure of government policy.

## 7. SUMMARY AND FUTURE RESEARCH DIRECTIONS

The key differences between the new approach to budgeting and past practice in Alberta are easily summarized. First, both public consultation and the reports of expert panels have had a significant effect on the government's overall direction and also on the budget process itself. The discussions at the Red Deer Roundtable provided concrete evidence to all parties that voters were willing to endorse harsh measures to eliminate the deficit over a short time horizon. The report of the Financial Review Commission underlined the urgency of dealing with the deficit and proposed far-reaching changes in financial reporting that facilitated the implementation of the business-planning approach to budgeting.

Second, the legislative constraints embodied in the DEA laid out the government's fiscal plan and provided a method for the government to build credibility internally and with the public by systematically meeting pre-announced targets. As well, the Act furnished a mechanism for the government to deal with the long-standing problem—revenue volatility.

Third, the business-planning approach to budgeting over a three-year horizon departed from past practice by expanding the focus to include the results of government programs as well as the costs. Although still in its early stages, performance measurement may provide a practical framework for assessing the success of departments in achieving their stated objectives.

Finally, political monitoring of the budget process has been expanded considerably with the review of department business plans by the Standing Policy Committees. This review has forced ministers to be more accountable to their caucus colleagues and, in turn, has made backbench MLAs more accountable for the government's overall success or failure in achieving its goals.

Given that we have relatively little experience with these innovations in budgeting, it is too soon to evaluate their overall impact. However, a number of interesting research questions arise. For example, can we demonstrate a difference in budgetary outcomes across jurisdictions that can be attributed to differences in the budget process? What criteria should be used to compare the relative value of alternative approaches: ability to meet stated goals? accountability to voters? meeting financial targets? overall cost of providing government services? A key element in any future research in this area will be measurement of output. One thing already clear is that the Alberta experiment in budgeting has provided researchers with fertile ground upon which to expand our understanding of the public sector.

## NOTES

1. The views expressed in this chapter are my own and should not be attributed to any other individual or institution. I am grateful to Rich Goodkey, Bob Stothart, and Al O'Brien for many helpful discussions on this topic. Allan Tupper provided thoughtful comments on an earlier version. This research was supported by a grant from the Donner Canadian Foundation.

2. For example, see Thomas (1982), Hartle (1989), Tupper and Doern (1989), and Boothe (1995). In Chapter 4, Kneebone reviews some recent international studies that are more supportive of a relationship between changes in the budget process and the level and mix of government spending.

3. In reality, given quarterly reporting and the use of performance measures to monitor non-financial performance, the business-planning process at the department level is ongoing.

4. As well, the roundtable also affected the election strategy of the Liberal Party, which was to form the official opposition following the June 1993 general election.

5. For a discussion of this phenomenon in 1986–7, see Chapter 5 of Boothe (1995).

6. See Kneebone and McKenzie, Chapter 7, for further discussion of this problem and an attempt to measure the size of the government's response to unexpected revenue windfalls.

7. The political incentives may also favour the use of prudent assumptions rather than current forecasts in budgeting. Finance ministers and provincial treasurers are routinely criticized by the media when budget forecasts of key macro variables vary from subsequent actualities. In 1993, the federal finance minister convened a special meeting of economists from across Canada to provide him with a consensus forecast on which to base his 1994 budget. The use of prudent assumptions, which differ explicitly from best-guess forecasts, may remove macro forecast accuracy as an issue over which to criticize government budgets and their political authors.

8. The best-known popular example is Osborne and Gaebler (1993). For a sample of critical reviews, see Peters and Savoie (1993) and Trebilcock (1994).

9. See, for example, Capital Health Authority (1994).

10. See Alberta (1994).

11. In business plan parlance, 'what gets measured gets done'.

12. The government's 'core' businesses, in business-planning jargon.

13. See Capital Health Authority (1995).

14. In the first review of business plans, this question was assigned to a select subcommittee of the Standing Policy Committee, which reviewed the technical aspects, including overall feasibility, of departments' business plans. Select subcommittees were typically made up of eight members, including a private-sector member, a senior official (e.g., an assistant deputy minister) from another department, as well as backbench MLAs and Treasury and Executive Council officials.

## REFERENCES

Alberta (1994), *A Better Way: A Plan for Securing Alberta's Future*. Edmonton: Alberta Treasury.

———— (1995), *Measuring Up: First Annual Report by the Government of Alberta*. Edmonton: Alberta Treasury.

Boothe, P. (1995), *The Growth of Government Spending in Alberta*. Toronto: Canadian Tax Foundation.

Capital Health Authority (1994), *A New Direction for Health*. Edmonton: Capital Health Authority.

———— (1995), *A Year in Review*. Edmonton: Capital Health Authority.

Hartle, D.G. (1989), 'Perceptions of the Expenditure Budget Process: Survey of Federal and Provincial Legislators and Public Servants', *Canadian Public Administration* 32 (3): 427–48.

Osborne, D., and T. Gaebler (1993), *Reinventing Government*. New York: Plume.

Peters, G., and D. Savoie (1993), 'Reinventing Osborne and Gaebler: Lessons from the Gore Commission', Canadian Centre for Management Development working paper.

Robson, W. (1994), 'Digging Holes and Hitting Walls: Canada's Fiscal Prospects in the Mid-1990s', Toronto: C.D. Howe Institute Commentary, No. 56 (Jan.).

Thomas, P.G. (1982), 'Public Administration and Expenditure Management', *Canadian Public Administration* 25 (4): 674–95.

Trebilcock, M. (1994), *The Prospects for Reinventing Government*. Toronto: C.D. Howe Institute.

Tupper, A., and G.B. Doern (1989), 'Alberta Budgeting in the Lougheed Era', in A.M. Maslove, ed., *Budgeting in the Provinces*. Toronto: Institute of Public Administration of Canada.

# CHAPTER 7

# Alberta's Budgetary Response to Fiscal Shocks ∎

*Ronald D. Kneebone and Kenneth J. McKenzie*

## 1. INTRODUCTION[1]

Over the course of the past 25 years, the finances of the province of Alberta have been particularly volatile. This volatility is in large part because the Alberta economy is heavily reliant on the extraction of fossil fuels.[2] Thus, the economy boomed following the oil price increases of the mid- and late 1970s and crashed following the drop in these prices in 1986. The volatility is also due to the Alberta government's heavy reliance on energy royalties to finance its expenditures: in 1984/5 energy royalties comprised 43 per cent of provincial revenues, but by 1986/7 they made up only 26 per cent. As a result, the health of the provincial government's balance sheet has closely mirrored the price of fossil fuels. This is reflected in the fact that since the crash in energy prices in 1986, the Alberta government's balance sheet has very rapidly moved from a healthy net asset position (equal to 25 per cent of provincial GDP) to a net debt position (equal to approximately 15 per cent of GDP by 1995).

The volatility of Alberta's finances makes it an interesting laboratory in which to investigate how governments respond to fiscal shocks. The purpose of this chapter is to do precisely that. In particular, we extend an approach used in Poterba (1994) to investigate US state responses to fiscal crises. In section 2, we briefly describe the approach used by Poterba and discuss why his approach must be modified to investigate the response to fiscal crises by Canadian provincial governments. In section 3, we present that modified model and in section 4 we present estimates of the model's coefficients. In section 5 we discuss empirical results. Finally, in section 6 we offer concluding comments and speculate on how the government's past experiences with fiscal shocks may have influenced the Klein government to introduce changes in its budget process, changes described by Paul Boothe in Chapter 6.

## 2. STATE VERSUS PROVINCIAL BUDGETS

Poterba (1994) makes use of an interesting data set provided by the National Association of State Budget Officers (NASBO) to investigate how US state governments respond to unexpected fiscal shocks. This data set, based on a NASBO survey, measures, by fiscal year and for virtually all 50 states, changes to state government tax revenues and spending that occur during the fiscal year but *after* the state budget has been announced. With this information, Poterba shows that it is possible to construct an estimate of a *revenue shock*, defined as the difference between what would have been state revenues given actual economic conditions during the fiscal year and the tax regime in effect at the beginning of the fiscal year, and the revenues this tax system was forecast to collect during that fiscal year. The difference, of course, is an estimate of the unexpected change in revenues due to unexpected changes in economic conditions. In a similar way, Poterba can generate an estimate of state *expenditure shocks*.

Having identified estimates of these shocks, Poterba measures the revenue and spending responses in a fiscal year relative to revenue and expenditure shocks occurring in that same fiscal year. That is, he estimates how state governments alter tax and expenditure regimes during the fiscal year in which shocks are experienced.

Availability of the NASBO data is crucial for measuring US state responses to fiscal shocks because virtually all states are prevented to varying degrees from running deficits. These restrictions take many forms. Most require that legislatures pass balanced budgets and eliminate any unexpected deficit within a certain specified period. All but six states require any such deficit to be eliminated in the following fiscal year.[3] As a result of these requirements, states must typically respond to revenue and expenditure shocks during the fiscal year in which they occur. The NASBO data allow one to obtain a true measure of state revenue and expenditure shocks and thereby obtain estimates of state responses to unexpected shocks.

Unlike US states, provincial governments in Canada have not faced constitutional restrictions on the size of the deficits and debts they may incur. As well, until very recently, no provincial government faced any legislated requirements for a balanced budget.[4] The implication of this is that provincial governments are not required to respond to fiscal shocks with changes to tax and spending legislation during the fiscal year in which the shock is experienced. Provincial governments can instead hold tax and expenditure rates constant in the face of shocks and simply allow these shocks to affect the size of their realized budget deficits, responding in the next budget cycle as they see fit. This means that we must modify Poterba's approach to study the response of provinces to fiscal shocks. This is the subject of the next section.

## 3. THE MODEL

We assume there is inertia in government expenditures and revenues in the sense that, once implemented, tax systems and expenditure programs tend to resist change. Part of the reason for this inertia is simply due to the fact that much of what government spends involves meeting statutory commitments. However, political reasons for inertia are also often cited. That is, there is a generally held notion that a new expenditure program quickly finds a constituency to defend it so that, once instituted, it is difficult to change. Wilsford (1994) and North (1990) both discuss the idea that institutions and spending programs evolve along path-dependent trajectories.

In an interview survey of Alberta politicians and public servants, Boothe (1995) provides a good deal of anecdotal evidence to support this assumption with respect to provincial expenditures in Alberta. A number of participants in the survey noted that the fast formation of constituencies to defend new programs made them difficult to cut, once introduced. Another problem often cited by survey participants was that the Treasury Board[5] typically focused on incremental changes in expenditures and thereby institutionalized spending inertia. This kind of spending inertia caused former Premier Don Getty to liken the process of changing government spending to 'turning the Queen Mary'.

We present a model explaining *changes* in provincial government revenue and spending.[6] We assume that the government bases its revenue and expenditure forecasts for fiscal year t on what it believes will happen to real provincial GDP during the coming fiscal year. In forming this forecast, the government uses information available at the end of the previous fiscal year—fiscal year t-1. Since we are modelling the change in the budget from the previous fiscal year, the expected change in the budget must be determined in part by unexpected shocks to its budget position that occurred during fiscal year t-1. Finally, we allow for the possibility that forecast budget changes may reflect political considerations. This is in consideration of political business cycle models that suggest incumbent governments may use the budget to influence voter preferences.[7] Thus, we allow for the possibility that elections influence budget choices.

With these assumptions, we model the government's forecast of the expected change in spending for fiscal year t as,

$$[E(t-1)S_t - S_{t-1}] = \alpha_0 + \alpha_1[RSHOCK_{t-1}] + \alpha_2[SSHOCK_{t-1}] +$$

$$\alpha_3[E(t-1)GDP_t - GDP_{t-1}] + \alpha_4 PV \qquad (1)$$

where $E(t-1)$ = the expectations operator conditional on information available in period t-1, $E(t-1)S_t$ = expected level of spending for fiscal year t, $S_{t-1}$ = observed spending in fiscal year t-1, $RSHOCK_{t-1}$ = unexpected change in government revenue during fiscal year t-1, $SSHOCK_{t-1}$ = unexpected change in government spending during fiscal year t-1, $E(t-1)GDP_t$ = the expected level of GDP for fiscal year t, and PV = a vector of 'political variables' to be defined. All variables are measured in real per capita terms. Equation (1) thus specifies that the change in spending budgeted for fiscal year t is a function of expected changes in economic conditions (measured by expected change in GDP), possible reactions to revenue and expenditure shocks in the previous year, and political considerations.

Observed spending in fiscal year t is,

$$S_t = E(t-1)S_t + e_t$$

where $e_t$ defines the unexpected shock to $S_t$. Substituting this into (1) and rewriting it, we have,

$$\Delta S_t = \alpha_0 + \alpha_1[RSHOCK_{t-1}] + \alpha_2[SSHOCK_{t-1}] + \alpha_3[E(t-1)GDP_t -$$
$$GDP_{t-1}] + \alpha_4 PV + e_t \tag{2}$$

where $\Delta S_t = [S_t - S_{t-1}]$. Note that the coefficient on $e_t$ is assumed to be unity. This reflects our assumption that the government makes no policy response to shocks that occur within the current fiscal year. Assuming shocks are random, we can treat $e_t$ as a white noise error term. In a similar way we can derive an equation for estimating the government's *revenue* response to shocks,

$$\Delta R_t = \beta_0 + \beta_1[RSHOCK_{t-1}] + \beta_2[SSHOCK_{t-1}] + \beta_3[E(t-1)GDP_t -$$
$$GDP_{t-1}] + \beta_4 PV + \epsilon_t \tag{3}$$

We define $RSHOCK_{t-1}$ and $SSHOCK_{t-1}$ as $[R_{t-1} - E(t-2)R_{t-1}]$ and $[S_{t-1} - E(t-2)S_{t-1}]$ respectively. Thus they measure the difference between the observed amount of revenue and spending that occurred in fiscal year t-1 and the amount that was expected, based on information available at the end of fiscal year t-2. Given our assumption that the province makes no substantial changes to spending and revenue rates during a fiscal year, this difference measures the unexpected change due solely to unexpected changes in economic conditions.

We assume that the government bases its revenue and expenditure forecasts, and its forecasts of GDP, on simple time series models. A number of alternative specifications for these forecasting equations were tried. The preferred form of the spending forecast involved two lags on spending and two on GDP. The spending forecast also included a dummy variable for fiscal year 1979/80. In that year, the provincial government purchased the debt of municipalities and thereby caused a large increase in planned expenditures. The preferred form of the revenue forecast involved two lags on spending and two on the real price of oil. The preferred GDP forecasting equation was a three-lag autoregression. It is worth noting that, as an alternative to using the NASBO data, Poterba estimated similar time series models to generate revenue and spending shocks. He found that replacing his data with these instrumental variables had little impact on his coefficients and no impact on his conclusions.[8]

## 4. INTERPRETING THE COEFFICIENTS

In this section we discuss the interpretation of the regression coefficients from our estimation of equations (2) and (3). We offer two alternative, but not mutually exclusive, interpretations.

Our first interpretation is based on the question of whether the government lets bygones be bygones. That is, does the government ignore past unexpected shocks to its spending and revenue when establishing its upcoming budget? Although we do not present a model of optimal stabilization policy, this idea is obviously related to the automatic stabilizer role of the budget. Thus, one interpretation of our empirical analysis is that it investigates the extent to which fiscal policy in Alberta has played this automatic stabilizing role. To understand the implications of letting bygones be bygones for our regression coefficients, consider the coefficients of the spending equation—equation (2). Suppose a positive shock to revenues occurs in fiscal year t-1 ($RSHOCK_{t-1} > 0$). A government that ignores past unexpected shocks would budget for no change in period t spending in response to that shock; thus we should expect $\alpha_1 = 0$. If in response to a positive revenue shock, the government increases its spending in fiscal year t, then $\alpha_1 > 0$ and we have evidence of a government not letting bygones be bygones. Now suppose there occurs a positive shock to expenditures in fiscal year t-1 ($SSHOCK_{t-1} > 0$). A government that ignores past unexpected shocks makes no adjustment to current period planned expenditures, $S_t$, in response to this shock. Since the positive shock to last period's expenditures is included in observations of $S_{t-1}$ and thus included in the dependent variable, making no change to $S_t$ implies the dependent variable will decrease dollar for dollar with every unexpected increase in $S_{t-1}$. Thus $\alpha_2 = -1$ for a government that ignores past shocks. Any value of $\alpha_2$ less than unity in absolute value indicates a government responding to past random shocks. If such a government increases $S_t$ dollar for dollar in response to the previous period's expenditure shock, there will be no change in the dependent variable in response to the expenditure shock and $\alpha_2 = 0$. Substituting these coefficient values into equation (2) (and ignoring the constant and political variables for now), we see that such a government would budget real per capita expenditures in the current period to be equal to budgeted real per capita expenditures last period plus an allowance for economic growth. In a similar way, we can determine that a government that lets bygones be bygones would behave in such a way that $\beta_1 = -1$ and $\beta_2 = 0$ in equation (3) so that such a government would budget revenues to equal what they were last period plus an allowance for growth in the tax base.

A second interpretation of the regression coefficients is based on the possibility that government ministers (the cabinet) have less than full faith in the forecasts of Alberta Treasury. Suppose, for example, the cabinet perceives that Treasury's forecast of revenues are understated by 10 per cent. Then $0.10 of every $1.00 of revenue 'shock' will be judged to be in fact a permanent change in revenue. If so, a cabinet that lets bygones be bygones would behave in a way such that we estimate $\beta_1 = -0.90$. That is, they budget for an increase in revenues equal to 10 per cent of the previous period's revenue shock. With this interpretation, the fact that $\beta_1$ is estimated to be less than unity in absolute value is a measure of the distrust cabinet has of Treasury forecasts. In a similar way, an estimated value of $\alpha_2$ less than unity in absolute value is indicative of the distrust cabinet has of Treasury's forecasts of spending requirements.[9]

A government that ignores past shocks should still find no reason to change $S_t$ in response to a revenue shock, even if it believes some of the revenue shock will prove to be permanent. Thus we should still find $\alpha_1 = 0$ for a government that is distrustful of forecasts. A positive value indicates the government has allowed spending to increase simply because revenue is thought to have permanently increased. Similarly, we should find $\beta_2 = 0$ from a government that is distrustful of forecasts.

The regression coefficient on the forecast of GDP also tells us something about government behaviour. In particular, in response to an expected $1 change in GDP, a government that lets bygones be bygones should budget for a change in revenue equal to the average value of its marginal tax rates. Thus, such a government allows tax revenues to play their automatic stabilizer role and we should expect $\beta_3$ to equal the average of its marginal tax rates. Similarly, such a government would budget to allow expenditures to respond automatically to expected changes in economic conditions. Thus, in response to an expected $1 increase in GDP, it should budget for a decrease in expenditures equal to the average of its marginal spending rates.[10] Significant departures from these values would indicate cabinet distrust of Treasury's GDP forecasts. If Treasury's forecasts of changes in GDP are also viewed with suspicion by the cabinet, this will affect the size of $\alpha_3$ regardless of whether the government ignores past shocks. In particular, if Treasury is believed to be underestimating positive GDP changes, the government will budget for a larger decrease in $S_t$ than otherwise, causing $\alpha_3$ to be larger in absolute value.

The regression constants also have an interpretation that tell us something about the fiscal behaviour of the government. Since we are estimating the *change* in revenue and spending in real per capita terms, the coefficients on the constants indicate the extent to which the Alberta government over time has sought to reduce the size of its average real per capita budget imbalance. Thus, other things being equal, the combination of a positive constant in the revenue equation and a negative constant in the spending equation would indicate that the government has sought to reduce the average size of its deficit. The opposite sign pattern would suggest a government seeking to increase the average size of its deficit and debt over time while two zero coefficients would indicate no effort to increase or decrease deficits over time.

Finally, it is useful to consider the definition and interpretation of our political variables. The political economy literature suggests many reasons why a government may find it advantageous to use its budget to try to influence election outcomes. The classic scenario is that government seeks to curry favour with voters by increasing spending and decreasing taxes before elections and then decreases spending and increases taxes afterward. This is based on the notion that voters are myopic and may therefore be 'bought' by increasing spending, decreasing taxes, and increasing the deficit just prior to elections. A number of other scenarios are also conceivable. It is possible, for example, that the government may increase spending in the years immediately following the election if it feels that it has been given a mandate to do so. Another possibility is that the government is seeking to appeal to the inherent fiscal conservativism of Albertans by decreasing spending prior to an election (thereby selling themselves as staunch fiscal conservatives) and then increasing spending following an election.

To investigate whether elections have influenced the budget behaviour of the Alberta government over our estimation period, we define an election dummy variable equal to one in fiscal years following an election. This approach allows for the possibility that spending and revenue are affected both before an election *and* after an election. Recall that our dependent variables are the *changes* in spending and revenue. Thus, if our dummy variable is equal to one for fiscal year t, the coefficient on that variable will measure the combined influence on spending in period t-1 (the year of the election) and in period t (the year after the election). If the government of Alberta has followed the classic scenario of increasing spending before an election and decreasing it afterward, we should therefore expect a negative coefficient on our election dummy. We would similarly expect a positive coefficient on the election dummy in the revenue equation. On the other hand, if the government has on average acted in one of the alternative manners suggested above—increasing government spending after an election—we would expect the opposite sign pattern to emerge.

## 5. EMPIRICAL RESULTS

Our estimates of changes in aggregate spending and revenue are derived from time series running from fiscal years 1970/1 to 1993/4. As mentioned, all variables are measured as real per capita values. All data are measured on a fiscal

**Table 1:** Summary Statistics on the Shock Variables, 1970/1–1993/4

|                           | RSHOCK    | SSHOCK  |
|---------------------------|-----------|---------|
| Mean                      | 8.7       | 20.0    |
| Standard Deviation        | 466.9     | 252.4   |
| Maximum Value             | 935.2     | 664.9   |
| Minimum Value             | −1,029.4  | −503.8  |
| Positive/Negative Values  | 10/14     | 14/10   |

year basis and are based on Statistics Canada national income accounting conventions. Total spending, S, excludes debt service costs and is thus program spending only. See Appendix 1 for a more complete description of the data.

Summary statistics on our RSHOCK and SSHOCK variables are presented in Table 1. The means of RSHOCK and SSHOCK are not significantly different from zero, and the correlation coefficient between them is −0.28. The other summary statistics in the table bear witness to the volatility of Alberta's economy and the resulting volatility in revenues and spending.

The RSHOCK and SSHOCK data are graphed in Figure 1. The spikes in RSHOCK mainly correspond to energy price shocks, but they also reflect our assumption that revenue forecasts are backward-looking. Thus, the large positive shock that followed the equally large negative shock due to the collapse of energy prices in 1986 reflects in part the partial recovery in energy prices but also reflects the forecasting method that puts significant weight on events in the recent past.

Support for our measures of spending and revenue shocks comes from the interviews of budget-makers in Boothe (1995). Budget-makers describe the steady increase in energy prices that occurred from 1973 to 1985 as being generally expected to be a permanent fixture. Thus the 45 per cent decline in the Alberta crude oil well-head price that occurred in 1986/7 was a rather unexpected and jolting shock. They also describe the recovery in energy prices in the following year and the increase in revenues due to the discovery of a large natural gas field near the town of Caroline as unexpected. The fact that our RSHOCK data describe these perceptions of budget-makers is thus encouraging. It is also encouraging that the plot of SSHOCK describes a spike in 1982/3. Boothe (1995) identifies an increase in expenditures in that fiscal year as being due to the introduction of the federal government's National Energy Program (NEP) and the response of the province to increase rebates to the energy industry to cushion the program's effects.

Our strategy is to estimate equations (2) and (3) using OLS (Ordinary Least Squares) and subject these estimates to specification tests. The results from

**Figure 1:** Revenue and Spending Shocks

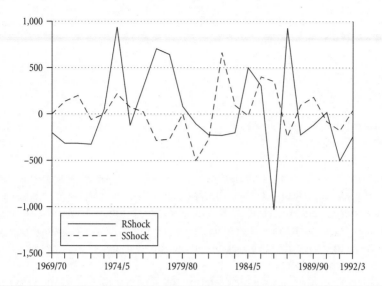

these regressions are presented in the table in Appendix 2. In these regressions, we could not reject the null hypothesis of the independence of residuals and for the most part the null hypothesis of the RESET specification test could be accepted. Given our interest in obtaining precise coefficient estimates, we tested for whether or not we were statistically able to omit variables so as to derive a more parsimonious specification. In choosing variables for possible omission, we limited our attention to variables whose t-statistic in the unrestricted regressions were less than unity. Columns (3) and (4) of the table in Appendix 2 show the OLS estimates and summary statistics of the preferred specification. Because of the likelihood of contemporaneous correlation of disturbances in the spending and revenue equations, we then estimated the model using the seemingly unrelated regression (SUR) approach. The SUR results are presented in Table 2.

We found that we could easily accept the null hypothesis of zero coefficients on the effect of revenue shocks in the spending equation and spending shocks in the revenue equation. These zero coefficients are consistent with the behaviour of a government that lets bygones be bygones. The coefficients on the expected change in real GDP are also consistent with this interpretation; this variable has no significant effect on spending and the effect on revenue easily falls within a range of values we expected for the average value of the province's marginal tax rates. In neither equation do we find evidence of a long-term trend towards larger or smaller spending or revenue collection per capita; that

**Table 2:** SUR Estimates

| Dependent Variable | Constant | Revenue Shock | Spending Shock | Expected $\Delta$GDP | Election Dummy |
|---|---|---|---|---|---|
| $\Delta S_t$ | 6.37 (81.33) | | −0.80 (0.27) | | 307.75 (151.10)* |
| $\Delta R_t$ | 136.54 (112.09) | −0.45 (0.22)* | | 0.29 (0.12)* | −468.70 (201.14)* |

NOTE: Standard errors are in parentheses. Asterisks indicate significance of a t-test at the 5 per cent level. On shock terms, the null hypothesis of the t-test is that the coefficient is *minus one*. On all other terms, the null hypothesis is that the coefficient is *zero*.

is, the constant terms are not significantly different from zero. In the spending equation, we cannot reject the null hypothesis that the response to a spending shock experienced in period t-1 has no effect on budgeted spending in period t. Thus, with respect to its aggregate spending behaviour, we cannot reject the hypothesis that the Alberta government has, on average, let bygones be bygones and ignored past shocks.

The results for the revenue equation are less supportive of the hypothesis that the government ignored past shocks. The coefficient measuring the response of revenue budgeted for period t in response to revenue shocks experienced in period t-1 is significantly smaller than unity in absolute value (t = 2.53). This suggests that approximately half of every extra dollar of revenue that is unexpectedly gained (lost) in period t-1 is built into the budget of period t. This indicates, then, that the government has, on average, allowed past revenue shocks to influence its current budgeting choices.

Our alternative interpretation of why revenue shocks in period t-1 may yield a coefficient significantly different from minus one is that ministers do not trust the revenue forecasts of Alberta Treasury. Anecdotal evidence supporting this possibility again comes from Boothe (1995). In particular, Boothe cites former Premier Don Getty as saying he felt Treasury consistently underestimated revenues during the period of rising energy prices. A number of other officials Boothe interviewed suggested this consistent underestimation caused Treasury to lose credibility in the eyes of Treasury Board members.

The coefficient on our election dummy proved to be significantly different from zero at the 5 per cent level in both equations. The *significance* of the coefficients suggests the presence of a political business cycle. The *signs* of the coefficients suggest that governments in Alberta have not typically followed the classic scenario of increasing expenditures and decreasing revenues prior to elections and then doing the opposite after elections. Instead, on average, the opposite pattern comes through. The parameter estimates in Table 2 suggest that in Alberta the provincial government has typically decreased spending and increased revenue prior to elections and increased spending and cut revenues afterward.

The sign pattern on the election dummy suggests two interpretations. One is that the provincial government has tended to respond to the inherent fiscal conservatism of Albertans[11] by decreasing spending, increasing revenues, and decreasing the deficit prior to an election (thereby selling themselves as staunch fiscal conservatives), and then increasing spending, decreasing revenue, and increasing the deficit following an election. Another possibility is that the government responded to the mandate it was perceived to have received from the electorate to increase spending. The interview study by Boothe (1995) offers anecdotal evidence in support of the latter interpretation. Peter Lougheed, premier over much of our estimation period, from 1971 to 1985, stated that one of the key aims of his Conservative government was to modernize and reform the social programs it had inherited from the past, programs that had been introduced by the very conservative Social Credit Party that had governed the province since the mid-1930s. Our estimates suggest he preferred to ratchet spending upward only on receiving a new mandate to do so—a sensible policy, perhaps, given a very conservative electorate.

One of the claims made by the budget-makers interviewed by Boothe is that positive revenue shocks tended to derail deficit reduction efforts because they were often judged to be permanent. In Table 3 we present estimates of a variation of our model that allow us to investigate whether the government has, on average, reacted differently to positive versus negative shocks.[12] In preliminary regressions (see columns 5 to 8 in Appendix 2) we again found support for a parsimonious specification where revenue shocks exert no influence on budgeted spending and spending shocks exert no influence on revenue plans.

The previous result—that we cannot reject the null hypothesis of the government ignoring past shocks in current budgeting on the spending side—continues to hold true; neither positive nor negative spending shocks in period t-1 elicit any statistically significant response in period t spending plans. On the revenue side, we now see evidence of a different response to positive versus negative shocks. An unexpected *loss* in revenue in period t-1 (a negative shock) has no influence on period t revenues. If, however, there is an unexpected *gain* in revenue in period t-1 (a positive shock), revenues in period t are budgeted for an estimated increase of $0.92 for every $1.00 revenue shock. In other words, our estimates suggest that bad news with respect to revenues is ignored while good news is seen to be permanent and incorporated into future budgets. Thus the perception of the budget-makers in the Boothe interviews—that positive revenue shocks tended to be viewed as permanent—finds empirical support in these coefficients. Not revealed in the interviews, but seen here, is the size of this response to positive revenue shocks and the fact that negative revenue shocks were typically ignored. If the response of positive revenue shocks was due to ministers distrusting Treasury's revenue forecasts as being too low, then these results are particularly interesting because of the asymmetry in ministers'

**Table 3:** SUR Estimates

| Dependent Variable | Constant | Revenue Shock (+) | Revenue Shock (−) | Spending Shock (+) | Spending Shock (−) | Expected ΔGDP | Election Dummy |
|---|---|---|---|---|---|---|---|
| $\Delta S_t$ | −51.33 (106.27) | | | −0.49 (0.45) | −1.17 (0.53) | | 295.03 (150.35)** |
| $\Delta R_t$ | −34.43 (160.44) | −0.08 (0.32)* | −1.04 (0.46) | | | 0.31 (0.12)* | −491.46 (195.70)* |

NOTE: Standard errors are in parentheses. Asterisks indicate significance at the 5 per cent (*) and 10 per cent (**) levels. On shock terms, the null hypothesis is that the coefficient is *minus one*. On all other terms, the null hypothesis is that the coefficient is *zero*.

perceptions. That is, while Treasury's forecasts of positive shocks may have been seen to be too low, its forecasts of negative shocks were not, on average, perceived to be underestimates.

## 6. SUMMARY AND CONCLUSIONS

The purpose of this chapter was to study the budgetary response of the Alberta government to unanticipated shocks to its revenues and expenditures. We tested the null hypothesis that over the 1970/1 to 1993/4 period the government let bygones be bygones when budgeting: that is, that it ignored past revenue and spending shocks when making current budget choices, allowing the government deficit to play an automatic stabilizer role. Using a methodology motivated in part by Poterba (1994), we found that we could not reject this hypothesis with respect to the government's spending behaviour. On average, past shocks to spending and revenues did not affect current expenditures. In contrast, we can reject the null hypothesis with respect to the government's budgeting with respect to revenue. We found that, on average, approximately half of unexpected changes in government revenues were incorporated into current revenue plans. Further investigation revealed that this behaviour was limited to positive revenue shocks. While an expected loss in revenue in the previous period had no impact on current revenue budgeting, for every dollar in unexpected revenue gained, $0.92 was incorporated into the current budget. We also found evidence of a rather interesting political business cycle in Alberta, in which government spending increased (fell), revenues fell (increased), and deficits increased (decreased) in the year immediately following (prior to) an election.

Since coming to power in late 1992, the Klein government has introduced a large number of changes to the budget process. These are detailed by Paul Boothe in the previous chapter. It is interesting to ask to what extent these changes might be viewed as a response to the experience the Alberta government has had with fiscal shocks. For example, the Deficit Elimination Act (DEA) requires that higher than planned revenues must be used to reduce debt. This might be judged a response to our finding that unexpected revenues have in the past tended to be built into next year's revenues, virtually dollar for dollar. Similarly, the requirement in the Balanced Budget and Debt Reduction Act (BBDRA) that corporate income tax and natural resource revenues be budgeted to be the lesser of 90 per cent of forecast or the five-year moving average of past revenue from these sources might be viewed as a response to the tendency to build unexpected revenue increases into the next budget's revenues. Using the average of the past five years of revenue from these two relatively volatile revenue sources will require budget-makers to weight such shocks less heavily than they have shown a tendency to do in the past.

One aspect of the changes to the budget process introduced by the Klein government is not explained by our empirical results. The reduction in the power of 'spending' ministers that has accompanied the introduction of Standing Policy Committees, three-year business plans, and the DEA and BBDRA would seem to suggest an experience with ministers responding to unexpected increases in spending by building them into next year's budget. Our results show that no such response has typified aggregate spending over the 1970/1–1993/4 period. The effort to limit spending choices may therefore indicate that looking at aggregate spending is misleading because it hides a response that appears only in certain departments at certain times and that the current government judges to be undesirable. We intend to address this possibility in future research.

Finally, an important element of the BBDRA is the requirement for annually balanced budgets. As discussed at the beginning of the chapter, unlike most US states, Canadian provinces in general, and Alberta in particular, have historically not had to budget in an environment where they are restricted by statute from running a deficit. This gives rise to the possibility that unexpected spending and revenue shocks can be cushioned by the deficit (surplus), so that governments can choose to let bygones be bygones. The introduction of balanced budget legislation substantially restricts the government's flexibility in this regard, particularly when viewed in conjunction with the move towards consolidated financial accounting, which makes it difficult to hide government expenditures off-budget.[13] The BBDRA effectively requires that positive revenue shocks be used to pay down the debt, while negative revenue shocks must be met with either an increase in tax rates or a reduction in spending. Both positive and negative spending shocks must be similarly offset on either the spending or revenue side. Thus, with the exception of positive revenue shocks, which are required to pay down the debt, the BBDRA explicitly does not allow the government to let bygones be bygones.

To some extent, this problem has been addressed in the BBDRA by the requirement that the government budget natural resource and corporate income tax revenues conservatively. This provides the government with a revenue cushion designed to absorb unexpected shocks. In essence, then, the Klein government has simply restricted the automatic stabilizer role of the budget to the size of these revenue cushions. For the fiscal year 1996/7, the government has budgeted a revenue cushion of $545 million. Our measures of spending and revenue shocks indicate that over the 1970/1–1993/4 period, the average unexpected increase in the deficit was only $38.7 million but with a maximum shock of $1,745 million (both measured in 1994 dollars). Thus, while on average the revenue cushion will prove sufficient to act as an automatic stabilizer, it will sometimes prove to be too small and require spending cuts and tax increases. Whether this is a good or bad thing is a matter open to judgement. Against the cost of possibly having to change spending and tax rates in a pro-cyclical way should shocks exceed the revenue cushions, one must weigh the benefit of limiting the likelihood of budget deficits growing too large, too quickly. Whether the Klein government has restricted the automatic stabilizer role of the budget by an amount deemed acceptable to voters will only be answered with time. In particular, this will only be answered after Albertans have experienced a spending cut and/or a tax increase resulting from an unexpected shock, such as that experienced in 1986, which increased the deficit by an amount exceeding the revenue cushions.

## APPENDIX 1: DATA SOURCES AND MEASUREMENT

Government spending and revenue data come from Statistics Canada (Cat. Nos. 68–512 and 68–212). The price of oil, measured as the price of Alberta crude oil at the wellhead, was kindly provided by Paul Boothe. Government revenue and expenditure data are measured on a fiscal year basis. These data were deflated using a measure of Alberta's CPI (Consumer Price Index). This series was constructed from monthly observations on the 'all items' CPI for Edmonton and Calgary (62–010). These indexes were weighted by these cities' relative populations and then used to create a fiscal year measure. All data were further adjusted to become per capita measures using monthly data on Alberta's population (91–001), which was used to create fiscal year data. Provincial nominal GDP data (13–213) are only available on a calendar year basis. To generate a fiscal year series, we calculated $GDP_t = 0.75^*Q_{t-1} + 0.25^*Q_t$, where $Q$ = output measured on a calendar year basis and GDP = output measured on a fiscal year basis. Our election year dummy variable was set equal to one for the first fiscal year following each provincial election. Fiscal years run from 1 April to 31 March and are defined for the year ending 31 March. Elections were held in August 1971, March 1975, March 1979, November 1982, May 1986, March 1989, and June 1993. Our dummy variable was set equal to one for fiscal years 1973, 1976, 1980, 1983, 1987, 1990, and 1994.

The real per capita data were subjected to various Dickey-Fuller tests for non-stationarity. All series were found to be integrated of order one, indicating the need first to differentiate the data. We thank Shelley Radway for performing these tests.

## APPENDIX 2: OLS ESTIMATES

| Dependent Variable | $\Delta S_t$ (1) | $\Delta R_t$ (2) | $\Delta S_t$ (3) | $\Delta R_t$ (4) | $\Delta S_t$ (5) | $\Delta R_t$ (6) | $\Delta S_t$ (7) | $\Delta R_t$ (8) |
|---|---|---|---|---|---|---|---|---|
| Constant | 10.64 (93.81) | 138.85 (126.27) | 6.45 (86.95) | 138.02 (123.04) | −24.89 (182.01) | 48.56 (243.35) | −42.28 (117.57) | −13.37 (184.35) |
| Revenue Shock | 0.15 (0.19) | −0.41 (0.26)* | | −0.40 (0.25)* | | | | |
| Revenue Shock (+) | | | | | −0.06 (0.31) | −0.04 (0.42)* | | −0.10 (0.37)* |
| Revenue Shock (−) | | | | | 0.35 (0.42) | −0.94 (0.57) | | −0.93 (0.53) |
| Spending Shock | −0.73 (0.32) | −0.07 (0.44) | −0.81 (0.30) | | | | | |
| Spending Shock (+) | | | | | −0.22 (0.67) | −0.42 (0.89) | −0.56 (0.50) | |
| Spending Shock (−) | | | | | −1.28 (0.73) | 0.28 (0.98) | −1.13 (0.59) | |
| Expected $\Delta$GDP | 0.004 (0.10) | 0.29 (0.14)* | | 0.29 (0.14)* | 0.06 (0.14) | 0.28 (0.18) | | 0.33 (0.14)* |
| Election Dummy | 280.05 (169.65) | −470.06 (228.36)* | 308.40 (161.56)** | −475.12 (220.46)* | 265.84 (176.47) | −475.47 (233.73)** | 298.08 (164.77)** | −496.55 (220.20)* |
| $\overline{R}^2$ | 0.22 | 0.20 | 0.26 | 0.24 | 0.18 | 0.17 | 0.24 | 0.25 |
| LM (1) | 0.12 | 2.92 | 0.59 | 2.67 | 0.02 | 4.44* | 0.95 | 4.17* |
| LM (2) | 0.06 | 1.45 | 0.28 | 1.38 | 0.02 | 2.24 | 0.49 | 2.31 |
| RESET (1) | 1.78 | 0.87 | 2.07 | 0.66 | 0.77 | 1.56 | 3.28** | 1.32 |
| RESET (2) | 2.32 | 5.57* | 2.67** | 5.50* | 2.38 | 2.47 | 3.03** | 2.03 |
| F-test on Zero Restrictions | | | 0.39 | 0.02 | | | 0.48 | 0.90 |

NOTE: LM is a test of the null hypothesis of no serially correlated disturbances. RESET is a test of the null hypothesis that the given specification is correct against the alternative that some unspecified alternative is correct. Each of these tests was performed for one and two terms. Asterisks denote rejection of the null at the 5 per cent (*) and 10 per cent (**) levels. Standard errors of regression coefficients are in parentheses. Asterisks on standard errors denote significance at the 5 per cent (*) and 10 per cent (**) levels on a t-test. On coefficients measuring the response to Spending (Revenue) Shocks in regressions where the dependent variable is $\Delta S$ ($\Delta R$), the null hypothesis of this test is that the coefficient is equal to *negative one*. For all other coefficients, the null hypothesis is that the coefficient is *zero*.

## NOTES

1. We thank Herb Emery and Dan Gordon for comments on an earlier draft and Shelley Radway for research assistance. We are, of course, solely responsible for errors.

2. The correlation coefficient between real per capita GDP in Alberta and the real price of oil is 0.62.

3. See the discussion in Kneebone, Chapter 4, for more details.

4. Growing voter dissatisfaction with and concern over government deficits has recently caused a number of provinces to introduce balanced budget legislation. See Boothe, Chapter 6, for discussion.

5. Treasury Board is a cabinet committee primarily responsible for budgetary matters.

6. This choice was dictated by the time series properties of the data. Various Dickey-Fuller tests for non-stationarity were performed and these indicated the need to first difference the data.

7. See McKenzie and Kneebone, Chapters 3 and 4, respectively, for discussion of political business cycle models.

8. An alternative to estimating our own revenue and spending forecasts is to use the government's forecasts published in budget papers. Shocks, then, are simply the difference between budget projections and observed data. The problem with this approach is that it is not uncommon for governments to make no budgetary provisions for certain expenditures. In his interviews with Alberta budget-makers, for example, Boothe (1995) notes that participants drew attention to the fact that it was common for the government to make no provision for public-sector wage settlements in order to protect the government's bargaining position. Others noted that conservative spending assumptions were often used to keep budgeted amounts smaller. For reasons such as these, we preferred to derive independent measures of shocks.

9. This is conditional on the presumption that the autoregressive forecasting approach discussed above is a reasonable approximation of Treasury forecasts.

10. By regressing $\Delta R$ on the change in real GDP we get a guesstimate of the government's marginal tax rate to be 0.28 with a standard error of 0.05. Thus we judge

0.23 > $\beta_3$ > 0.35 to indicate that the government has ignored past shocks and had confidence in Treasury's GDP forecasts. Regressing $\Delta S$ against $\Delta$GDP yields a zero coefficient with a large standard error.

11. For more on this, see the analysis of Archer and Gibbins in Chapter 13.

12. We defined a dummy variable, RDUM, equal to unity in fiscal years when revenue shocks are positive and zero otherwise. We then created two variables, R(+) = RDUM*RSHOCK and R(−) = RSHOCK − RDUM*RSHOCK, to represent data on positive and negative revenue shocks respectively. With this approach the estimated coefficients on R(+) and R(−) measure the separate influence of positive and negative shocks on budget choices. The same approach was followed to create data on positive and negative spending shocks.

13. For more on this, see Boothe, Chapter 6.

## REFERENCES

Boothe, P. (1995), 'Economic Reality and the Perceptions of Budget Makers', in Boothe, *The Growth of Government Spending in Alberta*. Canadian Tax Paper No. 100. Ottawa: Canadian Tax Foundation.

North, D. (1990), *Institutions, Institutional Change and Economic Performance*. Cambridge: Cambridge University Press.

Poterba, J. (1994), 'State Responses to Fiscal Crises: The Effects of Fiscal Institutions and Politics', *Journal of Political Economy* 102 (4).

Wilsford, D. (1994), 'Path Dependency, or Why History Makes It Difficult but Not Impossible to Reform Health Care Systems in a Big Way', *Journal of Public Policy* 14 (3): 251–83.

# PART III

# Implementation by Department

# CHAPTER 8

# Family and Social Services, the Alberta Deficit Elimination Program, and Welfare Reform

*M.S. Shedd*

## 1. INTRODUCTION[1]

During the 1992 election campaign, the Progressive Conservatives under Ralph Klein promised that, if elected, they would eliminate the provincial government deficit. After winning the election the Klein government proceeded to work towards fulfilling this promise. Initially, all government departments were asked to develop plans to cut their spending by approximately 20 per cent. While the final implementation of the budget cuts have allowed some variation in the level of cuts, all departments have had to make substantial cuts. The Department of Family and Social Services (FSS) was not exempt—between 1992/3 and 1994/5 its budget was reduced by 21.42 per cent. This paper considers the effects of the balanced budget policy and the concomitant welfare reforms on FSS.

Under its mandate, FSS is responsible for the administration of a number of programs. In its *Business Plan 1994–95 to 1996–97* it groups these responsibilities under a number of general areas. These areas are:

- income and employment support;
- services to people with disabilities;
- child welfare;
- family support services;
- aboriginal affairs.

Of these various responsibilities, the first requires the largest share of the department's total budget. While the level of spending is not an index of the importance or worth of a program, it is relevant for our consideration of the Alberta provincial budget-cutting process under the Klein government. Table 1 gives actual expenditures for FSS for the 1992/3 fiscal year.

**Table 1:** FSS Operating Budget 1992/3 (millions of dollars)

| | |
|---|---|
| Income and Employment Programs | 1,156.7 |
| Services to People with Disabilities | 187.6 |
| Child Welfare Services | 157.6 |
| Day Care | 71.1 |
| Office for the Prevention of Family Violence | 7.3 |
| Premier's Council in Support of Alberta Families | 0.5 |
| Métis Settlements Accord | 7.1 |
| Balance of Department | 76.9 |
| Statutory Expenditure | 30.0 |
| Total Operating | 1,694.8 |

SOURCE: Department of Family and Social Services, *Business Plan 1994–95 to 1996–97*, Edmonton.

The largest line entry is for income and employment support. The programs included here made up 68.2 per cent of the total budget. Since this paper deals with the budget-cutting process, most of the discussion will be directed at these programs. Most of the expenditures within this line item could be simply referred to as social assistance or welfare. This emphasis on welfare is even more appropriate because the projected 1997/8 budget targets cited in the department's *Business Plan 1995–96 to 1997–98* call for modest increases in most of the other areas. In a very real sense it is just welfare spending that has been cut in Alberta.

## 2. HISTORICAL BACKGROUND AND INTERPROVINCIAL COMPARISONS

The province has provided some form of social assistance since the Great Depression. In general, Alberta's expenditures on direct relief have been near or above the national average. Table 2 provides data on the development of direct relief payments in Alberta for selected years.

As Table 2 shows, welfare payments in Alberta increased dramatically between 1961 and 1993. The largest percentage increased occurred between 1961 and 1966. The federally funded Canada Assistance Plan (CAP) was introduced in 1966. The CAP was intended to replace the hit-and-miss provincially funded programs by establishing national standards with federal funding. It resulted in a significant increase in the level of social assistance. Direct relief

**Table 2:** Alberta—Direct Relief Payments for Selected Years

| Year | 1981 dollars per capita | Per cent of GDP |
|------|------------------------|-----------------|
| 1961 | 7.15   | 0.1 |
| 1966 | 48.64  | 0.5 |
| 1971 | 83.72  | 0.8 |
| 1976 | 100.32 | 0.6 |
| 1980 | 94.89  | 0.4 |
| 1981 | 103.04 | 0.5 |
| 1982 | 130.45 | 0.6 |
| 1983 | 155.01 | 0.8 |
| 1984 | 149.57 | 0.7 |
| 1985 | 163.76 | 0.7 |
| 1986 | 179.03 | 1.0 |
| 1987 | 207.59 | 1.2 |
| 1988 | 208.91 | 1.2 |
| 1989 | 206.62 | 1.2 |
| 1990 | 199.76 | 1.1 |
| 1991 | 216.87 | 1.3 |
| 1992 | 241.15 | 1.4 |
| 1993 | 251.01 | 1.3 |

SOURCES: Calculated from data in Statistics Canada, *Provincial Economic Accounts* (various years) (13–213); and *Canadian Economic Observer, Historical Statistical Supplement* (various years) (11–210), Ottawa.

payments both in real dollar value and as a per cent of GDP rose sharply in the 1960s. This trend did not continue into the seventies. Direct relief payments per capita increased only slightly more than $11 between 1971 and 1980. As a percentage of GDP, direct relief payments actually fell 50 per cent during the same period. It is also possible to see a hint of a cyclical pattern. Welfare payments rose significantly in 1983. Similarly, assistance payments rose in the early 1990s. However, there is only a very slight decrease in payments following the recession of the early eighties. In fact, by 1985 welfare was increasing again. Whether this same 'ratcheting effect' would have occurred after the recession of the early nineties is impossible to say because the budget-cutting of the Klein government forced welfare payments down.

**Table 3:** Average Monthly Caseloads in Alberta 1980/1–1992/3

| Year | Caseload |
|------|----------|
| 1980/1 | 30,010 |
| 1981/2 | 31,561 |
| 1982/3 | 42,175 |
| 1983/4 | 45,070 |
| 1984/5 | 47,896 |
| 1985/6 | 54,868 |
| 1986/7 | 62,813 |
| 1987/8 | 68,014 |
| 1988/9 | 67,732 |
| 1989/90 | 67,214 |
| 1990/1 | 66,989 |
| 1991/2 | 76,935 |
| 1992/3 | 88,978 |

SOURCE: Compiled by Carol Sharman of the Alberta Department of Family and Social Services Library, Edmonton.

Of course, two factors affect the level of assistance payments. These are the number of recipients and the rate at which they are paid. Table 3 shows the average monthly caseload for Alberta by fiscal years between 1980/1 and 1992/3.[2] Over that period the number of recipients increased by nearly 300 per cent.

The caseload figures show the same ratcheting as was evident in per capita direct relief payments. There was a sharp increase in the average monthly caseload in 1982/3 but no corresponding decline in the caseload following the recession. There was another sharp increase in the caseload with the onset of the recession of the early nineties. Again, it is impossible to say what would have happened to the caseload after the recession because of the change in government policy. It is interesting to note that the increase in caseload was proportionally greater than the increase in direct relief payments per capita.

As mentioned earlier, Alberta direct relief payments per capita have generally been near or even above the national average. A number of variables could determine the level of direct relief payments provided by a province. The most important factors are likely to be the level of need, the preferences of the voters, and the ability to pay. While the level of need is subjective, it is possible to agree on a standard definition. Interestingly, the CAP does not attempt to provide any such uniform definition. One might suppose that the level of need would be highest in a province with high long-term unemployment or with a large proportion of its population with low incomes. Assuming that a satisfactory definition of need can be agreed upon, the level of social assistance is going to depend on a willingness and ability to pay. With regard to the ability to pay one would assume that the three 'have' provinces, Ontario, Alberta, and British Columbia, would have the greatest ability to pay. On the other hand, the 'have-not' provinces, particularly Newfoundland, would have the least ability to pay. In effect, even with federal cost-sharing under the CAP, the provinces with the greatest need would be the provinces with the least ability to pay. Table 4 compares the level of direct assistance for all provinces for selected years since 1961. Provincial payments are given as index numbers with the Canadian per capita level of assistance being defined as 100 for each year.

In 1961 there was substantial variation in the level of support by province. Two provinces, Prince Edward Island and New Brunswick, provided no direct relief at that time. At the other extreme, Newfoundland provided support at 11 times the national average. The implementation of the CAP in 1966 resulted in greater uniformity. Newfoundland's level of support dropped to less than five times the national average and Prince Edward Island began making payments for the first time. New Brunswick began welfare the following year. By 1971 payments were far more uniform across Canada. Still, substantial variation does exist. From 1980 to 1993 four provinces consistently provided more direct relief per capita than the national average. Of these, two (New Brunswick and Quebec) are provinces that might be defined as 'have-not' provinces and two (Alberta and British Columbia) might be referred to as 'have' provinces. In light of Alberta's history of relatively generous welfare payments, the Klein cuts might be regarded as a marked change in policy. Moreover, Table 4 seems to indicate that, in relative terms at least, Alberta had some room to manoeuvre in terms of cutting direct assistance. However, as discussed below, this may be somewhat misleading. Ontario, on the other hand, has traditionally had the lowest per capita level of welfare payments. The recent cuts in that province do not represent a new policy but perhaps just a return to past policy.

While per capita direct relief payments serve as an index of the total level of welfare support in a province, it is determined by two variables—the number of recipients and the level of assistance. A province may have a high per capita expenditure on welfare because of a relatively large caseload or a relatively generous payment to those on welfare. Table 5 compares the levels of welfare payments for all provinces for 1986 and 1989–94. The values are based on basic levels of assistance. As can be seen, even before the Klein cuts, the level of individual support in Alberta was relatively low compared to most other

**Table 4:** Level of Provincial Direct Assistance per Capita (Canada = 100)

| Year | NF | PE | NS | NB | PQ | ON | MB | SK | AB | BC |
|------|------|-----|-----|-----|-----|-----|-----|-----|-----|-----|
| 1961 | 1,169 | — | 218 | — | 30 | 9 | 351 | 59 | 122 | 122 |
| 1966 | 485 | 126 | 92 | — | 114 | 36 | 160 | 175 | 239 | 52 |
| 1971 | 216 | 113 | 77 | 145 | 151 | 57 | 96 | 133 | 109 | 58 |
| 1976 | 144 | 113 | 87 | 142 | 132 | 69 | 75 | 170 | 107 | 85 |
| 1980 | 136 | 167 | 84 | 153 | 146 | 56 | 61 | 123 | 93 | 121 |
| 1981 | 117 | 143 | 80 | 154 | 158 | 54 | 68 | 117 | 98 | 104 |
| 1982 | 101 | 146 | 75 | 145 | 144 | 51 | 61 | 131 | 110 | 142 |
| 1983 | 92 | 101 | 68 | 132 | 145 | 48 | 59 | 121 | 113 | 161 |
| 1984 | 82 | 92 | 67 | 132 | 142 | 49 | 60 | 120 | 104 | 165 |
| 1985 | 82 | 85 | 65 | 130 | 145 | 50 | 58 | 153 | 110 | 150 |
| 1986 | 83 | 82 | 65 | 140 | 149 | 51 | 59 | 189 | 121 | 141 |
| 1987 | 88 | 91 | 68 | 141 | 134 | 57 | 64 | 111 | 142 | 140 |
| 1988 | 86 | 96 | 72 | 145 | 126 | 64 | 67 | 101 | 145 | 133 |
| 1989 | 91 | 97 | 76 | 143 | 121 | 69 | 68 | 91 | 145 | 128 |
| 1990 | 102 | 104 | 75 | 139 | 116 | 78 | 72 | 82 | 132 | 120 |
| 1991 | 92 | 101 | 73 | 127 | 117 | 86 | 70 | 77 | 123 | 121 |
| 1992 | 99 | 78 | 70 | 119 | 111 | 88 | 61 | 73 | 120 | 124 |
| 1993 | 102 | 96 | 73 | 108 | 112 | 86 | 59 | 81 | 119 | 126 |

SOURCE: Calculated from data in Statistics Canada, *Provincial Economic Accounts* (various years) (13–213), Ottawa.

provinces. For example, in 1986 Alberta ranked seventh in the level of support for single employables. In 1990 Alberta had the lowest level of assistance for a single disabled. In 1992 Alberta ranked seventh for single employables, tenth for single disabled, ninth for a single parent with one child, and fifth for a couple with two children. Since Table 4 shows that Alberta had above average expenditures on welfare, the province must have had a relatively large caseload. That is, in the past the province appears to have maintained a policy of granting relatively low benefits to a large number of people. As will be discussed below, the reforms to the welfare system can be viewed as a direct response to this characteristic of social assistance in Alberta.

**Table 5:** Welfare Benefits by Province, Selected Years

| | 1986 | 1989 | 1990 | 1991 | 1992 | 1993 | 1994 |
|---|---|---|---|---|---|---|---|
| **NEWFOUNDLAND** | | | | | | | |
| 1 Employable | 4,429 | 4,270 | 4,249 | 4,181 | 4,387 | 4,335 | 4,326 |
| 1 Disabled | N/A | 8,602 | 8,520 | 8,259 | 8,438 | 8,327 | 8,310 |
| 1 Adult, 1 Child | 11,104 | 10,871 | 10,861 | 10,977 | 11,422 | 11,285 | 11,262 |
| Couple, 2 Children | 12,845 | 12,576 | 12,559 | 12,150 | 12,361 | 12,210 | 12,186 |
| **PRINCE EDWARD ISLAND** | | | | | | | |
| 1 Employable | 8,226 | 7,956 | 7,926 | 7,919 | 8,029 | 7,972 | 7,160 |
| 1 Disabled | N/A | 9,259 | 9,173 | 9,038 | 9,143 | 9,066 | 8,952 |
| 1 Adult, 1 Child | 11,340 | 10,967 | 11,064 | 10,971 | 11,138 | 11,074 | 10,860 |
| Couple, 2 Children | 16,617 | 16,335 | 16,349 | 16,436 | 16,629 | 16,504 | 16,183 |
| **NOVA SCOTIA** | | | | | | | |
| 1 Employable | 6,046 | 6,738 | 6,435 | 6,117 | 6,022 | 5,916 | 5,904 |
| 1 Disabled | N/A | 8,870 | 8,822 | 8,690 | 8,568 | 8,417 | 8,568 |
| 1 Adult, 1 Child | 10,470 | 10,782 | 10,712 | 10,580 | 10,575 | 10,389 | 10,560 |
| Couple, 2 Children | 12,603 | 13,715 | 13,117 | 12,672 | 12,681 | 12,497 | 12,472 |
| **NEW BRUNSWICK** | | | | | | | |
| 1 Employable | 2,980 | 3,223 | 3,177 | 3,108 | 3,109 | 3,066 | 3,084 |
| 1 Disabled | N/A | 8,444 | 8,319 | 8,073 | 8,078 | 8,028 | 8,096 |
| 1 Adult, 1 Child | 8,950 | 8,737 | 8,608 | 8,412 | 8,470 | 8,497 | 8,844 |
| Couple, 2 Children | 9,682 | 9,452 | 9,299 | 9,208 | 9,504 | 9,531 | 9,876 |
| **QUÉBEC** | | | | | | | |
| 1 Employable | 3,137 | 4,028 | 5,721 | 5,938 | 6,114 | 6,132 | 6,000 |
| 1 Disabled | N/A | 7,242 | 7,518 | 7,729 | 7,962 | 7,960 | 8,088 |
| 1 Adult, 1 Child | 10,555 | 9,787 | 10,437 | 9,547 | 10,835 | 11,287 | 11,528 |
| Couple, 2 Children | 13,642 | 12,781 | 12,516 | 12,879 | 13,311 | 13,707 | 13,524 |
| **ONTARIO** | | | | | | | |
| 1 Employable | 6,704 | 7,204 | 7,871 | 8,075 | 8,350 | 8,323 | 8,326 |
| 1 Disabled | N/A | 10,401 | 11,104 | 11,344 | 11,528 | 11,463 | 11,466 |
| 1 Adult, 1 Child | 12,006 | 12,928 | 14,499 | 14,849 | 15,113 | 15,091 | 15,098 |
| Couple, 2 Children | 14,944 | 16,314 | 19,024 | 19,370 | 19,784 | 19,734 | 19,562 |
| **MANITOBA** | | | | | | | |
| 1 Employable | 6,651 | 6,898 | 6,993 | 6,906 | 7,044 | 7,054 | 6,642 |
| 1 Disabled | N/A | 7,501 | 7,409 | 7,283 | 8,952 | 8,062 | 7,997 |
| 1 Adult, 1 Child | 10,276 | 10,066 | 9,952 | 9,782 | 10,830 | 9,716 | 9,636 |
| Couple, 2 Children | 15,569 | 16,337 | 17,590 | 17,590 | 18,096 | 16,805 | 17,097 |
| **SASKATCHEWAN** | | | | | | | |
| 1 Employable | 5,568 | 5,570 | 5,448 | 5,284 | 5,483 | 5,772 | 5,760 |
| 1 Disabled | N/A | 9,076 | 8,796 | 8,454 | 8,374 | 8,297 | 8,280 |
| 1 Adult, 1 Child | 11,424 | 11,376 | 11,060 | 10,643 | 10,517 | 10,402 | 10,381 |
| Couple, 2 Children | 16,026 | 15,785 | 15,338 | 14,738 | 14,977 | 14,772 | 14,800 |
| **ALBERTA** | | | | | | | |
| 1 Employable | 7,923 | 5,504 | 5,254 | 5,713 | 5,753 | 5,423 | 4,728 |
| 1 Disabled | N/A | 6,807 | 6,498 | 6,841 | 6,793 | 6,595 | 6,568 |
| 1 Adult, 1 Child | 11,601 | 10,321 | 9,853 | 10,336 | 10,306 | 9,896 | 9,192 |
| Couple, 2 Children | 17,248 | 15,206 | 14,516 | 15,998 | 16,010 | 15,421 | 14,472 |
| **BRITISH COLUMBIA** | | | | | | | |
| 1 Employable | 5,781 | 6,342 | 6,483 | 6,380 | 6,573 | 6,598 | 6,754 |
| 1 Disabled | N/A | 8,752 | 9,052 | 8,843 | 9,228 | 9,295 | 9,500 |
| 1 Adult, 1 Child | 10,410 | 11,457 | 11,577 | 11,343 | 11,851 | 11,898 | 12,176 |
| Couple, 2 Children | 14,219 | 14,310 | 14,407 | 14,072 | 14,993 | 15,089 | 15,527 |

NOTE: Separate rates for single disabled persons were not available for 1986. It is assumed that at a minimum, they would have qualified at the single employable rate.

SOURCE: National Council of Welfare, *Welfare Income 1994* (Ottawa: 1995).

## 3. THE BUDGET CUTS IN FAMILY AND SOCIAL SERVICES

The changes in FSS were strongly influenced by the opinions of Mike Cardinal, the department's minister. Cardinal's experiences, both as an aboriginal and as a social worker, had led him to believe that FSS should shift its emphasis from the provision of financial assistance to the provision of counselling and education for those who needed assistance entering (or returning to) the labour market.

The first step in this change was to divide welfare recipients into two groups: those who were considered to be capable of functioning in the competitive labour market and those who were not. The latter group was composed primarily of children and the disabled. Funds to this group were left virtually unaffected. Total expenditures on child welfare programs[3] decreased by $29.4 million, or 7.3 per cent, between the 1992/3 and 1995/6 budget years, and expenditures on support for the disabled[4] increased by $37.5 million, or 9.7 per cent, over the same period. In contrast, expenditures on programs for those who were considered capable of working decreased by $321.7 million, or 35.9 per cent (Alberta Family and Social Services, 1996).

The latter reduction resulted from three changes to FSS policy: a reduction in the value of benefits available to welfare recipients, a transfer of clients to the Department of Advanced Education and Career Development, and a tightening of the eligibility rules for collecting welfare payments. Table 6 summarizes some of the most important changes made to welfare benefits between 1992/3 and 1995/6. Single employable adults suffered the largest percentage reduction, 18.8 per cent, but the smallest absolute reduction, $106 per month. The cuts left both single parents and families with more income from FSS than they could have received from one individual working 40 hours per week at Alberta's minimum wage of $5.00 per hour. (At that wage, an individual would earn $866.67 per month for a 40-hour week.) Nevertheless, Table 6 indicates that these reductions did not have an appreciable effect on Alberta's relative standing in Canada between 1992 and 1994, partly because many other provinces also reduced their benefits during that period.

At the beginning of the period of restructuring, May 1993, FSS recorded 47,646 caseloads receiving funds for 'employment and training'. Many of those individuals, however, were obtaining their training in programs operated by the Department of Advanced Education and Career Development (AECD). Approximately 9,000 of these cases and $60 million of funding (approximately 20 per cent of the reduction in funding to FSS), were transferred to AECD.

Eligibility requirements for those deemed capable of working were also tightened considerably. A more active role is now taken to assist those with adequate training to enter or re-enter the job market. These individuals will now receive social assistance if they enter one of a number of re-employment

**Table 6:** Welfare Benefit Comparison (Pre- vs. Post-welfare Reform)

| Type of Client | Benefit | 1992/3 | 1995/6 | Difference | |
|---|---|---|---|---|---|
| Single employable adult | Standard and Shelter | $470 | $394 | ($76) | −16.2% |
| | Supplementary and Medical | $95 | $65 | ($30) | −31.6% |
| | Monthly Total | $565 | $459 | ($106) | −18.8% |
| Single parent with 1 child | Standard and Shelter | $842 | $766 | ($76) | −9.0% |
| 0–11 yrs | Supplementary and Medical | $191 | $129 | ($62) | −32.5% |
| | Monthly Total | $1,033 | $895 | ($138) | −13.4% |
| Family—two adults with | Standard and Shelter | $1,308 | $1,206 | ($102) | −7.8% |
| 1 child less than 12 yrs | Supplementary and Medical | $240 | $152 | ($88) | −36.7% |
| 1 child greater than 12 yrs | Monthly Total | $1,548 | $1,358 | ($190) | −12.3% |

SOURCE: Alberta Family and Social Services, *Alberta Welfare Reforms Progress Report* (1996).

training programs, most of which have a duration of less than four months. These programs include: a job placement program, which concentrates on such job-finding skills as résumé writing and interview techniques; an on-the-job training program, which provides subsidies of up to $220 per week for as long as six or seven months; and an 'employment alternatives program' for hard to employ clients, which provides life skills training, short-term job-specific education, academic upgrading, and work experience.[5] Those who are deemed to lack sufficient education to function well in the labour force are eligible for two years of support while they upgrade their high school education and may be eligible for grants to supplement student loans if they enter post-secondary education. In each of these cases, however, FSS encourages students to become self-supporting as soon as possible, most educational funding is contingent on student performance, and strict limits are set on students' ability to take more than one educational program.

Finally, funds for transitional support were reduced substantially. Of particular importance was a change in eligibility for single parents. Whereas employable single parents could previously obtain social assistance if they had children under two years old, it is only parents of children less than six months old who are now eligible for this support.

The effect of these changes can be seen in Tables 7 and 8. Table 7 shows the dramatic decline, which occurred virtually on a month-by-month basis, from 1993 to 1995. The monthly caseload dropped more than 50 per cent between the date of the reforms, March 1993, and October 1995. Furthermore, the December 1995 caseload of 49,001 was more than 50 per cent lower than the previous peak caseload of 98,642, experienced in December 1992.

Table 8 indicates that the largest proportional reduction in support came in the 'transitional support' category (the category affected by the reduction in eligibility for single parents). This reduction is particularly remarkable when it

**Table 7:** Alberta Welfare Monthly Caseload Figures

| Month | 1993 | 1994 | 1995 |
|---|---|---|---|
| January | 96,275 | 66,519 | 53,114 |
| February | 95,048 | 64,050 | 52,285 |
| March | 94,087 | 62,394 | 52,243 |
| April | 91,835 | 59,471 | 50,456 |
| May | 89,602 | 59,069 | 51,566 |
| June | 87,641 | 58,564 | 50,947 |
| July | 86,241 | 58,289 | 51,900 |
| August | 83,769 | 57,521 | 52,681 |
| September | 75,991 | 52,731 | 49,105 |
| October | 70,486 | 50,064 | 46,715 |
| November | 68,118 | 50,384 | 47,429 |
| December | 66,883 | 51,799 | 49,001 |
| Average | 83,831 | 57,571 | 50,620 |

SOURCE: Alberta Family and Social Services, *Alberta Welfare Reforms Progress Report* (1996).

is recognized that approximately 8,000 to 9,000 of the 27,198 reduction in the 'employment and training' program represented cases transferred to AECD. Finally, as Table 8 indicates, the number of individuals on 'assured support' increased by more than 20 per cent, from 9,162 to 11,027.

## 4. THE IMPACT OF BUDGET CUTS

While the deficit-cutting policies of the Klein government have generally been popular with Albertans (see the chapter by Archer and Gibbins), there have been criticisms. One of the more commonly voiced criticisms has been that cuts were across the board as opposed to being selective. As discussed by Kneebone and McKenzie in Chapter 5, although there is perhaps a public perception that the cuts were across the board, in point of fact there were large differences across areas. This is also true *within* FSS. The 1997/8 target for the department calls for a total operating expenditure of $1,368.6 million. Based on the actual 1992/3 operating expenditure, that figure represents a reduction of $326.2 million or just over 19.2 per cent. Over the same period the cuts in income and employment programs are projected to be $435.5 million or 37.7 per cent. Combined expenditures on other programs under FSS will actually

**Table 8:** Caseload Composition by Welfare Program Category, 1992/3 vs. 1995/6

| | Program Category | March 1993 | December 1995 | Caseload Change |
|---|---|---|---|---|
| **Expected to Work** | Supplement to Earnings | 13,630 | 10,049 | (3,581) |
| | Employment and Training | 47,646 | 20,448 | (27,198) |
| | Transitional Support | 23,649 | 7,477 | (16,172) |
| | Subtotal | 84,925 | 37,974 | (46,951) |
| **Not Expected to Work** | Assured Support | 9,162 | 11,027 | 1,865 |
| | Total | 94,087 | 49,001 | (45,086) |

Source: Alberta Family and Social Services, *Alberta Welfare Reforms Progress Report* (1996).

increase over the 1992/3–1997/8 period, from $538.1 million to $647.5 million, or by 20.3 per cent. Clearly, FSS has not engaged in simple across-the-board budget-cutting.

A second common criticism of the Klein revolution is that the budget cuts have disproportionately affected the poor, the aged, women, and children. To the extent that the poor are women, children, and the aged the criticism is true, although it is important to recognize that this criticism is normative (subjective). Barring an extraordinary degree of administrative inefficiency, it is impossible to cut welfare without disproportionately hurting the poor and, by extension, women, children, and the aged.

The Minister of Family and Social Services in the Klein government, Mike Cardinal, has long advocated major reforms of social assistance. Recently, in an interview, he indicated that when he was an employee of FSS he was frustrated by the welfare system. His inability to change the system from within was one of the reasons he entered politics. This is consistent with the view that FSS is pursuing two goals—to contribute to the deficit elimination policy of the government and to reform the welfare system. While welfare reform and deficit elimination are not always viewed as complementary, some aspects of the reforms in Alberta are consistent with the policy of deficit elimination. It is also possible that many of the changes within FSS would not have occurred without the prod of deficit reduction. If FSS had two goals, its performance cannot be judged simply in terms of its contribution to the deficit-cutting process. It must also be judged in terms of its welfare reforms.

Social assistance is the main tool in the government's arsenal of tools for the redistribution of income. Progressive (or regressive) taxes and the provision of in-kind income can also be used by a government to affect the distribution of income. There is no objectively right distribution of income. Each individual has his or her own idea of the best possible distribution of income.

That view is embedded within that individual's welfare function. It is normative. In theory, societies might be able to reach a consensus of the best overall
state of society and therefore have an agreed-upon social welfare function
(SWF). That SWF would be an ordering of all possible states of society with
respect to the distribution of income, the level of income, the level of expenditure on all possible goods and services, the degree of individual freedom, and
so forth. More likely, an elected government will have an implicit SWF that is
acceptable to its supporters. The set of SWFs acceptable to the voters that supported the Klein government is likely different from the set of SWFs acceptable
to the voters who supported New Democrat or Liberal candidates. Whether a
change in the system of social assistance or other responsibilities of FSS is an
improvement or not depends on what that individual believes represents an
improvement in society. Each individual's ranking of all possible states of society is based on that particular individual's values. Again, it is normative.
Different individuals will have different ideas about what constitutes improvement in social assistance. Clearly, it is therefore impossible to determine objectively whether the welfare reforms instituted by FSS are better or worse than the
previous system. The voters will have to do that when there is another election.

While the voters will have to make the subjective evaluation of the Klein
budget-balancing policy, it is possible for economists to make some useful
observations about the proposed path of FSS. Four criteria can be used to judge
welfare programs: economic efficiency, distributive efficiency, administrative
efficiency, and invasiveness. I will discuss each of these separately.

The first criterion is economic efficiency. Given limited resources, how
does society maximize the value of its output? When applied to welfare, it
means that a given program has minimal disincentive effects. A program to
redistribute income can reduce the incentive to work or to save. If a program
decreases the incentive to work, it reduces the potential labour supply and
therefore the level of output. Welfare payments can reduce the labour supply if
they change the price of leisure. If the cost of leisure is reduced, one would
expect that there would be a substitution of leisure for other goods or services.
In an extreme, but sometimes relevant case, welfare payments can reduce the
cost of leisure to zero. If the number of hours of leisure is increased, the supply
of labour is reduced and the payment has had a disincentive effect. Welfare payments are low enough that individuals who have the ability to earn even mod-
erately high wages are not likely to be affected directly; however, the
disincentive effect may also occur to those who have relatively high income.
Extra tax revenue will be required to fund the transfer. The additional taxes will
reduce the cost of leisure for those required to pay. Again, a disincentive effect
is possible. In addition to the substitution effect, if leisure is a normal good,
there would be an income effect. The greater this effect, the less effective the

program is in terms of this criterion. Thus, it is possible that a welfare program could cause a disincentive even if it did not change the price of leisure.

The supply of labour is not the only economic variable that can be affected by the existence of a welfare program. Savings can also be affected. Individuals save for a variety of reasons. Typically, an individual will save for 'a rainy day'. If a welfare program exists, it will help with 'rainy days' and there is less incentive to save. This may result in there being less investment and a lower growth rate. Again, the greater the effect, the less effective the program is in terms of this criterion. While this criterion may seem straightforward, it is generally difficult to test performance. The results of the New Jersey and Manitoba experiences with negative income tax were not at all conclusive.

The second criterion is distributive efficiency. This criterion has been discussed considerably in recent years. Universal programs are not distributively efficient. They bestow benefits without regard for any qualifying conditions. There has been pressure in recent years to develop programs that aid only those who demonstrate need. If this criterion is to be applied, it is first necessary to identify a target group. The targeted group will have certain characteristics— for example, income below a specified level, physical disabilities, or the old 'no man about the house' rule. The choice of characteristics is normative. The members of this group are considered deserving. If some of the redistributed money goes to non-members of the deserving group, that is distributive inefficiency. The better the subset that receives funding corresponds to the subset that deserves funding, the higher the level of distributive efficiency. Under this criterion there are two possible errors that can be made. First, funds can go to non-deserving recipients. Second, deserving recipients may be denied funding (or receive inadequate funding).

The third criterion is administrative efficiency. A welfare program is designed to redistribute income. It takes money from one group and gives money (or income in kind) to another group. There are bound to be some administrative costs. The lower the administrative costs the better the program (all else being equal). Inefficiency can develop because the administrators do their job poorly. However, this is not the only reason for administrative costs. If a program is designed with a large number of qualifying conditions, the caseworker will be required to spend more time investigating each claim to determine if the recipient is deserving. The administrative cost is thus increased. A universal program is administratively very efficient, but generally not very efficient distributively. A program that is distributively efficient targets only recipients who meet certain requirements, but it is not likely to be administratively efficient.

The last criterion is not easily quantified and is more subjective than the first three. I have chosen to refer to it as invasiveness. It is sometimes referred to as the human dignity goal. Basically, this criterion requires that income transfers involve a minimum of government interference in the lives of recipients. It would also require that there be a minimum of embarrassment. Historically, many welfare programs have been designed to 'brand' recipients. Welfare cheques were more difficult to cash than family allowance cheques. Some believed that the shame would deter all but the truly needy. Welfare in kind, such as food banks, is often criticized on the ground that it treats recipients as unable or too irresponsible to make free choices.

Ideally, any welfare reform would do well in terms of the four criteria given above. However, that is impossible. The four criteria are not mutually compatible. As we have already seen, the administrative and distributive efficiency criteria can be mutually exclusive. The requirement that assistance be granted only to deserving recipients requires additional administrative investigation to check the eligibility of claimants. There are other possible conflicts. If society decides that anyone with an income below a certain level ought to have assistance, for instance, that individuals would be guaranteed an income of $1,000 a month, then anyone earning less would receive the difference between what they earned and their entitlement. For low-wage workers, this could be a strong disincentive to work. For them the cost of leisure would be zero or very little. Unless the work itself had some utility for the worker, the tendency to substitute leisure for earned income would be very high. The program would score low marks for economic efficiency. Such a program would ensure that everyone had an income of at least $1,000 per month. There would be no distributive inefficiency. Only individuals earning less than $1,000 per month would receive benefits. The program would score high marks in terms of distributive efficiency. Since the only characteristic required to be deemed deserving is an income less than $1,000, it should be possible to integrate the welfare scheme into the income tax system and the administrative cost would be low. In that case the program would score reasonably well in terms of the third criterion. It is difficult to assess the program in terms of the fourth criterion. It would depend to some degree on how the general public reacted. However, it is likely that there would be some stigma attached to recipients. On the other hand, the government would not have to pry into the lives of recipients except to determine their income.

Assume that we now change the system discussed above. Again each individual is still guaranteed $1,000; but under our reformed system individuals will not lose their welfare entitlement on a dollar-for-dollar basis if they earn income. Their income will be taxed back at a 50 per cent rate. Such a program is called a negative income tax. Such a change would decrease the disincentive to work because the recipients would keep half of their earned income. That would be an improvement in terms of the first criterion but would result in some individuals with incomes over $1,000 a month still receiving welfare. That is, some 'non-deserving' individuals would benefit. Both programs ought to be relatively efficient in terms of administrative costs. The second program might be slightly less invasive because more individuals would receive assistance and having a 'welfare' cheque would not necessarily mean that the individual was not working. Whether or not this change represents an improvement or not depends mainly on whether it is judged in terms of the first or second criterion. If economic efficiency is much more important than distributive efficiency the change would be a good reform. On the other hand, if distributive efficiency is much more important, the change would be a poor reform.

Just as in the case of the hypothetical reform, it is possible to judge the welfare reforms in Alberta in terms of the four criteria cited above. Moreover, any judgement about the performance of FSS should be made in terms of the stated goals.

Before proceeding with the discussion of welfare reform, we should remember that the government is pursuing two goals: deficit reduction and welfare reform. It is relatively easy to judge the performance of FSS with regard to the elimination of the budget deficit. The department is more or less in line with the required expenditure cuts. Barring unforeseen circumstances, it is likely that the deficit will be eliminated by the end of the 1995/6 fiscal year and that FSS will have contributed its share to the attainment of that goal.

The most obvious source for a statement of goals for FSS is its annual business plans. In its *Business Plan 1995–96 to 1997–98*, FSS states the following:

> We must identify specific outcomes or results for our Programs. These outcomes will be based on the Department's mission: Help Families to be Responsible and Accountable; Help Adults be Independent; and Keep Children Safe.
>
> Based on this mission, the Department has identified three key result areas:
>
> 1. Safety and Security of Children
> 2. Safety and Security of Disabled People
> 3. Client Self-Sufficiency

We can measure our programs by determining whether they have an effect on these three areas. Some of the measures for program outcomes will be:

- Percentage of day care centres which meet the five most important government standards.
- Percentage of children who stay free from injury or neglect following department intervention.
- Percentage of children in custody of Child Welfare whose needs are being satisfactorily met in their placement.
- Supports for Independence (welfare) caseload per 1,000 population.

- Percentage of closed Supports for Independence cases that remain closed after 12 months.
- Percentage of agencies serving the disabled that meet government standards. (FSS, 1995)

The first two of the 'key result areas', ensuring the safety and security of children and providing a guarantee for the disabled, are so non-controversial as to constitute 'motherhood' statements. It is not clear, however, what 'safety' and 'security' mean. The proposed measurements seem to imply safety and security from abuse. Some might suggest that security could include the provision of an adequate diet. Nevertheless, this official statement does provide a starting place for analysis. Clearly, the first two key result areas, those dealing with children and the disabled, are regarded very differently from the last. There are those to be protected and those to be directed to self-sufficiency.

Based on a number of sources it would appear that the government regards the first two criteria as having the highest priority. For example, in an interview Cardinal indicated that welfare reforms were undertaken in three phases: (1) reforms designed to get healthy, young individuals into the workforce; (2) reforms to children's services; and (3) reforms to programs for persons with disabilities.

One goal, obviously, is to get employable recipients working. This is consistent with the reduction of the disincentives in the system and with the evidence presented above that in the past Alberta caseloads have been disproportionately high. It also implies that healthy young individuals are not deserving, but children, the elderly, and the disabled are. The FSS *Business Plan 1995–96 to 1997–98* supports this view. Support for independents is scheduled to drop from $726.8 million in 1993/4 to $483.5 million in 1997/8. During the same period assured income of severely handicapped people is slated to increase from $162.5 million to $180.8 million. That represents a decrease of over 33 per cent for independents and an increase of over 11 per cent for the severely handicapped. An increase of $3.3 million, or about 39 per cent, is planned for the widows' pension program. If the deserving group is defined in this way the first two criteria appear to be compatible. If there is no welfare available to young healthy workers, there can be no disincentive to work. Either you work or you are on your own. Those in the deserving group eligible for assistance are effectively deemed unable to work. They are either too young to work (children) or disabled. If they cannot work anyway, the provision of welfare cannot be a disincentive.

In reality, being young and healthy is not a sufficient condition to be employable in a modern economy. In such an economy, the number of jobs for untrained workers is very limited. Consequently, there could be individuals who do not fall into the deserving set and who are not employed, not because of the disincentive effect of welfare but rather because they lack the skills to gain employment. The welfare reforms attempt to deal with this eventuality.

In an article in the *Fraser Forum*, Cardinal said: 'The other area that we concentrated on was to get people back into training, and back into the work-force by providing over $60 million in the first year to train over 11,000 individuals to take life-skills and academic upgrading to grade 12 level' (1995: 7). The role of training is clearly indicated in the department's plans. In its business plan it gives the following strategies for support for independents for 1995/6:

- increase employment support; extend Job Corps urban centres
- work with the Student Finance Board to support former welfare recipients in upgrading. (FSS, 1995a: 7)

FSS budget projections are consistent with its stated goal of increasing employment support. For fiscal 1992/3, FSS spent $10.8 million on employment initiatives—such as the Alberta Community Employment and Environmental Employment Program and Employment Skills Program—for the unemployed. In 1993/4 employment initiatives had increased to $27.1 million dollars. The 1995/6 budget calls for $45.1 million. Thereafter, FSS targets annual expenditures of $45.0 million.

Cardinal contends that at least the initial evidence proves that the training is working:

Interestingly we were criticized when the training program ended in June. People said, 'What are you going to do with the 11,000 students that will come back on your payroll July 1st?' You know what happened? The caseload continued dropping. None of the 11,000 came back on the public welfare roll. That just shows you that given the opportunity, people will participate in the work force. (1995: 7)

The minister seems to think that education not only increases an individual's employability but also serves as an incentive to work. He is quoted as having said, 'People are motivated through exposure, by being educated and by change' (FSS, 1995b). It is certainly possible that one of the functions of education is to provide motivation. There is, however, another possible explanation. In 1994 a single employable in Alberta received $4,728 per year in basic social assistance (National Council of Welfare, 1995). A full-time job at $5.00 per hour would have paid only about $10,000 per year. The opportunity cost of a year's leisure would have been $5,272 or $2.64 per hour. A better-educated worker could have earned a higher wage. At $10.00 per hour the opportunity cost of a year's leisure nearly triples, to $15,272 or $7.64 per hour. It is not necessary to accept Cardinal's assertion that education motivates. Increased education in and of itself decreases the disincentive effect of welfare by increasing the opportunity cost of leisure.

An important feature of the welfare reforms appears to have been a redefinition of the 'deserving' set. It includes not only those unable to work because of age or disability, but also those temporarily unable to work because of inadequate training. The latter are eligible for assistance conditional on undertaking further education. Clearly, one can define the deserving group in any manner one wants so the distributive efficiency criterion is not violated by this change. Supporting the able-bodied while they retrain does not violate the economic efficiency criterion either. It can be seen as correcting a market failure.

Many of those unable (or unwilling at the low wages they could command) to work might have undertaken additional training on their own if they had adequate information about the labour market and rates of return on human capital, and if there existed perfect capital markets so private lenders would have financed their program. FSS can correct the first cause of the market failure by providing the required information through its counselling. It can also 'correct' the fact that loan officers at Canada's chartered banks have proven unwilling to lend money to welfare recipients at reasonable rates of interest either by directly supporting eligible individuals or through its policy of working with the Student Finance Board.

There is one additional benefit from targeting welfare to only the deserving. A part of the funds saved by reducing welfare payments to the able-bodied can be used to increase funding for the deserving group. This redistribution has in fact taken place. The department's business plan does call for some increase in funding for service to individuals with disabilities. Cardinal is quick to emphasize this benefit: 'Our changes in the first year allowed us to redirect over $100 million to persons with disabilities, widows, the elderly, and children in need of protection' (Cardinal, 1995).

While it seems clear that the Klein government has chosen to place its priorities on the first two criteria, it is reasonable to discuss the reforms in terms of the last two criteria as well. To a certain degree, of course, the criteria are not mutually compatible and therefore it is impossible to design a program that performs well in terms of all four. The third criterion was administrative efficiency. Clearly, the reforms have reduced administrative efficiency as we have defined it. The fact that employment in FSS declined less than 7 per cent between 1992/3 and 1994/5, while the caseload has fallen about 44.5 per cent, is certainly consistent with this conclusion.

It appears that FSS is willing to trade off administrative efficiency to gain great distributive and economic efficiency. However, this seems to be at odds with the first of a number of efficiency measures cited in the *Business Plan 1994–95 to 1997–98*. The plan gives as its first efficiency measure: 'Cost per case for Income Support, Child Welfare, Services to Persons with Disabilities'. Is it possible that FSS is simply being inconsistent?

The remaining goal is harder to quantify. It relates to human dignity and government invasiveness. One of the problems is defining individual dignity. Many would claim that there is more dignity in working than in collecting welfare. Therefore, by forcing able-bodied individuals back into gainful employment, FSS is in fact performing well in terms of this criterion. Others would argue that working at a poor-paying job and having to go to the food bank to supplement one's budget is degrading. The 'right' answer is no more knowable than whether or not one ought to like mustard on a hot dog. However, there may well be some measurable gains in this area. If the public is convinced that only deserving recipients are collecting welfare payments there may be less stigma attached to social assistance. If that is the case, recipients might find it easier to cash their welfare cheques, to rent suitable accommodations, and, in general, to be treated with respect.

There is another important dimension to this criterion. Arthur Okun's (1975) discussion of why societies establish 'inefficient' rights is relevant here. In defending the universality of rights he wrote:

> To the advocate of laissez-faire, many rights protect the individual citizen against the encroachment of the state, and thus convey benefits that far outweigh any cost of economic inefficiency. Freedom of speech and religion must be universal and unconditional; regulation, limitation, or discrimination with respect to them would vest discretionary authority in the government. Any condition for eligibility to vote that cannot be settled by the presentation of a birth certificate would give powers to some public official who might have an interest in keeping certain people out of the polling booth. Even if a literacy test administered by an objective deity would be desirable, one administered by a bureaucracy would be intolerable. The nice thing about universality and equality is that they are identifiable and objective criteria and hence hard to abuse. (Okun, 1975: 10–11)

While many will not accept that welfare is a right, the same principle can be applied. The standard for being deserving may seem clear-cut; however, someone must make a judgement as to whether or not a particular individual is deserving. In most cases that means determining whether or not that individual has a disability sufficiently severe to prevent him/her from working. Stephen Hawking is severally disabled yet he is not only capable of earning a good living, but also of making an invaluable contribution to society. The determination of whether or not a person is too disabled to work is a judgement call. A caseworker faced with such a call may make a mistake or, worse, an arbitrary decision based on personal bias. In this respect, the welfare reforms may be questioned in terms of the last criterion. It is important to emphasize that any non-universal program is bound to run afoul of this criterion. Again, trade-offs must be made. The difficulty can be minimized. First, the selection criteria must be as objectively measurable as possible. Second, there must be an established appeal procedure that ensures public scrutiny. The latter requirement will increase the administrative cost—another trade-off.

Earlier I indicated that most of the discussion would be about cuts to social assistance. This was in part because welfare payments made up over two-thirds of the FSS budget and, generally speaking, the spending cuts were going to come out of social assistance. However, FSS is responsible for a number of other programs. Not surprisingly, they are related to social assistance. I will discuss each of these programs briefly and try to integrate the changes in each into the reforms discussed so far.

Of the other areas of responsibilities under FSS, the largest budget entry is for services to persons with disabilities (SPD). Its budget will be increasing over the period from 1993/4 to 1997/8 from \$236.0 million to \$276.5 million. SPD can be regarded as providing income in kind to the disabled. As such, it is in line with the goal of providing assistance to the targeted group. It is also consistent with the goal of economic efficiency. For those too disabled to work, there can be no disincentive. In addition, SPD is intended to support self-sufficiency. One might reasonably assume that that means to support employment for those not too disabled to work.

The next largest budget entry for FSS is child welfare. Again, the budget targets provide for increased funding—from \$164.0 million in 1993/4 to \$194.9 million in 1997/8. That represents a 19.3 per cent increase. Clearly, in this area the criteria must be different. While it could be argued that FSS is redistributing income in kind to children, it would not be a very useful starting point for analysis. FSS proposes major changes in this area. *The Business Plan 1994–95 to 1997–98* states: 'Major changes are being made to the child welfare system in Alberta—and they are being made at a rapid pace. The department's short term plan for Reshaping Child Welfare has identified 32 actions that will allow us to provide quality service within our budget.'

The first priority (Commissioner of Services for Children, 1994) is the safety, well-being, and healthy development of children. However, if the safety of a child is not endangered, the government will try to avoid removing her or him from the family setting. Parents and other family members will be expected to assume the main responsibility for child care. There is also a desire to decentralize the government's responsibility for children and make it more community-based. In general, this would mean less involvement by Edmonton bureaucrats and greater involvement by the local community. In the case of aboriginal children this would mean more involvement by the native population.

The general approach to child welfare is not inconsistent with the government's approach to social assistance. It emphasizes individual responsibility. However, while that approach to social assistance resulted in substantial cuts in welfare payments, it did not result in a reduction in the budget for child welfare. There are two possible explanations for increased expenditures in this area in a period of substantial budget cuts. One is that the present government actually does place a high priority on child welfare. The other possibility is that the government sees money spent in this area as money invested in lower future welfare payments. Children raised in safer, more responsible homes are more likely to become productive members of society as adults.

While the government proposes to increase expenditures on SPD and child welfare, it plans to decrease expenditures on day care. The FSS *Business Plan 1993–94 to 1997–98* projects a decrease in day care from $73.8 million to $60.2 million. This proposal is consistent with the desire to increase parental responsibility. However, it is at odds with the goal of support for independents. Single-parent families have historically made up a significant proportion of all welfare cases. Reducing government support of day care can only make it more difficult for single parents to enter the labour force.

The remaining responsibilities of FSS involve very small amounts of spending. They include the Office for the Prevention of Family Violence, Children's Advocacy, and the Commissioner of Services for Children, plus three programs related to aboriginal and Métis affairs. While the total amount budgeted for these responsibilities during the 1995/6 fiscal year is only $16.5 million, or a little over 1 per cent of the FSS budget, they are an important responsibility. Obviously, though, they could not play a significant role in the budget-cutting process. It is possible to argue that these programs play a preventive role. Single-parent families and native people make up a disproportionate share of those on social assistance. Considering that fact might lead one to ask why the government is spending so little in these areas.

Some additional changes in income redistribution programs are important. These changes will have significant effects on many seniors. First, the Alberta Assured Income Plan (AAIP) is being eliminated. In the 1993/4 budget it amounted to $49.6 million. About 40 per cent of Alberta seniors received some benefits. While the maximum benefit was only $95 per month, it did represent a significant benefit to low-income seniors. For 1994/5 only $13.2 million is budgeted for AAIP. Thereafter there will be no benefits, though some seniors may qualify for some benefits under Alberta Seniors Benefit. Seniors will also lose part or all of a number of other benefits. In the past, regardless of income, all seniors who lived in their own homes were eligible for a property tax reduction of up to $1,000 per year. All seniors who rented were eligible for up to $1,200 a year in rental assistance. This was reduced to $600 for those who rented subsidized units. Finally, all seniors were eligible for a number of bene-fits related to health care. They were exempt from paying Alberta Health Care premiums (presently $768 for a couple and $384 for a single person). In the future only lower-income seniors will receive this benefit. Couples will receive the full benefit if their annual income does not exceed $24,657. The subsidy will then decrease with income. Couples with income of $27,500 per year will be required to pay the full amount. The cut-offs for singles are $16,791 for full benefit and $18,200 for partial benefit.

A number of other medical and housing benefits for seniors were either reduced or eliminated. While some of these changes involved the loss of cash grants, others meant either the loss of tax expenditures or the increase in user fees. These changes can, in general, be seen as part of the government's pursuit of the second criterion. They are targeting benefits to 'deserving' recipients. Higher-income seniors are not defined as deserving and therefore lose benefits. There has been some criticism of the levels the government chose for target cut-offs, but this does not mean that the government has done poorly in terms of this criterion. The effects in terms of economic efficiency are harder to judge. Because most of the benefits are now income-tested as opposed to universal, it is possible to argue that they will have a modest disincentive effect on both the supply of labour and possibly savings. However, since the majority of those affected will have left the labour force anyway, possibly forced into retirement, it is likely that the policy will have no effect on the supply of labour.

In general, the government has seemed less concerned with its perfor-mance with respect to the last two criteria; however, these criteria may be important to others in passing judgement on Alberta's reforms. It is likely that the consolidation of a number of programs into the Alberta Seniors Benefit and the outright elimination of other programs will improve administrative effi-ciency. The fact that the eligibility conditions (age and income level) are objec-tive means that there is relatively little additional administrative cost. After all, it is substantially easier to determine income and age than it is to determine if a back injury is severe enough to prevent employment. These changes probably do not fare well in terms of the fourth criterion. As long as all seniors qualified for benefits, there was no stigma attached to receiving them. Now seniors who receive benefits are identified as 'poor'. Even the argument that being self-sufficient creates its own dignity is less applicable. Twenty-five-year-olds would have to believe the world owed them a living to think that they deserve support regardless of their own efforts. Many seniors believe that they have already earned the benefits based on their past contribution to society. The reduction of seniors' benefits may prove one of the least popular of FSS reforms.

Before concluding, one other element that has run through the FSS reforms needs mention. It is consistent with the government's general trend to decentralization. This trend is unlikely to have any significant effect on economic efficiency; however, it could have significant effects on the second criterion. Local authorities may have a different perception of social welfare from the province as a whole. If that is the case, the definition of 'deserving' could vary from location to location. To the extent that services are privatized, the problem could be more serious. The delivery of some social services may vary according to the recipient's affiliation with religious or ethnic groups. This could mean that the definition of 'deserving' is no longer consistent with the general view of the population but only with that of the specific group charged with the administration of the program.

## 5. CONCLUSIONS

We have seen that FSS has been able to cut its social assistance budget substantially and at the same time reform welfare in a manner that appears to be, in general, consistent with its goals as revealed in its own business plans. There are, however, some inconsistencies: the reduction in day care and the stated goal of minimizing administrative cost per case while the caseload per worker dropped significantly, and the stated goal of increasing support to the disabled. While there has been a slight increase in absolute level of support to those with disabilities, by 1994 Alberta had actually dropped to the lowest level of support for disabled singles of all the provinces. With the exception of FSS support for the disabled, the author does not see these inconsistencies as a serious problem. Essentially, FSS has tried to reform social assistance in two ways: (1) to reduce disincentives by requiring all able-bodied recipients to find employment or to retrain; (2) to target payments only to 'deserving' applicants. The 'deserving', in this instance, are those unable to work because of disability or age. The reforms appear to have been successful. The number on social assistance has fallen by almost 50 per cent. Indeed, given that a perceived problem with social assistance in Alberta in the past has been relatively high caseloads and low benefit levels, the sizeable reduction in caseloads and only modest reductions in benefit levels may be viewed by some as indicative of a successful change in policy. Those who have completed training programs do not seem to have reappeared on welfare rolls. There have been charges of busloads of 'welfare refugees' fleeing to British Columbia. In point of fact, British Columbia's caseload is up substantially (*The Globe and Mail*, 1995). However, there is little evidence that such migration is actually occurring. *The Globe and Mail* states:

> It is a popular myth that B.C. is flooded with émigrés from Alberta and Ontario attracted to the more lenient welfare system. B.C. does attract a good number of westward-heading Canadians, but only 0.3 percent say that they came to B.C. for handouts.

There is also the anecdotal evidence of increases in the number of homeless and panhandlers in Calgary and Edmonton. On the other hand, the evidence that the reforms are making a long-term difference is not that much more convincing. Information on welfare recipients is confidential, so it is not possible to check what happens to recipients. More importantly, the dramatic success in reducing welfare roles has corresponded to an economic recovery in which there was significant job creation. Between 1992 and June of 1995, the number employed in Alberta increased from 1,285,000 to 1,375,000 and unemployment dropped from 9.5 per cent to 7.3 per cent. The number of jobs created is about double the number who dropped out of social assistance. The real test of the system will only come with the next recession.

## NOTES

1. The author would like to thank Doug Allen (Simon Fraser University), Chris Bruce, Ron Kneebone, Ken McKenzie, Shelley Radway (University of Calgary), Susan Easton, Carol Sharman, Anne Marie Kingston (FSS), and the Donner Canadian Foundation for their assistance. None of the above are in any way responsible for opinions expressed in this paper.

2. A 'caseload' does not always refer to an individual but in some situations refers to a family. FSS advises me that an average caseload would consist of 2.1 individuals.

3. These programs include Community Services for Children, Widow's Pension, Day Care, Family Violence Prevention, Children's Advocacy, Aboriginal, Métis, and Commissioner's Office.

4. This support includes Services for Persons with Disabilities, Assured Income for the Severely Handicapped, and Personal Supports.

5. On average, individuals remain in the employment alternatives program for four to five months, but may continue for up to two years.

## REFERENCES

Alberta Family and Social Services (1994), *Business Plan 1994–95 to 1996–97*. Edmonton.

———— (1995a), *Business Plan 1995–96 to 1997–98*. Edmonton.

———— (1995b), *Welfare Reform*. Edmonton.

————— (1996), *Alberta Welfare Reforms Progress Report*. Edmonton.

*Calgary Herald* (1994), 'Alberta Seniors' Benefit', 9 Mar.: B3.

Cardinal, M. (1995), 'Welfare Reform in Alberta', *Fraser Forum* (June): 5–8.

Commissioner of Services for Children (1994), *Focus on Children*. Edmonton: Government of Alberta.

*The Globe and Mail* (1995), 'Why the rise in B.C. welfare cases?' 20 Sept.: A20.

National Council of Welfare (1995), *Welfare Incomes 1994*. Ottawa.

Okun, A.M. (1975), *Equality and Efficiency*. Washington: The Brookings Institution.

Radway, Shelley (1995), 'Interview with The Honourable Mike Cardinal' (mimeograph).

Statistics Canada, *Provincial Economic Accounts* (various years), Cat. No. 13–213. Ottawa.

# Comments on Chapter 8　　■

*Douglas W. Allen*

## 1. INTRODUCTION

Welfare is often a difficult topic for an economist to analyse because direct or indirect voluntary transfers of wealth from one group of individuals to another grind against the fundamental economic assumption of maximization. Economists are faced with the puzzle of private individuals being made better off by 'giving' some of their income to society. The puzzle is not confined to welfare, but also manifests itself in private charities, international aid, and most public transfer schemes. To date, unobservable social welfare functions notwithstanding, there is no generally accepted economic theory of transfer payments. Whether income is given to avoid theft or revolution (Johnsen, 1986; Eaton and White, 1991), or out of acts of altruism, we simply do not know.

However, if we take as given that a society wants to transfer income to the poor, economics still remains useful in evaluating how we do this. Economics is useful because economic theory points out the incentives and linkages of a welfare scheme and hopefully raises the level of debate. If we could all think fast enough, there would be no need of economic theory—unfortunately, we need economic theory. What economics cannot do, never has done, and never will do, is spit out some answer like 'X is the optimal welfare plan.' Economics is simply a method of argument, or as McCloskey would say, a rhetoric. In debates on welfare it is important to keep economic theory in its rightful place.

In his chapter, Shedd provides a framework for discussing the Alberta welfare reforms that both provides economic theory with more authority than it deserves on some issues and yet neuters it in the discussion of others. For Shedd, there are positive economic arguments to be made and normative judgements to be avoided. Fortunately for the chapter, this nineteenth-century methodological distinction only distracts the analysis without derailing it. However, I feel that to deal with the Alberta reforms properly, this distinction must be dealt with first.

Throughout the chapter Shedd constantly makes reference to statements that are 'normative' in nature. For example, he tells us that 'The choice of the characteristics [of a target group] is normative', and that 'Each individual has his or her own idea of the best possible distribution of income. That view is embedded within that individual's welfare function. It is normative.' Quite often the implication is that as economists we can have nothing to say about such issues. Sometimes, he suggests that no answer is even possible.

In discussing the effect of work on human dignity, he states that 'The "right" answer is no more knowable than whether or not one ought to like mustard on a hot dog.' We are told 'There is no "right" distribution of income.' And finally that: 'Clearly, it is therefore impossible to determine objectively whether the welfare reforms instituted by FSS are better or worse than the previous system.' One almost wonders what the point of any public debate is.

On the other hand, Shedd makes a number of statements with a much more scientific ring to them. Though private citizens are left with their subjective values, economists are able 'to make some *useful* observations' (emphasis added).

We are told that there are four criteria to judge welfare programs: economic efficiency; distributive efficiency; administrative efficiency; and invasiveness. In discussing these four criteria, statements are made that imply a unique meaning to all of these things.

What Shedd fails to realize is that all statements are normative, no matter what their scientific dressings. As Kuhn (1962) and Feyerabend (1965) pointed out long ago, and as McCloskey (1985, 1988) has nailed home many times, all observation is theory-laden, and all theory is value-laden. There is no escaping this, and there is no point in dressing an argument up as scientific and rigorous when you are attempting to address an issue on which many individuals hold different theories of the world. Economic theory, along with every other theoretical construct, is normative.

For example, the notion of efficiency used in the chapter is presumably economic efficiency, which is built on a neoclassical model of value. Many individuals outside our discipline simply do not accept this view of the world, and as a result will reject this definition of efficiency. Many of the implicit weights used in the chapter to access various outcomes are purely normative and should be explicitly recognized as such. Discussions of 'deserving' are also value-laden and beg the question, how does the author or province come up with such definitions?

This is not to say that the economist should ignore the questions of welfare. Far from it. We need to articulate our model carefully, justify the definitions we use, and analyse the problems at hand. What we must not do is lend our models authority they do not deserve. We must not divide the issue up into a normative vs. positive debate—it is all normative. If Shedd decides that the four criteria are important, then he should argue as such; economic theory on its own provides no answer.

Personally, I think Shedd has hit on the key issues in the debate. For Shedd, economic efficiency essentially refers to the disincentive effects caused by welfare; distributive efficiency refers to the success of transferring payments to the target group; administrative efficiency refers to the resources used in the process of transfer; and invasiveness is Shedd's way of talking about social stigma and other personal costs of using a welfare system. I would argue that these four categories, for analytical purposes, are easier to think about simply in terms of costs and benefits. As a society, we find a benefit in transferring income to a target group. In doing so we create costs in terms of disincentives, administration, and stigma. As one who has done a little work in the area, it is my impression that administration costs are quite trivial and that most of the problems with welfare regard incentives. What makes economics a useful tool in this debate is that incentives are tied to targeting and to stigma. What is missing from Shedd's chapter is an attempt to quantify these costs and benefits.

## 2. THE ECONOMICS OF WELFARE PARTICIPATION

The economics of welfare on participation and other incentives is very straightforward.[1] Consider the decision to participate in welfare. Not everyone who is poor collects social assistance. Welfare has social stigmas and may be perceived to adversely affect one's children, future earnings potential, or human capital skills.[2] Regardless of the reason, individuals do not automatically participate in welfare when their income under welfare is higher on than off the system. We could say that people have different 'tastes' for welfare, and we could define these tastes as:

$$\theta = U^* (1, p, \bar{I}) - U^* (0, p, I)$$

That is, our taste or distaste for participating in welfare is the difference in utility when we are on or off welfare. Here, $U^*$ is the indirect utility function, $p$ is the price of goods, $\bar{I}$ is the level of money income with welfare, and $I$ is the level of income when not on welfare. Individuals will participate in welfare when $\theta > 0$.

An important implication of this model is that changes in welfare income lead to higher participation rates, given that:

$$\delta\theta/\delta I = \lambda^1 > 0$$

where $\lambda^1$ is the marginal utility of money income and is positive given non-satiation. The following figure gives a graphical explanation.

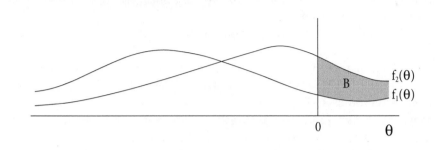

Prior to the rise in $\bar{I}$, the number of participants in welfare equalled the area below $f_1(\theta)$ and where $\theta > 0$. Increases in $\bar{I}$ shift everyone's $\theta$, and as a result participation increases by an amount equal to area B.

Shedd is careful and correct in noting these incentives to participate in welfare. In addition, he notes that since participation requires low income, welfare reduces the labour supply. Also, because welfare acts as a form of insurance and because individuals are allowed only minimal levels of liquid assets, savings rates are reduced. Finally, Shedd notes that welfare requires financing through taxation, and that these taxes also produce distortions elsewhere in the economy.[3]

What Shedd fails to consider, however, is the effect welfare can have on family structure. Changes in marital status that increase welfare payments will increase theta and will therefore increase participation in welfare among this group. However, to the extent that welfare income depends on marital status, the presence of children, or other endogenous factors, these choices are also influenced by the level of welfare income. Hence, the *structure* of welfare payments implies that some categories of the poor are more likely to participate in welfare and that some individuals will substitute into categories favoured by the welfare structure. For example, Becker (1981: 230) has stated: '[AFDC (Aid to Families with Dependent Children)] raises separation and divorce rates among eligible families in that the incomes of divorced and separated persons are raised relative to the incomes of married persons. These programs, in effect, provide poor women with divorce settlements that encourage divorce.' Welfare changes the relative cost of family structures to some individuals by basing payments on marital status. Changes in relative costs lead utility maximizers to substitute into new living arrangements.

In a recent C.D. Howe study, Ross Finnie notes that divorce is a major factor in the poverty of women and children. On the one hand, it makes sense to provide more income to single parents, but at the same time this encourages marginal marriages to break down (Allen, 1993). Hence, targeting and incentives are directly linked.

The welfare system in Canada is one of last resort. To collect welfare payments one must be poor: liquid assets must be depleted, and expenditures on certain types and levels of food, shelter, and clothing must be greater than one's income. As a result, for most Canadians (Albertans included) θ is well below zero and has no effect on choices made regarding participation and marital status. However, for those people near the margin (theta close to zero), the implications are clear. Shedd is correct in constantly pointing out the trade-offs involved in welfare policy. On the one hand we want to assist the poor, and yet to do so implies that more individuals end up on welfare. A hard-headed but soft-hearted approach to welfare would seem to suggest targeted payments, with stumbling blocks to prevent employable individuals from joining.

## 3. SPECIFIC COMMENTS ON THE ALBERTA REFORMS

The problem in designing welfare policy is how the government transfers income to the 'deserving' poor without inducing large amounts of substitution into welfare participation. In cutting back the overall expenditures of welfare payments but increasing the amounts directed to the disabled, it strikes me that the recent cuts and restructuring make a great deal of sense.

The most remarkable statistic reported by Shedd is that a 20 per cent reduction in welfare payments led to a 44 per cent fall in the welfare caseload. This is much higher than the elasticity I measured nationally.[4] The large change in welfare caseload is almost certainly due to a reduction in employable individuals on the caseload.[5] As such, it would be incorrect to assume that a second 20 per cent cut would lead to a further drastic reduction. However, the point remains—welfare participation is very elastic with respect to payments. This is extremely significant because a large elasticity essentially determines the best design of a welfare scheme.

For example, as Shedd addresses, should welfare be given to 'the deserving only' or should it be 'universal'? First, it should be noted that under the Canada Assistance Plan, we have a universal welfare program. Anyone who is poor can apply for welfare; one does not need to fit any specific category of poor. On the other hand, every province decides what the relative payments should be for various categories. Alberta, like most provinces in Canada, treats single employable individuals differently from single parents or poor couples. In this sense, the province has always moved away from a purely universal system of payments. Shedd argues for maintaining universal coverage. He quotes Okun in defence of universality. Okun was arguing that universality protects the individual from the state and the discretion of the bureaucrat. Okun was also talking about individual rights stated in the American constitution, such as the right to vote, free expression, and the freedom of religion. Although many individuals believe that State welfare entitlements are legal rights, they are not, and the issue here is, does universality hinder the State's ability to transfer wealth to the deserving poor? The answer is yes, it does. It provides the opportunity for large amounts of substitution from the labour force to the welfare roles. The huge reduction of participation in light of the recent cuts is evidence of this.

One key feature of the Alberta reforms has been to redirect funds from employable to unemployable individuals. This is a further movement away from universality and a movement in the right direction, given how sensitive participation is to payments. The one note of caution is that single parents are often classified as unemployable, and increases here must be made with consideration. This category already has the highest real per capita payments that are attractive to low-income earners.[6] Also, there is a large elasticity of single parenthood with respect to welfare payments (Allen, 1993), which implies large substitution effects. Finally, given the extensive length of time it takes to raise children, this is the category that suffers most from the fall in human capital due to being absent from the labour force.

Related to the issue of universality is the question of caseworker discretion versus fixed rules in determining the level of support. Shedd again argues, along with welfare advocates like the National Council of Welfare, that rules provide more dignity to the recipient. This may be true, but rules are also easy to exploit and again allow for illegitimate substitution. There is a huge information asymmetry between the applicant, the caseworker, and the welfare bureaucracy in favour of the applicant. There is simply no way for an office of the Crown to design a transfer scheme that is not universal that would not be exploitable. Allowing the caseworker some discretion, the ability to interview, and the powers to investigate and check information is essential to avoid fraud and mispayment.

## 4. CONCLUSION

Research over the last five years related to welfare in Canada suggests that incentives to substitute out of the labour force and into welfare participation are quite strong for able-bodied individuals. Furthermore, given the extra benefits provided single parents, the Canadian safety net, at the margin, has encouraged births out of wedlock and divorce. This incentive effect creates the welfare policy dilemma: assisting poor individuals creates incentives that contribute to poverty. Hence, higher welfare benefits not only remove people from productive activities, lower work effort on the part of the employed through higher taxes, and contribute to the relocation of firms to avoid taxation, they would appear to fail in their stated goal as well. By removing low-income individuals from the workforce, welfare participation accelerates the depreciation of human capital among those with the least amount of human capital to begin with.

If the elasticity of substitution into welfare were negligible, none of these problems would be significant. However, outcomes like those in Alberta suggest otherwise. When a 20 per cent fall in payments leads to a 44 per cent fall in participation, we have a large elasticity, indeed. The efforts by the government of Alberta to reduce the payments to the employables and to raise the payments to the disabled (and other groups with low elasticities of substitution) would appear to be the best strategy.

## NOTES

1. This section draws heavily from Allen (1993).

2. Herrnstein and Murray, in *The Bell Curve*, suggest a more radical reason for the failure of most eligible individuals to participate in welfare. They argue that a low intelligence level is the best predictor of participation. Given that welfare almost always makes recipients worse off than they would otherwise have been, they claim that intelligent people shy away from the program.

3. Allen (1993) provides empirical evidence from the 1986 census for some of these effects. David Brown (1995) also provides evidence that incentive effects matter a great deal for welfare participation.

4. Allen (1993) estimates a participation elasticity of .39. However, this is measured relative to the poverty line and at the mean level of participation—not at the margin. It makes sense that at the margin the response to changes in participation would be larger. Hence, though there is a huge difference, the results then are still consistent with each other.

5. Lippert (1994: 26) argues that the Klein effects led to no significant change in British Columbia's welfare roles.

6. For example, Sarlo (1994: 54) argues that though a single parent of two in BC receives $16,395 per year, once in-kind benefits, tax considerations, and child-care expenses are considered, this amounts to an income of about $25,000 per year. Once the value of leisure time is considered, the welfare benefit may be equivalent to $30,000 per year. Brown (1995) shows that these benefits rose throughout the 1980s relative to full-time wages and that this relative wage effect is the best explanation for the surge in welfare participation in the past 10 years.

## REFERENCES

Allen, D.W. (1993), 'Welfare and the Family: The Canadian Experience', *Journal of Labor Economics*.

Becker, G. (1981), *A Treatise on the Family*. Cambridge, Mass.: Harvard University Press.

Brown, D. (1995), 'Welfare Caseload Trends in Canada', in J. Richards and A. Vining, eds, *Helping the Poor: A Qualified Case for Workfare*. Toronto: C.D. Howe Institute.

Eaton, B.C., and W. White (1991), 'The Distribution of Wealth and the Efficiency of Institutions', *Economic Inquiry* (Apr.).

Feyerabend, P.K. (1965), 'On the Meaning of Scientific Terms', *Journal of Philosophy*, 62.

Herrnstein, R., and C. Murray (1994), *The Bell Curve: Intelligence and Class Structure in American Life*. New York: Free Press.

Johnsen, D.B. (1986), 'The Formation and Protection of Property Rights Among the Southern Kwakiutl Indians', *Journal of Legal Studies*, 15 (1).

Kuhn, Thomas (1962), *The Structure of Scientific Revolutions*. Chicago: University of Chicago Press.

Lippert, O. (1994), *Change and Choice: A Policy Vision for British Columbia: Welfare Reform*. Vancouver: The Fraser Institute.

McCloskey, D. (1985), *The Rhetoric of Economics*. Madison: University of Wisconsin Press.

——— (1988), 'The Limits of Expertise: If You're So Smart, Why Ain't You Rich?' *The American Scholar* (Summer).

Sarlo, C. (1994), 'Poverty In Canada—1994', in *Fraser Forum* (Feb.).

# CHAPTER 9

# The Role of Health Care Reform in the Reinventing of Government in Alberta

*Richard H.M. Plain*

## 1. INTRODUCTION

Far-reaching health care reforms are being implemented at a rapid pace in Alberta. The success or failure of these reforms will determine the future quality of health services, the cost-effectiveness of the health care system, and the accessibility Albertans will have to medically required health care services. The impetus for the health care reforms arose from fiscal concerns regarding the growth of the provincial debt and the seeming inability of the provincial government to balance its budget. Health care accounts for approximately one-third of total provincial spending. Balancing the budget by markedly reducing government spending must from necessity result in major reductions in health care funding. This in turn implies that major health care reforms must be implemented to allow the health care needs of the population to be met with a markedly lower level of provincial government spending. If the reform process fails even partially, the access of services to the population as a whole will fall and the health status of the population will either worsen or remain unchanged, depending on whether or not spending on health care services is deemed to have a positive or negligible effect on the health status of the people of the province. In the main, it is generally believed that health care spending and health status are positively linked. This means that economic efficiency has to be introduced into a health care system in a way that preserves its quality and the equity objectives contained in the Canada Health Act (Health Canada, 1985) while maintaining the existing case flow. This is not an insurmountable task; however, it is not easy one.

The Canada Health Act is one of the major pillars of social policy legislation currently existing within the nation. It effectively stops provincial governments from using the price mechanism as a vehicle for allocating resources within health care markets. Hospital user fees and extra-billing by doctors over and beyond a provincial fee schedule lead to dollar-for-dollar penalties being imposed on any province permitting medical practitioners or hospital authorities to levy such charges. In addition, hospital and medical insurance plans must be publicly administered. The *de facto* prohibition of the use of the price mechanism as a means of allocating resources in the markets for medically required health care goods and services, coupled with the widespread market failure resulting from the marked asymmetry of information between the provider and consumer of goods and services, creates a set of conditions in Canadian health care markets markedly different from those in the United States and even Britain, where changes in health care policy have altered the egalitarian basis of the National Health System and permitted two-tier medicine and private health care insurance options for those in the population who have the ability to pay. Health care economic efficiency and equity issues are linked to a degree in Canada that is not encountered to the same degree in any of the other major Western industrialized nations. The failure to understand this point has led to a great deal of confusion regarding the health care policy options that can be effectively pursued by provincial governments within Canada.

Sections 2 to 6 of this chapter deal with the origin of the health care reforms implemented by the Klein government, the role of business plans in the government of Alberta, and the fiscal dimensions of the Alberta health care business plan, including the economic effectiveness of Canadian-style medicare plans in facilitating major changes and reductions in health care spending. Sections 7 and 8 describe how major changes in the organization and governance of the health system were co-ordinated with the health care financial plan to bring about the major changes outlined within the three-year Department of Health business plan. Section 9 provides an overview of the major effects of the health reforms on hospitals and medical practitioners. Section 10 consists of an overview and critique of the major health goals and performance measures contained within the business plan. Certain unique features of the Alberta plan with respect to the measurement of the output and outcome of the health care system are identified and discussed. Sections 11 and 12 focus on the relationship between health status and health care spending. A formal basis for this relationship is established with models drawn from health care economic theory. The specific form of the equation relating life expectancy at birth to real per capita health care spending is estimated. The policy implications stemming from the identification of an excellent relationship between a mortality-based health indicator such as life expectancy and health care spending are explored in terms of their health reform implications. Section 13 examines the economic merits of allowing price discrimination to be introduced into the Alberta medicare system. The violations of the Canada Health Act contained in the attempt to legitimize this type of pricing scheme are identified.

Section 14 identifies 12 recommendations and conclusions arising from the review of the health care reform process within Alberta.

## 2. THE ORIGIN OF THE HEALTH CARE REFORMS IN ALBERTA

It is important at the outset to realize that the majority of the health care reforms currently being implemented in Alberta have not arisen from major new policy initiatives devised by the current government. This is not meant to be deprecatory. The fact is, the Alberta health care delivery system is not being reinvented. It is simply in the process of being further restructured and reorganized at a much faster rate than anything experienced to this point in time.

The bulk of the current health care reforms being implemented within the province are a product of the recommendations contained in: (1) the 1989 *Rainbow Report* produced by the Premier's Commission on Future Health Care for Albertans, which recommended among other things the regionalization of the health care delivery system (nine regional authorities were proposed, 17 have been established); (2) the provincial government's response to the *Rainbow Report, Partners in Health*, which articulated the general principles of health care that are still largely being followed today; and (3) the in-depth reviews and studies of provincial health care systems undertaken by the neighbouring provinces of Saskatchewan and British Columbia. In addition, international attention has been focused on the health care reforms carried out in New Zealand and the United Kingdom.

Ralph Klein assumed the leadership of the Progressive Conservative Party in Alberta in December 1992 and obtained an impressive mandate in the provincial election held in June 1993. The Klein government decided, and Albertans supported the proposition, that the fiscal affairs of the provincial government had to be 'put in order'. The budget had to be balanced and a plan had to be developed to pay down the debt. It was also agreed these reforms should come from expenditure-side reductions and not tax increases. The new government initiated a series of public roundtable discussions in September and October of 1993 where they requested the participants to focus on health care reform and advise the government on ways to make major reductions in health care spending (Alberta Planning Secretariat, 1993). The summary of the findings from the roundtables and the tabling of *Health Goals for Alberta* by the Ministry of Health in December 1993 form the basis for most of the health care reforms currently being implemented. The major conclusions reached from the roundtable process were as follows:

> (1) It is an understatement to say Albertans value their health services system. The fact is they care deeply about it, and consider access to a quality health system a defining characteristic of being Canadian;

(2) Albertans appear to understand the province's serious financial situation and that with health consuming 30 per cent or nearly $4B of the annual provincial budget, spending reductions in health care must occur. At the same time, however, Albertans caution that reductions and changes must be done with careful planning;

(3) Almost unanimously, consumers and health providers agree the health system can be reformed. Many examples of waste, inefficiency, duplication and overexpenditure were cited during the roundtables;

(4) Our current health system has been built in a random manner with an acute lack of accountability. This structure has allowed the preservation of bureaucracy to take priority over the true needs of health consumers;

(5) A new Alberta health system must place the needs of consumers as a priority;

(6) No discernible results are expected from the system for the billions of dollars taxpayers invest annually. Today, system performance is currently based on 'inputs'— the more dollars invested, the more hospitals built, the more care beds available, the better the system must be. Insufficient consideration is given to the general health of consumers as an outcome;

(7) Albertans want decisions on system reform to be made within their communities. (Ministry of Health, 1993)

Health care reform as it is occurring in Alberta is not centred on reinventing government but on the general public becoming sufficiently concerned over the fiscal state of the province to elect politicians who are willing to accelerate a number of badly needed economic reforms. Reinventing government as it relates to health care could be applied to a situation such as the introduction of a Canadian-style health care system (publicly financed and privately delivered) into the United States. Health care reform within Alberta builds on past trends and ideas borrowed from neighbouring provinces but is not based on a new and innovative path for public health care.

### 3. ALBERTA GOVERNMENT BUSINESS PLANS

Some system obviously had to be devised to transform the often general and at times vague and somewhat contradictory health care policy positions accumulated in the late 1980s and early 1990s into a set of operational programs capable of markedly reducing health care spending and effecting major reform. Three-year business plans were identified as the vehicle to be used to change and manage not only health but also all of the other provincial government reforms:

These plans detail the goals, strategies and actions to be taken over the next three years. They outline the specific spending targets for each department . . . they begin the important step of outlining expected results and the performance measures that will be used to measure our progress towards meeting the goals we've set.

> Our goal is to secure Alberta's future . . . to maintain essential programs and our quality of life. . . . We will not be able to reach our goal of a secure future unless we take steps now to balance the budget. (Alberta Ministry of Health, 1994a: 1)

Five so-called 'core businesses' were identified as the focal point of provincial government resources and efforts. These are: (1) investing in people and ideas; (2) building a strong, sustainable, and prosperous province; (3) providing essential services for the health and well-being of Albertans; (4) maintaining a quality system of roads and highways, telecommunications, and utilities; (5) providing law, order, and good government (Alberta Ministry of Health, 1994a: 2). Clearly, health care falls into the third of the five core businesses.

## 4. SELECTED FINANCIAL HIGHLIGHTS OF THE ALBERTA HEALTH BUSINESS PLAN

### 4.1 Expenditure Reduction, Revenue Enhancement, and Net Budgeting

The first three-year Alberta Health Business Plan was released in February 1994. It was designed to cover the 1994/5–1996/7 period. The second plan, for 1995/6–1997/8, was released a year later. It is important to note that while the official business plan was not promulgated until February 1994, steps had already been taken prior to the election in June 1993 to curb provincial health care spending. In effect, a four-year financial plan was put into force before the three-year business plans were prepared and implemented. This implies approximately two years of cutbacks in health care expenditures had occurred before the Regional Health Authorities (RHAs) were operationalized on 1 April 1995. Figure 1 provides an overview of actual and estimated provincial health care spending derived from provincial government sources for the fiscal years 1980/1 to 1997/8. As Figure 1 indicates, if the three-year business plans of the provincial government materialize, spending on health care in Alberta will have reached its historical high at approximately $4.17 billion in 1992/3.

The effects of the actual and proposed expenditure cutbacks originated by the current government are reflected in a decrease in total nominal health care spending from the 1992/3 peak to $3.43 billion in 1996/7—a decline of approximately $740 million or 17.8 per cent. Provincial health care spending is held at 1996/7 levels for 1997/8, the last year of the new three-year plan.[1] Figures 1 and 2 indicate that the expenditure reduction target built into the financial plan is accompanied by a revenue enhancement initiative that will raise the medicare premium revenue of the province by $214 million in 1996/7, an increase of approximately 50 per cent over 1992/3.

The total expenditure cuts will be finished by 1996/7; however, the total medicare premium take is slated to be increased by a further 6.3 per cent between 1996/7 and 1997/8.[2] In short, net health care spending in 1997/8 will

**Figure 1:** Provincial Government Health Spending, 1980/1–1997/8 ($ billions)

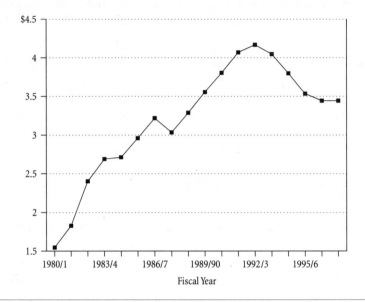

Fiscal Year

SOURCE: *Provincial Government Revenue and Expenditure Series*, Alberta Treasury, August 1993.

**Figure 2:** Total Medicare Premium Revenue, 1992/3–1997/8 ($ millions)

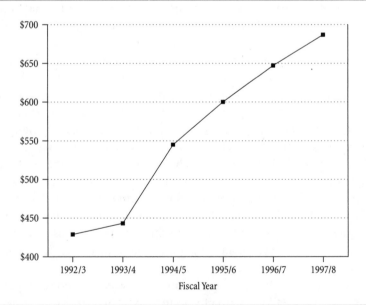

Fiscal Year

SOURCE: *A Three-Year Business Plan (1995–96 to 1997–98)*, Alberta Health, February 25, 1995.

be reduced by $1 billion per annum relative to 1992/3 ($3.735 billion versus $2.74 billion). Three-quarters of the $1 billion per annum decline in health spending will be achieved by expenditure reductions and one-quarter will be achieved through a revenue (medicare premium) enhancement.[3] The assignment of a $1 billion per year reduction in net health care spending seemingly arose from the fact that health care accounted for approximately one-third of provincial spending in 1992/3—a year in which the province experienced a $3.4 billion budget deficit (the second highest to occur between 1980/1 and 1994/5).[4]

## 4.2 Adjusting for Population Growth and Inflation

Figure 3 adds some additional important dimensions to the expenditure overview. First, surprising as it may seem, no formal discussion is made of the role population growth plays in the fiscal portion of either of the Alberta government's two health care business plans. If a five-year moving average is used as the basis for creating a population projection, it can be shown that the total population of Alberta would have increased by approximately 5.8 per cent (154,000 people) between 1992/3 and 1996/7 or by 7.4 per cent (197,000 people) between 1992/3 and 1997/8. This implies the total nominal Alberta government health care spending per person can be expected to decline from $1,572.70 in 1992/3 to $1,223.30 in 1996/7—a reduction of $349.40 per person or 22.2 per cent. The reduction in per capita spending between 1992/3 and the end of the current health care plan (1997/8) amounts to 23.4 per cent or $367.82 per capita. Obviously, this cutback in the level of support is markedly steeper than the 17.8 per cent change in total health care spending noted in the first three-year plan. The size and composition of the population matters when health care spending issues are being considered. Both total and per capita breakdowns are required if the general public is to have a clear understanding of what is included within the provincial or regional health care budget plans.

The second point to note is that the incorporation of even a mild rate of inflation (1.0 per cent per annum) further exacerbates matters. Reference to Figure 3 indicates the level of provincial health care spending per capita expressed in terms of constant 1986 dollars can be expected to fall from $1,242.20 in 1992/3 to $930.50 in 1996/7—a decline of $311.70 or approximately 25 per cent as compared to a nominal decline of 22.2 per cent. Third, if the period under consideration is extended to the end of the current planning horizon (1997/8), then the level of real per capita health care spending support will have declined by 27 per cent. This is almost a 50 per cent greater cut in the health care resources available to meet the health care needs of Albertans than is conveyed by the approximately 18 per cent reduction in total nominal health care spending noted in the Alberta government's three-year business plans.

**Figure 3:** Provincial Government Per Capita Health Spending, 1980/1–1997/8

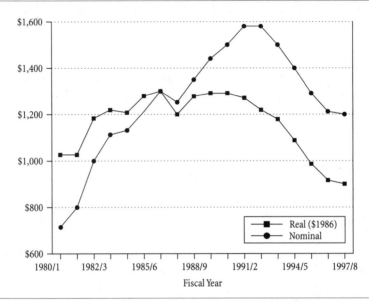

SOURCE: Alberta Health.

Lastly, it is useful to gain an understanding of the longer-run trend in spending on health care carried out by successive provincial governments. Reference to Figure 3 indicates real per capita provincial health care spending peaked at approximately $1,300 in 1986/7 and hovered in the $1,200 to $1,300 range until 1992/3—the year the major cutbacks in spending were initiated. It is evident from a perusal of the graph that if all of the major effects of the spending reforms in the nineties are implemented, real provincial per capita spending on health care in 1997/8 (the end of the second business plan) will be driven down to a level approximately 12 per cent below that existing in 1980/1. This would be a truly remarkable achievement if reasonable access to a high-quality health care system is maintained and a large portion of the costs required to operate that system are not simply being shifted onto businesses and the segment of the Alberta population requiring health care.

## 5. THE COST-CONTROL AND REVENUE-RAISING EFFECTIVENESS OF A CANADIAN-STYLE HEALTH CARE SYSTEM

A decrease of approximately 20.4 per cent in the real level of provincial government health care spending per capita will have been achieved between 1992/3 and 1995/6. Approximately 25.1 per cent will be obtained by 1996/7 and the full 27 per cent per capita change ($1,242 to $904) built into the second plan will be achieved in 1997/8. This means that approximately 76 per cent of the total real per capita cuts contained in the Alberta Health business plans will be completed by the end of this fiscal year. Four years is the normal length of the provincial political cycle in Alberta. This suggests the first three-year health plan (1992/3 to 1996/7) will be the one the current government will be judged on by the electorate. Given this assumption, approximately 81 per cent of the total provincial health care cuts planned by the current group of policy-makers will have been implemented by the end of the year. The ability to impose expenditure reductions of this magnitude on an entire health care system is a clear-cut demonstration of the effectiveness of the cost-control mechanisms built into a system where medically required hospital and physician services are publicly financed and privately delivered and the provincial government is the sole payer for such services. The rapidity and magnitude of this level of reduction in spending could only occur in a system where an extremely powerful public payer of health services was in charge of the system. Hybrid private and public systems made up of a number of private and public payers and insurance companies such as those existing in the United States could never achieve such an outcome in such a short space of time unless a major economic depression occurred or a national emergency was declared.

The reasonableness of large, unilaterally imposed reductions in health care spending will always be subject to debate and the changes in the Alberta system have certainly stimulated discussion among the general populace as well as various user groups over the merits of carrying out such a downsizing in such a short time frame. However, the Alberta experience demonstrates that few if any other systems in the Western industrialized world can match the cost-controlling abilities of a Canadian province operating within the confines of the national medicare (Canada Health) Act once the province has developed the political intestinal fortitude required to reduce health care costs markedly. The critics of medicare who have argued that a purely publicly funded plan could not control health care costs have just been handed a severe setback. Not only is the Canadian medicare system capable of controlling costs, the real concern among provider groups is that the various provincial public plans will be far too effective once they get started. The impacts on the incomes and employment of thousands of professional and non-professional health care providers in Alberta has not been lost on other health care providers in other parts of Canada as they consider with alarm the effect that an Alberta-style cost-cutting exercise will have on their livelihoods.

Most of the attention in Alberta has been focused on health care cuts; however, as noted earlier, a major initiative was undertaken by the provincial government to increase health care premium revenue. Figure 4 provides a per capita breakdown of the rise in the medicare premium take of the provincial government between 1992/3 and 1997/8. Increases of approximately 41.4 per cent and 48.1 per cent are expected between 1992/3 and 1996/7 and 1992/3 and 1997/8, respectively. The burden of the medicare premium increases has been absorbed to this point in time with a minimum of political fuss other than for the concerns evidenced mainly by senior citizens' groups. The Alberta experience suggests the Canadian population as a whole may be willing to contribute significantly more funds in areas where the service is deemed to be extremely beneficial, the contributions are tied, and the provincial government is perceived to be making a determined attempt to reduce spending and improve the economic efficiency of the public service as well as simply asking for more funds to maintain the viability and quality of a specific service. The ability of the Alberta government to raise a significant amount of non-tax revenue for health care purposes in a very short period of time is a facet of the Klein revolution that is often conveniently ignored in certain discussions of the major changes implemented within the public sector of Alberta.

## 6. TRENDS IN THE ALBERTA HEALTH CARE/GDP RATIO

Figure 5 provides an overview of the movement in the ratio of provincial government health care spending relative to GDP for the period 1981/2 to 1998/9. This ratio is useful for tracing the major trends in total public spending relative

**Figure 4:** Medicare Premium Revenue Per Capita in Alberta, 1992/3–1997/8

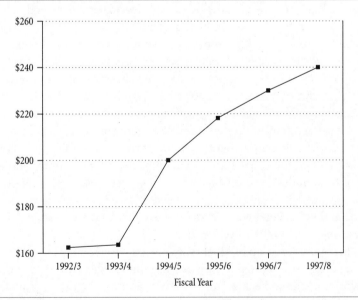

Fiscal Year

SOURCE: Alberta Health.

to total economic activity in the Alberta economy; however, it cannot shed any light on the important issue of determining whether or not shrinking public-sector activity is accompanied by expansion, contraction, or no change at all in the relative size of private-sector spending within the province. As matters presently stand it is clear the major reduction in provincial health care spending set out in the Alberta health care plan would, other things being equal, drive the provincial health care expenditure ratio down close to the 3.5 per cent of GDP level existing in the early 1980s. If the circumstances were similar one could also predict that the total health care/GDP ratio would be markedly lower and the Alberta government's health care expenditure plan would return all of Alberta, not just the provincial government, to that 'best-of-all-worlds' position the province as a whole enjoyed between 1977 and 1981.[5]

The problem with assuming the provincial government's health care plan will also drive down total health care spending relative to GDP is that anecdotal evidence is beginning to emerge from organizations such as the Consumers' Association of Canada (Alberta), other consumer groups such as Friends of Medicare, senior citizens' organizations, and various provider groups such as the United Nurses of Alberta that a significant shifting of costs onto the sick and the ill, their immediate family members, and employers is well under way in certain jurisdictions. The RHA cost shifts arise from pre-operative and early discharge patients being required to pay for drugs and other hospital supplies that used to

**Figure 5:** Provincial Government Health Care/GDP Ratio, 1981/2–1998/9

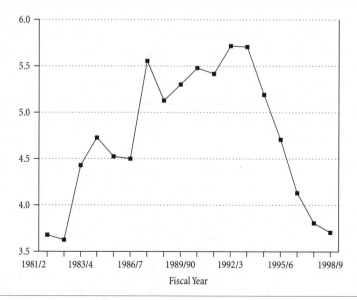

SOURCES: Alberta Treasury and Alberta Health.

be provided within the in-patient hospital component of an episode of illness. In addition, charges for home care appear to be rising and many of the costs of caring for the chronically, terminally, and mentally ill are seemingly being borne by their families. Out-of-pocket physician cost shifts are incorporated in the facility fees charged for certain services. Charges are also being levied for services that were traditionally included as part of the customary physician service package. The signing of school excuse slips for missing an examination, the renewal of a prescription over the phone, and the discussion of a patient's medical condition with family members, for instance, all became billable once the province began to reduce the gross revenues of physicians (Alberta Medical Association, 1995). Private health insurance costs for extended benefit plans are also increasing as the government reduces its coverage or excludes certain individuals from receiving certain extended benefits. Insurers respond in time-honoured ways by increasing their premiums, co-payments, or deductibles. Despite these shifts, the sheer magnitude of the public-sector cutbacks in the health care business plan are so large relative to any private-sector increases that the total as well as the public health care/GDP ratio inevitably will fall between 1992/3 and 1997/8. This observation is further buttressed by the fact that the Canada Health Act effectively prevents the provincial government from shifting a major portion of its hospital and physician costs onto the users.

## 7. GOVERNANCE OF THE HEALTH CARE SYSTEM: THE REGIONAL HEALTH AUTHORITIES

The use of business plans as the vehicle for identifying specific targets and mobilizing resources to achieve certain ends is primarily aimed at improving the management and accountability of the health care system; however, even well-designed business plans would have faltered and failed unless specific attention was directed towards reforming the governance structure of a highly fragmented unco-ordinated health care delivery system.[6] Alberta followed the lead of Saskatchewan, New Zealand, and the United Kingdom and established a regional health care system for governing the activities of local hospital boards (general acute and auxiliary), public health units, home care, and other related long-term care organizations.[7] Seventeen of these Regional Health Authorities, along with two temporary authorities for cancer and mental health, were created.[8] This was markedly less than in Saskatchewan (30) and markedly more than in New Zealand (4) and the UK (14).

A number of permanent regional funding and service delivery problems arise when regional boundaries are based primarily on political grounds rather than on health care service considerations and when a so-called population- or needs-based funding system is used. Residents located within a properly designed health care region are able to access a comprehensive range of health care services. The interregional flow of patients is minimized and the need to establish a complicated health care accounts resolution mechanism to settle interregional health care payments among sovereign RHAs is eliminated. A highly fragmented and incomplete set of health care regions is inevitable if health care service issues are subordinated to accommodate the political and economic interests of local and provincial politicians. A large number of health care regions incapable of meeting the needs of the population placed within their jurisdiction results in: (1) massive cross-border movements between regions in close proximity to each other; (2) the establishment of areas that have low population densities and an extremely limited number of health care facilities separated by long distances and inadequate financial resources to cope with their needs; and (3) the development of interregional funding settlement schemes that reward regions for diverting the number of patients as well as altering the case mix of patients flowing from one region to another.

All of these issues currently exist in Alberta or are in the process of being built into the new regional funding scheme (Ministry of Health, 1995b). For example, enormous variations exist in the census populations of the RHAs. The population of the Calgary RHA is 795,750 while the Northwestern RHA has a population of only 16,551 people. Only two RHAs (Calgary and the Capital region) have the capability of providing a full range of health care facilities to their citizens and even those regions are not large enough by themselves to provide the resources needed to provide the care needed in certain very highly specialized tertiary care areas. Approximately one-quarter of the regions provide hospital care for less than approximately 60 per cent (40 per cent in one region) of the people who reside within their region. Clearly, the census population is not representative of the actual proportion of the population of certain regions served by the health care facilities and health care professionals located within the region. This inability to sort out the population actually being served from the population contained within the administrative boundaries of the region results in the wrong population measure (census population) being used for health care region planning and administrative purposes.[9] All sorts of fictional inequities are alleged by local regional interests who continually relate their actual funding to their census population rather than to their service population.[10]

Regional Health Authority funding wars and the diversion of significant funds from the delivery of health care services towards protecting existing budgets and manipulating regional accounting systems are almost inevitable given the way the regional health care system has been set up in Alberta. One way to minimize the diversion of funds from patient-care to the establishment of more elaborate and resource-consuming information and administrative systems is simply to revise the regional boundaries in accordance with the existing health care services delivery patterns. Another is to eliminate the Funding Advisory Committee's proposal that the interregional movement of patients must be settled by a complicated province-wide costing of all of the services provided by RHAs (Ministry of Health, 1995b). There is a pressing and extremely practical reason for rejecting the comprehensive costing proposal as a basis for settling interregional servicing costs. The Province of Alberta does not have a credible costing system in place which could be used to evaluate the interregional flow of resources between RHAs. The population-based funding system is slated to be implemented in November of 1996, even though the costing system needed to implement properly the Funding Advisory Committee's recommendations has not been fully developed or operationalized. Unfortunately, this does not mean that some type of piece-meal incomplete costing system will not be 'cobbled' together and used to settle regional accounts. As matters presently stand, little is known about the actual costs of operating the multiplicity of long-term care, community care, prevention, promotion and protection, community rehabilitation, laboratory service, and ambulatory care programs for the entire Alberta health care system. Considerable effort has been expended in trying to develop a reasonable in-patient hospital costing system; however, the costing of the entire system is another matter. A lack of economic credibility destroyed the old Alberta Hospital Performance Index system, which was used in a valiant attempt to introduce a greater degree of economic efficiency among Alberta hospitals. Matters have an excellent chance of becoming worse at a much earlier stage with the proposed system unless certain of the obvious pitfalls are avoided.

Despite these weaknesses, the Alberta RHA system, which is still being phased in, is perceived to be a marked improvement over the old highly decentralized system. From a provincial government perspective the establishment of the 17 RHAs has meant that approximately 169 hospital boards (200 boards in total) have been able to be replaced or controlled more effectively than in the past.[11] This has resulted in the elimination of a large number of senior and middle management personnel. This consolidation gives the provincial government the opportunity to hold one local body responsible for the planning, management, and delivery of health care within a region. Each RHA has been required to prepare a coherent health care business plan for developing what will hopefully turn out to be an integrated, cost-effective way of delivering high-quality health care.

The emergence of strong local authorities with the ability to restructure the health care system has been viewed with concern by a number of health care providers. Some physicians who are quite active in the Alberta Medical Association (AMA) have complained long and loudly that they have not been consulted adequately in the major restructuring of the system. This outcry is seemingly in direct proportion to the degree that the managers of the RHAs have moved to make physicians accountable for how they use the region's resources. The majority of physicians have adapted and have worked quite diligently in making the new system work. It is not too unfair to suggest that the charge of 'lack of medical involvement and the lack of physician representation on the RHAs' orchestrated by the AMA has a great deal to do with physician concerns regarding the effect that their loss of control over the public health care system will do to their status, bargaining power, earnings, and ability to limit the entry of more paramedical personnel into the delivery of primary medical care.[12] (Protecting their turf is one of the most ancient of all the medical traditions.) On the other hand, it is also fair to say that claims of a marked deterioration in the quality of health care made by physicians and other health care providers are partially supported by anecdotal evidence emerging from media reports documenting alleged cases of maltreatment or neglect of patients. Patient surveys have indicated that the majority of the people using the system are satisfied with the quality of the care they have received (Capital Health Authority, 1995). In short, there is a high degree of ambiguity concerning the degree, if any, to which the quality of health care may have deteriorated as a result of the major cuts and reforms.

Certain of the RHAs (the Capital Health Authority, for example) have started to provide reports to the general public that can be used to commence monitoring the quality of the care being delivered.[13] Public rallies to save hospitals slated for closure or to prevent a change in their status from a higher level acute care to a community facility have resulted in thousands of people protesting the proposed changes; however, after the furore has died down the reforms have still been implemented. The reaction to the 15,000 marchers who protested the proposed change in the focus of the Grey Nuns (a 500-bed general acute care hospital located in Edmonton) from a full-service general acute care hospital to a community facility is a case in point. Surprisingly, both the provincial government and the RHAs have followed their business plans and stood up quite well under intense political pressure exerted by local medical providers and local community groups who were determined to 'save their hospital'.

The streamlining of the management and planning structure of the facilities and programs within a region and the development of a strong local health care authority have troubled smaller communities, which have felt they have been stripped of the input and control they previously enjoyed when their local facility was controlled by people resident within their community.[14] The provincial government anticipated this pressure and required each RHA to establish community health councils to keep the regional authority board appraised of local needs and concerns. The establishment of these councils has just commenced. The Capital Health Region, which encompasses the cities of

St Albert and Edmonton, has proposed that nine community health councils should be appointed by the RHA. The terms of reference of these community councils are currently unclear and their effects for better or for worse will only be known with the passage of time.

## 8. HANDS-OFF AND HANDS-ON:
## THE PROVINCIAL GOVERNMENT'S DILEMMA

From a 'top-down' perspective it appears the Ministry of Health has delegated a considerable amount of its authority. This is only partially true. All of the members of an RHA are appointed by the government and the minister of health still retains all of the sovereignty of the Crown in terms of overseeing and directing the activities of an RHA. Each RHA's business plan must conform to the business plan prepared by Alberta Health and each plan has to be approved by the minister. Regional advisers who ostensibly perform liaison work for the Health ministry are attached to each RHA. In addition, the minister of health has created a provincial health council with a technical advisory board composed solely of health providers[15] to report on the way the RHAs and other groups in the health care system are performing. Just recently the premier appointed a Special Standing Committee chaired by a physician MLA to investigate the activities of the RHAs and assist them in resolving certain perceived problems. In effect, the provincial government is schizophrenic when it comes to RHAs. On the one hand, it wants a strong local government capable of managing, planning, and delivering health care; on the other hand, it seems unwilling to establish broad guidelines and to grant the RHAs the autonomy to operate freely within such a framework. Health care providers, particularly physicians, are concerned that the new regional authorities will introduce new lines of economic accountability, price competition, managed care, and a monitoring of their activities that previously were either absent from the system or directly or indirectly under the control of providers. This has resulted in concerted physician lobbying of the provincial government to constrain the powers of the local authorities and place physicians on the boards of the RHAs. The minister of health has held off physicians in this regard, but some of the RHAs have invited physician representatives along with the heads of certain local governments to sit on their boards as non-voting participant observers.[16]

In short, the governance of the regional health care system is becoming confused and blurred as the provincial government and the local RHAs have begun to buckle under the demands for a sharing of power evidenced by a host of vested interest groups ranging from local government officials, health care provider groups, and the government's own backbench MLAs. The blurring of the lines of authority and the number of intermediate bodies and groups established to watch over and monitor the activities of the RHAs suggest that the effectiveness of the RHAs is in danger of becoming seriously impaired before they have had an opportunity to prove themselves. Indeed, it is suggested that the straw that will break the back of the RHAs will be contained in the government announcement indicating whether RHA board members will be elected or appointed by the minister. An RHA board made up of elected representatives will inevitably pit RHAs against the provincial government as two elected bodies express conflicting views over how a health care system should be run. In certain regions matters could become quite heated. The RHAs are empowered to spend and manage the money given to them by the province; however, the government has not granted the RHAs the authority required to access the tax base and raise the revenue required to meet the needs of the populace within their respective regions.

Government-RHA relationships will also take a turn for the worse if low turnouts at the polls result in the election of RHA boards largely beholden to various vested interest groups.[17] A functional democratic system could be created if the government was willing to create a local government structure for health care. This would markedly reduce provincial power and modify the RHA (appointed board) model. The creation of a fully democratic regional government along Scandinavian lines, with the RHAs directly elected and fully accountable to the people they served and having access to the provincial tax base required to fund a regional health care system, is an interesting alternative to the master-servant relationship presently built into the RHA structure.[18] A reasonable turnout at the polls and a careful scrutiny of the candidates could be expected if the population had to elect RHA boards that were both requisitioning and spending authorities.[19]

## 9. THE IMPACT OF HEALTH CARE REFORMS ON GENERAL ACUTE CARE HOSPITALS AND DOCTORS

### 9.1 Hospital Reforms

Outlays on hospitals and physicians are the two largest items of expenditure in the Alberta provincial health care budget. They amounted to 58 and 22 per cent, respectively, of total provincial health care spending in 1992/3. Major cutbacks are concentrated in both of these areas. General acute care hospitals account for almost 80 per cent of total hospital spending and they have accordingly borne the brunt of the cuts in funding. Approximately 44 per cent of the general acute care hospital beds within the province are slated to be closed as the system moves from an average of 4.3 to a target of 2.4 beds per 1,000 population (Ministry of Health, 1995a). It is evident, given the magnitude of the proposed reduction in the stock of beds, that major changes must also occur in the number of admissions and the length of stay if reasonable access to acute care services is to be maintained.

These two factors are captured in a single variable—the patient-day target established by the Health ministry. The three-year health plan envisages a reduction in the number of patient-days from 1,083 to 745 per 1,000 population—a decrease of approximately 33 per cent. The shock factor associated with closing 44 per cent of the acute care hospital beds has tended to detract from the fact that the patient-day target established by Alberta Health is quite credible. It lies within the range of what certain other provinces are already trying to do. For example, British Columbia and Ontario have targets of 850 patient-days per 1,000. The current British Columbia rate is around 931. Note that the patient-day targets set for Ontario and British Columbia are approximately 14 per cent higher than the Alberta target. This suggests that Alberta may experience greater degrees of difficulty (increasing marginal costs to the system and diminishing benefits to patients) as it attempts to move below the targets set by a province such as British Columbia, which has had more time to develop and has had more experience in operating a more fully integrated health care system that functions successfully with a relatively low level of general acute care beds available to back up its out-patient surgeries, early discharge, and chronic care programs.

Alberta can learn a great deal from Saskatchewan. Both Saskatchewan and Alberta started with a relatively high number of acute care beds per 1,000 population and both provinces have adopted a regional model that focuses on the development of an integrated health care delivery system with markedly lower levels of acute care in-patient stays. The major difference is that Saskatchewan started the experiment sooner and has exerted less financial pressure on its system in the process of carrying out its reforms (52 small rural hospitals have been closed).

Figure 6 is based on recently released Alberta Health data. It serves to illustrate that the health care reform process had been initiated and was working towards rationalizing the stock of hospital beds within the general acute care hospital system in Alberta long before the current three-year plan was conceived or initiated. It will be interesting to see what the total change in the stock of general acute care beds will actually be between 1990 and 1998 after the reforms in the early and late nineties have worked their way through the system and the political realities of hospital bed closures have been dealt with in rural Alberta.

### 9.2 Physician Reforms

A proposed reduction of approximately 20 per cent in medical expenditures is built into the three-year business plan. Total medical services spending is to be

**Figure 6:** Total Number of Beds: Calgary, Capital, and Other RHAs

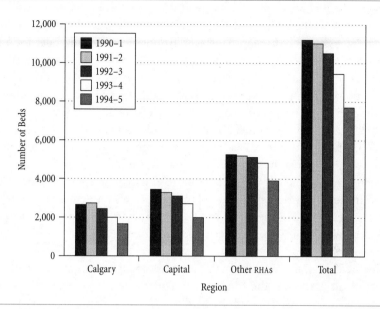

SOURCE: Alberta Health.

reduced from approximately $907 million in 1993/4 to $707 million in 1996/7 after allowances are made for the existing agreements and the factoring in of the medical profession's participation in the 5 per cent across-the-board roll-back in wages and salaries. This is an impressive reduction that has no precedent in the history of physician-provincial government bargaining relationships in the province of Alberta. It may also be unique in Canada. No other provincial government has ever taken on organized medicine and attempted to roll back total medical payments to such a degree. The $200 million worth of medical expenditure reductions are to come from a variety of initiatives, such as restructuring the laboratory system, de-insuring certain medical services, restricting the number of billing numbers issued within a given year, establishing clinical practice guidelines, tightening the payment rules for items such as third-party services, introducing alternative payment schemes for practitioners, educating the public with a view towards reducing their demand for medical services, etc. (Ministry of Health, 1994b: 7)

In the foreword to its second three-year business plan, Alberta Health stated: 'The new plan builds on the accomplishments from 1994–95, the most notable of which are: . . . An "omnibus" agreement with the Alberta Medical Association to reduce expenditures on physician services . . .' (Ministry of Health, 1995a: 1). In a news release dated 4 May 1994 the minister of health claimed that 'The agreement we have reached in principle with the AMA achieves virtually half of that target [the 20 per cent objective]'. In effect, an agreement was reached regarding one-half, or $100 million, of the $200 million planned expenditure reduction. However, trouble was brewing over the next $100 million, and in a news release dated 17 August 1994 Alberta Health noted: 'The Minister expressed disappointment with the progress of negotiations so far. Alberta Medical Association proposals to date would result in savings of approximately $6M over four years, far short of the government's objective. On July 25, the Alberta Cabinet reinforced its continued commitment to the original business plan target.' Matters are currently at an impasse between the minister of health and the AMA. Letters and last-minute appeals to all MLAs have been made by the AMA in an attempt to engineer an end-run around the health minister. The premier countered this ploy by announcing that he would attempt to clear up all of the major health care problems sitting on the government's desk within 90 days, in effect, by Christmas (*Edmonton Sun*, 21 Sept. 1995: 5).

The fiscal dilemma faced by both the government and organized medicine stems from the fact that the total stock of physicians accessing the Alberta medicare plan increased by approximately 34 per cent between 1984 and 1994 while the population increased by only 11 per cent and total nominal medicare spending increased by roughly 79 per cent. Figure 7 indicates that the physician/population ratio was relatively constant between the early 1970s and 1980s and has more or less stabilized in the late eighties and early nineties. Unfortunately, the physician boom of the eighties coincided with one of the most troubled decades in the fiscal history of the province.

Agreements have been reached to issue medicare billing numbers in line with the medical needs of each RHA in the province; however, no medical targets have been explicitly identified in the plan that would allow a needs-based system to work effectively. The establishment of physician targets to complement the hospital bed and patient-day ratios would help to rectify matters in the long run; however, a $100 million solution has to be found in the short run. A policy to use attrition coupled with severe restrictions on entry into what are viewed to be oversupplied RHAs such as Calgary and the Capital RHA could have been used to help alleviate a portion of the short-run problem over the first two years of the plan. Such a policy initiative seems to run up against what appears to be a tacit agreement between the province and the medical profession to guarantee sufficient openings at least to accommodate new graduates emerging from the two medical schools located in Calgary and Edmonton. This policy is quite at odds with respect to what has happened in nursing, the other health care occupations, and the rest of the university community within the province.

**Figure 7:** Physician/Population Ratio Trend, 1970–1993

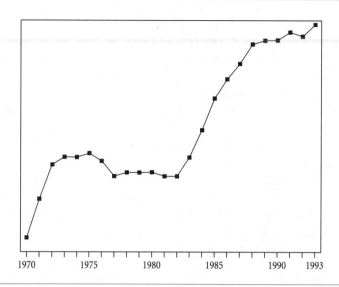

SOURCE: Alberta Health.

The $100 million fiscal objective of the government is crystal clear; however, if an agreement fails to materialize, the government will either have to admit failure and back down on the fulfilment of the physician component of its three-year health care plan or unilaterally implement policies that would lower total medical spending. A general roll-back in medical fees could be instituted. Other options exist, such as setting specific caps on billings by specialty and/or initiating a marked reduction in the excess stock of physicians located in Edmonton and Calgary. Exercising any of these options would be politically painful. The 'backing-down' option, which entails only piecemeal reform of the health care system without restructuring the delivery of medical services or significantly changing the financial incentives built into fee-for-service medicine, would not augur well for future cost-effectiveness, nor would it sit well with the rest of the health care labour force, which has had to bear the full burden of the cutback.

## 10. HEALTH CARE GOALS AND PERFORMANCE MEASURES

### 10.1 Measurement Problems and the Missing Link

No single measure exists to provide an unambiguous assessment of the success or failure of a health care delivery system. The bottom line of the private-sector firm, which indicates whether a profit or loss has been incurred, is missing from the Alberta health care business plan. This is not unique to Alberta. It is a common problem faced by every health care system in the civilized world. No common metric can be used to value all the benefits derived from the use of health care goods and services. Net health care benefits, the counterpart of profits and losses, are missing and the ability to evaluate the economic performance of a system can become an extremely complex and at times frustrating task for unwary analysts. It is all too easy to become bogged down in a bewildering array of often conflicting intermediate output and input measurements. Considerable progress has been made by health care researchers in identifying and resolving the methodological and practical difficulties of output measurement in health care; few would deny, however, that a great deal of work remains to be done. Drummond (1994: 98–114) provides a succinct overview of various types of output measures that are useful for dealing with certain health care economic resource allocation issues. He argues that QALYs (Quality Adjusted Life Years), despite their limitations, are a marked improvement over cases treated or various measures of mortality as far as an assessment of health outcomes are concerned. He concludes:

> there needs to be more comparisons of clinical measures, disease-specific scales, general scales and utility measures within clinical trials. Since there is no 'gold standard' for the measurement of health-related quality of life, it is important to explore the convergent validity of the various measures. . . . there needs to be more exploration of the differences between the alternative approaches to utility measurement. . . . there needs to be more research into the nature of choice at the level of health care policy.

Drummond's comments are sensible and to the point; the reality of the matter, though, is that various funding authorities have to use some measure or standard to guide them in determining whether there is any justification for expanding or contracting or leaving the funding to the total public health care system unchanged. The QALY approach has not been developed sufficiently, even if there were agreement that it would be the suitable instrument for such a purpose (see Mooney and Olsen, 1994).

Operational measures of health care outcomes are a mandatory feature of Alberta's three-year business plan process. The allocation of billions of dollars of health care funds within the provincial budget framework is based on short-run macroeconomic considerations. Any health care plan developed by the provincial government must be able to cope with short-run economic fluctuations. It must, by necessity, focus on highly aggregated segments of the health care system that are far removed from the resource allocation decisions made by individual health care providers and administrators as they attempt to meet the specific needs of Alberta society. It is useful, given this state of affairs, to consider the goals and performance measures the Alberta government has established to monitor and evaluate the success or failure of the province's three-year health care business plan. This matter is of particular interest since it is the first time in Canadian history that a provincial government has attempted to evaluate the performance of an entire health care system.

## 10.2 Setting the Goals and Identifying the Outcomes in the Three-Year Alberta Health Care Business Plan

Four major health care goals are identified within the three-year Alberta health care plan:

(1) Maintain a continuum of affordable, accessible and appropriate high-quality health services in appropriate settings and locales that ensure a client-oriented focus;

(2) Increase the ability of Albertans to lead healthy and independent lives;

(3) Increase financial contributions from Albertans, based on ability to pay for health programs where premiums or other charges are currently levied; and

(4) Increase the ability of partners in the health system to demonstrate accountability for the use of health resources and outcomes achieved.[20] (Ministry of Health, 1995a)

Each of the above goals has a number of strategies and performance measures linked to it. These are too numerous to be dealt with in their entirety here; however, it is useful to note certain of the key measures identified for goals 1 and 2, which are focused on affordability, accessibility, health care quality, and the improvement of the health of Albertans. Goal 3 and its performance measures are centred on raising revenues via the existing health care premium system. Goal 4 and its measures 'involve developing tools for use under other goals. Consequently, the measure of success under Goal 4 is often simply the proof that the tool has been developed and employed' (Ministry of Health, 1995a: 23). This is a curious statement given that certain of the measures listed deal with items such as the monitoring of physician visits per 100 residents, the public's rating of the health care system, and the development of indicators that are supposed to measure the public's ability to use the health care system appropriately.[21]

### Goal 1: The Affordability Measures

The performance measures associated with affordability have a set of indicators to track provincial government health care spending relative to GDP and various provincial health care budget targets, and also indicate some undefined shift from fee-for-service to some alternative method for paying doctors (Ministry of Health, 1995a: 18). Affordability focuses on the government as an entity acting separately and apart from its citizens. Affordability is perceived in terms of the Health department meeting or bettering the expenditure reductions set out in the current year's budget. The use of affordability within this context is most unusual. The affordability of health care in a Canadian system where the state has been charged with the responsibility for raising the revenue required to fund the provision of medically required services by hospitals and physicians must in some sense be centred on the issue of the affordability of the health care system by its citizens. The lack of consideration of the burden health care spending places on individual Albertans relative to their incomes or a consideration of the tax burden borne by Albertans arising from public health care spending is a serious omission from any properly constituted monitoring system designed to focus on how the affordability of the provincial portion of a health care system changes in response to a set of reform plans designed to reduce significantly the flow of funds to the system over a relatively short period of time. For example, it would be extremely useful, from a citizen's perspective, to know that total provincial health care spending per capita fell by 9.8 per cent between 1993 and 1994 while total personal income per capita rose by 1.3 per cent (Health Canada, 1996; Department of Finance, 1995). From an affordability perspective this implies that the ratio of provincial health care expenditures to personal income ratio fell by approximately 11 per cent in one year. Surely such a marked improvement in the affordability of the health care system is worth tracking and including within a health care business plan. Meeting a budget target is one thing; improving the affordability of the health care system is another. Comparisons of Alberta spending on health care relative to other provinces, as well as a comparison of spending to income and the health care tax burden borne by residents of other provinces, should also be considered. Affordability has many dimensions. The Alberta government's business plan has been highly selective and lacking in focus in its choice of the performance measures used to monitor this component of its plan.

*Goal 1: The Accessibility Measures*
The performance measures related to accessibility focus on commonly employed supply-side and utilization-based measures such as the number of acute care beds, long-term beds, patient-days, home-care services, Caesarean-sections, palliative facilities, etc., within a region. A need for interregional comparisons is identified; however, no targets are established for the majority of the performance indicators. Acute care and long-term beds and patient-days per 1,000 population are the exceptions in this regard (Ministry of Health, 1995a: 18). Another omission emerges from a review of the accessibility performance measures. Not one of the 16 accessibility performance measures deals with the effect increases in user fees have on patient access to various types of health services. This is a singular accomplishment. One of the longest-running controversies between various provincial governments and the federal government concerning health care matters over the past two decades has centred on the effect that out-of-pocket charges have on the access to medically required services of modest-income Canadians. Alberta was at the forefront during the

1980s in contravening the Canada Health Act provisions banning extra-billing and the implementation of various user fees by hospitals. Currently, Alberta is being fined approximately $430,000 per month for allowing doctors to levy facility fees for services provided within the confines of their private clinics. In addition, a whole set of new and existing charges have been implemented for health care services that seemingly lie mostly outside the purview of the Canada Health Act. These charges range from increased co-payment charges for the Blue Cross Drug Plan to the shifting of hospital costs from the hospital to individuals because of the creation of programs that lead to the treatment of patients at home as well as within an institutional setting. Such shifts in costs matter to private individuals and businesses.

It is difficult to believe Alberta Health simply overlooked the need to monitor the effect user fees have on patient access to health care services. User fees do restrict access to the use of health care services for modest-income users. Health care is one of Alberta's major social programs and the distributive consequences stemming from the implementation of user fees are of major importance in terms of maintaining the well-being of a significant portion of the population. Under medicare, altruism and equity have outweighed economic efficiency in the provision of hospital and medical services. A number of Alberta's health reform initiatives have challenged the equity efficiency trade-off by attacking the accessibility criterion with various types of user pay initiatives. If some understanding of the effects of user fees on access to services had been communicated to the RHAs, and if a careful monitoring of outcomes had been insisted upon, more of the problems experienced by patients could have been markedly reduced or eliminated.

### Goal 1: Appropriateness and Quality of Health Care

Six performance measures are identified in this section (Ministry of Health, 1995a: 19). Two of the six indicators focus on quality of health care issues. One is a measurement of patient satisfaction with the services provided by the health care system. The other quality measure centres on the development of an index to measure rates of avoidable hospitalization. The remaining variables deal with various appropriateness indicators that seek to measure whether patients are receiving care in the least costly setting. (Same-day surgery, long-term care residence classification mix, and percentage of patients receiving home care are examples of the indicators being used.) The quality of care performance measures clearly are weak at this stage. It is important to note, however, that the quality of care rendered is not necessarily dependent on what is set out in a provincial health care business plan. The major portion of the work in the quality assurance area is of a micro nature and has always been done by hospitals and various professional groups. The major criticism of the Alberta health care business plan is that no apparent direction has been given towards identifying the minimum quality of care that the RHAs and professional bodies are responsible for monitoring and making available to the public.

### Goal 2: Performance Indicators: Measuring the Improvement in the Health of Albertans

From an economic perspective, this is the most important of the four goals set out in the Alberta Health business plan. By focusing on the improvement in the health status of the population as the performance measure, it is relatively easy to accept the proposition that increases in health care expenditure that improve health status can also be assumed to improve the welfare or well-being of the population. No such claim can be made for any of the other goals, which use a variety of health care utilization or expenditure measures as their performance indicators. The relationship between health status and health care utilization and spending is not answered by such indicators. Will increases or decreases in health care spending, which may expand or contract health care use, lead to an enhancement or reduction in health status or no change at all? The second goal is what makes the Alberta health care business plan unique. The Alberta government has established an explicit mechanism for linking health care use and its associated health care spending to improvements in the health status and well-being of the Alberta population. While improvements in health status are a source of utility to patients, health care in and of itself is a source of disutility —more needles, drugs, and surgical procedures cannot be viewed as sources of satisfaction to a normal, sane individual (see Evans, 1984).

### Monitoring the Health Status of Albertans

How will the province monitor changes in the health status of the Alberta population? The answer is found in the following list of performance measures:

> Life expectancy, life expectancy in good health (disability-free life expectancy), infant mortality rate, age and sex-standardized mortality rates by major causes of death, age and sex-standardized injury rates by major categories, age and sex-standardized disability rates, age and sex-standardized rate of bed days, restricted activity rate, age and sex-standardized rate of Health Status Index scores, the percentage of Albertans who report their health to be very good or excellent and the percentage of Albertans over 75 who live independently at home. (Ministry of Health, 1994b: 20)

The above measures are a mix of mortality- and morbidity-based health status measures accompanied by self-assessment gleaned from a survey of the general population. The issue of determining how the health status of a population is to be obtained from this host of performance indicators is not discussed in the business plan. Clearly, all of these health status criteria could not be given equal weight. For example, the infant mortality rate provides a measure of how the death rate for an important subset of the population changes; however, the self-assessed health status measure covers the majority of the population and it involves the consideration of a range of health factors that greatly transcend mortality. The mortality-based status measures are derived from a data base that is updated annually (the provincial death files) and can generally be viewed to be reliable, inexpensive, and capable of being broken down into small regional subsets. Other more comprehensive health status indices require census data. This creates such time discontinuities that the index cannot be used for annual budgeting and performance evaluation purposes. The age- and sex-standardized health status index suffers partially from this type of information problem. It is evident that the selection of one or more of the health status criteria to measure changes in the Alberta population has not been resolved as far as the health care business plan is concerned. A list of health status performance measures or criteria exists, but the problem of resolving conflicting indicators or weighting or selecting an operational composite index has yet to be solved.

## 11. HEALTH STATUS AND HEALTH CARE SPENDING

### 11.1 The Alberta Health Business Plan Perspective

The Alberta Health business plan states that 'Over a three-year period the overall health of Albertans is expected to stay approximately the same or improve slightly. In the long term, it should improve' (Ministry of Health, 1994b). Two important points can be drawn from this statement. First, Alberta Health predicts that the health status of Albertans is expected to remain the same or even improve slightly over the course of a three-year business plan designed to bring about a 25 per cent real per capita (18 per cent total) reduction in provincial health care spending. Second, after the cuts are finished the health status of the population is assumed to continue rising. The basis for the long-run increase in health status is not specified. Attention is now directed to determining what the theoretical and empirical basis is of the relationship between the health status of a population and the level of health care spending. In short, how do the designers of the Alberta Health business plan claim that a marked decrease in health care spending can be associated with an improvement in the health status of the population?

### 11.2 The Theoretical Basis for Health Status and Health Care Spending Relationships

It is commonplace in health care economic lectures to set out one or more models linking health status outcomes to health care resource inputs. These models are used to highlight the strengths and weaknesses of the medical needs approach employed by health care professionals in allocating scarce health care resources. Meeting the health care needs of the populace, coupled with often heated debates centred on the under- or over-utilization of health care services, is at the heart of almost all health care policy discussions (Evans, 1984: 18). R.G. Evans (1984: 28) sets out four models depicting the possible relationships between health status improvements and health care spending. These models are derived from earlier work done by A.J. Culyer and are reflected again in Culyer's work in the late eighties on health care spending in Canada (Culyer, 1988).

The common point that all of these models share is that, initially, increases in health care spending are associated with positive increases in the health status of the population. The models are differentiated from each other on the basis of different assumptions regarding what happens at the margin to health status as spending increases. Diminishing or constant health status changes for each increment in health care spending give rise to the 'ever-increasing needs' class of models, which are curvilinear or linear in nature. The inverted 'U-shape' of a health status, health care spending curve includes the diminishing returns case and the possibility that health care spending could be taken to the point where additional spending on health care could actually reduce the health status of the nation. Lastly, an inverted 'L-shape' curve depicts a system where the change in health status relative to increased health care spending remains constant until all the needs of the population are met—health status reaches its maximum. Additional expenditures beyond the break in the straight line are viewed as over-utilization or flat-of-the-curve medicine. The change in health status is zero for each additional unit of health care spending.

### 11.3 Understanding the Alberta Health Care Status and Spending Relationship

Health care economic theory indicates that a number of possible curves depicting various types of medical needs models can be postulated. Theory alone cannot be used to select the 'right' model. The appropriate health data bases must be used to estimate the specific form of the health status and spending relationship that characterizes the health care system in Alberta. Virtually all policy-makers, administrators, professional groups, health care unions, and analysts knowingly or unknowingly have one of the models described by Culyer and Evans in mind as they advance various viewpoints regarding what they believe will happen if health care spending is reduced, expanded, or left unchanged. This is also true of the individuals who collectively formulated the Alberta Health three-year business plan. In effect, the Alberta government knowingly or unknowingly has incorporated one variant or other of the theoretical models described earlier. It is important to determine what the nature of this relationship might be, given the major differences in health care outcomes that result from changes in health care spending in certain of the health care models that have been identified.

### 11.4 Selection of the Health Status and Health Care Expenditure Criteria

The performance measures listed under the second Alberta Health goal were mostly mortality- or morbidity-based measures of health status. As noted above, however, no work had been done in determining how conflicting results obtained from a wide variety of health status variables were to be rationalized or whether some composite index of some of these variables, suitably weighted, could be created. Given these problems, I have used combined (male and female) life expectancy from birth as the health status criterion and total health care spending (public and private) per capita in constant 1986 dollars as the health spending measure. Two reasons exist for the selection of the life expectancy variable: (1) reliable data are available for mortality-based health status for the period 1975–92 and (2) a mortality-based health status measure has been employed for almost two decades in the funding of regional health authorities in Britain—the forerunner of the RHA system currently being developed in Alberta (Carr-Hill et al., 1994). The reason for focusing on total real health care spending on a per capita basis is quite straightforward. Private-sector spending needs to be included with public-sector spending because the cost of prescription drugs, exclusive of welfare recipents and the aged, tends to be the responsibility of individuals and their employers in most Canadian provinces where a publicly insured comprehensive drug plan has not been put into place. In addition, there are numerous expenditures on health care professionals and paramedical personnel, personal health care, care for the elderly, non-prescription drugs, and the like, all of which are part and parcel of the mix of health care goods and services used by the public.

### 11.5 The Specific Form of the Life Expectancy/Health Status Relationship in Alberta

Figure 8 depicts the relationship between the combined life expectancy at birth and total real per capita health expenditures for Alberta between 1975 and 1992, the latest date for which life expectancy data were available. The plot showing the actual values for various levels of real per capita health care spending and the life expectancy of the population is overlaid by a line estimated by means of an ordinary least-squares regression analysis.[22]

It is useful to explore the health care economic policy import of these results. First, a solid link exists between the life expectancy of Albertans and the level of total real per capita spending on health care. Quite surprisingly, the relationship is linear. Ever-increasing needs is the medical needs model that fits

**Figure 8:** Life Expectancy and Health Care Spending

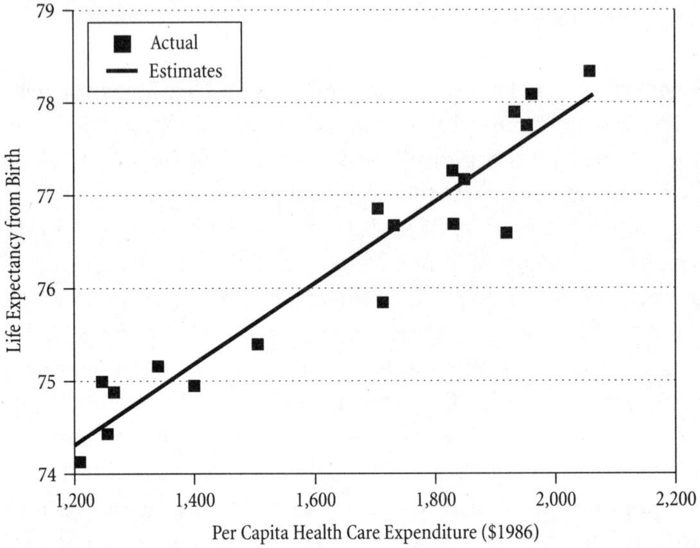

SOURCES: Health Canada, *National Health Expenditures in Canada 1975–94*, Ottawa, 1996; Statistics Canada, 'Births and Deaths', Cat. Nos. 82–003, 84–206, and 84–211.

the Alberta health care system. No diminishing returns are encountered. Much of the economic policy in Alberta has assumed that the Alberta health status health expenditure curve was represented by a non-linear reciprocal function (the inverted 'L' shape). In effect, it has been assumed for all practical purposes that no discernible change in health status could be detected for any change (increase or decrease) in provincial spending. Alberta was assumed to lie somewhere on the flat of the curve or a reasonable approximation to it. Health cutbacks in the flat-of-the-curve portion would not result in any significant change in the health status of the population.

Figure 8 has a different story to tell. If all other things remain equal, the linear model indicates the reduction in the level of health care expenditures envisaged in the Alberta plan would result in a significant lowering of the life expectancy of the population. Cutbacks without health care reform would reduce the health status of the population. If all goes well (if the health care reform plan works), all other things will not remain equal. More specifically, the health care reform plan envisages an increase in economic efficiency arising from the restructuring and reorganization of the system. All of the theoretical models assume that the most economically efficient way of providing health care is being used. If this is not the case then a higher level or the same level of health status can be expected with a lower level of health care spending. This means that the life expectancy/health care expenditure line shown in Figure 8 is expected to shift upward. In the best of all worlds real per capita health care spending would fall as specified under the health care reform plan and economic efficiency changes would be so successful that the line would shift upward at a rate that would improve, or at worst leave the life expectancy of the population unchanged. The key question is: Will the upward shift in the regression line be sufficient to offset the fall in life expectancy involved in moving along the 'x axis' as real per capita health care spending is lowered? This cannot be answered definitively until the new data on the health care reform period are made available.

Of course, the possibility also exists that the line could shift downward. This pessimistic view would be based on the assumption that the health care system is becoming less and less efficient as the reforms progress. Chaos brought about by extremely rapid changes and disruptions within the system would be viewed as lowering the economic efficiency of the health care system. Clearly, a combination of increasing economic inefficiency coupled with declining real per capita health care expenditures would maximize the rate of decline in the health status of the Alberta population. Such a pessimistic outlook would not be supported by most experienced observers at this stage in the Alberta health care reform process. However, new information systems at both the RHA and provincial government levels are just beginning to come on-line, and no comprehensive up-to-date data base currently allows any definitive assessment to be made of the overall economic efficiency gains or losses that the entire system has experienced as a result of the reforms.[23] All of the preliminary evidence[24] suggests there have been major gains; however, given the depth of the cutbacks it cannot be ruled out that some health status losses have also occurred.

It is worth noting, as an aside, that the upward sloping straight line implies that health care providers are not wrong in arguing that spending more on health care will improve the health status of the population. The problem is that there is no level of health care spending where the needs of the population will be met. Well-intentioned health care providers will always be able to find more needs and to justify more spending. If health care needs are unlimited (the needs of the population can never be met), then it is clear that individuals other than health care providers have to make the decision when 'enough is enough' as far as spending is concerned. The opportunity cost of providing additional health care is measured in the benefits forgone in employing resources in their next best endeavour. Health care providers may be able to claim special knowledge with respect to the beneficial outcomes from certain health care services being used in certain ways; however, they have absolutely no ability beyond that of the average citizen in determining whether more or less resources should be allocated to health care vis-à-vis other areas of human activity.

## 12. CROSS-SECTIONAL AND TIME SERIES HEALTH STATUS AND HEALTH CARE SPENDING RESULTS

The countries and provinces that have implemented a population-based funding system have decided on *a priori* grounds that if they don't have a good relationship between health care spending and the health status of the people, then they are going to remedy matters by employing a needs-based funding system that will eventually ensure that spending is closely linked to the health status of the population. Interestingly enough, it is possible for a nation or a province to have major inequities (a poor correlation) between the health status of the population and health care spending within various regions at a particular point in time and still have a relatively good relationship (high correlation) between the health status of the population and the level of health care spending of a nation over time. This paradox is easily explained once it is noted that relative inequities among regions may remain unchanged while the absolute aggregate health status of each region or the nation taken as a whole is steadily rising in response to increases in the level of real per capita health care spending.

This observation implies that two aspects of the issue in Alberta must be kept in mind as far as health care reforms are concerned. One involves keeping a watchful eye on the effect cutbacks in health care funding will have on the health status of the total provincial population, given the existing distribution of health care resources. The other is focused on ensuring that the provincial health care transfer payments are allocated to regions in accordance with their medical needs. Because of the magnitude of the Alberta cuts, provincial policy-makers and administrators have to be aware of the possibility of improving matters by relating health care funding more closely to the health status of the population in each region while reducing total funding to such a point that overall health status is lowered. The point of the brief discussion here is to highlight the fact that the Alberta Health three-year business plan requires a considerable amount of health care economic work if it is to be made operational. In particular, work must be done to establish explicit links between spending and certain of the key health status measurements. An example in terms of estimating the specific form of the life expectancy/health care spending relationship was given to show how this could be done and how important such results are for articulating and focusing the reforms being carried out.

## 13. PRICE DISCRIMINATION AND REASONABLE ACCESS TO HEALTH CARE SERVICES

Section 12 of the Canada Health Act sets out the criterion respecting accessibility. The health care insurance plan of a province 'must provide for insured health services on uniform terms and conditions and on a basis that does not impede or preclude, either directly or indirectly whether by charges made to insured persons or otherwise, reasonable access to those services by insured persons.' Twelve key principles have been set out by Alberta for establishing the hybrid public/private system it wishes to establish for the provision of medical services within the province. Among these are that the system should 'ensure reasonable access to a full range of appropriate, universal, insured services, without charge at point of service'; that 'private clinics should have the option of becoming completely private (patient pays), or allowing them to enter into a variety of funding arrangements with the public sector to cover the full costs of insured services'; and that 'physicians can receive payment from both the public funded system and fully private sources' (Ministry of Health, 1996). The following points should be noted:

(1) Price discrimination pays. Charging different prices to different patients for a service that costs the same allows a medical practitioner to capture a portion of the consumer surplus that otherwise would accrue to the public if only a single price (an agreed-upon medicare fee) was charged for the service. If other things remain equal, price discrimination allows a medical doctor to maximize his or her profits. In short, price discrimination allows the physician to benefit at the patients' expense.

(2) Manipulation of the waiting list is the vehicle for operating the price discrimination scheme built into Alberta's 'Key Principles' proposal. Price discrimination is the tool employed today in the facility fee scheme concocted by certain of Alberta's medical providers. The only difference between the current scheme and the proposed new scheme is that the medical practitioner will not be paid by both the medicare plan and the patient. The demand for most surgical services is highly inelastic; therefore, levying the full fee should reduce volumes somewhat and lead to the establishment of a new fee that could even be as high or higher than the combined current (regulated) medicare and (unregulated) facility fee. Interestingly, the ability of private practitioners to shift the demand for services to their facilities is great because of the current cutbacks in health care funding and the misleading statements from certain providers over the length of the waits being experienced within the public sector.

(3) What does Alberta mean by reasonable access to a full range of medical services? As matters presently stand, the Consumers' Association of Canada (Alberta) surveys have shown that the longest waits for cataract services are in practices where the physician is associated with or owns a private clinic. Reasonable access from an Alberta perspective seemingly means that a physician who is allowed to operate in both the private/public or public setting can manipulate his or her waiting list to best suit his/her income maximizing objectives. Equating waiting times will not resolve the access issue. Physicians (and their clinic receptionists) are the primary source of the patients' waiting list

information. An individual private clinic may not know or may not inform the patient correctly regarding the length of the waits being experienced by patients who have been placed on the medicare and private practice waiting lists of other physicians. In addition, the markets for many medical services in Alberta are very thin. Equal medicare and private clinic waiting times for each physician would be an improvement over the existing system; however, the operation of an equitable waiting list system would have to be policed and regulated. This would be a never-ending and thankless task that would probably involve the College of Physicians and Surgeons or some other physician-controlled quasi-regulatory group. Clearly, the best way of solving the access issue is to eliminate the principle that allows doctors both public and private-fee services, and give physicians the choice of either remaining totally within or opting totally out of the medicare plan.

## 14. CONCLUSIONS AND RECOMMENDATIONS

The reforms contained in the three-year Alberta Health business plan are playing a key role in helping the government achieve its deficit elimination objectives. The majority of the health care reforms being implemented needed to be carried out irrespective of whether the provincial budget was balanced, in deficit, or in a surplus. The breakneck pace at which the reforms are being implemented is another matter. Excellent arguments can be advanced that 'the fiscal cart' has been placed too far in advance of the 'health-care reform horse'. It is doubtful, however, if some of the more intransigent of the powerful vested interest groups controlling the health care industry could have been moved without massive fiscal pressure being applied. In any case, the niceties of incrementalism versus the cold-turkey approach to health care reform are matters that will be left for economic historians to resolve.

The following conclusions can be drawn regarding the health care reforms currently being implemented:

(1) The overwhelming bulk of the health care reforms in Alberta were not invented by the current government. They are an outgrowth of a number of other key reports and studies which were prepared by previous Alberta governments or by neighbouring provinces.

(2) The existing evidence suggests the fundamental nature of the Alberta health care system, centred on the private provision and public financing of medically required hospital and physician services, does not appear to have been significantly altered by the existing government as far as the consumer is concerned. This has primarily been due to the provisions of the Canada Health Act, the renewed determination of the federal government to enforce the Act, the wishes of the electorate, strong consumer advocacy groups, and the general

desire of the provincial government to control the costs of health care services. Major changes have occurred in various labour markets and in the private versus public provision of intermediate goods and services (laundries, preparation of meals, provision of laboratory services, etc.), which have not been fully documented or analysed. The facility fee issue is still outstanding and while it currently is small *vis-à-vis* total health care spending, it is major in regard to the preservation of the future integrity and control over the costs of the Canadian medicare system.

(3) The establishment of the boundaries of the RHAs on political grounds has led to a number of problems with the size, mix, and viability of certain RHAs that need to be addressed immediately. Particular urgency should be directed towards sorting out matters in the Capital region.

(4) The proposed population-based funding formula needs to be reviewed. Health status variables need to be incorporated into the formula and a different scheme needs to be established for adjusting to interregional patient flows.

(5) A careful analysis needs to be undertaken of the distributional effects stemming from the more intensive use of premiums as a vehicle for funding the health care system. The replacement of the tax-funded portion of the medical care insurance plan (the federal portion financed by tax points) with medicare premiums will seemingly shift a greater portion of the burden of financing the medical services portion of the Alberta health care plan onto the shoulders of lower-income Albertans. An increase of approximately 28 per cent in the number of individuals who have opted out of the medicare plan (fiscal 1993/4 versus fiscal 1994/5) is quite worrisome given that medicare premiums are continuing to rise. The access to medical services is impaired among the opted-out group unless one assumes that only multimillionaires have opted out (everyone else is medically indigent in the face of major and extremely costly health care interventions), and the universality provision of the Canada Health Act is violated. The numbers of people involved (101) are quite small at this point in time.

(6) The Alberta Health plan does not make any adjustment for population growth or inflation. Once these adjustments are carried out it can be shown what is touted to be a 17.8 per cent decrease in total health care spending really amounts to a 25 per cent per capita decline. It is totally unacceptable for Alberta Health to present a business plan that ignores population growth in its calculations. Such an omission destroys public confidence in the government and its planning process. Few businesses would ignore the fact that their customer base had grown by almost 200,000 people between 1992/3 and 1997/8 in the course of preparing their financial and business plans.

(7) The bed-population and patient-day targets chosen by Alberta Health are not unreasonable. Major difficulties may be experienced, however, in

attempting to attain the lowest levels in the country within such a short period of time.

(8) The physician component is one of the most ill-defined segments of the plan. Specific targets need to be set and articulated and the primary care segment of the medical service market needs to be reformed. Physician cost and utilization trends need to be analysed much more closely and medical manpower issues need to be addressed within a wider framework that includes the substitution of paramedical for physician personnel in the delivery of primary care.

(9) Anecdotal evidence suggests that significant cost shifts are occurring. It is believed that substantial out-of-pocket charges are being borne by certain types of individuals using the Alberta hospital system. In the acute care system these charges appear to be materializing in the form of 'pre-op' outlays required of patients before they are admitted for treatment and 'post-op' charges as they are moved from the hospital to the home while still undergoing active medical/nursing treatment. Reasonable access to medically required services can be assumed to be impeded by significant out-of-pocket charges levied on individuals and the inability of a significant portion of the population to purchase supplementary private insurance. Conclusion 2 above will have to be rescinded if the worst fears of a number of observers are confirmed over the next months and more evidence is gathered to show that portions of the publicly insured medically required services previously provided under the hospital insurance plan have been effectively de-insured by changes in the organizational structure of the health care system. In particular, new evidence seems to be turning up daily showing that in certain of the RHAs publicly insured hospital services are being replaced by private insurance with a 30 per cent co-payment and a $5,000 maximum risk provision. If this is shown to be pervasive and a part of the provincial/RHA policies within this area, then serious breaches of the fundamental principles underlying the Canada Health Act are occurring. As matters presently stand there is a morass of conflicting cost-shifting policies within and among the RHAs. Matters should be clarified in 1996 or 1997 as the RHAs get a better handle on things and either end or attempt to further extend the *ad hoc* user-fee policies initiated by various hospitals and community care programs.

(10) The Alberta Health business plan is suffering from the problems encountered by a number of other plans. A large number of intermediate output and input measures have been listed; however, the ministry has not been able to link its means of health care measurement (outcomes) at the macro level with the total level of spending. An analysis has been provided that demonstrates that health status (life expectancy) and health care spending relationships can be established for Alberta. (Some preliminary work has been done on the other Western provinces and some tentative first-run results have been

obtained for Québec, Ontario, and the Atlantic provinces.) The establishment of these relationships provides valuable information for provincial governments seriously interested in measuring the macroeconomic performance of their respective health care systems. In addition, the establishment of the specific form of various health status functions can be of marked assistance in firming up the population-based funding formulas used in allocating provincial financial resources among various regions. Matters are still at a preliminary stage, but if a full investigation of all the provinces is carried out the possibility exists that needs-based funding could be considered and possibly introduced as one of the elements to be included in the new health care funding formulas under discussion in the current round of federal-provincial health care transfer payment negotiations. The possible trade-off between health care cutbacks and the magnitude of the reductions in life expectancy, the increase in mortality rates, infant mortality, and other indicators does not appear to have been fully appreciated by a number of the parties to these debates. Major cuts in health care funding can have significant health status consequences under certain circumstances. This basic fact has seemingly been forgotten or ignored in much of the current debate.

(11) What has happened to the quality of care within specific programs in the province is an extremely important question that no one can fully answer at this time. Patient survey responses received at the provincial level indicate that the quality of care that patients receive is satisfactory. However, only one RHA (Capital) has released a detailed report monitoring a number of key quality-of-care variables. Close attention needs to be paid to changes in a number of key health status indicators and much more feedback is required.

(12) Horizontal equity (equal access to patients with equal health care needs) should be maintained within the medicare plan. Alberta's twelve 'Key Principles' violate this fundamental medicare principle. Forcing physicians to opt totally in or out of medicare would resolve matters. No physician should be allowed to participate in medicare and levy out-of-pocket charges, full or partial, on so-called private patients for medically required services.

**NOTES**

1. It should be noted that the second three-year plan extends beyond the current political mandate of the government, assuming that a four-year election cycle is followed. This is an interesting phenomenon. As each year expires in the current mandate, more and more of the future plans of the political party in power are revealed to the electorate. This suggests that sooner or later the opposition parties are going to have to focus on each of these plans and show the populace what an alternative set of three-year business plans would look like. It will be fascinating to see whether such

a wealth of economic information will have any significant effect on the political outcome of the next provincial election. The three-year government plans that bridge the government mandate have to be credible since the planning of all the local and provincial sectors as well as that of a significant portion of the private sector will be locked into them. An election surprise bestowing a generous across-the-board increase in the next fiscal year would destroy the credibility of the three-year planning process and eventually the political credibility of the party that tried to implement it. The old political cycle would have been re-established and the rationale for introducing multi-year budgeting and business plans would have been destroyed.

2. A significant change has occurred in the medicare premium policy. Under the old system the policy was to raise premium revenue to the point where premiums would account for 50 per cent of the medical payments provided under the auspices of the Alberta Health Care Insurance Plan (AHCIP). The basis for this policy rested on the 50–50 cost-sharing relationship between the provinces and the federal government when the provincial medical care insurance plan was first implemented on 1 July 1969. The provincial medical services fiscal plan was quite simple. The federal government would pay for approximately one-half of the cost of the provincial medical plan and Albertans would pay the other half through premiums. Ideally, no demands would be placed on the provincial treasury. During the seventies and eighties the budget surpluses created by the oil boom allowed the provincial government to expand its funding of physicians and other practitioners without increasing the premium-financed share of the plan. In addition, changes in federal transfers led to a relative reduction in the federal share of funding as the rate of growth in provincial health plan spending outstripped the growth in federal payments. The fiscal illusion was created in Alberta that a rapid expansion in medicare spending could be accommodated without concomitant increases being experienced in medical premiums or provincial taxes, or without financial constraints being imposed on physician spending. Consequently, the provincial treasurer became the major funder of the AHCIP and the original fiscal policy the medical services plan was based on was shattered. The new policy set out in the three-year health care business plan does not stop at reinstating the old policy. The new medicare premium policy breaks the linkage between premium revenue and the funding of professional (primarily physician) services. All provincial health care spending (hospitals, home care, public health, drugs, equipment, etc.) is now included in the set of services that will be partially financed by medicare premiums. By 1997/8, 20 per cent of the total health ministry's expenditures will be funded by medicare premium contributions. It is estimated the funds generated under this new policy will cover almost 95 per cent or so of the total medical services payments made to physicians. This is far in excess of the old 50–50 medical services target. This means that virtually all of the federal government health care transfer payments (tax

points plus cash payments) given to Alberta by the federal government to pay for medical services has been freed up and is available to be applied to other health or non-health expenditure areas of importance to the provincial government.

Both the provincial and federal governments derive an additional benefit from the increased use of medicare premiums as a means of financing provincial health care expenditures. This stems from the fact that for taxation purposes medicare premiums are treated as taxable benefits. In effect, most Albertans with the exception of the self-employed will experience a rise in their taxable benefits and subsequently an increase in their taxes as their employers pay the higher premiums mandated by the provincial government.

3. It is also interesting to note that the tax points granted to the province by the federal government to assist in paying for medical and hospital services are just another set of anonymous tax points as far as the provincial treasurer is concerned. They can be applied to any expenditure area. Medicare premiums, on the other hand, are deemed not to be a tax and are specifically tied to health care as a part of the new net budgeting stratagem. If a consistent approach was followed, then the tied tax points plus the tied medicare premiums would be summed and netted against the actual item of expenditure—medical service (physician) expenditures. Of course, if this was done it would demonstrate that the revenue sources assigned to defray the cost of medical services by the two levels of governments were generating a major surplus as far as medical services are concerned. Such information would be of major interest to taxpayers, who are willing to earmark increases in taxes and premiums to cover deficits or to meet increases in the costs of a valued program but are unwilling to make payments of a magnitude to create surpluses that could be transferred to other programs. The treatment of medicare premiums plus the federal medicare transfer payment revenue is a fine example of provincial fiscal legerdemain.

4. With the benefit of hindsight a number of readers might wish to debate government policy-makers over the economic and social merits of seizing upon the second highest deficit in the past two decades as the basis for assigning debt reduction targets to various departments. It is quite legitimate to pursue this line of argument; however, it will be shown later on that major expenditure reductions in health care can be justified solely on health care reform grounds. Interestingly, no one has ever considered whether the magnitude of the cutbacks on health care spending contained in the three-year business plan would match or fall short or be larger than the cutbacks recommended by health care economic reformers.

5. Alberta's total health care/GDP ratio during this period was lower than any of the G-7 nations—Japan, the United Kingdom, Germany, France, Italy, the United States, and Canada itself. This placed Alberta in a most favourable position relative

to a number of its major trading partners. The opportunity cost of meeting the health needs of its citizens measured in terms of forgone consumption and investment opportunities was markedly smaller than in any of the other major high-income nations (regions) of the world.

6. The old health care delivery system was highly decentralized. The provincial Department of Health had to negotiate a budget with literally hundreds of individual general acute care, auxiliary, and public health boards. A so-called global budgeting system ensured that a prospective rather than a retrospective payment system was used. A significant amount of duplication and overlap occurred among the large hospitals located in the major urban centres.

7. The Alberta and Saskatchewan RHAs have no control over the delivery of primary medical care by physicians with the exception of a relatively small number of doctors employed in public health and community clinics. The bulk of physicians are paid on a fee-for-service basis and their budgets are negotiated separately from those of the RHAs. As matters presently stand, health care reform in these two provinces has not led to any significant reform in the way physicians deliver medical care. This is in marked contrast to the experiment being carried out in the United Kingdom.

8. The decision to create 17 regional authorities was purely a political decision. No attention was paid to the concerns raised regarding the fact that the administrative boundaries of the RHAs did not match the boundaries of any known health service boundaries in existence since the province was created. It is interesting to speculate that by creating 17 RHAs, rural MLAs may have believed that they would be better able to maintain control of their health care systems 'closer to home'.

9. Both dimensions of this problem have to be kept in mind. Certain of the regions are so small they can only offer very basic health care services. This means they will never be able to deliver a comprehensive set of services. The second aspect of the service problem is that the residents of their regions may refuse or prefer not to be treated by the doctors or to use the hospital facilities available within their regions. In effect, the consumer of health care services may not be knowledgeable or sovereign in most medical matters; however, she/he still has the right to select which physician to entrust with her/his care. This means the population has largely ignored certain of the new RHAs and continued to use the health care system as in the past.

10. The desire of local authorities to retain more funds in their communities is quite understandable. This is particularly true in a period when total funding is being slashed, facilities are closing, and health care jobs are being lost. A number of

smaller communities within a number of RHAs feel they are fighting for their economic life when a proposal is made to close their local hospital.

11. Certain voluntary hospital boards run by religious orders and other voluntary agencies have been allowed to remain intact. They have no real budgetary power; however, they do have the ability to complicate and increase the costliness of administration within an RHA and also impede access of the public to certain health care services. On the other hand, these boards could also benefit a particular facility. No evidence exists at the present time to draw any firm conclusions regarding the pros and cons of hospitals with two governance structures existing side by side; however, creating two parallel administrative structures within the capital region between the Catholic hospitals and the Capital RHA deserves to be scrutinized very carefully.

12. Physicians are not the only group concerned over the possible introduction of other personnel into areas hitherto reserved for them. The nursing profession and various leaders of nursing unions have expressed concerns regarding the substitution of non-nursing for nursing personnel. In addition, interchanges have occurred between various nursing groups regarding the substitution of licensed practical nurses for registered nurses within various areas of the delivery system.

In hindsight, individual hospital boards can be viewed as being much more amenable to understanding the physicians' perspective than RHAs, which are determined to eliminate duplication and overlap in the new regional hospital systems. The old hospital systems were deliberately designed with major excess capacity and duplication of activities built into them. This was done with the express purpose of minimizing the time physicians spent in treatment, consultation, and training and research. Elimination of this costly duplication within a regional hospital system by moving to a system of specialized programs located in institutions spread throughout a region and the granting of privileges throughout an RHA rather than to a particular hospital has markedly increased physician travelling time. The desire to have physicians granted more powers in terms of advising and influencing RHA decisions may be a direct function of the rise in non-billable hours physicians spent in transit between various RHA facilities.

13. The difficulties inherent in measuring the quality of health care in different sectors of the system, coupled with the time involved in building the proper data bases, suggest a lengthy period of time will have passed before reliable quality-of-care indices will be available for monitoring the system.

14. Numerous news reports on the CBC television station in Edmonton, as well as those provided by other private stations during 1994 and 1995, bear vivid witness to the

concerns expressed by local communities regarding the problems encountered when the RHAs have made decisions to downsize or close hospitals. The problems faced by the Westview RHA, which borders on the Western boundary of the Capital RHA and stretches to the British Columbia border, is a classic case in this regard.

15. The reinstatement of the provider groups, which have such a strong vested interest in identifying more health care needs and increasing expenditures (expenditures are the incomes received by health care providers), will place the citizen representatives on the Provincial Health Council under enormous pressure. Their 'technical' advisers will almost assuredly find shortcomings in any of the activities of the RHAs that inhibit their earnings or threaten their positions of privilege and power. Exceptions may arise when different provider groups vie with each other for additional shares of the health care market.

16. The Capital Health Authority has invited a representative from the University of Alberta, a physician (AMA) representative, a technical/professional representative, and representatives from the Edmonton and St Albert city councils to sit on its board in a non-voting capacity. This arrangement is subject to review.

17. The most costly elections in the province are those held for the position of mayor in Calgary and Edmonton. Numerous MLA and MP seats are contained within each city's boundaries. This minimizes the costs provincial or federal candidates incur; however, a candidate for mayor must cover the expenses involved in running a city-wide campaign. Any backbench member of the legislature or the House of Commons earns far more than the chair of the health authorities. This implies that donations made by various vested interest groups—corporate, professional, or union—may play a major role in determining the successful candidates in RHA elections that transcend the boundaries of each of the major cities. A similar observation holds true if a number of board members are elected at large.

18. A reform of this nature would be quite far-reaching, and would be challenging to a number of elected provincial representatives. The influence of provincial MLAs would tend to be diminished if a strong local government structure was introduced.

19. The very low turnout in the recent Saskatchewan election of regional health board members suggests that a number of the concerns expressed here have a great deal of practical relevance.

20. None of these goals explicitly requires the province to comply with the provisions of the Canada Health Act. The lack of any explicit commitment in this regard within the three-year business plan has resulted in the development of provincial

policies *ultra vires* of the Act—facility fees are a case in point. The Alberta government has indicated on numerous occasions that it does intend to comply with the Canada Health Act. The seeming confusion over what constitutes compliance may stem from the lack of formally incorporating the Canada Health Act principles in its health care plan.

21. Only the goals and the performance measures are discussed here. It should be noted that various strategies are identified for each goal.

22. LEX = 69.1 + 0.004362*HEXCAP   Adj $R^2$ = 0.91, F = 170, DW = 1.43, n = 18
    (t = 123.0)  (t = 13.0)
    where LEX is the life expectancy of the population at birth and HEXCAP is total health care expenditure per capita in Alberta expressed in terms of 1986 dollars.

    The estimates of the parameters of this equation are all significant at the 1 per cent level of significance as far as the standard t, F, and Durbin Watson statistics are concerned. The Box-Cox results are not reported above; however, they support the selection of the linear model over the inverse or any of the other standard functional forms. The elasticity of life expectancy with respect to per capita health care spending calculated at the means is 0.094. Comparable elasticities by gender are 0.0691 for females and 0.1079 for males. Each of these equations passes muster at the 1 per cent significance level. It is interesting to note that the life expectancy responsiveness of the males is so much higher than for the females. This may simply reflect the fact that the average life expectancy of females in Alberta is approximately 6.8 years greater than for males. In effect, the gain in an already markedly longer life span per dollar spent is smaller than for the relatively younger males.

23. The substitution of day surgery for in-patient surgery has had a significant impact on the economic efficiency of the Alberta system. Individual micro studies are available; however, a comprehensive reliable data base that could be used to analyse the effects of out-patient and ambulatory care activities on the whole system is still in a developmental stage.

24. The reduction in the length of stay from 3.5 days to one day in maternity wards for a straightforward, uncomplicated delivery is a further illustration of changes in the length of stay for conventional in-patient hospital procedures, which permit the same volume of services to be delivered with a markedly smaller number of beds and in-patient staff. Similarly, the reduction in the number of long-term patients treated in general acute care hospitals is another relatively major source of economic efficiency gain. The extent of any trade-offs in the quality of care as these individuals are dealt with in private homes or other institutional settings is currently unknown.

## REFERENCES

Alberta Medical Association (1995), 'Guide to Direct Billing for Uninsured Services' (June).

Alberta Planning Secretariat (1993), *Starting Points: Recommendations for Creating a More Accountable and Affordable Health System* (Dec.).

Canada, Health and Welfare (1994a), *Preliminary Estimates of Health Expenditures in Canada, 1987–1991* (Feb.).

―――― (1994b), *Provincial Government Health Expenditures and Related Federal Contributions, Canada, the Provinces and the Territories* (July).

Canada, Health Canada (1985), Canada Health Act, 1984.

―――― (1996), *National Health Expenditures in Canada, 1975–94*. Ottawa (Jan.).

Capital Health Authority (1995), 'Detailed Performance Report: A Background Document to the Public: A Year in Review'. Edmonton (27 Sept).

Carr-Hill, R.A., et al. (1994), 'Allocating Resources to Health Authorities: Development of Method for Small Area Analysis of Use of Inpatient Services'. *British Medical Journal* 309 (Oct.): 1046–9.

Culyer, A.J. (1988), *Health Care Expenditures in Canada: Myth and Reality, Past and Future*. Ottawa: Canadian Tax Foundation, No. 82.

Department of Finance (1995), *Economic Reference Tables*. Ottawa (Aug.).

Drummond, M.F. (1994), 'Output Measurement for Resource-Allocation Decisions in Health Care', in A. McGuire, P. Fenn, and K. Mayhew, eds, *Providing Health Care: The Economics of Alternative Systems of Finance and Delivery*. Oxford: Oxford University Press.

Evans, R.G. (1984), *Strained Mercy: The Economics of Canadian Health Care*. Toronto: Butterworths.

―――――, and G. Stoddart (1994), 'Producing Health, Consuming Health Care', in R.G. Evans, M.L. Barer, and T.R. Marmor, eds, *Why Are Some People Healthy And Others Not? The Determinants of Health of Populations*. New York: Aldine De Gruyter.

Ministry of Health (1991), *Partners in Health: The Government of Alberta's Response to the Premier's Commission on Future Health Care for Albertans* (Nov.).

——— (1993), *Health Goals for Alberta: Progress Report* (Dec.).

——— (1994a), *A Better Way: A Plan for Securing Alberta's Future* (24 Feb.).

——— (1994b), *Healthy Albertans Living in a Healthy Alberta: A Three-Year Business Plan* (24 Feb.).

——— (1995a), *A Three-Year Business Plan (1995–96 to 1997–98)* (25 Feb.).

——— (1995b), *Funding Regional Health Services in Alberta: Preliminary Report of the Health Services Advisory Committee* (21 June).

——— (1996), 'Private Clinics: Key Principles' (Feb.).

Mooney, G., and J.A. Olsen (1994), 'QALYs: Where Next?' in A. McGuire, P. Fenn, and K. Mayhew, eds, *Providing Health Care: The Economics of Alternative Systems of Finance and Delivery*. Oxford: Oxford University Press: 120–40.

Premier's Commission on Future Health Care for Albertans (1989), *Rainbow Report: Our Vision for Health*, vol. 1 (Dec.).

# Comments on Chapter 9: The Effects of Institutional Changes on Health Care Reform

*R.G. Beck*

## 1. INTRODUCTION

The health care policy debate in Canada has been virtually uninterrupted since the formation of the Hall Commission, which reported in 1964.[1] What is new to the current situation, as Richard Plain points out, is the public preoccupation with the size of the public debt and a seeming willingness to entertain both an accelerated rate of change and radical change in the institutions and agencies that govern the sector. Thus, Plain is correct when he points out that closures of hospital beds, declining average lengths of stay, day surgeries, minimal access surgery, nursing-home care, medical personnel restrictions, practice guidelines, alternative methods of payment, and the like were all policies that were either in progress or under active consideration for a long period of time. What is new, and is the focal point of this volume, is the extent to which the institutions of governance themselves, both structures and functions, are undergoing radical change. In the health care setting this takes the form of regionalization, which we may take to mean a pervasive change in the relationship of the provincial government and its Department of Health to the constituent agencies and boards in the health sector. Under the impetus of controlling the debt, governments generally, and the Alberta government specifically, intervened with this governing structure ostensibly as a means of accelerating the adoption of policies that already had been the subject of extensive analysis and debate in the health care sector.

The theme of the impact of governing structure on the process of reform poses a particular problem for Plain in the Alberta setting. As Plain points out, the Alberta case is somewhat like the cart before the proverbial horse because reductions in funding levels preceded structural reforms. The Klein government assumed power in Alberta in December 1992 and, as Plain's Figure 1 illustrates, Alberta Health expenditures plummeted thereafter. Klein's government was determined to solve the deficit problem by reducing government expenditures rather than by increasing revenues. But it was not until April

1995 that Alberta's Regional Health Authorities were created. Accordingly, Plain's analysis must focus on the role of the business plans and a variety of commissions and roundtable public discussions—the government's *modus operandi* with respect to spending generally. The business plans are generally symbolic documents rather than specific operational plans. They seem directed to garnering public support through the illusion of orchestrated consultation. The Alberta government, through its central departments, dictated the specific health policy actions in this period.

Could the same pattern of policy outcomes have been achieved in another way and with less public friction? We will draw on the Saskatchewan experience, and that of the Saskatoon District Health Board, to highlight the differences in approach, some of the relevant issues, and the differences in allocative outcomes.[2] We begin with an overview of the public-sector problem as perceived in the two provinces. Next we characterize institutional reform in the health care sector. Attention is then turned to regionalization specifically, as part of institutional reform. Selected issues relating to regionalization are discussed, including effectiveness and efficiency of regions, appropriateness of boundaries, jurisdictional problems, and intraregional co-ordination issues. Before concluding, the structure of resource reallocation under the Saskatoon Health District is presented as a comparative reflection of what has been achieved under Saskatchewan's approach.

## 2. THE PUBLIC-SECTOR PROBLEM

Shortly before Ralph Klein assumed the leadership in Alberta, in October 1991 Roy Romanow's NDP government replaced Grant Devine's Conservative government in Saskatchewan. The Conservative government passed on to the NDP what the Alberta Conservatives passed onto themselves and their new leader— a significant public debt and deficit.[3] The NDP election campaign drew attention to the deficit and the high level of taxation as Romanow expressed the widely reported opinion that the public had been 'taxed to death'.[4] However, as a first order of business after the election the Romanow government appointed the Gass Commission to look into the province's debt and into some of the financial dealings giving rise to it. The Commission and the publicity attending its deliberations (fuelled by the prospect of disclosure of financial scandals) had the effect of conditioning the electorate for what was to follow. Under the guise of deficit terrorism the Romanow government opted to increase revenues through taxes, licenses, and charges and to restrict, but not necessarily reduce, government expenditures. Health expenditures were maintained at their nominal dollar 1990/1 level of approximately $1.5 billion through 1995/6. Obviously, the situation in real dollar terms would depend vitally on the ability to restrict wage increases because of the large share of health care spending accounted for by the wage bill. But there were significant changes in the institutional relationships in the public sector.

## 3. INSTITUTIONAL REFORM IN HEALTH CARE

Drawing on the health care policy debate the Saskatchewan government concluded that it is possible to spend more wisely by accelerating the rate of reform in the public sector. In a dramatic move, sweeping changes were made in the local governing structures. Some 450 boards were replaced in 1993 by 30 regional health boards. In addition, the fiscal relationships between the Health Department and its constituent agencies/boards were changed. The Health Department abandoned detailed line budgets as the vehicle of management. Instead, the regional boards would receive funding in essentially four separate envelopes—acute care, nursing-home care, home care, and rural health initiatives.[5] In addition, funding levels in the envelopes were to be 'performance-based' or 'needs-based'. The age/sex population structure of the regions, together with life expectancy and mortality ratios, would be the primary determinants for distributing envelopes among the regions.[6] The level of funding in the acute care envelope was reduced by 10 per cent in nominal dollars. Regional boards were permitted to transfer funds between the envelopes but they could not transfer funds into the acute care envelope.

The Saskatchewan government also introduced the health care equivalent to Alberta's business plan in the form of the 'Wellness Model'. This euphemistically titled document had two effects. First, it was designed to change public expectations about the medical system—a 'limits to modern medicine' notion that is frequently associated with Cochrane in the UK.[7] Second, it challenged people's perceptions of responsibility for health care by suggesting both that people may affect their own health[8] and that some remedial care can be provided by families in their own homes.[9] The government's commitment to change was given dramatic emphasis by its announcement that 52 small rural hospitals would be closed. In 1991/2 Saskatoon had approximately 3.1 beds per 1,000 population. The ratio for the province as a whole was 7.2 beds per 1,000. Clearly the rural bed allotment had to pull up the provincial average.[10] This was a particularly courageous political decision given the nature of rural gerrymander common to the Prairies.[11] Thus the general strategy and policy directions were set, though the specific details of implementation were to be left to the individual regional boards.

## 4. REGIONALIZATION AND REGIONAL BOARDS

While the regional boards were given implementation responsibilities, they had little difficulty in 'reading the government's lips'. A by-product of regionalization was that previously existing government-appointed (élite?) boards were dismissed, destroying formal and informal lines of communication and influence. In addition, employees and managers of the constituent institutions were put to the trouble of reapplying for their jobs where the number of new positions was less than the number of old jobs. Nothing gets the attention and allegiance of senior and junior management more effectively than the simple expedient of saying that you are all dismissed. Thus the task of building the regional institutional framework was taken on with considerable zeal—or at least with muted criticism.[12] It is to specific aspects of the process of regionalization that we now turn.

## 4.1 Effectiveness and Efficiency Issues

Whether or not the regional organizational approach is a more cost-effective arrangement in the health sector is difficult to say and indeed may be unknown.[13] What is more generally agreed upon is that regional organization, which brings together elements of previously separately administered programs, has some scope for more effective and efficient program delivery. For example, the health care literature routinely lamented the 'medicalization of the aged' under which people were admitted to acute care hospitals when they could have been equally well cared for in a less expensive setting, such as nursing homes or even, with assistance, in their own homes. There were at least two impediments to this approach. First, the other programs operated under different agencies, thereby making resource reallocation difficult to achieve. Hospitals could save beds and resources only at the expense of increased expenditures in the other programs. Placing administrative and fiscal responsibility for all substitute services under a single roof would enhance the prospects for cost-saving substitutions. Second, care of the aged may have been medicalized because as a society we could not define and sell a program that made the difficult distinction between when the state should assume responsibility for the aged and when it should remain a private responsibility. Using public funds to pay for changing grampa's storm windows is saleable if it is achieved through reduction in acute care hospital beds. The public sees the trade-off between home-care expenditure and acute care costs. Moreover, it is administered in a framework that continuously emphasizes the substitution process. In addition, the public may have more confidence in such decisions when they are administered at the (relatively) local level since the program must rely heavily on professional discretion rather than rules. Thus, a critical dimension of the regionalization process is that the regional boards should have control over the appropriate range of programs and facilities so that effective substitution in care modalities can take place.

It is important to note that regionalization and local or decentralized decision-making are not always synonymous. In one respect regionalization in

Saskatchewan conferred greater centralization in decision-making. Some 4,000–5,000 appointed people serving on some 450 boards were replaced by approximately 300 appointed people serving on 30 boards. In this dimension there is less local input, not more. Yet in another respect some programs that were centrally administered by the Department of Health were (or would be) shifted to the regions. Thus, the regional boards would have broader planning authority than the boards of the fragmented jurisdictions they replaced. In this respect regionalization involved decentralization. Therefore, depending on the exigencies of political rhetoric, the process of regionalization can be described as involving less local input or more local input.

### 4.2 Appropriateness of Boundaries Issue

The importance of service substitution in the regionalization process has implications for another issue—the appropriateness of regional boundaries. Ideally, the region should have an administrative jurisdiction that facilitates service substitution. If a patient is to be moved from an acute care bed to a nursing home or to home care, this obviously can be accomplished more easily if the single authority controls all the service facilities. Let us define the service population of a region as one that actually receives services in the region's facilities. The census population of the region includes all who reside within the geographic boundaries of the region. Accordingly, the more closely the ratio of the service population to the census population approaches one, the greater the region's capacity to implement effective service substitution. Moreover, we would expect that referral centres would have ratios greater than one and referring centres would have ratios less than one.[14] If we were to examine the frequency distribution of the ratio of service to census population, the less the variance of the distribution the more efficient the regional boundaries in the sense described above. This conclusion is also consistent with the 'needs-based' approach to funding the regions. In theory at least, a region's funding is linked to its impact on life expectancy and mortality of its census population. These performance indices are calculated on the *census* population, so the more closely the census population approximates the service population the more accurately the indices capture the region's achievements.

Probably no one would argue that either Saskatchewan's or Alberta's regional boundaries are ideal. Indeed, Richard Plain points out that a quarter of the Alberta regions provide hospital care for less than 60 per cent of their census population. The Saskatoon Health District provides 46 per cent of its services to patients outside its census region. In Chapter 5 in this book, Ron Kneebone and Ken McKenzie suggest similarities between school board programs and boundaries and the health boards.[15] However, compared to health programs, school programs are relatively homogeneous.[16] Health involves a hierarchical vertical referral pattern. General practitioners refer to specialists. Moreover, sufficient volumes to support specialized programs are only achievable in the referral centres.

Obviously, in each province some equilibrating process must occur with respect to regional borders. The Saskatchewan regions were originally formed on a somewhat voluntary basis with opportunities for regions to amalgamate voluntarily, so there is scope for the equilibration process.

### 4.3 Jurisdictional Problems

We now turn to the jurisdictional relationship between the regions and the government. From a public accountability point of view, it should be clear which decision agency is responsible for what. The District Health Act (Saskatchewan), which provides for the creation of the regional boards, offers little guidance with respect to accountability. If one were to contrast this legislation with that governing institutions of higher learning, the District Health Act would seem to have given little consideration to the special characteristics of health—in particular, the role of professionalism. University legislation restricts lay boards to permissive decisions, particularly in areas related to academic judgement and academic freedom. The District Health Act is innocent of such considerations. Indeed, the Act is so generally written that the boards and government can play handball with the public regarding accountability.

On 10 October 1995, the Saskatchewan district health boards signed a 'framework' agreement with the government. The agreement was alleged to address the assignment of responsibilities.[17] Nevertheless, there remains the fundamental question of whether one level of governance (the boards) that relies almost exclusively for funding on another level of government can in fact exercise real authority.[18] One way of liberating health boards from the chains of fiscal subservience is to let them develop their own programs and priorities through elected health boards. Elected candidates whose campaigns featured particular operational plans would have greater claim to legitimacy and authority. Early on, the Saskatchewan government declared its intention to move to elected boards. Some would argue that they moved with deliberate slowness, for the first elections did not occur until 25 October 1995. Moreover, the government reserved to itself a right to appoint approximately one-third of each board's members after the election. The government's reticence in moving to elected boards was undoubtedly linked to its desire to accelerate reform and to keep the process focused. Board elections—susceptible as they are to single interest groups, to the timing of visible decisions like hospital closures, and to the unevenness with which political rhetoric services decision-making—might possibly derail the entire reform process. Alternatively, if one takes the view that health policy should be properly determined by the government responsible for raising the taxes and that implementation within the policy framework is the mandate of the regional boards, then elections may be stillborn.[19] Most members of the public have little experience with a wide range of health services (women are hospitalized for maternity) and the depth of detail that attends implementation decisions is not easily grasped. Thus, the elections could easily become sterile events, as many believe the Saskatchewan elections were. The turnout was extraordinarily poor for Saskatchewan; the candidates all declared themselves to be 'for medicare' so voters were left to throw a dart. What effects the elections will have on the focus and cohesiveness of the District Health Boards remains to be seen. Probably the best that can be said at this time is that district health senior executives will continue to work for their salary.

### 4.4 Intraregional Co-ordination Issues

Within their own jurisdictions the health districts faced some intraregional jurisdictional problems. In the larger regions particularly, separate union contracts provided facility-specific seniority and bumping rights. The provincial government was reluctant to interfere with the labour contracts. However, the issue eventually was resolved with the unions endorsing transfer rights throughout the region, thereby facilitating effective use of human resources.

A little more problematic is the issue of credentials. Determining the competence of physicians to practise in a hospital was formerly left in the hands of a lay board. While this might seem surprising, it must be remembered that the monopoly control of the single hospital board was tempered by opportunities for physicians to move elsewhere. In rural and remote areas the difficulty of retaining and recruiting physicians probably worked perversely in the sense that scrutiny might be lax. In any event, with the formation of the health districts monopoly, control over credentials was extended to the entire region. Surprisingly, the decision process, the use of (former) hospital by-laws, was retained as well. At least two concerns arise in regard to this issue. First, we have to consider the impact on the scope for medical innovation.[20] A physician seeking to introduce minimal access surgery, for example, might find the opportunity blocked in one hospital but another independent hospital might endorse the program. Monopoly control over accreditation, in the absence of refinements in the process, might reduce the scope for innovation.

The second concern relates to the extent to which physician services are to be integrated into the region's mandate. Presently in Saskatchewan neither the drug program nor physicians' services have been transferred to the regions. However, the health policy debates in Canada feature calls for alternative methods of payment for physicians, and capitation in particular.[21] If we are to contemplate integrating physician services into the regional framework a number of complex issues arise, to say the least. We need note here only that accreditation that relates to qualifications may then become synonymous with employment. Employment decisions involve a much wider range of issues, especially with regard to satisfactory performance, job security, etc. Suffice it to say, the accreditation issue should probably not reside with a lay board, or at least the board's power should be tempered by the process.

## 5. THE COMPLEXION OF SERVICES UNDER A REGIONAL BOARD

The Saskatoon Health District is the largest in Saskatchewan. Its budget is the second largest in the province, second only to the provincial government itself. The environment within which the board has functioned from 1993 to 1995 has been set out above. The government provided funding in program envelopes, including reduced funding of approximately 10 per cent for acute care. Over the period home-care funding increased roughly 100 per cent, though it began from a relatively modest base of $30 million for the province. Unlike Alberta, no specific bed targets or service volumes were dictated by the Health Department. It is interesting, therefore, to observe the results of the new institutional decision-making process.

Without attempting to be precise about different start dates for different programs, we can see the following structural changes in the Saskatoon Health District roughly between 1992 and 1994/5.[22] There was a 21 per cent decline in acute care beds. Patient-days in hospital declined 25 per cent, while through-put (number of cases) declined 13 per cent. Separations per 1,000 population declined from 110 in 1991/2 to 95 in 1994/5. Average length of stay in hospitals continued its long-term decline, dropping 15 per cent over the same period. By 1995 the Saskatoon District Health Board had achieved a beds per 1,000 population ratio of 2.2 as compared with 3.1 in 1991/2. Home-care units of service increased 62 per cent. In long-term care there was a compositional change. Level I and level II patients, those requiring minimal supervisory care and assistance, were decanted to home care. Long-term patients who were in acute care beds in hospitals were moved into nursing-home facilities. Thus, the strategy featured downloading. However, the district boards were given administrative responsibility for the facilities so that the strategy could be implemented with some confidence.

## 6. CONCLUSIONS

Clearly, some rather significant structural changes have taken place in Saskatchewan. Whether the magnitude of these structural shifts sheds any light on the reasonableness of the Alberta targets reported in Plain's chapter is difficult to say. What is particularly relevant to the issue of reinvention of government is that Saskatchewan's restructuring was achieved through the regional boards and with far less social discontent than appears to have attended the Alberta experience. The scant attention given to health in Saskatchewan's recent election and the low turnout for the district health board elections would suggest that the public is at least not outraged. Romanow has claimed that the public trusts the NDP to reform health.[23] Maybe he is right. Then again, maybe reform was just done right by introducing the facilities to accommodate downloading concurrent with the reduction in acute care bed availability.

It would be irresponsible to conclude without noting that the 'outcome' of the health care system is not measured in the structural terms that we have presented above. As Richard Plain stresses, *health status* is the outcome of the health care system. Plain presents a simplified though surprising relationship between life expectancy as a measurement for health status and real per capita spending on health care. He notes that the positive relationship indicates that large cuts in health care spending may be attended by significant reductions in life expectancy. This, of course, would not sit well with those who believe that the marginal product of health resources is small or even that we are on the 'flat of the curve'. However, the proponents of needs-based funding must surely have reason to pause. The reverse of the needs-based funding argument is that if funding is not forthcoming health status will deteriorate.

The white-knuckle part of the experiment in both Alberta and Saskatchewan is what the ultimate impact of the expenditure reductions on health status will be. In the Alberta case, as Plain's Figure 4 indicates, real per capita health care spending rose from approximately $1,040 in 1980/1 to a peak of about $1,300 between 1986 and 1990, and then is predicted to fall in 1997 to $930, or 12 per cent *below* its 1980/1 level! The Saskatchewan case is focused on 'spending smarter', since in nominal terms per capita spending remained roughly constant since 1990/1. Moreover, 25 per cent of the Alberta reduction in real per capita expenditure occurs in the four-year period from 1992/3 to 1996/7. The health status effects of changes of this magnitude should be detectable even if the marginal product is small. It is imperative that these policy changes be accompanied by vigorous efforts to evaluate the impacts on health.[24] In the absence of measurement of the outcome effects, we are simply in no position to argue persuasively that efficiency and effectiveness have been achieved in either provincial setting, though clearly the burden of proof is of a different order of magnitude in the Alberta case.

## NOTES

1. The views expressed herein are solely those of the author.

2. The Saskatchewan and Alberta situations were somewhat different. In 1991 beds per 1,000 in Saskatchewan and Alberta were 7.2 and 4.7 respectively. Saskatchewan

had the highest ratio in the country, with the Canadian average beds per 1,000 at 4.7 and New Brunswick following Saskatchwan at 6.0 beds. Government per capita expenditures on health were $1,395 in Saskatchewan, $1,523 in Alberta, and $1,537 in Canada. 'Interprovincial Comparisons: Provincial/Territorial Health Services and Selected Data', Health Planning and Policy Development Branch, Saskatchewan Health, revised June 1995.

3. In Saskatchewan's case the debt in terms of the productive capacity of the province was in fact far more burdensome than Alberta's.

4. Promises to restrict or reduce taxes in elections are like leveraged buyouts in the corporate world; they appeal to many.

5. These labels are meant to be illustrative. The shifting of responsibility for programs and services to the regional boards was to be phased in over time. However, acute care, nursing-home care, and home care were immediate candidates for reasons that shall be shown.

6. Note that the term 'needs-based' is misleading in the sense that the mechanism is used to distribute a given level of funding among the regions rather than to figure prominently in establishing the aggregate level of funding.

7. A.L. Cochrane, *Effectiveness and Efficiency: Random Reflections in the Health Services* (Oxford: Nuffield Provincial Hospitals Trust, 1972).

8. M. Lalonde, *A New Perspective on the Health of Canadians* Ottawa (April, 1974). This government White Paper popularized and officially recognized the importance of lifestyle determinants of health.

9. An alternative interpretation of this perspective was put forward by Dr. M. Shokier, who argued that it also blames the sick for their situation, thereby absolving public responsibility. 'Health Care Reform and Academic Medicine', 90th Saskatchewan Anniversary Conference, University of Saskatchewan, Saskatoon, 23 Sept. 1995.

10. It is recognized, of course, that population density is a legitimate consideration. Beds can be more efficiently deployed in areas of high population density. But many would argue that this factor alone could not justify the excess supply of beds in rural Saskatchewan.

11. By contrast, the brunt of the Alberta government's cost-cutting, at least in the initial stages, appears to have fallen on the urban settings.

12. The contemporary management guru's touting of 'downsizing' is the private sector's means of getting people to reconsider the mission.

13. See McKenzie, Chapter 3, for an extensive survey of the public choice literature as it relates to the issue of governance. One is reminded of Jonathan Swift's 'big end'ians' and 'little end'ians'.

14. In addition to supply-side factors, demand-side considerations might affect the ratio. If a region's preference function included the desire to offer highly technical services—pride in its kidney transplant unit, for example—the region's ratio might be greater than one. It is also possible to define the ratio for categories of services where the ratio for primary care, for example, might be expected to approximate one for all regions, but secondary and tertiary care ratios might have different frequency distributions.

15. See Kneebone and McKenzie, Chapter 5.

16. Education is not completely homogeneous, of course. Urban settings are often able to offer specialized programs, computer labs, for example, which smaller rural settings are unable to support. But the degree of vertical referral in health is much greater.

17. The chairperson of the organization comprised of the health districts, Saskatchewan Association of Health Organizations, described the document in this fashion to the press. However, examination of the document, 'A Framework of Accountability: The Minister of Health and District Health Boards', reveals it to be little more than a lesson in civics. It is difficult to see in the document what could have been 'negotiated'. Also, it is interesting to note that this framework agreement was concluded before the board elections but was not released to inform the electoral debate. Thus far there is no indication that it will be released to the public.

18. One interesting example was the Regina District Board's attempt to implement hospital hotel fees for the dying. When the story reached the public the deputy minister of health at first correctly stated that it was within the board's powers to do so. However, within days, as the political fires warmed, the deputy wrote to all health district boards informing them that such charges are unacceptable.

19. The provincial government might establish the policy framework for the regional boards in the same sense that the Canada Health Act establishes a framework for the provinces.

20. Some might argue that the scope was too broad and that further randomized controlled trials are needed, but this relates more to the nature of the evidence than to the decision process itself.

21. See the Kilshaw Report to the Provincial Deputy Ministers of Health, Fall 1995.

22. These figures were obtained from personal communication with Lorraine Skene, Manager of Health Information, Saskatoon District Health Board. Her data were precise respecting start and end dates for each statistic but the picture presented above is generally consistent with the stylized facts.

23. The Saskatchewan government implemented significant structural reform in the health sector. It is doubtful, however, that Premier Romanow would claim to have 'reinvented' government or even to have revolted against common sense.

24. Paul Boothe advises that the Capital Region Health Board in Edmonton, of which he is a member, has published a document containing statistics on adverse events in the region's facilities. The publication of such information is important because the performance of public institutions can only be evaluated with full and open disclosure of information. However, examination of the document *Detailed Performance Report: A Background Document to the Public Performance Report*, Capital Health Authority, Edmonton, 27 Sept. 1995, was a disappointment. The evidence presented is based on satisfaction questionnaires, which are not particularly persuasive in this context.

CHAPTER 10

# New Directions? Government Spending Cuts and Alberta's Institutional Resilience in Advanced Education

J.C. Herbert Emery

## 1. INTRODUCTION

'Greatest accessibility at the lowest cost' is the Klein government's announced objective for advanced education in the Province of Alberta.[1] To meet this objective, as outlined in the Klein government's business plan document *A Better Way* (Alberta, 1994a), government grants to Alberta's post-secondary institutions are scheduled to fall by 19.5 per cent over the three years 1994/5 to 1996/7. Students are to pay a higher share of the cost of their education. Accessibility is to be maintained through the imposition of enrolment corridors, through enrolment opportunities created with funds targeted at innovative new programs, and through a revamped student loans program. The Klein agenda also seeks to create a more market-oriented system of higher learning, with greater accountability to the taxpayers of Alberta.

This chapter examines how Alberta's institutions of higher learning have dealt with the new directions and assesses the consequences of the Klein agenda for higher education in Alberta. The analysis highlights several themes discussed in earlier chapters (primarily Chapters 4 and 5): the role of conflict avoidance in retrenchment strategy; the role of 'crisis' in effecting institutional change; and the roles of horizontal competition and decentralization in generating efficiency gains within universities and colleges in Alberta.

The Klein government's agenda for advanced education in Alberta is consistent with developments in advanced education across Canada. More responsive and accountable institutions with a greater share of cost borne by students are policy goals advocated by many observers of advanced education in Canada (Kesselman, 1993; Maxwell, 1994). Hardy (1996: 3), in her study of financial retrenchment strategies of Canadian universities in the 1980s, refers to these developments as part of a general move towards 'managerialism' in university administration—a concept that 'advocates greater accountability, centralized authority and objective resource allocation to improve performance'. In terms of reduced expenditures on advanced education, Alberta has lagged behind other provinces as Alberta's reductions in expenditures on advanced education have come a decade later than those in other provinces. Not even the magnitude of the spending cut over a brief time horizon (a 19.5 per cent reduction in government grants over three years) is exceptional given the experiences of universities in Québec and British Columbia in the 1980s.[2]

Generally, the outcome of retrenchment in Alberta universities is consistent with Hardy's conclusions for Québec universities that faced similar reductions in government funding in the 1980s—cuts to government funding have not resulted in any radical reallocation of resources. As such, the pessimistic forecasts for the future of advanced education in Alberta under the provincial government's 'New Directions' (Alberta, 1994b) appear to have been overstated. What we can conclude is that the objective of lowering the cost of advanced education to the taxpayer has been met; students pay higher tuition, hence a greater share of the cost of their education; new programs have been introduced; and there are fewer full-time faculty and larger class sizes. The existing level of services should not be fundamentally different, with perhaps the exception of capital-intensive programs like the sciences.

Section 2 of the chapter describes advanced education in Alberta and the details of the business plan for the Department of Advanced Education and Career Development. Section 3 provides the arguments as to whether the Klein government's initiatives will be a detriment or a benefit to Alberta's universities and colleges. Section 4 presents a case study of the University of Calgary's retrenchment strategy aimed at addressing the reduction in government grants of 19.5 per cent over three years. The discussion is then extended to demonstrate similarities and differences between institutional retrenchment strategies in Alberta. Section 5 discusses the nature of changes within Alberta's universities and colleges since the Klein government implemented its plan; the section focuses on the move to higher tuition fees and the move towards a more responsive, market-oriented system. Section 6 presents concluding comments.

## 2. GOVERNMENT FUNDING OF ADVANCED EDUCATION IN ALBERTA

Alberta's post-secondary education system is comprised of four provincially administered colleges, 11 public colleges, four private colleges, two technical institutes, five hospital-based schools of nursing, the Banff Centre, and four universities (Alberta, 1993). The Alberta post-secondary system is a regional system where access to a broad range of programs and services is available throughout the province. Albertans can participate in academic upgrading and certificate, diploma, and university transfer programs through the college system in their home region. Of the Alberta Department of Advanced Education and Career Development's 1993/4 budget of $1.2 billion, $980 million (82 per cent) was provided to post-secondary institutions in Alberta; operating funds for the institutions totalled $890 million in 1993/4. Of this latter figure, operating grants for the University of Alberta, the University of Calgary, and the University of Lethbridge totalled $460 million.

Universities and colleges in Alberta receive annual grants through a base grant system. Any change from year to year is prescribed by the provincial government. Although special funding can be approved for individual programs, the annual base grant to an institution reflects factors such as new programs, new space needs, and special circumstances (Kitchen and Auld, 1995: 64). This base grant arrangement remains largely unchanged to date. The Klein government's major initiatives are to reduce the base operating grants for colleges and universities by 11 per cent from 1993/4 to 1994/5, a further 7 per cent in 1995/6, and finally 3 per cent for 1996/7—overall, a 19.5 per cent reduction in expenditures (Alberta, 1994a: 3). The reduction in institutional operating grants plays a large part in cutting overall gross expenditures by Alberta's Department of Advanced Education and Career Development from $1,305 million in 1992/3 to $1,099 million by 1996/7 (a reduction of 14.2 per cent in the department budget).

Beyond the operating grant reductions for the three years, institutional operating grants and capital renewal grants have been combined. No funds are to be provided for new capital construction in the three-year period 1994/5 to 1996/7. Thus, the decision to upgrade or maintain capital is largely left to the discretion of the institution according to its own priorities.[3] As such, institutions could deal with the loss in operating grants by 'consuming' their capital.

The Alberta government generally placed few restrictions on how institutions could achieve their budget targets. One notable exception, however, is that, as for all government departments in Alberta, the Klein government strongly encouraged that employers and employees 'reduce compensation by 5 per cent' for 1994/5. The requirement for a 5 per cent reduction in compensation is itself very broad in that salaries could be reduced, benefits given up, or positions eliminated.[4] Given that salaries and benefits can account for up to 80 per cent of an institution's operating expenses,[5] this cut to compensation represented substantial potential savings in operating expenditures. The 5 per cent cut in compensation was not straightforward to implement, however, as salaries and benefits in Alberta's universities and colleges must be amended through collective bargaining. At the same time, the 'encouragement' for the compensation reduction coming from outside the university administration may have simplified the bargaining process by focusing bargaining efforts on how to meet the 5 per cent cut rather than on whether there would be a cut to compensation.[6]

The Klein government also imposed 'enrolment corridors' with associated financial penalties to discourage institutions from meeting their budget targets by reducing enrolment. For the six largest urban institutions,[7] if enrolment falls more than 2 per cent below their 1993/4 enrolment, then financial penalties of $1,500 per student are imposed via a further reduction in the operating grant to the institution. For the remaining institutions, the colleges located in more rural areas, there is a 5 per cent enrolment corridor.[8]

The enrolment corridors are of some consequence since demographic forecasts for Alberta suggest only slight growth in enrolments and possibly even enrolment decreases, independent of institutional actions (Alberta, 1992). Because of the enrolment corridors, institutions are aggressively advertising their programs. At the University of Calgary, admission standards have fallen and the university initiated an aggressive (and controversial) advertising campaign. The 'Grab Your Seat' campaign notified prospective students that a matriculating average from high school of 65 per cent guarantees an individual admission to the University of Calgary's General Studies faculty.

As a result of the enrolment corridor, the University of Alberta suffered financial penalties in 1995 when its enrolment fell by almost 5 per cent from the institution's benchmark (and record high) enrolment of 1993. Initial unofficial estimates suggested that the University of Alberta would lose an additional $2 million in operating grants for 1995/6.[9] The University of Alberta ultimately suffered a penalty of just over $300,000 in 1995/6 and is projected to lose an additional $550,000 for 1996/7.[10] The combined two-year grant reduction of $850,000 is substantially less than the penalty initially projected.

With the enrolment corridors and the 5 per cent compensation cut in place, the government stated that it expected that reduced funding would push institutions to be 'more efficient and effective'. It anticipated that 'centres of specialization will be encouraged to enhance quality and to realize economies of scale and eliminate duplication' (Alberta, 1994a: 10). Interviews with university and college administrators suggest that the enrolment corridors may circumvent this latter goal because institutions could be unwilling to give up programs to other institutions due to the loss in enrolment that would result.[11] It is worthy of note, however, that the government is sensitive to this concern. When the Southern Alberta Institute of Technology (SAIT) gave up five of its programs, the government adjusted the enrolment target accordingly.[12]

The government allocated $47 million to create the Access Fund, which over the three-year budget period is intended to create 10,000 new student enrolment opportunities by 1996/7. Essentially, the Access Fund represents a contingent portion of institutional operating grant that is awarded on the basis of perceived innovation and responsiveness to the labour market on the part of institutions. The Access Funds are to be awarded on a competitive bid basis. An advisory board made up of public- and private-sector members will be created to 'suggest areas where more graduates will be required in the labour market'. All universities, public and accredited private colleges, and technical institutes are eligible to apply to the Access Fund. Priority is to be given to 'innovative proposals that increase the long-run effectiveness and efficiency and meet labour market needs' (Alberta, 1994a: 7). Funds gained through the Access Fund cannot be used to hire full-time faculty.

In its first year, $9 million of the Access Fund was distributed. Half of all proposals submitted were accepted. Of the institutions in Calgary, the University of Calgary received $3 million in extra funding, Mount Royal College received $1 million, the Southern Alberta Institute of Technology received $474,000, the privately owned Henderson College received $280,000, and Alberta Vocational College received $63,000. The Access Fund money is expected to create 2,000 enrolment places in the city's institutions in the coming year. The Access Fund money for the University of Calgary is intended to expand the enrolment of transfer students from Mount Royal College and to expand work-experience opportunities for students.[13] Mount Royal College received Access Fund money to set up applied degree programs in small business and entrepreneurship and in communication, as well as a joint Bachelor of Commerce degree with the University of Calgary. At SAIT the funds will go towards expanding programs in hotel and restaurant management, electrical engineering technology, computer technology, and applied degree programs in petroleum and information systems.[14]

Another major change in advanced education in Alberta is the increase in the proportion of education costs to be borne by the student. Up until 1993/4, fees for instruction could account for a maximum of 20 per cent of an institution's net operating expenses. After 1993/4, an institution's revenue from tuition can account for up to 30 per cent of an institution's net operating expenses.[15] To prevent rapid escalation in fees, the 30 per cent limit on tuition fee revenues cannot be reached before the year 2000. The maximum annual average increase in tuition fees for universities was set at $200 in 1991 and is indexed each year for inflation. Thus, for 1994/5, the maximum average increase was $215.50. For colleges and technical institutes, the maximum was set initially at $100 in 1991 (Alberta, 1994b). Subsequently, annual tuition increases for colleges and technical institutes were increased to the same level as universities, $200 plus inflation (Alberta, 1995).

To ensure that financial need is not a barrier to accessing higher learning in Alberta, the government has expanded and revamped its student assistance program. The value of outstanding loans held by students is expected to increase from $260 million in 1994 to $460 million by 1996/7. Grants are to be replaced by loans except for the most needy students. Loans are to be brokered by commercial banks, not the government, hence banks will identify students as their customers rather than having the government dictate who the customers are. Debt limits for students are to be increased, but maximum student debt levels will also be established. It is expected that maximum student debt upon graduation will increase to $20,000 for a four-year undergraduate program by 1997/8. The Alberta government also intends to make loan repayments more sensitive to a student's income and ability to pay; hence, the government recently announced an income-sensitive loan repayment plan and an interest relief program.

The student loans program will also have three other features. First, no student loans will be available for programs whose students have had high default rates in the past. Programs that demonstrate 'no reasonable employment prospects for the student' will not be fundable through student assistance. Second, to be eligible for loans and grants, students who have four months to work over the summer will be required to have minimum savings of $1,350. Finally, parents will be expected to assist with their children's education costs for the first four years after high school graduation. For married students, spouses will be expected to share in the financial responsibility for education.

The final element of the new directions for the Department of Advanced Education in Alberta is the implementation of Key Performance Indicators to increase accountability for the use of resources and for outcomes achieved. At this point, the KPIs are still being developed and have not been implemented.

## 3. FOR BETTER OR WORSE?

As mentioned earlier, the Klein government expects the changes to advanced education outlined in A Better Way to result in 'more efficient and effective' institutions. At the same time, many Albertans have raised concerns that the reduction in government spending on advanced education will undermine the levels of services provided by Alberta's colleges and universities.

Level of service in the context of advanced education has both quantity and quality dimensions—how many students are being educated and the quality of education a given student receives. The quantity dimension has been addressed explicitly in the government's objectives. To prevent Alberta's universities and colleges from absorbing the reduced government grant by decreasing places for student enrolment, enrolment corridors of 2 and 5 per cent were imposed. If an institution's enrolment falls by more than what is allowed under the enrolment corridor policy, the government imposes financial penalties. Institutions can only eliminate programs if the minister of advanced education signs off on the proposal. Thus, the main avenue for lower levels of service in advanced education rests in reduced quality of programs offered.

Of the ten Canadian provinces, Alberta has had among the highest per capita and per student government expenditures on advanced education. In 1991/2, only Québec had higher per capita expenditures (Alberta, 1993; Statistics Canada). Since 1986, expenditures per student in Alberta began to approach the national average as the growth of Alberta's spending slowed relative to the growth of spending in other provinces. The Klein government's spending reductions on advanced education should leave Alberta's expenditures per student at about the national average for universities and above average for colleges. The regression towards the mean of Alberta's spending on advanced education may be temporary, however, as universities and colleges in other Canadian provinces, like Ontario, are bracing for large reductions in government spending as well.[16]

If we believe that quality of education is directly related to government expenditures, then Alberta's students have enjoyed a level of services above the national average. In this sense any quality decline should lower Alberta's advanced education to be on par with the rest of the country. As pointed out earlier, universities and colleges in other provinces have already experienced large reductions in government expenditures on advanced education, particularly in the 1980s. In this light, the Klein cuts to advanced education are part of a trend in Canada, with Alberta experiencing these changes relatively late.

An alternative interpretation is that despite the high levels of Alberta government expenditures on advanced education, the quality of services provided was only as good as the national average, so that Alberta's institutions will fall behind those in other provinces. Higher than the national average expenditures may have been necessary for Alberta's post-secondary system to meet the quality of services provided in other provinces. First, the regional nature of the system means that programs may be offered on smaller scales at many locations, which raises the costs relative to more centralized post-secondary systems.

Second, relative to universities in Ontario and Québec, Alberta's universities may have to pay 'wage premiums' to attract top academics. The premium wages are required to compensate the academics for the professional isolation of Alberta, or perhaps to compensate for any disamenities of Edmonton, Calgary, or Lethbridge relative to alternative work locations.[17] Given that salaries and benefits of teaching faculty account for the majority of university operating expenses, building and maintaining academic institutions in Alberta may be more costly than in other provinces. This notion is consistent with the University of Alberta's recent announcement that cutbacks have resulted in the university falling from the second highest average salary for faculty in Canada to fifteenth.[18] University of Alberta adminstrators argue that this development has jeopardized the ability to attract, and retain, top faculty. The University of Calgary faces similar problems. Ultimately, losses and non-replacement of full-time faculty may undermine program viability for both institutions.[19]

The impact of the Klein agenda for advanced education on the continued leading research role of Alberta's two main universities has also been raised as a concern. In a report to Alberta Advanced Education Minister Jack Ady, Gilles Cloutier suggests that the increasing difficulty in attracting and retaining top researchers, insufficient funds to cover the maintenance and purchase of equipment, and public doubts over the value of research are undermining the institutions. Cloutier called on Ady to 'clarify and promote the importance of university research'.[20] Before condemning the government on this point, however, it should be noted that the federal government has also drastically cut back on research support. Hence, it may be the case that in the face of shrinking federal sources of research funding, more pressure is being put on shrinking provincial sources of funding.

Most arguments as to the detrimental impacts of the Klein agenda on advanced education focus on the loss of government operating grant revenue. Implicitly, it is assumed that more money means a better system. Many observers of advanced education in Canada challenge this assumption and argue that more dollars spent have not translated into improved quality. In their view, the status quo of advanced education in Alberta and Canada is not optimal. Maxwell (1994) argues that much of the existing post-secondary system in Canada was the legacy of rapid growth in the 1960s and 1970s, growth that was clearly not sustainable given the necessary financial restraints of the previous 15 years. Maxwell also argues that universities in Canada are in 'desperate need of innovation' because little incentive exists for innovation or structural change to deal with problems of staffing, program redundancy, or overcapacity that (Maxwell feels) plague Canadian universities.

From this perspective, the Alberta initiatives would appear to be in the right direction. The 5 per cent reduction in compensation means that the same levels of service could be provided at a lower cost. Dale Landry, president of the Southern Alberta Institute of Technology, has claimed that the use of business plans, which inform institutions as to what their operating grants for the next three years will be, has made the planning process easier. As discussed in Chapter 4, horizontal (interinstitutional) competition for students and for contingent funding through initiatives like the Access Fund could push institutions towards greater efficiency and innovation in program delivery. The enrolment corridors and consequent competition for students could provide further incentive for institutions to improve on program delivery. Greater accountability of universities and colleges to Alberta taxpayers should make it more difficult for inefficient practices to persist. Kesselman (1993) argues that higher tuition fees should create pressure for institutions to innovate and to take their teaching role more seriously. As students pay a larger share of their educational cost they will demand better value for their money. Institutions that deliver low-quality programs would find it difficult to attract students. Reflecting this mechanism of market discipline resulting from competition between universities (and even between universities and colleges) for students, students are often referred to as customers or stakeholders.[21]

Maxwell (1994) believes that there is clearly a need for more 'sticks and carrots' in advanced education to improve the system. As budgets for universities and colleges shrink, institutions performing beneath their potential become harder to tolerate for taxpayers, students, and, in many cases, university and college faculty and administration (Kesselman, 1993). Thus, it appears as though the Alberta government has taken positive steps towards improving advanced education in Alberta. Whether or not the desired changes will be achieved, however, cannot be determined *a priori*.

## 4. THE BOTTOM LINE TO GOVERNMENT SPENDING CUTS: THE UNIVERSITY OF CALGARY EXPERIENCE

On 31 January 1994, President Murray Fraser outlined at a campus meeting the impact of the 11 per cent reduction in the government grant to the University of Calgary (UC) for 1994/5, which amounted to an $18 million reduction in revenues.[22] Fraser expected that a tuition fee increase approved for 1994/5 would make up $4.5 million of the loss; $7 million in costs would be eliminated through position abolition, early retirements, and other cost-cutting initiatives.[23] Thus, the bottom line for the University of Calgary after these initiatives was the remaining $6.5 million that would have to be cut as a result of the reduced provincial grant. A sizeable portion of this $6.5 million was to be met with a one time 5 per cent reduction in compensation to faculty and support staff at UC. Since the provincial government had only 'strongly urged', and not legislated, the 5 per cent reduction in compensation, the UC administration had to bargain with the faculty association. Fraser argued that the collective bargaining process would have 'a major impact on our ability to balance the budget'. Despite the size of the government cut, Fraser ended his address optimistically, saying he believed in the university's future and its ability to respond to rapid change and reduced resources. Fraser urged the UC community to 'resist the urge to shoot each other'. This latter point was of some importance given the 7 per cent and 3 per cent reductions to the government grants to follow in 1995/6 and 1996/7.

Viewed from 1993/4, the 11 per cent reduction in government funding looked daunting, particularly the $6.5 million shortfall in revenue. For 1992/3, the financial condition of the university seems to have been much the same (Table 1). In the absence of a $5 million increase in fee revenues for 1993/4, the total UC budget would have been the same in 1993/4 as in 1992/3. Since the grants to universities and colleges were not cut until 1994/5, the $5 million increase in tuition fee revenues in 1993/4 represented a 3 per cent budget increase. Expenditures for 1993/4 rose accordingly. The tuition fee increases in 1993/4 are of some significance given that tuition fees are politically difficult to raise and the annual sizes of increase are institutionally limited. Once the fee increases of 1993/4 (one year before the 11 per cent cut) are accounted for, UC really only had to make up for a $1.5 million shortfall relative to 1992/3. What this represents is that a $12,305,600 reduction in the government grant from 1993/4 to 1994/5 reported in the UC operating budgets[24] was offset by an increase in annual fee revenues of $9,550,400 implemented over 1993/4 and 1994/5, not just 1994/5 (see Table 1). Thus, total revenues for the 1994/5 budget year were essentially the same as total revenues in 1992/3. Only the composition of revenues was substantially changed. As such, with the increase in tuition fees, the reduced government grant effectively amounted to more of a freeze on revenues *vis-à-vis* 1992/3 rather than a reduction.

The last column of Table 1 presents the revenues forecasted for academic budget year 1995/6. The government grant to the University of Calgary was reduced by $10,237,300 from the 1994/5 grant. Again, revenues from fees rose, by $3,911,000, partially offsetting the reduction in the government grant. The change in total general revenues for the University of Calgary was a reduction of $4,080,010, representing a projected 2 per cent decrease in revenues from 1994/5. The actual reduction in the 1995/6 budget over 1994/5 was in fact less

**Table 1:** Revenues for the University of Calgary, 1992/3 to 1995/6 (dollars)

| Revenue Source | 1992/3 | 1993/4 | 1994/5 | 1995/6 |
|---|---|---|---|---|
| Government Grants | 163,276,400 | 164,098,700 | 151,793,100 | 141,555,800 |
| Adjusted Grant | 169,414,000 | 169,765,400 | 151,793,100 | 141,555,800 |
| Fees | 34,242,000 | 39,199,640 | 43,792,400 | 47,703,500 |
| Interest and Other Revenues | 3,480,000 | 2,894,665 | 3,158,755 | 2,758,500 |
| Total | 200,998,400 | 206,193,005 | 198,744,255 | 192,017,800 |
| Total General Revenues | 201,507,005 | 207,705,855 | 199,010,710 | 194,930,700 |
| Adjusted Total General Revenues | 207,644,605 | 213,372,555 | 199,010,710 | 194,930,700 |

SOURCE: University of Calgary, *Capital and Operating Budgets*, 'Operating Budget, University Summary', p. 1. Adjusted grant and adjusted total general revenues are the 1992/3 and 1993/4 operating grants and total general revenues inclusive of capital renewal allocations that are included in the operating grant revenues as of 1994/5.

than 2 per cent due to an unanticipated increase in enrolment and UC's success in acquiring $3 million in revenues through the Access Fund.

Table 2 presents the scheduled percentage change in government grants compared to the effective percentage change in total revenues. The percentage changes are calculated from the figures in Table 1. Two sets of numbers are presented: unadjusted and adjusted revenue numbers. The 'adjusted grant' numbers in Table 1 are the operating grants for 1992/3 and 1993/4, including the capital renewal grant.[25] Both the adjusted grants and unadjusted grants are presented since it is not clear which set of numbers is more appropriate for this analysis. The grant reductions beginning in 1994/5 are applied to the combined operating grant and capital renewal grant, which suggests the adjusted grant numbers may be more appropriate. On the other hand, the capital renewal grants before 1994/5 are not completely comparable to the capital renewal grants after 1994/5 since the university has had more flexibility in how to spend the capital renewal funds after 1994/5.

If we assume that revenues reported in the 1995/6 UC budget are realized values, then from 1993/4 to 1995/6 government grants to UC have fallen by 18 per cent but the total (unadjusted) university revenues have fallen by only 6.2 per cent (Table 2). Relative to 1992/3, however, the reduction in total university revenues has been only 3.2 per cent because tuition fee revenue increases in 1993/4, prior to the 1994/5 government grant reduction, raised total revenues by 3 per cent. An 18 per cent reduction in government spending over two years will amount to a 3.2 per cent reduction (unadjusted numbers, or a 5.9 per cent reduction using adjusted numbers) in the institution's budgeted revenues relative to 1992/3. Clearly, focusing on the reduction in government transfers to the institution grossly overstates the potential impact of the Klein agenda on advanced education.

The Alberta government intended that the reduced operating grants would pressure institutions to be 'more efficient and effective'. The government's ability to pressure fundamental institutional change by 'shocking the system' is clearly weakened when the institution is allowed to pass the burden of the reduced government grant on to the students.[26] This observation does not only apply to UC, and it need not only apply to tuition fee increases. In Québec, universities could not raise tuition in response to reduced government grants in the 1980s, but they could, and did, run deficits (Hardy, 1996). In British Columbia, the sizes of cuts to government grants to universities were not as large as in Québec in the 1980s or Alberta after 1993, but Hardy describes the fiscal restraint in British Columbia as 'severe' compared to Québec. One reason for this may be that universities in British Columbia could not run deficits and may have had limited scope for raising tuition fees.

So far we have seen that much of the loss in government grant revenue was recouped through tuition fee increases beginning in 1993/4. By 1995/6, ignoring

**Table 2:** Percentage Change in Government Grants and Total General Revenues at the University of Calgary, 1992/3 to 1995/6

| Percentage Change in: | 1992/3 to 1993/4 | 1993/4 to 1994/5 | 1994/5 to 1995/6 |
|---|---|---|---|
| Government Grant–Scheduled | 0 | –11 | –7 |
| Government Grant–Actual | 0.5 | –7.5 | –6.7 |
| Government Grant–Adjusted | 0.002 | –10.6 | –6.7 |
| Total General Revenues | 3 | –4.2 | –2 |
| Total General Revenues–Adjusted | 2.8 | –6.7 | –2 |

NOTE: 'Scheduled' refers to change scheduled in Alberta, 1994a. Difference between actual and scheduled reduction in government grant reflects part of the capital renewal budget being included in the operating budget after 1993/4. Hence the 11 per cent reduction was applied to the 1993/4 operating grant plus an adjustment for the inclusion of the capital renewal budget. Data from Table 1.

the Access Fund revenue, we will see a UC budget smaller by 3 to 6 per cent. Even this reduction may not be a 'real' budget reduction given the UC administration's success in achieving the 5 per cent reduction in compensation (salaries and benefits) to faculty and support staff. Looking at only academic salaries (not including benefits), we find that salaries to full-time academic positions were reduced by $4,460,860 from 1993/4 to 1994/5, roughly a 4.9 per cent reduction. This reduction came about through the loss of 20 full-time academic positions (from 1,372.57 full-time positions in 1993/4) and a $2,200 (3 per cent) reduction in average salary (from $69,400 in 1993/4) paid for full-time academic positions.[27] These savings alone are well over the needed $1.5 million for the 1994/5 revenue shortfall over 1993/4.

Reducing compensation to faculty and support staff in a faculty association (union) setting is not a simple task. Realistically, an administration would only have one opportunity to negotiate a pay roll-back. A 5 per cent reduction to compensation achieved cost savings greater than UC needed for 1994/5, hence, the one-time reduction was large enough also to cover some of the revenue shortfall from 1994/5 following the 7 per cent reduction to the government grant in 1995/6.

The bottom line for the University of Calgary is that total budgeted revenues for 1994/5, 1995/6, and 1996/7 are essentially the same as in 1992/3. Losses in government grant revenues were largely recouped through sizeable tuition increases beginning in 1993/4 and money from the Access Fund. Reduced payroll costs should mean that the same dollars go further, even after accounting for general inflation in the economy over the same period.[28] Indeed, it is possible that in real terms, the UC budget will be larger than in 1992/3 after funds are returned through the Access Fund. The UC Board of Governors has approved a balanced budget for 1996/7 of $204 million. This budgeted amount includes the final scheduled (3 per cent) reduction in the government operating grant.[29] If this reported budget size compares directly with budget numbers reported in Table 1, then at $204 million this budget is 1.2 per cent larger than the unadjusted total budgeted revenues for 1992/3 and is 2.6 per cent larger than the university's budget for 1994/5.

Despite this apparent lack of change in the size of the UC budget, faculty operating budgets for 1994/5 are an average of 4 per cent lower than in 1992/3. As part of the university's long-term planning process, all faculties had been asked to absorb target cuts of 17 per cent. Thus, from the outset, many interpreted the UC retrenchment strategy as an across-the-board approach, where all faculties have shared in the pain. Keith Winter, UC vice-president of finance and services, would not characterize the implementation of budget cuts as across the board:

> As part of our long-term planning, all areas have been asked to absorb target cuts of 17 per cent for academic units and 20 per cent for administrative units, but in the annual budgeting process each area is considered individually. Since we began this process the cuts have ranged from zero per cent in some cases to 100 per cent in others. There were no across-the-board cuts.[30]

Only the Faculty of Graduate Studies experienced an increase in its operating budget (by 4 per cent) from 1992/3 to 1994/5. The smallest budget reductions over 1992/3 to 1994/5 were in the faculties of General Studies (no change), Social Work (1 per cent), Environmental Design (2 per cent), and Science (2.5 per cent). The largest budget reductions from 1992/3 to 1994/5 were in the faculties of Law (8.7 per cent), Continuing Education (7.5 per cent), Humanities (7.3 per cent), and Management (7 per cent). Given that the faculties' net expenditures are reduced but the overall budget is not, a greater proportion of university resources must be directly under the control of the administration rather than faculty deans and department heads. At UC, there was no explicit strategic plan for implementing selective cuts to academic units. As discussed later in the chapter, the differential sizes of the faculty budget reductions may reflect differential faculty attrition rates, where attrition has been one of the major cost-saving initiatives.

One final consideration for interpreting the bottom line of universities in Alberta needs to be highlighted. Although the budgeted revenues are relatively unchanged for Alberta's universities, the institutions face some important financial challenges as operating costs continue to rise. The likely outcome of this squeeze, however, appears not to be fundamental restructuring, but instead, the non-replacement of lost faculty and the consumption/degradation of capital. Cloutier's report on research identified this as an undesirable direction of change if Alberta's universities are to maintain the quality of their research.

Institutions appear to have taken advantage of the option to consume their capital following the consolidation of the operating and capital renewal budgets. Libraries on various campuses in Alberta are examples of capital that has been seriously compromised by real cuts to library budgets. For capital-intensive faculties like Engineering and Science, technological advances in lab equipment and other teaching and research institutional infrastructure may raise costs much more than in low-tech faculties like Humanities and Social Sciences. Hence, these faculties may face a much greater financial squeeze. On the other hand, the nature of the research produced by Engineering and Science faculties may mean that these faculties have an easier time obtaining financial support for programs and research from sources external to the university.

For purposes of a summary, several aspects of the UC strategy for dealing with the reduced operating grants deserve note. First, President Fraser's address emphasized the collegial nature of the UC retrenchment strategy. Budget cuts through the UC faculties and departments were initiated following more of an across-the-board approach rather than an approach of strategically determined selective cuts. No obvious fundamental restructuring occurred. Considerable cost savings were achieved through attrition of faculty and early retirement initiatives. Finally, tuition fee increases have played an important role.

## 4.1 How Representative is the Calgary Experience?

Budget figures for the University of Lethbridge (UL) and the University of Alberta (UA) suggest that the UC experience is representative. Like UC, both UA and UL had substantial increases in fee revenues in 1993/4, the year prior to the 11 per cent cut. In 1994/5, UL total revenues were almost $8 million higher than in 1992/3, after the 11 per cent cut to the base grant.

For UA, the government operating grant in 1994/5 was $20 million less than in 1992/3 and 1993/4, but fee revenues in 1994/5 were about $8 million higher than in 1992/3, representing a net decrease of $12 million (see Table 3). If one accounts for the 5 per cent compensation cut in 1994/5, operating expenses at UA would be roughly $13 million lower in 1994/5 than in 1992/3 and 1993/4.[31] Thus, UA may be able to meet the 11 per cent cut through tuition fee increases and the 5 per cent compensation cut. The 7 per cent cut for 1995/6, however, still has to be met. Again, tuition fees are projected in the budget to increase by $6 million, but the operating grant will fall by $13 million from 1994/5 to 1995/6, leaving a reduction of total operating revenues of about 5 per cent from 1992/3 to 1995/6 (see Table 4). Financial penalties for violating the enrolment corridor will exacerbate the problem. At the same time, success in securing money from the Access Fund will obviously help the UA situation.

The difference in the UC and UA financial situations may explain the extent of the differences in how the two institutions dealt with the Klein cuts. At UC,

**Table 3:** Revenues for the University of Alberta, 1992/3 to 1995/6 (dollars)

| Revenue Source | 1992/3 | 1993/4 | 1994/5 | 1995/6 |
|---|---|---|---|---|
| Government Grants | 259,903,000 | 260,361,000 | 239,666,000 | 226,524,000 |
| Adjusted Grant | 269,773,300 | 271,022,000 | 239,666,000 | 226,524,000 |
| Fees | 52,141,000 | 60,440,000 | 64,034,000 | 70,304,000 |
| Total | 312,044,000 | 320,801,000 | 303,700,000 | 296,828,000 |
| Total General Revenues | 321,012,000 | 327,701,000 | 313,010,710 | 304,693,000 |
| Total General Revenues–Adjusted | 330,882,300 | 338,362,000 | 313,010,710 | 304,693,000 |

SOURCES: Unaudited schedules and audited financial statements; 1995/6 board-approved operating budget. Excludes ancillary operations. Adjusted grant and adjusted total general revenues are the 1992/3 and 1993/4 operating grants and total general revenues inclusive of capital renewal allocations that are included in the operating grant revenues as of 1994/5.

**Table 4:** Percentage Change in Government Grants and Total General Revenues at the University of Alberta, 1992/3 to 1995/6

| Percentage Change in: | 1992/3 to 1993/4 | 1993/4 to 1994/5 | 1994/5 to 1995/6 |
|---|---|---|---|
| Government Grant–Scheduled | 0 | −11 | −7 |
| Government Grant–Actual | 0.2 | −7.9 | −5.5 |
| Government Grant–Adjusted | 0.5 | −11.6 | −5.5 |
| Total General Revenues | 2.1 | −4.4 | −2.7 |
| Total General Revenues–Adjusted | 2.3 | −7.5 | −2.7 |

NOTE: 'Scheduled' refers to change scheduled in Alberta, 1994a. Difference between actual and scheduled reduction in government grant reflects part of the capital renewal budget being included in the operating budget after 1993/4. Hence the 11 per cent reduction was appplied to the 1993/4 operating grant plus an adjustment for the inclusion of the capital renewal budget. Data from Table 3.

funding reductions for programs occurred largely for ancillary programs not considered part of the university's core. Funding was either eliminated or drastically reduced for the sports program, the Nickle Arts Museum, campus recreation, the design office, the university press, special events, the conference office, university health services, the Student Employment Centre, and printing services.[32] The sports program has not been eliminated but instead has been made fully self-funding. At UA, university-wide restructuring of faculties, departments, and programs coincided with the reductions in the government grant. The number of departments at UA has been reduced from 86 in 1990/1 to 62 by 1995/6.[33] One of the more notable changes was the elimination of dentistry as an independent faculty as the School of Dentistry was merged with the School of Medicine. The intent of such restructuring could be to economize on administration resources and to allow for more flexible budgeting with the reduction in the number of budget entities explicitly entitled to budget funds. Or, as Hardy (1996: 120) points out, cuts to ancillary programs at UC, and restructuring at UA, have both a cost-saving component and a symbolic component. They are highly visible and often highly publicized changes, which may signal to the government and taxpayers that the institutions are serious about responding to provincial concerns.

On the surface, it would appear that the larger funding shock to UA relative to UC accomplished what the Alberta government had intended—greater efficiency in program delivery represented by the extent of restructuring. This would suggest that governments can use financial 'sticks' to beat the inefficiency out of the institutions. If this is in fact true, universities must be incredibly responsive institutions if fundamental restructuring occurs as a result of a 2 per cent to 5 per cent reduction in revenues. As it turns out, there is an alternative, and better, explanation for the differences between UA's and UC's observed changes after 1992/3—different administrative visions. Both institutions had plans for dealing with expected and emerging budgetary squeezes before the Klein government was elected.

UA's more selective approach to expenditure cuts reflected a direction established as early as 1991 in a document titled 'Maintaining Excellence and Accessibility in an Environment of Budgetary Restraint'. As Richard Peter, Dean of Science at UA, puts it, 'in one way, the budget reductions have been extremely hard, but they've also provided an opportunity for change. . . . We've undergone considerable restructuring . . . the impetus was academic as well as economic.'[34] The threat of budget cuts prompted UC's president, Murray Fraser, in 1993 to direct academic units to plan for 17 per cent reductions in funding over five years. Joy Calkin, vice-president academic at UC, suggests that 'the goal was to create a pool of unallocated funds that would "allow the U of C to protect its key priorities in tough times." When the province cut funding even deeper than expected, the plan was viewed as a lifesaver by many on campus.'[35]

Among Alberta's colleges, the Southern Alberta Institute of Technology warrants discussion. At SAIT, cost recovery initiatives, an increasing market orientation, and lotteries to raise money have offset and even surpassed the magnitude of the cut to the government grant. As with the universities, however, SAIT's cost reduction and revenue generation initiatives had little to do with the Klein government's changes to advanced education.

SAIT in many ways appears to have been the government's model for advanced education in Alberta. As a result of a large debt ($8 million) incurred in 1990, SAIT was forced to undertake massive financial restructuring. Programs like Fashion Design and Process Piping Drafting were eliminated, 15 departments were amalgamated, and services such as caretaking of buildings and grounds were contracted out. Decisions to eliminate programs were based on such factors as student enrolment, student applications (required minimum of 2.5 applications per enrolment place), and employability of graduates (stipulated goal: 90 per cent of graduates to be employed within six months of graduation). Hence, programs with low demand from students or prospective employers were eliminated. SAIT is also moving away from a department-based structure to a 'program module' structure. In this sense, faculty positions follow programs; if a use for the position cannot be found, the position can be eliminated. Rather than across-the-board budget reductions, 39 per cent of staff were laid off over a three-year period. Enrolment increased by 17 per cent over the same period. SAIT senior executives have five-year, performance-based contracts.[36] To be less reliant on government funding, SAIT has approached potential industry clients and created and administered customized training programs. SAIT also earns revenues by taking on applied projects for the private sector.[37]

The key point to note is that SAIT undertook all of these initiatives well before the government's announced changes to advanced education in 1993/4. Thus, the government initiatives did not push SAIT in this direction. Illustrating this point is the fact that when the government encouraged the 5 per cent cut to compensation, SAIT was one of the only institutions that did not cut salaries 5 per cent since they had already cut staff levels by 39 per cent.

Beyond the case of SAIT, the impacts of the Klein government's initiatives for colleges are harder to determine since current revenue figures for colleges are difficult to obtain. In some cases, colleges have resorted to fee increases to offset the decrease in the government grant. In other cases, for example, at Olds College where fees have been extremely low, administrators did not take this route. Clearly, in cases where fee revenue increases are not as easy to implement, the financial squeeze may be greater. Where revenues are awarded through the Access Fund, colleges in Alberta may be able to deal with the reduced operating grant much as the universities have.

## 5. NEW DIRECTIONS?

The Klein government intended that the reduced operating grants would pressure institutions into more efficient and effective delivery of programs much in the way SAIT's debt forced its executives to undertake fundamental restructuring. In other words, the grant reductions were 'sticks' intended to encourage innovation and efficiency. For these gains to be achieved it must be the case that resources within an institution can be reallocated to enhance areas of emerging strength and diminish declining, or redundant, programs. To address this point, we need to look more closely at how institutions have sought and been able to reallocate resources in a socially desired direction. The government has identified the socially desired direction for reallocating resources as the market oriented allocation. An integral part of strengthening market signals has been to raise tuition fees.

## 5.1 Creating More Responsive Institutions

The Klein government's agenda for advanced education embodied the notion that the education and training provided by universities and colleges had to become more relevant for the needs of Alberta's society and economy. Thus, the attempt to make Alberta's universities and colleges more responsive to labour market demands, and the needs of the market in general, has been a prominent part of the Klein agenda for advanced education. Ironically, the main vehicle for encouraging the market focus is the Access Fund, run by an advisory board, which essentially plays the role of a central planner. The advisory board is mandated to determine what labour market demands are and to allocate Access Fund resources accordingly. Implicitly, students are considered insensitive to market rates of return to various education or training options; hence, shepherding them into programs is required.

Access Fund money represents a relatively small share of total revenues in an institution. As such, the emphasis on a market focus has not likely had a large influence on institutions in Alberta, with the exception of SAIT. Consistent with this argument is the observation for UC that the scheduled $2.1 million reduction in salaries for teaching positions for 1995/6 over 1994/5 is all due to the budgeted elimination of 61 full-time equivalent teaching positions in the part-time and other category. The 1995/6 budget for UC did not include the $3 million in Access Funds, which is primarily to be used to hire part-time instructors. Thus, UC's Access Fund success may allow for these positions to be retained.

The greatest barrier to having more market-oriented, responsive institutions is the long-term employment arrangement of university and college faculty. Universities and colleges have always been market-responsive to some degree, but the responses were asymmetric between increases in student demand and decreases in student demand. It is easier to expand an institution through hiring than it is to shrink an institution or reallocate resources from one program to another within an institution, unless you can lay off faculty. Staffing levels of university programs or departments today may reflect enrolment trends of two previous decades rather than current demand.

To be responsive to changes in labour market demands, an institution must be able to both hire and fire (not renew). The fundamental trade-off in moving to a more market-oriented system may be between full-time/tenured faculty and part-time/sessional contract instructors. For some time, institutions in Alberta and Canada have been moving towards a greater reliance on part-time teachers, hence becoming more capable of responding to change in student demand. Maxwell (1994) argues that when university budgets tightened with declining government financial support starting in the late 1970s, the quality of university programs declined as class sizes increased and greater delegation of teaching to teaching assistants and inexperienced part-time lecturers occurred.[38] Interestingly, Table 5 suggests that part-time teaching faculty positions (Full-Time Equivalents or FTEs) at UC have been stable over the period under study, not increasing. The perception that full-time faculty are being replaced by part-time sessional instructors therefore does not appear to be true. The perception of increased reliance on part-time sessional instructors reflects instead the fact that not all full-time faculty are being replaced, so that the proportionate use of sessional instructors has increased.[39] Thus, the only conclusion we can make is that class sizes in Alberta must be larger since enrolment has not declined with staffing levels.

Given that this relative shift to part-time and inexperienced instructors over full-time faculty has been accentuated in Alberta as institutions seek to meet their budget targets, the increasing market orientation of institutions will worsen program quality, not improve it, if Maxwell's arguments are reasonable. Finally, contract employment for the purpose of teaching only could mean that universities are moving away from their research orientation.

The primary way in which universities in Alberta have sought to reallocate resources is through attrition and early retirements. As full-time faculty resign or accept an early retirement package, the faculty positions they occupied can be closed. The power to return a position to a department or faculty is left to the discretion of the institution's administration. In this way, programs with

**Table 5:** Academic Salaries for Full-Time and Part-Time and Other, Full-Time Equivalent Teaching Positions at the University of Calgary, 1992/3 to 1995/6

|  | 1992/3 | 1993/4 | 1994/5 | 1995/6 |
|---|---|---|---|---|
| **Full-time (FTEs)** | $87,961,755 | $88,007,605 | $84,470,795 | $84,692,235 |
|  | (1,284.9) | (1,258.64) | (1,247.96) | (1,237.69) |
| **Part-time and Other (FTEs)** | $9,710,230 | $9,778,865 | $9,371,140 | $7,038,290 |
|  | (311.36) | (299.62) | (303.07) | (242.00) |
| **Total (FTEs)** | $97,671,985 | $97,786,470 | $93,841,935 | $91,730,525 |
|  | (1,596.26) | (1,558.26) | (1,551.03) | (1,479.69) |

SOURCE: University of Calgary, *Capital and Operating Budgets,* 'Operating Budget, Teaching Summary', p. 3. These are gross figures that are not adjusted for academic recovery of salaries and FTEs.

declining demand/enrolment can be reduced and the resources released can be reallocated to other faculties or departments, or the expenditure on the position can be eliminated. Table 5 shows the impact of the early retirement strategy on teaching faculty positions for UC. Over the period 1992/3 to 1994/5, the number of full-time teaching full-time equivalent (FTE) positions has declined from 1,284.9 to 1,247.96. A large number of early retirements are still due to occur through 1997/8.

Attrition and early retirement have been the primary way in which financially squeezed universities have sought to reduce expenditures (Hardy, 1996). Hardy points out, however, that it is not clear how much of a saving was actually achieved. Early retirements are an expensive way to reallocate institutional resources and do not provide the soundest of bases for such reallocation. UC has already spent millions of dollars on early retirement pay-outs and still faces the problem of coming up with $5 million for early retirement pay-outs in 1997/8.[40] With early retirements, resources released for reallocation are freed up on the basis of staff demographics, not strategic planning. Reduction in faculty largely reflects which departments or programs had the greatest growth in positions 20 or 30 years earlier, even if those programs or departments are not ones in which decline in demand has been the greatest. Different demographics of faculties at UC may explain the differences in budget reductions reported above. Hardy suggests that for McGill and the University of Montreal, most institutional savings were achieved in areas populated with older professors. At the University of British Columbia, where attrition of faculty was a major component of the university's cost-saving strategy, an administrator was quoted by Hardy (1996: 91) as saying that 'the lucky departments are the ones that don't have anyone retiring or resigning around the time of the budget cuts.'

The alternative way to reduce full-time faculty would be to lay-off/fire faculty or eliminate positions at the decision of an institution's governors.[41] This approach requires governors/administrators to make 'tough' choices and decide where resources should be reduced and where resources should be increased. SAIT used objective indicators of student demand for enrolment and employer demand for graduates to determine where positions should be eliminated. Of course, this approach may have high costs for an institution resulting from the concerns over job security among remaining faculty. Higher salaries may be required to retain faculty to compensate them for the reduced job security.

There are at least two explanations for the use of faculty attrition and early retirement packages (carrots) over firing (sticks) for reducing or reallocating budgeted resources. If university administrators seek to avoid conflict as discussed in Chapter 4, then they would cut positions in the politically easiest manner. Hardy (1996: 91) quotes a UBC administrator: 'It [using attrition to reduce costs] makes management look pretty weak—the line of least resistance. But when you have to cut on short notice, it is an expedient way of cutting.'

Another possibility raised by Maxwell (1994) is that university presidents/administrators lack the necessary power to use sticks, hence they must resort to the more costly, and probably less efficient, carrots. Hardy finds that powerful deans can limit what higher levels of university government can accomplish, but she also finds that more centralized power does not lead to more success with retrenchment. Hardy (1996: 144) argues that power appears to have been more centralized at the University of Toronto than at the University of British Columbia, and concludes that, counter to what one might expect, retrenchment plans were implemented more successfully at UBC where power was less centralized.

Hardy resolves the previous counter-intuitive conclusion by raising a factor that may be the most important of all for effecting change—crisis. She suggests that the University of Toronto was unsuccessful in implementing its retrenchment plan in the 1980s because it lacked a perceived crisis to create a mandate for change. UBC did not suffer the same disadvantage:

> The perceived crisis caused by the government's attack on tenure helped to legitimize the administration's action. Many people felt 'something had to be done'. . . . The crisis may also help to explain why the deans were agreeable to at least some form of cutbacks: they too had become 'aware of the corporate problem.' (Hardy, 1996: 90)

Consistent with this view on the importance of perceived crisis is the observation that the most radical institutional changes in Alberta occurred at SAIT, where President Dale Landry was given a powerful mandate in 1991—to get rid of SAIT's debt by whatever means necessary.

Given the relatively small reductions in institutional budgets in advanced education in Alberta since 1993/4, it may be that the most important role of a reduced government operating grant for an institution is that the perceived financial crisis associated with the funding cut gives administrators the opportunity to increase their executive power. Donald Savage, executive director of the Canadian Association of University Teachers, argues that across Canada 'we have a number of institutions who want to exploit the financial situation to increase their executive power and decrease the power of staff and faculty'.[42] Consistent with this argument are the 'words of advice' from Alberta's universities for universities elsewhere facing cuts to operating grants—'use the budget reductions to make some much needed changes'.[43]

## 5.2 Higher Tuition Fees

Higher tuition fees in Alberta's institutions have allowed university and college budgets to be maintained, at the same time lowering the cost of advanced education for taxpayers. One of the motivating principles behind the higher tuition policy was that students should have to pay their 'fair' share of the cost of their education since they are the primary beneficiaries of the educational investment. What constitutes a fair share has changed in just the last three years. Originally, 20 per cent was considered to be a fair share, but as of 1994/5, 30 per cent was established as the fair share. How the fair share has been determined appears to be the outcome of 'gut' feeling, opinion, recognition of inter-provincial competition for students, and political feasibility.[44]

Higher tuition fees were also argued to be a potential source of efficiency gain in the advanced education system by forcing students to take their educational investment choices more seriously. With fees uniformly higher across all programs, this is unlikely to be the case. Kitchen and Auld's (1995) survey of the literature on private rates of return to post-secondary education[45] suggests that rates vary considerably across a student's chosen area of specialization and across occupations of graduates. For example, they report that in 1985 the private rate of return for a male with a bachelor's degree in arts or science was 4 per cent while a male with a degree in dentistry realized a private rate of return of 22.4 per cent. Uniformly higher tuition costs may direct students towards areas that have higher private rates of return after graduation. Thus, demand for business schools and professional programs could increase at the expense of the humanities and social sciences. The increase in training of professionals could result in an oversupply of business graduates, lawyers, and the like. An alternative tuition fee policy could be to differentiate tuition fees according to the private rate of return associated with the degree or diploma, with some programs such as business schools charging for full cost recovery. Whereas uniform tuition fees and fee increases distort market signals for students, differentiated tuition fees and fee increases would allow labour markets to signal which degrees students should be pursuing.[46]

One final argument for high fees reflects the potential for efficiency gains arising from student exit from poor programs or 'voice' disciplining substandard programs or institutions. Students presumably would take more interest in the quality of their programs when the personal cost to them is higher. In Alberta, however, students, while newly identified as customers or stakeholders, have not displayed heightened interest in program quality. Part of the explanation for this has to be the fact that students have always shown an interest in program quality independent of the levels of their fees. The real difference in the customer-oriented college or university must lie in the heightened awareness of responsibility for quality programs by university and college faculty. Presumably, not too many instructors would feel comfortable shirking on their teaching responsibilities given the financial commitment students must make to get their educations. Unfortunately, too many may have done so in the past, and now current students must pay to 'discipline' institutions for perceived sins of the past.

## 6. CONCLUSIONS

Two unambiguous conclusions can be drawn about the impact of the Klein agenda for advanced education in Alberta: taxpayers in Alberta pay less for advanced education, while students (and their parents) pay more for their educations. What is not clear is how different Alberta's advanced education system is following the Klein government's initiatives. After reductions in government operating grants to institutions of 19.5 per cent since 1993/4, the sizes of institutional budgets are much the same as before. If the institutions are relatively unchanged, then the main impact of the Klein agenda has been to reallocate the burden of education finance from taxpayers to students. Administrators of institutions may also have gained executive power over institutional resources at the expense of faculty members. In terms of this latter suggestion, we cannot conclude if this development is to the benefit or detriment of students and taxpayers.

There are indications, however, that universities and colleges have been scarred despite their maintenance of total budgets. Capital has not been renewed and faculty have not been replaced. With enrolment levels maintained, class sizes must be larger or, if teacher substitutes are employed, faculty-student contact must be reduced. Thus, whatever has been gained may have come at a price.

We have also seen from the Alberta experience that the extent of restructuring is not necessarily related to the size of the financial 'stick'. As restructuring may reflect 'administrative visions', restructuring results in change. We cannot say, however, whether the changes represent improvement or deterioration in Alberta's system of advanced education.

Finally, the question must be raised as to what lessons the Alberta experience can provide for institutions in other provinces or for Alberta's institutions in the future. There are few lessons of this sort from the Alberta experience. Given that the government spending cuts on advanced education in Alberta lagged behind those in other provinces, the lessons to be learned are more likely to come from jurisdictions that have dealt with shrinking government support for a longer period of time. In all likelihood, there was some financial slack in Alberta's universities and colleges. Once that slack is eliminated, however, we cannot predict the impact of further government spending cuts on the institutions.

## NOTES

1. Prepared for 'A Government Reinvented: A Study of the Alberta Deficit Elimination Program', sponsored by the Donner Canadian Foundation. I thank Peter Malcolm of Alberta's Department of Advanced Education and Career Development for data and information he provided. I thank Ken McKenzie, Ron Kneebone, Jonathan

Kesselman, and Dale Landry, president of SAIT, for comments and information. I am solely responsible for any errors.

2. Beginning in 1981, the Québec government announced funding to universities would be reduced by 11.3, 5.9, and 5.9 per cent over the following three years. The total budgets cuts were thus 23.1 per cent over three years. British Columbia universities had their operating grants frozen for 1983/4 and reduced 5 per cent per year for the next two years (Hardy, 1996). For Alberta, the reductions in operating grants of 11, 7, and 3 per cent total 21 per cent. The 19.5 per cent over three years reflects that the 7 and 3 per cent reductions are assessed on previously reduced operating grants. Despite the smaller total percentage cut, Hardy (1996: 116) characterizes the cuts to British Columbia universities as more 'severe and dramatic' than in other provinces, including Québec, since universities in British Columbia relied on government funding for 85 per cent of their operating revenues. The characterization seems odd given the larger percentage cut in Québec, where the University of Montreal relied on government funding for 88 per cent of operating revenues according to Hardy's Table 2.2 (p. 34). In Alberta, government operating grants accounted for 80 per cent or more of total budgeted revenues before 1993/4.

3. Dale Landry, president of the Southern Alberta Institute of Technology, has pointed out to the author that a capital funding policy was circulated to the colleges in Alberta.

4. At the University of Calgary the 5 per cent reduction in compensation was met through some direct reduction in salaries, the imposition of seven unpaid days (similar to 'Rae Days' in Ontario), and the elimination of benefits like travel allowances, tuition fee waivers for faculty spouses and dependents, and the elimination of the subsidy paid for membership in the campus recreation facilities. Notably, merit pay was retained and paid out after the salary reduction, which helped to feather the cut. Professional allowances were also retained.

5. Keith Winter, Vice-President (Finance and Services), University of Calgary, 'Notes on Special Joint Committee Meeting of Dean's Council, 1994-01-24'; Hardy, 1996.

6. Hardy (1996) describes the difficulties some universities encountered in the 1980s negotiating even pay freezes, let alone pay reductions, in a collective bargaining setting. At McGill, non-unionized staff were willing to forgo 5 per cent in pay increases to help the university reduce expenditures. At the University of Montreal, the unionized faculty would not negotiate salary concessions, in part because of perceptions that administrative costs could be reduced instead.

7. These are the University of Calgary, the University of Alberta, the Southern Alberta Institute of Technology, the Northern Alberta Institute of Technology, Mount Royal College, and Grant MacEwan Community College.

8. Interview with Jack Ady, Alberta Minister of Advanced Education, conducted by Chris Bruce and Ken McKenzie of the Department of Economics, University of Calgary. Subsequent to this interview, rural colleges were allowed a two-year grace period to meet the enrolment corridor. Many colleges experienced difficulties maintaining enrolment through no fault of their own. Information provided by Alberta's Department of Advanced Education and Career Development. The Banff Centre is excluded from the enrolment corridor policy.

9. 'Calgary is Target of U of A Enrolment Campaign', *Calgary Herald*, 18 Sept. 1995: B4.

10. Information on grant reductions as a result of the enrolment corridor policy provided by Alberta's Department of Advanced Education and Career Development.

11. Interviews with administrators at the Universities of Alberta and Calgary, Southern Alberta Institute of Technology, Red Deer College, and Olds College conducted by Christopher Bruce, Ronald Kneebone, and Kenneth McKenzie of the Department of Economics, University of Calgary.

12. Information provided by Dale Landry, president of the Southern Alberta Institute of Technology.

13. The University of Calgary already had a Co-operative Education program, which did not receive Access Fund money because it was not a new program. To some extent, the work experience and applied programs supported by the Access Fund may be reinventing existing programs.

14. 'Advanced Education Gets $9-million Boost', *Calgary Herald*, 5 May 1995: A1.

15. In 1991/2, fees at the University of Calgary accounted for 15.3 per cent of total operating expenditures and by 1994/5 they accounted for 20.9 per cent of total operating expenditures. *University of Calgary Calendars*.

16. 'Campuses in Turmoil Over Job Security', *Globe and Mail*, 18 Oct. 1995: A1.

17. As most academics are not originally from Alberta, isolation from family and social networks are two examples of locational disamenities.

18. 'U of A Says Wages Too Low', *Calgary Herald*, 7 Sept. 1995: A17.

19. In the case of maintaining the viability of existing programs, there is little discussion of whether these programs should be offered, only the implicit argument that a program must be worth maintaining because it has been offered up until now. Many programs offered are to some extent the result of 'historic accidents' in hiring faculty in the past rather than the product of design. Instead of dictating hiring priorities, it may be that programs should be retired with the loss of core faculty members.

20. 'Alberta Universities' Role Seriously Challenged', *Calgary Herald*, 8 Sept. 1995: B16.

21. One example of this customer-oriented approach was the use of 'greeters' for students arriving on campuses in Alberta this fall, much like the greeters for customers at Wal-Mart.

22. 'Summary of President Murray Fraser's Jan. 31, 1994 Campus Meeting Regarding Provincial Budget Cuts to the U of C', retrieved from the UC GOPHER site.

23. Some of the cost-cutting initiatives were part of the university's own budget reduction plans that had been implemented prior to the announced Klein cuts.

24. The discrepancy with UC President Fraser's figure of an $18 million reduction is explained by the lower figure reflecting an adjustment for the inclusion of the capital renewal budget in the government operating grant as of 1994/5.

25. I wish to thank Peter Malcolm of the Department of Advanced Education and Career Development for providing the adjusted grant numbers.

26. Of course, as Kesselman (1993) argues, this change may indirectly lead to pressure for change from students paying higher fees.

27. University of Calgary, *Capital and Operating Budgets*.

28. The UC administration may have squandered this possibility by not freezing salaries after 1993/4. With the 5 per cent compensation cut, average salaries fell by only 3 per cent. Merit pay was left in place, hence most of the loss in salary was recouped by full-time faculty in the same year. The continuance of merit pay has allowed salaries to increase each year. Non-replacement of full-time faculty and non-renewal of university capital may be the consequence of the decision not to freeze salaries at UC.

29. 'Balanced Budget in Record Time', *University of Calgary Gazette*, 25 Mar. 1996: 1. The budget document for 1996/7 was not available at the time this chapter was written.

30. Ibid.

31. Assuming that salaries and benefits account for 80 per cent of the total operating budget, $13,108,040 = 0.05*0.8*327,701,000$, where $327,701,000 was UA's total operating revenue for 1993/4, excluding ancillary operations.

32. Information provided by A.P. Chambers, Associate Director, Budgets, Office of the Vice-President (Finance and Services), University of Calgary.

33. Although not on the same scale, such changes have occurred at UC. For example, departmental mergers ocurred within Bio-sciences and the Faculty of Education.

34. 'Facing the Budget Crunch', *University Affairs*, Oct. 1995: 9–11.

35. Ibid.

36. SAIT's Board of Governors has extended President Landry's contract to the year 2001 because 'he's performed well beyond expectations'. Since Landry assumed the president's seat, SAIT's enrolment has increased by 29 per cent and SAIT has accumulated a $12 million surplus in its current $90 million budget. 'SAIT President Wins Five-Year Vote of Confidence', *Calgary Herald*, 23 Nov. 1995: B7.

37. Southern Alberta Institute of Technology, *Annual Report 1994*. Information also obtained in interview with Dale Landry (SAIT president) and Keith Pederson (SAIT vice-president) conducted by Chris Bruce and Ron Kneebone of the Department of Economics, University of Calgary.

38. Maxwell appears to assume that program quality declines as class sizes increase. She also appears to assume that part-time sessional instructors are inferior teachers to full-time faculty members. Maxwell does not provide any empirical support for these assumptions. Empirical evidence as to the validity of her assumptions is inconclusive.

39. Also contributing to the perception of increased reliance on part-time sessional instructors is the fact that they teach predominantly first- and second-year courses with large class sizes. As such, sessional instructors may teach larger numbers of students than full-time faculty whose teaching is concentrated at the senior undergraduate and graduate levels.

40. 'Slightly Ahead of the Buzz Saw: Cost Increases Keep Budget Situation Precarious', *University of Calgary Gazette*, 10 Oct. 1995: 3.

41. A redundancy agreement was ratified through collective bargaining at the University of Calgary in 1995. This agreement was needed in the event that the university administration chose to eliminate programs.

42. 'Campuses in Turmoil Over Job Security', *Globe and Mail*, 18 Oct. 1995: A6.

43. 'Facing the Budget Crunch', *University Affairs*, Oct. 1995: 9.

44. Interviews with administrators at the Universities of Alberta and Calgary, Southern Alberta Institute of Technology, Red Deer College, and Olds College conducted by Christopher Bruce, Ronald Kneebone, and Kenneth McKenzie of the Department of Economics, University of Calgary.

45. The private rate of return to a university degree reflects the difference in earnings between a university graduate in a given program and the average earnings of high school graduates. This increase in earnings is compared to the student's own costs of education (tuition, books, etc.) and forgone earnings while at university to derive the private rate of return.

46. An anonymous referee pointed out that both the University of Western Ontario and the University of Toronto plan to charge higher, differential fees for professional programs.

## REFERENCES

Alberta (1992), Advanced Education, 'High School Graduates and Enrolment Demand to the year 2005'. Edmonton.

———— (1993), Advanced Education and Career Development, 'Profile of Adult Learning in Alberta: Current Context and Selected Trends Affecting Public Post-Secondary Education and Labour Market Training', Background Discussion Paper. Edmonton.

———— (1994a), Advanced Education and Career Development Business Plan 1994–95 to 1996–97, *A Better Way: A Plan for Securing Alberta's Future*. Edmonton.

———— (1994b), Advanced Education and Career Development, 'New Directions for Adult Learning in Alberta', Oct. Edmonton.

———— (1995), Advanced Education and Career Development Business Plan 1995/96 to 1997/98, *A Better Way II: A Blueprint for Building Alberta's Future 1995/96–1997/98*. Edmonton.

Cloutier, G.G. (1995), 'Towards a Policy Framework for University Research: A Discussion Paper'. Edmonton: Department of Advanced Education and Career Development.

Hardy, C. (1996), *The Politics of Collegiality: Retrenchment Strategies in Canadian Universities*. Montreal and Kingston: McGill-Queen's University Press.

Kesselman, J.R. (1993), 'Squeezing Universities, Students, or Taxpayers? Issues in Designing a Canadian Income-Contingent Loan Program', in S.T. Easton, ed., *Ending the Squeeze on Universities*. Ottawa: Institute for Research on Public Policy.

Kitchen, H., and D. Auld (1995), *Financing Education and Training in Canada*. Canadian Tax Paper No. 99. Ottawa: Canadian Tax Foundation.

Maxwell, J. (1994), 'More Carrots, Please: Education, Training and Fiscal Federalism', in K.G. Banting et al., eds, *The Future of Fiscal Federalism*. Kingston: School of Policy Studies, Queen's University.

Southern Alberta Institute of Technology (1994), *Annual Report 1994*.

Statistics Canada, *Education in Canada* (ongoing serial publication), Cat. No. 81–229. Ottawa.

University of Alberta (1991), 'Maintaining Excellence and Accessibility in an Environment of Budgetary Restraint', Feb.

———— (1993), 'Degrees of Freedom: A Strategic Plan for the University of Alberta to the Year 2005', Nov.

———— (1994), 'Quality First', Feb.

University of Calgary (various years), *Capital and Operating Budgets*.

University of Calgary, Office of Institutional Analysis (various years), *University of Calgary Fact Books*.

# Comments on Chapter 10:
# Advanced Education Policies in Canada:
# Restraint for What Purpose?

*Jonathan Kesselman*

## 1. INTRODUCTION

The careful case study by Herb Emery offers a guardedly positive assessment of the Alberta experience of financial restraint for advanced education. It may be reassuring to policy-makers to learn that Alberta's advanced education system has had the slack and resilience to absorb large cuts in public funding without severe impacts on the quality or quantity of services. In my view, this is a potentially dangerous message for the other provinces unless some critical qualifications and discussion are appended. Emery does note many of these points, but I believe they warrant further amplification.

First, Alberta's cuts have merely moved the province close to the national average for advanced education from a position well above that. Hence, the Alberta experiment in this field may have very limited relevance to the other provinces. To wit, would we expect the same resilience and minimal effects to Alberta advanced education if additional cuts of 20 per cent were imposed beyond those already implemented and forthcoming? In most other provinces, real levels of public funding per university and college student have declined sharply over the past 10 to 15 years. This marks an unusual example of increased 'efficiency' and 'productivity' in a major area of the public sector. The result has been larger class sizes, increased teaching loads, lower relative faculty pay, and declining resources for ancillary but essential functions such as library services. It is unlike the patterns of rising real spending in the areas of basic education and health care, both relatively favoured in the political arena.

What are the limits to and implications of further moves to reduce public funding for advanced education? In discussing this issue, I shall draw on the British Columbia and in particular the UBC experience, including that of my own Economics Department, just as Emery has focused on Alberta and his own University of Calgary. My comments here will investigate the economic and social consequences of pushing the financial restraints on advanced education significantly further than Alberta has already done. Unless effectively questioned, that will be the natural course of all the fiscally pressed provinces.

I shall explore three major and interrelated dimensions of the impacts on advanced education of further public financial restraint:

- greater reliance on tuition finance, with associated issues about the structuring of loans;
- cost and quality of education, especially at the undergraduate and vocational levels;
- other outputs of universities, especially research but also graduate education, community service, and industry liaison.

My analysis will then turn to methods of improving efficiency in the supply of advanced education, focusing on undergraduate education and research outputs. Finally, I shall consider the use of the Alberta methods of Access Funds and Key Performance Indicators.

Throughout my discussion, the Klein government's announced objective for Alberta advanced education—'greatest accessibility at the lowest cost'—should be kept in mind. This slogan does not refer to the qualitative aspect of advanced education, which is perhaps the critical aspect. It further begs the questions of cost to whom and accessibility to what.

## 2. GREATER RELIANCE ON TUITION FINANCE

A basic issue in the finance of advanced education is the relative role of public and private funding. As the president of the University of British Columbia, David Strangway, has succinctly stated, 'Society, the taxpayer and the university must establish the appropriate balance between government funding on the one hand, and the funding that comes from tuition on the other' (*Vancouver Sun*, 13 Oct. 1995: B1).

Based on the economic analysis of public finance, tuition charges should reflect the benefits from advanced education that accrue to the individual student from higher lifetime earnings as well as social status and personal enjoyment. Society generally should bear the portion of costs attributable to social benefits such as better functioning labour markets and a better informed citizenry. Of course, the social versus private benefits are difficult to distinguish in practice and, indeed, are closely linked in their production. However, it is known that students derive above-market rates of return on their private investments in advanced education, and these high returns have shown no sign of abating.[1]

Students and their families currently bear a percentage of the total instructional costs that ranges from the mid-teens to the mid-twenties. However, at universities much faculty time associated with research or community or professional service may not be separated from teaching activities. If that is the case, then students' share of the direct teaching costs may be understated. For example, if students are reported as paying 20 per cent of their costs but those costs include one-third that should be allocated to non-instructional services, then students are actually paying 30 per cent of their true educational costs.

Reducing the public share of financing advanced education and increasing the private share, through higher tuition fees, potentially could make institutions more responsive to students and parents as consumers. These benefits could be manifested in a variety of ways, such as faster shifting of resources into programs that are more in demand, improved and more relevant curriculum, and reduced costs of educational programs.

The failure of Alberta advanced education to exhibit many gains of these kinds, as noted by Emery, could be attributed to several factors. First, the financing changes in Alberta have been in place for less than two years. Second, even though students' share of their educational costs will ultimately rise to a ceiling of 30 per cent from the previous 20 per cent, policy-dictated limits will keep annual tuition increases below 8 per cent and delay the total impact for several years. Third, institutional rigidities in tuition differentials across programs with very different costs have further retarded the desired adjustments.

The Alberta experience with tuition fees can be contrasted with recent developments elsewhere in Canada. A couple of business schools at major universities have already begun MBA programs that will charge tuitions set to cover their full costs, which is several times the traditional tuition levels in Canada. Equally striking, the University of British Columbia has adopted a new policy for setting future tuition levels intended to insulate the institution's budget from any future shortfalls in provincial grants.[2]

The UBC policy will set tuition fees so as to maintain the university's real resources. This policy could bring very sharp tuition increases, much more rapid than Alberta will be allowing, in the event of even modest cutbacks in the provincial grants. For example, if UBC students now pay for 20 per cent of their education, a 5 per cent cut in the provincial grant (or 4 per cent of total budget, which is 5 per cent of the other 80 per cent) combined with a 2 per cent increase in general operating costs would imply a one-year hike in tuition levels of about 30 per cent (4 plus 2 per cent divided by the original 20 per cent share).[3] This is far above the rates of tuition increase being permitted in Alberta.

One might question the new UBC tuition fee policy in that it attempts to insulate the institution from pressures to rationalize and reduce costs. Yet, if tuition charges do jump sufficiently, natural market-type pressures on all suppliers of advanced education will arise. Prospective students will shop more carefully across programs and institutions to find the package that satisfies them, at a price they are prepared to pay. Competitive considerations of enrolment and quality of students will enter more directly into suppliers' planning.

Of course, any major move towards higher tuition charges in Canada will require a revamping of student loan and aid policies. Federal and provincial loan provisions will be affected.[4] To make the higher tuition charges viable, both in affordability and in equitable maintenance of accessibility, loans will have to be made on an income-contingent repayment basis. Emery notes that the Alberta government has recently announced an 'income-sensitive loan repayment plan', and it will be interesting to learn the details of this plan.

## 3. COST AND QUALITY OF UNDERGRADUATE EDUCATION

Central to attempts to improve the advanced educational system are the cost and quality of undergraduate education. For present purposes, I shall take this term to include the pre-university, vocational, and technical programs offered at the colleges. However, some of the issues concerning undergraduate education are unique to the universities on account of their multiple mandates, including research and graduate education.

If tuition charges are allowed to rise substantially, at both colleges and universities, one question is whether this will place economizing incentives on the suppliers. Another is whether it will produce a broader range of types and qualities of programs, with prices to match the varying production costs. And will many students pay a premium to obtain a higher-quality but higher-cost form of education? Experience in the United States, which has perhaps the world's most diverse forms of advanced education and also the highest rate of participation, is at least somewhat promising on most of these issues.

My analysis here will focus on the likely impacts of further financial restraint, even if partially offset by tuition hikes, on the cost and quality of undergraduate education. Mostly by considering how institutions have adapted to funding pressures over the past decade, one can obtain a rough forecast of future responses.

The main channels for adaptation have included the following: (1) increased numbers of students in classes; (2) reduced offerings of courses with smaller enrolments; (3) higher teaching loads for some staff; (4) reduced compensation for faculty members relative to their peers in the professions and public service; and (5) the substitution of lower-paid staff such as sessional lecturers, early retirements, and filling vacancies with junior staff. Given the heavy labour intensity of advanced education, it is only natural that the focus of cost-saving would be on the quantity and cost of the teaching input.

A key question associated with these economizing moves is whether the quality of the instruction or the programs has been significantly affected. Though hard to quantify, the evidence shows clearly that quality has deteriorated. In entry-level and intermediate-level courses, growing class sizes mean that students have less opportunity to ask questions in class and to consult with teachers out of class. Essays and research papers that were assigned in such courses in previous years are less often assigned because of limits on the instructors' time for marking. Small enrolment courses at the upper undergraduate level have been eliminated or have seen their enrolments rising, both of which seriously undermine the quality of the educational experience.

Compensation to teaching staff also has an impact on the quality of undergraduate education, although this is likely a much more critical issue for the quality of research and graduate education. Even at the undergraduate level, the education of students majoring in a field can be disproportionately influenced by a small number of exceptional teachers, who usually are engaged in frontier research. Substantially higher salaries are needed to attract and retain the best academic talents as opposed to those who are solely teachers.

Since high-quality faculty are vital for successful programs of research and graduate training, one might query whether the requisite salary premiums should be assigned to the costs of undergraduate instruction. Conversely, one might ask about the quality of undergraduate training in departments where little or no research of significance is taking place. In the end, it seems appropriate to assign a part of the extra costs of higher-quality faculty to the undergraduate instruction as well as to the other functions for which they are vital.

The presence of faculty engaged in substantial research affects the costs of providing education in a second way, beyond the salary premiums that must be paid. A portion of the faculty member's time, typically ranging from 30 to 40 per cent of total year-round time, would be applied to research and therefore would not be available for teaching and related duties.[5] This in part explains why the teaching loads of faculty at major research universities are much lower than the loads of college instructors.

My observations suggest that an institution that lacks significant depth in the research function should be thought of as a college rather than a university, whatever its formal title may be. Pressures to reduce the costs of undergraduate education at universities by major de-emphasis on research would, in effect, convert them into colleges. Such institutions have an important role in the overall system of advanced education, but one should not view moves in this direction as having little impact on the quality of undergraduate studies.

The quality of undergraduate education has a particular salience for Canada, which suggests that it should not be left to provincial policy alone. Young people with the best minds are randomly dispersed across the country;

with the proper opportunities, they will become the future national leaders in business, politics, media, arts, and the professions. Given the low cross-provincial mobility of undergraduate students and the absence of élite private universities in Canada, it is essential for the country's future that each province or region offer opportunities for high-quality undergraduate studies.

## 4. OTHER OUTPUTS OF ADVANCED EDUCATION

My comments on undergraduate education have already flagged the significance of the research output of advanced education. Research is even more vital in several other major outputs of the university branch of the advanced educational system. These fall under the headings of graduate and professional education, the advancement of general knowledge, scientific research with special local applications, applied research relevant to local policies, high-tech business stimulus, and the cultural environment.

Graduate and professional education are important to society in providing an adequate supply of quality specialists to serve business and consumers. Further, in many graduate and professional fields the expertise has some provincial or regional content, so that simply importing people trained elsewhere in Canada or abroad is not a good substitute for home-trained talents. Insofar as these areas are typically high-paying, most provinces would also like to give their own residents a chance to fill them.

Provinces may be less eager to fund research that leads to the advancement of general knowledge, since this can be simply and cheaply borrowed from elsewhere. Yet, any university that wishes to have strength in applied research also needs to have a complement of theorists and pure researchers. Graduate students cannot be well trained without a solid theoretical grounding. And applied researchers need colleagues who are expert in the more theoretical ends of their disciplines. As a specialist in applied economics, I cannot imagine working in a department without several theorists and econometric experts to consult as the need arises. And one could not employ top theorists unless they have a major research function.

Both economic/social policy research and scientific/technical research have important applications that are specific to the needs of particular provinces and regions. One cannot always import experts on a contract basis who are sufficiently knowledgeable about local circumstances, and even then they are not always sensitive to local conditions and culture. Applied research oriented to the public policy, geographical, industrial, or cultural needs of a particular province will for the most part not be undertaken elsewhere.

A province that does not maintain one or more high-quality research-oriented centres of advanced education will lose out on all of the benefits described above. It will not have expertise available on its public policies in areas ranging from business regulation to law reform to domestic violence. It will not have depth of knowledge about environmental control processes that are suited to its unique set of industries and geography.

Major research universities are also critical in the process of stimulating knowledge-intensive industries and high-tech start-ups. Little needs to be said about the importance of such developments for a healthy economy, with high rewards both to individual workers and to society through tax revenues, job stability, and quality of life. It is also a fact that even the research universities that excel in applied science have breadth in areas other than science. MIT and the California Institute of Technology, for example, have top departments in areas such as economics, linguistics, and political science.

Universities frequently serve in another capacity, as centres for cultural activities and places where persons serving cultural industries obtain training. They can also host major speakers and visiting cultural events of interest to the broader community. These aspects can help to make a locality attractive for senior managers and businesses seeking to relocate.

To recapitulate one of my basic points, restraint in the public financing of advanced education and seeking minimal costs will undermine many of the important economic and social outputs. Local or regional colleges offer few of the benefits described here for major research-oriented universities. They may be the cheapest way of supplying a baseline level of advanced education or vocational training, but they offer little beyond that.

## 5. EFFICIENCY IN THE ADVANCED EDUCATION SYSTEM

Despite my support for a high-quality form of undergraduate instruction and a major continuing research role for advanced education, I would not argue that the current system is perfect. Public authorities and taxpayers have a reasonable expectation that all public services, including advanced education, be supplied with economy and accountability. Voters also have a right to determine what quantities and qualities of any public service they want—be it undergraduate education or research.

These two areas—undergraduate education and research—will be the focus of my analysis of ways to improve efficiency in the advanced education system. In each case I shall consider ways of reducing the total costs of providing the service at a given level of quality or of reducing the quantity of the service while maintaining a core level of quality. Emery's review of developments in Alberta suggests that few of these issues have been explicitly considered by policy-makers there. I shall also consider the Access Fund and Key Performance Indicators that are part of the Alberta strategy for advanced education.

## 5.1 Efficiency in Undergraduate Education

To reduce the costs of undergraduate education without sacrificing quality, technological changes and systemic rationalization will be needed. One must distinguish between simply trying to squeeze more work, or different kinds of work, out of the existing academic staff and changes in student/faculty ratios that are combined with technological changes to maintain educational quality and simultaneously maintain all the other outputs of the system. Examples include multimedia instruction, computer labs, and automated language labs that allow teachers to serve more students better in the same time frame.

Systemic rationalization of undergraduate education would include greater program specialization across the institutions in a region or province. To achieve this will require a higher authority to overcome the natural resistance of existing administrative entities and their staff. This will entail closing some departments and programs and relocating and releasing some staff. It is ironic that the 'enrolment corridors' imposed on institutions in Alberta will retard this kind of adjustment.

Potential benefits of such rationalization would include not only lower total costs but also a broader selection of courses in the surviving or consolidated programs. This kind of consideration also applies to graduate education. It is hard to explain why, for example, there should be multiple institutions in some provinces and even in some metropolitan areas offering the same program, when each has limited course offerings and very small enrolments in some courses. Offset against the concentration of programs at fewer institutions would be the increased costs faced by students who would have to commute long distances or live away from their family home to study.

Given the financial pressures, it will likely be necessary to eliminate some programs of study entirely in particular provinces or regions. This result may arise where even a consolidated program does not meet a critical size to achieve scale economies. It may also arise where a program is deemed to be of insufficient value for learning and for preparing for further studies and the workplace. Failure to make judicious program cuts will only compromise the finances for the rest of the educational enterprise.

Other key issues relating to undergraduate studies revolve around the total numbers of students and their allocation by program or discipline. Anyone who teaches at a college or university in Canada can attest that a significant portion of students lack the abilities and ambitions to benefit fully from the program. Institutions attempt to control the quality of students by admission thresholds and in some cases, at the program level, by quotas.

While quotas are putatively applied for purposes of controlling quality, they may also be used to compensate for the lack of internal flexibility within educational institutions. At UBC, for example, the Commerce faculty many years ago instituted quotas for admission to its undergraduate program. More recently, the Economics Department instituted its own quotas because we were getting increasing numbers of students unable to gain entry to Commerce. Now students who cannot get into Economics reputedly go into International Relations and other areas, which at some point may need quotas of their own.

If the funding within the institution were more flexible, departments and programs in greater demand would increase, and those in lesser demand by students would decline. Then quotas could be used much more sparingly. One must also ask about the acceptable minimum level of ability to allow a student to undertake any particular program. Even mediocre bricklayers can be employable and productive members of the workforce, but is there a reason to use public funds to train mediocre historians, classicists, or economists?

These considerations suggest that we may be educating too many young people in the liberal arts and too often the wrong individuals. It is hard to justify the expenditure of large public funds on students who are doing mediocre work or worse in their studies. The problem lies in identifying the individuals with the best likelihood for success in advanced education at the point of admission. Some students who are admitted are in fact less able than some applicants who are denied admission.

I would suggest that colleges and universities apply a higher standard for students to continue after their first and second year of studies. More individuals would be asked to suspend their studies for a couple of years or to depart permanently from the institution. That would leave more room to admit additional students to the first year of studies and give more young people a chance to pursue an advanced education. In the face of limited funding, allowing even marginal performers to continue their studies effectively deprives others of having a chance to begin studies.

Another approach would channel a much higher proportion of students wishing to pursue university studies through the colleges for their first year or two. Only the best applicants would be admitted from the outset to university. This approach would save on total educational costs and also provide more diversified academic-vocational programs for many students who would in the end not be pursuing the full university route.

A basic issue in advanced education policy is how much resources to allocate to the universities as against more vocationally oriented college programs and basic education at the primary and secondary levels. In British Columbia, the balance in recent years has shifted more toward the other levels at the expense of universities. Given my observations about problems of quality and job relevance for many university students, this is likely the proper general direction for public policy to pursue.[6]

Universities in Manitoba and Nova Scotia are currently engaged in disputes over management demands for much greater flexibility in staffing, such as lay-offs on short notice based on course enrolments. This would move educational institutions much closer to a traditional factory model of worker management. Given the state of the job market, some colleges may find they can get away with this strategy, but for research universities this is not a viable method to contain costs.

Any moves towards reduced job security for university faculty would have long-term effects on the ability to hire and the quality of staff. Individuals are willing to specialize in areas of research and instruction based on the understanding that they will have security over the long term. Once that implicit contract is broken, universities will find it harder and more costly to attract the best talents in specialized areas of knowledge that do not have widespread application to other lines of employment.

Similarly, salary reductions may also have adverse longer-term effects beyond the reduced ability to hire and retain quality members of faculty.[7] The great majority of current faculty members will not depart, on account of their local ties by way of family, housing, and spouse's work. But some faculty may exert themselves less assiduously, and others will divert their energies to supplementing incomes, from consulting to textbook writing.

### 5.2 Efficiency in Research

I now turn to efficiency issues related to the research function of advanced education, and hence I again focus on universities. If society decides that too much research is being publicly funded, either in general or in specific fields, then several alternatives exist for public policy. An important point on this topic is that the provinces bear the lion's share of research costs associated with the faculty members' time, since few of the national granting agencies cover the costs to release researchers from teaching duties. Average teaching loads at the universities are set at levels that assume substantial research activities.

One approach would be to have fewer or smaller universities and more colleges. A variant would be to make some or all universities more like colleges by having all faculty members teach substantially more and research less or not at all. The latter approach would clearly not be feasible if one wanted to retain a quality research university or even solid graduate programs. It would drive away the best faculty researchers in short order.

Another approach would be to have some departments or faculties within a university as research entities with graduate programs and make others purely undergraduate teaching entities. Teaching loads per faculty member in the latter units would be much higher than in the research units. In fact, the research in some departments at many universities is not of a level or quality that would justify continued public support, yet by association with the university milieu these research activities continue to be funded through reduced teaching.

A final approach is to differentiate the teaching loads of faculty members within each department based on their research productivity. My own department has explored this approach over the past year and found that the practical problems of measuring individual research productivity and the resultant loss of collegiality could outweigh any potential gains.[8] Still, some departments have either formal rules or informal procedures to allocate differential teaching loads inversely to perceived or measured research output. Any scheme is vulnerable to problems of assessing quality and biases against certain types of research, but this is hardly grounds for ignoring the issue in its entirety.

To the extent that research outputs are related to pure or fundamental research, one might expect the provinces to offer only limited support. Any strong applied research department or graduate program requires its complement of pure researchers and theorists. Beyond this level, any further support for pure research should come directly from the federal research granting agencies. This could be dispensed either as block grants to the universities or to individual grantees as a teaching release component of research grants.

## 5.3 Access Fund and Key Performance Indicators

Two elements of the Alberta strategy for improving performance and reducing costs in advanced education are the Access Fund and Key Performance Indicators. These are attempts to intervene in decisions about the production and delivery of educational services with a less blunt instrument than sheer budgetary cutbacks. Emery describes the use of the Access Fund and notes that the performance indicators are still being designed.

The use of these policy interventions is justified by the observation that educational institutions find it very hard to reform themselves. Emery astutely notes that the Access Fund, intended to encourage a market focus, is itself an example of central planning. The reasons for institutional rigidity stem from traditional outlooks, bureaucratic structures, and ordinary vested interest that characterize all entities in the public and private sectors.

Alberta's Access Fund is not a completely novel institution. Other provinces with financially restrained advanced education have partially offset the budgetary restraint with targeted funds for specified programs and purposes; BC has done this for over a decade. While such funds may serve a useful purpose in stimulating innovation in the design and delivery of educational services, they cannot replace a more fundamental change in the incentives, culture, and decision processes of the advanced educational system.

Improvements in the efficiency and productivity of advanced education cannot easily be imposed from outside. Institutional and incentive structures are needed that will induce the principal actors—teachers and researchers—to devise the appropriate innovations. One reason is that only those actors understand what changes are needed and how to implement them. Another is that externally imposed changes will meet great resistance. To succeed, the changes must be initiated from within.

One example of a way to restructure institutions is to make it clear that the gains from increased productivity will be shared with the faculty who undertake them. Contrary to Emery's forecast of ever-decreasing faculty pay, there should be means by which salaries can recover their real losses over the past decade.[9] Only with appropriate incentives will faculty and their representatives bring forward and implement the ideas needed for effective reform. After a decade of rising teaching productivity combined with slipping real salaries, faculty are rightfully suspicious of co-operative strategies.

Key Performance Indicators are to be part of the managerial monitoring system for Alberta advanced education, but the indicators have not yet been released. At this point one can merely express apprehensions about their possible form and application, especially for universities. Indicators could be applied at the level of the institution, department or program, and individual faculty member.

The outputs of university departments and professors are complex and long-term, whether they are related to undergraduate or graduate education or research. Any attempts to measure these outputs quantitatively and bureaucratically are bound to distort behaviour away from excellence. Formalized measures of research will cause individuals to increase the quantity of publications at the expense of quality and will discourage long-term basic research. In contrast, peer assessment is capable of gauging the qualitative aspects.

Similarly, assessing undergraduate arts and sciences education based on the short-run outcomes for graduates will provide the wrong performance cues. Liberal arts education is an essential basis for future leaders in the professional, business, and science communities. Attempts to quantify the success of such instruction, even if based on short-term student assessments, are not likely to lead to excellence and intellectual challenge.

Universities are the archetypal form of the modern knowledge-intensive enterprise. They have flat hierarchies, with junior faculty performing most of the same functions as senior faculty, peer assessment, collaborative work, long-term outcomes, little supervision and high autonomy, and emphasis on performance rather than status. These are precisely the properties espoused by modern management gurus. It is dubious whether externally devised and imposed performance indicators will improve rather than worsen affairs.

## 6. CLOSING THOUGHTS

There are ways to reduce the costs of advanced education, but many of them also involve serious compromises to the quality of undergraduate education, research, or other outputs of the sector. It is not yet clear how many of these adverse effects have arisen in the Alberta advanced education system. But there can be little doubt that further financial restraint would cause negative fallout unless offset by still higher tuition revenues.

Major savings from the advanced education sector are more likely to come from difficult decisions about the numbers and minimum acceptable quality of students receiving university training as against other, less costly, and often more work-relevant forms of advanced training. Savings through reduced research activities at universities will require decisions about how much, what type, and the minimum acceptable quality of research. As Emery suggests, across-the-board cuts in public grants to educational institutions are not in and of themselves likely to produce many of the needed changes.

The requisite reforms will face stubborn resistance if imposed from outside the university. Indeed, they cannot be effectively and sensibly implemented without faculty co-operation. Hence, the challenge is to find ways—including new reward structures and cultural changes—that will facilitate the evolution of advanced education to serve society's needs at a price that society is prepared to pay.

## NOTES

1. F. Vaillancourt, 'The Private and Total Returns to Education in Canada, 1985', *Canadian Journal of Economics*, 28 (Aug. 1995): 532–54.

2. As a result of campaign promises made by the New Democratic Party in 1996, tuition fees were in practice frozen for the following two years.

3. The impact on needy students would be offset by the allocation of one-third of the additional tuition revenues for student aid; however, this might require an even larger hike in fees to maintain the university's real resources.

4. For a study based on the BC loan system, see J.R. Kesselman and M.J. McGlenen, 'Reforming Student Loans in British Columbia', Discussion Paper 35 (Vancouver, BC: UBC Centre for Research on Economic and Social Policy, May 1996).

5. Research includes related activities such as attending conferences, presenting seminars, refereeing for journals, and preparing and reviewing grants. About 40 to 50 per cent of total time would be taken by teaching, including preparations, marking, advising, and graduate student supervision. The remaining 15 to 25 per cent of time would typically be consumed by administrative functions and public service.

6. Essentially this view was argued by the British Columbia Labour Force Development Board in their report, *Training for What?* (Vancouver, BC, 1995); for an effective response to this view, see R.C. Allen, 'The Economic Benefits of Post-Secondary Education and Training in BC: An Outcomes Assessment', Discussion Paper 34 (Vancouver, BC: UBC Centre for Research on Economic and Social Policy, April 1996).

7. Emery reports that Alberta's faculty and staff accepted compensation cuts of about 5 per cent. Given the further freezing of nominal salaries over the three-year period, the total real losses are nearly 12 per cent in view of annual inflation running somewhat above 2 per cent.

8. A minority view was that if financial restraint became so severe as to threaten my department's research quality, the issue of differential teaching loads should be revisited.

9. For those who may believe that Canadian academics are still overpaid, I note that a majority of my departmental colleagues could raise their real take-home pay by 25 to over 100 per cent by moving elsewhere in North America. They have stayed at UBC for a variety of reasons, including family and community attachments and institutional loyalty, but one cannot rely on these bonds forever.

# CHAPTER 11

# Education: Meeting the Challenge ■

*Christopher J. Bruce and Arthur M. Schwartz*

## 1. INTRODUCTION

In the last school year before the deficit elimination program was introduced (1992/3), Alberta had one of the highest pupil/teacher ratios in Canada and one of the lowest expenditures per pupil outside the Atlantic provinces (Tables 1 and 2). It is perhaps not surprising, then, that one of the clearest recommendations to arise from the series of public roundtables the government held in the fall of 1993 was that Education be spared the deep cuts to spending that were generally anticipated at that time. Indeed, whereas the budgets of the other 'core' departments—Advanced Education, Family and Social Services, and Health—were cut by 17 to 21 per cent, the Education budget was cut by only 6.2 per cent. Furthermore, as virtually all employees of the Department of Education took a 5 per cent wage cut, the 'real' impact was only 1.2 per cent.

As a result, the deficit elimination program provided the Education ministry with less incentive to restructure its operations than was provided to the other departments. In spite of this, senior officials in Alberta Education indicated in interviews with us that they had particularly ambitious plans to overhaul their department. This raises the question of whether dramatic changes can be made as easily in an agency not experiencing significant reductions in its budget as can be made in those experiencing more sizeable cuts. This question underlies the analysis of this chapter.

Specifically, we will attempt to trace the relationships among voters, the provincial cabinet, senior civil servants in Alberta Education, and officials in the individual school districts to determine how preferences were revealed and conflicts were resolved. Can the changes in policy be traced directly to the budget cuts, or did the budget cuts act as a catalyst to bring the goals of various interest groups to the front of the political agenda? Did senior civil servants act to undermine the wishes of the government, as many theories of bureaucracy suggest,[1] or did they take the opportunity to introduce changes they believed would improve the delivery of educational services? And how did school

**Table 1:** Pupil/Teacher Ratio, Canada and the Provinces: 1985/6 to 1992/3

| Academic Year | Canada | NF | PE | NS | NB | PQ | ON | MB | SK | AB | BC | YT | NT |
|---|---|---|---|---|---|---|---|---|---|---|---|---|---|
| 1985/6 | 18.11 | 17.51 | 19.30 | 16.73 | 19.16 | 16.18 | 18.91 | 17.68 | 18.93 | 18.51 | 20.19 | 16.38 | 19.54 |
| 1986/7 | 18.30 | 17.22 | 19.25 | 16.89 | 18.53 | 17.53 | 18.50 | 17.47 | 18.77 | 18.79 | 19.97 | 16.46 | 18.83 |
| 1987/8 | 17.98 | 16.91 | 18.77 | 16.63 | 17.94 | 17.55 | 17.80 | 17.26 | 18.93 | 18.93 | 19.64 | 17.80 | 17.99 |
| 1988/9 | 17.80 | 16.48 | 18.64 | 16.59 | 17.76 | 17.64 | 17.37 | 17.35 | 18.66 | 19.29 | 19.31 | 16.31 | 16.75 |
| 1989/90 | 17.56 | 16.33 | 17.83 | 16.26 | 17.36 | 17.88 | 16.98 | 16.75 | 18.58 | 18.92 | 18.79 | 16.03 | 16.67 |
| 1990/1 | 17.30 | 15.87 | 17.86 | 15.89 | 16.41 | 17.67 | 16.55 | 16.73 | 20.43 | 18.96 | 18.41 | 15.96 | 16.13 |
| 1991/2 | 17.54 | 15.73 | 17.92 | 16.59 | 16.93 | 17.64 | 17.13 | 17.35 | 18.77 | 19.90 | 18.34 | 14.48 | 14.43 |
| 1992/3 | 17.75 | 15.65 | 17.95 | 16.42 | 16.96 | 18.17 | 17.34 | 16.66 | 19.64 | 19.07 | 18.49 | 15.09 | 14.64 |

**Table 2:** Expenditure Per Pupil (Thousands of Dollars), Canada and the Provinces: 1985/6 to 1992/3

| Academic Year | Canada | NF | PE | NS | NB | PQ | ON | MB | SK | AB | BC | YT | NT |
|---|---|---|---|---|---|---|---|---|---|---|---|---|---|
| 1985/6 | 4.45 | 3.27 | 3.30 | 3.87 | 3.99 | 5.14 | 4.35 | 4.37 | 4.20* | 4.62 | 3.92 | 6.71 | 7.20 |
| 1986/7 | 4.75 | 3.42 | 3.58 | 4.11 | 4.30 | 5.36 | 4.75 | 4.84 | 4.47 | 4.80 | 4.02 | 7.13 | 7.49 |
| 1987/8 | 4.84 | 3.87 | 3.74 | 4.28 | 4.59 | 5.28 | 4.83 | 4.99 | 4.85 | 4.84 | 4.26 | 8.32 | 9.54 |
| 1988/9 | 5.31 | 4.16 | 4.00 | 4.67 | 4.93 | 5.83 | 5.46 | 5.21 | 4.72 | 5.00 | 4.70 | 8.67 | 9.18 |
| 1989/90 | 5.57 | 4.50 | 4.23 | 4.88 | 5.05 | 5.70 | 5.89 | 5.68 | 4.90 | 5.15 | 5.08 | 9.07 | 10.21 |
| 1990/1 | 5.97 | 4.73 | 4.61 | 5.13 | 5.41 | 6.11 | 6.29 | 6.06 | 5.13 | 5.42 | 5.82 | 10.67 | 11.44 |
| 1991/2 | 6.40 | 4.97 | 4.98 | 5.26 | 5.47 | 6.51 | 6.90 | 6.30 | 5.32 | 5.70 | 6.14 | 11.94 | 11.79 |
| 1992/3 | 6.52 | 5.31 | 5.23 | 5.24 | 5.57 | 6.74 | 6.89 | 6.34 | 5.47 | 5.86 | 6.28 | 14.80 | 15.53 |

SOURCE: Calculated from data in Statistics Canada, *Education in Canada*, Cat. No. 81–229 (various issues).

boards, principals, and teachers react? Were they consulted? Did they seize the opportunity to overhaul the system? Or did they see changes as a challenge to their authority?

We begin, in section 2, with a description of the legislative and budgetary changes imposed on Education as a result of the deficit elimination program. The goal of many of these changes was to provide more power to parents, teachers, and principals through the introduction of school-based management and school councils and the provision of greater parental choice among schools (including the establishment of charter schools). Section 3 summarizes the academic literature concerning these changes to identify the impact they could be expected to have on educational quality. Finally, in section 4, we report on the extent to which the deficit elimination program has led to a transference of power to the local level.

## 2. LEGISLATIVE AND BUDGETARY CHANGES

### 2.1 Public Input

In the election of 15 June 1993, the government won a mandate to eliminate the provincial deficit within three years. It immediately announced that this would require an average cut of 20 per cent per department. Recognizing that cuts on this order of magnitude were likely to produce significant resistance from the public, particularly once the details of the cuts became apparent, the government moved quickly to co-opt special interest groups by obtaining broad-based input into the decision-making process. The government brought together over 300 members of the educational community in the fall of 1992, at what were called the Fiscal Reality meetings, to discuss alternative delivery strategies. Alberta Education incorporated the opinions expressed at these meetings into a 'workbook' that was used as the basis of discussion at two public roundtables held in October 1993.[2] In addition, eight regional meetings concerning financial planning were held with 'stakeholder' groups such as school boards, the teachers' association, school trustees, and parent associations.[3] The government also received 17,000 public submissions, most of which were form or generic letters (16,338) or petitions (85). Nevertheless, 552 responses (representing 1,933 individuals) to the government workbook were received and 25 responses (2,239 individuals) to an Alberta Teachers' Association workbook were received (Mann, 1993).

Several common themes can be identified from these sources. We have divided the recommendations into two rough categories—those that responded directly to the need to reduce the Department of Education budget and those that took the opportunity to suggest changes to the structure of the educational system.

*Budget Reduction*
- The 20 per cent cut initially proposed for Alberta Education's budget was universally considered to be too great.
- It was widely felt that the school system was over-administered.
- Most participants recommended that the number of school boards be reduced significantly; and some recommended that Education be amalgamated with Advanced Education.
- The roundtables suggested that support services be contracted out.
- Although opinion was divided, most groups supported a government-mandated across-the-board reduction in wages. The most commonly heard recommendation was for a 5 per cent cut.
- A number of groups felt that funding for programs that fell outside 'basic education' should be reduced. Included in this category were grade 12 students upgrading their university entrance marks, programs of English as a second language, and Early Childhood Services (ECS—Alberta's kindergarten equivalent). ECS was not universally derided, however. Over 95 per cent of the public responses received concerning this issue indicated that ECS was 'essential'.[4]

*Structural Changes*
- The roundtable discussions produced a call for improvements in the methods of evaluating teachers and students.
- Approximately 50 per cent of school funding was derived from local taxes, with the other 50 per cent coming from the provincial government. As some school districts had much higher tax bases than others, this led to inequities in local funding. Virtually all public participants called for reductions in these inequities.[5]
- It was widely argued that 'Decisions should be made closest to the place where implementation happens. This means that teachers, principals, students, and parents need to be involved in decision-making and resource-allocation' (Alberta Education, 1993a: 21). More specifically, it was often argued that increased power should be given to 'school councils'—groups composed of teachers, parents, and community representatives.
- A number of respondents recommended that a greater portion of school funding be based on per pupil grants than had been the case in the past. Apparently, the basis of this recommendation was the view that schools would be more responsive to student and parent concerns if transfers of students among schools had more serious financial implications for individual schools than they had previously.

## 2.2 Alberta Education's Response
There was a close correlation between the changes in regulations made after the public discussion and the recommendations that resulted from that process.

Two hypotheses are consistent with this observation. One is that officials in Alberta Education listened carefully to the views presented to them. The second is that the questions put to the public were framed in such a way as to elicit responses sympathetic to the views held by senior officials in the government and Alberta Education. Some evidence for the latter hypothesis was provided in one of Alberta Education's own publications, in which it reported that some respondents to the workbook felt that 'the wording and direction of the [questions] *directed* their answers' (Mann, 1993: 37; emphasis added). It should be noted, however, that many of the recommendations discussed in the workbook appear to have been derived from earlier public discussions and that the government continued to seek public input well after it had made its initial announcements concerning proposed policy changes.[6]

What we can say with virtual certainty, however, is that Alberta Education's response to the threat of budget cuts was not to thwart movement towards significant structural change. Rather, the reverse appears to have been true. Our interviews, not only with senior officials in Alberta Education but also with school board employees, school trustees, principals, and teachers, suggest strongly that senior officials saw the turmoil created by the budget-cutting process to be a providential opportunity to introduce significant changes. Some of these changes appear to have been politically motivated—an attempt to increase the central administration's power at the expense of local school boards, for example—but more often the motivating factor appears to have been a desire to introduce a number of reforms that had become popular in the United States over the preceding decade, such as site-based management, parental choice, school councils, and charter schools.

We list here the major changes announced, beginning with those that appear to have been made primarily in response to the need to cut the department budget, then moving progressively to those whose justification derives less from budgetary pressures and more from a desire to introduce fundamental changes to the structure of the educational system.

**a. General cut:** On 17 January 1994 the government announced that Alberta Education's budget was to be cut by 12.4 per cent, down from the 20 per cent figure that had been the basis of discussion during the fall of 1993 and the lowest reduction among all government departments. (The next lowest was Health, at 17.6 per cent.) Furthermore, as half of the school districts' budgets derived from municipally levied taxes, which were not affected by the provincial cuts, the net reduction in the total budget for Education was approximately 6.2 per cent.[7] We were unable to obtain a definitive answer to the question of why Education received this favourable treatment. However, the strong objections to the 20 per cent cut expressed in the public consultation process appear to have been crucial. In addition, any deeper cuts would have meant significant reductions in wages or increases in pupil-teacher ratios, both of which were protected in contracts with the teachers' union.

**b. Wage roll-backs:** The preceding point notwithstanding, the government did obtain a 'voluntary' 5 per cent wage roll-back from all of its civil servants, including the teachers. Two factors seem to have provided the government with the leverage to obtain these concessions without the necessity of introducing legislation. First, because all government employees, including elected officials, were asked to take the same cut in the interests of meeting a goal that had the clear support of the electorate—the elimination of the deficit—individual public-sector employees could not argue that they had been singled out for inequitable treatment. Second, the request came following a decade in which there had been a number of dramatic, well-publicized lay-offs in the private sector. The electorate was not in the mood to listen sympathetically to complaints about wage roll-backs from a public sector that had been spared the effects of these lay-offs.

**c. Reduction in the number of school boards:** The number of operating school boards was reduced from 141 to 68 (by March 1995). The stated objective for this move was always that it reduced excessive administrative expenses. Nevertheless, it also had the effect of reducing the power of school trustees in districts that had previously been small enough that trustees were able to exert influence on a school-by-school basis. These trustees had earned the ire of participants both 'below' them—principals and teachers—and 'above' them—provincial politicians and senior civil servants.

**d. Early Childhood Services:** Funding for ECS was cut from 400 hours per child per year (or approximately one-half day per school day throughout the year) to 200. Although ECS had been targeted for cutbacks by many of the public focus groups, this was clearly the most unpopular change made to the education budget. The outcry was strong enough that funding was increased to 240 hours in the 1994/5 budget.

**e. Block funding:** Each school board's budget was divided into three categories or 'blocks'. Of these, the largest is the *instruction block*, which is to provide for the cost of operating schools—that is, the costs of 'principals, teaching staff, learning resources, and supplies, equipment, and furnishings used in the instructional program' (Alberta Education, 1995b: 10). The second is the *support block*, which provides for the 'costs of plant operations and maintenance, board governance, system administration, student transportation, and the equipment and facilities related to these programs' (Alberta Education, 1995b: 17). Finally, the *capital block* is to fund major capital expenditures on school buildings and equipment.

A number of constraints were placed on shool boards' abilities to direct funds to these blocks and to transfer funds among them. The most important constraint was that funds for board governance and system administration (within the support block) were not to exceed 4 per cent of the sum of the funds available for instruction, plant operations and maintenance, and student transportation.[8] Also, school boards could not transfer more than 2 per cent of the funds in the instruction block to plant operations and maintenance and student transportation; and no more than 1.6 per cent of the sum of the funds available for the instruction block, plant operations and maintenance, and student transportation could be used for 'system based instructional support' (e.g., curriculum development, special education teachers, and psychological testing).[9] These restrictions could be justified by reference to the public consultation process, where most groups called for reductions to administration. Nevertheless, it was clear from our interviews with senior officials that the primary motivation was to prevent school boards from protecting their own positions by passing budget cuts on to the most politically sensitive arena, the classroom. As one official commented, it had not 'been the trend' for school boards to act 'responsibly' in this regard. Clearly, these officials considered their board members to be 'Niskanen-type' bureaucrats.[10]

As an example of the impact of the restrictions placed on administrative expenses and on ECS, in its 1994/5 budget, the Calgary Board of Education cut 155.7 positions from instructional support and 23.8 positions from ECS. These figures together represented approximately 2.7 per cent of the previous year's staffing total of 6,755.2 (Calgary Board of Education, 1994: 9).

f. **Centralization of revenue collection:** School boards had raised approximately half of their revenues through local property taxes. As tax bases differed significantly among districts, mill rates and revenues per pupil also differed significantly. In part to overcome these inequities, the provincial government centralized the assessment and collection of educational taxes. Mill rates are to be equalized across districts and all locally collected taxes are directed to a central fund, the Alberta School Foundation Fund (ASFF). School boards are now not allowed to levy their own taxes[11] but are paid from the ASFF and from general revenues according to a formula based on: their respective levels of enrolment; the number of students in such special categories as those with severe disabilities, natives, and those studying English as a second language; the number of enhanced oportunity programs for disadvantaged students; and transportation costs. (The 1996/7 funding formula is described in greater detail in Appendix 1 to this chapter.) It should be noted, however, that officials in Alberta Education also perceived the removal of the school boards' taxing powers to be a method of ensuring that the boards would not thwart the government's tax restraint goals by raising local taxes. Again, the government appeared to expect school board officials to behave like Niskanen bureaucrats.

**g. School councils:** The School Act was initially amended in the spring of 1994 to require that a 'school council', composed of parents, principal, students, and community representatives, be established for each school.[12] In the initial amendment proposal, Section 17 (3) of the Act indicated that:

A school council shall

(a) *advise* the principal and the board respecting any matter relating to the school,

(b) *perform* any duty or function delegated to it by the board . . . ,

(c) *ensure* that students in the school have the opportunity to meet the standards of education set by the Minister,

(d) *ensure* that the fiscal management of the school is in accordance with the requirements of the board . . . .

(Alberta, 1994; emphasis added)

Although this amendment was introduced as part of the overall deficit-reduction package, little attempt was made to use the deficit-reduction program as a justification for the new legislation. Rather, school councils appear to have been part of a larger set of reforms that senior officials in the government and Alberta Education had been trying to introduce for over a decade. These reforms centred on the provision of greater local control over schools, particularly by parents and community representatives but also by teachers and principals. Interviews with participants in the education system make it clear that Alberta Education seized the opportunity provided by teacher and school board concentration on budgetary issues to introduce its own agenda concerning decentralization of authority.

To a certain extent the enthusiasm of senior officials for these reforms may have been based on their desire to reduce the power of local school boards. But as the reforms also weakened the power of central administrators, a more plausible hypothesis is that senior officials were convinced that decentralization was in the public interest. In short, the deficit-reduction program was used as an opportunity to introduce reforms that had, in less turbulent times, met with resistance. On the one hand, if this hypothesis is correct, it should offer comfort to those who are concerned that bureaucrats will respond to budget cuts simply by protecting their positions. On the other hand, it raises the concern that the policies that bureaucrats introduce during periods of upheaval may not be in the public interest, either because bureaucrats have interpreted the public preferences incorrectly or because they have chosen to introduce policies they know to be contrary to those preferences.

**h. Charter schools:** A further element in the movement towards decentralization was taken by amending the School Act to allow for the incorporation of charter schools. Under this legislation, any group can 'charter' a school if it can convince its local school board or, failing that, the minister of education that a sufficient number of students[13] can benefit from a type of educational environment not being offered currently by the public system. The charter will describe the educational service the school will provide, the manner in which the school will operate, and the indicators of success it proposes to employ. Charter schools will not be allowed to charge fees; rather, they will be funded by the province according to the same formulas that apply to public school boards in regard to block funding. Each charter school will be operated by its own board of directors, independently of local school boards, and will be allowed to hire its own teachers.[14]

It was the clear intention of the government that this provision would create competition among schools within the public system.[15] As parents could threaten to move their children to charter schools, or to establish charter schools where they had not previously existed, public schools would be forced to be more responsive to parental concerns.

**i. Site-based management:** To allow principals to respond to the pressures that school councils and charter schools place on them, they will be given greater control over school budgets beginning in the 1996/7 school year. This policy—which is known in the literature variously as 'site-based management', 'school-based management', and 'local management of schools'—is intended to provide schools with greater flexibility to meet local demands. Although the details of the policy have yet to be finalized in Alberta, it is anticipated that schools will be given lump-sum budgets and the authority to spend those budgets as they wish, subject only to general guidelines from Alberta Education. They may be allowed, for example, to purchase their own supplies, contract for caretaking services, select textbooks, choose teaching styles, hire, train, supervise, promote, and fire their own teaching and support staffs, and determine which optional courses will be offered.

**j. Parental choice:** In addition to establishing charter schools, Alberta Education also hopes to foster competition by encouraging greater student mobility among public schools. No explicit provisions were made for this *within* school districts, as most school boards already had policies that allowed students to move among schools and for funds to 'follow' students to their new schools (although school boards typically would not pay for transportation to schools other than those the boards had directed students to attend). At the most, moral suasion was applied to encourage districts to ease within-district transfers. Competition among school boards was encouraged, however, by tying school board funding to the number of students. Thus, if a student moves from one district to another, funds will now follow the student to the new district. (Given the geographical size of school boards in Alberta, it is unlikely that this provision will create a significant degree of competition.)

**k. Achievement tests and Key Performance Indicators:** Finally, in order to allow parents to make informed choices among schools, the government announced that it would encourage school boards to develop and publish performance indicators.[16] These were to include factors such as: the results of surveys of parent and student satisfaction, student-teacher ratios, numbers of students transferring into and out of the school, incidences of vandalism, graduation rates, average scores on provincial tests, and percentages of students meeting provincial test standards (Alberta Education, 1995a). Ultimately, the government announced that it would only require schools to report information concerning: parental satisfaction, student satisfaction, and student results on achievement tests and diploma exams (Alberta Education, 1995d: 8). In light of the latter requirement, Alberta Education also increased the number of provincial achievement tests it administered. Previously it had tested students in each of grades 3, 6, and 9 on one of mathematics, English, social studies, or science each year (on a rotating basis). Beginning in the 1994/5 school year, it began to administer annual tests to grade 3 students on all three of reading, writing, and arithmetic and to grade 6 and 9 students on all four of the 'core' subjects—English, mathematics, social studies, and science.

## 3. DECENTRALIZATION: THE THEORY

In its analysis of the Canadian education system, *A Lot to Learn*, the Economic Council of Canada (1992: 13) concluded that 'achievement can be improved in the public-school system by reducing interference, increasing the principal's freedom, disseminating the results of assessments, and increasing parental freedom of choice among schools.' The education roundtables suggest that few provinces in Canada have more avidly received this message than Alberta. Albertans clearly indicated that they wanted to feel more involved in the decision-making processes at their children's schools; and there was strong support for the view that school quality would be increased if there was an increase in competition among schools. Alberta Education responded with a number of initiatives to decentralize decision-making: school councils, school-based management, school choice, and charter schools. In section 4 of this chapter we will investigate the impact these initiatives have had on Alberta's education system. Before we do so, however, it will be useful to review briefly the literature concerning the costs and benefits of decentralization. It is our hypothesis that opposition to these initiatives is more likely to succeed, the weaker are the arguments in their favour.

### 3.1 School Councils/School-Based Management

The introduction of both school councils and a system of school-based management was designed to provide parents and principals (and, to a lesser extent, teachers and community leaders) with greater control over local decision-making. Two broad arguments have been made in favour of providing this control. First, it has been argued that in a democratic society citizens have an inherent right to the greatest participation possible. Second, it has been hypothesized that schools constrained by decisions made by centralized bureaucracies will be less flexible than locally controlled schools and, therefore, less able to take advantage of local opportunities for quality improvement or to experiment with new instructional techniques. Proponents of decentralization conclude that school systems that allow local control will be more effective than centrally managed systems. We will review here the evidence concerning the latter claim.

It is argued that decentralization will both reduce school costs and increase student achievement. Costs can be lowered because local staff observe the impacts of spending decisions more closely than do central administrators and, therefore, are in a better position to recommend cost-saving changes. Also, staff will be motivated to search for additional cost-reducing techniques if the savings from those techniques can be used to fund other aspects of school spending. Parents and community representatives may also be able to suggest improvements drawn from their experiences outside the school system. And parents may be willing to agree to reductions in expenditures in some programs if the funds can be diverted to other, preferred uses.

Student achievement may be improved if the increased responsibility given to teachers and principals improves staff morale. Also, funds may be directed away from programs that are found to be irrelevant to the student population and into programs that will be more productive. And individual schools may be able to move more quickly than school boards to introduce new, innovative techniques.

In spite of these theoretical arguments, research has not found significant gains from decentralized decision-making. A number of factors intervene to thwart the good intentions of the participants. First, parents and community representatives often lack the knowledge to make informed decisions about budgets and curricula. As a result, most important decisions remain with school staff, particularly with principals. School councils rarely address central issues. Rather, research suggests that they 'develop procedures for handling disruptive student behavior, set times for parent conferences, adjust school schedules, sponsor fund raising projects, make facility improvements, [and] augment extra curricular activities.' Even in undertaking these activities, they 'characterize their involvement as "listening", "advising", "endorsing decisions others have already made", [or] taking "rubber stamp" or "token" action' (Malen, Ogawa, and Kranz, 1990: 305).

Second, teachers and principals are often less knowledgeable about recent educational developments than are school board subject specialists. Thus, although they may be able to react more flexibly than can school boards once they become sufficiently informed, it may take them longer to obtain that information. Similarly, individual schools will be less able than central boards to obtain cost concessions from suppliers and may be less informed than school boards concerning innovative techniques for reducing costs.

Third, all participants in school-based management complain about the amount of time that local decision-making requires. Parents find that they cannot afford to devote sufficient time to become fully informed. As a result, they are forced to leave the most important decisions to the school's staff. But staff find that they devote so much additional time to school management that their class preparation time and teaching begin to suffer. It is not surprising that, although an initial period of improved morale often follows the introduction of school-based management, disillusion soon sets in and both morale and motivation decline (Malen, Ogawa, and Kranz, 1990: 313).

In an extensive survey of the empirical literature, Malen, Ogawa, and Kranz (1990) concluded that school-based management could not be said to have produced improvements in scholastic achievement, to have altered power relationships among parents, teachers, and principals, or to have resulted in any consequential changes in instructional activities. It may be that school councils and school-based management serve other purposes, such as providing parents and teachers with some control over local schools, and it may be possible to find a form of local decision-making that would produce improvements in scholastic achievement. None the less, current knowledge in this area suggests that the potential gains are small enough that there is unlikely to be strong support for change.

### 3.2 School Choice/Charter Schools

What is missing from proposals for school-based management and school councils is a means of providing participants with a strong incentive to invest in innovation. Both proposals require that teachers and principals increase their attention to administrative functions, yet both offer little compensation for these efforts. Similarly, in a school council system the amount of time that community and parent representatives have to spend to become informed about educational policy issues is disproportionate to the benefits most of them expect to receive.

It has been suggested that one method of providing the desired incentives would be to introduce an element of competition to the school system. Two specific proposals are: to provide 'school choice'—that is, to allow parents to send their children to any public school of their choice—and to create charter schools—that is, to allow parents to establish their own schools within the public system. In both cases it is anticipated that the threat of dissatisfied parents transferring their children to other schools within the system, or establishing their own schools, will act as an incentive to principals and teachers to be more responsive to parental concerns. The similarity between school choice programs and competitive product markets has led many to refer to such programs as 'market-driven' systems (Kearney and Arnold, 1994). Indeed, should the analogy prove strong enough, school councils and other forms of mandated parental involvement should become superfluous, for much the same reason that one rarely observes customer advisory panels to retail establishments.

Like school councils and school-based management, however, school choice and charter schools have proven less successful in practice than they promised in theory. Two factors have inhibited widespread use of school choice. First, most school boards cannot afford to pay for transportation costs outside the student's home district. Second, as distance increases from the home district, parents have less and less information about the programs of other schools. As a result, most parents are reluctant to send their children to out-of-district public schools, in turn making it difficult for principals to offer specialized programs. Although unique programs might attract students across boundaries, principals have to be careful that they do not upset the parents of the in-district students for whom their schools were established.

A partial solution to this problem has been the creation of charter schools, which are designed to be unique and, hence, have no in-district groups that must be satisfied. Nine states in the United States (Arizona, California, Colorado, Delaware, Massachusetts, Michigan, Minnesota, New Hampshire, and Texas) have strong charter school legislation, in the sense that they allow non-local board sponsorship of such schools or an appeal process[17] (Bierlein, 1995: 16). Also, Great Britain has had legislation since 1988 allowing for a type of charter school known as a 'grant-maintained school'[18] (Wohlstetter and Anderson, 1994).

The experience in these jurisdictions has been that those charter schools that have been established have been successful. The concern that charter schools would become élitist institutions, catering primarily to bright children of well-educated parents, has not proved to be well founded in the United States. For example, five of the 17 schools scheduled to open in Massachusetts in 1995, and two of the 14 charter schools operating in Colorado, are targeted at students 'at risk'. Furthermore, the remaining Colorado schools accommodate a broad spectrum of educational programs. None of the first 39 charter schools established in California was targeted at gifted students, while five were aimed specifically toward at-risk students and two were for special education students (Mauhs-Pugh, 1995: 35). And one indicator of success in Great Britain is that none of the 693 grant-maintained schools had been closed by 1994 (Wohlstetter and Anderson, 1994: 489).

This is not to say, however, that charter schools have lived up to their initial promise. Their primary failing has been that they are sufficiently difficult to establish that there are not yet enough of them to offer serious competition to the public school system. Great Britain has only 693 for the whole country. California, in which there is a limit of 100 for the state, has only 39. The Massachusetts Education Reform Act allows a maximum of 25 schools, enough for only three-fourths of 1 per cent of Massachusetts students (Mauhs-Pugh, 1995: 43), and Minnesota allows no more than 20 charter schools (Nathan and Ysseldyke, 1994: 687). Furthermore, that a large percentage of charter schools are aimed at children with special needs further reduces the number available to compete with most public schools.

The British experience also suggests that, as schools tend to be chartered on an individual basis, they may lose many of the economies of scale available to school boards. As Wohlstetter and Anderson (1994: 490) note, 'the individual school can be too small to keep a school psychologist on staff or to offer employee health insurance or to afford high-priced information technology systems.' And charter schools may be at a disadvantage collecting and disseminating information about new ideas and educational practices. In Britain, grant-maintained schools have begun to address some of these problems through the establishment of staff networks. But such networks offer greater promise in a densely populated country such as the United Kingdom than in a province such as Alberta, or even in states such as California and Massachusetts that have sufficient population bases but very few charter schools.

Only in Minnesota can investigators claim to have identified a positive effect of charter schools on the public school system. One school district was reported to have moved quickly to implement features like team teaching, block scheduling, and heightened parental involvement in response to the 'threat' of a K-12 charter school (Hopchin, 1994: 19). Another Minnesota school district introduced a non-charter Montessori school soon after a private group had applied to charter such a school (Kolderie, 1993), and Kolderie claims that many secondary schools became much more responsive to parental pressure to increase the quality and quantity of advanced placement courses once the threat of charter schools became apparent. To our knowledge, however, no formal studies have been conducted of Minnesota's experience. Only anecdotal evidence is available. Furthermore, it appears to us to be unlikely that charter schools could have had a significant impact in a state that limits the number of such schools to 20.

To conclude, the charter schools that have been established have clearly filled an important need for their students and may have provided some spur for innovation in public school boards. Nevertheless, the chartering process requires sufficient dedication and resources that charter schools have not accounted for more than a tiny percentage of the schools in any jurisdiction in which they have been allowed. Once again, these drawbacks reduce the amount of political pressure that can be expected to be exerted on their behalf.

## 4. IMPLEMENTATION

School boards in Alberta, as in the other provinces, are in every sense of the word creatures of the province, whose power to legislate over education is limited only by two constitutional provisions: denominational minority rights protected under Section 93 of the British North America Act (*Constitution Act, 1867*), and minority official language rights protected under Section 23 of the Canadian Charter of Rights and Freedoms (Constitution Act, 1982). While Alberta's boards of education may be creatures of the province, confrontation between local trustees and district-employed senior officials, on the one side, and the provincial government and centrally employed officials, on the other side, has been a consistent feature of the operation of the provincial education system. Contestation and legal challenges to provincial authority have marked the current restructuring process.[19]

### 4.1 School Finance

Details of the new *Framework for Funding School Boards* were announced in February 1995, to take effect in the 1995/6 school year. Without direct access to local property tax bases, school boards have lost the capacity to spend more on schools and educational programs than is provided by provincial grants, corporate benevolence and local fund-raising apart. This will substantially reduce the previous fiscal disparities, which reflected differences among districts in the size of their local tax bases and thus in the amounts that could be raised with the same tax effort. Districts that previously were disadvantaged because of their low tax bases and consequent inability to raise funds locally will see this disadvantage offset by increased provincial grants. Wealthier districts will lose their past advantage and will be able to spend less on the programs they offer. To the extent that money buys quality, what they offer may be downgraded from a 'better education' of more than basic quality, paid for by local tax effort, to what the provincial government refers to as 'quality *basic* education' (Alberta Education, 1995b; emphasis added). Just what 'quality' means in this usage remains to be determined.

Table 3 shows the distribution of increases and decreases in school district funding for 1995/6 over 1994/5. Full provincial funding was to the benefit of 30 of the 68 districts funded for 1995/6. Their estimated grants from the province were up to 14 per cent greater than revenues from grants and local property tax had been the year before. Twenty-nine districts have reduced revenues under the new funding framework, and 9 are unchanged from the previous year.

**Table 3:** Changes in District Revenues under Full Provincial Funding, 1994/5 to 1995/6

|  | Number of Districts | |
| --- | --- | --- |
| Range | Increase | Decrease |
| 1–2% | 6 | 8 |
| 3–5% | 9 | 6 |
| 6–9% | 10 | 15 |
| 10–14% | 5 | — |
| Subtotals | 30 | 29 |
| Unchanged | 9 | |
| Total districts funded | 68 | |

SOURCE: Alberta Education, 1995b.

The restriction on spending for system administration, coupled with limitations on inter-block transfers, responds to the perception that school districts had become top-heavy, with unnecessarily large central bureaucracies. The larger school districts, especially the large urban districts, will be more severely affected by these restrictions than will the smaller districts. Faced with the needs of large and increasingly diverse urban populations, and with the economy-of-scale advantages their student numbers provide, these boards have developed centrally based ancillary and suppport staff who provide services to schools in areas such as curriculum development, diagnostic and classroom support services for children with special needs, and central library services. Staff who work in these areas but are not school-based are generally not considered as part of the instruction block under the new grant scheme and cannot be funded out of the limited system administration block. While there have been examples of creative accounting as districts attempt to save what they have developed in the past, many such positions have disappeared from larger districts in the current school year.

### 4.2 Reduction in Number of School Boards

The intention to reduce the number of school boards from 141 to 'about 60' was announced in January 1994, although the general intent was not a surprise. Existing boards were encouraged to negotiate amalgamations (existing boards to be absorbed by others) or combinations of boards into new 'regional school divisions', all subject to ministerial approval. While voluntarism was encouraged, there was no ambiguity about the government's intentions. In February 1994, Alberta Education presented three alternative regionalization scenarios to a meeting of school board representatives and other stakeholder groups. While not all existing jurisdictions would be affected, central planning for a reduction in the number of operating districts was under way.

The new larger boards meant a reduction in the number of trustees in the province and in the number of board-employed senior officials and secretary-treasurers. Many former senior staff of dissolved boards were 'grandfathered' or protected in various ways in the new districts. Individual severance arrangements were negotiated with those who left, with the financial costs being part of the price of restructuring. News releases at intervals announced the formation of more and more amalgamated and new regional jurisdictions. A news release on 13 October 1994 identified a total of 57 school boards that would be operating in the province by January 1995. An additional three newly created francophone regional divisions later raised the total to 60. Ministerial intervention had been required to bring some of the new arrangements into being.

The short-term effects of amalgamation/regionalization on schools in those districts involved were indirect, if not minimal. Reorganization of school bus routes and thus attendance patterns occurred in some areas as parents and communities pressed to have their children moved to other schools more to their liking than previous arrangements had allowed.

The overall numbers of senior and district-based staff fell. Differences in teacher and support staff contracts had to be reconciled, although not all support staff were unionized. There were some bitter disputes as non-unionized and contract staff were let go. With new organizations to be developed and a steady stream of provincial directives to be absorbed and responded to, superintendents and other senior officials found their time increasingly taken up with district-level administrative and managerial tasks. They had less and less time available for work in and with schools on educational matters.[20] The closure during the 1994/5 school year of two regional offices of Alberta Education and staff reductions in the remaining regional offices effectively eliminated central consulting services for rural schools and small districts. Over the preceding decade, however, the practical access of small jurisdictions to such services had already been substantially reduced as the role of regional office staff had progressively changed from consultation and assistance for small jurisdictions and their schools to evaluation and monitoring of district and school operations.

At the end of September 1995, the new format *1994/95 Alberta Education Annual Report* was released together with the province's public accounts for the same year. Included in the press release accompanying the report was a table of school district expenditures for that year on superintendent offices' salaries and benefits, with a statement by the minister that many of the offices included in the table no longer existed as a result of the reduction in number of school boards.

School superintendents, by the nature of their work and responsibilities as chief executive officers of their employing boards, earn civil service executive salaries, although some of the school districts listed were small and severance pay had been included in listed expenses for districts that no longer existed. Media reports focused on the larger figures in the table, indirectly emphasizing the extent to which the province was reducing administrative costs by eliminating school districts.

For superintendents and other senior staff who remained in the regionalized/amalgamated school districts, the year was a taxing one. They had to build new corporate identities and corporate consciousness among trustees brought together, in some cases unwillingly, from different jurisdictions with different organizational cultures and even different understandings of what an effective school looked like and what constituted good teaching. They had to build common organizational cultures among teaching and non-teaching staff from different jurisdictions who had been working amidst the trustee differences referred to above. Many were demoralized by salary and benefit cuts and by what teachers in particular regarded as continuing government attacks on themselves, their profession, and education generally.

Reorganization did not always proceed smoothly. The legislative framework had first been set with the introduction of Bill 8 in September 1993, followed by Bill 19 at the end of March 1994, with a package of government amendments following in May. The amended bill was then passed and assented to at the end of May, with closure used by the government to cut off debate. School boards protested strongly against their loss of taxing power. Catholic boards were particularly vigorous in their protest. The Calgary Catholic Board, in protest against what it felt was underrepresentation at the government's sessions, held its own public roundtables simultaneously with the provincial meetings in October 1993, followed by a series of well-attended protest rallies beginning in January 1994 and running into the period of legislative debate. Those public meetings, held in arenas and high school gymnasiums, were coordinated with similar events in other cities. The series of large-scale protests culminated on 14 April with electronically linked rallies in the five major urban centres of the province.

When finally passed, Bill 19 made concessions to the Catholic concerns, allowing separate (but not public) boards the right to opt out of the proposed new funding arrangements and retain their taxation powers, although they could not set a mill rate lower than that set by the province. Where an opted-out board raised a lower sum per student through local taxation than the Alberta School Foundation Fund would provide, the Fund (i.e., the province) would make up the difference. Any excess raised locally over the provincial grant would revert to the Fund. These concessions were not enough. A number of Catholic school boards, along with the Alberta Catholic School Trustees Association and a number of individuals, have petitioned for and been granted an injunction restraining the government from putting its proposed regionalization of Catholic school boards into place, pending the resolution of a full-scale court challenge. The plaintiffs intend to argue that the provincial restructuring proposals are unconstitutional because they take away from the educational rights granted to the denominational minority under the 1901 Ordinances of the North-West Territories, which are thus guaranteed by the Alberta Act (1905) that created the province. Those rights include the power to tax separate school supporters, to petition for the establishment of new separate school districts, and to retain the boundaries of existing districts unless the government can demonstrate that proposed boundary changes will not prejudicially affect the rights of existing ratepayers. This case has not yet been heard in court.

The concessions granted to Catholic boards have given rise to still another case arguing constitutional rights against the government's restructuring proposals. Here the Public School Boards Association of Alberta (representing the larger boards) and the Edmonton Public School Board, with the support of the Alberta School Boards Association and the Alberta Catholic School Trustees Association (i.e., all school boards in the province), took a different constitutional position. They argued that granting the right to opt out of the new financing arrangements to Catholic but not to public school boards was discriminatory and thus unconstitutional. They also argued that the restructuring generally—and, specifically, the denial of taxation powers and the requirement that the minister of education approve the appointment by boards of their superintendents—is contrary to an implicit constitutional guarantee of autonomy for local government. Judgement in this case was delivered in the Court of Queen's Bench in November 1995. In a complex ruling, the court rejected the local autonomy argument, but found that public boards must be allowed the same rights as the Catholic boards; i.e., to opt out of the Alberta School Foundation Fund and retain their local taxation powers. The government was subsequently granted a stay of the order to implement that ruling pending the results of appeal.

In November 1996 and January 1997, the Court of Appeal also heard arguments from the Alberta School Boards Association and the Public School Boards Association concerning consolidation of school districts, local government autonomy, and religious discrimination. No decision had been announced at press time.

## 4.3 Early Childhood Services

The reduction in funding for, and thus in the ability of school boards to provide, Early Childhood Services was another of the most contentious issues, and one on which Alberta stood virtually alone among the provinces, as it ignored published research and conventional wisdom on the value of age-appropriate structured educational experience for children of kindergarten age. Educators universally decried the scheme to cut the availability of programs in half: from 400 hours (i.e., half-days throughout the school year) to 200 hours (half-days for half the year). It is ironic that in February 1994, as the controversy over the ECS proposal heated up in Alberta, the minister of education for Newfoundland, a province beset by financial crisis far greater than any claimed for Alberta, announced his government's intention to increase its provision of kindergarten programs to double what Alberta's had been before the cuts. Ontario's Royal Commission on Learning (1994: 169) had highlighted as the first and key recommendation in its December 1994 report:

> That Early Childhood Education (ECE) be provided by all school boards to all children from 3 to 5 years of age whose parents/guardians choose to enrol them. ECE would gradually replace existing junior and senior kindergarten programs, and become a part of the public education system.

Lisac (1995) recounts that when Alberta's minister of education tabled in the legislature a bibliography of more than 1,000 studies purporting to demonstrate the inconsistency of research findings on ECS and similar programs, many of the titles were found to be irrelevant. The research argument was subsequently dropped from ministerial pronouncements. Grounds other than expenditure reduction could not be found to justify the cuts in ECS programs and provincial funding for ECS programs was later increased to cover 240 hours.

School boards reacted in a variety of ways. The Calgary Catholic Board announced its intention to continue to offer a 400-hour program with no fees. The Calgary Public Board determined that programs beyond 200 hours would continue to be available, but fees would be charged for the period over 200 hours, with partial or full remission of fees for parents in financial need. Other boards reacted with a mix of full provision and partial provision with or without fees, or a mix of public and private services.

### 4.4 School Councils

The evolution of policy dealing with school councils, from the initial discussion in the 1993 *Roundtable Workbook* (Alberta Education, 1993a) to the 1995 School Act amendments, provides a demonstration of the tension that can develop between a government keen to bring schools under community control and both educators and parents who are concerned about the rapid pace of change being thrust upon them.

In the mid-1980s a committee of MLAs reviewing existing school legislation echoed the conventional wisdom on the role of parents in the education of their children but did not refer to a role for parents in the operation of schools. Rather, the committee called for:

> the creation of School Councils or Advisory Committees in which the School Principal should be a key participant. While these would not be autonomous bodies, their authority in influencing board decisions will determine the extent of community input. (Alberta, Policy Advisory Committee, 1985: 44)

There was no consideration of autonomy in this proposal, nor any significant role for such bodies, in the operation of schools. Rather, the consideration was one of possible influence on school board decisions—a more general matter of policy, and at a level removed from the individual school. The resulting 1988 legislation allowed parents the option of forming a school council on which they would hold a majority, and gave that council an advisory role at best, at the same time making it subordinate to the school board:

> 17(3) A school council may
> (a) advise the principal of the school and the board respecting any matter relating to the school, and
> (b) perform any duty or function delegated to it by the board in accordance with the delegation. (Alberta, 1988).

The discussion in the 1993 *Roundtable Workbook* referred to the 'limited' roles that most school councils had played up to that moment and called for legislative changes to enable boards to delegate to school councils authority over matters such as evaluation of school programs, financial allocations, special needs programming, and attendance boundaries, among other things (Alberta Education, 1993a: 35–6).

Bill 19, containing the 1994 amendments to the School Act, was first introduced in the Legislative Assembly in March 1994. It called for significant change in the role and powers of school councils. They were no longer to be optional; there would have to be a council with a parent majority for each school:

> 17(1) A school council shall be established in accordance with the regulations for each school operated by a board.
> (2) The majority of the members of a school council shall be parents of students enrolled in the school.

In previous legislation school councils had the option of advising the principal and performing duties delegated by the board, but now those tasks were to be mandatory. Councils were also to be given significant responsibilities for overseeing both educational and financial operations of the school, as well as for creating and implementing educational and financial policy for the school:

17(4) A school council shall

(a) advise the principal and the board respecting any matter relating to the school,

(b) perform any duty or function delegated to it by the board in accordance with the delegation,

(c) ensure that students in the school have the opportunity to meet the standards of education set by the Minister,

(d) ensure that the fiscal management of the school is in accordance with the requirements of the board and the superintendent, and

(e) do anything it is required to do under the regulations.

(5) Subject to the regulations, a school council may make and implement policies in the school that the council considers necessary to carry out its responsibilities under subsection (4) including but not limited to policies respecting

(a) the nature of programs offered,

(b) the expenditure of money,

(c) the educational standards to be met by students, and

(d) the management of the school.

Nothing up to that moment indicated exactly how councils were to carry out the 'ensuring' responsibilities given them in 17(4)(c) and (d). Not merely were these tasks likely to be onerous for lay people as well as for professional educators, they were also likely to conflict with the responsibilities of principals. Section 15 of the School Act sets out those duties and responsibilities. As amended by Bill 19, it reads as follows:

15. A principal of a school must

(a) provide instructional leadership in the school;

(b) ensure that the instruction provided by the teachers employed in the school is consistent with the courses of study and education programs prescribed, approved or authorized pursuant to this Act;

(c) evaluate or provide for the evaluation of programs offered in the school;

(c.1) ensure that students in the school have the opportunity to meet the standards of education set by the Minister;

(d) direct the management of the school;

(e) maintain order and discipline in the school and on the school grounds and during activities sponsored or approved by the board;

(f) promote co-operation between the school and the community that it serves;

(g) supervise the evaluation and advancement of students;

(h) evaluate the teachers employed in the school;

(i) subject to any applicable collective agreement and the principal's contract of employment, carry out those duties that are assigned to the principal by the board in accordance with the regulations and the requirements of the school council and the board.

Both the school council, in 17(4)(c), and the principal, explicitly in 15(c.1) and implicitly in other subsections, were given equivalent educational responsibilities; there were similar potential overlaps with respect to financial matters. Section 15(i) made it clear that duties were also to be assigned to the principal by the board, but nevertheless those duties had to be carried out in accordance with the 'requirements of the school council'. Section 17(5) would have given the school council additional powers both to make and to implement policies dealing with financial expenditure, educational matters, and school management.

Many principals were apprehensive. The wording of the 'shall ensure' subsections made their relationships with the new councils problematic. Both principal and council were to be responsible for the quality of a school's educational program; the exact locus of responsibility for financial management appeared uncertain. And the draft legislation made responsibilities mandatory—school councils would be required by law to exercise a presence in these areas.

Principals were accustomed to working with interested parents and dealing with individual parent complaints and requests. Many had established and promoted effective parental advisory groups for their schools. But the new school councils were to be much more than parent-teacher groups or home-and-school associations. They looked more like the individual school governing bodies established by reform legislation in the United Kingdom and New Zealand, where 'governors' or 'trustees' for individual schools were the employers of teachers and principals and had significant powers to oversee school operations. In some communities, principals feared the possibility of factional attempts to take over their schools through the manipulation of school council elections. While board members did not necessarily share principals' concerns over close supervision, many questioned whether there would continue to be a place for district-level school boards if parent bodies were given the roles suggested by the draft legislation.

In the interim, the MLA Implementation Team on Roles and Responsibilities in Education held public meetings in regional centres across the province to hear representations about school council functions and powers. It subsequently released a synthesis of concerns expressed to it (Alberta Education, 1994b) and then a position paper (Alberta Education, 1994c). The synthesis report makes it clear that the preference of those contributing to the discussion was strongly in favour of an advisory and consultative role for school councils, rather than the more substantive decision-making and even executive role suggested in Bill 19. The School Act was again amended, by Bill 37, in May 1995. Subsections (4) and (5) of section 17 were repealed, and new subsections were substituted:

(4) A school council may, at its discretion,

(a) advise the principal and the board respecting any matter relating to the school,

(b) perform any duty or function delegated to it by the board in accordance with the delegation,

(c) consult with the principal so that the principal may ensure that students in the school have the opportunity to meet the standards of education set by the minister,

(d) consult with the principal so that the principal may ensure that the fiscal management of the school is in accordance with the requirements of the board and the superintendent, and

(e) do anything it is authorized under the regulations to do.

(5) Subject to the regulations, a school council may make and implement policies in the school that the council considers necessary to carry out its functions.

A new subsection (7.1) was also added, requiring boards to establish 'an appeal process or conflict resolution procedure' for dealing with disputes between principals and their councils. School councils are once again to be advisory bodies, with involvement at their own discretion. Like Bagehot's constitutional monarch, they may have no legal powers other than 'the right to be consulted, the right to encourage, the right to warn'. But the attention generated by the original provisions of Bill 19 and the Implementation Team reports will make them important parts of education in Alberta for the foreseeable future. Principals are being made aware of the differences between consultation and collaboration, as well as the difficulties they are likely to face in reclaiming control of decisions once that control has been ceded to a 'consultative' body of parents.

Perhaps ironically, the increased involvement of parents in school councils, even if only in a consultative role, may come back to haunt government when further rounds of funding cuts are announced. Informed school councils can easily become activists against funding cuts and for grant increases. The UK experience might be salutary in this respect. Many school governors there have not sought second terms and replacements have been difficult to find, as the task of running schools with inadequate levels of funding has become more and more onerous. In March 1995, the National Governors Council, a representative body of school governors, demonstrated against further budget cuts in front of the House of Commons in London (*Times Educational Supplement*, 1995).

Late in June 1995, Alberta's minister of education announced that a sum of $1.9 million had been set aside to fund regional consortia to co-ordinate training for school councils and teacher professional development with respect to school-based management. Six regional consortia have been established across the province, each with an executive director and a board of directors representing the various educator, parent, and community interests. A 'School

Council Resource Manual' was issued in November 1995, and a series of development workshops for school councils was held across the province in the winter of 1996. By the autumn of 1996, the various consortia had developed schedules of professional development workshops and seminars for teachers, school officials, and school council members, as well as an active communications network. In at least their earliest stage of development, the consortia seem to be 'going concerns', offering the services they were established and funded to provide (Alberta Home and School Councils Association, 1995).

## 4.5 Charter Schools

The idea of alternative forms of schooling under school board auspices was not new when the 1993 *Roundtable Workbook*'s charter school proposals emerged. Various forms of 'alternative' schools had been operated by school boards in different parts of the province for a number of years: bilingual/bicultural programs in the Edmonton public schools; schools with a focus on fine arts in the Calgary Catholic and Foothills public systems; schools organized around First Nations cultures in a number of jurisdictions; small, informal high school programs for students having difficulty in regular large high schools; and programs for gifted and talented students in a variety of segregated and non-segregated settings. In each of these cases the school was operated and funded as part of a school district but retained a degree of program uniqueness and some operational autonomy. In each case, the program had been established after a period of internal advocacy from within the district, and with the support of influential senior officials and/or trustees. In most such programs, there was a degree of precariousness. Their continuity was not assured and there was always the question of whether funding would be available in the next budget or after the next school board election. Educational causes go out of fashion from time to time.

The province proposed to regularize such programs and, through individual charters, to grant them a greater degree of autonomy from direct control by school district officials than had been the case with alternative schools. School boards will nevertheless carry a degree of responsibility for at least approving the concept underlying a charter school, through the requirement that the proposing group make its first approach for a charter to a school board. Only when a board has rejected such a request can the charter seekers apply for a ministerial charter.

The Alberta Teachers' Association was particularly hostile to the idea of charter schools, at least in part because of the possibility that Association membership would not be required of charter school teachers. There was also the implication that the very existence of charter schools as a matter of government policy insinuated that public and separate schools were not meeting the needs of their communities. Trustees tended to share the latter concerns, if not the former. The draft *Charter School Handbook* issued in November 1994 sought to mollify concerns over teacher quality, if not ATA membership, by requiring teacher certification. Active membership in the Association would not be required of charter school teachers. However, teachers employed by boards who worked in charter schools while either on leave or secondment would be allowed to retain their ATA membership.

There were also concerns from within the educational community that charter schools would be selective, élitist, and private in everything but name and that they were intended primarily as a device for further diverting public funds to private purposes. In part to forestall these concerns, both the draft and the final *Charter School Handbook* (Alberta Education, 1995d) specified that tuition fees could not be charged, that except for those chartered by a separate school board charter schools could have no religious affiliation, and that access could not be denied to prospective students as long as space and resources were available. Provision would have to be made in a school charter for a selection process to be used when applications exceeded program capacity. The process would have to be one 'that ensures openness and fairness'. In light of the élitist critique, it is interesting to note the findings of a study of the charter school experience in the United States. In a preliminary discussion of his findings, Mauhs-Pugh (1995a) observed:

> The evidence is inconclusive, but . . . suggests that charter schools may be more geared toward the hard to educate student, than not. . . . Those who see a need to provide for those who have been served poorly by regular public schooling are strongly motivated to create a school with a clear commonality of purpose.

While there may have been a number of initial expressions of interest, there has not been much of an uptake of the charter school idea in its first year in Alberta. The final *Handbook* was not issued until April 1995. The complexities of the required charter proposal, the difficulties of organizing a school on short notice, and the lack of start-up funding kept the number of actual proposals down. By fall 1996 only eight charters had been granted, five by school boards and three by the minister of education. Three of the eight schools opened in September 1995, one in January 1996, and four in September 1996. All are in urban or suburban areas. Two were to serve gifted children, one was to 'integrate a basic education with a music curriculum centered on the Suzuki methodology', another would focus 'on academic and personal excellence', one is 'directed toward meeting the needs of disadvantaged students, aged 12–19 years, who have been unable to succeed in the mainstream education system', one will focus on children for whom 'English is a second language', a seventh hopes to attract students with 'high academic expectations', and the last is aimed at 'increasing opportunities for individual learning'. (Alberta Education,

1995h and 1996). It will be a few years yet before the Alberta jury can report on charter schools.

## 4.6 Accountability

Under the restructuring proposals, schools and school districts will have to issue annual report cards on themselves, beginning in the fall of 1995. Following a year of consultations and public meetings by the MLA Implementation Team, a policy framework setting out the reporting requirements and specifying the performance indicators to be used was issued in June 1995 (Alberta Education, 1995e). The objectives are to hold schools and school boards accountable to parents and students for their accomplishments and failures, and to promote informed choice of schools by parents in an open-boundary educational system.

There is an implicit conflict between the policy objective of promoting informed school choice by parents and the objection by school-based educators to the idea of 'box scores' or 'league standings' that rank schools one against the other in terms of student achievement scores. Educators argue that because student achievement is in large measure dependent on social, demographic, and cultural factors in the individual family, schools drawing their students from a diversity of communities cannot be compared fairly on the basis of student achievement alone. Any comparison limited to such indicators will by its very nature be simplistic, unfair, and misleading. The argument runs that it is not possible, for example, to make a valid comparison based on achievement scores alone between a school with a high rate of transience (student turnover between the beginning and end of a school year) and another school with a stable population.

The Alberta scheme takes some of these concerns into account. Beginning in November 1995, individual schools were required to report to their parents and communities in the fall of each year on such indicators of the previous year's performance as:

- provincial achievement test and diploma examination results;
- ratings of parent and student satisfaction;
- student turnover during the year;
- other indicators of local interest chosen with school council involvement.

By April 1997, schools will have to provide annual plans keyed to provincial goals and to district and locally developed objectives. School boards will be required to report:

- provincial achievement test and diploma examination results, including participation rates;
- ratings of parent and student satisfaction;
- percentage of jurisdiction spending on instruction;
- spending per student.

Boards will not be required to report school-by-school results. They were required to submit an interim one-year educational plan in September 1995 and a three-year plan in April 1996, to be updated annually thereafter. These plans are to be keyed to provincial goals and should state locally developed objectives. Annual reports will be required to reflect progress towards provincial goals and locally developed objectives.

While box scores may be avoided in provincially specified terms of reference for accountability reports, one can easily foresee media compilations from individual school data, whether on the city pages of major urban newspapers or in other publications such as the *Rocky View Five Village Weekly*. The extent to which these compilations will in fact enable informed choice remains to be seen.

## 5. INTERPRETATION

The models of bureaucratic behaviour that McKenzie surveys in Chapter 3 are generally based on the assumption that civil servants act in their own financial interests. These models predict, for example, that civil servants will respond to budget reductions by cutting peripheral programs, by offering generous early retirement packages (particularly to senior managers), and by soliciting the support of special interest groups to oppose government policy.

What our study of Alberta Education revealed is that the factors motivating civil servants can be much more complex than is presumed in these standard, or naïve, models. Although events at the school board level appeared consistent with the predictions of the naïve view, the actions of the central administration of Alberta Education were not. Officials in the deputy minister's office appeared to be motivated by two non-financial factors. First, there appears to have been a genuine desire to improve the educational system—by introducing greater competition among schools, by increasing parental and community involvement, and by reducing disparities in school board funding. Second, central administrators clearly wished to redress what they perceived to be a shift of power from Alberta Education to the school boards.

Our interpretation of the events to date is that the central administrators in Alberta Education seized the 'excuse' of budget cuts to impose changes they had lacked the political power to introduce during less turbulent political times. Once teachers had accepted a 5 per cent wage roll-back, the 6.23 per cent

## Appendix 1: 1996/97 School Board Funding Formula (Selected Data)

### 1. INSTRUCTION BLOCK

#### 1.1 Basic Instruction

| | |
|---|---|
| Basic instruction | $3,686 per full-time equivalent student |
| Severe disabilities | $8,910 per funded student |
| English as a second language | $644 per funded student |
| Sparsity and distance | Sparsity rate $500; distance rate $0.40 per km |
| Home education | $990 per student plus 50% of the cost of Alberta Distance Learning Centre courses to a maximum of $990 for grades 7–12 |
| Learning Resources Credit | $9.30 per enrolled student |

#### 1.2 Projects/Contracts

| | |
|---|---|
| Enhanced opportunities | per approved project |
| Native education | per approved project |
| Institutional support | per approved contract |
| Regional assessment services | per approved contract |

#### 1.3 Early Childhood Services

| | |
|---|---|
| Basic ECS program | $1,182 per child with a minimum of 400 hours of instruction |
| Program enhancement projects | $165 per child for 15% of eligible enrolment; $20,000 maximum per project |
| Mildly or moderately disabled | $1,360 per child |

| Number of Children in a Program Unit | Maximum |
|---|---|
| 1 | $19,000 per unit |
| 2 | $22,800 per unit |
| 3 | $26,600 per unit |
| 4 | $30,410 per unit |
| 5 | $34,200 per unit |
| 6 | $37,970 per unit |
| 7 or more | $37,970 + $6,330 for each additional child |

| | |
|---|---|
| Transportation of disabled ECS children | $8.65 per round trip |

### 2. SUPPORT BLOCK

| | |
|---|---|
| Plant operations and maintenance | $413 per full-time equivalent student; and $10.35 per square metre |
| Board governance/administration | Percentage of instruction block and plant operations and maintenance and student transportation allocation: |

- 6% if fewer than 2,000 full-time equivalent students
- 4% if more than 6,000 full-time equivalent students
- Between 6% and 4% on a sliding scale if between 2,000 and 6,000 full-time equivalent students

## Appendix 1: (Continued)

Transportation
Urban $345 per eligible passenger
Rural $1,710 per expected special passenger

| Capacity | Annual Bus Support | Rate per km |
|---|---|---|
| 12 | $ 6,894 | $0.61 |
| 13–24 | 8,664 | 0.74 |
| 25–36 | 10,690 | 0.74 |
| 37–54 | 11,274 | 0.76 |
| 55–66 | 11,892 | 0.77 |
| 67+ | 12,273 | 0.77 |

| Special vehicles other than school buses | Horse-drawn vehicle | $6,739 per year |
|---|---|---|
| | Car | $1,092 per passenger per year to a maximum of $3,276 |
| | Station-wagon/van | $1,092 per passenger per year to a maximum of $4,368 |

Route distance allowance for:
Special vehicles $0.40 per km
Parent provided up to $0.17 per km

Special (for students with disabilities) $1,710 per funded student
Weekend $2,782 per funded student

### 3. CAPITAL BLOCK

Current school building projects | As approved by the school buildings board
Debt retirement | Full funding for the debt owing on school building projects supported by Alberta Education

SOURCE: Alberta Education, *Funding for School Authorities in the 1996–97 School Year.*

---

reduction in the Education budget created little need for significant changes in the delivery of services. Nevertheless, central administrators reduced the number of school boards, equalized funding across districts, introduced charter schools and school councils, and used block funding to impose significant constraints on local authority spending. Future developments in the modelling of government bureaucracies will have to take into account the possibility of such opportunistic behaviour.

## NOTES

1. See section 4 of Chapter 3.

2. One roundtable was held in Calgary on 15–16 October and one was held in Edmonton on 22–23 October. Each roundtable was attended by 120 individuals selected by the government (Alberta Education, 1993b).

3. The eight meetings were held in: Fairview (20–21 September), Westlock (22–23 September), Red Deer (27–28 September), Edmonton (29 September), St Paul (29–30 September), Taber (5–6 October), Strathmore (6–7 October), and Calgary (13 October). In total, 557 individuals participated (Alberta Education, 1993c).

4. School boards had not been required to offer ECS programs. Most, but not all, had chosen to do so, meeting the costs out of various combinations of provincial grants specific to that purpose, other revenues, and fees charged to parents. In a few jurisdictions, ECS services had been provided entirely by private firms.

5. Nor was this a new concern. The current provincial treasurer, Jim Dinning, had repeatedly drawn attention to these inequities during his tenure as minister of education in the previous government.

6. Particularly notable were five 'implementation teams' composed of government MLAs. These committees held public meetings concerning (i) regionalizing and amalgamating school boards; (ii) redefining roles and responsibilities; (iii) creating a framework for funding school boards; (iv) developing an accountability framework and performance measures; and (v) improving business involvement and technology integration.

7. By the time the 1996 budget estimates were tabled, Education's projected budget for 1996/7 was 6.23 per cent less than that of 1992/3; Health's budget was projected to fall by 11.27 per cent over the same time period. (See Table 1 in Chapter 1.)

8. An exception was made for school districts with fewer than 6,000 students. Those with less than 2,000 students could spend as much as 6 per cent; and those with between 2,000 and 6,000 could spend between 6 per cent and 4 per cent on a sliding scale.

9. This allocation is to decrease to 1.2 per cent in 1996/7 and to 0.8 per cent in 1997/8.

10. See section 4 of Chapter 3.

11. There is an exception. School boards are allowed to impose a special school tax levy, not exceeding 3 per cent of the budget of the board, if such a levy is approved by a plebiscite in a general election. There were no such plebiscites in the October 1995 school board elections.

12. Parents of children attending the school must compose a majority of the individuals on each school council (Alberta Education, 1995e: 6).

13. At school opening, the minimum number of students is 75 (Alberta Education, 1995c: 14).

14. A charter school may 'second' teachers from the local school board. But if it employs its own teachers, they may not be active members of the provincial teachers' union, the Alberta Teachers' Association.

15. The use of intragovernmental competition to encourage innovation is discussed by McKenzie in section 4 of Chapter 3.

16. These proposals were developed by an MLA implementation team on Accountability in Education (see Alberta Education, 1995a, 1995d).

17. Eleven other states (Alaska, Arkansas, Georgia, Hawaii, Kansas, Louisiana, Missouri, New Mexico, Rhode Island, Wisconsin, and Wyoming) have 'weak' legislation (Bierlein, 1995: 16).

18. Such schools had also been part of British education prior to the 1988 reforms.

19. The discussion in this section is based primarily on a series of interviews with school district senior officials and school principals (both urban and rural) conducted during the spring and summer of 1995.

20. Coleman and LaRocque (1990), in their important study of effectiveness at the district level, point out that senior officials make significant contributions towards the educational quality of school districts through their work with schools and school staff, and through the importance placed on such work as part of school district norms, practices, and ethos.

## REFERENCES

Alberta (1988), School Act 1988.

——— (1993), School Amendment Act 1993 (Bill 8), 10 Nov.

——— (1994a), School Amendment Act 1994 (Bill 19), 25 May.

——— (1994b), Amendments to Bill 19, School Amendment Act 1994: Government Amendment. 16 May.

——— (1995), School Amendment Act 1995 (Bill 37), 17 May.

Alberta, Policy Advisory Committee for the School Act Review (1985), *Partners in Education: Principles for a New School Act.*

Alberta Education (1993a), *Meeting the Challenge: An Education Roundtable Workbook.*

———— (1993b), *Meeting the Challenge: What We Heard.* Nov.

———— (1993c), *A Summary Report of Alberta Education's Eight Meetings with Stakeholders.* Nov.

———— (1994a), *Meeting the Challenge: Three-Year Business Plan 1994/95–1996/97.*

———— (1994b), MLA Implementation Team on Roles and Responsibilities in Education, *Roles and Responsibilities in Education in Alberta: A Synthesis of Public Input.* 24 Aug.

———— (1994c), MLA Implementation Team on Roles and Responsibilities in Education, *Roles and Responsibilities in Education: A Position Paper.* Dec.

———— (1995a), *Accountability in Education: Discussion Paper.* Jan.

———— (1995b), '1995/96 Education Funding Announced', news release, Feb.

———— (1995c), *Framework for Funding School Boards in the 1995–96 School Year.* Feb.

———— (1995d), *Charter School Handbook.* Apr.

———— (1995e), *Accountability in Education: Policy Framework.* June.

———— (1995f), *School Councils Handbook.* June.

———— (1995g), *90th Annual Report: 1994–1995.*

———— (1995h), 'Five Charter Schools Approved for Alberta', news release, 10 Oct.

———— (1996), 'Three Charter Schools Given Green Light for 1996/97', news release, 7 Aug.

———— (1997), *Funding for School Authorities in the 1996–97 School Year.*

Alberta Home and School Council Association (1995), *School Council Resource Manual.* Edmonton: AHSCA.

Bagehot, W. (1867), *The English Constitution.*

Bierlein, L. (1995), 'Charter Schools: A New Approach to Public Education', *NASSP Bulletin* 79, 572 (Sept.): 12–20.

Calgary Board of Education (1995), *'94 Budget: 1994–95 Approved Operating Budget, 1994–97 Capital Budget and Forecasts.* Sept.

Coleman, P., and L. LaRocque (1990), *Struggling to be 'Good Enough': Administrative Practices and School District Ethos*. London: Falmer.

Economic Council of Canada (1992), *A Lot to Learn: Education and Training in Canada*. Ottawa.

Hopchin, B. (1994), 'Charter Schools: Theory and Practice', *The ATA Magazine* 75, 1 (Nov./Dec.): 19–22.

Kearney, C.P., and M. Arnold (1994), 'Market Driven Schools and Educational Choices', *Theory Into Practice* 33, 2 (Spring): 112–17.

Kolderie, T. (1993), 'Answering the Challenge: Minnesota's Charter Schools', An Address to the 1993 Conference of the American Education Finance Association, Albuquerque, New Mexico.

Lisac, M. (1995), *The Klein Revolution*. Edmonton: NeWest.

Malen, B., R. Ogawa, and J. Kranz (1990), 'What Do We Know About School-Based Management? A Study of the Literature—A Call For Research', in W.H. Clune and J.F. Witte, eds, *Choice and Control in American Education*, vol. 2. Philadelphia: Falmer: 289–342.

Mann, L. (1993), *Meeting the Challenge: The Public Response*. Edmonton: Laura M. Mann Consulting Services, 20 Dec.

Martinez, V., K. Thomas, and F. Kemerer (1994), 'Who Chooses and Why: A Look at Five School Choice Plans', *Phi Delta Kappan* 75, 9 (May): 678–81.

Mauhs-Pugh, T. (1995), 'Charter Schools 1995: A Survey and Analysis of the Laws and Practices of the States', *Education Policy Analysis Archives* 3, 13 (12 July): 1–58.

Nathan, J., and J. Ysseldyke (1994), 'What Minnesota Has Learned About School Choice', *Phi Delta Kappan* 75, 9 (May): 682–8.

Ontario, Royal Commission on Learning (1994), *Learning: Our Vision for Schools*, vol. 2. Toronto: Queen's Printer.

*The Times Literary Supplement* (1995), 'Governors' Council Issues a Cry for Help', 24 Mar. 1995 (No. 4108).

Wohlstetter, P., and L. Anderson (1994), 'What Can U.S. Charter Schools Learn from England's Grant-Maintained Schools?' *Phi Delta Kappan* 75, 6 (Feb.): 486–91.

———, and A. Odden (1992), 'Rethinking School-Based Management Policy and Research', *Educational Administration Quarterly* 28, 4 (Nov.): 529–49.

# Comments on Chapter 11  ∎

*Stephen B. Lawton*

'Education: Meeting the Challenge' is a description and analysis of recent educational reforms in the province of Alberta that accompanied a significant reduction in educational funding in the province. The description is helpful since, all too often, descriptions of policy reforms in Canada are neither documented nor assessed. For students of public policy, in general, and educational policy, in particular, this is a constant source of irritation. Polemics are easy to find; solid data are not. For this reason alone, I welcome this chapter.

Overall, the chapter is solid and useful. The proposed reforms are cogently described, as are the processes followed by government in refining and, ultimately, implementing them. As the authors make clear, there was significant movement from the proposed 20 per cent cut in funding, creation of powerful school councils, and highly autonomous charter schools, to the final legislation, which included a 12.7 per cent reduction in provincial funding (including the 5 per cent roll-back in wages, for a net roll-back at the school board level of just 1 per cent since provincial funds are 50 per cent of education funding), maintenance of advisory councils for schools, and weak charter school legislation. What was not weakened significantly were the school finance 'reforms' that revoked the independent taxation powers of school boards and created an apparently uniform allocation formula for all school systems in the province. The failure of the authors to describe the nature of this allocation formula is the one factual shortcoming that I perceive.

Beyond my appreciation of the descriptive contribution of the chapter, I am somewhat less satisfied. The main thesis of the authors seems to be that Ministry of Education bureaucrats took the opportunity created by the dramatic decrease in funding to implement a number of pet changes that were not required by the economics of the situation; these changes included, I believe, more authority to school councils, the creation of charter schools, the reduction in the number of school boards, and the reduction in the authority of the 'middle level' of the educational system—the elected school trustees and their appointed superintendents. This scheme of greater centralization to the ministry and decentralization to schools seems to be one the authors believe is faddish (following US reforms) and unrelated to real problems. Research is cited 'proving' the ineffectiveness of school-based management and school councils. Although the authors do not list it as such, the centralization of school finance in the ministry to 'remove' inequities among school boards is one policy with which they seem to agree, although they do not recount any data demonstrating that this will improve effectiveness or efficiency. Given that much North American research in economics (e.g., Hanushek, 1981) demonstrates no consistent relationship between expenditures per pupil and student achievement, I find this surprising. Curiously, in the conference version of this chapter they commented, 'While there have been examples of creative accounting as districts attempt to save what they have developed in the past, many such positions [e.g., curriculum development, diagnostic and classroom support services for special needs children, and central library services] have disappeared from larger districts [read: Calgary and Edmonton] in the current school year. Thus, while the disparities in per student funding available to districts have been substantially reduced by the new funding framework, the effects of redistribution on the range of services provided and thus on the ability of boards to meet student needs, may not have been equitable' (p. 19).

Just what did the authors expect when funding in public urban boards with higher assessments was reduced by 6–9 per cent while it was increased by up to 14 per cent in lower assessment rural and Roman Catholic school boards (Table 3)? (The attribution of public and Roman Catholic, urban and rural, is my own deduction; such a breakdown was not provided by the authors.) Robin Hood policies—also known as rewarding 'relative deprivation' or 'the politics of greed'—work that way. If you take from A and give to B, then A has less to spend. Services in A decline; services in B increase. Why, though, do they suddenly suggest this 'may not have been equitable'? Are they having second thoughts? Maybe the authors are beginning to wonder if plundering the fortunes of those who created the wealth in order to reward those who were either not as successful or not as ambitious is not a good policy. If they are beginning to question it, they have good company.

The virtual collapse of the Metro Toronto economy after having been consistently drained to support bankrupt Atlantic provinces and rural/northern Ontario in the name of equity does suggest that 'redistribution' results not only in reduced services in the 'giving' jurisdiction, but also a decline in its ability to produce wealth. This is called 'killing [or at least maiming] the golden goose'. Urbanologists such as Jane Jacobs (e.g, in *The Economy of Cities*, 1969) have written on this phenomenon, and a growing literature posits the notion that the international economy is now driven by competition among 'city-states', not nation-states. Toronto competes with Boston, San Francisco, Montreal, etc. New York competes with London, Hong Kong, Tokyo, Paris, etc. And Calgary competes with Edmonton, Spokane, and Salt Lake City. Draining cities of their wealth to 'raise' the standard of living in their respective hinter-lands is foolish; in the end, both will lose. 'Redistribution' policies that act as if wealth is a pie to be cut, rather than a spring to be used for careful irrigation, are a menace to our collective, long-term well-being wherever they are found—in school finance policies, in monopoly power granted to provincial and national unions that extract high wages in low-income jurisdictions, etc.

In my view, then, the economy that Peter Drucker refers to as 'post-capital-ist' (1993) calls for an entirely different set of public policies and structures than did the industrial economy. High taxation, big bureaucracies and their partner unions, uniform standards of service, and the like are obsolete. More fluid, market-like, and organic forms must replace them. Those who redesigned the New Zealand system of education understood this; at least some of those cur-rently redesigning governance structures in the Greater Toronto Area (GTA) and Metro Toronto understand this. However, I do not find a sense of this need for a new paradigm of governance and public service clearly evident either in the paper by Bruce and Schwartz or in most of the reforms by the Klein government (or in the McKenna government in New Brunswick, which is also touted as reformist and cost-effective). Bruce and Schwartz suggest that reforms such as stronger school councils and charter schools were pet projects of bureaucrats and unrelated to fundamental reform. They seem to view the creation of power-ful, more tightly controlled, downsized bureaucracies as the primary govern-ment aim—and seem to support steps reflecting such changes as defensible.

I would argue, on the other hand, that the essence of genuine reform is composed of the formation of a deregulated system of education with more control given to those at the production level—teachers, principals, parents, and community members—and financed through a more decentralized (rather than centralized) system. Elements of such reforms were evident in some proposals, but established bureaucrats, political interests, and unions appear to have defeated these elements—or at least greatly weakened them. Ironically, elements of decentralization previously in the system—local taxation and independent appointment of school superintendents—were removed, resulting in the formation of one of the most highly centralized edu-cation systems in Canada.

The moves towards stronger centralized school systems are now evident in British Columbia, Alberta, Prince Edward Island, Newfoundland, Ontario, and Nova Scotia. I have come to suspect that, through the Council of Ministers of Education, an agreement or protocol has been reached among ministers of education (1) to blame excessive educational costs and weak effectiveness on school trustees and local superintendents, and (2) to take control of education at the provincial centres. If such an agreement does not exist, then at least the diffusion of a centralized model has occurred.

This is a tragic outcome. The most centralized system of education in Canada, that of Québec, is demonstrably the worst. The dropout rates for young males there now approaches 50 per cent; the overall dropout rate is about 35 per cent (Simpson, 1995). Strong provincial teachers' unions define education (and are a major source of Québec independence rhetoric) and threaten province-wide strikes. Rather than removing such powers of unions, as they should, current reforms are strengthening them.

The current fiscal crises of Canadian governments are providing the last chance in this generation to genuinely reform Canadian education to meet the challenges of the knowledge-driven, post-industrial economy. The reforms recounted by Bruce and Schwartz indicate to me that we are losing this opportunity. I regret that the analysis provided by Bruce and Schwartz fails to embrace a different vision of reform and interprets what should have been the crucial foundations of genuine reform—strong school councils and charter schools—as incidental initiatives of a few ministry officials.

## REFERENCES

Drucker, P.F. (1993), *Post-capitalist Society*. New York: HarperCollins.

Hanushek, E.A. (1981), 'Throwing Money at Schools', *Journal of Policy Analysis and Management* 1 (1): 19–41.

Jacobs, Jane (1969), *The Economy of Cities*. New York: Vintage Books.

Simpson, Jeffrey (1995), 'Quebec's Education Minister Takes a Step in the Classic Direction', *Globe and Mail*, 9 Nov.: A12.

# CHAPTER 12

# Rethinking the Delivery of Government Services

*Christopher J. Bruce*

## 1. INTRODUCTION

Throughout our interviews with cabinet ministers and senior government officials, we heard repeatedly that the Alberta government was committed to reviewing all of its services to determine whether each was an essential component of the 'business of government'. Each service had to meet the test that it was appropriate that the government be responsible for its provision—the government would provide only 'core' services. Furthermore, it had to be decided whether services for which the government was to be responsible would be provided by the government itself or by third parties funded by the government. Finally, even when the government was to continue providing a service, a critical review was to be conducted to determine whether improvements could be made in the way the service was delivered. No government agency was to be immune from this review.

In short, it was the clear intention of the government and its senior officials that the method of delivering government services be rethought completely. The purpose of this chapter will be to investigate this review in order to identify whether it was successful. The analysis comprises four sections. Section 2 develops a model of direct public provision of services; section 3 identifies a number of alternative methods of delivering government services; and section 4 identifies the relative advantages and disadvantages of employing these methods. Section 5 applies the analysis to a review of the Alberta government's privatization program over the last two years. Section 6 offers a conclusion.

## 2. AN ECONOMIC MODEL OF PUBLIC-SECTOR BEHAVIOUR

The advantages and disadvantages of private-sector production can only be measured by contrasting them with public-sector provision of the same service. The first step in analysing the effectiveness of government restructuring, therefore, must be to develop a model of the operation of public-sector agencies. That will be the purpose of this section.

The model developed here is based on the survey of government behaviour provided by Ken McKenzie in Chapter 3. It is useful in the development of such a model to identify four groups of interested parties, each of which is presumed to seek to maximize utility subject to its own constraints. These groups are: the elected official who is responsible for overseeing the government agency (here called 'the minister'), the general electorate (voters), direct consumers of the agency's products or services (consumers), and employees of the government agency (civil servants).

### 2.1 The Minister

In the model to be developed here, it is assumed that the primary goals of the minister are to maximize the probability that he or she will be re-elected and to satisfy his/her own views concerning the appropriate role of government. Of these goals it is assumed that the former is the more important, for the same reason that profit-maximization is generally assumed to dominate the other goals of competitive firms. That is, if a minister does not actively seek re-election, then he or she, along with his/her policies, can expect to be defeated.

The minister's ability to maximize votes is constrained by two major factors: the willingness of voters to pay taxes and limitations on the minister's ability to obtain and digest information. Whereas the constraint imposed by the voters' willingness to pay taxes is clear, the constraint imposed by the cost of obtaining information is more subtle. The primary problem faced by a government minister in this respect is that he/she is responsible for a very large, complex bureaucracy. It would require enormous investments of time and energy to become familiar with anything more than the most rudimentary basics of how the agency functioned. These investments would have to come at the expense of competing uses of the minister's time, such as dealing with voters, the press, the legislature, and his/her own family. In order to respond to these competing demands, the minister is often forced to obtain information from the agency's senior employees—individuals who can be expected to have different goals from the minister and who, therefore, may have an incentive to present to the minister only that information which suits their purposes. The result is that the minister is not able to influence more than the broad outlines of the government agency's policies, in many respects becoming a captive of the civil service.[1]

### 2.2 Voters

Each voter is assumed to maximize utility subject to his/her income constraint. With respect to government-provided goods and services, this implies, first, that the consumer will wish to direct additional resources to the public sector only as long as the value of a (tax) dollar spent on public goods equals or exceeds the value of a dollar spent on private goods; and, second, that he/she will wish to ensure that the maximum amount of utility is obtained from the total tax bill. Attainment of these goals will be constrained by the costs of obtaining information about the operation of the public sector and by the 'public' nature of government-produced goods and services. For example, assume that expenditure of $10,000 on the investigation of government efficiency could be expected to produce a gain of $20 for each of 1,000 voters. Although the total expected gain of $20,000 clearly exceeds the cost, no individual taxpayer would be willing to mount such an investigation (and the 'free-rider' problem would make it difficult to organize sufficient taxpayers to cover the $10,000 cost). Accordingly, it is to be expected that voters will devote very little of their time and resources to the monitoring of government activities. Extensive monitoring, by voters, will only occur with respect to those government activities that have major impacts on individuals—such as public education—and with respect to those functions that can be observed at little cost—such as street-cleaning.

## 2.3 Consumers

As those who consume the product of a government agency are also voters, they have the same goals, and are subject to the same constraints, as are voters in general. They differ, however, in two important ways. First, as they are affected directly by the actions of the agency, they will have more information about the agency's operations, and will be willing to spend more money obtaining additional information, than will the average voter. For example, truckers and bus drivers could be expected to have more information about highways than would most voters and could be expected to derive greater benefits from purchases of additional information. Second, users of a public service have an incentive to 'free ride' on other taxpayers by exaggerating the benefits the service provides. Assume, for example, that in a jurisdiction of 1,000,000 taxpayers an expenditure of $100,000 would provide a benefit of $100 to each of 500 consumers. If those consumers could convince the government that they each benefited by $300 (for a total of $150,000), and thereby could convince the government to spend the required $100,000, the consumers would each obtain a benefit of $100 in return for an increase in their average tax bills of only $100,000/1,000,000 = $0.10.

The government agency does not always confer benefits on consumers; it may also impose external costs on some. Those who value unspoiled wilderness, for example, may object to the development of government campgrounds in national parks—both because of their direct effects, through the construction of roads, felling of trees, etc., and because of their indirect effects, through the attraction of visitors to areas that would otherwise be left unblemished. Like those who benefit from government production, those who suffer from the effects of external costs may attempt to employ their superior knowledge about the issues to sway public opinion. Environmentalists and animal rights activists, for example, can be expected to exaggerate, or at least emphasize, both the benefits of wilderness areas and the harms being inflicted on those areas by campers, hikers, and skiers.

### 2.4 Civil Servants

Finally, it is usually assumed that civil servants attempt to maximize personal utility, which in turn is a function of such factors as income, fringe benefits, and security.[2] The constraints on this goal are those placed by the government. These constraints may include: control of the size of the agency's budget; direct controls on salary levels, educational requirements, and numbers of employees; incentive schemes to encourage increased productivity; legislated limits on the scope of the agency's functions; and codes of conduct. On the other hand, agency employees will be able to use their superior access to information (about their own activities) to thwart government attempts to control them. Also, agency employees will normally have a greater vested interest in the outcome of attempts to constrain their actions than will the minister who is their nominal head. Thus, they can be expected to be willing to spend more to protect their positions than the minister will be willing to spend to criticize them.

### 2.5 Hypotheses

Employing these assumptions about the goals of the various interest groups, it is possible to develop a number of hypotheses concerning the functioning of government agencies.

*(a) Employee compensation will be higher in the public than in the private sector.* Early models of the government sector (see, especially, Niskanen, 1971) assumed that because politicians and voters had little information concerning the day-to-day functioning of government agencies, civil servants would be left to set their own salaries and working conditions (subject to fairly broad guidelines). An obvious criticism of these models in Canada is that the salaries of most junior civil servants are set by collective bargaining. Thus, anyone who wishes to obtain information concerning these salaries can do so simply by reading the collective agreements or by reading the summaries of those agreements in publications such as Labour Canada's *Collective Bargaining Review*. And the salaries of civil servants as senior as deputy ministers are often reported in newspapers. Therefore, it would be expected that the government would receive pressure from voters to keep civil servants' salaries in line with what voters perceived to be 'fair' levels.

If a clearly defined labour market rate of pay existed for each occupation employed by the government—for example, if all private-sector secretaries received exactly $1,500 per month—this pressure from voters could be converted into simple government guidelines, such as: all government secretaries are to be paid exactly the same salaries as are private-sector secretaries. But market rates of pay are not clearly defined, in part because levels of productivity vary across workers within the same occupation and in part because many public-sector positions have no private-sector equivalents with which they can be compared. As a result, government efforts to control civil service salaries are not likely to achieve more than the establishment of a rough ceiling on those salaries.[3]

This will leave civil servants with a considerable amount of leeway to capture some elements of their agency's budget. For example, by exaggerating the complexities of their jobs, civil servants may be able to convince the government to set their salaries at the top end of the market distribution of earnings. Or, because fringe benefits are less easily monitored than salaries and because, typically, few details are known about the fringe benefits offered by private-sector employers, civil servants may be able to extract part of the budget surplus in the form of fringe benefits. If voters and government members have difficulty monitoring the productivity of civil servants, civil service salaries could be raised, *de facto*, by promoting workers into jobs for which they were not qualified. Some of the agency's budget also may be captured in the form of overstaffing, that is, the government agency might hire considerably more workers than necessary, thereby lightening the workload for each of them. Or, in a similar vein, senior civil servants might reduce their own workloads by hiring assistants with higher qualifications than those that would normally be required for private-sector assistants. Thus, this model of the government sector predicts that:

- civil servants' salaries will be above the average of private-sector salaries;
- civil servants will receive considerably more fringe benefits than their private-sector counterparts;
- government agencies will be overstaffed; and
- the average level of qualifications required for civil service jobs will exceed that required for private-sector jobs.

*(b) Government agencies will provide services of 'excessive' quality and quantity.* The consumers of government services—such as users of public campgrounds or law courts—will find it in their interests to lobby the government to provide more facilities, and facilities of much higher quality than

would have been provided by the private sector. The reason for this is that voters at large, and not consumers in particular, pay for these facilities. If the government spends $600,000 instead of $300,000 developing campgrounds or courtrooms, for example, the benefits to the individual consumer will increase by 100 per cent, whereas the costs to that consumer, as a voter/taxpayer, will increase only infinitesimally. Because the majority of the costs are transferred to someone else, the consumer has an incentive to ask the government to continue production *beyond* the point at which the value of additional production falls below its cost.

This theory suggests why the government is often observed to produce more facilities, of higher quality, than does the private sector. It is *not*, as many commentators incorrectly assume, because the private sector reduces quality and quantity below the socially desired level in an effort to cut costs, but because the public sector produces excessive quality and quantity in response to demands from those who expect to benefit from such excesses without having to pay for them in full.

*(c) Consumers will not 'get what they want'.* It is generally argued that, in competitive markets, firms are induced by the profit motive always to 'give consumers what they want'. For example, if there are consumers willing to pay more to obtain higher quality than is currently being offered by most firms, or who would rather pay less because they would prefer to obtain lower quality, it will be to at least one firm's advantage to respond to this demand. As a result we observe that private firms offer a wide variety of qualities of products. Overnight accommodation, for example, ranges from the most basic of roadside motels to the most luxurious of resort hotels; and restaurants range from simple coffee shops and fast-food joints to five-star purveyors of cordon bleu.

Such is not the case with respect to government-provided services. Instead, these services tend to be of uniform quality. The reason is twofold. First, as was seen above, because customers pay for only a fraction of the costs of government services, they press for high quality. And, second, as the government finds it difficult to justify offering higher-quality services to one set of 'customers' than to another, all services tend to be of the same quality.

This failure of government production is rarely recognized. Almost all studies that compare public- and private-sector producers concentrate on the relative costs of producing the 'same' product. But voters may be just as poorly served by a government agency that produces at a low cost but forces them to 'buy' a higher-quality good than they want as one that produces what they want but does so at a high cost. They might, for example, be no more satisfied with a government-operated automobile industry that was run efficiently but produced only Cadillacs as one that was run inefficiently but provided a wide selection of models.

(d) *Insufficient resources will be devoted to innovation and experimentation.* Public-sector agencies have less incentive than private firms either to devise new products or to adopt new products devised elsewhere. The reason for this is that there are often considerable risks involved in both of these processes. In the private sector these risks are offset to some extent by the promise of significant profits if the new product is successful. In the public sector, however, the government is generally unable to monitor employees closely. As a result, there is only a loose connection between the level or quality of the output an agency produces and the salaries paid to its employees. Employees perceive, therefore, that the risk of failure associated with innovation is only imperfectly balanced by promises of rewards for success and they opt for the 'safe' approach.

Furthermore, not only does imperfect monitoring mean an imperfect correlation between the efforts and the salaries of employees, it also means that there will be an imperfect correlation between the efforts and the budgets of agencies as a whole. Assume, for example, that the park service is responsible for running a profitable attraction, such as a hot spring, or for negotiating the lease with a profitable park tenant, such as a hotel or ski resort. Assume also that the park service will earn a profit even if it puts relatively little effort into these activities. As the minister will have little information about the amount of profit that would be earned in the absence of a significant effort, he/she will be unable to determine how much extra profit would have been generated had the park service devoted a considerable amount of time and effort either to improving the operation of its attractions or to extracting additional revenue from its tenants. The result is that it may be difficult for the minister to 'reward' extra effort on the part of the agency, meaning that the agency will have little incentive to make that effort.

(e) *The public agency will not operate at minimum cost.* For the same reasons that public agencies can be expected to underinvest in expenditures on innovation, they can also be expected to devote inadequate efforts to the reduction of costs. That is, as the minister will not be well informed concerning the lowest costs that could have been obtained by the public agency, he/she will be unable to reward the agency for reducing costs and the agency's employees will be provided with little incentive to devote effort to that activity.

Furthermore, the minister will generally be at less of an 'information disadvantage' relative to his/her civil servants with respect to proposals for new programs than with respect to existing programs. For this reason, it can be expected that ministers will scrutinize requests for changes in programs much more carefully than they will requests for renewals of existing programs, thereby discouraging civil servants from bringing forward proposals for significant restructuring, even when such restructuring would result in cost savings.

In many cases, the tendency for government agencies to make requests for only marginal changes in programs will just slow their progress towards the cost-minimizing set of policies. In others, however, this tendency may lead the agency to move away from the cost-minimizing strategy. For example, it is not uncommon to find that the growth of small towns has left post offices short of post boxes while it has increased the market value of the post office buildings dramatically. The cost-minimizing policy would appear to be to sell the building, transferring the post box and mail-sorting operations to less central locations, where additional space could be purchased, and the retail sales operations to smaller facilities. Because such a policy would require a dramatic restructuring, however, it is likely to attract much greater attention from the minister than would a less ambitious proposal such as increasing the level of door-to-door delivery services (while maintaining the existing building). The incremental approach in this case will force the post office into offering more and more delivery services even if the cost-minimizing policy is to offer additional post boxes at a decentralized location.

## 3. ALTERNATIVE METHODS OF DELIVERING GOVERNMENT SERVICES: A TYPOLOGY

The general purpose of this chapter is to identify whether the Alberta government chose to undertake those restructurings for which the net advantages were the greatest. Two steps must be taken before this question can be answered: the alternative forms of delivery of government services must be identified; and the relative advantages and disadvantages of these forms must be investigated. The former step is taken in this section; the latter in section 4.

### 3.1 Public-Sector Agencies
Clearly, one possibility is that government services could be provided by the public sector. But the public sector is not a monolithic organization. Within that sector, a number of alternative methods of delivering services are possible. I consider four here, in roughly ascending order of the percentage of the agency budget that is obtained from users of the service. In each of these cases, a distinction is drawn between 'the government'—by which I mean elected members of the legislature and their senior advisers—and 'the public agency'—by which I mean the branch of the civil service established to perform a particular public function.

#### Contract Monopoly
At one extreme is the situation in which the public agency acts as a government-operated monopoly. In this model, the public agency may be thought of as

receiving a 'contract' from the government in return for a fixed sum—the 'budget'—to be the sole provider of a government service. These contracts contain general instructions concerning how the budget is to be spent. But there are no other constraints or incentives, except those provided by the implicit threat that if funds are not spent wisely this year, the budget may be reduced in the future. A police department's mandate to preserve the peace represents an example of this type of relationship between the government and one of its agencies.

## Regulated Monopoly

One of the problems that arises when public agencies are operated as contract monopolies is that only very broad, non-specific incentives are provided to the agency to pursue government policy. In some situations it might be possible to minimize the resulting problems by establishing a reward/incentive system. I call this form of public agency a 'regulated monopoly' as the government is able to use this incentive system to regulate the behaviour of its employees.

Two types of incentive system have been suggested. In the first, public agencies are allowed to keep some portion of the revenues they collect—with the amount retained sometimes being based on the size of the differential between revenues and costs. Such systems have been used only rarely in Canada as they reduce the control the legislature exerts over government spending. In particular, when agencies that collect revenues are allowed to retain those revenues, the legislature no longer has full control over the distribution of funds among departments. Nevertheless, a number of experiments are currently being conducted in Canada, particularly by the federal government, in which agencies are 'rewarded' for reducing costs or increasing revenues.

A second form of regulation has been popularized by the New Zealand government (Boston, 1992). There, senior government officials—primarily at the deputy minister level—have been hired on a contract basis. These contracts, which normally run for five years, specify in some detail what the government's expectations are to be for the individual over the duration of the contract. The underlying principle behind these contracts is that the salaries of senior government officials are to be tied to the performance of their agencies. Also, their salaries are to be competitive with those of their private-sector counterparts.

## Intragovernmental Competition

One way of obtaining the advantages of competitive bidding without contracting services to the private sector is to encourage public-sector agencies to compete among themselves. Such competition is easiest to arrange when, for geographical reasons, numerous regional and local agencies offer similar services. For example, hospitals within a region could compete with one another to offer specialized services such as cardiac surgery; small hospital districts could contract with larger ones to perform specialized procedures; small school districts could 'hire' larger ones to provide specialized testing or curriculum development; and one social service district could pay another to provide training or residential care for its more difficult cases.

### Competitive Firms

Finally, some government services could be operated like private firms, obtaining all of their funds from user fees charged to customers and paying for all of their expenses out of those funds. The three hot pools operated by Parks Canada in the Rocky Mountain parks represent a clear example. These pools are now run as 'enterprise units'. Instead of sending their revenues to Ottawa and receiving in return a budget set by a central agency, the hot pools now retain their revenues, which they use to pay for all of their costs, including capital expenditures. The government of Manitoba is also experimenting with a similar model, which it calls 'special operating agencies'.

### 3.2 Contracting Out to Private Firms

A second alternative is to contract services to private firms. These contracts can be categorized in at least three ways: by the degree of competition allowed; by the manner in which the contract is negotiated; and by the nature of the remuneration to be paid.

### Competition

In most circumstances the contractor will become the sole supplier of the service in question—the janitorial firm that cleans the government agency's offices or the construction company that builds a particular stretch of highway, for example. In others, however, the agency might contract with more than one supplier and allow its employees to choose among those suppliers. An agency might, for example, allow its employees to choose from among two or three office supply companies or printing firms. Similarly, some agencies might give 'vouchers' to their clients to allow them to choose among private suppliers. A social welfare department might, for example, allow food stamps to be used at a large number of supermarkets; and a school board might allow parents to use educational vouchers at any certified private school.

### Method of Negotiation

If it appears that only one private-sector firm is capable of performing a particular service, the government might negotiate solely with that firm over the nature of the contract. More commonly, however, more than one firm will be willing to bid for the government contract. Two alternative approaches to negotiating the terms of the contract appear possible. First, the agency could establish a contract price in advance and either accept all bids, or decide among bids on the basis of some non-price criterion such as quality of service. Alternatively, the agency may employ a competitive tendering or auction process in which businesses compete on some combination of price, quality, and quantity of a service to be provided to the agency—as in the case of firms competing for a contract to provide janitorial or accounting services.

### Pricing

Two types of pricing policies are possible—fixed and variable. In a fixed price contract between a government agency and a private firm, one party agrees to pay the other a pre-arranged fee. When a municipality hires a firm to collect garbage, for example, the contract normally specifies that the firm is to be paid a fixed price per household or per month. Similarly, when a private firm obtains the right to provide a profit-making service, such as a campsite in a provincial park, the contract may specify that the firm is to pay a fixed annual rent. Alternatively, the contract may tie the level of remuneration to some measure of the private firm's success. For example, the fee payable by a hospital board to a clinic that has contracted to provide day surgery may depend on factors such as the number of operations performed or a measure of patient satisfaction.

## 3.3 Privatization

Under the contracting-out alternative, the government agency retains the responsibility to provide a service but hires a private firm to perform that service on its behalf. In contrast, when the government privatizes a service, it sells that service to the private sector. Normally, the private sector will only pay a positive price for such services if those services are sold directly to the public. Some common examples of services that might be privatized include: the publication branches of many government departments; nursing home facilities; day-care and kindergarten services; public campgrounds; leisure centres; and commercial garbage disposal. Some government administrative services, such as motor vehicle licensing and safety inspections, may also be privatized as long as the government maintains a regulatory role and users are required or are willing to pay a fee for those services.

## 3.4 Non-Profit Organizations

An alternative often given less attention than it deserves is to tender services to non-profit organizations. At least three methods of accomplishing this are evident.

### Grants

The public agency could provide grants to organizations that agreed to provide services the agency had previously operated at a loss. For example, a municipality might pay an environmental or historical group to run a local museum.

*Bids*

Where a service could be expected to generate a profit, non-profit organizations could be asked to tender bids to be allowed to operate that service. For example, the parks service might allow a hostelling, cross-country skiing, or mountaineering society to operate an alpine hostel.

*Creation of New Organizations*

A third, closely related alternative would be to establish or encourage the establishment of non-profit organizations to undertake activities that would otherwise have been provided by the government. Local volunteers might be organized, for example, to provide routine maintenance activities at city parks; charitable organizations might be given assistance in establishing food banks or hostels for the homeless; and producers' organizations might appropriate the government's role in the regulation of industry safety or licensing.

### 3.5 Abandonment

Finally, the public agency might simply cease to provide a service it had previously performed, on the assumption that if it was sufficiently valued by user or special interest groups, those groups would step in and re-establish the service themselves. An example might be the provision of a provincial or municipal tourist information booth. If the government were to abandon responsibility for such a function, it is quite possible that local businesses might form an association to provide a substitute service.

### 4. ALTERNATIVE TYPES OF GOVERNMENT SERVICES AND THEIR OPTIMAL METHODS OF DELIVERY

### 4.1 Contracting Out

One of the most important characteristics to be taken into account when analysing the merits of contracting out is the extent to which production of the service requires investment in capital goods specific to that service. Two problems are created when capital is specific in this way. If the capital is owned by the government but used by a private contractor, incentives must be provided to ensure that the contractor maintains the capital properly. If the capital is to be provided by the contractor, either some mechanism must be provided to ensure that the contractor is compensated for that investment at the end of the contract or the contract must be of sufficient duration to allow the contractor to recoup its investment. To simplify the discussion, I will deal first with those cases in which no investments are required in specific capital. The complications that arise when capital is specific are dealt with later.

*Non-Specific Capital*

The capital employed in a project may be considered to be 'non-specific' if it can be transferred easily to another project at the conclusion of a contract. Even goods as specialized as fire trucks and city buses will fit this category if there is a second-hand market for such products. Buildings may also prove to be non-specific if they can be converted to private use following completion of a government contract.

Contracts involving non-specific capital will be easier to write and to enforce if the service to be provided is easily measured than if the service is of a more nebulous nature. It will be easier, for example, to specify the product of a contract to clear snow from a specified set of streets than the product of a contract to provide food services to a large hospital.

***Output is easily measured.*** If the service the government agency wishes produced is easily measured and the private-sector firms that offer those services operate in competitive industries, there would appear to be a strong argument for contracting out. The government agency could announce the precise specifications of the product it wished provided and then take bids from firms to supply that product. Because the firms would be competing with one another, there would be an incentive for each firm to provide its services at the lowest possible cost—unlike a public-sector supplier whose incentive to economize would be blunted by its monopoly position. Furthermore, because the quality and quantity of the firm's production are easily identifiable, the agency would be able to ensure that the firms that provided the winning bids fulfilled their contractual obligations, thereby avoiding any problems arising from conflicts between the goals of the government and those of the contractors.

These results could not be predicted as confidently if any of the contractors were the sole suppliers of their products. In such a case, the assumption that competition would keep costs to a minimum would not hold (although the probability that other firms would consider entering competition would increase as the price charged to the government increased). This is not to say, however, that the government agency could be expected to provide the service at a lower cost than the private firm. As the agency would also be a monopolist in such a circumstance, it also would be protected from competitive pressures to keep its costs down.

A number of alternative policies present themselves in this circumstance. One might be to require that the government agency contract out the service and maintain vigilant supervision over the contractor's costs. A second would be to encourage competition among different government agencies to provide the service, or to introduce incentives for the government agency to minimize costs or improve service, such as bonuses to agency heads who meet pre-specified goals.

A third method of increasing competition when there is only a limited number of private firms is to encourage the government agency to compete with the private firms in the tendering process. For example, if a municipality was to seek to contract out the provision of garbage collection, it might encourage its existing public works department to compete with private bidders. To obtain the maximum benefits from this policy, the agency tendering the contract must ensure that the internal (government) and external (private) bidders are treated equally. Otherwise, the external bidders will come to perceive that they are at a disadvantage in the tendering process and they may, in the long run, withdraw from that process.

Equality requires that the external bidders be given access to the same information about the service to be tendered as is available to the employees of the internal bidder. It also requires that if the bid tendered by the external bidder proves to be the winning bid, the internal bidder should not be offered the option of meeting that bid. The reason for this is that the cost savings or quality improvements offered by the external bidder may result from ideas or information concerning the restructuring of the agency that had not been known to agency employees. If the agency is allowed to 'borrow' these ideas from the private bidder without compensation, potential bidders will learn that there will be little or no return on their investments in the preparation of government tenders. In the long run, therefore, they will refuse to bid on government contracts and the advantages of competitive tendering will be lost.

***Output is not easily measured.*** When the quantity and quality of output cannot be measured easily, there may be an incentive for contracting firms to produce at the lowest quantity and quality levels consistent with the wording of their contracts. If a janitorial contract requires that floors be cleaned once a week, there may be an incentive for the contractor to apply a very loose interpretation of the word 'clean'; and if a contract calls for the provision of nutritious food to a hospital, the contractor may attempt to minimize its costs by meeting nutritional requirements at the expense of variety or palatability. A number of alternative methods are apparent for ensuring that the quality of privately provided services is maintained.

First, detailed controls over quality could be written into contracts with private suppliers. As there will be substantial fixed costs of writing such contracts, this policy would appear to be most attractive in situations in which the government can spread the costs of contract-writing across a large number of similar contracts. For example, a rural school board that hired a different busing contractor in each of a large number of small towns might develop a standard contract for such services. Where this can be done, the pressures of competitive tendering would be expected to lead to production at lower cost than would have been achieved by the government had it provided the service itself.

Second, if there is competition among private providers of a service, it might not be necessary to impose tight controls to ensure that they provide the desired quality. For example, if more than one firm was willing to provide janitorial services, an agency dissatisfied with the quality of service it was receiving from a private contractor could credibly threaten to take its business to another company when its current contract expired. This policy is more likely to be successful if the average duration of contracts is short—that is, the more frequently contractors are subjected to competitive forces. Thus, as firms employing non-specific capital will require shorter contracts than firms employing specific capital—because the latter require a sufficient period over which to repay their investments—the threat of competition will be more credible in the former type of market than in the latter.

If the private sector is not competitive and it is prohibitively expensive to write contracts that specify quality and quantity expectations clearly, three options remain: the service can, nevertheless, be contracted to the private sector; the government can continue to provide the service itself; or competition can be created by allowing the existing agency's employees to bid against the private firm for the contract to provide the service. Of these options, the former appears the least desirable. Although it was argued in section 2 of this chapter that government agencies could not be expected to be operated efficiently, the prime argument in support of that view was that the government does not face competitive pressures. As a private monopoly would be equally sheltered from competition, there is not a strong reason for believing that such a firm would be operated more efficiently than a government agency. Further, as the owners of a private firm will be in a better position to benefit personally from cost savings than will the employees of a public agency, private operators face a comparably greater incentive to sacrifice quality in order to reduce costs. For these reasons, it may be preferable to leave monopoly production with a public agency when the quality of the product is not easily measured.

This does not mean, however, that private production should be rejected altogether in these circumstances. The optimal policy may be to create competition by allowing the public agency to bid against the (monopoly) private firm. It can be determined immediately that such a policy would require that if the private firm is the successful bidder, it cannot be allowed to replace the agency's senior personnel with its own. If it were to do so, the replaced individuals could not reasonably be expected to remain a cohesive group for long enough that they would represent a serious competitive threat when the private firm's contract was concluded. To maintain the level of competition created by allowing government employees to bid against private-sector firms, a winning private-sector bidder must only be allowed to obtain a management contract.

When provision is made for such contracts, the advantages of private-sector production of services over public production increase significantly. Most importantly, competitive bidders have an incentive to obtain information concerning potential sources of improved efficiency and provide that information to the elected officials who are responsible for the operation of the tendered service. This obviates two of the primary sources of government inefficiency: the inequity in information between elected officials and civil servants; and the lack of incentive on the part of civil servants to propose innovative ideas. Indeed, the tendering of management contracts appears sufficiently attractive that it is difficult to imagine a government service that could not be offered in this way to the advantage of the government.

### Specific Capital

In many cases, investment in long-term capital is a pre-condition for the provision of a public service. If this capital is specific to public-sector production—that is, it cannot easily be transferred to alternative uses—one of two obstacles to contracting out arises. On the one hand, if the government offers a contract of sufficient duration that the private investor is able to recoup its investment, the advantages of competitive bidding will be lost during the term of that contract. On the other hand, if the government offers only short-term contracts, some method will have to be found to ensure either that the contractor receives a fair price for its investments when the contract is terminated or that the contractor is provided adequate incentive to provide upkeep for its investment during the term of the contract.

For example, assume that a school board is considering building an elementary school in a new subdivision. In the absence of an agreement concerning a fair transfer price for investments in the school building, a private firm might bid on the construction (and operation) of the school only if the contract offered to it was as long as 20 years or more. Such a contract is sufficiently long that it gives the private operator significant monopoly powers with respect to the school board, powers the board could mitigate by building and operating the school itself. Alternatively, the private firm could be given a contract shorter than the useful life of the building—say, three or four years—in order to maintain the advantages of competitive tendering. In this case, adequate incentives would have to be offered to the contractor to ensure that it did not allow the building to deteriorate. Two general approaches can be taken to reach this objective: the school board could build the school itself and employ a private contractor to operate the building on its behalf or the private firm could be employed to build the school and the contract could specify a method for ensuring that the firm received a fair market value for the building when its contract expired. I consider each of these options in turn.

*Investments in specific capital are made by the government agency.* There are numerous situations in which it would be possible for government agencies to contract the operation of their facilities to third parties. A simple example of such a situation is that in which the parks service hires a private contractor to operate a government-owned campground. The roads, campsites, toilet facilities, electrical hookups, etc. have been built by the parks service and the contractor's responsibility may include the setting of campground fees, admission of customers, maintenance of order, and repair of the grounds, in return for which it may be expected to remit a fee to the parks service. Other similar facilities might include schools, fire departments, museums, and swimming pools.

Two problems arise when contracting out such services to private firms. First, as was noted above, some incentive has to be provided to ensure that the facilities are maintained. Second, a method has to be found to ensure that the desired quality of service is obtained. A great many alternative techniques have been suggested for dealing with these problems. Five of these will be considered here—in the first three of these, private firms operate the facility; in the fourth the operator is a non-government, non-profit agency; and in the fifth the public agency operates the facility itself.

*(i) Short-term tendering.* As has been noted previously, one method of ensuring that private operators both maintain the quality of a facility's capital assets and offer the desired quality of service would be to tender only short-term contracts. In this way, if it became apparent that the operator was not living up to the government's expectations, the contract could be awarded to a different firm at the end of the current term—provided only that there was a competitive market in the production of the service. Not only would this approach provide an incentive for operators to maintain quality, the government would not have to monitor the facility closely as competing firms would find it in their interests to do so—in order to argue that they, and not the incumbent, should be awarded the next contract.

*(ii) Long-term contracts for services sold in competitive markets.* It may also be possible to maintain the quality and quantity of public services within long-term contracts as long as contractors obtain a significant portion of their revenues from sale of the service in competitive product markets. For example, if a public campground was one among a large number of campgrounds in a particular area, competition among them could be expected to force the operators of the public campground to offer the quality of service demanded by customers. The operators would, for example, be induced to ensure that employees were courteous and that the campsites were kept clean. Thus, it would not be necessary to offer short-term contracts in order to obtain the desired level of quality. In turn, this would allow the use of long-term contracts, thereby minimizing the possibility that the operator would have little interest in maintaining

the facility's capital assets. Any deterioration in a campground's buildings or roads, for example, would lead to a reduction in the operator's long-run profits in much the same way as if the operator had owned those assets.

The primary drawback to this technique—other than the prerequisite requirement that there be a competitive market—arises when the services demanded by customers differ from those desired by the government agency. As the private operator of the government facility will respond to customer demand, a tension between public and private goals may be created. For example, the private operator of a campground in an environmentally sensitive area might be less vigilant about blocking campers' access to that area than would be the parks service, particularly if campers were more willing to stay in a campground that allowed such access than in one that did not. Thus, in those cases in which it was difficult for the government agency to monitor the private operator's activity, it might be preferable to rely on a technique other than the awarding of long-term contracts.[4]

*(iii) Long-term contracts for services that are not sold to the public.* It is difficult to conceive of a situation in which it would be to the government's advantage to issue a long-term contract to a firm to operate a government facility funded primarily from government revenues. First, there is no advantage to issuing a long-term contract in such a case relative to a short-term contract. Second, a private firm operating under a long-term contract has a greater incentive to reduce the quality of service than would civil servants providing the same service. Whereas civil servants find it difficult to direct the cost savings from quality reduction to their personal benefit, private operators are able to capture such savings in the form of management fees or dividends. In short, it is not expected that long-term contracts of this type would be observed.

*(iv) Contracts with non-profit agencies.* In those cases in which it is difficult to measure quality, the government agency might subcontract the service to an interest group whose goals were known to be consonant with those of the agency. For example, although it might be difficult to write a contract for the operation of a museum in such a way as to ensure that a private firm would provide the desired level of service, a local historical society might ensure that such a level of service was provided even in the absence of controls. A contract with an interest group of this type will need to include only terms concerning easily verified factors such as price and numbers of worker-hours to be provided. Similarly, operation of a tourist information centre might be subcontracted to a chamber of commerce.

*(v) Government production.* The preceding analysis suggests that the primary circumstance in which government operation of a government facility would be superior to private operation is that in which there is no competitive market in either the production or consumption of the service.

*Decisions concerning investments in specific capital are made by private firms.* If decisions concerning investments in specific capital are made by the government, the potential gains from competitive tendering of the capital project are lost. The government may, therefore, wish to involve the private sector in both the design and operation of capital projects.

*(i) Management contracts with capital design.* Instead of calling for bids to manage a facility after it has been built, the government agency could call for a joint bid to design, build, and manage the facility. For example, a hospital that wished to construct a laundry might call for a joint bid to design and operate it. The government would pay for the construction. If management contracts were of sufficiently short duration, then subsequent tenders could call for bidders to suggest revisions that could be made to the existing capital stock. The primary drawback to this approach is that it is not clear how decisions concerning investments to be made *during* the contract would be negotiated.

*(ii) Depreciation.* An alternative method of encouraging a private firm to make capital investments is to agree to purchase the equipment from the firm, at its depreciated value, upon the completion of the contract. The depreciated value can be calculated by using accounting procedures, by establishing a contractual agreement with the contractor, or by obtaining an estimate of the asset's market value. The disadvantage of the first of these approaches is that, in many cases, the 'book value' of the asset will not vary with the asset's 'use value'. That is, regardless of the amount of repairs and maintenance carried out by the owner, the resale value of the capital will remain unchanged. Thus, the owner will be given inadequate incentive to maintain the asset unless the parties agree to compensate the contractor for expenditures made during the term of the contract—expenditures the agency would have to approve. The disadvantage of the market value approach is that there may only be a 'thin' market for the asset in question. Thus, evaluators will have inadequate reference points on which to base an estimate of the asset's value.

*(iii) Auctions.* It might appear that it would be possible to place a value on the asset by auctioning it. Unfortunately, such an auction cannot be organized. The reason for this is that, at the end of the contract, the government agency wishes to auction both the asset and the contract to manage that asset, and the two cannot be disentangled. For example, assume that a private firm has built and operated a rural hospital under contract to the local hospital board. At the completion of the contract, the hospital board will wish to auction the hospital facility and tender the management contract. The minimum price that bidders for the management contract will accept, $P$, equals the present discounted value of their operating costs, $C$, plus the amount they have agreed to pay the original contractor for the purchase of its assets, $A$. That is:

$$P_{min} = C + A$$

But the maximum value that bidders are willing to offer for the original contractor's capital assets equals the difference between P and C. That is:

$$A_{max} = P - C$$

As this equation is simply a rearrangement of the first one, there are two unknowns, P and A, and only one equation. In such a situation, it is not possible to obtain unique values for both the minimum contract bid and the maximum capital asset price.

*(iv) Capital leasing.* A final possibility is that capital investments approved by the government agency, and made by the private contractor, could be financed through a long-term capital lease with a financial institution. In this way, if the original contractor was not the successful bidder in a later round, the new contractor could assume the lease. Under this approach, contract bids would be composed of an amount to cover the cost of making the lease payments plus an amount to compensate the bidder for the cost of operating the assets over the term of the contract.

There are two advantages to this approach over that in which the ownership of the assets vests in the agency. First, financial institutions have expertise in both evaluating appropriate schedules of lease payments and in establishing appropriate schedules of repairs and maintenance to be followed by the lessee. The government agency would not need to negotiate these schedules itself. Second, the contractor would have less incentive to suggest unprofitable capital expenditures than if the capital was owned and paid for by the government agency.

### 4.2 Alternative Methods of Producing Government Services
Section 3 identified a number of methods of delivering government services in addition to contracting out. These methods will be discussed briefly here.

*Public-Sector 'Regulated Monopoly'*
The government could obtain some of the benefits of private contracting by offering incentives to its employees to improve government efficiency. The government might allow agencies to retain funds generated through cost savings, for example; or it might require that its senior employees agree to employment contracts with performance goals. Most such arrangements are inferior to private contracts with competitive firms, however. The New Zealand government has found, for example, that it is extremely difficult to set out clearly the goals of senior civil servants ahead of time. As a result, it becomes very difficult to discipline civil servants *ex post facto* for failing to meet those goals. Only the

most egregious failures can be penalized or self-evident successes rewarded.[5] Schemes to encourage departments to reduce costs by allowing them to retain some of the funds saved also encounter problems with misdirected incentives.

Whereas employee incentives must be spelled out very carefully in advance, usually with respect to goals that are not easily specified, competition among potential contractors ensures that private firms have a strong incentive to meet the government's objectives. Hence, it would be expected that incentive schemes would only be employed in those situations in which private production was inferior to public—such as the case in which only one private firm was willing to provide a service that required major capital investments.

### Intragovernmental Competition

In cases where it is not possible to obtain competitive bids from the private sector, some of the benefits of competitive tendering may be obtained by encouraging government agencies to bid against one another to produce government services. Such a policy requires that there are no significant economies of scale in production, as otherwise the government may be able to reduce costs by concentrating all of its production in one agency.

### Non-Profit Organizations

That voters as a group do not consider the benefits of a service to exceed the costs does not imply that there is no subgroup of citizens who would be willing to pay for that service. Thus, in cases in which the electorate has voted not to fund an activity, the government may be able to find a non-profit group that would be willing to provide that activity either for free or in return for a subsidy.

### Privatization

The arguments presented earlier suggest that, all else being equal, private-sector firms will produce at a lower cost than the public sector. In most cases, therefore, if a private firm is willing to provide a service at no cost to the government—by charging users for its services—there is a strong presumption that that service should be privatized (that is, sold to the private sector). The primary exceptions to this conclusion occur when the private firm is a monopolist or when production of the service in question produces an externality.

If the private firm enjoys monopoly power in the sale of its product, there will be no incentive for it to sell its product at the lowest possible price. Thus, although the desire to maximize profits may lead it to produce at low cost, the benefits of those savings will not be passed on to consumers. In contrast, whereas a public agency might not be expected to produce efficiently, taxpayers will not be asked to pay a monopoly profit surcharge on top of its costs. It is possible, therefore, that private and public monopolies will produce at roughly the same cost to the public and that there would be little to choose between them on this ground. This balance between the two can be altered, however, if the pricing policies of the private firm can be regulated by a government agency. Examples of this type of privatization/regulation include electrical utilities, railways, and airlines.

A second criticism of private firms is that they ignore external costs—costs they impose on society for which they are not required to pay—and, therefore, 'overproduce' the cost-imposing activity. Common examples include air and water pollution. Those who levy this criticism often implicitly assume that if the activity had been produced by the government, the externality would not have been generated. Both the models developed in section 2 of this chapter and observations of government behaviour suggest that this assumption cannot easily be defended. Furthermore, even if government agencies are less likely to create externalities than are *unregulated* private firms, it may well be the case that *regulated* private firms will produce fewer externalities than government agencies. The reason for this is that a government department established to regulate the production of externalities will have no greater incentive to monitor other government agencies than it will to monitor private-sector producers and, indeed, may be less willing to impose sanctions on 'fellow workers' than on an outside agency. In short, as there is no strong reason to believe that regulated private firms will produce more external costs than government agencies, and as private firms can be expected to operate more efficiently than government agencies, the presumption in favour of privatization is maintained.

*Abandonment*

'Abandonment' is merely a form of privatization in which the government charges no fee to the private firm for the right to provide a service that was previously provided by the government. Hence, the analysis is identical to that of privatization.

### 4.3 Conclusion

Economic theory suggests that a far wider variety of government services could be sold or contracted out to the private sector than has been the case in the past. Furthermore, a number of recent experiments have suggested that when services are provided by the government, improvements in efficiency can be obtained by encouraging intragovernmental competition, writing performance-based contracts with senior government employees, or allowing departments to retain some portion of the funds they save through cost-saving procedures. Given the Alberta government's stated goal of reducing budget deficits without impinging on the delivery of government services, it would be expected that significant changes would have been made to the manner in which those services are delivered. It is to a review of the Alberta experience that this chapter now turns.

## 5. THE ALBERTA EXPERIENCE

Although it is clear that the Alberta government is committed to a thorough rethinking of how it delivers government services, decisions about how revisions are to be put into effect have been left, for the most part, to civil servants within the various agencies. We surveyed a wide range of government agencies to determine how quickly and thoroughly they had revised their operational procedures. The responses to this survey are reported in this section. Three broad types of policy are identified: encouraging competitive behaviour within the government sector; contracting out government services; and privatizing government services.

### 5.1 Encouraging Competitive Behaviour within the Government

Section 3 introduced four methods of encouraging government agencies to act like private firms: allow agencies to retain funds they have saved by reducing costs; write performance contracts with senior civil servants; encourage competition among government agencies; and require that government agencies compete directly with the private sector. The Alberta experience with respect to each of these policies will be discussed here.

*Reward for Cost Reduction*
The Alberta deficit elimination program has not generated proposals to reward agencies for reducing costs. The reason for this may be seen by contrasting two approaches to deficit reduction. In one, the government attempts to induce agencies to reveal where cuts can be made most easily by offering rewards to those agencies that are most successful in reducing their expenditures. In the second, a central body decides how much is to be cut from each agency's budget and decrees that these cuts are to be made. In the latter program, incentives would be superfluous—except to the extent that civil servants have to be induced to make the required cuts—because no leeway has been provided to the agencies involved. As the Alberta experience most closely reflects the latter approach, it is not surprising that reward-based techniques for inducing cost savings have not been commonly proposed.

*Performance Contracts*
We found only one clear case in which senior civil servants had been given performance-based contracts. After the Southern Alberta Institute of Technology (SAIT) suffered a serious financial loss in the early 1990s, a new

president was hired. His contract required that he eliminate SAIT's debt within the term of his contract. SAIT's experience with this type of contract was sufficiently positive that it now plans to write limited-term performance-based contracts for all of its vice-presidents.

Two explanations may be given for why SAIT introduced these contracts when other agencies did not. First, unlike most government agencies, SAIT's goals are easily enunciated. Its purpose is to train students to fill clearly identified vacancies in the job market. The school actively and continuously monitors the numbers of applicants for each program, surveys employers to identify occupations in which there are currently, or are expected to be, shortages of qualified applicants, and follows graduates to determine whether they obtained jobs in the occupations for which they were trained. As a result, the success of the senior administrators at SAIT can be measured readily against the school's ability to meet the demands of the market for its graduates. This contrasts with most other government agencies, where it proves difficult to determine objectively whether the goals of those agencies have been met and, therefore, to determine whether senior civil servants should be rewarded.

Second, many agencies feel that three-year business plans, which were introduced as part of the deficit elimination program, substitute in many ways for individual-specific performance contracts. As the business plans contain detailed specifications of agency goals, they can and have been used to develop criteria against which the agencies are measured. To the extent that these business plans constitute implicit contracts with either the agencies or their employees, they may act as close substitutes for explicit performance contracts. In this light, the use of three-year business plans may represent a 'second-best' solution to the difficulty governments encounter in writing enforceable performance contracts with senior civil servants.

It should also be mentioned that, in recognition of the difficulty of establishing clear goals for civil servants, the government is attempting to develop Key Performance Indicators for each sector. Although the government currently intends to use these indicators to evaluate the performance of departments, a strong possibility exists that they may also be used to evaluate individual administrators.

*Intragovernmental Competition*
Major experiments with intragovernmental competition are being planned in two Alberta departments: Education and Health. In Health, the practice had previously been to fund individual hospital boards, and sometimes individual hospitals, on an *ad hoc* basis. Any one of the 200 hospital boards could make a request for funds, with the likelihood of success depending not only on the inherent benefits of the proposal but also on factors such as the availability of

funds and the political power of the particular board. It is commonly asserted that inequities in funding and duplication of services resulted.

In an effort to rectify these problems, Alberta Health replaced the hospital boards with 17 Regional Health Authorities (RHAs). Furthermore, the RHAs are to be funded primarily on a per capita basis, with funding to be determined by density of population and demographic factors. There will be no requirement, however, that RHAs spend all of their funds within their own districts. It is anticipated that only a few hospitals will specialize in low-volume, highly capital-intensive procedures such as heart surgery. Two methods have been proposed for compensating the RHAs that provide these procedures. One possibility is that when one RHA sends patients requiring these procedures to a hospital in another district, the funds will 'follow' the patient directly. Alternatively, if sufficient patients are observed to be moving from one RHA to another, Alberta Health may adjust its formula to increase the funds being paid to the RHA performing the specialized procedures. In either case, the possibility exists that RHAs may compete with one another to attract patients from other districts. Although most participants implicitly assume that the Calgary and Edmonton hospitals will ultimately offer most of the specialist services, smaller cities may attempt to attract patients into hospitals whose facilities would otherwise be underutilized.

Alberta Education also encourages intragovernmental competition (see Chapter 10). First, like RHAs, school boards are funded on a per capita basis. If a student who lives in one school district chooses to attend a school in another district, the per capita grant applicable to that student is transferred to the district of instruction. Second, and perhaps more importantly, parent groups have been allowed to establish charter schools which are funded by the province yet in which parents determine the curriculum and hire the teachers (provided both meet provincially established standards). Although only three of the first 14 applications for such schools were accepted, the threat implied by charter schools may have a competitive impact on the existing school system—particularly on urban school boards.

### Government Competition with the Private Sector

It is also possible that government agencies could operate like private firms, in direct competition with the private sector. We are unaware of any situations in which a government agency in Alberta has responded to the deficit elimination program by establishing a branch whose purpose is to compete with the private sector. This is not surprising given the government's frequently stated preference to restrict government activities to those that cannot be provided privately.

## 5.2 Contracting Out

With few exceptions, decisions concerning contracting out were left to the individual agencies. Very little direction was provided from the political arm of the government. A Niskanen-type model (see Chapter 3) would predict that, in such a circumstance, employees would attempt to restrict the number of contracts issued in order to preserve their own jobs and influence. In most cases, Niskanen's predictions were verified. If the Department of Labour is excluded, departments can be divided into two broad categories: those with little experience of contracting out prior to 1993, and those that had been contracting out an increasing number of services prior to 1993. Although both increased their levels of contracting out, neither made significant changes.

*Departments with Little Experience of Contracting Out*
Agencies that had done little contracting out before 1993 included hospital boards (now Regional Health Authorities), school boards, and Treasury.

Our survey found that most of the health authorities in the smaller regions were not even considering contracting out their services. In some this was because they felt constrained by union contracts; in others it appeared that they simply had not had time to consider the matter. The larger regions indicated that they had been inundated with private-sector proposals for contracting out services but also had not had the time to give these proposals serious consideration. The only major contract we were able to identify was issued by the Calgary RHA to provide ophthalmological surgery. The remaining contracts were for secondary programs such as laboratory and dietary services. Nevertheless, budget-cutting pressures in Health are sufficient that we expect to see significant moves towards contracting out once the current restructuring of the hospital system is completed. Contracts to private surgical units, to private long-stay hospitals, and to private nursing supply agencies are all being considered.

School boards have also made little progress towards contracting out. Prior to the deficit elimination program, many had contracted out transportation services, computer programming (in central administration), and caretaking. But almost no change has occurred as a result of the deficit elimination program. Some school boards indicated that contracting out was simply not under consideration while others felt themselves to be restricted by the provisions of their collective bargaining agreements. Furthermore, in some cases in which boards had discussed the contracting out of caretaking services, the boards' own employees had offered to match the bids made by private firms and had been allowed to continue providing those services.

The school boards suggested that little contracting out had occurred because very few services *could* be contracted out—typically, caretaking, busing, cafeteria services, computer programming, and psychological testing were mentioned as the only services considered. An equally plausible explanation is that the budget cuts to Education were simply not deep enough to encourage serious evaluation of more fundamental changes. No consideration was given to contracting out the provision of teaching services, for example. Yet, ECS had been provided by private operators for many years before it was absorbed by the government. And the operation of public schools has now been contracted out in some jurisdictions in the United States (Hill, 1995; Evans and Carroll, 1995). Although school boards' ability to contract out these services is constrained by their collective bargaining agreements with the teachers' association, this issue could have been resolved if the incentives had been strong enough.

Treasury has contracted out the operation of a number of administrative systems. These include the government's payroll and accounts payable processes (including computer operations); the systems development and maintenance functions of Tax and Revenue Administration; and the operation of the Tax and Revenue Administration computer centre. Of these, the first two required capital investments by the contractor. Nevertheless, no provision has been made to compensate the contractors for these investments should their contracts not be renewed three years hence.

### Departments with Prior Experience of Contracting Out

Public Works, Transportation, and Agriculture all reported that their policies had been to increase the extent of contracting out well before the deficit elimination program was introduced in 1993. Although some contracts may have been issued earlier than they might otherwise have been, officials indicated that there had been no change in their departments' long-term plans. Both Public Works and Transportation provided evidence that such long-term plans had been in effect prior to 1993. For example, Public Works, which had contracted out 95 per cent of its architectural and engineering design prior to 1993, increased that figure to 'virtually 100 per cent', and it increased the portion of property management conducted privately from 35 to 50 per cent. After having contracted out the operation of its water bombers in 1986, it sold its helicopter fleet in 1993 and 1994. Most of its warehousing operations had been phased out in the 1980s through the use of standing offers, direct delivery, and local purchases, and in August 1994 all remaining warehouse operations were discontinued. Finally, the move to contracting out courier services, which has accelerated since 1993, began in the 1970s.[6] This information from Public Works, and similar information from Transportation, suggests strongly that the decision to contract out an increasing number of government services was not closely related to government budget cutbacks.

Three initiatives to contract out public services, however, appeared to arise in response to the deficit elimination program. First, the Department of the Environment contracted out the operation of a number of provincial park campsites to private operators. Second, it was proposed that the operation of penal institutions be contracted out. This proposal was taken seriously enough that legislation permitting such a contract was introduced. It was withdrawn before the third reading, however. Because privatization of penal institutions is a relatively new phenomenon, the government felt that it could not take the risk of privatizing more than one or two institutions, on a trial basis. Officials within the Department of Justice argued that the short-run financial gains from such a policy would be negligible. Instead, they proposed that a concerted effort be undertaken to identify areas within the existing system in which costs could be reduced. This policy has been adopted, and the privatization of prisons has been placed in abeyance. Finally, the Department of Labour provides mediation services to employers and unions engaged in contract disputes. Whereas the department had previously provided these services using its own employees, it now contracts out mediation services to private individuals (primarily former employees). The department pays the mediator directly for the first two days of mediation; the parties pay for all subsequent services at a rate of $75 per hour.

## 5.3 Privatization

There have been three major initiatives to privatize government services in Alberta since 1993. First, the sale of alcohol was transferred to private firms. All Alberta Liquor Control Board (ALCB) retail outlets were either closed or sold to private operators. Additional outlets could be established under ALCB regulation, provided alcohol was not sold in supermarkets.

Second, the sheriff's office in the Department of Justice serves legal documents and seizes property from delinquent debtors. As of 1 January 1996 these activities are provided by private firms that charge fees directly to the firms benefiting from them—generally, law firms and banks.

Third, many of the registry functions formerly performed by Municipal Affairs are now provided by private firms. These functions include registration of motor vehicles, administration of driving exams, issuance of motor vehicle license plates, and registration of land titles. For each service, the fee charged by the private registry is composed of two parts: a government-set tariff that must be remitted to Municipal Affairs and a commission the registry keeps for itself. If the service is considered to be 'essential', such as the issuance of a driver's license or license plate, the commission is fixed by the government, usually at $4.00. If the service is 'non-essential', however, the registry is free to set its own commission.

There have also been two other 'privatizations' resulting from government abandonment of programs. The Department of Energy had offered an Energy

Efficiency Program in which it conducted energy efficiency audits of commercial establishments, provided information to schools, and operated a telephone hotline called 'Energy Matters'. Government support for the program was discontinued, but most of the former employees have remained employed in this field, continuing to provide the program's services directly to the public. Finally, Municipal Affairs privatized the assessment of residential properties for the purpose of municipal taxation. The assessors who had previously been employed by Municipal Affairs were encouraged to form their own agencies to provide this service directly to individual municipalities.

### 5.4 Delegated Administrative Organizations: The Department of Labour

The Department of Labour has developed some of the most innovative responses to the deficit elimination program.[7] These responses have generally fallen under the heading of what it calls 'the third option'. The department's position is that traditionally there have been two options for the delivery of public services—the government can provide those services itself, or it can arrange for the private sector to provide them (through contracting out or privatization). It argues that a new, third option should be considered in situations in which the government's role is regulatory, such as in the enforcement of health and safety standards. In such situations, the regulated sectors could be encouraged to form private enforcement bodies—which the Alberta government calls Delegated Administrative Organizations (DAOs)[8]—to deliver the services traditionally provided by government employees. Under this system, the government would restrict its role to developing regulations and monitoring the DAOs.

The Department of Labour has enthusiastically adopted this third option.[9] The DAOs it has established to date have followed two broad formats: a contract format[10] and a privatization format. Under the contract format the government delegates its responsibilities to an industry association, but funding for that association continues to be provided by the government. An example of this arrangement is the Propane Inspection Program, in which the Propane Gas Association has been contracted to supervise the conversion of motor vehicles from gas to propane.[11]

Under the privatization format, the DAO is funded by the regulated industry. Three examples of this arrangement have been incorporated to date. In the first of these, the boiler and pressure vessel industry has incorporated a nonprofit organization, called the Alberta Boilers Safety Association, to enforce government safety regulations concerning pressure vessels. The association is funded from annual registration fees (levied on each boiler registered in the province) charged to firms for the inspection of boilers[12] and from fees charged to individuals who wish to obtain registration as pressure welders or power engineers. The association may select its own fee schedule in each case, subject to the approval of the Minister of Labour.

Similarly, the retail and wholesale gasoline sector has formed the Petroleum Tank Management Association of Alberta (PTMAA) to regulate fuel storage tanks, and an Alberta Elevating Devices and Amusement Rides Safety Association has been formed to regulate elevators, lifts, hoists, and amusement rides. Both are funded from annual, per unit registration fees levied on owners. (For example, separate fees are levied for each petroleum tank and for each elevator.) One of the anticipated future functions of the PTMAA will be dealing with lawsuits concerning environmental contamination. In this light, the association has proposed that the government impose a fuel tax, the proceeds of which would be used by the association for remediation of aging tank sites.

A number of other DAOs are under consideration by the Department of Labour. The department is close to approving the formation of a corporation, composed of members from the pension industry and pension holders, to administer pension legislation. This corporation would be funded from a registration fee based on each pension's assets. There are also preliminary proposals to form a DAO for 'rope tow' (ski hill) operators; and the Department of Labour has established, at arm's length, a Safety Codes Council that is responsible for developing safety standards in nine areas: amusement rides, boilers, buildings, electrical installations, elevators, fire prevention, gas, plumbing, and passenger ropeways. One of the primary responsibilities of the Safety Codes Council has been to delegate building, electrical, fire, gas, and plumbing inspections to accredited organizations (including many muncipalities).

The government's contention that DAOs represent a third option is based on two arguments: that DAOs are the first 'private' organizations to be given the power to perform government regulatory functions and that, by providing the affected industries with some 'ownership' of the regulatory function, DAOs encourage innovation in service delivery. The first of these arguments can easily be seen to be questionable. The methods used to delegate powers to the DAOs are very similar to those traditionally used to obtain private provision of government services from the private sector—privatization and contracting out. The DAOs may not be for-profit firms, like office supply companies or engineering consulting firms, but they are private none the less. Furthermore, not all private agencies that have contracted with the government in the past have been for-profit. Social Services has traditionally contracted with a number of charitable organizations, for example.

Rather, if DAOs are to be considered unique, the transfer of decision-making from government-appointed regulators to representatives of the regulated industries must be the focus. Our initial investigations suggest that DAOs have been able to respond much more quickly and appropriately to industry concerns than would have been possible under the former system. For example, all three of the industries now regulated by DAOs had complained that, under the Department of Labour, delays in certification and inspection procedures had become unacceptably long. In each case, one of the first steps was to hire sufficient staff to reduce these delays significantly and, in some cases, to offer incentive schemes to employees to increase productivity.[13] Delays have also been reduced by certifying companies with reliable safety records to conduct their own safety checks (subject only to audits from the relevant DAO). In addition, the DAOs were able to borrow in order to upgrade their information systems; and cost-effectiveness studies have been undertaken to determine whether certain services could be rationalized.[14]

Critics have argued that DAOs will become 'captives' of the industries they are intended to oversee and, therefore, will be less diligent in the regulation of those industries than the government would be. This criticism may be an example of the 'grass is greener fallacy'. It does not follow that because private regulation falls short of some theoretical ideal that it must be less satisfactory than government regulation. First, if government regulators are overworked or succumb to intense lobbying pressures by private firms, the government may fail to ensure that the legislated regulations are enforced. Second, DAOs will be closely monitored both by government officials and by the government's political opponents. Furthermore, industry associations will have a strong incentive to ensure that the regulatory function is not withdrawn from their DAOs because the latter, as private organizations, can be expected to have greater incentive to respond to industry demands for cost and quality control than would government regulators. Finally, many of the practices regulated by DAOs are now subject to scrutiny by the courts. Firms that own pressure boilers, for example, may be liable for substantial fines should failure of those boilers be found responsible for property damage or personal injury. These firms are not seeking less regulation of their industries. Indeed, it is usually in their private interests to have greater numbers of safety inspections and more rapid certification processes than are provided by government agencies. It is not clear, therefore, that the 'captive' hypothesis can be supported.

This hypothesis suggests that DAOs may interpret government regulations too leniently. A more telling criticism is that they may interpret them too harshly. A policy of rigid enforcement of the regulations could be motivated by a desire to restrict entrance into the industry, thereby reducing competition for existing firms. It is unlikely that government audits would restrain this behaviour as audits are designed primarily to deal with underenforcement. Furthermore, the legislated requirement that all proposed changes to DAO regulations be approved by the minister may fail to curb entry-preventing enforcement activities.[15] As industry representatives will be better informed than the minister concerning the impact of new regulations on the industry, it will be difficult for the minister to evaluate industry proposals objectively. Also, even if the minister maintains complete control over the establishment of regulations, the DAO may be able to restrict entry by 'following the letter of the law' when applying regulations to new entrants. If DAOs are to be successful, a method may have to be found to curb these restrictive activities.

## 6. CONCLUSION

It appears that if there is to be a significant restructuring of the way the Alberta government does business, that restructuring will come primarily from changes to systems for offering incentives to civil servants, not from contracting out or privatizing. With few notable exceptions—the privatization of Alberta Liquor Control Board outlets and the introduction of the Delegated Administrative Organizations, for example—most contracts or privatizations have been for peripheral services such as caretaking, computer maintenance, and print services. This lack of movement towards devolution appears to have arisen in many departments because the budget cuts were not deep enough to force them to reconsider how they do business—although some agencies, particularly the Regional Health Authorities, may rely more extensively on contracting out once they have had more time to evaluate their programs.

The most far-reaching changes arose from the introduction of three-year business plans and Key Performance Indicators, the development of the DAO model, and the expansion of intragovernmental competition—for example, through the establishment of charter schools. Importantly, none of these innovations could be characterized as having been made by departments attempting to deal with the impact of budget cuts. Rather, three-year business plans and Key Performance Indicators were imposed by the government; and DAOs and charter schools were introduced by senior civil servants who used the political turmoil surrounding the deficit elimination program to introduce policies with little direct relation to the budget-cutting process.

## NOTES

1. Note that this conclusion is not inconsistent with the view put forward by writers who argue that voters are able to exert pressure on ministers to change the behaviour of government agencies. There is nothing in these writers' models to suggest that voters will be able to influence more than the broad outlines of government policy.

2. The approach taken here is based on what McKenzie (Chapter 3) has called the 'Niskanen model'.

3. In a study of Canadian workers, Gunderson (1979) found that male government employees received earnings 9.3 per cent higher than their private-sector counterparts, while female government employees received earnings 22.3 per cent higher than private workers. He also estimated that one-third of the male differential, or 3.1 per cent, resulted from higher skill levels among government workers than private, and that two-thirds of the female differential, or 13.7 per cent, resulted from the same effect. Thus, he concluded that government workers received between 6.2 (male) and 8.6 (female) per cent more than private workers after allowance had been made for differences in skill levels. Two recent studies by Shapiro and Stelcner (1987 and 1989), using data from the 1981 census, provide support for Gunderson's findings. Their results suggest that of the six major industry classifications, the government sector has the second highest earnings. Only the transportation industry pays more than the government. Thus, on average, salaries are higher in the public sector than in the private. They also found that, between 1970 and 1980, public-private sector wage differentials did not, on average, decrease. (Although the gap for females increased, the gap for males decreased.)

4. It should be noted, however, that a firm with a long-term contract would have a great deal to lose if it was found to have violated an agreement to keep campers out of an environmentally sensitive area. This threat may be adequate to ensure the private firm's compliance with government standards. Also, it may be possible to use arbitration procedures to enforce compliance.

5. Nevertheless, Leslie Siedle (1996) concludes that British 'Executive Agencies' have experienced 'modest but positive' success. The innovation introduced by these agencies was to separate the policy-*making* branches of government agencies from the policy-*delivering*. As the New Zealand government discovered, it is difficult to establish performance criteria for policy-making but it is much less difficult to develop performance measures for policy delivery.

6. The source of the information in this paragraph was a memo dated 24 Aug. 1995 provided by D.H. Bader, acting deputy minister, Public Works, Supply, and Service.

7. Information for this section was drawn from Ford (1995) and Alberta (1994). Additional information can be obtained from Bruce and Woytowich (1997).

8. The concept of DAOs was developed by officials who were, at the time, in the Alberta Department of Consumer and Corporate Affairs (now called Municipal Affairs). Subsequently, two of those officials transferred to the Department of Labour. They are Robin Ford, currently deputy minister, and Don Woytowich, currently executive director of finance and administration in that department.

9. Although the Department of Labour has been a leader in this field, other departments have also initiated DAOs. The Alberta Insurance Council, for example, now operates a licensing program that used to be provided by the Treasury Department.

10. The Department of Labour does not classify contract-based organizations as DAOs. However, as both the structure of DAOs and the terminology used to describe them are still evolving, I have taken the liberty of including them here for ease of exposition.

11. This initial responsibility has since been expanded.

12. Government regulation requires that new and renovated boilers must be inspected before they can be used and that all boilers must be inspected annually.

13. Incentive schemes are generally not available to government employees.

14. For example, the Alberta Boilers Safety Association had been holding certification examinations for welders and power engineers every two to three weeks. It is now considering reducing this frequency to once every four to six months.

15. It was clear from my interviews with officials from the DAOs that large firms, with their greater public profiles, often followed safety regulations more carefully than did small firms. Large firms saw their influence over the DAOs as a means of insisting that small firms adopt the same standards they were following. This insistence may not have been designed as an entry-deterring policy, but it is likely to have that effect.

## REFERENCES

Alberta (1994), *Delegated Administrative Organizations: A 'Third Option'*. Edmonton.

Bruce, C., and D. Woytowich (1997), 'Delegated Administrative Organizations: Alberta's "Third Option"', in Robin Ford and David Zussman, eds, *Alternative Service Delivery*. Toronto: Institute of Public Administration of Canada.

Evans, K., and T. Carroll (1995), 'Why We Did It', *American School Board Journal* 44 (Mar.): 44.

Ford, R. (1995), 'The Third Option', presentation to The Workshop on Civil Service Reform for Private Sector Development: Visions and Strategies, Cairo, Egypt, 16–17 Sept.

Gunderson, M. (1979), 'Earnings Differentials Between the Public and Private Sectors', *Canadian Journal of Economics* 12 (May): 228–42.

Hill, P.T. (1995), *Reinventing Public Education*. Santa Monica: Rand Institute on Education and Training.

Niskanen, W. (1971), *Bureaucracy and Representative Government*. Chicago: Aldine Autherton.

Shapiro, D.M., and M. Stelcner (1987), 'The Persistence of the Male-Female Earnings Gap in Canada, 1970–1980: The Impact of Equal Pay Laws and Language Policies', *Canadian Public Policy* 13 (Dec.): 465–76.

——— (1989), 'Canadian Public-Private Sector Earnings Differentials, 1970–1980', *Industrial Relations* 28 (Winter): 72–81.

Siedle, L. (1996), *Rethinking the Delivery of Public Services*. Montreal: Institute for Research on Public Policy.

# Comments on Chapter 12                                    ∎

*Douglas S. West*

My first comments are directed at the hypotheses concerning the functioning of government agencies, in particular, on the hypothesis that with respect to government-provided services, 'consumers will not get what they want'. Bruce suggests that private firms will offer a wide variety of qualities of products in response to consumer demands, whereas government-provided services tend to be of uniformly high quality and all services tend to be of the same quality. One problem with this hypothesis is that quality as such is frequently hard to measure. It will often be difficult to define measurable quality variables for government services, and obtaining data for these variables might also be very costly or impractical (if not impossible). For example, there seems to be little agreement on the definition of quality health care, and there are clearly different dimensions to the quality of education, quality of municipal services, etc., many of which would be hard to quantify.

A second problem with this hypothesis is that casual empiricism suggests that it is false. For example, it is unlikely that the quality of government services in rural and urban areas is the same. Scale economies in the provision of government services in urban areas can be exploited, so that a given quality of service can be produced at lower average cost in urban areas than in rural areas. Given this lower average cost, certain services can be provided in urban areas that would be prohibitively costly to provide in rural areas.

A third problem with this hypothesis is that it does not recognize the possibility that governments might find it in their best interests to manipulate the quality of government services in order to alter the demand for them. For example, by lengthening the waiting periods for certain health care services, or by increasing a consumer's transportation costs that need to be incurred before obtaining a government service, a consumer's total acquisition costs for the service are increased. At some point, a consumer will seek out less costly alternatives for the government-provided service (if such alternatives exist). The point here is that while consumers might demand high-quality government services, quality is costly to provide and governments, concerned about their budget deficits, might reduce quality to reduce demand.

My second set of comments revolves around contracting out as an alternative method of delivering government services. In the case where a public agency acts as a government-operated contract monopoly, Bruce suggests that the agency receives general instructions concerning how the budget is to be spent, but no other constraints or incentives are imposed, except perhaps the threat of a reduced budget if the agency does not spend its funds wisely. The government can, however, exercise more control if it wishes to do so by monitoring agency resource allocation and organizational plans. It can also require that the agency obtain government approval for a detailed business plan and any restructuring proposals.

Contrary to what Bruce suggests, the government might wish to invest more resources in monitoring a public versus a private contract monopoly given the different incentives affecting the two. The owner of a private contract monopoly, as residual claimant, has an incentive to operate efficiently in order to maximize its profits. To the extent that it does not minimize costs, it risks losing the contract to a lower bidder at contract renewal time. The public contract monopoly would not have the same incentive to operate efficiently, although the prospect of losing the contract and the associated jobs at contract renewal time might enhance efficiency incentives.

Bruce suggests that in the case where output is not easily measured, because the owners of a private firm will be in a better position to benefit personally from cost savings than will the employees of a public agency, private operators face a comparably greater incentive to sacrifice quality in order to reduce costs. However, this may not be the case given that the private firm might rely on repeat purchases by consumers, and reductions in quality can reduce the repeat purchase probability. Future sales and profits could fall as a result. This will be especially true if the private firm has a monopoly only on the delivery of a service within a public institution, but still faces competition from outside the institution. An example would be where a university food service is contracted out to a single private firm but faces competition from off-campus restaurants. In the case where a private firm has a real contract monopoly on the provision of a service and there are no close substitutes for it, quality standards of some sort can still be written into the contract along with a termination clause for unsatisfactory performance. Incentives for efficient operation would thereby be enhanced, particularly if the private monopoly could be replaced at low cost and with little delay by either another private firm or a public operation.

Besides any differences in quality that might arise depending on whether the contracting out is to a public or private firm, there can also be differences in quality depending on whether it is a public agency or private firm that is doing the contracting out. Two reasons why a private firm contracts out particular services (such as accounting and legal) or particular parts of its production are to achieve lower costs or higher-quality services and products. The lower costs could be in the form of lower transportation or transaction costs or they could arise from the exploitation of scale economies by the contract recipient (that might produce output for a number of firms) that would not be obtained in the absence of contracting out.

The public agency that contracts out might be doing so to avoid the cost of providing a specific good or service and/or to have the good or service provided more efficiently. This would seem to be laudable, but the danger is that the public contractor might not follow up the contracting out with an appropriate level of monitoring of the performance of the contract recipient. After all, the failure to monitor will not necessarily affect the public agency's revenues or the compensation of the public agency's managers. If the monitoring is known to be inadequate or ineffective, then quality standards and termination clauses written into the contract cannot be expected to induce efficient behaviour on the part of the contract recipient. As an example, a university or hospital food service can be contracted out. But unless there are either close substitutes for these services available nearby or the ongoing monitoring of food and service quality (and the possibility of contract termination for unacceptable performance), there will be an incentive to shirk on quality.

One can still imagine cases where the products and services to be contracted out are so complex or hard to measure that writing enforceable contracts could be extremely difficult. In these cases, a private-public joint venture might be a reasonable alternative method for the delivery of the service. (A joint venture is also thought to be a reasonable alternative when there is a high degree of asset specificity and performance uncertainty; see Kogut, 1988.) The possible benefits of a private-public joint venture include: (1) keeping the public sector involved in the provision of the service so that it can retain the knowledge of how to supply the service (and be prepared to use this knowledge in the event of private-sector failure); (2) ensuring that certain services get provided to certain areas that a private-sector operator might find unprofitable to serve; (3) improving the ability to realize scale economies and rationalization of a publicly provided service, and exploitation of any private-public sector synergies; (4) improving the ability to monitor the private-sector provision of the good or service; (5) resolving the problem of incomplete contracts and reducing the possibility of opportunistic recontracting; and (6) risk-sharing.

There are also some possible costs associated with private-public joint ventures, including (1) conflicting interests and conflicting objective functions on the part of the private and public sectors, resulting in slow and possibly poor decision-making; (2) reduced private-sector incentives to be efficient and minimize costs if this can lead to reduced revenue from the funding body; (3) persistent disagreements over the division of costs and income between the parties to the venture; and (4) in the absence of competitive bidding, less opportunity to discover at what price the private sector would be willing to provide the service. (Discussions of the costs and benefits of joint ventures can be found in Harrigan, 1988; Kogut, 1988; and Shapiro and Willig, 1990.)

While Bruce does not include joint ventures in his list of alternative delivery methods for government services, a joint venture should probably be considered when evaluating alternatives. Even if its costs are such as to make a joint venture an infrequently chosen alternative, the consideration of it at least requires that some important questions about service delivery get asked. One might find, for example, that despite some of the benefits that a joint venture could deliver in a particular setting, the lack of competitive bidding to offer the service makes it an unacceptable alternative.

Bruce notes in his discussion of contracting out that a competitive tendering or auction process is one approach to choosing the provider for a government service. In the right circumstances, competitive bidding can allow the government to find the lowest price at which a given service can be supplied, and also the most efficient method for providing the service. However, problems can arise if there is a small number of bidders (collusion and the submission of higher than expected bids being one). In this case, the government may have a maximum amount it is willing to pay for a given level of service. The question then becomes one of whether the successful bidder is willing to provide the specified level of service at the set price, and whether the government can establish performance measures and a monitoring system to ensure that the service is supplied according to the terms of the contract.

A different problem can arise in a competitive bidding process that is open to both private firms and government agencies. This is the problem of the so-called 'level playing field'. Bruce discusses some aspects of this problem, noting that the public agency tendering the contract must ensure that internal and external (private) bidders are treated equally. However, to get an efficient outcome, it is also necessary that capital and overhead costs of offering a particular government service be properly accounted for by both public and private bidders. This can be difficult if the public bidder shares facilities with other government operations and if the public bidder owns capital that is used to produce services in addition to the ones that are up for bid. Nevertheless, it is important that every effort be made to ensure that the public bidder does not understate its true costs, since inappropriate decisions could be the result.

Finally, I have a few comments regarding the use of non-profit organizations as an alternative method of delivering government services. There are reasons why certain services have traditionally been provided by government. One is that the private sector will either not provide the service or will provide less than the socially optimal amount of it. Before turning over the provision of a government service to a non-profit organization, one must be certain that the organization has a long-term interest in providing the service and that it has the incentive to supply the socially optimal amount of the service. Even if the non-profit organization's goals are consonant with those of the government agency, the individuals working for the non-profit organization may not have the same long-run commitment to providing the service (especially if many of them are unpaid volunteers) as would the government agency. The non-profit organization will also face ongoing funding problems, and these problems might be most severe and sap the energies of organization staff precisely at those times when demand for its services is greatest.

## REFERENCES

Harrigan, K.R. (1988), 'Joint Ventures and Competitive Strategy', *Strategic Management Journal* 9: 141–58.

Kogut, B. (1988), 'Joint Ventures: Theoretical and Empirical Perspectives', *Strategic Management Journal* 9: 319–32.

Shapiro, C., and R.D. Willig (1990), 'On the Antitrust Treatment of Production Joint Ventures', *Journal of Economic Perspectives* 4: 113–30.

# PART IV

# Public Opinion and Commentary

# CHAPTER 13

# What Do Albertans Think? The Klein Agenda on the Public Opinion Landscape

*Keith Archer and Roger Gibbins*

## 1. INTRODUCTION

Our analysis begins with two points of emphasis. The first is that interpretations of the Klein agenda must pay particular attention to the political factors underlying it. In short, we reject any premise that the actions of the Alberta government were driven solely by 'economic realities'. As we saw with the 1995 referendum debate in Quebec, economic realities seldom prevail within the political arena, and there is no reason to assume that they did so in this case. The Alberta government had options as to the depth, speed, and targets of its cuts, and choices were made with a view to electoral considerations and ideological aspirations as well as to the dictates of sound economic management. Thus, the character of public opinion is critical in figuring out why the government acted as it did, and where it might go from here.

The second point takes us to the heart of our empirical analysis. The Klein government has performed what is little short of a political miracle. It has imposed massive spending cuts while maintaining, and perhaps even enhancing, its electoral support. And, it has managed to do this despite the fact that a majority of the electorate feels that the budget cuts have created more losers than winners and disagrees with many of the specifics of the Klein agenda. It is important to explain the government's success in this respect if we are to consider what lessons other governments might draw from the Alberta experience.

## 2. THE ALBERTA SURVEY

In late April and early May 1995 we surveyed 1,004 respondents, 18 years of age or older, from across Alberta. Respondents were randomly drawn from Alberta Government Telephone and Edmonton Telephone subscriber lists. A sample of this size has a margin of error of plus or minus 3 per cent, 19 times out of 20. The interviews were conducted by telephone and were approximately 15 minutes in length. The survey covered a wide range of public policy issues, although little attention was paid to what might be considered the moral side of the Klein agenda. (There were no questions, for example, on the appropriateness of public funding for abortions.)

In the analysis to follow, we will first sketch in the broad contours of public support for and opposition to the central components of the Klein agenda. Second, we will examine the extent to which variations in support and opposition can be explained by the socio-demographic characteristics of respondents. In short, are there cleavages within the provincial society that reinforce, or might potentially reinforce, the political debate over debts and deficits? Third, we will explore how outlooks on the Klein agenda reflect partisan dispositions and respondent assessments of the province's political leaders. This will take us to the partisan and leadership dynamics of the Klein agenda, and to the role played by those dynamics in the political success of Alberta's Progressive Conservative government.

We should also note an important caveat before we begin. The analysis to follow tries to untangle the political and partisan dynamics of the contemporary scene in Alberta, and does so through the window provided by an extensive survey of public opinion. However, it is not our intention to provide a critical analysis of the Klein agenda.[1] Rather than asking whether the government *should* or *should not* have taken the actions it did, we will try to explain why it was able to act as it did without paying a serious political price. Whether the Klein agenda makes sense as economic policy, or as social policy more broadly defined, we leave to other contributors to this volume.

## 3. BASIC CONTOURS OF PUBLIC OPINION

When the Alberta government moved to address the province's budget deficit and ballooning public debt, it made every effort to sell its program to the electorate as an economic necessity. In this effort, the government was backed by nearly a decade of argumentation from economists and the business community that the deficit was a serious problem that had to be brought under control. The government argued, and clearly did so effectively, that its political hands were tied; there was no choice but to attack the deficit, and to do so aggressively. Our data show that a strong majority of Albertans accepted this argument.

> As you probably know, the Alberta government plans to eliminate the deficit by next year. In general, do you strongly support, support, oppose, or strongly oppose the government's goal of eliminating the deficit?

Across the province, an overwhelming 80.8 per cent of the sample supported the government's goal, and 34.6 per cent did so strongly; 16.6 per cent opposed the deficit elimination goal, and only 5.0 per cent did so strongly. This is a remarkable level of support, given that many people, as we shall soon see, opposed the specifics and depth of the program cuts. The government, therefore, scored a major success: it convinced the electorate that deep program cuts were essential. This finding also exposes the major, indeed, crippling dilemma confronting opposition parties in the province: how does one oppose a government whose primary policy objective enjoys such widespread public support?

The dilemma facing the opposition parties gets only worse when we find equally broad public support for the means chosen by the government to eliminate the deficit. As Table 1 shows, the government's basic strategy of spending cuts, no increase in personal tax rates, and no provincial sales tax enjoys strong, indeed sweeping, public support. While it is true that the government may be open to attack if it increases user fees, and while there would be support for higher corporate tax rates, opposition parties do not have a lot of room to carve out a distinctive but still attractive deficit elimination strategy.

We also asked respondents if they approved or disapproved of 'the Klein government's performance'. Given the high level of approval for the central plank of the government's agenda, it is not surprising that a majority of respondents (56.8 per cent) approved, with 16.5 per cent approving strongly. However, approval ratings for the government were not as strong as approval for the government's deficit elimination goal; 40.1 per cent of the respondents disapproved of the government's performance, and 16.0 per cent did so strongly. None the less, for a government to slash program funding by approximately 20 per cent and still enjoy the support of a solid majority of the electorate is no mean feat.

But here comes the puzzling part of the survey findings. When we move to the specifics of the government's agenda, opposition quickly mounts. For

**Table 1:** Deficit Elimination Strategies

*'The government could balance the budget in a number of ways. I am going to read several options, and for each one, please tell me whether the government should or should not do this to balance the budget.'*

|  | Should % | Should Not % |
|---|---|---|
| Cut spending | 89.8 | 8.6 |
| Increase personal tax | 19.4 | 78.3 |
| Increase corporate tax | 66.9 | 28.3 |
| Increase user fees | 46.5 | 49.0 |
| Have a sales tax in Alberta | 16.2 | 81.9 |

example, when we asked respondents whether the government was moving too fast, too slow, or just about right in trying to balance the budget over a three-year period, a majority (54.3 per cent) felt it was moving too quickly, while 41.1 per cent felt the pace was just about right. Interestingly, only 3.3 per cent felt the government was moving too slowly, which suggests that the government has positioned itself at one pole of the deficit reduction debate; there is no room on the public opinion landscape for a party favouring an even more aggressive approach. While an argument can be made, as New Zealand's former finance minister, Roger Douglas, has done, that rapid action is the only way in which sweeping change can be accomplished, Albertans at large have not been convinced.

When governments cut programs as broadly and deeply as the Alberta government has done, it would be foolish to expect the cuts to affect everyone equally; a more realistic view would be that cuts will produce winners and losers. We therefore asked respondents whether each of 15 groups was a winner or a loser in the budget-cutting exercise. As Table 2 shows, virtually all groups were seen as losers; the only clear winner was 'big business'. A narrow plurality see future generations as winners, while the biggest losers were perceived to be students, senior citizens, the poor, government workers, and young people. Particularly striking is the finding that a majority of respondents saw average Albertans as losers. The fact that over 80 per cent of Albertans approve of the government's deficit-cutting agenda even though so many see the poor and senior citizens as losers suggests a rather tough edge to the public opinion environment.

We also asked respondents a 'three bears' question: had budget cuts in a number of specific areas been too big, too small, or just about right? As Table 3 shows, a clear majority of Albertans felt that the cuts to education, universities and colleges, and health care were too big. Public opinion was aligned with government policy only when it came to cuts to social services and welfare, a finding that again underscores Alberta's hard-edged public opinion climate.

In both Tables 2 and 3, we find a public opinion environment that appears to offer little support for the government's agenda. However, in Table 4, which explores public support for a number of specific policy initiatives, we find a more mixed and complex opinion environment. Clearly, many of the government's initiatives enjoy substantial public support; of particular note is majority support for privatization, job retraining, and a reduction in the number of school boards and hospital boards, and plurality support for lower payments for social services. At the same time, there are marked areas of vulnerability on the education and health care fronts. Public support for a number of important elements of the government's plans for health care restructuring is especially weak.

**Table 2:** Perceptions of Winners and Losers

*'It is hard to cut the provincial budget without some people being hurt, and without others coming out ahead. In short, there are bound to be winners and losers. I will read out a list of groups. For each one, please tell me whether they have been a winner or a loser in the budget cuts, or whether the cuts have had neither a positive nor a negative effect on this group.'*

|  | Winner % | Loser % | No Effect % |
|---|---|---|---|
| Average Albertans | 23.9 | 52.6 | 18.4 |
| Big business | 58.9 | 11.9 | 20.1 |
| Senior citizens | 8.2 | 79.0 | 9.3 |
| College and university students | 6.4 | 79.7 | 9.1 |
| Children | 12.2 | 60.0 | 22.0 |
| Women | 11.8 | 44.7 | 33.4 |
| Union members | 12.9 | 47.8 | 19.9 |
| Government workers | 16.6 | 67.9 | 9.2 |
| Doctors | 26.5 | 40.9 | 24.5 |
| Young people | 14.4 | 62.8 | 15.9 |
| People in rural areas | 23.1 | 34.3 | 26.3 |
| The poor | 9.1 | 74.0 | 11.8 |
| Teachers | 17.3 | 58.5 | 17.0 |
| Future generations | 42.1 | 41.4 | 7.8 |
| Small entrepreneurs | 33.7 | 38.4 | 15.9 |

In summary, the data reveal many areas where public opinion is at odds with government plans and actions, yet specific public concerns apparently do not translate into general opposition to the Conservative government or to the central plank of the Klein agenda. Why? Three possible answers suggest themselves. The first may be that opposition to the Klein agenda has not coalesced around recognizable social groupings within the electorate, but that it is unanchored and therefore politically impotent. The second and related answer is that while opposition to the Klein agenda or at least to many specifics of that agenda certainly exists, it has not been mobilized by opposition parties. It is therefore latent and ineffective. Third, Albertans may have bought into the wartime psychology fostered by the provincial government, a psychology that urged all Albertans to carry their share of the load in an unavoidable battle with

## Table 3: Reactions to Specific Budget Cuts

*'Now I'd like to ask you a few questions about some specific budget cuts. As you may know, spending on programs is being cut by varying amounts. For each of the following programs, do you think the cuts have been too big, too small, or just about right?'*

|  | Too Big % | Too Small % | Just Right % |
|---|---|---|---|
| Primary and secondary education | 56.6 | 3.8 | 37.3 |
| Universities and colleges | 57.0 | 4.2 | 31.8 |
| Health | 64.5 | 6.2 | 26.4 |
| Social services and welfare | 34.3 | 18.5 | 39.0 |

## Table 4: Support for Specific Policy Initiatives

|  | % Support | % Opposed |
|---|---|---|
| Mandatory job retraining for welfare recipients | 85.2 | 11.3 |
| Stronger parent councils to encourage more parental involvement in the school system | 81.8 | 14.7 |
| Less administration in the school boards | 78.7 | 17.0 |
| Significant reduction in the number of school boards | 74.0 | 20.7 |
| More community-based and home-based health care | 65.0 | 28.1 |
| Increased privatization of government services | 55.0 | 37.8 |
| Charging user fees for kindergarten/ECS | 52.7 | 44.3 |
| Creating 17 large Regional Health Authorities to determine how the health care budget will be spent | 47.1 | 41.9 |
| Lower payments for social services | 44.7 | 41.9 |
| Less money for kindergarten/ECS | 39.8 | 56.5 |
| Creation of charter schools | 39.4 | 42.2 |
| Fewer hospitals | 36.8 | 58.5 |
| Encouraging the creation of private user-pay health care clinics | 35.0 | 59.2 |
| Higher tuition at colleges and universities | 27.7 | 67.9 |
| Mandatory job retraining for welfare recipients | 85.2 | 11.3 |
| Fewer teachers and professors at colleges and universities | 27.7 | 60.2 |
| Fewer doctors and nurses | 20.0 | 72.1 |

the deficit and debt. Albertans, in other words, may recognize that most people will be losers, but still believe that the price has to be paid, although this line of reasoning does not address the finding that a majority find the cuts to education, universities, and health care to be too big.

Let us turn now to the first and second possibilities, upon which we can shed some empirical light. We return to the third possibility in conclusion.

## 4. SOCIO-DEMOGRAPHIC EXPLANATIONS

The story line with respect to socio-economic factors is relatively straightforward and can be told without a great deal of elaboration. First, variations in personal income play a very modest role in explaining support for or opposition to the Klein government and its deficit reduction policies. To be sure, relatively wealthy Albertans are most supportive of the government and its policies, but the differences are neither huge nor consistent. Only the small number of respondents (15.2 per cent of the sample) with annual family incomes of less than $20,000 stood out in their opposition. Second, no consistent differences in opinion can be systematically traced to the educational background of respondents. For example, respondents with university degrees are not particularly receptive to the plight of the universities, their faculty, or their students.

Third, little variation can be traced to age differences. Although age proves to have a substantial impact on a range of community identifications that one might expect to be implicated in the government's agenda,[2] it is only weakly linked to opinion towards the key elements of the Klein agenda. It is interesting to note, however, that the highest levels of support tend to come from those between 25 and 49 years of age, a group that benefits the least from government programs while facing the heaviest tax load. It is not surprising, therefore, that a mix of program cuts and tax relief finds a ready audience within this age bracket.

Fourth, and again not surprisingly, place of residence looms large as a source of variation. On question after question, Edmontonians stand apart from other respondents in their opposition to the Klein government and its agenda. For example, only 44 per cent of Edmonton respondents approved of the government's performance, compared to 63 per cent of Calgarians and 60 per cent of those living elsewhere in the province. Only 31 per cent of Edmontonians said they would vote Conservative in the next provincial election, compared to 45 per cent across the rest of the province. To date, then, the Klein revolution has not carried 'Redmonton'. Whether it may have greater success in doing so now that Edmontonians have elected a mayor much more in tune with the provincial government remains to be seen.

Finally, and of greatest importance, there are strong gender differences across a range of questions relating to the performance and agenda of the provincial government.[3] Such differences are not unexpected given that neo-conservative agendas have a greater impact on women than they do on men. Women experience proportionately greater benefits from income security and social services programs, and therefore shrinking the welfare state is of greater consequence for women than it is for men.[4] Moreover, the gendered division of labour in the private and public sectors means that women are more affected by job losses in the public sector, benefit less from infrastructure jobs created by public funding in the private sector, and assume most of the workload in the home, for example, when patients are released earlier from hospital or when extended care facilities for the infirm are curtailed. In ideological terms, women tend to be more liberal than men, and therefore are less positively inclined towards the form of neo-conservatism embedded in the Alberta government's public policy agenda. Finally, there is sharp ideological tension between feminism and neo-conservatism; the modern welfare state, which neo-conservatives are trying to roll back, has been an important vehicle for aspects of the feminist agenda such as employment equity.[5] For all of these reasons, gender differences should be expected.

When we turn to the data, we indeed find that the gender of respondents has a marked impact on opinion towards the Klein government and its deficit reduction agenda. Overall, 48 per cent of women disapprove of the government's performance, compared to 33 per cent of men who disapprove. Voting intentions reveal the same gender patterns. Only 34.9 per cent of the female respondents indicate an intention to vote for the Conservatives in the next provincial election, as compared to 51.1 per cent of the men. The Liberal opposition is favoured by 28.5 per cent of the women but by only 19.6 per cent of the men. Men and women differ in their *intensity* of support for the government's goal of eliminating the deficit in three years; 44.8 per cent of men report 'strong support' compared to 27.5 per cent of women. Differences between men and women are also evident in attitudes towards the urgency of deficit reduction: 62.9 per cent of women, but only 45.6 per cent of men, feel the government is moving too quickly. Finally, men and women differ significantly in their perceptions of the effects of the government's agenda on women. When asked if women would be winners or losers under the Klein government, 56.4 per cent of the female respondents said 'losers', as opposed to 41.5 per cent of the men.

The Alberta survey asked respondents to rate their 'closeness' to feminists on a 10-point scale.[6] As expected, support for feminism is correlated with opposition to neo-conservatism. This is seen in assessments of the Klein government's performance: 57.8 per cent of the strong identifiers with feminism disapprove or strongly disapprove of the government. More generally, approval decreases as support for feminism increases. This pattern is also seen in voting intentions for the next provincial election: as support for feminism increases, Conservative support decreases. Of those displaying the lowest identification with feminism, 51.4 per cent intend to support the PCs in the next election, whereas only 25.7 per cent of strong feminist identifiers have the same intention. A feminism gap also emerges with respect to the economic policies of the Klein government. Strong support for deficit elimination decreases as support for feminism increases, dropping from 42.2 per cent to 25.4 per cent. However, 75.4 per cent of even the strong identifiers with feminism demonstrate some support for deficit elimination, a finding that illustrates how widespread public support is for deficit elimination in Alberta. Identification with feminism is related to *lower* levels of support for deficit elimination rather than with opposition to this goal.

In summary, there are socio-economic variations in support for the Klein government and its policy agenda, with those relating to gender and feminism tending to overshadow the rest.[7] However, socio-economic effects tend more to shade or moderate levels of support than to polarize the electorate. In ideological terms, most Albertans are neo-conservatives who find themselves in agreement with the broad outlines of the Klein agenda. They may be neo-conservatives of varying hues, but they are neo-conservatives none the less. It should be stressed, furthermore, that socio-economic cleavages within the electorate become relevant to the determination of public policy only if they are articulated and mobilized within the political process. It is to this aspect of the public opinion landscape that we now turn.

## 5. PARTISAN DYNAMICS

Although the Klein government controls a majority of legislative seats in Alberta, one should not forget how narrow was its margin of victory in the 1993 provincial election. In what was by far the closest contest in recent memory, the Conservatives won 44.5 per cent of the vote compared to 39.7 per cent for the Liberals.[8] The New Democrats, who had been the official opposition heading into the election, won only 11 per cent of the vote and no seats. The data from our survey indicate that, reminiscent of the era of Conservative Party dominance under the leadership of Peter Lougheed, once again the Conservatives are pulling ahead of the opposition.[9]

We asked respondents, 'If a provincial election were held tomorrow, for which party would you vote?' Among the electorate as a whole, the Conservatives have the support of 41.5 per cent of voters, compared to 24.1 per cent who support the Liberals and only 7.5 per cent who support the New Democrats (see Table 5). However, and not unexpectedly at a time when the election may be a full two years away, almost a quarter of the respondents either did not know who they would vote for or indicated they would not vote. Excluding the non-voters and undecideds, the Conservatives have a commanding lead over the Liberals, with 54.9 per cent compared to 31.8 per cent of the decided vote. A comparison of the reported vote in 1993 with current vote intention reveals that one in five Liberal voters in 1993 would now vote for the Conservatives, and a further one in six are undecided about how they would vote.

An examination of the demographics of party support reveals a number of consistent patterns in how various segments of the electorate align with the parties. One important difference is between men and women. Men favour the Conservatives over the Liberals by a margin of 2.5 to 1, whereas women are almost evenly divided in their support for the two parties. Conservative support also peaks among the younger middle-aged respondents (25 to 49 years) and among those earning over $40,000 per year. Among occupational groups, the self-employed and full-time workers are the strongest supporters of the Conservative government. The demographic difference that counts the most in elections is simple geography, because electoral constituencies are all based on territory. In Edmonton, the Liberals and Conservatives are tied at 43 per cent of the vote. In Calgary and in other parts of the province, the Conservatives lead by a two-to-one margin. Thus, if an election were held tomorrow, the Conservatives would sweep Calgary and all other areas outside Edmonton, and they would give the Liberals a run for the Edmonton seats. As the baseball philosopher Yogi Berra once said, it would be *déjà vu* all over again.

In the eyes of a majority of Albertans, the Klein government has been a success, or at least enough of a success to earn their votes. However, it is one thing to identify a success; it is quite another to explain it. Election contests are

**Table 5:** Vote Intention

*'If a provincial election were held tomorrow, for which party would you vote?'*

| Party Would Support | Per cent | Adjusted Per cent |
|---|---|---|
| Conservative | 41.5 | 54.9 |
| Liberal | 24.1 | 31.8 |
| New Democrat | 7.5 | 9.9 |
| Other | 2.6 | 3.5 |
| None/would not vote | 4.3 | (excluded) |
| Don't know/refused | 20.0 | (excluded) |
| Total | 100.0 | 100.1* |

*Does not sum to 100 due to rounding.

often described as 'horse-races', and in fact the racetrack may be a useful metaphor for political analysis. There are countless factors at play in explaining the outcome of a horse-race—what is the condition of the track, who is the competition, how has the horse been training lately, what is the weather like? All of these factors have a role to play in the outcome. But most analysts, and a host of bettors, agree that the most important factors are the qualities of the horse itself and of the jockey. Similarly in politics, although many factors play a part in explaining election outcomes, the two most important are the party's campaign platform and election issues (the horse) and the party leader (the jockey).[10] Our data indicate that with Ralph Klein, the Conservatives have the best jockey. We are not so sure about the horse.

## 6. LEADERSHIP DYNAMICS

Respondents were asked to rate the leaders of the three main political parties in Alberta, along with Prime Minister Jean Chrétien and Reform leader Preston Manning, on a 100-point feeling thermometer (Table 6). The data indicate that Ralph Klein is by far the most popular of the three provincial leaders. Although Klein's average score was only a middling 53.2 out of 100, it was significantly higher than the 40.7 awarded to Liberal leader Grant Mitchell and the 35.5 given to New Democrat leader Ross Harvey. Klein also scored higher than Manning (47.9), although he was four points shy of Chrétien (57.6), who was the most popular among the leaders.[11] Klein enjoys two advantages over Mitchell and Harvey. First, as premier, almost everyone knows him. In contrast, almost one in six respondents do not have an opinion about Mitchell, and almost one in three do not know Harvey. Second, attitudes towards Klein are much more likely to be positive than attitudes towards Mitchell and Harvey. For example, 52.1 per cent of respondents rate Klein on the positive side of the scale (over 50), compared to only 16 per cent and 10 per cent for Mitchell and Harvey, respectively. There is also a strong pocket of Albertans who hold very negative attitudes towards Klein (23.6 per cent), a figure much higher than for Chrétien. However, despite the presence of a significant hostile group, support for Klein overall is highly positive compared to his provincial opposition. So, although he was a controversial choice for Conservative Party leader back in December 1992, Klein has given the Conservatives the top jockey.[12]

Consistent with the earlier discussion on attitudes towards the deficit reduction agenda, the data on leadership assessments indicate that the socio-demographic characteristics of respondents have a limited impact on attitudes towards the party leaders.[13] Table 7, based on the same feeling thermometer, indicates that, with very few exceptions, Ralph Klein enjoys higher leadership evaluations among Albertans in terms of almost all characteristics than do the

**Table 6:** Attitudes Towards Party Leaders—100-point Feeling Thermometer

| Description | Klein | Mitchell | Party Leader Harvey | Chrétien | Manning |
|---|---|---|---|---|---|
| Cold (0–25) | 23.6 | 21.9 | 25.3 | 9.9 | 24.4 |
| Cool (26–49) | 10.2 | 17.8 | 12.5 | 11.9 | 13.2 |
| Tepid (50) | 12.7 | 29.3 | 21.1 | 18.7 | 14.7 |
| Warm (51–75) | 25.6 | 14.4 | 8.1 | 41.3 | 30.7 |
| Hot (76–100) | 26.5 | 1.6 | 2.0 | 15.6 | 13.3 |
| Don't know | 1.4 | 14.9 | 31.1 | 2.6 | 3.6 |
| Mean | 53.2 | 40.7 | 35.5 | 57.6 | 47.9 |

other provincial party leaders. For example, although men tend to rate Klein more positively than women (59.2 versus 48.1), note also that women rate Klein more positively than either Mitchell or Harvey (48.1 versus 42.9 and 37.5, respectively). Thus, while gender is related to assessments of Klein, the overall impact of gender on partisan choice in Alberta is likely to be quite limited because women are even less impressed with the other party leaders. A similar portrait emerges when looking at the place of residence. Assessments of Klein are quite positive in Calgary and in other areas of the province outside of Edmonton, and the Premier enjoys a substantial lead over the other leaders in these areas. However, although assessments of Klein are much more negative in Edmonton (41.8), even in the provincial capital the premier's rating is as high or higher than that of the opposition leaders.

And perhaps most telling of all, the premier inspires a level of support among his own partisans that far exceeds that of the other party leaders. For example, Klein's rating among those who intend to vote Conservative is 75.8, more than 40 points higher than Liberal and New Democrat voters' evaluation of him. In contrast, provincial Liberals rate Mitchell at only 51.1, only 10 points higher than Harvey, the ND leader, and just 20 points higher than the Conservative leader. Finally, and a point to which we shall return, assessments of the party leaders are relatively flat among the undecided voters, whose evaluations of Klein, Mitchell, and Harvey were 42.9, 39.8, and 37.6, respectively. This latter group, which at the time of our survey comprised almost one in four voters, is of critical importance to the political future of the province.

A clearer indication of the impact of socio-demographic characteristics and partisan leanings on assessments of party leaders is obtained in Tables 8 and 9, which use multivariate models. Table 8 examines the impact of the six socio-demographic variables of gender, education, age, income, employment status, and area of residence on attitudes towards the three party leaders; Table 9 repeats the analysis with the addition of vote intention variables. Elaborating

**Table 7:** Ratings of Party Leaders by Vote Intention and Various Socio-demographic Characteristics

| | Party Leader | | | |
| | Klein | Mitchell | Harvey | No. |
| --- | --- | --- | --- | --- |
| *Vote Intention* | | | | |
| Conservative | 75.8 | 35.5 | 28.7 | (411) |
| Liberal | 31.2 | 51.1 | 40.4 | (236) |
| New Democrat | 28.3 | 41.4 | 51.8 | (73) |
| Other | 53.9 | 35.2 | 32.4 | (26) |
| None/undecided | 42.9 | 39.8 | 37.6 | (220) |
| *Gender* | | | | |
| Male | 59.2 | 38.2 | 33.1 | (450) |
| Female | 48.1 | 42.9 | 37.5 | (533) |
| *Education* | | | | |
| Less than high school | 50.8 | 38.3 | 31.6 | (180) |
| High school grad./college | 56.6 | 39.5 | 34.4 | (413) |
| University | 50.9 | 43.1 | 38.2 | (388) |
| *Age* | | | | |
| 18–24 years | 50.5 | 46.6 | 45.6 | (125) |
| 25–34 years | 58.5 | 45.5 | 40.5 | (201) |
| 35–49 years | 54.8 | 38.4 | 32.9 | (338) |
| 50–64 years | 48.7 | 38.2 | 33.8 | (179) |
| 65+ years | 50.8 | 36.9 | 26.5 | (138) |
| *Income* | | | | |
| < $20,000 | 45.1 | 42.2 | 36.1 | (149) |
| $21,000–$40,000 | 52.2 | 40.9 | 35.9 | (257) |
| $41,000–$60,000 | 56.7 | 39.9 | 34.1 | (225) |
| $61,000–$80,000 | 55.3 | 40.5 | 36.4 | (115) |
| $81,000+ | 54.6 | 38.5 | 33.6 | (108) |
| *Employment Status* | | | | |
| Full-time | 56.8 | 41.2 | 34.8 | (405) |
| Part-time | 47.9 | 41.5 | 38.2 | (127) |
| Retired | 49.9 | 37.9 | 29.5 | (160) |
| Unemployed | 47.2 | 39.5 | 37.6 | (53) |
| Self-employed | 61.4 | 36.8 | 28.3 | (101) |
| Student | 44.1 | 51.1 | 50.0 | (61) |
| Homemaker | 51.6 | 37.2 | 40.9 | (68) |
| *Area of Residence* | | | | |
| Calgary | 58.7 | 42.9 | 36.8 | (280) |
| Edmonton | 41.8 | 41.1 | 37.5 | (268) |
| Other | 56.7 | 39.1 | 33.5 | (441) |

on the previous analysis, Table 8 illustrates the overall weakness of socio-demographic determinants of leadership assessments. Statistically significant predictors of attitudes towards Klein are gender and area of residence within the province. A weaker, but also statistically significant negative predictor is a high level of education. Since the Klein variable is a 100-point feeling thermometer, and the independent variables are 'dummy' variables, the

**Table 8:** The Effect of Socio-demographic Characteristics on Party Leader Ratings

| | Party Leader | | | | | |
|---|---|---|---|---|---|---|
| | Klein | | Mitchell | | Harvey | |
| Criterion Variable | b (se) | | b (se) | | b (se) | |
| Constant | 54.7 | (4.1)** | 34.8 | (2.6)** | 28.4 | (3.0)** |
| *Gender* | | | | | | |
| Female | −13.5 | (2.7)** | 5.2 | (1.7)** | 5.3 | (2.0)** |
| *Education* | | | | | | |
| Less than high school grad. | −3.9 | (4.0) | −5.3 | (2.5)* | −2.8 | (2.9) |
| University | −8.1 | (2.9)** | 1.4 | (1.8) | 2.7 | (2.1) |
| *Age* | | | | | | |
| 18–24 years | 1.7 | (4.6) | 6.6 | (2.9)* | 9.9 | (3.3)** |
| 25–34 years | 6.0 | (3.4) | 5.3 | (2.2)** | 6.7 | (2.5)** |
| 50–64 years | −3.7 | (4.0) | 1.9 | (2.6) | 1.6 | (2.9) |
| 65+ years | 4.6 | (5.7) | −2.6 | (3.6) | −6.0 | (4.2) |
| *Income* | | | | | | |
| < $20,000 | −1.3 | (4.7) | −0.1 | (3.0) | 0.0 | (3.4) |
| $21,000–$40,000 | −4.7 | (3.4) | 2.1 | (2.2) | 2.7 | (2.5) |
| $61,000–$80,000 | −1.7 | (4.2) | −2.6 | (2.7) | 2.4 | (3.1) |
| $81,000+ | −1.5 | (4.3) | −1.7 | (2.7) | −0.2 | (3.1) |
| *Employment Status* | | | | | | |
| Part-time | −8.1 | (4.2) | −1.9 | (2.7) | 4.2 | (3.1) |
| Retired | 1.3 | (5.4) | −6.3 | (3.5) | −1.0 | (4.0) |
| Unemployed | −4.4 | (6.1) | −5.4 | (3.9) | 2.1 | (4.5) |
| Self-employed | 3.8 | (4.4) | −5.2 | (2.8) | −5.4 | (3.2) |
| Student | −6.7 | (6.0) | 9.0 | (3.8)* | 12.1 | (4.4)** |
| Homemaker | −3.3 | (5.8) | −5.0 | (3.7) | 2.4 | (4.2) |
| *Area* | | | | | | |
| Calgary | 17.8 | (3.6)** | 6.2 | (2.3)** | 0.1 | (2.6) |
| Rural | 16.0 | (3.1)** | 1.6 | (2.0) | −2.9 | (2.3) |
| Adjusted R-square | .13** | | .10** | | .11** | |

*p<.05; **p<.01
b: regression coefficient
se: standard error of estimate

NOTE: The adjusted R-square statistic indicates the proportion of the variance in people's attitudes towards the party leaders that can be explained by one's gender, education, age, income, employment status, and area of residence. Thus our results indicate that 13 per cent of the variation in people's attitudes towards Klein can be explained by these factors. In brackets beside the regression coefficients are standard errors. When marked with a single asterisk, a standard error is of a magnitude sufficient that one can judge the probability of the coefficient having a value of zero to be less than 5 chances in 100. Two asterisks indicate this probability is even lower; only 1 chance in 100.

**Table 9:** The Effect of Vote Intention and Socio-demographic Characteristics on Party Leader Ratings

| Criterion Variable | Klein b (se) | | Mitchell b (se) | | Harvey b (se) | |
|---|---|---|---|---|---|---|
| Constant | 41.4 | (3.8)** | 34.6 | (3.0)** | 31.2 | (3.4)** |
| *Vote Intention* | | | | | | |
| Conservative | 29.7 | (3.8)** | −3.1 | (2.1) | −6.6 | (2.4)** |
| Liberal | −13.1 | (3.0)** | 9.7 | (2.4)** | 1.4 | (2.7) |
| ND | −14.3 | (4.0)** | 1.2 | (3.2) | 13.1 | (3.6)** |
| *Gender* | | | | | | |
| Female | −8.3 | (2.1)** | 4.0 | (1.7)* | 4.1 | (1.9)* |
| *Education* | | | | | | |
| Less than high school grad. | −3.1 | (3.1) | −5.6 | (2.4)* | −2.9 | (2.8) |
| University | −3.3 | (2.3) | 0.5 | (1.8) | 1.2 | (2.0) |
| *Age* | | | | | | |
| 18–24 years | 4.2 | (3.5) | 6.1 | (2.8)* | 9.3 | (3.2)** |
| 25–34 years | 4.2 | (2.6) | 5.9 | (2.1)** | 7.4 | (2.4)** |
| 50–64 years | −0.8 | (3.1) | 1.2 | (2.5) | 1.6 | (2.9) |
| 65+ years | 3.8 | (4.5) | −2.4 | (3.6) | −4.8 | (4.1) |
| *Income* | | | | | | |
| < $20,000 | 2.1 | (3.6) | 0.2 | (2.9) | −1.5 | (3.3) |
| $21,000–$40,000 | −1.5 | (2.7) | 1.7 | (2.1) | 1.4 | (2.4) |
| $61,000–$80,000 | −4.9 | (3.2) | −1.6 | (2.6) | 2.4 | (3.0) |
| $81,000+ | −2.0 | (3.3) | −1.4 | (2.6) | −0.3 | (3.0) |
| *Employment Status* | | | | | | |
| Part-time | −2.8 | (3.3) | −2.7 | (2.6) | 2.1 | (3.0) |
| Retired | 2.0 | (4.2) | −6.5 | (3.4) | −2.0 | (3.9) |
| Unemployed | 5.1 | (4.8) | −7.0 | (3.8) | −1.0 | (4.3) |
| Self-employed | 0.3 | (3.4) | −4.4 | (2.7) | −4.8 | (3.1) |
| Student | 0.6 | (4.7) | 6.3 | (3.7) | 10.9 | (4.3)* |
| Homemaker | 0.0 | (4.5) | −5.6 | (3.6) | 1.9 | (4.1) |
| *Area* | | | | | | |
| Calgary | 13.9 | (2.8)** | 6.8 | (2.2)** | 1.3 | (2.5) |
| Rural | 10.9 | (2.5)** | 2.6 | (2.0) | −1.6 | (2.2) |
| Adjusted R-square | .47** | | .16** | | .16** | |

*p<.05; **p<.01

interpretation is that all other things being equal, females gave a rating to Klein 13.5 points lower than did males, and residents of Calgary and other areas outside Edmonton gave ratings to Klein 17.8 and 16.0 points higher than did Edmonton residents. Overall, however, these 19 variables explain only 13 per cent of the variance in attitudes towards Klein. Furthermore, note that these variables are even weaker predictors of attitudes towards Mitchell and Harvey; for each, females gave significantly higher evaluations than did men, but the effect of region of residence dissipated or disappeared altogether.

When the analysis was repeated including the three vote intention dummy variables, the performance of the models changed sharply. Note that for the vote intention variables, the suppressed category is undecided voters, so the coefficients compare the effect of partisan leaning with no partisan leaning. Vote intention is powerfully related to assessments of Klein, with all coefficients being very strong, and in the expected direction. Note also the dramatic improvement in performance of the model, which now explains 47 per cent of the variation in Klein's ratings. However, the addition of the vote intention variables had a much more muted effect on assessments of Mitchell and Harvey. Although the explanatory power of these models also improved (to an R-square of .16), the overall impact of party leanings on feelings towards the leaders was far more muted than for Klein. In short, neither Mitchell nor Harvey has the same drawing power as Klein. Furthermore, there are few groups in the electorate for whom the opposition party leaders have particular appeal, although women and youth hold some promise for both the opposition party leaders.

## 7. THE DYNAMICS OF VOTING

Thus far we have discussed opinion towards the Klein government's budget-balancing agenda and assessments of party leadership. These factors, while important in and of themselves, are also important for the role they play in explaining patterns of political support. It is to this ultimate question in democratic and electoral politics—for whom would you vote?—that we now turn.

First we examine the impact of socio-demographic characteristics. The data, presented in Table 10, are reasonably unambiguous—socio-demographic factors, with several notable exceptions, have little purchase in explaining voting patterns in Alberta. Women, the highly educated, and the unemployed are all less likely to vote Conservative than are their comparison groups (i.e., men, those with a 'middle' level of education, and full-time workers). In addition, living in an area outside the two large cities has a positive impact on Conservative voting, and residence in Calgary is just shy of achieving statistical significance. Overall, however, these factors explain only 9 per cent of the variance in Conservative voting. Furthermore, they explain virtually none of the variance

**Table 10:** The Effect of Socio-demographic Characteristics on Vote Intention

| | Party Would Vote For | | | | | |
| --- | --- | --- | --- | --- | --- | --- |
| | Conservative | | Liberal | | ND | |
| Criterion Variable | b (se) | | b (se) | | b (se) | |
| Constant | 0.56 | (.07)** | 0.20 | (.06)** | 0.05 | (.04) |
| *Gender* | | | | | | |
| Female | −0.13 | (.04)** | 0.08 | (.04)* | 0.01 | (.03) |
| *Education* | | | | | | |
| Less than high school grad. | −0.02 | (.06) | 0.03 | (.06)* | −0.01 | (.04) |
| University | −0.11 | (0.5)* | 0.05 | (.04) | 0.06 | (.03)* |
| *Age* | | | | | | |
| 18–24 years | −0.07 | (.07) | 0.03 | (.07) | 0.01 | (0.4) |
| 25–34 years | 0.05 | (.05) | 0.00 | (.05) | −0.03 | (0.3) |
| 50–64 years | −0.10 | (.06) | 0.05 | (.06) | −0.05 | (.04) |
| 65+ years | −0.03 | (.09) | −0.02 | (.08) | −0.11 | (.06)* |
| *Income* | | | | | | |
| < $20,000 | −0.11 | (.08) | −0.07 | (.07) | 0.07 | (.05) |
| $21,000–$40,000 | −0.08 | (.06) | 0.01 | (.05) | 0.05 | (.03) |
| $61,000–$80,000 | 0.10 | (.07) | −0.07 | (.06) | 0.05 | (.04) |
| $81,000+ | 0.02 | (.07) | −0.02 | (.06) | 0.02 | (.04) |
| *Employment Status* | | | | | | |
| Part-time | −0.12 | (.07) | 0.03 | (.06) | 0.10 | (.04)* |
| Retired | 0.03 | (.09) | 0.01 | (.08) | 0.10 | (.05) |
| Unemployed | −0.24 | (.10)* | 0.08 | (.09) | 0.11 | (.06) |
| Self-employed | 0.10 | (.07) | −0.05 | (.06) | 0.01 | (0.4) |
| Student | −0.15 | (.10) | 0.23 | (.09)** | −0.01 | (.06) |
| Homemaker | −0.11 | (.09) | 0.02 | (.08) | −0.01 | (.06) |
| *Area* | | | | | | |
| Calgary | 0.10 | (.06) | −0.03 | (.05) | −0.04 | (.04) |
| Rural | 0.12 | (.05)* | −0.07 | (.05) | −0.03 | (.03) |
| Adjusted R-square | .09** | .02 | | .02 | | |

*p<.05; **p<.01

in Liberal and New Democrat voting intention. To the extent that opposition to the Klein agenda is distributed differentially among groups in the electorate, the data indicate the opposition parties have been singularly unable to link themselves with those socio-economic pockets of discontent.

Although the data indicate the limited explanatory power of socio-demographic factors, they also indicate the important role played by attitudes towards deficit reduction and by leadership assessments in explaining vote intentions. Table 11 illustrates a fascinating pattern of attitudes towards the deficit and partisan support. As we noted previously, there is overwhelming support in Alberta for reducing the deficit. But the intensity of support for

**Table 11:** Attitudes Towards Budget-Balancing by Vote Intention

| | Party Would Vote For | | | |
| --- | --- | --- | --- | --- |
| | Conservative | Liberal | ND | Undecided |
| **a. Deficit elimination** | | | | |
| strongly support | 60.4 | 14.3 | 12.9 | 18.3 |
| support | 34.7 | 58.9 | 55.7 | 57.8 |
| oppose | 4.9 | 16.9 | 21.4 | 16.1 |
| strongly oppose | 0.0 | 10.0 | 10.0 | 7.8 |
| N | 409 | 231 | 70 | 218 |
| Cramer's V = .28** | | | | |
| **b. Pace of balanced budget in three years** | | | | |
| too fast | 28.5 | 81.7 | 68.9 | 70.6 |
| too slow | 4.4 | 1.3 | 4.1 | 2.7 |
| just about right | 67.2 | 17.0 | 27.0 | 26.7 |
| N | 411 | 235 | 74 | 221 |
| Cramer's V = .33** | | | | |

| | Conservative | Liberal | ND | Undecided | Cramer's V |
| --- | --- | --- | --- | --- | --- |
| **c. Support the following to balance the budget** | | | | | |
| i. cut spending | 96.8 | 87 | 84.5 | 88.8 | .18** |
| ii. increase personal tax | 11.9 | 30.9 | 35.2 | 17.9 | .23** |
| iii. increase corporate tax | 61.8 | 77.7 | 81.9 | 73.7 | .17** |
| iv. increase user fees | 63.6 | 36.8 | 31.3 | 39.8 | .26** |
| v. have sales tax | 9.9 | 25.2 | 26.0 | 17.6 | .19** |

*$p<.05$; **$p<.01$

NOTE: N defines the number of respondents. The Cramer's V statistic is a measure of association for nominal data. It takes on values between 0 and +1. The higher the value of this statistic, the stronger the relationship between the two variables.

budget-balancing, together with assessments of the appropriate pace for budget-balancing, provides important distinctions along lines of party support in Alberta. For example, whereas 60 per cent of Conservatives 'strongly support' deficit elimination, this high intensity of support drops to less than 15 per cent among Liberals and New Democrats and to 18 per cent among the undecided voters. However, for each of the latter three groups, differences with Conservative voters represent differences of degree rather than differences in kind, with a further 50 per cent or more supporting deficit elimination. The difference between the parties is founded on rather dramatic differences in perceptions of how quickly the budget should be balanced. Almost 7 in 10 Conservatives think that three years is about right, whereas 8 in 10 Liberals and 7 in 10 New Democrats think three years is too fast. Again, it is noteworthy that undecided voters are much more similar to the supporters of the opposition parties than they are to supporters of the government in their assessment of this item. Furthermore, whereas the data indicate substantial differences among party supporters on the pace of budget-balancing, the differences are more muted when it comes to selecting the instruments to be used for balancing the budget. The greatest agreement among supporters of the different parties is over cutting spending, increasing corporate taxes, and opposition to a sales tax. Partisans are more divided on the utility of higher personal taxes and more user fees. In each case, the differences are in the anticipated direction.

Much of the explanation for the political success of the Klein government can be found in Table 12. These data present the 100-point feeling thermometer scores for the three party leaders according to one's position on the deficit reduction agenda. There is a strong positive impact of attitudes towards deficit elimination on assessments of Klein, and a much weaker negative impact on assessments of Mitchell and Harvey. Furthermore, recall that fully 80.7 per cent of respondents either strongly support or support deficit reduction, the two categories in which the premier enjoys a substantial lead in overall assessments. Note also that whereas attitudes towards the pace of budget-balancing are strongly related to assessment of Klein, the relationship is much weaker for Mitchell and Harvey. Those who feel the cuts have been too slow or just about right have much higher evaluations of Klein, whereas assessments of the party leaders are quite indifferent among those feeling the three-year time frame is too fast. These general trends hold as well for assessments of the various techniques for balancing the budget. The conclusion to be drawn from Table 12 is that, once again, Klein has far greater mobilizing potential among supporters of his policies than do the opposition leaders among opponents of the Klein agenda. The result is that opponents of the Klein agenda either support the Liberals and New Democrats in spite of their misgivings about the party leaders, or they 'float' as part of the large group of undecided voters.

The final attitudinal analysis of the determinants of voting in Alberta is provided in Table 13. The story that emerges is both simple and profound. Conservative vote intention is explainable first and foremost by assessments of Ralph Klein, who is by far the party's greatest asset. Linked with assessments of Klein are support for the principle that the budget should be balanced in three years and opposition to the introduction of a sales tax. In addition, belief in the principle of deficit elimination strongly predicts Conservative support. Furthermore, this simple attitudinal model explains 48 per cent of the variance in Conservative voting. For the Liberals, the leadership effect is much more limited, and the only significant issue effect is the pace of budget reduction. Overall, the model explains only 26 per cent of the variance in Liberal voting, a proportion that drops to 11 per cent for New Democrats and 3 per cent for the undecided voters. Thus the distribution of party support presents a portrait of an electorate that is only half aligned. Conservatives have a strong evaluation of their leader, and the key principles of deficit elimination and moving quickly to balance the budget resonate with strong effects on Conservative Party support. Much of the remainder of the electorate, however, appears to be unaligned. The effect of the other party leaders is either

**Table 12:** Attitudes Towards Party Leaders by Deficit Reduction Attitudes

|  | Party Leader | | |
|---|---|---|---|
|  | Klein | Mitchell | Harvey |
| **a. Deficit elimination** (mean thermometer rating) | | | |
| strongly support | 72.1 | 36.3 | 29.4 |
| support | 47.6 | 41.9 | 36.8 |
| oppose | 34.4 | 47.8 | 44.7 |
| strongly oppose | 27.9 | 43.5 | 45.8 |
| N | (963) | (832) | (673) |
| Eta-squared | .23** | .04** | .05** |
| **b. Pace of balanced budget in three years** (mean thermometer rating) | | | |
| too fast | 39.7 | 43.6 | 38.5 |
| too slow | 70.5 | 37.1 | 25.7 |
| just about right | 69.9 | 37.7 | 33.0 |
| N | (975) | (844) | (684) |
| Eta-squared | .24** | .02** | .02** |

**c. Support the following action to balance the budget** (mean thermometer rating)

|  | Klein | | Mitchell | | Harvey | |
|---|---|---|---|---|---|---|
|  | support | oppose | support | oppose | support | oppose |
| i. cut spending | 55.3 | 37.0** | 40.5 | 39.7 | 34.8 | 42.5* |
| ii. increase personal tax | 40.8 | 56.4** | 45.3 | 39.7** | 43.0 | 33.6** |
| iii. increase corporate tax | 49.4 | 61.1** | 42.1 | 37.7** | 37.5 | 31.1** |
| iv. increase user fees | 61.6 | 45.3** | 39.1 | 42.7** | 32.3 | 38.6** |
| v. have sales tax | 42.6 | 55.3** | 43.2 | 40.1 | 41.1 | 34.2** |

*p<.05; **p<.01

NOTE: The eta-squared statistic is a measure of association when one of the variables is nominal and the other is interval. Its value ranges from 0 to +1. The higher the value of this statistic, the stronger the relationship between the two variables. Thus attitudes towards deficit reduction explain 23 per cent of the variance in ratings of Klein, but only 4 per cent in ratings of Mitchell.

**Table 13:** The Effect of Leader Evaluations and Attitudes Towards the Deficit on Vote Intention

|  | Party Would Vote For | | | | | | | |
|---|---|---|---|---|---|---|---|---|
|  | Conservative | | Liberal | | ND | | Undecided | |
| Constant | −.089 | (.170) | .778 | (.176)** | .002 | (.123)** | .288 | (.186) |
| **Party Leaders** | | | | | | | | |
| Klein | .077 | (.001)** | −.004 | (.001)* | −.002 | (.000)** | −.000 | (.001) |
| Mitchell | −.002 | (.001)* | .005 | (.001)** | −.002 | (.001)* | −.001 | (.001) |
| Harvey | −.001 | (.001) | −.002 | (.001)* | .003 | (.001)** | .001 | (.000) |
| **Issue Attitudes** | | | | | | | | |
| Deficit elimination | −.070 | (.026)** | −.016 | (.027) | .026 | (.019) | .068 | (.029)* |
| Pace of balancing budget | .188 | (.041)** | −.195 | (.043)** | .043 | (.030) | −.037 | (.047) |
| Spending cuts | .001 | (.067) | −.063 | (.070) | .099 | (.048)* | −.067 | (.075) |
| Increase personal tax | .008 | (.042) | −.025 | (.044) | −.016 | (.030) | .033 | (.048) |
| Increase corporate tax | .003 | (.039) | −.006 | (.041) | .004 | (.028) | .011 | (.043) |
| Increase user fees | −.060 | (.036) | .032 | (.037) | −.009 | (.025) | .043 | (.039) |
| Introduce sales tax | .132 | (.046)** | −.022 | (.047) | −.032 | (.033) | −.094 | (.050) |
| **Adjusted R-square** | .48** | | .26** | | .11** | | .03* | |

*p<.05; **p<.01

substantially more muted or, in the case of undecided voters, non-existent. Even on the core policies of the Klein agenda, opposition parties have been unsuccessful in hitching themselves to the substantial elements of opposition that exist. It is in the lack of partisan focus of its opponents, coupled with its own clarity of support, that the Conservative government continues to find its political success.

## 8. CONCLUSIONS

The political public opinion landscape in Alberta is one on which partisan and leadership effects loom large, and on which socio-demographic effects other than those associated with gender are relatively subdued. It is also a landscape where many of the most important differences are in the degree of support for the Klein agenda. We see less a landscape of polarized camps than we do a landscape characterized by enthusiastic and moderate supporters of balanced budgets, program cuts, government restructuring, and, more broadly defined neo-conservative policies. The absence of polarization makes the landscape a very difficult one for opposition parties and leaders, as large groups of discontented voters are difficult to find, categorize, and mobilize.

What lessons does the Alberta experience hold for other provinces and countries? First, neo-conservative governments can minimize the possibility of inflaming opposition by avoiding direct responsibility for specific program cuts. The Klein government has done this by passing the responsibility for specific cuts down to school districts, hospital boards, and universities. Opposition parties are then placed in a difficult position. If they attack the government's broad economic objectives, they face public opposition, but if they target specific cuts, they find themselves in conflict with local authorities. Second, the opposition that does exist, such as that attributable to feminist and gender-based resistance to neo-conservatism, will only be effective if it is cultivated and orchestrated by opposition parties. To date, this has not been the Alberta experience. Although latent gender and feminism gaps exist in the electorate, they remain dormant, in part because opposition parties have not sought to exploit them. Such a strategy could well be effective—this study found that the cleavages of gender and feminism were among the strongest within the Alberta electorate. If articulated and nurtured by opposition parties, these cleavages could grow. In the face of strong popular support for the broad economic principles of neo-conservatism, such a strategy may be one of a very few options available to opposition parties.

Finally, what lessons does the Alberta experience hold for neo-conservative politics in Canada's largest province, Ontario, where a new Progressive Conservative government has embarked on a neo-conservative trajectory similar to that adopted by Alberta in 1993? In answering this question, we must first put aside the common assumption that the Alberta experience, indeed any Alberta experience, is too idiosyncratic to generalize to the Canadian heartland. In this case, there is little that is idiosyncratic about the primary forces at work; ideological currents of neo-conservatism and the public policy pressures generated by public debt and deficits are not unique to Alberta. While opposition parties may be notoriously weak in the province, the current legislative strength of the opposition Liberals easily rivals that of opposition parties in Ontario. We would argue, therefore, that lessons for Ontario can be drawn from the Alberta experience. If neo-conservative governments move rapidly across a broad policy front, if they stick to an economic agenda, and if they offload the responsibility for specific cuts to local authorities, boards, and institutions, then the Alberta experience suggests that opposition to specific aspects of the government's agenda need not generate an unmanageable electoral threat.

## NOTES

1. For a generally critical assessment, see T. Harrison and G. Laxer, eds, *The Trojan Horse: Alberta and the Future of Canada* (Montreal: Black Rose Books, 1995). For a much more positive assessment, see B. Cooper, *The Klein Achievement* (Toronto: University of Toronto Press, 1995).

2. For a detailed discussion, see R. Gibbins and J. Stewart-Toth, 'Globalization, Community Attachment and Provincial Down-Sizing: The Alberta Experience', paper presented at the annual conference of the Atlantic Provinces Political Studies Association, Fredericton, NB, 13–15 Oct. 1995.

3. For an extended discussion of differences related to gender and feminism, see L. Youngman and R. Gibbins, 'Gender and Neoconservatism: Public Policy Implications of the Alberta Experience', paper presented to the annual meeting of the New Zealand Political Studies Association, Wellington, New Zealand, 30 Aug. 1995.

4. See G. Dacks, J. Green, and L. Trimble, 'Road Kill: Women in Alberta's Drive Toward Deficit Elimination', in Harrison and Laxer, eds, *The Trojan Horse*, 270–85.

5. There is also considerable tension between feminism and the moral agenda of neo-conservatives, although our data do not illuminate this tension.

6. Respondents were asked, 'On a scale of one to ten, where one is not very close at all, and ten is very close, how close do you feel to feminists?' The same question was also asked with reference to environmentalists, territorial identifications, class, and religion. Interestingly, closeness to feminism is not correlated with the gender of respondents.

7. The effects of gender and feminism are additive, and therefore a measure that takes both into account provides a powerful tool for interpreting the Alberta public opinion landscape. See Youngman and Gibbins, 'Gender and Neoconservatism'.

8. Alberta, *Report of the Chief Electoral Officer*, 1993.

9. For a discussion of partisan dynamics in Alberta, see K. Archer, 'Voting Behaviour and Political Dominance in Alberta, 1971–1991', in A. Tupper and R. Gibbins, eds, *Government and Politics in Alberta* (Edmonton: University of Alberta Press, 1992).

10. See, for example, R. Johnston, A. Blais, H. Brady, and J. Crête, *Letting the People Decide: Dynamics of a Canadian Election* (Montreal and Kingston: McGill-Queen's University Press, 1992); H. Clarke, J. Jenson, L. LeDuc, and J. Pammett, *Absent Mandate: Interpreting Change in Canadian Elections* (Toronto: Gage, 1991).

11. Parenthetically, it is interesting to note that Jean Chrétien is evaluated more positively than Preston Manning among this sample of Albertans. This finding is consistent with data for the 1993 Canadian National Election Study. It is at odds with simplistic views of political support that see Preston Manning and the Reform Party dominating contemporary politics in Alberta.

12. For a discussion of Klein's selection as Conservative Party leader, see K. Archer and D. Stewart, 'Democracy, Representation and the Selection of Party Leaders in Alberta', paper presented to the 1995 meeting of the Atlantic Provinces Political Studies Association, University of New Brunswick, 1995; J. Stokes and K. Archer, 'The De-Klein of Government in Alberta', paper presented to the annual meeting of the Canadian Political Science Association, University of Quebec at Montreal, 6–8 June 1995; and D. Stewart, 'Electing the Premier: An Analysis of the 1992 Alberta PC Leadership', paper presented to the annual meeting of the Canadian Political Science Association, University of Calgary, 2–4 June 1994.

13. The relative weakness of socio-demographic determinants of political attitudes has been a recurrent theme of research on Canadian voting behaviour. Canadians' partisan ties are only weakly related to their long-term socio-demographic charac-

teristics. As a result, Canadians' political attitudes and partisan ties are highly fluid and variable. This partisan fluidity facilitates significant, and at times even dramatic, reversals of party fortunes, such as occurred in the 1993 federal election. For a discussion of the weakness of socio-demographic determinants of political behaviour, see L. LeDuc, H. Clarke, J. Jenson, and J. Pammett, 'Partisan Instability in Canada: Evidence from a New Panel Study', *American Political Science Review* 78 (1984): 470–83. For an application to Alberta politics, see K. Archer, 'Voting Behaviour and Political Dominance in Alberta, 1971–1991'.

# Comments on Chapter 13

∎

*Linda Trimble*

The Archer/Gibbins chapter addresses a question that has been vexing Alberta political scientists since the Klein government made the first of a series of dramatic program spending cuts in 1994: how can a government that has done such unpopular things retain its fairly high level of popularity? The authors present data gleaned from a public opinion survey conducted in April and May 1995 and provide a two-part answer.

First, while Albertans don't like many of the Klein government's policies, especially spending cuts to health care and education, they overwhelmingly approve of the government's overall policy direction (deficit elimination). In other words, many Albertans oppose the specifics while supporting the big picture. The second part of the answer is that the fairly high level of discontent with the government's performance, and the high level of concern about many of the specific deficit reduction policies, have not yet been effectively mobilized. In particular, the huge, unprecedented gender gap in public opinion—at 15 to 17 points on most measures—has yet to be either recognized or used as a strategy by opposition parties. This is not surprising as gender is typically overlooked by politicians and political scientists. I applaud Archer and Gibbins for including gender as a variable and taking it seriously. On the whole, their two-part answer is based on sound hypotheses and is well supported by the data.

I have only three quibbles with the chapter. The first is that the authors refer to the Klein agenda as a neo-conservative agenda. I agree that the Klein agenda is neo-conservative but it is *also* neo-liberal. These are divergent, though not incompatible, ideological perspectives, and it is important to keep the distinction in mind[1] when analysing government policy and public opinion. The *neo-liberal agenda* is an economic agenda with political implications. Its overriding goal is to promote the freest possible market for increasingly fluid transnational capital. Neo-liberals support minimum government in general and minimum regulation of corporate activity in particular; thus, they promote privatization, deregulation, and the dismantling of the welfare state. A smaller, less regulatory state eliminates barriers to transnational capital, such as social programs, which are considered 'subsidies'. The neo-conservative agenda is a political and moral agenda premised on support for hierarchical and authoritarian social relations. The neo-conservative believes in order, stability, and authority, and therefore supports 'law and order' generally and 'getting tough on youth crime' in particular. The neo-conservative supports the patriarchal family and other supposedly 'natural' societal hierarchies. So, for the neo-conservative, the fact that there is a massive gap between the rich and the poor is of little concern to the government as those who work hard are well off, those who slack off or fail to 'make something of themselves' are poor, and it is silly and counterproductive for the state to intervene in this 'natural' process. Neo-conservatives, therefore, are in favour of 'cracking down on welfare fraud' and dramatically cutting social assistance payments. For the neo-conservative, gender inequality is also not a concern of government because inequities in wages, power, and economic status are 'natural' outcomes of 'innate' gender differences.

Clearly, the Alberta government's policies reflect both neo-conservatism and neo-liberalism. I'm not so sure about the electorate, though. According to the Archer/Gibbins data, there is support for privatization and for 'less government' in the sense that people support consolidation of school boards and so on. But there is opposition to the withering away of the welfare state, as Archer and Gibbins show. Albertans are acutely concerned about the nature and pace of dramatic spending cuts to kindergarten, health care, schools, and universities. The public values public health care and education and does not support privatization in these sectors. As for neo-conservatism, because the study did not delve into moral issues, there isn't much to go on here. Respondents seemed fairly mean-spirited with respect to welfare recipients; most supported cuts to social welfare payments and mandatory job retraining. On the whole, though, the authors do not have enough data to assert that, 'in ideological terms, most Albertans are neo-conservatives who find themselves in agreement with the broad outlines of the Klein agenda.'

My second comment is that the authors discuss the gender gap and the feminism gap in public opinion, but don't sufficiently distinguish between the two. The distinction is implicitly made, as an aside or afterthought, in a footnote (note 6). The gender gap means that women are significantly more likely than men to disapprove of the government's performance, and women are significantly less likely than men to support the premier and the governing Conservative Party. Archer and Gibbins also discover a feminism gap, with people who identify themselves as feminists less likely to support the Klein government and to approve of the government's agenda. It would be easy to conclude that the gender gap and the feminism gap are one and the same thing, but as the authors point out (in the note referred to above), support for feminism is not correlated with gender. Therefore, the gender gap can't be explained by saying that women are more likely to be feminists, and the Klein government can't easily dismiss the gender gap as a creation of feminist 'special interest groups'.

There is evidence that the gender gap is widening. A University of Alberta Population Research Lab survey found a gender gap with respect to levels of concern about the impact of program spending cuts, but the percentage difference did not exceed 10 points.[2] The Archer/Gibbins survey finds a gender gap between 15 and 17 points on measures such as overall assessment of the government's performance, concern about the speed of the spending cuts, and voting intentions. The high levels of concern among women are not surprising given the fact that women encounter, firsthand, the effects of the cuts, especially in education and health care. Women form the majority of workers in these sectors and are more likely than men to interact with schools, doctors' offices, and hospitals. Women are also more likely than men to provide services no longer provided by government and to 'pick up the slack' due to service and program deterioration. Alberta women are volunteering in schools and communities, taking care of the sick and elderly, and generally performing unpaid and unrecognized work in an attempt to mend the social safety net. My prediction is that, unless the Alberta government begins to rethink the 'reinvented' education and health care systems, the gender gap will grow.

Finally, I disagree with the conclusion of the chapter, which asserts that the new Ontario government will likely be able to follow in Alberta's footsteps by slashing program spending and enjoying continued public support none the less. Ontario doesn't share Alberta's 'one party state' characteristics, especially the discomfort with opposition evidenced here. Ontario has a history and tradition of strong opposition parties, and a three-party legislature; Alberta doesn't. In many ways, Alberta *is* idiosyncratic. In Alberta, opposing the government is viewed as unseemly, anti-Albertan, and, to some extent, traitorous. Remember when the premier went to Texas and the Liberals faxed their 'Kleindex' to a few newspapers? This move, which would have been regarded as fair-game politics in any other province, was soundly condemned by the press and the public; it wasn't fair to criticize the premier and his government when they were out trying to promote Alberta, people said. It's as if criticism of the government is seen as criticism of Alberta itself. The Alberta legislature is arguably the most opposition-unfriendly legislature in Canada.[3] For instance, the Liberals have been scoring some political points recently, especially on the health care system. Indeed, the opposition party has been effective enough that the Tories kept the fall 1995 session extraordinarily brief to avoid continued criticism in the legislature and bad press. In short, I wouldn't tell the Ontario government to expect an easy ride. It is likely that opposition will be mobilized much more quickly and effectively in Ontario.

In conclusion, I would like to reiterate my overall assessment of the chapter. The research is relevant and interesting, and the data and analysis are presented in a clear and straightforward fashion. If I were a government or opposition party strategist, I would study the results very carefully. Perhaps Alberta political parties will absorb a key conclusion of the chapter, which is that women's realities shape opinion formation and voting intentions. Perhaps the next election will be conducted as if women matter.

## NOTES

1. This distinction is drawn by G. Dacks, J. Green, and L. Trimble in 'Road Kill: Women in Alberta's Drive Toward Deficit Elimination', in T. Harrison and G. Laxer, eds, *The Trojan Horse: Alberta and the Future of Canada* (Montreal: Black Rose Books, 1995): 270–1.

2. K. Hughes, G. Lowe, and A. McKinnon, 'Albertans' Experiences with Cuts to Health Care, Education and Public Sector Employment', Edmonton: University of Alberta Population Research Lab Discussion Paper No. 111, September 1995.

3. See F. Engelmann, 'The Legislature', in A. Tupper and R. Gibbins, eds, *Government and Politics in Alberta* (Edmonton: University of Alberta Press, 1992): 137–66.

# CHAPTER 14

# A Government Reinvented?  ∎

*Christopher J. Bruce, Ronald D. Kneebone, and Kenneth J. McKenzie*

## 1. INTRODUCTION

The goal of *A Government Reinvented* has been to shed light on the question of *how* the Alberta government was able to implement such a massive downsizing of the government in such a short period of time. As indicated in the introductory chapter, by the end of fiscal year 1998/9, real per capita government expenditures are projected to have been reduced by approximately 38 per cent from 1992/3 levels. This is a substantial reduction by any standard; the time frame makes it all the more remarkable. The answer to the question of how the Alberta government has accomplished what it has done will prove important in determining whether the Alberta experience can provide lessons for other jurisdictions considering reducing their budget deficits or restructuring their service delivery. In this concluding chapter, we present our view on what others may learn from the Alberta experience.

We organize these insights according to a very loose 'public choice' framework. That is, in keeping with the literatures surveyed by McKenzie (Chapter 3) and Kneebone (Chapter 4), we conceive of the political process as a complex multiple principal-agent 'game' played among four groups of actors. In this game, the dominant group, 'the government', consists of the elected members of the party in power. While the government can be thought of as the agent of the electorate, once elected it tends to dominate the game in the sense that it has first-mover advantage, setting the political agenda to which the other groups react. The second group is composed of 'civil servants'. Their function is to provide information to, and act as agent for, the government. However, as stressed in the principal-agent approach, it is also recognized that civil servants have their own goals that may conflict with those of the government, and they may attempt to realize these goals if adequate constraints or incentives are not established. A third group is 'voters', who wish to maximize their own utility levels subject to the constraints placed on them by the necessity to pay taxes and by the cost to them of obtaining information. Voters can be viewed as the ultimate principal in the principal-agent framework, counting on governments to represent their interests. Finally, we also identify a group we call 'consumers' or 'stakeholders'. These are the individuals who benefit directly from particular government programs. With respect to Advanced Education, for example, this group would be composed primarily of students and instructors at post-secondary institutions (such as universities and colleges); with respect to Health, it would be composed primarily of health professionals, the elderly, and the ill.

In the deficit elimination game played by the Alberta government, we presume that the government's goal was to obtain the civil servants' co-operation in reducing the deficit with as little reduction in the quantity and quality of government services as possible, at the same time maintaining the support of the majority of voters and minimizing the strength of the objections raised by consumers. In the remainder of this chapter, we assess the policies the Alberta government followed with respect to each of these groups. As we have stressed throughout the volume, the purpose of this assessment is *not* to determine whether or not the government should have attempted to eliminate its deficit or to undertake a major restructuring of the way it provided services to the public. Rather, the goal is to provide a critical review of the methods chosen to achieve these ends.

## 2. CIVIL SERVANTS

In some chapters in this volume, it was suggested that the government appeared inconsistent at times in the way it dealt with the civil servants charged with implementing the cuts. At the very least, it appears that the government held a number of possibly conflicting hypotheses regarding the behaviour of civil servants and their reactions to the budget cuts. First, it seems that there was a prevailing belief that most agencies were operating sufficiently inefficiently that substantial budget cuts could be absorbed without causing a significant reduction in the quality or quantity of services delivered. Thus, the government felt that a cut in expenditures that averaged 20 per cent across departments was feasible without dramatically affecting quality. Second, the government recognized that civil servants (broadly defined), in order to protect their own salaries and positions of authority, might attempt to thwart government objectives (although perhaps not overtly). This perception was most clearly visible in the government's treatment of Education. But, third, it also seemed to believe that a model based on the presumption that government employees would act only to further their own goals might be overly simplistic. Some employees, perhaps driven by professional standards of conduct, could be expected to adopt a public-spirited attitude. In addition, the government often appeared to take the view that in many cases civil servants were in a better position than were its own members to identify efficiency-improving measures. This latter perception was most clearly in evidence in the government's treatment of Advanced Education.

One view is that these different hypotheses are mutually exclusive and therefore irreconcilable. Another, which we prefer, is that the bureaucracy is complex, and that any approach to structural reform inevitably involves trade-offs. Moreover, the margins along which these trade-offs occur are likely to differ across different agencies within the bureaucracy, depending on the amount of information the politicians possess *vis-à-vis* civil servants, the ability and cost of monitoring, etc. As such, what may appear on the surface to be an inconsistent approach to policy-making both within and across agencies may in fact represent differences among these trade-offs. If so, the government was faced with a complex balancing act with respect to its relationship with civil servants.

In the remainder of this section, we discuss four ways in which the government appears to have tried to juggle its wishes to increase efficiency *vis-à-vis* its relationship with the civil service.

## 2.1 Devolution of Power

One of the distinguishing characteristics of Alberta's deficit elimination program was the degree of authority provided to individual government agencies in making both budget-cutting and restructuring decisions. Indeed, an important lesson that arose from our study was the role played by delegation and devolution in the restructuring process. With a few important exceptions (discussed below), the government provided little in the way of detailed direction concerning how the cuts were to be implemented; agencies were told what their overall budgets were, and then, aside from fairly broad policy objectives, were left to determine for themselves how best to make the required cuts.[1]

The success of this approach seems to have been a function of two factors: the size of the cut imposed on the agency and whether or not the agency had previously studied proposals for a restructuring (which may reflect different informational advantages on the part of different agencies). The latter factor seems to have been particularly important. A critical lesson for other governments contemplating a substantial budget cut and restructuring of services is to begin the process by consulting the civil service at every level. This is particularly important in complex areas such as health care and social services, where agency employees may have a substantial informational advantage. The civil service has likely already accumulated a substantial stock of innovative ideas. Moreover, the civil service is in many cases much more knowledgeable than the government about the nature of the services to be delivered and about alternative delivery mechanisms. Thus, the job of a new government may be less to create new ideas than it is to induce its employees to reveal the ideas already in their possession.[2] Moreover, as discussed by McKenzie in Chapter 3 and

Kneebone and McKenzie in Chapter 5, involving civil servants in the restructuring process right from the beginning might also encourage them to 'buy in' to the reforms, making it more likely that they are implemented in a way that is consistent with the government's agenda.

It seems, however, that for previously studied innovations to be implemented, a large cut to the agency's budget was required. Those agencies whose revenues were reduced the least, including schools and universities, tended to rely on options such as early retirement plans and reductions in support staff to produce only minor modifications to the delivery of services, very much as principal-agent theory would predict.[3] As well, proposals for change were often delayed significantly by extensive consultative activities and by reference to committees. Emery discusses some of these issues with respect to Advanced Education in Chapter 10.

The agencies that suffered the greatest reductions in government financing, however, introduced the most creative changes, which may lead to improved efficiency. By the end of fiscal year 1995/6, for example, Alberta Health had reduced its budget by over 22 per cent in real per capita terms in just three years and in the process replaced a maze of small hospital boards with 17 Regional Health Authorities (RHAs), closing and rationalizing numerous hospitals in the process. Although broad goals and general guidance were provided by Alberta Health, the RHAs were given substantial latitude in deciding how to achieve the budget cuts requested of them. As discussed by Plain in Chapter 9, it is too early to analyse the long-run impact of the resulting changes; however, it seems clear at this time that some efficiencies were realized. Similarly, the Department of Labour introduced Delegated Administrative Organizations and Family and Social Services cut its welfare roles by half by encouraging 'employable' recipients of special assistance to accept greater responsibility for their own support.

In each of these cases, and in many more that were investigated, agencies were able to move quickly because the ideas that were introduced had been under consideration, at least internally, for some time; the relevant agencies had simply been waiting for an opportunity to put these ideas into effect. The need for restructuring suggested by drastic budget cuts provided such an opportunity.

As pointed out by Archer and Gibbins in Chapter 13, devolving the responsibility for administering the cuts down to the agencies may not only make 'economic' sense but also 'political' sense—it takes some of the heat off the government and places it on the agencies themselves. This may well explain Archer and Gibbins's finding that the general support for the government's deficit elimination program is high, while the support for specific elements of the program is low.

The devolution of decision-making power has not been without problems, however. In Chapter 12, Bruce argues that empowering the bureaucracy may introduce a bias against contracting out and privatization. Although there have been instances when the civil service was the source of privatization proposals, this has not been widespread. In general, civil servants have little apparent incentive to initiate programs that contract out their jobs to private-sector employers. Hence, a possible weakness of the Alberta experiment is that the government did not institute a mechanism to counter this bias and encourage greater consideration of contracting out.

Devolution also raises the possibility that the civil service will present programs that are not consistent with the government's objectives. An example of this problem was observed when the initial business plans were presented to the Standing Policy Committees (SPCs). The plans of a number of agencies were not consistent with the restructuring objectives of the SPCs and were therefore sent back for more work. This is indicative of a bureaucracy that, if left to its own devices, may have chosen a different route than that preferred by the government. The government seemed to recognize the potential for this problem and in some cases, presumably where the government thought the likelihood of the problem arising was most prevalent, established mechanisms to deal with it.

## 2.2 Monitoring and Incentives

Although the Alberta government was willing to provide its employees with a great deal of leeway in implementing the budget cuts, it was unwilling to give them complete *carte blanche*. Rather, it introduced various monitoring and incentive schemes and imposed administrative limits to ensure that civil servants did not make decisions inconsistent with the government's broad goals. Three types of incentive schemes were employed: three-year business plans, Key Performance Indicators (KPIs), and intragovernmental competition.

Instead of providing an annual budget, each government agency is required to produce a rotating three-year business plan, setting out its long-term goals and identifying how it proposes to meet those goals. One of the objectives of these plans is to establish broad criteria against which the performance of senior civil servants can be measured. However, as Bruce notes in Chapter 12, when the New Zealand government attempted to write performance-based contracts with its senior civil servants it discovered that 'performance' was extremely difficult to measure. The Alberta government may have mitigated this problem in part by having its agencies establish their own broad goals as set forth in the business plans (subject to the approval of the relevant SPC). As such, the three-year business plans provide a monitoring and incentive mechanism for the government. A unique aspect of these plans is that they are also made available to the public. This facilitates monitoring by the public, which may well prove to be more effective than internal monitoring by the government.

As discussed by Boothe in Chapter 6, the three-year plans also moved departments away from the 'spend it or lose it' attitude often associated with short-term, line-item budgeting. The three-year plans provided agencies with the flexibility to move budget items both across time and across uses.[4] For example, as discussed by Shedd in Chapter 8, Family and Social Services redirected money away from welfare rolls towards services for the disabled. Similarly, in Chapter 9, Plain discusses how Alberta Health moved money away from acute care and towards community care programs.

In recognition that the goals associated with three-year business plans are stated in very general terms, the government has also required that its agencies develop KPIs. These indicators are designed to establish specific criteria against which each agency's performance is to be measured. For example, Regional Health Authorities might be evaluated by measures such as the length of waiting lists for elective surgery, the survival rate of newborns, and the number of patients who must be readmitted following hospital treatment; and universities might be evaluated by the numbers of students receiving national or international scholarships or by the satisfaction rating given by graduating students. As one might expect, the government is struggling with the definition of appropriate and meaningful performance indicators. At this point, then, KPIs are viewed as more of an information and monitoring mechanism for both the government and the public than as an incentive device. However, within some specific areas the government has proposed distributing and allocating funds on the basis of performance as measured in the KPIs; this has been proposed, for example, in Advanced Education (see Emery, Chapter 10).

Finally, the regionalization of areas such as health and social services has created an environment conducive to experimentation and competition across the province. The health authorities, for example, have been encouraged to monitor one another's experiments with new technologies and service delivery mechanisms. As the 17 RHAs operate largely independently of each other, there is considerable scope for cross-fertilization of ideas. Also, to a lesser extent, competition among agencies has been encouraged. Within Education, for example, parents were given permission to establish government-funded charter schools to compete with the existing school system; and provincial funding now 'follows' students who move from one school district to another. Within Advanced Education, an Access Fund was created for which colleges and universities compete for additional funding.

## 2.3 Administrative Limits

A concern of any government that imposes significant budget cuts is that civil servants may give preference to proposals that preserve the salaries and jobs of government employees, at the expense of the users of government services. In a small number of cases, the Alberta government introduced administrative limits to constrain such activities. For example, to ensure that some part of the budget cuts was borne by civil servants, the government used moral suasion to induce virtually all of its agencies to accept a 5 per cent wage roll-back. Also, out of concern that school boards would protect administrative positions at the expense of resources devoted directly to teaching, the government imposed strict limits on the percentage of school board budgets that could be devoted to administration. And in Advanced Education, where administrators might be tempted to pass some of the cuts on to students in the form of higher tuition fees, limits were set on both the rate at which tuition could be increased and the absolute percentage of the school's budget that could be financed from tuition.[5]

All of these provisions acted specifically to constrain agencies from acting in ways contrary to those desired by the government. In most cases, constraints of this type were established in areas where the direct control over the decision-making process was not fully in the hands of the government. For example, university and college administrators are largely autonomous from the government and may pursue different objectives. Similarly, at the basic education level, locally elected school boards may have other objectives and serve a narrower constituency than the government. Indeed, in the interviews with policy-makers reported in Chapter 5 by Kneebone and McKenzie, it was indicated that the government had previous experience with school boards following an agenda different from its own.

## 2.4 Cutting Horizontally and Simultaneously

Not only did the government impose significant cuts on every department (including the salaries and pensions of MLAs), it announced all of those cuts virtually simultaneously. One effect of this policy was to defuse opposition, both internally and externally, to the government's program. If one department's budget had been cut much earlier than others', or by a much greater amount, that department might have been able to organize other departments in its support. When all departments were affected simultaneously, however, each became too self-absorbed to be able to lend support to others. Thus, although in many cases the government did not have in place a detailed plan as to how all of the budget cuts were to be met, the general size of the cuts across functional areas was established early and simultaneously. From one perspective this may have been politically risky—consider the implications of not being able to meet the announced cuts. On the other hand, it did send a clear signal to the bureaucracy.

A potential drawback to a policy of cutting all departments at the same time was that they might respond by forming a common front against the deficit-elimination program. Indeed, it is difficult to see how the government could have prevented such a feeling of commonality from forming. However, it appears that the government was relatively successful in this regard, as the across-the-board nature of the cuts seemed at least to defuse the opposition within the civil service to some extent.

## 3. VOTERS

One of the greatest challenges facing a government in a period of dramatic budget retrenchment is maintaining the support of the electorate. As pointed out by Archer and Gibbins in Chapter 13, one of the distinguishing features of the budget-cutting process in Alberta has been the ability of the government to maintain a remarkably high level of public support. Important elements of the government's strategy in this respect concern the gathering of information about voters' preferences and the dissemination of information regarding its policies.

### 3.1 Gathering Information

As Kneebone (Chapter 4) notes, some political economy models assume that politicians seek to minimize the political costs and maximize the political benefits associated with spending and tax changes. To do so requires that they monitor public opinion closely. Key elements of the government's strategy in this regard were the use of public roundtables and an increased role for backbench MLAs in the policy process.

As soon as it was elected, the government organized a series of public roundtables to which both informed laypersons and representatives of various special interest groups were invited. These large, well-publicized meetings dealt with broad issues concerning general aspects of the budget cuts. These were followed by smaller roundtables that sounded out public opinion on detailed issues. In Education, for example, five implementation teams held public meetings concerning (i) regionalizing and amalgamating school boards, (ii) redefining roles and responsibilities, (iii) creating a framework for funding school boards, (iv) developing an accountability framework and performance measures, and (v) improving business involvement and technology integration. While the roundtables served to inform the public of the government's intentions, perhaps their most important role was to reaffirm to the government that the public was generally supportive of the thrust of the deficit elimination program.

In addition, backbenchers in the Conservative caucus were given increased power through the use of Standing Policy Committees. (For a discussion of these committees, see section 4 below, and Boothe in Chapter 6.) Some argue that individual MLAs are closer to their constituents than are cabinet members. To the extent that this is true, these committees can act as an important conduit through which grass-roots opinion can reach the cabinet.

### 3.2 Dissemination of Information

With some exceptions, the Alberta government did not devote a great deal of effort to keeping voters informed about the specific details of the changes it was implementing. In many cases, this led to misinformation. For example, there seemed to be a public perception that the cuts had affected particular services dramatically even when close examination proved these claims to be exaggerated. The areas of basic and advanced education provide a good example of this. As illustrated by Bruce and Schwartz in Chapter 11, total school budgets were cut by only 6.2 per cent on average, with much of that cut being made up with the 5 per cent roll-back of teachers' salaries. Similarly, in Chapter 10 Emery shows that some universities used tuition increases and salary cuts to offset a large portion of their budget reductions. Yet, as shown by Archer and Gibbins in Chapter 13, the public perception seems to be that these areas suffered huge cuts.

This public misperception may have acted to promote the government's objectives in a curious sort of way. Although on the one hand the government had to face perhaps unfounded criticism in these areas, on the other hand, inequities *across* departments were less apparent. Given that an important element of the government's strategy was to give the *impression* of across-the-board cuts in which everyone shared the pain, it may well have chosen to face what it considered the lesser of two evils. Archer and Gibbins describe what they refer to as a sort of 'siege mentality' on the part of the electorate. Their survey results suggest that while Albertans are very supportive of the general budget-cutting exercise, they are more critical of the details. As such, voters seem to have bought into the general message delivered by the government that broad across-the-board cuts are painful but necessary. The government may well have been loath to address misinformation regarding specific areas for fear of upsetting this delicate balance.

### 4. CONSUMERS (STAKEHOLDERS)

Although most members of the group we call consumers are also voters, they differ from other voters in two important respects: they possess more information than other voters about the government services they consume; and the excess of the benefits they receive over the taxes they pay is greater than it is for other groups of voters. Consequently, they may dominate the public debate about particular services.

Our analysis suggests that the Alberta government adopted two strategies to deal with these special interest groups: it gave increased power to some groups to encourage them to accept responsibility for the changes that were introduced and it took steps to dissipate the bargaining power of other groups.

## 4.1 Co-option

Individuals may be less likely to criticize the decisions of a public body if they have been 'co-opted' into the decision-making process. This is true both because they will feel some responsibility for those decisions and because the decisions will reflect more closely the preferences of the affected groups.[6] The Alberta government's approach to stakeholders seems to reflect both of these considerations.

One example of this policy was the establishment of school councils and community health councils. In each of these cases, increased power was given to representatives of those groups most affected by government decisions. For example, parents will be less likely to argue that budget cuts have been implemented unfairly if they have been involved in the decision-making process.

The roundtable process was also oriented towards the co-option of special interest groups. Although laypersons were invited to the roundtables, most of the participants were drawn from those who were immediately affected by the relevant government policies. The Education roundtables, for example, were dominated by representatives from school boards, teachers, and school trustees.

Finally, the Delegated Administrative Organizations established by Consumer Affairs and Alberta Labour may be considered to be an extreme form of co-option. By giving industry associations the responsibility for enforcing the statutes that regulate them, the government has induced those associations both to select the means by which regulatory budgets were to be cut and to accept the rulings made with respect to regulatory affairs.

Co-option can also enable the government to design policies that conform to public preferences and in so doing develop more efficient policies. One of the announced objectives of the government was to move decision-making authority closer to the relevant stakeholders, perhaps circumventing some of the agency problems that can arise when government policy is developed and implemented through several layers of bureaucracy. In this way the government could achieve perhaps conflicting ends. For example, as discussed previously, the government was obviously concerned with how elected school boards would deal with the budget cuts. Thus, strict constraints were imposed on how grant money could be spent and the taxing power of local school boards was curtailed. At the same time, however, in non-budgetary matters some decision-making authority was devolved to individual schools and school councils.

In this way, issues of a local nature that do not have broad implications for tax-payers at large can be handled by those most affected by them, while budgetary matters, which have broader implications, are more tightly controlled by the government.

### 4.2 Dissipation of Power

Two aspects of the Alberta government's approach to budget-cutting may have acted to constrain the power of special interest groups. First, the three-year business plans, by establishing intermediate-term budgets and goals, make it difficult for any group to obtain incremental concessions. Second, the across-the-board nature of the cuts made it difficult for consumers of specific government services to argue that they had been treated inequitably and that the services they used should be restored to their previous levels. As all groups were seen to be 'in the same boat', there was little sympathy for groups seeking special consideration.

## 5. GOVERNMENT

Any sign of weakness of resolve by one party may be exploited by its adversaries; thus, commitment can be an important element for the parties to a game. In terms of the deficit-elimination game, the government must convince voters, civil servants, and consumers that it is serious both about reducing the deficit and about holding the debt at the lower level that has been achieved. Otherwise, opponents of the deficit elimination program will be encouraged to increase the intensity of their opposition and proponents of the program may reduce their support for the government. To combat these outcomes, the government must present a consistent face to the public both across individual members of the government and across time.

### 5.1 Internal Consistency

One of the greatest challenges facing a government that makes dramatic changes to public policy is maintaining cohesion among its own members. We believe that, in large part, the success of the Alberta government in maintaining this cohesion may be attributed to the establishment of the Standing Policy Committee system. Under this system, all caucus and cabinet committees were collapsed into four Standing Policy Committees, each of which is composed of eight cabinet ministers and eight government backbenchers.[7] All proposed legislation and all budget allocations must pass through at least one of these committees.

These SPCs have played an integral part in the policy-making process in Alberta. As discussed by Kneebone and McKenzie in Chapter 5 and Boothe in

Chapter 6, committees of this type can be the source of many useful ideas, often from backbenchers who are perhaps in closer touch with their constituents than the executive (cabinet). Moreover, in Chapter 4 Kneebone reviewed evidence from OECD countries indicating that such committees can act as a brake on the spending proclivities of cabinet ministers who may be 'captured' by the relevant stakeholders. They can also reduce party in-fighting by ensuring that every backbencher has a stake in the success of the government's initiatives. And, because most MLAs sit on more than one committee, the committees can increase the degree of co-ordination among departmental budgeting processes. The SPC system implemented by the Klein government seems to capture all of these positive aspects.

However, there are potentially negative attributes of these committees as well. As discussed by McKenzie in Chapter 3, when these committees are able to initiate policy rather than merely act as a review or monitoring mechanism for executive decisions, policies may emerge that reflect the preferences of individual committee members rather than the government as a whole. This is not a problem so long as these preferences are well aligned, but it can be problematic otherwise. From the interviews discussed in Chapter 5 by Kneebone and McKenzie, it is apparent that the glue that bound government MLAs together was the need to eliminate the deficit quickly. The SPCs never lost sight of this objective, even though there were some indications that individual departments periodically did. As such, the SPCs played a key role in keeping the government on track.

Interestingly, the government in general, and the SPC system in particular, may end up being a victim of its own success. Now that the government has fulfilled its mandate of eliminating the deficit within three years, this has left a political vacuum. As we all know, like nature, politicians abhor a vacuum. After the excitement and turmoil created by the far-reaching changes introduced in its first term in office, the government appears to be at a loss to formulate a new electoral agenda. In the absence of the glue that binds them together, it may well be that some of the negative attributes of the SPC system will begin to emerge.

## 5.2  Intertemporal Commitment

The government adopted other commitment mechanisms as well. First, it established a commission of nine senior executives (mostly accountants) to investigate government accounting procedures and to provide an independent assessment of the province's financial position as of 31 March 1993. The procedures recommended by this commission, virtually all of which were subsequently adopted, made the government's financial position much m transparent. Hence, it became more difficult for the government to 'hi guise' expenditures, for example, by placing them in Crown corp failing to report the true financial impacts of future commitments such as government employee pension plans.

Second, as discussed above, the government required each government agency to establish a three-year business plan. The publication of these plans increased the cost of making *ad hoc* changes to agencies' long-term programs. A further effect of three-year plans, which has not gone unnoticed by members of the current government, is that any plans that are finalized immediately prior to an election may act to limit the actions of the new government throughout the early part of its term. (Elections are held approximately once every four years in Alberta.) Hence, a government concerned that it will lose a general election can, through judicious use of the budgeting process, impose important components of its fiscal agenda on its opponent into the future.

Finally, three pieces of legislation aimed at limiting both the expenditure and revenue sides of the budget were introduced: the Deficit Elimination Act (DEA) (1993), the Alberta Taxpayer Protection Act (ATPA) (1995), and the Balanced Budget and Debt Retirement Act (BBDRA) (1995). As discussed by Boothe in Chapter 6, the DEA commits the government to eliminate the deficit within three years, the ATPA prohibits the imposition of a sales tax without a public referendum, and the BBDRA sets out the government's plan to eliminate the provincial net debt over a 25-year period. Kneebone and McKenzie (Chapter 7) suggest that these Acts may have been spawned by the lack of conservative budgeting practices by previous governments, in particular the tendency to treat positive random shocks to revenues as permanent. Although none of this legislation binds future governments—the legislature is free to rescind it at any time[8]—it does send a strong signal to voters concerning the government's intentions and, therefore, may serve as a form of 'self-commitment'. That is, a government that writes its promises into formal legislation will find it more difficult to justify reneging on those promises than will a government that makes only verbal promises (during an election campaign, for example). Although Kneebone (Chapter 4) discusses empirical evidence that such 'tax and expenditure limits' do lead to reductions in government deficits as well as to more favourable treatment from bond markets, Kneebone and McKenzie in Chapter 7 note that balanced budget legislation also limits the automatic stabilizer role of the budget.

## 6. CLOSING THOUGHTS

The purpose of this volume was to provide a critical overview of the methods by which the Alberta government achieved its deficit elimination and restructuring goals. Certainly, the government has been successful in eliminating its deficit and it is well ahead of schedule in reducing its net debt. It has also dramatically restructured how government services are delivered to the public. We feel that other jurisdictions can learn from the Alberta experience, and we have summarized some of those lessons above. We also believe that analysts can learn from a comparison of the approach adopted by Alberta to the approaches adopted by other jurisdictions that have successfully eliminated deficits, such as Saskatchewan, New Brunswick, and Manitoba. Only by such a comparison can we begin to make a judgement of whether the approach adopted by Alberta is the most *desirable*. This, perhaps, will be the subject of future research.

The question of whether or not the approach taken by the Alberta government will prove to be effective in the long run is, of course, open to question and will only be answered in time. In particular, it is important to note that the Alberta government has been fortunate in that it has implemented dramatic changes during a period of relative prosperity. This has enabled it to eliminate its deficit sooner than anticipated and to provide Albertans with a quick reward for their sacrifices. We note, however, that the unexpectedly rapid elimination of the deficit carried with it the potential to upset the government's efforts. That is, it would have been easy for the government to deviate from its plan to cut expenditures by 20 per cent (in nominal terms) when it became clear that a smaller cut than this was sufficient to balance the budget. The fact that it stuck to its agenda and continued to restructure and rethink how it delivers services to the public is a sign of the value of the intertemporal commitment the government imposed on itself by way of legislation (the DEA and BBDRA) and the other methods of imposing fiscal discipline implemented by the government and described in this volume. We think it is also a sign that the approach taken by the Alberta government will prove to be effective in the long run.

Still, we think serious challenges to the government's restructuring efforts are on the horizon. In particular, it remains to be seen whether Albertans are prepared to accept the sacrifices that will be demanded by the DEA and BBDRA should the economy go into a recession serious enough that the government's revenue cushions prove too small to prevent tax increases and/or further expenditure cuts. It also remains to be seen whether the government and its restructuring efforts can survive the fact that the elimination of the deficit has also eliminated its *raison d'être*. Can restructuring efforts survive the loss of the focus that so effectively bound the government, civil servants, voters, and consumers to a common cause? Or will creeping incrementalism again lead to a growing public sector and future deficits?

## NOTES

1. For a detailed discussion of the methods employed to increase department autonomy, see Boothe, Chapter 6.

2. In general, the Alberta government did not find this a difficult task. In our experience, most civil servants, especially those in middle management, were eager to offer their opinions to anyone who asked. Indeed, some would say that they were too eager. After one official in the Department of Justice suggested to the minister that Alberta investigate the possibility of contracting out the management of penitentiaries, it took the department—which opposed this attack on its authority—almost a year to have the proposal withdrawn.

3. The debate concerning the optimal pace of reform—the 'incremental' versus the 'once-for-all' approaches—is discussed by McKenzie in Chapter 3.

4. See also the discussion by McKenzie in Chapter 3.

5. Emery, Chapter 10, provides evidence that the government's concerns were justified. He shows that the University of Calgary was able to replace most of its budget cuts by increased student fees.

6. This issue is discussed in some detail in McKenzie, Chapter 3.

7. See Boothe, Chapter 6, for a description of the responsibilities of each SPC. The number of SPCs was subsequently increased to five, with the addition of a 'health restructuring' committee to deal with public concerns about the pace of change in the hospital system. Previously there had been approximately 10 caucus committees and seven cabinet committees.

8. Kneebone, in Chapter 4, notes that British Columbia's Taxpayer Protection Act of 1991 was rescinded in 1992, immediately following the election of a new government.

# Notes on Contributors

**Douglas W. Allen** is Associate Professor of Economics at Simon Fraser University. He received his Ph.D. from the University of Washington, and has taught at Carleton University in Ottawa. His main research interest is the study of contracts, focusing on agriculture and family issues.

**Keith Archer** is Professor of Political Science and Associate Dean (Research) in the Faculty of Social Sciences at the University of Calgary, where he has taught since 1984. His research interests include voting and elections, and political parties in Canada.

**R.G. Beck** is Professor of Economics at the University of Saskatchewan. He obtained his Ph.D. from the University of Alberta. His primary research interests are in health economics.

**Paul Boothe** is Professor of Economics at the University of Alberta. His main areas of research are regional government finance and the economics of federalism.

**Christopher J. Bruce** is Professor of Economics at the University of Calgary, where he has taught since 1973. He obtained his Ph.D. from Cambridge University. His primary research interests are in labour economics and the economic analysis of law.

**J.C. Herbert Emery** has been Assistant Professor of Economics at the University of Calgary since 1993. His main areas of research are in economic history and labour economics.

**Roger Gibbins** is Professor of Political Science at the University of Calgary, where he has taught since 1973. His research interests include Canadian federal and constitutional politics, regionalism, and political belief systems.

**Jonathan Kesselman** is Professor of Economics at the University of British Columbia, where he also serves as Director of the Centre for Research on Economic and Social Policy. His primary research interests are the theory and policy of taxation and income security programs.

**Ronald D. Kneebone** is Associate Professor of Economics at the University of Calgary. His main areas of research deal with issues of government finance and fiscal federalism. In recent research he has investigated whether certain past efforts by Canadian governments to reduce their deficits proved more effective than others.

**Stephen B. Lawton** is Professor of Educational Administration in the Department of Theory and Policy Studies of the Ontario Institute for Studies in Education at the University of Toronto. His research focuses on both educational finance and economics, and continuous improvement programs in education.

**Robert L. Mansell** is Professor and Head of the Department of Economics at the University of Calgary. His main areas of research and teaching include regional/resource economics, the Alberta economy, and regulatory economics.

**Kenneth J. McKenzie** is Associate Professor of Economics at the University of Calgary. His primary area of research is public economics, with an emphasis on taxation and government finance.

**Kenneth Norrie** is Professor of Economics at the University of Alberta. His main research interests are Canadian economic history and contemporary economic policy.

**Richard H.M. Plain** is Associate Professor of Economics at the University of Alberta where he holds joint appointments in the Departments of Economics and Public Health Sciences. His main areas of research are in health care economics and local government finance. He is currently analysing the economic impact of proposed changes in the funding of Regional Health Authorities on the allocation of health care resources in Alberta.

**Bryne Purchase** is Chair, Executive and Professional Programs, School of Policy Studies, Queen's University. He has a Ph.D. in economics from the University of Toronto and is a former civil servant in the government of Ontario. His specialty is the design of public organizations and programs.

**M.S. Shedd** is Associate Professor of Economics at the University of Calgary. He obtained his Ph.D. from Southern Illinois University (Carbondale). His primary research interests are the economics of social policy and income distribution.

**Arthur M. Schwartz** is Associate Professor of Education at the University of Calgary. He obtained his Ph.D. from the Ontario Institute for Studies in Education at the University of Toronto. His primary research interests are the politics of education and education administration.

**Michael J. Trebilcock** is Professor of Law at the University of Toronto, and Director of the Law and Economics Program and the Centre for the Study of State and Market. His main areas of research are competition policy, international trade, government regulation, and privatization.

**Linda Trimble** is Associate Professor of Political Science at the University of Alberta where she has been teaching Canadian politics since 1989. Her research focuses on women and politics in Canada. She is co-editor, with Jane Arscott, of *In the Presence of Women: Representation in Canadian Governments* (Toronto: Harcourt Brace, 1997).

**Douglas S. West** is Professor of Economics at the University of Alberta, where he has taught since 1981. His earlier research included studies of pre-emptive and predatory locational behaviour by firms, competition among shopping centres, and pricing in automobile insurance and video rental markets. His current research interests include the economic effects of the privatization of liquor retailing in Alberta and the similarity of shopping centres.

**Stanley Winer** is Professor of Economics and Public Policy in the School of Public Administration at Carleton University. His research is primarily concerned with the relationship between collective choice and public finance.

# Index

■

# Acknowledgements ∎

Table 1, pages 2-3. Alberta Treasury Department. 'Expenditure Reductions by Ministry, 1992/3 to 1998/9' from *Agenda '96*, Alberta Government Budget, February 1996.

Table 5, page 256. National Council of Welfare. 'Welfare Benefits by Province, Selected Years' from *Welfare Income 1994*, National Council of Welfare, 1995.

Table 6, page 258. Alberta Family and Social Services. 'Welfare Benefit Comparison (Pre- vs. Post-welfare Reform) from *Alberta Welfare Reforms Progress Report*, Alberta Family and Social Services, 1996.

Table 7, page 259. Alberta Family and Social Services. 'Alberta Welfare Monthly Caseload Figures' from *Alberta Welfare Reforms Progress Report*, Alberta Family and Social Services, 1996.

Table 8, page 260. Alberta Family and Social Services. 'Caseload Composition by Welfare Program Category, 1992/3 vs. 1995/6' from *Alberta Welfare Reforms Progress Report*, Alberta Family and Social Services, 1996.

Appendix 1, pages 411-12. Alberta Education. '1996/97 School Board Funding Formula (Selected Data)'. Reproduced with the permission of the Minister of Education, Province of Alberta, Canada, 1997.

Alberta Family and Social Services. Quotes from *Business Plan 1995-96 to 1997-98*, Alberta Family and Social Services, 1995.

The Brookings Institution. Quote from *Equality and Efficiency*, A.M. Okun, Washington: The Brookings Institution, 1975. Reprinted by permission of The Brookings Institution.

Government Policy Consultants. Adaptation of Appendix, 'Significant Events for the Klein Government—December 1992 to December 1994' from *The Klein Government at Two: Staying the Course*, Government Policy Consultants, 1995. Reprinted by permission of Government Policy Consultants.